CONCORDIA UNIV
DA554.L481904
QUEEN VICTORIA NEW REV
Y0-CLJ-916

3 4211 000022158

WITHDRAWN

QUEEN VICTORIA

QUEEN VICTORIA AT THE AGE OF SEVENTY-EIGHT
From the original painting by BARON H. VON ANGELI, *now at Windsor Castle*

QUEEN VICTORIA

A BIOGRAPHY

BY SIDNEY LEE
EDITOR OF THE DICTIONARY OF NATIONAL BIOGRAPHY

WITH PORTRAITS, FACSIMILE, AND MAP

NEW AND REVISED EDITION

KLINCK MEMORIAL LIBRARY
Concordia College
River Forest, IL 60305

LONDON
JOHN MURRAY, ALBEMARLE STREET, W.
1904

FIRST EDITION (Smith, Elder & Co.)		-	*December*	1902
SECOND EDITION	,,	,,	-	*March*	1903
Reprinted	,,	,,	-	*March*	1903
Reprinted	,,	,,	-	*March*	1903
CHEAPER EDITION	,,	,,	-	*February*	1904

All Rights Reserved

PREFACE

TO

THE NEW EDITION

I AM grateful for the welcome which was accorded this work by the press and the public at home, in the Colonies, and in the United States of America, on its publication at the end of 1902. I hope that this cheaper edition may extend the ranks of its readers.

In revising the biography for re-issue I have taken advantage of the communications of correspondents who have been kind enough to send me some corrections and additional information. A few of these correspondents were in one capacity or another in close relations with the late Queen, and have given me the results of first-hand knowledge.

Of the new light which Mr. John Morley's lately published 'Life of Gladstone' has thrown on Queen Victoria's personal relations with the longest-lived of her Prime Ministers I have also availed myself in this revision of my work. Mr. Morley's volumes form a contribution of first-rate importance to the history of the Queen's reign, and they place all students of the subject under vast obligations. One or two other books, which illustrate in a comparatively small way episodes in the Queen's career, have come into my hands for the first time in the course of recent months. These volumes include ' The History of Lord Lytton's Indian Administration, 1876-1880,' by Lady Betty Balfour (1899) ; ' Recollections of a Royal Parish,' by Mrs. Patricia Lindsay (1902) ; and ' Letters of a Diplomat's Wife,' by Mary King Waddington (1903). Although the new details which I have derived from such sources are slight in themselves, they help, I think, to make my picture a little more complete.

During my absence in America through the first half of last year, my publishers found it necessary to omit a few passages from the third and fourth impressions of the book. These omissions did not affect the general narrative, but it was not possible for me at the time personally to supervise the making of them. This the present re-issue has given me the opportunity of doing.

None of the alterations or additions which the text has undergone since it was first presented to the public in any way affects the scheme or tone of the biography. My endeavour has been throughout to pay due respect alike to the honoured memory of the late Queen, and to those just and independent principles which alone give historical writing any value.

S. L.

January 2, 1904.

PREFACE

TO

THE FIRST EDITION[1]

THIS work is based on the biographical notice of Queen Victoria which was published in the third Supplementary Volume of the 'Dictionary of National Biography' in October 1901. I undertook that article at the earnest request of the public-spirited proprietor of the Dictionary, the late Mr. George Smith, who impressed on me the imperative need of observing in the notice of the Queen that sense of proportion and that regard for exact detail which distinguished other contributions to the 'Dictionary,' and were essential characteristics of its general scheme. I set to work on the memoir with some misgiving. I was fully conscious of its difficulty. But I did what I could to execute the task in the spirit in which it was confided to me.

The article in the 'Dictionary' was on its publication favourably received by the press and the public as a first serious attempt at an exhaustive account of

[1] A few words are omitted in this reprint of the original preface.

the Queen's long and varied life, and of her relations with public affairs. A general wish was at once expressed for the independent re-issue of the article, and with that wish I have here complied.

In order to fit the memoir for separate publication, I have found it necessary substantially to re-write it. The somewhat abrupt method of presenting facts and dates which is appropriate to a 'Dictionary' article is out of place in an independent volume. The 'Dictionary' memoir was exceptionally long, but the space at my disposal there did not enable me to utilise all the material that I had collected. The omitted detail or illustrative comment is now added. A few errors which readers of the article pointed out to me have been corrected. I have also incorporated much information which has only been recently at my disposal, and is, I believe, of first-rate importance.

In spite of all changes and additions, I have endeavoured to remain loyal throughout to the principles inherent in the aims of the 'Dictionary of National Biography.' I have sought to record clearly and with such conciseness as coherence would permit the main facts known to me concerning the Queen's personal history in the varied spheres of life in which she played her great part. It has been necessary for me to touch on the extended political history, and on the many vexed questions of politics at home and abroad, with which her long career was associated. But I have tried to avoid treating such topics in any fuller detail than was needful to make her personal experiences and opinions intelligible. The circumstance of politics is to a large extent the scenery of every sovereign's biography, but it is the duty of a biographer sternly to subordinate his scenery to the actor who is alone his just concern.

The sources whence I have derived my information are mentioned in the notes to my text and in the detailed bibliography which I give in the third appendix to the volume. I believe that I have examined all the printed memoirs in English, French, or German which could reasonably be expected to throw light on my subject, nor have I neglected newspapers of the time, and periodical publications like the 'Annual Register,' which collect methodically contemporary facts and dates. The printed records are abundant and detailed, but they are not all equally trustworthy, and the labour of reconciling the published evidence of the numerous witnesses has not been light.

Most of the printed testimony has the advantage of a remarkable frankness. The statesmen of the Queen's reign who gave their memoirs to the world showed little reticence in describing their intercourse with their sovereign. Nor were journalists holding responsible positions in the early and middle years of her career timorous in their notices of the Queen's life or in their comments on important passages of it. They interpreted very liberally the principle of the freedom of the press. As one turns over the pages of 'The Times' newspaper and other leading London journals of thirty years ago, one is impressed by the outspoken tone in which the actions of the Queen were then recorded and criticised. The editorial judgments may have been warped by prejudice, and many of them may now excite resentment, but the lack of reserve frequently enables the investigator to detect the cause and effect of the Queen's public conduct with a precision that greater urbanity and more respectful restraint would render impossible.

The Queen was a voluminous correspondent. Thousands of her letters to ministers, relatives, and friends survive. A great number of these, on both public and personal topics, were published with her permission in her lifetime in the biographies of distinguished subjects with whom she was on terms of intimacy. Many have been acquired as valued autographs by public libraries or museums, and are now placed freely at the public disposal. Other of her letters have from time to time been printed in volumes issued for private circulation only. Such fragments of the Queen's correspondence as I have been able to consult afford a rich mine of biographical material.

The Queen was rarely averse from taking her subjects into her confidence. She allowed Sir Theodore Martin to print many fragments of her diary in his 'Life of the Prince Consort.' Other portions she herself prepared for publication in the two volumes of 'Leaves' from her journal. The various letters of the Queen to which I have had access, combined with the available excerpts from her diary, have enabled me to present in her own words her opinions and experiences at some critical epochs of her reign. Wherever my sources of knowledge permitted it, I have endeavoured to let the Queen speak for herself.

I have also derived assistance from the reminiscences of several of her friends and associates. Some of those who came into most frequent intercourse with her in her later years have been good enough to communicate to me their recollections.

My endeavour has been at all points to present facts fully, truthfully, and impartially, but I hope that I may claim to have written in a spirit of sympathy as well as in a spirit of justice, and to have paid fitting consideration alike to the public and to the private interests involved. The inevitable candour of the historical biographer can never be unwelcome to those who honour the Queen's memory aright. Truth with her was an enduring passion. Not long before her death she contemplated the preparation of a biography which should give her people accurate knowledge of her career. Although that purpose was not fulfilled, her subjects may confidently cherish the thought that such a record would have testified in no grudging measure to her unquenchable 'delight no less in truth than life.'

To the gracious kindness of the King I am indebted for an autograph of Queen Victoria, which his Majesty has been pleased to lend me for reproduction in facsimile in this volume; it is the Queen's first draft of her letter summoning Mr. Disraeli to Windsor to form an administration in February 1874. By his Majesty's gracious permission I am also enabled to include two photogravure portraits of Queen Victoria, which have been reproduced from the originals in his Majesty's possession at Windsor Castle.

My thanks are due to my friend Mr. Thomas Seccombe for the valuable assistance he has rendered in reading with me the final proofs.

S. L.

November 24, 1902.

CONTENTS

I

PARENTAGE AND BIRTH

		PAGE			PAGE
	Queen Victoria's ancestry.	1	1819	Her place in the succession	11
	Her descent from King Alfred	1		*June* 24. Baptism	11
1714	The Hanoverian line	2		Baptismal names .	12
	Hanoverian marriages .	3		*Aug.* At Claremont	13
	George III.'s family	3	1820,	*Jan.* At Sidmouth	13
1817	Succession to the crown	4		*Jan.* 23. Death of Duke of Kent .	14
	George III.'s sons	4		*Jan.* 29. Death of George III.	14
1818	Three marriages .	4		Position of the Duchess of Kent .	14
	The Duke of Kent	5		Prince Leopold and his niece .	16
	May 29. His marriage	6		The Duchess of Kent's resolve	16
	The Duchess of Kent .	8		The Duke of Kent's influence	17
	Her family connections	8			
	Relations with France and Portugal	9			
1819,	*May* 24. Queen Victoria's birth	10			

II

CHILDHOOD

1820	Settlement at Kensington	19	1828	Knowledge of her rank.	24
1824	Fräulein Lehzen	20	1829	Country excursions . .	25
1827	Appointment of a preceptor	20	1826	Visit to George IV.	26
	The Princess's teachers	21	1827,	*Jan.* 5. Death of the Duke of York	27
	Homely life at Kensington.	23	1829,	*May* 28. The Princess and the Queen of Portugal	27
1828,	*May* 19. Sir Walter Scott's visit	24		Queen Victoria's sympathy with Portugal .	28

III

HEIR TO THE CROWN

		PAGE			PAGE
1830,	*June* 26. Death of George IV. and accession of William IV.	29	1834	Delight in music and the drama	39
	Heir-presumptive to the crown	29	1835	At Ascot	40
	Appointment of a governess	30		*July* 30. Her confirmation	40
1831,	*Sept.* 8. Absence from William IV.'s coronation	31		Further visits to the nobility	41
	Prince Leopold's removal to Belgium	32	1836,	*May.* First meeting with Prince Albert	42
	William IV.'s treatment of the Princess	33		Other possible suitors	42
	The Princess's early travels	33		Widening of the breach with William IV.	44
1832	Tour in Wales	35		*Aug.* 21. The King and the Duchess of Kent at Windsor	45
	Visits to the nobility	35	1837,	*May* 24. Coming of age	46
	Nov. 8. At Oxford	36		State ball in her honour	46
	Hospitalities at Kensington	37		Visits the Royal Academy	47
1833	Tour on the south coast	37		William IV.'s last communication to his niece	47

IV

THE ACCESSION TO THE THRONE

		PAGE			PAGE
1837,	*June* 20. Death of William IV.	48	1837	Dissemination of the name Victoria	52
	The Queen's accession	48		Public sentiment regarding her	53
	Lord Melbourne's first audience	49		Peel on her inexperience	53
	The first council	49		The hopes of Sydney Smith and Lord John Russell	54
	The proclamation	51			
	The second council	51			
	Her name as sovereign	52			

V

THE TUITION OF LORD MELBOURNE

		PAGE			PAGE
1837	The Queen and Hanover	56	1837	Lord Melbourne's instruction	58
	The Queen and the criminal law	57		His career	58

CONTENTS

		PAGE			PAGE
1837	His opinions and character	59	1837	Her foreign advisers	64
				Baron Stockmar	64
	The private secretaryship	60		The Baroness Lehzen	66
				The Duchess of Kent	66
	The Queen's preference for the Whigs	61		Public ceremonials	67
				First speech from the throne	67
	The formation of her household	62			

VI

THE CIVIL LIST AND COLONIAL AFFAIRS

1837	Removal to Buckingham Palace	69	1837,	*Nov.* 20. Opening of her first Parliament	77
	Aug 21. Opening of Victoria Gate, Hyde Park	70		The Civil List	77
				The hereditary Crown lands	78
	At the Pavilion, Brighton	70		William IV.'s income	78
	Private life	70		The duchies of Lancaster and Cornwall	79
	Innovations at Buckingham Palace	71		The first settlement	79
	Foreign guests	72		Civil List pensions	80
	Attitude to her kinsfolk	72		Radical criticism	80
				Provision for Duchess of Kent	81
	Court etiquette	73			
	The general election	74		The Queen pays her father's debts	81
	Tory attacks on the Queen	74		The British Empire in 1837	82
	Whigs affect suspicion of a Hanoverian plot	75		The revolt of Canada	83
	Whigs' small majority	75		Lord Durham's mission	84
	Nov. 9. At the Guildhall banquet	77		His recall	85
				The colonial policy of self-government	85

VII

THE CORONATION AND THE CRISES OF 1839

1838,	*June* 28. The coronation	87	1839	The episode of Lady Flora Hastings	93
	The ceremony in the Abbey	88		Outcry in the press	94
				Lady Flora's death	94
	The want of rehearsal	89		Hostility to the Court	95
	Close of the celebrations	91		*May*. First ministerial crisis	95
1838–9	The Queen's speeches in Parliament	92		Melbourne's resignation	96
1839	Crises of 1839	92			

xvi   QUEEN VICTORIA

1839	The Queen resists change in household	97
	May 10. The Queen's letter to Peel	98
	Melbourne's cabinet reconsiders its position	99
	His reconstructed ministry	100

1839	Admission of the Queen's error	100
	Tory attacks on the Queen	101
	General effect of the bedchamber crisis	102

VIII

MARRIAGE

1839	Adoption of penny postage	104
	Unreadiness to marry	105
	King Leopold's choice of Prince Albert	105
	Stockmar's co-operation	106
	English courtiers and German princes	107
	Her sense of isolation	108
	Oct. 10. Arrival of Prince Albert	108
	Oct. 15. Engagement to him	108
	Nov. 20. The public announcement	109

1839	Daniel O'Connell's congratulations	110
	Public criticism	111
	The Queen's demands	112
1840	Melbourne's dilemma	113
	Ministerial proposals	113
	Obduracy of the House of Commons	114
	The Queen's irritation	115
	Difficulties with the House of Lords	115
	The Prince's precedence	115
	The Queen's warrant	116
	The Prince's attendants	116
	Feb. 10. The marriage ceremony	117

IX

PRINCE ALBERT'S POSITION

1840	Prince Albert and his wife	118
	His character and influence on the Queen	118
	Popular dislike of the Prince	119
	The Prince's ultimate position	121
	Obstinacy of the public prejudice	122
	Changes in the palace	122
	The withdrawal of the Duchess of Kent	123
	Departure of Baroness Lehzen	123
	Stockmar remains at Court	123

1840	*June* 10. First attempt on the Queen's life	124
	June 12. The concert at Buckingham Palace	124
	Approaching birth of an heir	125
	The Regency Bill	125
	The nomination of Prince Albert	126
	Nov. 21. Birth of Princess Royal	127
1841,	*Feb.* 10. The baptism	127
1840	Political anxieties	128
	The Prince and foreign policy	128
	Palmerston at the Foreign Office	128

CONTENTS

		PAGE
1840	His impatience of the Prince's counsel	130
	Mehemet Ali and Turkey	130
	Political crisis with France	131
	Divisions in the cabinet	131
1841	Palmerston's triumphant action	132

		PAGE
1841	Defeat of Melbourne's Ministry	132
	June. The Queen at Oxford	133
	Her sympathy with Whig ministers	133
	Defeat of the Whigs at the polls	134

X

SIR ROBERT PEEL'S ADMINISTRATION

		PAGE
1841	The Queen's regrets	135
	Aug. Acceptance of Peel's ministry	135
	Cordiality between the Queen and Peel	136
	Change of attitude to the Tories	137
	Nov. 9. Birth of the Prince of Wales	138
1842	General rejoicings	138
	The sponsors	139
	The King of Prussia	139
	Popular fear of German preponderance	139
	Inconvenient display of loyalty at Brighton	140
	The London season	140
	The introduction of railways	140
	June. The Queen first travels by rail	141
	May 30. Second attempt on her life	141
	July 3. Third attempt on her life	142
	New legislation for her personal security	143
	Chartist agitation	143
	Aug.-Sept. First visit to Scotland	144
	Her Scottish hosts	145
	Her affection for Scotland	145
1844	Second visit to Scotland	146
1842	The Queen and Peel	146
	The disruption of the Scottish Church	146
1843,	*Jan.* The murder of Edward Drummond	147
	The Queen and Aberdeen	147

		PAGE
1843	Prince Albert's growing influence	148
	April 21. Death of the Duke of Sussex	149
	June 5. Baptism of Princess Alice	149
	The surliness of the King of Hanover	149
	Sept. The Queen's visit to Louis Philippe	150
	Question of a regency	151
	At the Château d'Eu	152
	The Queen in Belgium	153
	Oct. First visit to Trinity College, Cambridge	154
	Nov.-Dec. At Drayton Manor	155
	At Chatsworth	155
1844,	*Jan.* 29. Death of Prince Albert's father	156
	June. Visit of Tsar Nicholas I.	156
	The Queen and the Irish Union	157
	The Queen on parliamentary obstruction	157
	Peel threatens resignation	158
	Foreign affairs	158
	Aug. 6. Birth of Prince Alfred	159
	Oct. Louis Philippe's visit to Windsor	159
	Oct. 28. The opening of the Royal Exchange	160
1845	Visits to the nobility	160
	Jan. At Strathfieldsaye	161
	Jan. At Stowe	161
	First meeting with Disraeli	161

XI

THE QUEEN AND FREE TRADE

1845	The parliamentary session	163	1845,	*Dec.* 6. Peel's resignation 168
	The Queen and the Maynooth agitation . . 163			Lord John Russell summoned . . . 168
	Court entertainments . 164			Negotiations with Lord John 169
	Aug. Queen's first visit to Germany . . 164			The Queen's dread of Palmerston . . 169
	The King of Prussia's welcome . . . 165			Lord John's pertinacious appeals . . . 169
	Prince Albert's precedence . . . 165			Peel's return to power . 170
	Aug. 19. At Rosenau . 165		1846	The Queen's support of him 171
	Second visit to Louis Philippe . . . 166			Regrets for his difficulties 172
	The Queen's delight at visiting Coburg . . 166			*June* 26. His fall . . 172
	Peel and the corn laws 166			*May* 25. Birth of Princess Helena . . 172
	The Queen's support of Peel 167			The Queen's enthusiasm for free trade . . 173

XII

THE SPANISH MARRIAGES

1846,	*July.* Lord John's first ministry . . . 174		1846	Prince Albert and Prince Leopold of Saxe-Coburg 178
	The Queen and Lord John 174			Queen Christina's interference . . . 179
	His colleagues . . 175			Family conference at Windsor . . . 179
	Macaulay at Court . . 175			
	Difficulties with Palmerston 176			Palmerston's rash despatch . . . 180
	The Spanish marriages 177			French retaliation . . 180
	The Château d'Eu agreement . . 177			The Queen's indignation 181

XIII

THE YEAR OF REVOLUTION, 1848

1847	The 'season' of 1847 . 183		1847,	*July.* At Cambridge . 184
	Prince Albert Chancellor of Cambridge . 183			Third visit to Scotland . 185
			1848	Louis Philippe's dethronement . . 185

CONTENTS

		PAGE			PAGE
1848	The Queen's treatment of him	186	1848, *May* 13.	Princess Louise christened	188
	Welcome to his sons	187		Anticipated defeat of the Government	188
	Revolution in Germany	187			
	Mar. 18. Birth of Princess Louise	187	*Sept.* 5.	Parliament prorogued	189
	Chartist menaces	188			

XIV

PRIVATE LIFE AND RECREATIONS, 1848–54

1848	First stay at Balmoral	190	1842	Patronage of art	195
	Music and drama at Court	191		Education of the children	196
1842, *July*.	The Queen and Mendelssohn	191		The Queen's dislike of London	198
	Actors and actresses at Court	194	1844	Acquisition of Osborne	199
	The drama at Windsor	194	1848–52	Acquisition of Balmoral	200
	The Queen and Charles Kean	195		Modes of life at Balmoral and Osborne	200

XV

IRELAND AND LOSS OF FRIENDS

1849	First visit to Ireland	202	1850, *Aug.* 26.	Death of Louis Philippe	205
	State of the country	202	1849–50	Two assaults on the Queen	206
	Arrival at Queenstown	203			
	Oct. 30. Last royal water pageant	204	1850, *May* 1.	Birth of Prince Arthur	206
1848	*Nov.* 24. Death of Lord Melbourne	204		The Queen's robust health	207
1850, *July* 3.	Death of Peel	205			

XVI

THE DISSENSIONS WITH PALMERSTON

	Differences with Palmerston	208		Their respective attitudes towards Prussia	210
	Prince Albert's antagonism	208		Palmerston's offences	211
	Their respective attitudes towards Italy	209	1847	The Queen's private correspondence	212
				The appeal of the Queen of Portugal	212

		PAGE			PAGE
1847	Letter to the King of Prussia	213	1850	Prince Albert on Palmerston	217
	Palmerston's obduracy	214		Fresh dissensions	217
1850	Popularity of Palmerston's policy	215	1851	Papal aggressions	218
	The Queen's demands	215		Ministerial crisis	219
				Recall of Lord John	219

XVII

THE GREAT EXHIBITION AND PALMERSTON'S FALL

1851	The Great Exhibition	221	1851	Palmerston and Napoleon III.	225
	Court festivities	223		*Dec.* 19. Palmerston's fall	225
	The Queen at Liverpool and Manchester	224		Prince Albert's elation	226
	Nov. 18. Death of King Ernest of Hanover	224		The peril of dismissing a minister	227
	Palmerston and Kossuth	224			

XVIII

LORD ABERDEEN'S MINISTRY

1852, *Feb.*	Palmerston's revenge	228	1852	Coalition of Peelites and Liberals	234
	Lord Derby's first Government	229		Aberdeen's Whig colleagues	234
	Inexperience of its members	229		The Queen's satisfaction	235
	Early impression of Disraeli	229	1853, *April* 7.	Birth of Prince Leopold	235
July.	Defeat of Derby's Government	230		Military preparations	235
	Second visit to Belgium	231	*Aug.* 30.	Second visit to Dublin	236
	Neild's bequest	231	1852	Napoleon III.'s advances	236
Sept. 14.	Death of the Duke of Wellington	231		His matrimonial plans	237
Nov. 18.	His funeral	232		King Leopold's mediation between the Queen and Napoleon	237
Dec. 17.	Lord Derby's resignation	232		Napoleon's importunities	238
	The Queen's desire for a coalition ministry	232			
	Her appeal to Aberdeen	233			

XIX

THE CRIMEAN WAR

		PAGE
1853	Quarrel with Russia	240
	Palmerston's resolute views	240
	The Queen's dread of war	241
	Attitude of foreign sovereigns	241
1854	Popular suspicion of Prince Albert	242
	The Queen's resentment	243
	Feb. 28. War declared with Russia	244
	The Queen and the troops	244
	Hospitalities at Court	245
	June 10. Opening of the Crystal Palace at Sydenham	246

		PAGE
1854	The Queen protests against lukewarmness about the war	246
	Prince Albert at St. Omer	246
	Aug. 12. The Speaker harangues the sovereign for the last time	247
	Anxieties about the war	248
	Oct. 25. Battle of Inkerman	248
	Nov. 5. Battle of Balaclava	248
1854–5	The winter and its hardships	248
1855, *Jan.* 29.	Lord Aberdeen's defeat	249

XX

TRIUMPH OF PALMERSTON AND NAPOLEON III.

		PAGE
1855	The Queen's renewed dread of Palmerston	251
	Her appeal to Lord John	251
	Palmerston's omnipotence	252
	Feb. 15. The Queen accepts Palmerston	253
	Wounded soldiers	254
	Napoleon offers to go to the Crimea	254
	The Queen's distrust of her political associates	254
	April 16. Visit of Napoleon III.	255
	His agreeable demeanour	255

		PAGE
1855	His welcome by the people	256
	The Queen on the irony of royalty	256
	She reproves Lord John	257
	May 18. First distribution of war medals	257
	The Emperor's invitation	258
	Aug. 20–7. The Queen in Paris	258
	Her brilliant welcome	259
	First meeting with Bismarck	260
	Success of the Paris visit	261
	Relations with Napoleon	261

XXI

THE PEACE OF PARIS

	PAGE		PAGE
1855, *Aug.* The fall of Sebastopol	262	1856 The Victoria Cross	267
Sept. 29. The Princess Royal's engagement	262	*July* 14. The Duke of Cambridge Commander-in-Chief	267
Hostility in England	262	Court festivities	268
Views of Prussian statesmen	263	*May* 9. Ball at Buckingham Palace	269
Nov. Victor Emanuel visits the Queen	264	Reception of Sir Fenwick Williams and Florence Nightingale	269
She discourages him	265	Domestic hospitalities	269
1856, *March* 30. The peace of Paris	265	*Nov.* Death of Prince Leiningen, the Queen's half-brother	270
General rejoicings	266		
April 16. First visit to Aldershot	266		

XXII

INDIA AND THE PRINCESS ROYAL

	PAGE		PAGE
1857 Approach of the Indian mutiny	271	1857 Differences about the Balkan peninsula	276
March. Palmerston's defeat on China question	271	*Aug.* 19. Prince Albert and the Queen visit Cherbourg	277
April 14. Birth of Princess Beatrice	272	The Indian mutiny	277
April 30. Death of the Duchess of Gloucester	272	The Queen's urgency of counsel	278
May. Grant to the Princess Royal	272	*Sept.* Fall of Delhi and relief of Lucknow	279
Brilliant festivities at Court	273	*Nov.* Death of the Duchess de Nemours	279
Public functions	274	1858, *Jan.* 25. Marriage of the Princess Royal	279
Royal guests	274	Palmerston and the Orsini conspiracy	280
June 25. The title of Prince Consort	275	*Feb.* 19. Palmerston's fall	281
Relations with Napoleon III.	275		

XXIII

THE RESETTLEMENT OF INDIA

1858, *Feb.* Lord Derby's second cabinet . . 283
Aug. Second visit to Cherbourg . . 284
Aug. Tour in Germany 285
At Birmingham and Leeds 286
The first submarine cable 286
The resettlement of India 286
The Queen's objections to the Government Bill 287

1858 Her personal interest in India . . . 288
Her sympathy with the natives 288
Her attitude to her Indian subjects . . 289
Final form of the Queen's proclamation 290
The Order of the Star of India 290
The Queen's sense of imperial responsibility 291

XXIV

THE QUEEN'S FEARS OF NAPOLEON III.

1858, *Nov.* 9. Majority of the Prince of Wales . 293
1859, *Jan.* 27. Birth of the Queen's eldest grandchild (afterwards the German Emperor, William II.) . . . 293
Her appeal for peace to Napoleon III. . . 294
Napoleon's intervention in Italy 294
April. Austria declares war on Italy . . 295
Napoleon at war with Austria 295
The Queen's anxiety respecting Prussia . 296
Her efforts to localise the war 296
April 1. Lord Derby's resignation . . 297

1859, *June.* She sends for Lord Granville . . 297
Her confidence betrayed to 'The Times' . . 298
Lord John's obstinacy . 299
Palmerston again Prime Minister . . . 299
Differences with Lord John on the Italian question . . . 300
The peace of Villafranca 300
The Queen's quarrel with her ministry . . 300
Struggle for Italian unity 301
Anger with Napoleon . 302
1860 Heated protests against her ministers . . 302
The Queen and the Commander-in-Chief . 303

XXV

THE SECOND VISIT TO COBURG

1859 Military ceremonials . 305	1860, *Sept.–Oct.* Second visit to Coburg . . . 307
May. The Volunteers . 305	*Oct.* 1. Accident to Prince Albert . . 308
Domestic life . . . 306	Relations with Prussia . 309
1860 Engagement of Princess Alice 307	1861, *Jan.* 2. Accession of King William I. of Prussia 309
Feb.–Nov. Tour of the Prince of Wales in America . . . 307	

XXVI

DEATH OF THE PRINCE CONSORT

1861, *Jan.* Disraeli and the grant to Princess Alice 311	1861, *Nov.* At Windsor . . 315
Feb. 10. The twenty-first anniversary of the Queen's marriage . . 312	The Prince Consort's illness 315
March 16. Death of the Queen's mother . . 312	*Dec.* Affair of the 'Trent' 316
Disraeli's condolence . 313	Federals' attack on the Southern envoys . 316
The Queen and her mother's dependents . 313	Palmerston's peremptory tone . . . 317
Minor troubles . . . 313	Prince Albert's intervention . . . 317
Resumption of hospitalities 314	The gratitude of American democrats . . 318
Aug. Third visit to Ireland 314	Walt Whitman on the Queen's action . . 318
At Killarney . . . 314	*Dec.* 14. Prince Albert's death 319
Sept. The Prince Consort's last visit to Balmoral . . . 315	

XXVII

THE QUEEN'S GRIEF

1861 The Queen's widowhood 321	1861, *Dec.* Her movements after bereavement 324
Public sympathy . . 321	1862, *Jan.* Her ministers' reproof 324
Tennyson's elegy . . 322	Her resolves for the future 325
The Prince's reputation 322	The Prince's lasting influence on her . 325
Permanence of the Queen's grief . . 323	
Her sympathy with others' distress . 323	

XXVIII

FIRST ANXIETIES OF WIDOWHOOD

		PAGE				PAGE
1862	Her personal attendants in her widowhood	327		1862	Memorial to the Prince at Balmoral	332
	Friends in her household	327			*Sept.* Betrothal of the Prince of Wales	332
	Scottish sympathisers	327			The throne of Greece	333
	John Brown	328			Duke Ernest and the Greek throne	333
	The Queen's private secretaries	328			His appeal to the Queen	334
	Grey, Phipps, and Biddulph	329			Her replies	334
	Dean Wellesley	330		1863, *March* 30. Prince George of Denmark, King of Greece		335
	Jan. Public business	330				
	Her signature to officers' commissions	331			*March* 10. Marriage of the Prince of Wales	335
	Prince of Wales in the Holy Land	331			Hopes of the Queen's reappearance in public life	336
	July 1. Princess Alice's marriage	331				

XXIX

THE QUEEN AND PRUSSIA

		PAGE				PAGE
1863	Her views of foreign policy	337		1863,	*Aug.* 31. Visit of the King of Prussia	340
	Disagreements with ministers	337			Interview with the Emperor of Austria	341
	The Polish insurrection	338			The Queen's earnest appeal to him	341
	Visit to Coburg	339			*Sept.* At Darmstadt and Balmoral	342
	Depressed prospects of the Crown Prince	339			*Oct.* 13. Prince Consort's statue unveiled at Aberdeen	342
	The Queen's despair of Prussia	340				

XXX

THE SCHLESWIG-HOLSTEIN QUESTION

		PAGE				PAGE
1863	The Schleswig-Holstein question	344		1863	Efforts of Duke Frederick's allies	345
	Opinion in Germany	344			Intentions of Prussia	345
	Duke Frederick's claim	345			The Queen's divided interests	346

1863	Her sympathy with Germany . . . 346	1864,	*April* 20. The London conference . . . 351
1864	England's treaty obligations 347		Her zeal for neutrality . 352
	Differences in her family circle 347		Her tactful correspondence 352
	Her efforts for peace . 348		Her triumph . . . 353
	Ministry's support of Denmark . . . 348		*Jan.* 8. Birth of the Prince of Wales's son 354
	Her rejection of Duke Frederick . . . 350		Garibaldi's visit . . 354
	Feb. 4. Her declaration to Parliament . . 351		Unveiling of the Prince Consort's statue at Perth 354

XXXI

THE QUEEN'S SECLUSION

1864	Complaints of the Queen's seclusion . 355	1864	Explanation of her position 358
	Her interest in her subjects' welfare . . . 355		*Dec.* 14. Severity of 'The Times' . . 358
	Her neglect of ceremonial duties . . 356	1865,	*Feb.* Partial reaction in her favour . . 359
	Vehement attacks . . 357	1866,	*Dec.* 4. John Bright's defence of her . . 360
	April 6. The Queen's reply 358		Her refusal to leave her retirement . . . 360

XXXII

THE SEVEN WEEKS' WAR

1865,	*Aug.* Visit to Coburg . 362	1866	Grants to Princess Helena and Prince Alfred 368
	Betrothal of Princess Helena . . . 362		War between Austria and Prussia . . 368
	Aug. Dissolution of Parliament . . . 363		*March.* The Queen's offer of mediation . 369
	Oct. 18. Death of Palmerston . . . 363		The Queen and the Reform Bill . . . 370
	Lord Russell Prime Minister . . . 364		Her defiance of Lord Russell . . . 370
	Dec. 10. Death of the King of the Belgians 365		*June* 19. His resignation 370
1866,	*Feb.* 10. The Queen opens Parliament . 366		*July* 6. Lord Derby Prime Minister . . 372
	March-April. Visits to Aldershot . . . 367		*June* 28. Prussia seizes Hanover . . . 373
	June 12. Marriage of Princess Mary of Cambridge 368		*July* 3. Battle of Sadowa and end of the Seven Weeks' War . 374
	July 5. Marriage of Princess Helena . . 368		

XXXIII

THE PRINCE CONSORT'S BIOGRAPHY

	PAGE
1866, *Oct.* Rest at Balmoral	375
Oct. 16. The Queen at Aberdeen	375
Nov. 30. At Wolverhampton	375
1874–80 The biography of Prince Consort	376
Choice of (Sir) Theodore Martin as biographer	376
1874–80 Character of the work	377
Her faith in its utility	378
1874 Her dislike of the Greville Memoirs	378
1867 Publication of 'Leaves from a Journal'	378
Cordial relations with Lord Derby's ministry	379

XXXIV

FOREIGN AFFAIRS IN 1867

	PAGE
1867 Disraeli's Reform Bill	381
The Queen's distrust of Napoleon III.	381
May. The Luxemburg affair	382
June 20. Murder of Emperor Maximilian	383
1867 The Queen's horror	384
June. Foreign Sovereigns at Court	384
July. The Sultan's visit	385
Aug. 22. At Abbotsford	386
Continued depression	386

XXXV

DISRAELI'S FIRST ADMINISTRATION

	PAGE
1868, *Feb.* Disraeli Prime Minister	387
The Queen's growing respect for him	387
May 1. Gladstone and the Irish Church	388
The Queen's dislike of Disestablishment	388
Disraeli's offer of resignation	389
Attitude of the Opposition	389
May 5. The Queen elects to dissolve Parliament	390
Her constitutional rights	391
Her respect for parliamentary powers	391
1868 Public functions	392
Aug. First visit to Switzerland	392
Sept. Her retreat of Glassalt Shiel	393
Nov. Disraeli's defeat	393
Nov. 30. Her special mark of favour to him	394
Appointment of Archbishop Tait	394
Friendship with Tait	395
Her attitude to bishops	395
Her view of Church patronage	396
Interference in Church appointments	396
Her respect for the Scottish Church	397

XXXVI

GLADSTONE'S FIRST ADMINISTRATION

	PAGE
1868, *Dec.* Gladstone Prime Minister	399
Divergent views of foreign policy	400
The Government's legislative activity	401
Gladstone and the Queen's private affairs	402
Gladstone's colleagues	403
Feb.–May. The Irish Church Bill	404
The Queen's attitude	404
Her mediation with the Lords	405
1868, *June.* Her appeal to the Lords	406
1869, *Mar.* The Queen and sailors' beards	407
Public activities	407
Intercourse with men of letters	408
Tennyson	408
May. Meeting with Carlyle	409
George Eliot and Dickens	409
Dr. Samuel Smiles	410

XXXVII

ANXIOUS YEARS, 1870–1

	PAGE
1870, *July.* Lord Clarendon's death	411
July. The Franco-German war	411
The Queen's sympathy with Germany	411
Her pity for France	412
Oct. Bismarck resents her interference	412
Decline of British influence	413
French gratitude	413
Her care of the Empress Eugénie and Napoleon III.	414
Domestic politics	414
Dislike of Cardwell's army reforms	415
1871 Abolition of purchase in the army	416
1870 Continued complaints of her seclusion	417
Oct. Betrothal of Princess Louise	417
1871, *Feb.* 9. Queen opens Parliament	418
1871 Grants to Princess Louise and Prince Arthur	418
March 21. Princess Louise's marriage	419
Sept. The Queen's illness	419
Nov.–Dec. Illness of the Prince of Wales	420
1872, *Feb.* 27. Public thanksgiving	420
1871 Display of Republican tendencies	421
Popular censure of the Sovereign	421
Attacks on her income	422
Her reputed affluence	423
Nov. Falsity of public rumours	423
Official refutations	424
1872, *March* 19. Debate on the Civil List	424
Causes of her future popularity	424

XXXVIII

OLD FRIENDS AND NEW

1872, *March–April.* Visit to Germany . . . 426
Feb. 12. Assassination of Lord Mayo . . 426
June 16. Death of Norman Macleod . . 427
Sept. 23. Death of the Queen's step-sister . 427
1873, *Jan.* 9. Death of Napoleon III. . . . 427
1873, *Mar.* 12. Disraeli declines office . . 428
April 2. Visit to East London . . . 429
June–July. First visit of the Shah of Persia 429
Relations with Russia . 430
1874, *Jan.* 23. Marriage of the Duke of Edinburgh . 431
Its small political significance . . . 431

XXXIX

DISRAELI IN POWER

1874, *Jan.* Disraeli in power . 432
Strength of his position 432
The Queen's approval of his political views . . 433
His personal fascination 433
His recognition of his own responsibilities . 434
Church legislation . 435
Continued irritation with Gladstone . . . 436
1875, *Feb.* Prince Leopold's illness . . . 436
Queen's fear of another Franco-German war . 437
June. Her appeals to the King of Prussia . 437
End of the correspondence 438
New links with India . 439
Sept.–May 1876. Prince of Wales's Indian tour 439
1876, *May* 1. Empress of India 439
Aug. 21. Disraeli becomes Earl of Beaconsfield . . . 441
Public appearances, 1874–6 441
London engagements . 442
April. Visit to Coburg 442
At Balmoral and Osborne 443
Crisis in Eastern Europe 443
1876 The Queen's efforts for peace 443
1877, *Dec.* 21. At Hughenden 445
The history of the Crimean war . . . 446
The third volume of the Prince Consort's biography . . . 447
1878 The Queen seeks to protect Turkey . . . 447
Her support of Beaconsfield's policy . . 447
June. The Congress of Berlin 448
July. The Queen welcomes Lord Beaconsfield 448
Domestic incidents . . 449
Dec. 14. Death of Princess Alice . . . 449
1879, *Mar.* 13. Marriage of the Duke of Connaught 450
April. First visit to Italy 450
June 19. The Prince Imperial's death . 451
The ministry's difficulties 451
Indian wars . . 452
Gladstone's Midlothian speeches . . . 453
The Queen's devotion to Lord Beaconsfield . . 453

XL

GLADSTONE RESUMES OFFICE

	PAGE
1880, *Mar.* Visit to Germany	455
Betrothal of Prince William of Prussia	455
The general election	456
April. The Queen's perplexity	456
April 23. Gladstone resumes office	457
April 24. Marriage of the King of Hanover's daughter	460
July. Memorial to the Prince Imperial	460
Queen's active control of ministers	461
Burials Act	462
Distrust of ministerial measures	462
Afghanistan	463
July 27. Maiwand	463
Recall of Sir Bartle Frere	464
1881 The Transvaal	464
Feb. 27. Majuba Hill	464
Sympathy with the troops	465
1881, *April* 19. Death of Beaconsfield	465
Marks of respect for his memory	466
1882 Murders of Tsar Alexander II. and President Garfield	467
War in Egypt	467
The Queen's activity	468
Her urgency	468
Sept. 13. The battle of Tel-el-Kebir	469
Reception of the troops	470
Mar. 2. Fifth attempt on her life	470
Irish affairs	470
May 6. Murder of Lord Frederick Cavendish	470
First visit to the Riviera	471
Mar. 23. Grant to Prince Leopold	471
April 27. Prince Leopold's marriage	472
Epping Forest and the new Law Courts	472

XLI

GENERAL GORDON

1883–5 Years of gloom	473
1883, *Jan.* Appointment of Archbishop Benson	475
March 27. Death of John Brown	475
Publication of 'More Leaves'	476
The Queen's lameness	476
1884, *March* 28. Prince Leopold's death	476
The Soudan	477
General Gordon	478
1885, *Jan.* 26. The Queen's view of Gordon's death	479
Feb. 17. Her letter to Miss Gordon	479
March. The gift of Gordon's Bible	480
Gordon's diary	481
The affairs of the Soudan	482
1884, *July.* The Queen and the Franchise Bill	483
Oct. She mediates between the two Houses of Parliament	484
At Darmstadt	485
The Princes of Battenberg	486
Nov. 29. Princess Beatrice's betrothal	486
1885, *July* 23. Her marriage	487
The Queen and Prince Henry of Battenberg	487
June 8. Gladstone's fall	488
Negotiations between Lord Salisbury and Gladstone	489
1886, *June* 24. Lord Salisbury's first ministry	490

XLII

THE JUBILEE OF 1887

Year	Entry	Page
1886	The Session	492
	The Queen's hostility to Home Rule	492
	June 7. Gladstone's defeat	493
	The Queen objects to dissolution	494
	July. The general election	494
	Lord Salisbury's second ministry	496
	The Queen and Lord Salisbury	496
1886	The Jubilee of her accession	497
	The growth of imperialism	498
	Her imperialist zeal	499
1887	She learns Hindustani	500
	March. Long visit to London	500
	June 21. The Jubilee	500
	The women's gift	502
	The ceremonials	502
	Historic significance of the celebration	503

XLIII

THE QUEEN AND HER GRANDCHILDREN

Year	Entry	Page
1887	Illness of the Crown Prince	504
1888	The Queen's sorrow	504
	March 9. Death of the Emperor William I.	504
	April. Visits to Italy and Germany	505
	Family quarrel in Berlin	505
	Prince Alexander of Battenberg's betrothal to Princess Victoria of Prussia	506
	April 24. The Queen and Bismarck	507
	Royal banquet at Charlottenburg	507
	June 15. Death of the Emperor Frederick	508
	Public engagements in Scotland	508
1889,	*March* 27. The Queen in Spain	509
	April 6. Death of the Duchess of Cambridge	509
1889	Renewed interest in the drama	509
	Public activity	510
	The Queen and her grandchildren	510
	Request for pecuniary provision	510
	False reports of her wealth	511
	Parliamentary committee of inquiry	512
	Government's proposal	512
	Gladstone's intervention	513
	Grants to Prince of Wales's children adopted	513
	The Queen's savings	514
	July. Visit of the Shah of Persia	515
	Aug. Visit of the German Emperor, William II.	515
	His later visits	515

XLIV

DOMESTIC AFFAIRS, 1889–96

	PAGE
1889–1901 Mode of life	516
1889, *Aug.* Visit to Wales	516
1889–96 Provincial engagements	517
1890–9 Foreign tours	517
1890–5 Last visits to Germany	518
Gratitude for foreign courtesy	519
1890–1900 Revival of the drama and opera at court	519
1891, *Dec.* Betrothal of the Duke of Clarence	520
1892, *Jan.* 14. His death	520
1893 *July* 6. The Duke of York's marriage	521
The Duchy of Saxe-Coburg-Gotha	521
1894, *Nov.* 23. The marriage of the Tsar Nicholas II.	521
June 23. Birth of Prince Edward of York (afterwards Wales)	522

XLV

THE POLITICAL SITUATION, 1892–6

1892–4 Gladstone again in office	524
1893, *Sept.* 8. The fate of the Home Rule Bill	525
1894, *Mar.* 2. The Queen's farewell to Gladstone	526
1897, *Jan.* Last meeting with Gladstone at Cimiez	527
1898, *May* 19. His death	528
1894, *March* 3. Lord Rosebery Prime Minister	528
1895 The Queen's want of enthusiasm for his Government	529
June. His resignation	530
1895 Lord Salisbury's third Government	530
The Queen and Mr. Chamberlain	530
Her critical energy	531
Her signature to commissions	532
1890–9 Her continued interest in the army	532
1896, *Jan.* 20. Death of Prince Henry of Battenberg	533
April 21. The Victorian Order	534
Sept.–Oct. Visit of the Tsar Nicholas II.	534

XLVI

THE DIAMOND JUBILEE OF 1897

1897 The Diamond Jubilee	536
June 22. Service outside St. Paul's Cathedral	537
The beacons	537
1897 The festivities	537
Naval review	538
The people's passionate loyalty	538

XLVII

THE GREAT BOER WAR

	PAGE
1897-8 Military expeditions	539
1898 The Queen's interest in Netley	540
Reviews of troops	540
1899, *May* 17. The Victoria and Albert Museum	540
1891 The Queen and Cecil Rhodes	541
1899 Negotiations with the Transvaal	541
1899-1901 The Great Boer War	542
1899, *Dec.* The Queen and the reinforcements	542
Nov. The Emperor William II.'s visit	543
Cordiality of the Emperor's welcome	543
The Queen's sympathy with her soldiers	544
Her Christmas gift	544
1900, *Feb.–June.* The successes in South Africa	544
The Irish soldiers	545
April 4-25. Fourth visit to Ireland	545
Lord Roberts in South Africa	546
1900, *March.* The Federation of Australia	547
1901, *Jan.* 1. The inauguration of the Australian Commonwealth	548
1900, *Aug.–Dec.* Distresses of the war	549
July 29. King Humbert's murder	549
The Duc d'Orleans's insults	550
Oct. The new Unionist House of Commons	551
Changes in the ministry	551
1897-9 The Queen's latest bereavements	552
1900, *July* 30. Death of Alfred, Duke of Saxe-Coburg	552
Oct. 29. Prince Christian Victor's death	553
June. The Empress Frederick's malady	553
Nov.–Dec. Final migrations of the Court	553
Dec. 12. The Queen's last public appearance	553
Dec. 18. Last journey to Osborne	553

XLVIII

THE QUEEN'S DEATH

	PAGE
1900 The Queen's health in old age	554
1895-1900 Her ailments	554
1900 *June–Dec.* Physical decay	555
Last days at Osborne	556
1901, *Jan.* 2 & 14. Lord Roberts's audiences	556
Jan. 11. Mr. Chamberlain's audience	556
Jan. 22. The Queen's death	556
1901 Her age and length of reign	557
Jan. 24. Accession of Edward VII.	557
Feb. 1-2. The Queen's funeral	557
The universal sorrow	558
Causes of the loyalty to her person	559
The Queen and imperial unity	559

XLIX

THE QUEEN'S POSITION AND CHARACTER

	PAGE
Her attitude to business of State	561
The benefits of her experience and detachment	561
Her loyalty to the constitution	562
Increase of royal influence and decay of royal power	563
Her absence from Parliament	563
Foreign travels	564
The Queen and Ireland	565
The Queen's foreign kindred	565
Her views of war	566
Her temperament	567
Her wide sympathies	568
Her recreations	568
Her attitude to art	569
Her tastes in music	569
Her devotion to the drama	570
Her taste in literature	570
Her dress and carriage	571
Her conversation	572
Her dislike of obsequiousness	572
Her sense of her public services	572
Her religion	573
Her dislike of Women's Rights	573
Her Stuart sympathies	574
Her reliance on her personal sentiment	574

APPENDIX

I

THE QUEEN'S DESCENDANTS

	PAGE
The Queen's children	579
Surviving children	579
Grandchildren and great-grandchildren	580
Her grandchildren and the reigning families of Europe	580
Marriages in England	580
Marriages in Germany	580
Marriage in the fourth generation	581

II

THE QUEEN'S PORTRAITS

	PAGE
Defects of the portraits	582
Before accession	582
After accession	582
After marriage	583
Pictures of ceremonials	583
Sculptures	584
National memorial	584
The coinage	584
Medals	585
Postage-stamps and postcards	585

III

PUBLISHED SOURCES OF INFORMATION

	PAGE
General authorities	586
Sir Theodore Martin's Biography of the Prince Consort	586
The Greville Memoirs and Memoirs of Duke Ernest of Saxe-Coburg	587
German memoirs	587
Relations with France	588
English memoirs of early days	588
Domestic memoirs	588
Diplomatic affairs	588
Political memoirs	589
Personal reminiscences	589
Minor notices	589
The royal household	589

IV

GROWTH OF THE BRITISH EMPIRE, 1837–1901

	PAGE
Extent of the acquisitions	590
Population and area	590
Europe	591
Asia outside India	591
India	592
Africa	592
West Africa	592
East Africa	593
South Africa	593
The Transvaal and Orange Free State	594
Central Africa	594
North America	594
Australasia	595
The Pacific Islands	595

INDEX 597

ILLUSTRATIONS

QUEEN VICTORIA AT THE AGE OF SEVENTY-EIGHT . . . . *Frontispiece*

> *From the original painting by Baron H. von Angeli, now at Windsor Castle.*

QUEEN VICTORIA AT THE AGE OF TWENTY . *To face p.* 108

> *From the original sketch by Sir Edwin Landseer, now at Windsor Castle.*

AUTOGRAPH DRAFT OF QUEEN VICTORIA'S LETTER TO MR. DISRAELI INVITING HIM TO FORM AN ADMINISTRATION, FEBRUARY 17, 1874 ,, 432

> *Reproduced in facsimile from the original at Windsor Castle.*

THE DIAMOND JUBILEE MEDAL OF 1897 . ,, 537

> *From a specimen kindly lent by Messrs. Spink & Son.*

MAP OF THE BRITISH EMPIRE IN 1901 . ,, 590

QUEEN VICTORIA:

A BIOGRAPHY

I

PARENTAGE AND BIRTH

VICTORIA, Queen of the United Kingdom of Great Britain and Ireland and Empress of India, was granddaughter of George III., who was King of Great Britain and Ireland from his accession on October 25, 1760, until his death on January 29, 1820. George III.'s fourth son, Edward Augustus, Duke of Kent, was her father, and she was his only child.

Queen Victoria's ancestry.

The Hanoverian dynasty, to which Queen Victoria belonged, traces authentic descent from Alfred the Great, who was in the ninth century King of the West Saxons and overlord of all the English. One female descendant of King Alfred in the direct line married William the Conqueror, the first Norman wearer of the English crown; another female descendant was wife of the Conqueror's son and eventual successor, Henry I. Thus the blood of King Alfred flowed in no niggardly measure in the

Her descent from King Alfred.

veins of the progeny of Henry I., whence sprang the occupants of the English throne through the subsequent eight-and-twenty generations. The royal generations did not always succeed one another on the throne in regular hereditary sequence; some monarchs died without heirs, and the succession reverted to an elder generation. Many times, too, during the seven centuries that followed Henry I.'s death, there was matrimonial mingling of the English royal blood with new foreign strains, French, Spanish, Danish, and German. But save for the eleven years in the seventeenth century, when monarchy was temporarily exchanged for a republic, the ancient line knew no interruption. The enforced abdication of James II., Henry I.'s distant but direct heir, though it seemed to transmit the English crown to a foreigner, did not really divert the sovereignty from King Alfred's race, for James II.'s successor, William III., while hereditary Prince of the Dutch territory of Orange, was also son of James's sister, and Queen Mary, William's childless wife, was James's elder daughter.

The Hanoverian line. On the death without living issue in 1714 of Queen Anne, the younger of James II.'s daughters, the crown passed to her second cousin, Prince George of Hanover, the first Hanoverian King of England. Both Prince George's parents were born and bred in Germany. But his mother, the Electress Sophia, was daughter of James I.'s child and Queen Mary Stuart's grandchild, Elizabeth, the ill-fated English wife of Frederick V., Elector Palatine of the Rhine and the 'Winter King' of Bohemia. And Prince

George's father, who was Duke of Brunswick as well as Elector of Hanover and acknowledged the family surname of Welf or Guelph, boasted a direct ancestress in a daughter of the great English King Henry II. Thus George I. of England, despite his German birth and breeding and surname, was lineally connected, through both father and mother, with King Alfred's stock.

George I., George II., his heir, and Frederick, Prince of Wales, his eldest grandson (who died in his father's lifetime), all sought wives in Germany, the country in which each drew his first breath. George III., Queen Victoria's grandfather, as heir-apparent since the death in 1751 of his father, Frederick Prince of Wales, succeeded his grandfather George II. in 1760. He was the first of the Hanoverian line to be born in England, and he never set foot out of it. But, although he knew no other home than England, George III., like his immediate predecessors, chose a German wife. He married on September 8, 1761, the German Princess, Charlotte Sophia, second daughter of Charles Louis Frederick, the reigning Duke of Mecklenburg-Strelitz.

The marriages of the early Hanoverian kings.

George III.'s family.

George III.'s marriage proved a prolific union. Fifteen children—nine sons and six daughters—were born to the King and Queen between 1762 and 1783, and of these all but two survived infancy, and only one of the survivors died under thirty. Yet when George III.'s long reign—the longest known to English history before that of Queen Victoria—was nearing its end, fate seemed to have decreed that the old King's large family should maintain the succession to his throne through no more than a single generation.

The succession to the Crown in 1817.

On May 2, 1816, Princess Charlotte Augusta of Wales, only child of the Prince Regent (George III.'s heir), had married Prince Leopold of Saxe-Coburg, and on November 6, 1817, she died after the birth of a stillborn son. The crown was thereby deprived of its only legitimate representative in the third generation.

George III.'s sons.

Of the seven sons of George III. who reached adult years, three, at the date of Princess Charlotte's death, were bachelors, and the four who were married were either childless or without lawful issue.[1] Of the five surviving daughters of the King, three were married but had no children living, and two were elderly spinsters. With a view to maintaining the succession it was deemed essential after Princess Charlotte's demise that the three unmarried sons, all of whom were middle-aged—William, Duke of Clarence, the third son; Edward, Duke of Kent, the fourth son; and Adolphus Frederick, Duke of Cambridge, the seventh and youngest son—should marry without delay.

Three marriages.

In each case the bride, in conformity with family tradition, was chosen from a princely family of

[1] The dead Princess Charlotte was the only child of the Prince Regent by his wife, Princess Caroline. George III.'s second son, Frederick, Duke of York, had married in 1791 the Princess Royal of Prussia, Frederick William II.'s daughter, by whom he had no issue. The fifth son, Ernest Augustus, Duke of Cumberland, had married in 1815 his first cousin on the maternal side, Princess Frederica of Mecklenburg-Strelitz, and his only child by her, a son George, was not born till 1819; while the sixth son, Augustus Frederick, Duke of Sussex, had in 1793 contracted a marriage which violated the Royal Marriage Act and was declared null and void.

Germany. The weddings followed one another with rapidity. On May 7, 1818, the Duke of Cambridge, who was residing in Hanover as the representative of his father, George III., in the government there, married, at Cassel, Augusta, daughter of Frederick, Landgrave of Hesse-Cassel, who was to live longer than any of her generation. On June 11, 1818, the Duke of Clarence wedded in his fifty-third year Adelaide, eldest daughter of George Frederick Charles, reigning Duke of Saxe-Meiningen. In the interval, on May 29, the Duke of Kent, who was in his fifty-first year, married a widowed sister of Prince Leopold of Saxe-Coburg, the premature death of whose wife, Princess Charlotte, had induced so much matrimonial activity in the English royal house.

Edward Augustus, Duke of Kent, who was born at Buckingham House, London, on November 2, 1767, had been sent to Hanover in boyhood to complete his education, and his German tutor, Baron Wangenheim, a rigorous disciplinarian, kept him so short of pocket-money that he then contracted a fixed habit, which proved a lifelong embarrassment, of incurring debts that he could not discharge. His father, who showed the young prince little sympathy, destined him as a child for the military profession, to which, long before his marriage, he proved his devotion in trying circumstances. He filled many responsible military posts in the colonies, taking part in the reduction of St. Lucia in the West Indies in 1794. In the spring of 1799 he was granted an income of 12,000*l.* a year, and was created Duke of Kent. From May of that year till July of the next he was Commander-in-Chief

The Duke of Kent.

of the forces in British North America, and during 1802–3 he was Governor of Gibraltar. There he acquired undeservedly a bad reputation. A somewhat tactless endeavour to suppress undoubted abuses which infected the garrison roused a mutiny among the troops. The result was that his military career ended in 1805, when he was gazetted a field-marshal. Small blame attached to him for the outbreak of insubordination which clouded his government of Gibraltar, but he had ruled his men with a harassing and pedantic rigour, and an almost superstitious regard for minutiæ of etiquette and equipment rendered him unpopular even with the officers. He was a Liberal in politics and took an enlightened view of large questions affecting both military and civil policy ; but after 1803 he had no active employment and long lived in comparative retirement at Ealing. Finally, in 1815, he sought asylum in Brussels from the importunities of an ever-growing army of creditors whose demands he was unable to meet. Pecuniary anxieties continued to depress him to the end of his life.

Duke of Kent's bride.
The Duke of Kent's bride, who was commonly known by the Christian name of Victoria, although her full Christian names were Mary Louisa Victoria, was nearly thirty-two years old. She was fourth daughter and youngest of the eight children of Francis Frederick Antony (1750–1806), reigning Duke of Saxe-Coburg and Saalfeld.[1] The day of her birth (Aug. 17,

[1] In 1825, the pleasant province of Saalfeld on the banks of the Saal was, by an awkward family arrangement, exchanged with the Duke of Saxe-Meiningen for the less attractive and more distant

1786) was that of the death of Frederick the Great, whose wife was her great-aunt, and the coincidence implanted in her a dislike of the Prussians, because her family treated the anniversary of her birth as a season of mourning for the demise of their great kinsman and not as one of rejoicing for her arrival in the world. At a very youthful age she married. Her husband was Ernest Charles, reigning Prince of Leiningen, whose second wife she became on September 21, 1803, at the age of seventeen. This first experience of matrimony lasted less than eleven years. The Prince of Leiningen died on July 4, 1814, leaving by her a son and a daughter. For the son, who was born on September 12, 1804, she was acting as regent and guardian when the Duke of Kent proposed marriage to her. Her responsibilities to her children and to the principality of Leiningen made her somewhat reluctant to accept the Duke's offer. But her father's family of Saxe-Coburg was unwilling for her to neglect an opportunity of reinforcing those intimate relations with the English reigning house which the Princess Charlotte's marriage had no sooner brought into being than they were threatened with extinction by her premature death. The Dowager Princess of Leiningen consequently married the Duke of Kent, the ceremony taking place at the ducal palace of Coburg on May 29, 1818.

The Princess was a cheerful woman of homely

duchy of Gotha. The Dukes of Saxe-Coburg-Saalfeld were thenceforth known as Dukes of Saxe-Coburg-Gotha. Cf. King Leopold's Reminiscences in Grey's *Early Years of the Prince Consort*, p. 393.

intellect and temperament, with a pronounced love of her family and her fatherland. Her kindred was exceptionally numerous; she maintained close relations with most of them, and domestic interests thus absorbed her attention through life. Besides the son and daughter of her first marriage, she had three surviving brothers and three sisters, all of whom married, and all but one of whom had issue. Fifteen nephews and three nieces reached maturity, and their marriages greatly extended her family connections. Most of her near kindred allied themselves matrimonially, as she in the first instance had done, with the smaller German reigning families. Her eldest brother, Ernest, who succeeded to the duchy of Saxe-Coburg, and was father of Albert, Prince Consort of Queen Victoria, twice married princesses of small German Courts—in the first instance of Saxe-Gotha-Altenburg, in the second of Würtemberg. A sister, Antoinette Ernestina Amelia, married Alexander Frederick Charles, Duke of Würtemberg. At the same time some matrimonial unions were effected by the Saxe-Coburg family with the royal houses of two Latin countries—France and Portugal. One of the Duchess of Kent's nephews married the Queen of Portugal,[1] while there were no fewer than four intermarriages on the part of her family with that of King Louis Philippe. A brother and two

---

[1] Queen Victoria's first cousin, Ferdinand (1816–1853), eldest son of the Duchess of Kent's second brother, Ferdinand (1785–1851), married in 1836, as his second wife, Maria da Gloria, Queen of Portugal; he was father by her of two successive Kings of Portugal (Pedro V. and Luis), and was grandfather of Carlos the present King, the son of King Luis.

of her nephews married respectively the French king's eldest, second, and third daughters, and a niece married his second son, the Duc de Nemours.¹ Members of the Hanoverian family on the English throne had long been accustomed to seek husbands or wives at the minor Courts of Germany, but the private relations of the English royal house with those Courts became far closer than before through the strong family sentiment which the Duchess of Kent not merely cherished personally, but instilled in her daughter, the future Queen of England. For the first time since the seventeenth century, too, the private ties of kinship and family feeling linked the sovereign of England with the rulers of France and Portugal.

Relations with France and Portugal.

The Duke of Kent brought his bride to England for the first time in July 1818, and the marriage ceremony was repeated at Kew Palace on the 11th of that month. The Duke received on his marriage an annuity of 6,000*l.* from Parliament, in addition to the earlier annuity of 12,000*l.*; but his pecuniary position was irremediable, and his income, which was mortgaged to his creditors and was administered

---

[1] The Duchess of Kent's third brother, and Queen Victoria's uncle, Prince Leopold, married in 1832, after he became King of the Belgians, Louis Philippe's eldest daughter, Princess Louise Marie of Orleans; Queen Victoria's first cousin, Prince Augustus, younger son of the Duchess of Kent's second brother, Ferdinand, married in 1843 Princess Marie Clementine, Louis Philippe's third daughter, while Prince Augustus's sister, Victoria, married in 1840 Louis Philippe's second son, the Duc de Nemours; Duke Friedrich Wilhelm, son of the Duchess of Kent's second sister, the Duchess of Würtemberg, married in 1837 Louis Philippe's second daughter, Princess Marie Christine.

by trustees on their behalf, was wholly inadequate to his needs. His brothers and sisters showed no disposition either to assist him or to treat his Duchess, who was not congenial to them, with much personal courtesy. He therefore left the country for Germany soon after the second marriage ceremony, and accepted the hospitality of his wife, with whom and with whose children by her former marriage he settled at her dower-house at Amorbach in her son's principality of Leiningen.

Queen Victoria's birth, May 24, 1819.

In the spring of 1819 the birth of a child became imminent. There was a likelihood, although at the moment it looked remote, that it might prove the heir to the English crown; the Duke and Duchess hurried to England so that the birth might take place on English soil. Alderman Matthew Wood, a trustee of the Duke's encumbered estate, encouraged the plan, and made some urgent pecuniary provision. The Prince Regent allotted the Duke and Duchess apartments in the palace at Kensington, in the south-east wing, and there, on Monday, May 24, 1819, at 4.15 in the morning, was born to them the girl who was the future Queen Victoria.[1]

The infant and the crown.

The Duke of Kent, while describing his daughter as 'a fine healthy child,' modestly deprecated congratulations which anticipated her succession to the throne, 'for while (he wrote) I have three brothers senior to myself, and one (i.e. the Duke of Clarence) possessing every reasonable prospect of having a family, I should deem it the height of presumption to

[1] A gilt plate above the mantelpiece of the room still attests the fact.

believe it probable that a future heir to the crown of England would spring from me.' The child's maternal grandmother, the Duchess of Saxe-Coburg-Saalfeld, wrote of her as ' a Charlotte—destined perhaps to play a great part one day.' ' The English like queens,' she added, ' and the niece [she was both niece through her mother, and first cousin through her father] of the ever-lamented beloved Charlotte will be most dear to them.' Her father remarked that the infant was too healthy to satisfy the members of his own family, who regarded her as an unwelcome intruder.

The child held, in fact, the fifth place in the succession. Between her and the crown there stood her three uncles, the Prince Regent, the Duke of York, and the Duke of Clarence, besides her father the Duke of Kent. *Her place in the succession.*

Formal honours were accorded the newly born Princess as one in the direct line. The privy councillors who were summoned to Kensington on her birth included her uncle the Duke of Sussex, the Duke of Wellington, and the Marquis of Lansdowne, together with George Canning, the president of the Board of Control, and Nicholas Vansittart, the Chancellor of the Exchequer, two leading members of Lord Liverpool's long-lived Tory ministry, which had already been seven years in office. On June 24 the infant's baptism took place in the grand saloon at Kensington Palace. The gold font, which was part of the regalia of the kingdom, was brought from the Tower, and crimson velvet curtains from the chapel at St. James's. There were three sponsors, of whom the most interesting was the Tsar, Alexander I., the *Baptism, June 24, 1819.*

head of the Holy Alliance, and the most powerful monarch on the continent of Europe. The Regent and the Tory prime minister, Lord Liverpool, desired to maintain friendly relations with Russia, and the offer of Prince Lieven, Russian Ambassador in London, that his master should act as sponsor was accepted with alacrity. The second sponsor was the child's eldest aunt, the widowed Queen of Würtemberg (George III.'s eldest daughter and the Princess Royal of England). The third sponsor was the infant's maternal grandmother, the Duchess of Saxe-Coburg-Saalfeld, eldest daughter of Count Reuss von Elbersdorf XXIV. None of the three sponsors were present at the christening in person. They were represented respectively by the child's uncle, the Duke of York, and by her aunts, the Princess Augusta and the Duchess of Gloucester.

Her baptismal names.

The rite was performed by Dr. Manners Sutton, Archbishop of Canterbury, assisted by William Howley, Bishop of London. The Prince Regent, who was present, declared that the one name of 'Alexandrina,' after the Tsar, was sufficient. The Duke of Kent requested that a second name should be added. The Prince Regent suggested 'Georgina.' The Duke of Kent urged 'Elizabeth.' Thereupon the Regent brusquely insisted on the mother's name of Victoria, at the same time stipulating that it should follow that of Alexandrina. The Princess was therefore named at baptism Alexandrina Victoria, and for several years was known in the family circle as 'Drina.' But her mother was desirous from the first to give public and official prominence to her second name of Victoria.

When only four the child signed her name as Victoria, and the autograph is now in the British Museum.[1] The appellation, although it was not unknown in England, had a foreign sound to English ears, and its bestowal on the Princess excited no little insular prejudice.[2]

When the child was a month old her parents removed with her to Claremont, the residence, near Esher in Surrey, which had been granted for life to her uncle, Prince Leopold, the widowed husband of the Princess Charlotte, and remained his property till his death in 1865. In August 1819 the Princess was vaccinated, and the royal sanction, which was thus for the first time conferred upon the operation, greatly extended its popularity. Before the end of the month the Duchess of Kent learned from her mother of the birth on the 26th, at the ducal summer palace of Rosenau in Coburg, of the second son (Albert) of her eldest brother, the reigning Duke of Saxe-Coburg-Saalfeld (afterwards Gotha). Madame Siebold, the German accoucheuse, who had attended Princess Victoria's birth, was also

At Claremont and Sidmouth, Aug. 1819–Jan. 1820.

---

[1] Addit. MS. 18204, fol. 12.

The name was well known in the Roman Empire. It was borne by a Gaulish princess, who claimed in the third century A.D. imperial power over Gaul and the western provinces of the empire (cf. Gibbon, vol. i. ch. xi.). Subsequently under the italianised form of Vittoria it was widely used in mediæval and modern Italy. The Duchess of Kent seems to have been the first of the Saxe-Coburg family to bear it, but it was soon conferred, in compliment to her, on several of her nieces. It was found in at least one Anglo-Italian family before it achieved royal prestige in England. Vincent Novello, the music publisher of London, named his daughter (who became Mrs. Cowden Clarke) Mary Victoria, after his friend, the Rev. Victor Fryer; born ten years before the future Queen, she was in girlhood known solely as Victoria in her family circle.

present at Prince Albert's, and in the Saxe-Coburg circle the names of the two children were at once linked together. In December 1819 the Duke and Duchess of Kent went with their daughter to Sidmouth, where they rented a small house called Woolbrook Glen, which is still standing. The sojourn there did not lack incident. The discharge of an arrow by a mischievous boy at the window of the room which the infant was occupying went very near ending her career before it was well begun.

After a few weeks at Sidmouth the child's position in the State underwent momentous change. On January 20, 1820, her father, the Duke of Kent, fell ill of a cold contracted while walking in wet weather; inflammation of the lungs set in, and on the 23rd he died. Six days later, on January 29, 1820, her grandfather, King George III., who had long been blind and imbecile, passed away, and her eldest uncle, the Prince Regent, became King at the age of fifty-eight. Thus the four lives that had intervened between the Princess and the highest place in the State were suddenly reduced to two—those of her uncles, the Duke of York, who was fifty-seven, and the Duke of Clarence, who was fifty-five. Neither Duke had a lawful heir, or seemed likely to have one. A great future for the child of the Duchess of Kent thus seemed assured.

Deaths of Duke of Kent and George III., Jan. 1820.

Position of the Duchess of Kent.

The immediate position of mother and daughter was not, however, enviable. The Duke of Kent appointed his widow sole guardian of their child, with his friends General Wetherall and Sir John Conroy as executors of his will. Conroy, who had been ten years equerry to the Duke, and greatly in his confidence, thenceforth acted as major-domo for the Duchess, was constantly consulted by her, and lived under the same roof until the accession of the Princess, by whom he came to be cordially disliked. The Duchess was obnoxious to her husband's brothers, especially to the new King, and to her younger brothers-in-law, the Duke of Clarence, now heir-presumptive to the crown, and the Duke of Cumberland, who was the next heir to the throne after her daughter. Speaking later of her relations with the heads of the royal family, she said that on her husband's death she stood with her daughter 'friendless and alone, in a country that was not her own.' Not the least of her trials was her inability to speak English.

Although the Duke had made a will, he left no property to which his creditors had not a first claim. He had made a vain effort shortly before his death to reduce his embarrassments by applying to Parliament for permission to sell, by lottery, for the benefit of his estate, the property at Ealing which he had acquired in 1805. But the requisite permission was refused. In the result, he only bequeathed a heavy mass of debts, which the Princess, to her lasting credit, took in course of time on her own shoulders and discharged to the last penny.[1] Parliament had directed that the annuity of 6,000*l*. granted to the Duke on his marriage in 1818 should in the event of his death pass to his widow for her lifetime; apartments

Her pecuniary difficulties.

---

[1] See p. 81.

in Kensington Palace, which had been allotted to the Duke and Duchess on their arrival in England in 1819, remained at the Duchess's disposal; but she and her daughter had no other acknowledged resources.

Sympathy of her sisters-in-law.

The Duchess's desolate lot was not without mitigation. She had the sympathy of her late husband's unmarried sisters, Sophia and Augusta, who admired her self-possession at this critical period; and the kindly Duchess of Clarence, a German Princess, like herself, who could converse with her in her mother-tongue, paid her constant visits.

Prince Leopold and his niece.

But her main source of consolation was her brother Leopold, who proved an invaluable adviser and a generous benefactor. As soon as the gravity of the Duke's illness declared itself he had hurried to Sidmouth to console and counsel her. Deprived by death some four years before of wife and child, he had since led an aimless career of travel in England and Scotland, without any recognised position or influence. It was congenial to him to assume informally the place of a father to the Duke's child. Although, owing to his German education, he was never quite at home in English politics, he was cautious and far-seeing, and was qualified for the rôles of guardian of his niece and counsellor of his sister, which he at once assumed.

The Duchess of Kent's resolve.

It was Prince Leopold who impressed on the Duchess of Kent the destiny in store for her youngest child. Her responsibilities as Regent of the principality of Leiningen in behalf of her son by her first marriage weighed heavily upon her. But, strong as was her affection for her German kindred, anxious as she was to maintain close relations with them, and sensitive as she was to the indifference manifested to her at the English Court, she, under Leopold's influence, resigned the regency of Leiningen, and resolved to reside permanently in England. After deliberating with her brother, she chose as 'the whole object of her future life' the education of her younger daughter in view of the likelihood of her accession to the English throne. Until the Princess's marriage, when she was in her twenty-first year, mother and daughter were never parted for a day.

Of her father the Princess had no personal remembrance, but her mother taught her to honour his memory. She cherished, from childhood to old age, stories of his active career in the West Indies, in Canada, and at Gibraltar. When, as Queen Victoria, she presented new colours to his old regiment, the Royal Scots, at Ballater on September 26, 1876, she said of him: 'He was proud of his profession, and I was always told to consider myself a soldier's child.' Strong sympathy with the army was a main characteristic of her career. Nor were her father's strong liberal, even radical, sympathies concealed from her. At the time of his death he was arranging to visit New Lanark with his wife as the guests of the socialist, Robert Owen, with whose principles he had already declared his agreement.[1] The Princess's whiggish

The Duke of Kent's influence.

---

[1] Owen, *Autobiography*, 1857, p. 237. On June 26, 1819 (a month after Queen Victoria's birth), the Duke of Kent took the chair at a meeting held in the Freemasons' Hall for the purpose of appointing a committee to investigate and report on Mr. Owen's plan for

predilections in early life were not the least noteworthy part of her paternal inheritance.

providing for the poor, and ameliorating the condition of the working classes. The Duke commented ' on the anomalous condition of the country arising from the deficiency of productive employment for those who without it must be poor, in consequence of the excess to which manufactures had been extended by the late increase of machinery.' He expressed his belief in Owen's competency to devise measures to rectify the evil, drawing attention to the success of Owen's great experiment at New Lanark.

II

CHILDHOOD

It was in the spring of 1820 that the Duchess of Kent took up her permanent abode in Kensington Palace, and there, in comparative seclusion, the Princess spent most of her first eighteen years of life. Kensington was then effectually cut off from London by market gardens and country lanes, and formed a quiet rural retreat from the bustling activity of the capital. Besides her infant daughter the Duchess had another companion in her child by her first husband, Princess Féodore of Leiningen,[1] who was twelve years Princess Victoria's senior, and inspired her with deep and lasting affection. Prince Charles of Leiningen, Princess Victoria's stepbrother, was a frequent visitor, and to him also she was much attached. A child about her own age who was constantly with her in early days was the daughter of Sir John Conroy, chief of her mother's household; the Duchess had stood godmother to the little girl, and had conferred on her her own names of Victoria Maria Louisa.[2]

Chief among the permanent adult members of

Settlement at Kensington.

---

[1] Born December 7, 1807; died September 23, 1872.
[2] Miss Conroy married on March 10, 1842, Major Wyndham Edward Hanmer, and died February 9, 1866.

Fräulein Lehzen.

the Kensington household was Louise Lehzen, the daughter of a Lutheran clergyman of Hanover, who had acted as governess of the Princess Féodore from 1818. Princess Victoria's education was begun in 1824, when Fräulein Lehzen transferred her services from the elder to the younger daughter. Voluble in talk, severe in manner, restricted in information, conventional in opinion, she was never popular in English society; but she was shrewd in judgment and wholehearted in her devotion to her charge, whom she at once inspired with affection and fear, the memory of which never wholly left her pupil. Long after the Princess's girlhood close intimacy continued between the two, and, as long as Lehzen lived, they corresponded with each other and exchanged gifts with regularity. At Lehzen's death in 1870 the Queen wrote of her: 'She knew me from six months old, and from my fifth to my eighteenth year devoted all her care and energies to me with most wonderful abnegation of self, never even taking one day's holiday. I adored, though I was greatly in awe of her. She really seemed to have no thought but for me.'

Appointment of a preceptor, 1827.

The need of fittingly providing for the Princess's education first brought the child to the formal notice of Parliament. In 1825 Parliament unanimously resolved to allow the Duchess of Kent an additional 6,000*l*. a year 'for the purpose of making an adequate provision for the honourable support and education of her Highness Princess Alexandrina Victoria of Kent.'[1] English instruction was needful, and Fräulein Lehzen, who was never officially recognised to fill any posi-

---

[1] *Hansard*, new ser. xiii. 909-27.

tion except that of 'lady attendant on Princess Victoria,' was hardly qualified for the whole of the teaching. On the advice of the Rev. Thomas Russell, vicar of Kensington, the Rev. George Davys, a country clergyman in middle life, became the Princess's preceptor. He was at the time vicar of a small Lincolnshire parish, but was soon transferred to the Crown living of All Hallows-on-the-Wall, in the City of London. In 1827 he was formally appointed director of the Princess's education, and took up his residence at Kensington Palace. To reconcile Fräulein Lehzen to the new situation, George IV. in the same year, at the friendly suggestion of his sister, Princess Sophia, made her a Hanoverian baroness.

Davys did his work discreetly. He gathered round him a band of efficient masters in special subjects of study, mainly reserving for himself religious knowledge and history. Although his personal religious views were decidedly evangelical, he was liberal in his attitude to all religious opinions, and he encouraged in his pupil a singularly tolerant temper, which served her in good stead in after life. Thomas Steward, the writing-master of Westminster School, taught her penmanship and arithmetic. She rapidly acquired great ease and speed in writing, although at the sacrifice of elegance. As a girl she corresponded volubly with her numerous kinsfolk, and she maintained the practice till the end of her life. During her girlhood the Duchess conscientiously caused her daughter to converse almost entirely in English, but German was the earliest language

Her teachers.

Study of languages.

she learned, and she always knew it as a mother-tongue. She studied it grammatically, together with German literature, under M. Barez. At first she spoke English with a slight German accent; but this was soon mended, and in mature years her pronunciation of English was thoroughly natural, although refined. As a young woman she liked to be regarded as an authority on English accent.[1] She was instructed in French by M. Grandineau, and came to speak it exceptionally well and fluently. At a later period, when she was fascinated by Italian opera, she studied Italian assiduously, and rarely lost an opportunity of speaking it. She was naturally a good linguist, though she showed no marked aptitude or liking for literary subjects of study. She was not permitted in youth to read novels. First-rate literature never greatly appealed to her.

Her youthful devotion to music and art,

To the practical pursuit of the arts the Princess applied herself as a girl with persistency and delight, but she was not conspicuously endowed with artistic taste. Music occupied much of her time. John Bernard Sale, organist of St. Margaret's, Westminster, and subsequently organist of the Chapel Royal, gave her her first lessons in singing in 1826. She developed a sweet soprano voice, and soon both sang and played the piano with good effect. Drawing was first taught her by Richard Westall, the Academician, who in 1829 painted one of the earliest portraits of her; she afterwards studied under Edwin (afterwards Sir Edwin) Landseer. Sketching in pencil or water-colours was a lifelong amusement, and after her marriage she at-

---

[1] Lady Lyttelton, *Letters.*

tempted etching. In both music and the pictorial arts she continued to seek instruction till comparatively late in life. To dancing, which she was first taught by Mlle. Bourdin, she was, like her mother, devoted; and, like the Duchess, danced with exceptional grace and energy until middle age. She was fond of learning and of arranging country dances, and was an enthusiastic adept at dancing games, of which her favourites were called respectively 'Young and old come out to play' and 'The Grandfather.' She was also from childhood a skilful horsewoman, and enjoyed physical exercise, taking part in all manner of indoor and outdoor pastimes. Battledore and shuttlecock remained a frequent recreation when she was well advanced in womanhood. *dancing and games.*

The Princess grew up an amiable, merry, affectionate, simple-hearted child—very considerate for others' comfort, scrupulously regardful of truth, and easily pleased by homely amusement. At the same time she was self-willed and impatient of restraint. Her memory was from the first singularly retentive. Great simplicity was encouraged in her general mode of life. She dressed without ostentation. Lord Albemarle watched her watering, at Kensington, a little garden of her own, wearing 'a large straw hat and a suit of white cotton,' her only ornament being 'a coloured fichu round the neck.'[1] Charles Knight watched her breakfasting in the open air, well in sight of Kensington Gardens, when she was nine years old, enjoying all the freedom of her years, and suddenly darting from the breakfast-table *Homely life at Kensington.*

[1] Earl of Albemarle, *Fifty Years of my Life*, 1876, ii. 227.

'to gather a flower in an adjoining pasture.' Leigh Hunt often met her walking at her ease in Kensington Gardens, and although he was chilled by the gorgeous raiment of the footman who followed her, he noticed the unaffected playfulness with which she treated a companion of her own age.

Early visitors to Kensington.

The Duchess of Kent was fond of presenting her daughter to her visitors at Kensington, who included men of distinction in all ranks of life. William Wilberforce describes how he received an invitation to visit the Duchess at Kensington Palace in July 1820, and how the Duchess received him 'with her fine animated child on the floor by her side with its playthings, of which I soon became one.'[1]

Sir Walter Scott's visit.

On May 19, 1828, Sir Walter Scott 'dined with the Duchess' and was 'presented to the little Princess Victoria—I hope they will change her name (he added)—the heir-apparent to the crown as things now stand. . . . This little lady is educating with much care, and watched so closely, that no busy maid has a moment to whisper, "you are heir of England."' But Sir Walter suggested 'I suspect, if we could dissect the little heart, we should find that some pigeon or other bird of the air had carried the matter.'[2]

Her knowledge of her rank.

According to a story recorded many years afterwards by Baroness Lehzen, the fact of the Princess's rank was carefully concealed from her until her twelfth year, when, after much consultation, it was solemnly revealed to her by the Baroness, who

---

[1] R. I. Wilberforce and S. Wilberforce, *Life of William Wilberforce*, 1838, v. 71–72.

[2] J. G. Lockhart, *Memoirs of Sir Walter Scott*, 1900, v. 200.

cunningly inserted in the child's book of English history a royal genealogical tree in which her place was prominently indicated. The Princess, the Baroness stated, received the information, of which she knew nothing before, with an ecstatic assurance that she would be 'good' thenceforth. But there were many opportunities open to her previously of learning the truth about her position, and on the story in the precise form that it took in the Baroness Lehzen's reminiscence the Queen herself threw doubt. Among the Princess's companions were the daughters of Heinrich von Bülow, the Prussian Ambassador in London, whose wife was daughter of Humboldt. When, on May 28, 1829, they and some other children spent an afternoon at Kensington at play with the Princess, each of them on leaving was presented by her with her portrait—an act which does not harmonise well with the ignorance of her rank with which the Baroness Lehzen was anxious to credit her.[1]

The most fondly remembered of the Princess's recreations were summer and autumn excursions to the country or to the seaside. Visits to her uncle Leopold's house at Claremont, near Esher, were repeated many times a year. There, she said, the happiest days of her youth were spent.[2] In the autumn of 1824 she was introduced at Claremont to Leopold's mother, who was her own godmother and grandmother, the Duchess Dowager of Saxe-Coburg, who stayed at Claremont for more than two months. The old Duchess was

Country excursions.

---

[1] *Gabriele von Bülow*, a Memoir, English transl. 1897, p. 163.
[2] Grey, *Early Years of the Prince Consort*, p. 392.

enthusiastic in praise of her granddaughter—'the sweet blossom of May' she called her—and she favoured the notion, which her son Leopold seems first to have suggested to her, that the girl might do worse than marry into the Saxe-Coburg family. Albert, the younger of the two sons of her eldest son, the reigning Duke of Saxe-Coburg—a boy of Victoria's own age—was seriously considered as a suitor. Thenceforth the Princess's uncle Leopold was as solicitous about the well-being of his nephew Albert as about that of his niece Victoria. A little later in the same year (1824) the child and her mother paid the first of many visits to Ramsgate, staying at Albion House. Broadstairs was also in early days a favourite resort of the Duchess and her daughter, and on returning thence on one occasion they paid a first visit to a nobleman, the Earl of Winchilsea, at Eastwell Park, Ashford.

Visit to Geo. IV., 1826. In 1826 the Princess and her mother were invited for the first time to visit the King, George IV., at Windsor. He was then residing at the royal lodge in the park while the castle was undergoing restoration, and his guests were allotted quarters at Cumberland Lodge. The King was gracious to his niece, and gave her the badge worn by members of the royal family. Her good spirits and frankness completely won the monarch's heart. On one occasion she especially pleased him by bidding a band play 'God save the King' after he had invited her to choose the tune. On August 17, 1826, she went with him on Virginia Water, and afterwards he drove her out in his phaeton.

Next year died without issue the Princess's uncle, the Duke of York, of whom she knew little, although just before his death, while he was living in the King's Road, Chelsea, he had invited her to pay him a visit, and had provided a punch-and-judy show for her amusement. His death left only her uncle the Duke of Clarence between herself and the throne, and her ultimate succession to the crown was now recognised to be almost certain.[1] On May 28, 1829, she attended a Court function for the first time. It was at St. James's Palace. The ten-year-old Queen of Portugal, Maria II. (da Gloria), a protégée of the English Government, was on a visit to England, and a children's ball was given in her honour by George IV. 'It was pretty enough,' wrote the gossip Greville, who was to record many later impressions of the Princess, 'and I saw for the first time the Queen of Portugal and our little Victoria. . . . The Queen is good-looking and has a sensible Austrian countenance. Our Princess is a short, plain-looking child, and not near so good-looking as the Portuguese. However, if nature has not done so much, fortune is likely to do a good deal more for her.'[2]

Death of the Duke of York, Jan. 5, 1827.

The Princess and the Queen of Portugal.

Queen Maria, who was only a month older than the Princess, had already worn her crown three years.

---

[1] The Duke of Clarence had had by his wife two daughters, but neither long survived her birth; the elder, Charlotte Augusta Louisa, was born and died the same day, March 29, 1819, and the younger, Elizabeth Georgina Adelaide, born December 10, 1820, died March 4, 1821. No legitimate child had been born to the Duke for nearly ten years when he ascended the throne in 1830.

[2] *Greville Memoirs*, 1st ser. i. 209.

Queen Victoria's sympathy with Portugal. By the efforts of the constitutional party in Portugal, and under the virtual protection of England, she had ascended her throne in 1826, at the age of seven, when her father, the absolutist King Pedro I., was forced by his disaffected subjects to surrender his European crown for the uneasy independent sovereignty of Brazil. The persistence of rebellion in Portugal forced the child-queen to spend the first seven years of her reign in retirement in northern Europe, chiefly at Paris, where she was educated. Before her final return to her own country in 1834, she had further meetings in England with Princess Victoria, who was from the first attracted by her gentle bearing. Their last meeting seems to have taken place in the Isle of Wight in the autumn of 1833. Afterwards (April 9, 1836) Queen Maria entered the family circle of the Saxe-Coburg house by marrying Princess Victoria's first cousin, Prince Ferdinand Augustus of Saxe-Coburg.[1] The Portuguese sovereign's dynastic and matrimonial fortunes ran parallel to some extent with those of the English Princess, and Queen Victoria always took an eager and sympathetic interest in Queen Maria's career, her descendants, and her country.

[1] Cf. *supra*, p. 8, note 1.

III

HEIR TO THE CROWN

In June 1830 the last stage but one in the Princess's progress towards the crown was reached. Her uncle George IV. died on June 26, and was succeeded by his brother William, Duke of Clarence, who had no legitimate children alive. The girl thus became heir-presumptive. The public was roused to interest itself in her, and in November 1830 her status was brought to the notice of Parliament. A Bill was introduced by the Lord Chancellor, Lord Lyndhurst, and was duly passed, which conferred the regency on the Duchess of Kent, in case the new King died before the Princess came of age. This mark of confidence was a source of great satisfaction to the Duchess. Next year William IV. invited Parliament to make further 'provision for Princess Alexandrina Victoria of Kent, in view of recent events.' The Government recommended that 10,000*l.* should be added to the Duchess of Kent's allowance on behalf of the Princess. Two influential members, Sir Matthew White Ridley and Sir Robert Inglis, while supporting the proposal, urged that the Princess should as Queen assume the style of Elizabeth II., and repeated the old complaint that the name Victoria

Heir-presumptive to the crown, 1830.

did not accord with the feelings of the English people. The speakers were representative country gentlemen of insular breeding, who resented whatever savoured of foreign origin. The Princess had, however, already taken a violent antipathy to Queen Elizabeth, and always deprecated any association with her. Happily for her peace of mind, the opposition to her baptismal names was not pressed. A hostile amendment to reduce the new allowance by one half was lost, and the Government's recommendation was ultimately adopted without qualification.[1]

Appointment of a governess.

The Duchess of Kent regarded the addition to her income as inadequate to the needs of her position, but greater dignity was at once secured for her household. The Duchess of Northumberland (a granddaughter of the great Lord Clive) was formally appointed governess of the Princess,[2] and her preceptor Davys was made Dean of Chester. The King requested her to attend Court functions. On July 20, 1830, dressed in deep mourning with a long Court train and veil reaching to the ground [3] she followed Queen Adelaide at a chapter of the Order of the Garter held at St. James's Palace. A few months later she was present at the prorogation of Parlia-

[1] *Hansard*, 3rd ser. v. 591, 654 seq.

[2] The Duchess of Northumberland was second daughter of Edward Clive, Earl of Powis (Lord Clive's heir); she married in 1817 Hugh Percy, third Duke of Northumberland, a very moderate Tory, who was Lord-Lieutenant of Ireland under the Duke of Wellington in 1825–6. Greville describes her as 'sensible, amiable, and good-humoured, ruling her husband in all things.' She died childless on July 27, 1866.

[3] Bülow, p. 191.

ment. On February 24, 1831, she attended her first drawing-room, in honour of Queen Adelaide's birthday. The King, who studied her closely, complained that she looked at him stonily.

No love was lost between the King and the Princess's mother, and the Duchess contrived to make the Princess's future attendances at his Court as few as possible. The King made the irregularity of her appearances a serious grievance. She and her mother were naturally expected to attend his coronation on September 8, 1831, but they did not come. Inquiries as to the cause of their absence were made in Parliament, and ministers gave the evasive answer that the King was satisfied with the situation; they declined to give specific reasons. The facts were that the King, whose view of the Princess's dynastic position was somewhat ambiguous, insisted that she should follow instead of precede his brothers in the royal procession through Westminster Abbey. The Duchess of Kent retorted that the Princess as heir-presumptive must take her place next the Sovereign. Neither William nor the Duchess would give way, and the Duchess declined to suffer her daughter to be present at the ceremony. The Queen often told her children how deeply she felt the disappointment, and how copious were her tears on learning her mother's decision. 'Nothing could console me,' she said, 'not even my dolls.' *[Her absence from Wm.IV.'s coronation, Sept. 8, 1831.]*

With the apparent access of prosperity went indeed many griefs and annoyances which caused more than passing tears, and permanently impressed the Princess's mind with a sense of the 'sadness' and *[Youthful griefs.]*

'unhappiness' of her youth. In January 1828 her constant companion, the Princess Féodore of Leiningen, left England for good, on her marriage to Prince von Hohenlohe-Langenburg, and the separation deeply pained Victoria. In 1830 alarm was felt at Kensington at the prospect of Prince Leopold's permanent removal to the continent. Both mother and daughter trusted to his guidance implicitly. The Princess was almost as deeply attached to him as to her mother. But separation from him was imminent. Although he declined the offer of the throne of Greece in 1830, his acceptance next year, at the suggestion of the English Government, of the throne of Belgium grieved the Princess acutely. As King of the Belgians he watched her interests with no less devotion than before, and he was an assiduous correspondent; but his absence from the country and his subsequent marriage in 1832 with Louis Philippe's daughter withdrew him from that constant supervision of her affairs to which she and her mother had grown accustomed. Two deaths which followed in the Saxe-Coburg family increased the sense of depression. The earlier loss did not justify deep regrets. The Duchess of Kent's sister-in-law, the mother of Prince Albert, who soon after his birth had been divorced, died in August 1831. But the death on November 16 of the Duchess Dowager of Saxe-Coburg, the Duchess of Kent's mother and the Princess's godmother and grandmother, who took the warmest interest in the child's future, was a lasting sorrow.

The main cause, however, of the Duchess of Kent's

anxieties, which her daughter shared, was the hostile attitude that William IV. assumed towards the Duchess. There was no reason to complain of the unconventional geniality with which the King welcomed her daughter on her private visits to him, nor would it be easy to exaggerate the maternal solicitude which the homely Duchess of Clarence, now become Queen Adelaide, showed the Princess. But the King resented the payment to the Duchess or to her daughter of that public consideration which the Princess's station clearly warranted. The King seems to have been moved by a senile jealousy of the Duchess's influence with the heiress-presumptive to the crown, and by a fear that his position was compromised by the Princess's intrusions on public notice. He repeatedly threatened to remove the girl from her mother's care, with a view to increasing her seclusion. When the two ladies received, in August 1831, a royal salute from the ships at Portsmouth on proceeding for their autumn holiday to a hired residence, Norris Castle, Isle of Wight, William IV. requested the Duchess voluntarily to forego such honours in the future, and, when she protested, he prohibited them from being offered. Incessant wrangling between him and the Duchess continued throughout the reign. *Wm.IV.'s treatment of her and her mother.*

Although the Duchess's alleged dependence on the counsels of Sir John Conroy, her major-domo, exposed her to some ill-conditioned criticism from general society and gossiping newspapers, her conduct from a maternal point of view continued unexceptionable. She did all she could to impress her daughter with the eminence of her future responsibilities. *Early travels in England.*

D

With that end in view she sought to make her acquainted with places of historic interest or commercial importance in the country over which she was to reign. On October 23, 1830, the Princess opened at Bath the Royal Victoria Park, and afterwards inaugurated the Victoria Drive at Malvern. These were the first instances in which the name of Victoria was associated with English topography. From 1832 onwards the Duchess accompanied her daughter year by year on extended tours, during which they were the guests of the nobility, or visited public works and manufacturing centres, so that the Princess might acquire practical knowledge of the industrial and social conditions of the people. The arrangements were made by Sir John Conroy, who was always of the party. William IV. made impotent protests against these 'royal progresses,' as he derisively called them, and the Princess was herself often tried by the strictness of behaviour which was enjoined on her in order to lend them adequate dignity.

Despite the open avowal in some quarters of a hope that she might never rise above the position of 'plain Miss Guelph,'[1] the royal heiress was everywhere well received, and when she took part in public functions she invariably left a favourable impression. Municipal corporations always offered her addresses of welcome; and the Duchess of Kent, in varying phraseology, replied in the Princess's behalf that it was 'the object of her life to render her daughter deserving of the affectionate solicitude she so universally inspires, and to make her worthy of

[1] *Croker Papers*, ii. 176.

the attachment and respect of a free and loyal people.'

The Tour of 1832.

The first tour, which took place in the autumn of 1832, introduced the Princess to the principality of Wales. Leaving Kensington in August, the party drove rapidly through Birmingham, Wolverhampton, and Shrewsbury to Powis Castle, the early home of her governess, the Duchess of Northumberland. Thence the Princess crossed the Menai Bridge to a house at Beaumaris, which she rented for a month. She presented prizes at the Eisteddfod there; but an outbreak of cholera shortened her stay, and she removed to Plas Newydd, which was lent to her mother by the Marquis of Anglesey. She laid the first stone of a boys' school in the neighbourhood on October 13, and made so good an impression that 'the Princess Victoria' was the theme set for a poetic competition in 1834 at the Cardiff Bardic Festival.[1] Passing on to Eaton Hall, the seat of Lord Grosvenor, she visited Chester on October 17, and opened a new bridge over the Dee, which was called Victoria Bridge. From October 17 to 24 she stayed with the Duke of Devonshire[2] at Chatsworth, and made many excursions in the neighbourhood, including a visit to Strutt's cotton mills at Belper.

In Wales.

Subsequently the Princess and her mother stayed at a long series of noblemen's houses—an experience

Visits to the nobility.

---

[1] The candidates were two hundred, and the prize was won by Mrs. Cornwell Baron Wilson.

[2] The sixth Duke of Devonshire was at the time Lord Chamberlain under Lord Grey's Whig ministry. He was a great collector of books and pictures. He died unmarried in 1858.

of which the Princess always retained vivid memories.
Among her noble hosts of 1832 the third Earl of
Liverpool, half-brother of the late Tory Prime Minister,
impressed her most deeply. He invited her to his
seat, Pitchford,[1] in Staffordshire. The invitation was
probably due to the fact that the Earl's daughter,
Lady Catherine Jenkinson, now a young lady of
twenty-one, had lately joined the Duchess of Kent's
household as lady-in-waiting. Lord Liverpool, who
was known to Tory circles as a politician of ability
and insight, was a man of great natural kindliness, and
the Princess at once formed for him an almost filial
affection. She also visited during the same autumn
Shugborough,[2] Lord Lichfield's house, also in Staffordshire; Oakley Court, near Windsor, the seat of Mr.
Clive; Hewell Grange, near Bromsgrove, the seat of
Lord Plymouth; and Wytham Abbey, the seat of the
Earl of Abingdon.

At Oxford.
From Wytham she and her mother twice went
over to Oxford (November 8–9), where they received
addresses from both town and university; Dean
Gaisford conducted them over Christ Church; they
spent some time at the Bodleian Library and at the
buildings of the University Press, and they lunched
with Vice-Chancellor Rowley at University College.
Robert Lowe (afterwards Viscount Sherbrooke), then
an undergraduate, described the incidents of the visit

---

[1] She revisited Pitchford, an old house dating from the fourteenth century, in 1833, 1834, and 1835, always occupying the same small plainly furnished bedroom, which had no fireplace. In 1836 she visited Lord Liverpool at his residence at Buxted.

[2] Cf. Mrs. Bagot's *Links with the Past*, 1901, pp. 9, 10.

in a brilliant macaronic poem.[1] Leaving Oxford the royal party journeyed by way of High Wycombe and Uxbridge to Kensington. Throughout the tour the Princess dined with her mother and her hosts at seven o'clock each evening.

Henceforth social engagements multiplied rapidly. Much hospitality was practised at Kensington, and visitors of all kinds grew numerous. In November 1832 Captain Back came to explain his projected expedition to the North Pole. In January 1833 the portrait painters David Wilkie and George Hayter arrived to paint the Princess's portrait. On April 24 the Duchess of Kent, with a view to mollifying the King, entertained him at a large dinner party; the Princess was present only before and after dinner. In June, two of her first cousins, Princes Alexander and Ernest of Würtemberg, and her half-brother, the Prince of Leiningen, were her mother's guests. On May 24, 1833, the Princess's fourteenth birthday was celebrated at St. James's Palace by a juvenile ball given by the King in a rare burst of amiability.

Hospitalities at Kensington.

Another tour was arranged for the summer and autumn of 1833. The southern coast was the district

The tour of 1833.

---

[1] The poem is printed in Patchett Martin's *Life of Lord Sherbrooke*, i. 86–90. The opening lines run—

Dicite praeclaram, Musae, mihi dicite Kentae
Duchessam, Princessque simul Victoria nostro
Singatur versu, Conroianusque triumphus,
Et quàm shoutârunt Undergraduates atque Magistri,
Et quantum dederit Vice-Chancellor ipse refreshment.

'Conroianus triumphus' in the third line is a derisive reference to the presence of Sir John Conroy.

chosen. The royal party went a second time to Norris Castle, Isle of Wight, and made personal acquaintance with those parts of the island with which an important part of the Princess's after life was identified. She visited the energetic director of her mother's household, Sir John Conroy, at his residence, Osborne Lodge, on the site of which at a later date Queen Victoria built Osborne Cottage, and near which she erected Osborne House.[1] She explored Whippingham Church and East Cowes; but the main object of her present sojourn in the island was to visit national objects of interest on the neighbouring coast. At Portsmouth she went over the 'Victory,' Nelson's flagship. Crossing to Weymouth, on July 29, she spent some time at Melbury, Lord Ilchester's seat. On August 2 she and her mother arrived at Plymouth to inspect the dockyards. Next day the Princess presented on Plymouth Hoe new colours to the 89th regiment (Royal Irish Fusiliers), which was then stationed at Devonport. Lord Hill, the Commander-in-Chief, who happened to be at the barracks, took part in the ceremony. The Duchess of Kent on behalf of her daughter addressed the troops, declaring that her daughter's study of English history had inspired her with martial ardour. With the fortunes of the regiment the Princess always identified herself thenceforth. It was at a later date named the Princess Victoria's Royal Irish Fusiliers,[2] and twice again, in 1866 and 1889, she presented it with new

At Plymouth.

[1] See pp. 365 and 495.
[2] Cf. Rowland Brinckman's *Hist. Records of the Eighty-ninth (Princess Victoria's) Regiment*, 1888, pp. 83-4.

colours. The Princess afterwards made a cruise in the yacht 'Emerald' to Eddystone lighthouse, put in at Torquay, whence she visited Exeter, and thence sailed to Swanage.

The calls of public duty, to which she was loyally responding, at times caused her a sense of oppression, but she was enjoying at the same time enlarged opportunities of recreation. She frequently visited the theatre, in which she always delighted. But it was the Italian opera that roused her highest enthusiasm. She never forgot the deep impression that the great singers, Pasta, Malibran, and Grisi, Tamburini and Rubini, made on her girlhood. Grisi was her ideal vocalist, by whom she judged all others. All forms of music of the simpler melodic kinds, when artistically rendered, fascinated her. Her reverence for the violinist Paganini, after she had once heard him, never waned. In June 1834 she was an auditor at the royal musical festival that was given in Westminster Abbey. But of elaborate sacred oratorios she heard more than she approved, and she attributed to a surfeit in girlhood of that form of musical entertainment her distaste for Bach and Handel in later life. During her autumn holiday of 1833, when she stayed both at Tunbridge Wells and St. Leonards-on-Sea, she spent much of her time in playing and singing, and her instrument was then the harp.[1] In 1836 Lablache became her singing master, and he gave her lessons for nearly twenty years, long after her accession to the throne.[2]

Her delight in music and the drama.

[1] Cf. *Memoirs of Georgiana Lady Chatterton*, by E. H. Dering, 1901, p. 29.

[2] Luigi Lablache, a native of Naples, though the son of a French father, achieved the highest reputation on the continent of Europe

At Ascot, 1835.

Early in 1835, when she completed her sixteenth year, she suffered serious illness, happily a rare occurrence in her life. She had an attack of typhoid fever, but fortunately her recovery was rapid and complete. New and agreeable experiences were now crowding on her. In June she went for the first time to Ascot, and joined in the royal procession. The American observer, N. P. Willis, watched her listening with unaffected delight to an itinerant ballad singer, and thought her 'quite unnecessarily pretty and interesting,' but he regretfully anticipated that it would be the fate of 'the heir to such a crown as that of England' to be sold in marriage for political purposes without regard to her personal character or wishes.[1]

Her confirmation, July 30 1835.

On July 30, 1835, the Princess was confirmed at the Chapel Royal, St. James's. The address of the Archbishop of Canterbury (William Howley) on her future responsibilities affected her. She 'was drowned in tears and frightened to death.' Next Sunday, at the chapel of Kensington Palace, the Princess received the Holy Sacrament for the first time. The formidable Archbishop (Howley) again officiated, together with her preceptor, Davys, the Dean of Chester. In subsequent years she always fully appreciated the solemnity of the ceremony, though she was never a communicant on more than two occasions in each year and strongly objected to others taking the Sacra-

---

as an opera singer before he was first heard in London during the season of 1830. Thenceforth he was annually a leading performer in opera in London until his death at Naples in 1858, at the age of sixty-four.

[1] Willis, *Pencillings by the Way*, 1835, iii. 115.

ment more often. Until the end of her life, on the evening preceding the celebration she dined quietly with her family and ladies-in-waiting, and afterwards read with them religious books.

After a second visit in 1835 to Tunbridge Wells, where she stayed at Avoyne House, she made a progress through the north-east of England, which bore some resemblance to a triumphal procession. At York she remained a week at Bishopsthorp with Archbishop Harcourt, whose younger son, Colonel Francis Vernon Harcourt, was equerry to her mother.[1] She afterwards visited Lord Fitzwilliam at Wentworth House; thence she went over to Doncaster to witness the races, which attracted 'vast crowds of people.' She was next the guest of the Duke of Rutland at Belvoir Castle, and then, passing on to the Marquis of Exeter's at Burghley, was enthusiastically received by the people of Stamford on the road. Despite heavy rain, the civic authorities and crowds of the townsfolk met her and her mother outside the town and escorted them through it. An address was presented to the Duchess in behalf of the Princess, who was greeted as one 'destined to mount the throne of this realm.' Sir John Conroy handed a written answer to the Duchess 'just as the Prime Minister does to the King,' it was noted at the time.[2] A great ball at Burghley was opened by a dance in which the Princess's partner was her host the Marquis.

The tour of 1835.

---

[1] Col. Francis Vernon Harcourt married in 1837, after the Queen's accession, the Queen's close friend, Lady Catherine Jenkinson, Lord Liverpool's daughter, who was one of her mother's ladies-in-waiting.

[2] *Greville Memoirs*, 1st ser. i. 315–6.

The following day she reached Lynn on her way to Holkham, the Earl of Leicester's seat. The reception there was almost warmer than at Stamford. Navvies yoked themselves to the royal carriage and drew it round the town. Her last sojourn on this tour was at Euston Hall, the residence of the Duke of Grafton. After returning to Kensington, she spent the month of September at Ramsgate, making excursions to Walmer Castle and to Dover.

In 1836, when the Princess was seventeen, her uncle Leopold deemed that the time had arrived to apply a practical test to his scheme of uniting her in marriage with her first cousin, Prince Albert of Saxe-Coburg. The Prince had been carefully educated, and had grown into an intelligent, serious-minded youth. The Duchess of Kent was quite ready to second her brother's plan. Accordingly, King Leopold arranged with her that Albert and his elder brother Ernest, the heir-apparent to the duchy, should in the spring pay a visit of some weeks' duration to their aunt and her daughter at Kensington Palace.

First meeting with Prince Albert, 1836.

In May the two youths reached England, and Princess Victoria met Prince Albert for the first time. Varied hospitalities were offered him and his brother. William IV. and Queen Adelaide received them courteously, and they were frequently at Court. They saw the chief sights of London, and lunched with the Lord Mayor at the Mansion House.

Other possible suitors.

But William IV. was not likely to approve with warmth any scheme in regard to the Princess which his sister-in-law had adopted. Naturally he looked with small favour on Prince Albert as a suitor for his niece's hand. At any rate, he was resolved to provide her with a wider field of choice, and he therefore invited the Prince of Orange and his two sons as well as the young Duke William of Brunswick to be his guests at St. James's Palace during the same period that the Saxe-Coburg princes were with the Duchess and her daughter at Kensington. He somewhat maliciously gave the Princess every opportunity of meeting all the young men together. His own choice finally fell on Alexander, the younger son of the Prince of Orange. On May 30 the Duchess of Kent gave a brilliant ball at Kensington Palace, and found herself under the necessity of inviting Duke William of Brunswick and the Prince of Orange with his two sons, as well as her own *protégés*.[1] Among the general guests was the old Duke of Wellington, who paid the Princess every courtesy. She thus found herself the centre of an admiring throng, and betrayed no preference for any one of her admirers over another.

Some days later the Saxe-Coburg princes left

[1] Thomas Raikes wrote in his *Journal*, 1858, vol. i. p. 419, under the date May 30, 1836 : 'In England there are already arrived the Prince of Orange and his two sons, the Duke of Brunswick, and two Princes of Saxe-Coburg. They all attended a grand ball on Monday evening, given by the Duchess of Kent at Kensington Palace, perhaps with the hope of interesting our future Queen, the Princess Victoria. Indeed, as the Prince of Orange himself was formerly a candidate for the hand of the Princess Charlotte, it is not improbable that he has brought over his sons to England with that view ; but here again he meets with the two nephews of the hated Leopold, of whom he used to say, " Voilà un homme qui a pris ma femme et mon royaume."

England. Albert had constantly sketched and
played the piano with his cousin; but her ordinary
language, like that of those about her, was English,
which placed him at a disadvantage, for he had but
recently begun to learn it. The result of their visit
was vague and indecisive. Prince Albert wrote of
his cousin as 'very amiable,' and astonishingly self-
possessed, but parted with her heart-whole. The
Princess, however, had learned the suggested plan
from her uncle Leopold, whose wishes were law to
her, and on June 7, after Albert had left England,
she wrote ingenuously to Leopold that she commended the youth to her uncle's special protection,
adding, 'I hope and trust that all will go on prosper-
ously and well on this subject, now of so much importance to me.' Her views were uncoloured by
sentiment. Her personal inclinations hardly entered
into her estimate of the position of affairs. It was
natural and congenial to her to obey her uncle.[1]

Widening of the breach with Wm. IV.

In the early autumn of 1836 she paid another
visit to her friend, Lord Liverpool, who was then
living at Buxted Park, near Uckfield, and afterwards spent a quiet month at Ramsgate. The old
King was at the moment causing the Duchess of
Kent renewed disquietude. The Princess had altogether absented herself of late from Court, and the
King complained that he saw too little of her. At
the same time he neglected no occasion, however
inopportune, of advertising his growing dislike of her

---

[1] Cf. Raikes's *Journal*, i. 426, June 18, 1836 : ' I hear to-day that
the young Prince of Saxe-Coburg is the destined husband of our
Princess Victoria.'

mother. In August 1836 he invited mother and
daughter to Windsor to stay from the 12th for
eleven or twelve days; during the period both his
and the Queen's birthdays were to be celebrated.
The Duchess incensed the King by declining to come
before the 20th. On the arrival of the Duchess
and the Princess, the King greeted the Princess cordially, but angrily upbraided her mother with occupying, contrary to his orders, an excessive number of
rooms—seventeen in all—at Kensington Palace.
He neither understood, nor would, he said, 'endure
conduct so disrespectful to him.'

Next day, at the state banquet which he gave in
honour of his birthday, he publicly expressed the hope
that he might live till his niece came of age, so that
the kingdom might be spared the regency which Parliament had designed for the Duchess of Kent. He
described his sister-in-law, who sat beside him, as
a 'person' 'surrounded by evil advisers and incompetent to act with propriety.' 'I have no hesitation in
saying,' he proceeded, 'that I have been insulted—
grossly and continually insulted—by that person, but
I am determined to endure no longer a course of
behaviour so disrespectful to me. Amongst many
other things I have particularly to complain of the
manner in which that young lady [i.e. the Princess
Victoria, who was seated opposite the speaker] has
been kept away from my Court; she has been repeatedly kept from my drawing-rooms, at which
she ought always to have been present; but I am
fully resolved that this shall not happen again. I
would have her know that I am King, and I am

The King denounces the Duchess of Kent at Windsor, Aug. 21, 1836.

determined to make my authority respected, and for the future I shall insist and command that the Princess do upon all occasions appear at my Court, as it is her duty to do.' 'The Queen,' added Greville, who reported the singular oration, 'looked in deep distress, the Princess burst into tears, and the whole company were aghast. The Duchess of Kent said not a word.'[1] The breach between the King and the Princess's mother was complete.

Coming of age, May 24, 1837.
William IV.'s hope of living long enough to prevent a regency was fulfilled. Although his health was feeble, no serious crisis was feared when, on May 24, 1837, the Princess celebrated her eighteenth birthday, and thus came of age. At Kensington the occasion was worthily celebrated, and the hamlet kept holiday. The Princess was awakened by an *aubade*, and received many costly gifts. Addresses from public bodies were presented to her mother. To one from the Corporation of London the Duchess made, on behalf of her daughter, an elaborate reply. She pointed out that the Princess was in intercourse with all classes of society, and, after an indiscreet reference to the slights put on herself by the royal family, spoke volubly of the diffusion of religious knowledge, the preservation of the constitutional prerogatives of the Crown, and the protection of popular liberties as the proper aims of a sovereign. The King was loth to withdraw himself from the public rejoicing. He sent his niece a grand piano, and in the evening gave a state ball in her honour at St. James's Palace. Neither he nor

A state ball in her honour.

---

[1] *Greville Memoirs*, 1st ser. iii. 366 seq.

the Queen attended it, owing, it was stated, to illness. The Princess opened the entertainment in a quadrille with Lord FitzAlan, grandson of the Duke of Norfolk, and afterwards danced with Nicholas Esterhazy, son of the Austrian Ambassador.

The Princess's interests widened with her years, and with the prospect of independence that her coming of age brought with it. While her birthday was still in process of celebration, she paid two visits to the Royal Academy, which then for the first time held its exhibition in what is now the National Gallery, Trafalgar Square. She was the centre of attraction. On the first visit she shook hands and talked with Rogers the poet, and, hearing that the actor, Charles Kemble, was in the room, desired that he should be introduced to her. *Visit to the Royal Academy.*

A few days after the Princess's eighteenth birthday the King, in a letter addressed to the Duchess of Kent, proposed to form an independent household for the Princess. This the Duchess peremptorily declined 'in very unsatisfactory terms.' Thereupon the King sent directly to his niece an offer of 10,000*l.* a year to be at her disposal, independently of her mother. She accepted the proposal to her mother's chagrin. But the King's health was fast failing, and the project went no further. *The King's last communication to his niece.*

IV

THE ACCESSION TO THE THRONE

Death of Wm. IV., June 20, 1837.

No sooner had the celebrations of the Princess's majority ended than death put her in possession of the fullest rights that it could confer. Early in June it was announced that the King's health was breaking. On Tuesday, June 20, 1837, at twelve minutes past two in the morning, he died at Windsor Castle. The last barrier between Princess Victoria and the crown was thus removed.

Accession, June 20, 1837.

Howley, the Archbishop of Canterbury, who had performed the last religious rites at the bedside of the dying monarch, at once took leave of Queen Adelaide, and with Lord Conyngham, the Lord Chamberlain, rode through the early morning to Kensington to break the news to the new Sovereign. The distinguished messengers arrived there before 5 A.M. and found difficulty in obtaining admission. The porter refused to rouse the Princess. At length the Baroness Lehzen was sent for, and she reluctantly agreed to warn the Princess of their presence. The girl came into the room with a shawl thrown over her dressing-gown, her feet in slippers, and her hair falling down her back. Lord Conyngham dropped on his knee, saluted her as Queen, and kissed the hand she held towards him. The Archbishop did the like, addressing to her 'a sort of pastoral charge.' At the same time she was informed of the King's peaceful end. The Princess clasped her hands and anxiously asked for news of her aunt.[1]

The Prime Minister, Lord Melbourne, arrived before nine o'clock, and was at once received in audience. The Queen's uncle, the Duke of Sussex, and the Duke of Wellington, the most popular man in the State, also visited her. But it was from the Prime Minister, Lord Melbourne, alone that the constitution permitted her to receive counsel as to her official duties and conduct. *Lord Melbourne's first audience.*

The Privy Council was hastily summoned to meet at Kensington at 11 A.M. on the day of the King's death. On entering the room the Queen was met by her uncles, the Dukes of Cumberland and Sussex, and, having taken her seat, at once read the speech which Lord Melbourne had written for her some days before in consultation with Lord Lansdowne, the veteran President of the Council. She was dressed very plainly in black and wore no ornaments. She was already in mourning for the death of Queen Adelaide's mother.[2] After a reference to 'this awful responsibility imposed on me so suddenly and at so early a period of my life,' she spoke of herself as 'educated in England under the tender and enlightened care of a most affectionate mother; she had learned from her infancy to respect and love the constitution of her native country.' She would aim at securing the *The first Council.*

---

[1] Bunsen, i. 272.
[2] Louise, Duchess of Saxe-Meiningen, who died on April 30, 1837.

enjoyment of religious liberty and would protect the rights of all her subjects. She then took the oath, guaranteeing the security of the Church of Scotland. The ministers, including Lord Melbourne, First Lord of the Treasury, Lord John Russell, Home Secretary, and Lord Palmerston, Foreign Secretary, both of whom were to be among her future Prime Ministers, gave up their seals to her and she returned them to them. They then kissed her hand on reappointment, and the privy councillors took the oaths.

The Queen's bearing.

Although she was unusually short in stature (below five feet), and with no pretensions to beauty, her manner and movement were singularly unembarrassed, modest, graceful, and dignified, while her distinct and perfectly modulated elocution thrilled her auditors. 'I cannot describe to you,' wrote the Tory privy councillor Croker, by no means a lenient critic, 'with what a mixture of self-possession and feminine delicacy she read the paper. Her voice, which is naturally beautiful, was clear and untroubled, and her eye was bright and calm, neither bold nor downcast, but firm and soft. There was a blush on her cheek which made her look both handsomer and more interesting; and certainly she *did* look as interesting and handsome as any young lady I ever saw.'[1] 'She not merely filled her chair,' said the Duke of Wellington a few hours later, 'she filled the room.' Throughout the ceremony she conducted herself as though she had long been familiar with her part in it.[2]

[1] *Croker Papers*, ii. 359.
[2] Cf. Lane-Poole, *Life of Stratford Canning*, 1888, ii. 45 ; *Croker*

The admirable impression her composure created in the Council on her first public appearance as Queen was fully confirmed in the weeks that followed. Next day she drove to St. James's Palace to attend the formal proclamation of her accession to the throne. While the heralds recited their announcement she stood in full view of the public between Lord Melbourne and Lord Lansdowne, at the open window of the Privy Council chamber, looking on the quadrangle nearest Marlborough House. The crowd cheered vociferously, and prominent in the throng was the great Irish agitator, Daniel O'Connell, who waved his hat with conspicuous energy. 'At the sound of the first shouts the colour faded from the Queen's cheeks,' wrote Lord Albemarle, her first Master of the Horse, who was also an onlooker, 'and her eyes filled with tears. The emotion thus called forth imparted an additional charm to the winning courtesy with which the girl-sovereign accepted the proffered homage.'[1] *The Proclamation.*

After the proclamation the Queen saw Lord Hill, the Commander-in-Chief, Lord Cottenham, the Lord Chancellor, and other great officers of State. At noon her second Council was held at St. James's Palace, and all the cabinet ministers were present. Later in the day the Proclamation was repeated at Trafalgar Square, Temple Bar, Wood Street, and the Royal Exchange. *The second Council.*

Papers, ii. 359; Ashley, *Life of Palmerston*, i. 340. Disraeli gave in his novel *Sybil* (Book I., chapter vi.) a somewhat grandiloquent description of the scene from information supplied him by Lord Lyndhurst.

[1] Albemarle, *Fifty Years of my Life*, p. 378.

Her name as Sovereign.

Although the Queen signed the Privy Council register at her first Council in the name of Victoria only, in all the official documents which were prepared on the first day of her reign her name figured with the prefix of Alexandrina. In the Proclamation she was called 'Her Royal Majesty Alexandrina Victoria, Queen of the United Kingdom.' But, despite the sentiment that had been excited against the name Victoria, it was contrary to her wish to be known by any other. Papers omitting the prefix 'Alexandrina' were hastily substituted for those in which that prefix had been introduced, and from the second day of the new reign the Sovereign was known solely as Queen Victoria.

Dissemination of the name Victoria.

Thenceforth that name was accepted without cavil as of the worthiest English significance. It has since spread far among her subjects. It was conferred on one of the most prosperous colonies of the British Empire in 1851, and since on many smaller settlements or cities, while few municipalities in the United Kingdom or the empire have failed to employ it in the nomenclature of streets, parks, railway stations, or places of public assembly.[1]

Abroad, and even in some well-informed quarters

---

[1] Very early in the reign there was invented the light carriage on which the name Victoria was conferred. The London terminus of the London Chatham and Dover, and London Brighton and South Coast Railways was christened Victoria in 1846. The like cognomen—*Victoria regia*—was conferred on the great water-lily (of the order *Nymphæaceæ* and tribe *Nymphææ*) which was brought from Guiana to this country in 1838, and bloomed for the first time on English soil in 1849 when the flower was presented to the Queen.

at home, surprise was manifested at the tranquillity with which the nation saw the change of monarch effected. But the general enthusiasm that Queen Victoria's accession evoked was partly due to the contrast she presented with those who had lately occupied the throne. Since the century began there had been three kings of England—men all advanced in years—of whom the first was long an imbecile, the second won the reputation of a profligate, and the third was regarded as little better than a buffoon. The principle of monarchy was an article of faith with the British people which defects in the personal character of the monarch seemed unable to touch. But the substitution for kings whose personalities inspired no respect of an innocent girl, with what promised to be a long and virtuous life before her, evoked at the outset in the large mass of the people a new sentiment—a sentiment of chivalric devotion to the monarchy which gave it new stability and deprived revolution of all foothold. Although the play of party politics failed to render the sentiment universal, and some impolitic actions of the Queen herself, in the early and middle years of the reign, severely strained it, it was a plant that, once taking root, could not readily decay.

Public sentiment regarding her.

Politicians—of the high rank of Lord Palmerston, the Foreign Secretary in the Whig ministry, and Sir Robert Peel, leader of the Tories in the House of Commons—deplored the young Queen's inexperience and ignorance of the world. 'The personal character

Peel on the Queen's inexperience, July 5, 1837.

of a really constitutional king,' wrote Peel on July 5, 1837, 'of mature age, of experience in public affairs, and knowledge of men, manners, and customs, is, practically, so much ballast, keeping the vessel of State steady in her course, counteracting the levity of popular ministers, of orators forced by oratory into public councils, the blasts of democratic passions, the ground-swell of discontent, and the ignorant impatience for the relaxation of taxation. . . . But at this crisis of our fate we are deprived of this aid.'[1] Such dangers, however, as Peel associated at the moment with the immature age and character of his girlish Sovereign were, in a firmly established constitutional monarchy, more specious than real, and, as far as they were real, were capable of remedy by time.

The hopes of Sydney Smith and Lord John Russell.

Sydney Smith echoed more faithfully the national feeling, when, preaching in St. Paul's Cathedral on the first Sunday of her reign, he described the new Sovereign as 'a patriot Queen,' who might be expected to live to a ripe old age and to contribute to the happiness and prosperity of her people. 'We have had glorious female reigns,' said Lord John Russell, the Home Secretary under Melbourne, a few weeks later. 'Those of Elizabeth and Anne led us to great victories. Let us now hope that we are going to have a female reign illustrious in its deeds of peace—an Elizabeth without her tyranny, an Anne without her weakness.' The Whig leader added an earnest hope that in three ways at least—by the total abolition of

---

[1] *Croker Papers*, ii. 317.

slavery, by a more enlightened method of punishing crime, by the improved education of the people—' the reign of Victoria might prove celebrated among the nations of the earth and to our posterity.'[1]

[1] Walpole, *Life of Lord John Russell*, i. 284.

V

THE TUITION OF LORD MELBOURNE

The Queen and Hanover.

QUEEN VICTORIA's status at her accession was not in all respects identical with that of her predecessors. Owing to her sex, some changes in the position and duties of a British sovereign were inevitable. The Salic law rendered her incompetent to succeed to the throne of Hanover, which British sovereigns had filled since George the Elector of Hanover became George I. of England in 1714. Hanover had been elevated from an electorate to a kingdom by the congress of Vienna in 1814, and the kingdom now passed to the Queen's uncle, the next heir after her to the English throne, Ernest, Duke of Cumberland. The dissolution of the union between England and Hanover was acquiesced in readily by both countries. They had long drifted apart in political sentiments and aspirations.[1] The new King of Hanover was

[1] The severance of Hanover from England was, in the eyes of George III.'s surviving sons and daughters, one of the least agreeable results of their brother William's death, and of the succession of their youthful niece. Adolphus Frederick, Duke of Cambridge, George III.'s youngest surviving son, who had been Viceroy of Hanover for twenty-one years, was recalled, and Ernest, the new King of Hanover, was no favourite in his domestic circle. His sister, Princess Elizabeth (one of Queen Victoria's aunts), widow of Frederick, Landgrave of Hesse-Homburg, wrote dejectedly from Homburg July 1,

altogether out of sympathy with his royal niece. A man of violent temper and forbidding manner, he proved an illiberal and reactionary ruler. But Queen Victoria, in whom domestic feeling was always strong, took a lively and sympathetic interest, despite her uncle's surliness, in his personal affairs and in the fortunes of his family, and showed especial kindness to them in the trials that awaited them.[1]

At home the main alteration in Queen Victoria's duty as Sovereign related to the criminal law. Death had been the punishment awarded to every manner of felony until William IV.'s Parliament humanely reduced the number of capital offences to four or five. But capital sentences pronounced in London at the Old Bailey were still numerous, and it remained the custom for the Sovereign personally to revise these. At the close of each session they were reported to the Sovereign by the Recorder for final judgment. A girl was obviously unfitted to perform this repugnant task. Accordingly the Queen was promptly relieved of it by Act of Parliament (7 William IV.

The Queen and the criminal law.

1837, of the recent events: 'To me, dear Adolphus [Duke of Cambridge], leaving Hanover nearly kills me. I have not a doubt that my brother Ernest will do all in his power to do what is right and kind, but the whole thing is so changed, one's mind is quite overset.' *Correspondence of Princess Elizabeth of England*, edited by P. C. Yorke, 1898, p. 320. A subordinate effect of the separation of Hanover from England was the extinction of the Royal Guelphic Hanoverian Order, a decoration which had long been at the personal disposal of the British Sovereign as a reward of meritorious military or civil services.

[1] Some anecdotes illustrating King Ernest's repellent disposition and his jealousy of his royal niece are tactfully related by a daughter of his English equerry in *Tales of my Father*, by A. M. F., London, 1902.

and 1 Vict. cap. 77). Outside London the order of the Court to the Sheriff had long been sufficient to insure the execution of the death penalty. To that practice London now conformed, while the Home Secretary dealt henceforth by his sole authority with petitions affecting offenders capitally convicted, and was alone responsible for the grant of pardons, reprieves, or respites. Whenever capital sentences were modified by the Home Secretary, he made a report to that effect to the Queen, and occasionally it evoked comment from her; but his decision was always acted on as soon as it was formed. Thus, although the statute of 1837 formally reserved 'the royal prerogative of mercy,' the accession of a woman to the throne had the paradoxical effect of practically annulling almost all that survived of it.

Lord Melbourne's instruction.
But, while the Queen was not called on to do everything that her predecessors had done, she studied with ardour the routine duties of her station and was immersed from the moment of her accession in pressing business. The Prime Minister, Melbourne, approached his task of giving her political instruction with exceptional tact and consideration, and she proved on the whole an apt pupil, although from the outset she showed a wilfulness and a precocious self-reliance which at times embarrassed her tutor.

Lord Melbourne's career.
Lord Melbourne, who was fifty-eight years old at the Queen's accession, had had more than thirty years' active experience of politics. From 1806 to 1829 he had sat in the House of Commons. Thenceforth he filled his father's place in the House of Lords. He began his political career as a Whig, but joined

Canning's Tory administration as Irish Secretary in 1827, resigning the office after eleven months' trial of it. He subsequently identified himself exclusively with the Whig party, and rapidly became its leader. He was Home Secretary in Lord Grey's Reform ministry of 1830, and succeeded Lord Grey as Prime Minister on his resignation in 1834. At the end of that year he was the somewhat passive victim of the final encroachment which the wearer of an English crown ventured to make on the rights and independence of his chief minister. Melbourne and his colleagues, in November 1834, were dismissed by the personal act of Queen Victoria's predecessor, William IV., in consequence of an unreasoning fear on the Sovereign's part that the ministry designed an attack on the Established Church. This was the last occasion on which an English monarch shortened of his own motion the life of an administration. It proved in this instance of greater peril to the Crown than to its servants, and remained in permanence a deterrent example in the royal circle. Sir Robert Peel, who at the King's order replaced Lord Melbourne, at once dissolved Parliament, and the country expressed its view of the situation by returning a gigantic Whig majority. Peel hastily retired, and Melbourne resumed power in a far fuller measure than he had enjoyed it before. He retained it for six years continuously—two preceding and four succeeding Queen Victoria's accession.

Although Melbourne was a genuine Liberal, a firm believer in the virtues of the constitution, and a generous advocate of the great principle of religious *Melbourne's opinions and character.*

equality, he supported without conspicuous enthusiasm the recent legislation for electoral reform, and viewed with something like indifference some measures aiming at social amelioration which he helped to carry through Parliament. He was a champion of the Corn Laws and regarded the Radical programme of the day as the frothy chatter of troublesome agitators. Unconventional in manner and prone to use strong language, he was reckoned of cynical temperament, but his habitual tone of flippancy was probably assumed.[1] He found his main recreation in literature, and, despite his impatience of social restraint, was popular in ladies' society.

The private secretaryship. But Lord Melbourne was not merely the Queen's Prime Minister at the opening of her reign. Grave perplexities attached to the question of the appointment of a private secretary to the new Sovereign. Although former occupants of the throne had found such an officer absolutely essential to the due performance of their duties, the ministers feared the influence that one occupying so confidential a relation with a young untried girl might gain over her. With admirable self-denial Melbourne solved the difficulty by taking the post on himself for all public business. As both her Prime Minister and private secretary it was necessary for him to be always with the Court. For the first two years of her reign he was her constant companion, spending most of the

---

[1] His domestic affairs were unhappy. He had married in 1805 Lady Caroline Ponsonby, the only daughter of the third Earl of Bessborough; but soon after marriage his wife fell under the infatuation of Byron, and a separation followed some years later.

morning at work with her, riding with her of an afternoon, and dining with her of an evening. The readiness with which he adapted himself to the routine of the Court excited the surprise of his friends, but the paternal interest he obviously took in the Queen's welfare was acknowledged with gratitude alike by political allies and foes. He always treated the youthful Queen with a familiar, unembarrassed courtesy, which perfectly fitted his years and his confidential position.

As the Whig leader who had recently suffered humiliation through his Sovereign's imperfect apprehension of the royal place and power in the constitution, Melbourne was not backward in impressing on his royal pupil's attention those constitutional principles which denied the Sovereign genuine independence. It was with the Whigs that Queen Victoria's father had associated himself, and her mother had courted their favour at Kensington, while the bitter quarrel with William IV., an avowed patron of the Tories, was in progress. Association with the Whigs was personally congenial to her, and she made no secret of her preference for them over the Tories. None the less, her imperious and somewhat impatient temperament discouraged her from accepting too literally any political theories which trespassed on her sense of dignity or authority. She was naturally proud of her elevation and of the dignified responsibilities which nominally adhered to the Crown. While, therefore, receiving, for the most part without demur, her Whiggish instructor's warnings of the dependent place of a sovereign in a constitutional monarchy, she soon set her own interpretation on

The Queen's preference for the Whigs.

Her interpretation of Whig theories of monarchy.

the practical working of his doctrine. She was shrewdly conscious of her inexperience. She knew instinctively the ultimate need of trusting those who were older and better versed in affairs than herself. But she never unreservedly admitted, in word or thought, her subjection in any sense to her ministers. From almost the first to the last day of her reign she did not hesitate closely to interrogate her officers of state, to ask for time for consideration before accepting their decisions, and to express her own wishes and views frankly and ingenuously in all affairs of government that came before her. If her ministers expressed doubt as to what course to pursue, she rarely hesitated to point out that which she was prepared to follow. After giving voice to her opinion, she left the final choice of action or policy to her official advisers' discretion; but if she disapproved of their choice, or it failed of its effect, she exercised unsparingly the right of private rebuke.

The formation of her household.

The first duty of her ministers and herself was to create a royal household. The principles to be followed differed from those which had recently prevailed. It was necessary for a female sovereign to have women and not men as her personal attendants. She deprecated an establishment on the vast scale that was adopted by the last female sovereign in England—Queen Anne. A mistress of the robes, eight ladies of the bedchamber, eight women of the bedchamber, and eight maids of honour, she regarded as adequate. Her uncle Leopold wisely urged her to ignore political considerations in choosing her attendants. But she

The ladies of the household.

was without any close personal friends of the rank needed for the household offices; she had met some of the wives and daughters of the Whig ministers, and she accepted Lord Melbourne's injudicious advice to choose their first holders exclusively from them. She asked the Marchioness of Lansdowne to become mistress of the robes, and, although her health did not permit her to accept that post, the Marchioness agreed to act as principal lady of the bedchamber. The higher household dignity was filled (July 1, 1837) by the Duchess of Sutherland, who was soon one of the Queen's most intimate associates. Others of her first ladies-in-waiting were the Marchioness of Tavistock, the Countess of Charlemont, the Countess of Mulgrave, afterwards Marchioness of Normanby, and Lady Lyttelton. The Countess of Rosebery was invited, but declined to join them.[1]

In accordance with better established precedent, the gentlemen of her household were also chosen exclusively from orthodox supporters of the Whig ministry. The Queen only asserted herself by requesting that Sir John Conroy, the master of her mother's and

The gentlemen of the household.

[1] Cf. *Melbourne Papers*, 1889, p. 366; *Peel Papers*, ii. 460. The female portion of the Queen's household was finally constituted thus:—Mistress of the Robes: Duchess of Sutherland. Principal Lady of the Bedchamber: Marchioness of Lansdowne. Ladies of the Bedchamber: Marchioness of Tavistock, Countess of Charlemont, Countess of Mulgrave, Lady Portman, Lady Lyttelton, Lady Barham, Countess of Durham. Bedchamber Women: Lady Caroline Barrington, Lady Harriet Clive, Lady Charlotte Copley, Viscountess Forbes, Hon. Mrs. Brand, Lady Gardiner, Hon. Mrs. G. Campbell. Resident Woman of the Bedchamber: Miss Davys. Maids of Honour: Hon. Harriet Pitt, Hon. Margaret Dillon, Hon. Caroline Cocks, Hon. Miss Cavendish, Hon. Matilda Paget, Miss Amelia Murray, Miss Harriet Lester, Miss Mary Spring-Rice.

her own household, whom she never liked, should retire from her service; she gave him a pension of 3,000*l.* a year, but refused his request for an order and an Irish peerage.

<small>Foreign advisers.</small>

Melbourne's acceptance of the office of private secretary best guaranteed the Queen's course against pitfalls which might have involved disaster. Members of the family circle in which she had grown up claimed the right and duty of taking part in her guidance when she began the labour of her life. Owing to their foreign birth, it was in her own interest that their influence should be permanently counterbalanced by native counsel. King Leopold, the Queen's foster-father, who had hitherto controlled her career, and remained a trusted adviser till his death, had, as soon as she reached her majority, sent his confidential friend and former secretary, Baron Stockmar, to direct her political education. The Baron remained in continuous attendance on her, without official recognition, for the first fifteen months of her reign, and when the question of a choice of private secretary was first raised, the Queen expressed an infelicitous anxiety to appoint him. She felt genuine affection for him, and in later life often spoke of him as 'her dear old Baron,' whose worth was never, to her regret, adequately appreciated.

<small>Baron Stockmar.</small>

A native of Coburg, who originally came to England with Leopold in 1816 as his medical attendant, Stockmar was now fifty years old. Sincerely devoted to his master and to the Saxe-Coburg family, he sought no personal advantage from his association with them. Even Lord Palmerston, who bore him no affection, admitted that he was the most disinterested man he ever met. Intelligently read in English history, he studied with zeal the theory of the British constitution. There was genuine virtue in the substance of his reiterated advice that the Queen should endeavour to maintain a position above party and above intrigue. But, although sagacious, Stockmar was a pedant and a doctrinaire, and as a critic of English politics he cherished some perilous heresies. The internal working of the British government was never quite understood by him. His opinion that the Sovereign was no 'nodding mandarin' was arguable, but his contention that a monarch, if of competent ability, might act as his own minister was wholly fallacious. It was a dangerous doctrine to be instilled in Queen Victoria's ear.

The constant intercourse which Stockmar sought with her and her ministers was consequently felt by them to be embarrassing, and to be disadvantageous to the Queen. The English public generally resented his presence on the scene, and a hostile feeling against him quickly manifested itself. An impression got abroad that 'the German Baron' exerted on the Queen a mysterious anti-national influence 'behind the throne.' Abercromby, the Whig Speaker of the House of Commons, threatened in very early days of the reign to bring the subject to the notice of Parliament—a threat which Melbourne contemptuously ignored. But, when it was rumoured that Stockmar was acting as the Queen's private secretary, Melbourne circulated a peremptory denial.

Suspicions of Stockmar.

Public attention was for the time diverted from Stockmar. But he long remained a member of the royal circle, and never divested himself of the jealous suspicion which first attached to him in England.

The Baroness Lehzen.
The Queen's openly displayed fidelity to her old governess, the Baroness Lehzen, did not tend to dissipate the fear that she was in the hands of foreign advisers. But the Baroness's relations with her mistress were above reproach, and did credit to both. She had acted as her old pupil's secretary in private matters before she came to the throne, and she continued to perform the same functions after the Queen's accession. But public affairs were never brought by the Queen to her cognisance, and the Baroness loyally accepted the situation.

The Duchess of Kent.
With the Duchess of Kent, who continued to reside with her daughter, although she was now given a separate suite of apartments, the Queen's relation was no less discreet—far more discreet than the Duchess approved. She was excluded from all share in public business, an exclusion in which she did not readily acquiesce. For a long time she treated her daughter's emancipation from her direction as a personal grievance.[1] There was never any ground for the insinuation which Lord Brougham conveyed when he spoke in the House of Lords of the Duchess of Kent as 'the Queen-mother.' Melbourne protested with just indignation against applying such a misnomer to 'the mother of the Queen,' who was wholly outside the political sphere.

Public ceremonials meanwhile claimed much of

[1] *Greville Memoirs*, 2nd ser.

the Queen's attention. On June 27 she held her first levee at Kensington to receive the credentials of the ambassadors and envoys. She was dressed in black, but, as Sovereign of the Order of the Garter, wore all its brilliant insignia—ribbon, star, and a band bearing the motto, in place of the garter, buckled on the left arm.[1] There followed a long series of deputations from public bodies, bearing addresses of condolence and congratulation, to all of which she replied with characteristic composure. On July 17 she went in state to dissolve Parliament in accordance with the law which required a general election to take place within six months of the demise of the Crown, and in conformity with the then unquestioned practice which called for the Sovereign's presence at the closing as well as at the opening of each session of Parliament. For the first time she appeared in apparel of state—a mantle of crimson velvet lined with ermine, an ermine cape, a dress of white satin embroidered with gold, a tiara and stomacher of diamonds, and the insignia of the Garter.

Public ceremonials.

In a somewhat colourless speech from the throne she expressed her thanks for the congratulations that Parliament had offered her on her accession. The only Bill of importance that was submitted for her assent was one for the amendment of the criminal code and the further restriction of capital punishment. In that merciful aim she professed 'a peculiar interest.' 'It will be my care,' she said in conclusion, ' to strengthen our institutions, civil and ecclesiastical,

First speech from the Throne in Parliament.

[1] Bunsen, ii. 273.

by discreet improvement, wherever improvement is required, and to do all in my power to compose and allay animosity and discord.' She read the unpretending words with splendid effect. Fanny Kemble, who was present, wrote: 'The Queen's voice was exquisite. . . . The enunciation was as perfect as the intonation was melodious, and I think it is impossible to hear a more excellent utterance than that of the Queen's English by the English Queen.'[1] On July 19 the Queen held her first levee at St. James's Palace, and next day her first drawing-room. On both occasions the attendance was enormous.

[1] Fanny Kemble's *Letters*.

VI

THE CIVIL LIST AND COLONIAL AFFAIRS

On July 13, four days before her first appearance in Parliament, and within three weeks of her accession, the Queen left the home of her girlhood at Kensington for Buckingham Palace, the new official residence in London appointed for the Sovereign. The building had been begun by the architect John Nash for George IV., but was not completed until William IV. became King. He, however, disliked it, and preferred to remain at St. James's Palace. No monarch occupied Buckingham Palace before Queen Victoria, for whom it was for the first time put in order. A contemporary wag in ' The Times ' newspaper declared it was the cheapest house ever erected, having been built for one sovereign and furnished for another. But the inconvenience with which William IV. credited the edifice proved real, and it underwent radical alterations and additions at the instance of the Queen and Prince Albert before it was deemed to be adapted for its purpose. An east front was erected to form a quadrangle; the ground behind the house, to the extent of forty acres, was laid out as a pleasure-garden; a conservatory was converted into a chapel, and a ballroom was added as late as 1856.

Removal to Buckingham Palace.

The concert there, Aug. 17, 1837.

One of the first entertainments which were given at Buckingham Palace was a grand concert commanded by Queen Victoria on August 17, 1837, under the direction of Signor Costa. In honour of the occasion the Queen ordered the Court to go out of mourning for the day. The vocalists were Madame Grisi, Madame Albertazzi, Signor Lablache, and Signor Tamburini.

Opening of Victoria Gate, Hyde Park, Aug. 21.

The Queen's first official appearance out of doors took place on August 21, when she opened the new gate of Hyde Park on the Bayswater Road, and conferred on it the name of Victoria Gate. On August 22 she drove to Windsor to assume residence at the Castle for the first time. On September 28 she had her earliest experience of a military review, when the Guards in Windsor garrison marched before her in the Home Park.

At the Pavilion, Brighton.

After remaining at Windsor till October 4 she made acquaintance with the third and last of the royal palaces then in occupation, the pretentious Pavilion at Brighton, which George IV. had caused to be erected in a strange freak of fancy from the designs of his favourite architect, John Nash. Lord John Russell, the Home Secretary, together with his wife, stayed with her there. On November 4 she returned to Buckingham Palace.

Private life.

The Queen took a girlish delight in the sense of proprietorship. She actively directed her domestic establishments; the mode of life she adopted in her palaces was of her own devising. She exercised a constant and wide hospitality which had been long unknown in the royal circle, and was fond of con-

ducting a visitor over all parts of her houses, even
the kitchens. The entertainments were somewhat formal and monotonous; but, although she was zealous
for rules of etiquette, she was never indisposed to
modify them if she was thereby the better able to
indulge the kindly feeling that she invariably extended to her guests. Most of her mornings were
spent at work with Melbourne. In the early afternoon
when at Windsor she rode in the park or neighbouring country, with a large cavalcade often numbering
thirty persons. Later she romped with children,
some of whom she usually contrived to include
among her visitors, or played at ball or battledore and
shuttlecock with ladies of the Court—an exercise
which she continued till middle age—or practised
singing and pianoforte playing. Dining at half-past
seven, she usually devoted the evening to round
games of cards, chess, or draughts, while the Duchess
of Kent invariably played whist.

One of the Queen's innovations was the institution of a Court band, which played music during
and after dinner. When she was settled at Buckingham Palace she gave a small dance every Monday.
She found time for a little serious historical reading,
one of the earliest books through which she persevered
as Queen being Coxe's 'Life of Sir Robert Walpole,'[1]
and for the first time in her life she attempted novel-reading, making trial of three books by Sir Walter
Scott, Fenimore Cooper, and Bulwer Lytton respectively.[2] A little later she struggled through Hallam's
'Constitutional History' and Saint-Simon's 'Memoirs.'

Innovations at Buckingham Palace.

[1] Lady Lyttelton. [2] Bunsen, i. 296.

Foreign guests.

Relatives from the continent of Europe were in the first days of her reign very frequent companions. With them she always seemed most at ease, and she showed them marked attention. Vacant garters were bestowed on two of her German kinsmen who came on early visits to her—the first on her half-brother, the Prince of Leiningen, in July 1837, the next on her uncle, Prince Albert's father, in the year following. The King of the Belgians and his gentle Queen Louise spent three weeks with her at Windsor (August–September 1837), and the visit was repeated for years every autumn. Her first cousin Victoria, daughter of Duke Ferdinand of Saxe-Coburg, who in 1840 married the Duc de Nemours, was also often with her, and shared in her afternoon games.

Attitude to her kinsfolk.

Queen Victoria was not at the same time neglectful of her kinsfolk at home. Nothing could exceed the tenderness with which she treated the Dowager Queen Adelaide. On the day of her accession she wrote a letter of condolence, addressing it to 'the Queen' and not to 'the Dowager Queen,' for fear of adding to her grief. A very few days later, before the late King's funeral, she visited the widowed lady at Windsor, and she forbade, of her own motion, the lifting of the royal standard, then at half-mast, to mast-high, as was customary on the arrival of the Sovereign. When Queen Adelaide removed from Windsor Castle ultimately to settle at Marlborough House, her royal niece bade her take from the castle any furniture that her residence there had specially endeared to her, and until the old Queen's death the young Queen never relaxed any of her attentions.

To all her uncles and aunts she showed like consideration. She corresponded with them, entertained them, visited them, read to them, sang to them, and bore with little murmuring their recurrent displays of jealousy or ill-temper.[1] The Duchess of Cambridge, the last survivor of that generation, died as late as 1889, and no cares of family or state were ever permitted by the Queen to interfere with the due rendering of those acts of personal devotion to which she accustomed the aged Duchess from her youth. Even to the welfare of the FitzClarences, William IV.'s illegitimate children by the great actress, Mrs. Jordan, she was not indifferent, and often exerted her influence in their interests.

Consideration for uncles and aunts.

But the Queen was well able to repress domestic sentiment when points of Court etiquette to which

Court etiquette and domestic sentiment.

[1] The following simple autograph letter, addressed by her to her uncle, the Duke of Sussex, when he was unwell, is characteristic:—

'Buckingham Palace: December 29, 1837.

'MY DEAR UNCLE,—I grieve much to see by your kind letter, which I got yesterday, that you are still on crutches, and suffering. Under these circumstances, fearing that you might still be unable to leave the house at the end of this week, I wish to know if Tuesday, 12th, would suit you to drive with me. I trust then, dear uncle, that I shall find you quite recovered.— Believe me always, my dear uncle, your affectionate niece, VICTORIA R.'

On July 19, 1837, the Duke of Sussex, who was President of the Royal Society, formally introduced, according to custom, a deputation of the Fellows to present the Statutes to her, as Sovereign, and obtain her signature to them. 'She received the Duke of Sussex,' wrote Adam Sedgwick, a member of the deputation, 'without any of the formality of a Court, and seemed only to remember that he was her uncle. . . . He offered to bend his knee and kiss her hand (which is the regular form on such occasions), but she immediately stopped him, put her arm round his neck, and kissed his cheek.'—*Life and Letters of Sedgwick*, by Clark and Hughes, i. 511.

she attached importance seemed to her to require it. At her own table the Queen deemed it politic to give, for the first time, precedence to foreign ambassadors—even to the American envoy, Mr. Stephenson —over all guests of whatever rank, excepting only Lord Melbourne, who always sat at her left hand. For years she declined to alter the practice in favour of the dukes and duchesses of the royal family, although she ultimately made some exceptions.

The general election of 1837. Meanwhile the first general election of the new reign, and the third since the wide extension of the franchise under the Reform Bill of 1832, had taken place. The Whig leaders somewhat vaguely announced a moderate programme of domestic reform—the abolition of compulsory church rates and a further alleviation of Irish grievances. But the battle of the rival parties mainly raged round the position and prospects of the Queen. The Tories, who were the attacking force, and had been in a hopeless minority in the House of Commons for six years, bitterly complained that Melbourne and the Whigs in power identified the Queen with themselves, and that they used her and her name as party weapons of offence. Croker, a Tory spokesman, in an article in the 'Quarterly Review' (July 1837), denounced the policy of surrounding her with female relatives of the Whig leaders. Sir Robert Peel argued that the monarchy was endangered by the rigour with which she was ruled by Melbourne, the chief of one political party. Stress was laid on a letter sent by Lord John Russell to Lord Mulgrave, Lord-Lieutenant of Ireland, in which her personal sympathy was claimed

Tory attacks on the Queen's subjection to Whigs.

for the Whig policy in Ireland. Release of the Sovereign from Whig tyranny consequently became a Tory cry, and it gave rise to the epigram :—

> 'The Queen is with us,' Whigs insulting say;
> 'For when *she found us in* she let us stay.'
> It may be so, but give me leave to doubt
> How long she'll keep you when *she finds you out*.[1]

Whig wire-pullers, on the other hand, made the most of the recent conduct of the next heir to the throne, the new King of Hanover, the Queen's uncle Ernest, who had signalised his accession to the Hanoverian crown by revoking constitutional government in his dominions. A report was spread that the new King of Hanover was plotting to dethrone his niece in order to destroy constitutional government in England as well as in Hanover. A cartoon entitled 'The Contrast,' which was widely circulated by Whig election agents, represented side by side portraits of the Queen and her uncle, the Queen being depicted as a charming *ingénue*, and her uncle as a grey-haired beetle-browed villain.

Whigs' affected suspicion of a Hanoverian plot.

The final result of the elections was not satisfactory to either side. The Tories gained on the balance thirty-seven seats, and thus reduced their opponents' majority. But the estimated strength of parties at the close of the contest was Liberals 348 and Conservatives 310. In the new House of Commons the Whigs still led by thirty-eight, and Melbourne and his colleagues retained office. Their power, however, was small. They were in a clear minority in the House of Lords—a difficulty which was a chronic experience

Whigs' small majority.

[1] *Annual Register*, 1837, p. 239.

of the Liberal party throughout the reign. The Opposition in the House of Commons, under the experienced leadership of Sir Robert Peel, was alert and bellicose, and had been reinforced during the election, not merely by numbers, but by much enlightened ability and energy. The most notable of the recruits in the Tory army was Benjamin Disraeli, then widely known as a brilliant novelist, who was to play a commanding part in a later act of the drama of the Queen's public career. He had now, after two failures, won at Maidstone a seat in Parliament for the first time.[1] His future rival, with whom the Queen was also to be very closely associated, William Ewart Gladstone, was then also a promising member of the Tory party. He was for the third time returned in the Conservative interest for Newark, for which he had sat since 1832.[2] An Opposition, whose rank and file included men of the energy and intellect of Disraeli and Gladstone, was not one to be lightly disregarded.

[1] Born in London, December 21, 1804, of Jewish parents (his father being a laborious man of letters), Disraeli made a wide reputation as a novelist at the precocious age of twenty-two, and was thenceforth a familiar figure in London society, which he fascinated by his brilliant wit and foppish affectation. Literature was still his main occupation when he entered the House of Commons, and his reputation as a novelist was steadily growing. In the House of Commons he joined the Young England party, which sought to combine social reform with the unimpaired maintenance of ancient institutions. He rapidly became a leader of that clique.

[2] Gladstone, who was five years Disraeli's junior, was son of a substantial Liverpool merchant, had been educated at Eton and Christchurch, where he greatly distinguished himself, and had greatly impressed the House of Commons since he entered it in 1832 by his power of impressive oratory and the apparent strength of his convictions. Macaulay, in 1839, described him as the 'rising hope of the stern and unbending Tories.'

Before the new Parliament opened, the Queen made a formal progress through London, going from Buckingham Palace to the Guildhall to dine in state with the Lord Mayor. Her passage through the streets evoked an imposing demonstration of loyalty. Fifty-eight carriages formed the procession, in which rode many of the foreign ambassadors. The Lord Mayor, Sir John Cowan, with the Sheriffs, George Carroll and Moses Montefiore, and members of the Corporation of London, received the Queen at Temple Bar. The banquet lasted from 3.30 in the afternoon till 8.30 in the evening, when the City was ablaze with illuminations.[1]

At the Guildhall banquet, Nov. 9, 1837

On November 20 the Queen opened her first Parliament, reading her own speech, as was her custom until her widowhood whenever she attended in person. Reference was made to difficulties that were apprehended in Spain, which was torn by civil war, in Canada, where the French settlers were in revolt against English rule, and in Ireland, where agitators, under O'Connell's leadership, were loudly manifesting normal signs of discontent. But the leading business of the opening session was a settlement of the Royal Civil List.

Opening of her first Parliament, Nov. 20.

Financially the Queen's position since her accession had been a source of anxiety. She inherited nothing, and the Crown had lost the royal revenues of Hanover. She had complained to Melbourne of

The Civil List.

---

[1] A fine medal was struck from a design by William Wyon. The Queen's arrival at Temple Bar was pictured in a bas-relief on the monument that was erected on the site of the old gate after it was removed in 1878.

her lack of money for immediate private expenses. He had done little but listen sympathetically; but Messrs. Coutts, who had been bankers to various members of the royal family, came to her rescue with temporary advances.

The hereditary Crown lands.

In approaching the question of the Queen's income, the main question for the Government to consider was not merely the amount necessary to maintain the throne in fitting dignity, but the proportion of her income which might prudently be derived from the hereditary revenues of the Crown, i.e. revenues from the Crown lands. In return for a fixed annuity George III. had surrendered a large portion of these revenues, and George IV. yielded a further portion, while William IV. surrendered all but those proceeding from the duchies of Cornwall and Lancaster, which were held to belong to a different category. At the same time it was arranged, on the accession of William IV., that the general expenses of civil government, which had been previously defrayed out of the King's Civil List, should henceforth be discharged by the Consolidated Fund, and that of the income allotted to King William only a very small proportion should be applied to aught outside his household and personal expenses; the sole external calls were 75,000*l*. for pensions and 10,000*l*. for the Secret Service Fund. On these conditions King William was content to accept 460,000*l*. instead of 850,000*l*. which had been paid his predecessor, while an annuity of 50,000*l*. was bestowed on his Queen Consort. His net personal parliamentary income (excluding pensions and the Secret Service Fund) was thus 375,000*l*., with

Wm. IV.'s income.

some 25,000*l*. from the duchies of Lancaster and Cornwall.

Radical members of Parliament now urged Melbourne to bring the whole of the Crown lands under parliamentary control, to deprive the Crown of the control and income of the duchies of Lancaster and Cornwall, and to supply the Sovereign with a revenue which should be exclusively applied to her own purposes, and not to any part of the civil government. Treasury officials drew out a scheme with these ends in view, but Melbourne rejected most of it from a fear of rousing against his somewhat unstable Government the cry of tampering with the royal prerogative. In the result the precedent of William IV.'s case was followed, with certain modifications.

<small>The duchies of Lancaster and Cornwall.</small>

The Queen resigned all the hereditary revenues of the Crown, but was left in possession of the revenues of the duchies of Lancaster and Cornwall, of which the latter was the legal appanage of the heir-apparent. The duchy of Cornwall therefore ceased to be the Sovereign's property as soon as a lawful heir to the throne was born. It and the duchy of Lancaster produced during the first years of the reign about 27,500*l*. annually, but the revenues from both rose rapidly, and the duchy of Lancaster, which was a permanent source of income to the Queen, ultimately produced above 60,000*l*. a year.[1] Parliament now granted her, apart from these hereditary revenues, an annuity of 385,000*l*., being 10,000*l*. in excess of the net personal income

<small>The first settlement.</small>

---

[1] The duchy of Cornwall, which passed to the Prince of Wales at his birth in 1841, ultimately produced more than 66,000*l*.

granted by Parliament to her predecessor. Of this sum 60,000*l.* was appropriated to her privy purse, 131,260*l.* to the salaries of the household, 172,500*l.* to the expenses of the household, 13,200*l.* to the royal bounty, while 8,040*l.* was unappropriated. Repairs to the Sovereign's official residences and the maintenance of the royal yachts were provided for by the Treasury apart from the Civil List revenues.

The Civil List pensions. The annual payment from the Civil List of 75,000*l.* in pensions and of 10,000*l.* secret service money was cancelled, but permission was given the Crown to create Civil List pensions to the amount of 1,200*l.* annually, a sum which the Treasury undertook to defray independently of the royal income. This arrangement ultimately meant the yearly expenditure of some 23,000*l.*, but the pensions were only nominally associated with the Sovereign's expenditure, were wholly removed from the Sovereign's control, and were bestowed exclusively on persons in more or less needy circumstances who had distinguished themselves in literature, art, or the public service outside the sphere of politics.

Radical criticism. The Radicals, who steadfastly advocated rigorous economy in all departments of the State, resisted the arrangement on the score of its needless munificence. Joseph Hume, one of the leading Radicals in the House of Commons, moved, on the third reading of the Civil List Bill, a reduction of 50,000*l.*, which was rejected by 199 votes against 19. Benjamin Hawes, another member of the Radical section, vainly moved on like grounds a reduction of 10,000*l.*, which was supported by 41 members and opposed by

173. Lord Brougham severely criticised the settlement in the Radical sense on the second reading of the Bill in the House of Lords. He made searching inquiries respecting the incomes from the Crown duchies, and objected to the arrangement being made for the Queen's life. But no modification was accepted by the Government, and the Bill quickly became law. Although numerous additional grants, approaching a total of 200,000*l.* a year, were afterwards allotted to the Queen's children, the annual sum allowed her by Parliament on her accession was never altered during her reign of nearly sixty-four years, and proved amply sufficient for her needs.

At the same time as the Civil List Bill passed through Parliament, the Queen's mother, at the Sovereign's instance, was granted an annuity of 30,000*l.*; she formerly received 22,000*l.* a year, of which 10,000*l.* was appropriated to the care of her daughter while Princess. The Queen was well contented with the settlement. On December 23, 1837, the Queen went to Parliament to return thanks in person for what had been done. Christmas was spent merrily at Buckingham Palace, and next day the Court withdrew to Windsor. *Provision for the Duchess of Kent.*

The liberal allowance enabled the Queen to fulfil at once her resolve to pay off her father's debts. By the autumn of next year she had transferred to the late Duke's creditors from her privy purse nearly 50,000*l.*, and on October 7, 1839, she received their formal thanks. *The Queen pays her father's debts.*

Meanwhile the Queen's sympathy with her ministers increased. Difficulties beset them at every step. Through 1838-9 she followed their parliamentary movements with keen anxiety lest their narrow majority might prove inadequate to maintain them in office. Disturbances in Canada during the early months of 1838 roused differences of opinion in the House of Commons, which imperilled their position, and the crisis was prolonged. 'The Queen is as steady to us as ever,' wrote Palmerston on April 14, 1838, 'and was in the depth of despair when she thought we were in danger of being turned out. She keeps well in health, and even in London takes long rides into the country, which have done her great good.'[1] Under Melbourne's guidance, and in agreement with her own wish, she daily perused masses of despatches and official correspondence with exemplary diligence.

The British Empire in 1837.

The first great political question to which the Queen's ministers were compelled to direct her attention had a prophetic likeness to the last great political question which was to occupy her mind at the close of her long reign. It concerned her empire beyond the seas. The Queen's dominions outside the British Isles were to undergo vast extension and conspicuous consolidation in the course of her career. None the less the colonial inheritance to which she succeeded was of great dimensions. In 1837 the British possessions outside the United Kingdom (including those portions of the peninsula of India which were ruled by a chartered company of merchants in alliance with the British Government) covered some eight million square miles, more than

[1] Ashley, *Life of Palmerston*, i. 344.

six times the area of the mother country. But the future of this massive heritage looked doubtful when it first passed under her and her ministers' sway. Its past was sullied by the severance, some half a century before, owing largely to the impolitic conduct of the Queen's grandfather, George III., of the North American colonies, which had become the independent republic of the United States. From the shock of the American revolt the colonial empire of England took time to recover. The first signs of that renewal of colonial expansion, which was ultimately to convert the eight million square miles of colonial territory under Queen Victoria's sceptre into twelve millions, were plainly discernible during the last years of William IV.'s reign, especially in Australasia and the Southern Seas.[1] But Queen Victoria's Government had, when she ascended the throne, no considered policy which might be calculated to give lasting coherence to the constituent parts of a widely extended colonial empire and avert further experience of disruption.

The prestige of the mother country and of the Crown required that the colonists now and hereafter should accept contentedly and of their own free will the British allegiance. Happily, within a year of the

The revolt of Canada.

---

[1] South Australia had been first formed into a settlement in 1836, and there had begun emigration to New Zealand, which was formed into a colony in 1840. New South Wales (of which the territories afterwards named Victoria and Queensland also at first formed part), the Swan River Settlement (afterwards called Western Australia), and Van Diemen's Land (afterwards Tasmania), were of older birth, and were mainly used as penal settlements for criminals sentenced to transportation.

Queen's accession, the question of the relations in which the Sovereign and her ministers were to stand to colonial settlements across the ocean claimed a prompt and definite answer. The imperial topic involved Lord Melbourne's Government, with which the Queen identified herself, in a momentous struggle with the parliamentary Opposition throughout 1838. The battle raged round the colony of Canada, then the widest in extent of any of England's colonial possessions. The future of the British Empire largely depended on the issue of the Canadian conflict.

Canadian conditions. Canada was territory that had been colonised by France and ceded to England by treaty in 1763. French settlers of old standing multiplied there; English immigrants did not amalgamate with them, and the British Government imprudently added fuel to the mutual jealousy by consigning each race to a separate province. On each province a formal parliamentary constitution, which speciously resembled that of the United Kingdom, had been conferred, but executive power was exclusively in the hands of the governors representing the Crown. At the same time the United States watched with envious eyes the development of Canada, was prolific in threats of annexation, and encouraged disaffection among both French and English Canadians.

Lord Durham's mission. When the Queen's reign opened, the two races in Canada were alike impatient of British domination, and were at one in their desire for complete parliamentary self-government on an effective English pattern. They claimed that the governor should stand to freely elected colonial ministers and Parliament in the same relations of nominal ruler as the British Sovereign stood to British ministers and Parliament. Lord Melbourne's weak ministry hesitated to make the requisite concession, but when rebellion broke out in both the French and English provinces of Canada they did the next best thing. They suspended the existing constitution and despatched one of their supporters, Lord Durham, to report fully on the situation and to exercise in the meantime despotic authority. The rebellion was easily suppressed, but Lord Durham's autocratic procedure in re-establishing order gave the Opposition an excellent battle-cry, which was none the less effective because of its inconsistency with prescriptive Tory principles.

Yielding to agitation, the ministers recalled Lord Durham. The Tory triumph was extremely disconcerting to the Queen. Lord Durham's wife, a daughter of the second Lord Grey, was one of the ladies-in-waiting, whom she had invited at her accession to join her household. On her husband's dismissal from Canada, Lady Durham, to the Queen's regret, retired from her service. The Queen greatly respected her and her husband, and she bitterly lamented their untoward fate. *Lord Durham's recall.*

But Lord Durham had earned his Sovereign's sympathy more richly than the Queen then knew. Before his humiliation he had solved the problem of the future of the British Empire in the manner that best enhanced the prestige of the Crown. With the aid of his companions, Charles Buller and Edward Gibbon Wakefield, he had drawn up an elaborate report which *The colonial policy of self-government.*

proved that the grant of self-government to British colonies was the sole safeguard of a permanent colonial empire, and that allegiance to the throne voluntarily resting on the natural patriotic sentiment of the colonists, and on no prescribed or compulsory obligations, was the strongest, if not the only practicable, link wherewith to bind the distant dependencies of a monarchy to the mother country. This new principle of colonial policy Lord Durham offered his countrymen for their adoption at the outset of the Queen's reign, and they accepted it while they cashiered its author. Within two years Canada received practical autonomy at the hands of Lord Melbourne's ministry. That self-governing principle of colonial expansion which was to grow into the most distinctive characteristic of Queen Victoria's long reign was thus almost exactly of the same age as her own sovereignty.

VII

THE CORONATION AND THE CRISES OF 1839

WHILE the Canadian difficulties were in process of solution, the Queen's chief interest outside politics lay in the preparations that were in progress for her coronation and for the festivities accompanying it. Three state balls—one on June 18, the day of Waterloo, a choice of date which offended the French [1] —two levees, a drawing-room, a state concert, a first state visit to Ascot, and attendance at Eton 'montem' immediately preceded the elaborate ceremonial, which took place on June 28, 1838, eight days after the anniversary of her accession.

The Coronation, June 28, 1838.

The ministers had resolved to endow the ceremonial with exceptional splendour. For the expenses of William IV.'s coronation 50,000*l*. had been allowed. No less a sum than 200,000*l*. was voted by Parliament for the expenses of Queen Victoria's coronation. Westminster Abbey was elaborately decorated in crimson and gold. The royal procession to the Abbey was

Its splendour.

---

[1] Thomas Raikes, then at Paris, wrote of this episode: 'As the Queen gave a concert on that evening [of Waterloo day] to all the foreigners [who were in London for the coronation], the French construe it into an affront. Louis Philippe is in a peck of troubles about it, and, wishing to keep well with all parties, i.e. with England and with his ambassadors, *ne sait pas à quel saint se vouer*'! *Journal*, ii. 105.

revived for the first time since the coronation of George III. in 1761, and four hundred thousand persons came to London to witness it, many bivouacking in the streets the night before.

The royal procession.

At 10 A.M. on the appointed day, under a sunny sky, the Queen left Buckingham Palace in full panoply of state, passing up Constitution Hill, along Piccadilly, down St. James's Street, and across Trafalgar Square, which had just been laid out in Nelson's memory. The Abbey was reached by way of Parliament Street at 11.30. Among the numerous foreign visitors, who went thither in brilliant array in advance of the Queen, was Marshal Soult, the old rival of Wellington in the Spanish Peninsula and at Waterloo, now the special representative of France. The French general was received by the crowd with hardly less enthusiasm than her Majesty, and was greatly impressed by the generous warmth of his reception.[1] The great company of the Queen's German relatives included her uncle the Duke of Saxe-Coburg and her half-brother and half-sister of Leiningen.[2]

The ceremony in the Abbey.

When the Queen entered the Abbey, 'with eight ladies all in white floating about her like a silvery cloud, she paused, as if for breath, and clasped her

---

[1] Raikes's *Journal*, ii. 107 : 'Soult was so much cheered, both in and out of the Abbey, that he was completely overcome. He has since publicly said, " C'est le plus beau jour de ma vie, il prouve que les Anglois pensent que j'ai toujours fait la guerre en loyal homme." When in the Abbey he seized the arm of his aide-de-camp, quite overpowered, and said, "Ah! vraiment, c'est un brave peuple."'

[2] An amusing and spirited account of the great company of officials, relatives, and foreign guests was given by the Rev. Richard Barham, author of the *Ingoldsby Legends*, in his burlesque 'Account of the Coronation by Barney Maguire.'

hands.'[1] After she had been crowned, a ray of sunlight fell on her head as she knelt at the altar to receive the Holy Communion, and the Duchess of Kent burst into tears. The brilliance of the scene impressed every one.

There were, however, some drawbacks to the successful completion of the coronation rite. Harriet Martineau, who was present, wrote: 'The brightness, vastness, and dreamy magnificence produced a strange effect of exhaustion and sleepiness.' The Queen, too, suffered not only from natural emotion and fatigue, but from the hesitation of the officiating clergy as to the exact part she was to play at many points in the long ritual, and from the insufficient training that had been accorded her. Dr. John Ireland, the Dean of Westminster,[2] who had conducted the two preceding coronations of George IV. and William IV., was too infirm to attend (he had nearly completed his seventy-eighth year). His place was filled by the Sub-dean, Lord John Thynne. 'Pray tell me what I am to do, for they [i.e. the clergy] don't know,' she said at one solemn point to Lord John Thynne who stood near her. She complained that the orb which was unexpectedly put into her hand was too heavy for her to hold; and when the ruby ring, which had been made for her little finger, was forced by the Archbishop on to her fourth, she nearly cried out with the pain. The fear of betraying her nervousness intensified her

The want of rehearsal.

[1] Prothero and Bradley's *Life of Dean Stanley*.
[2] Dr. Ireland, who had been Dean since 1816, remained in office, despite his feeble health, till his death on September 2, 1842. He was succeeded by Thomas Turton, who left Westminster after two and a half years to become Bishop of Ely.

discomfort, but she never seemed to spectators to lose her composure, although the awkwardness of the other actors in the scene was patent to all. 'The Queen,' wrote the observant Disraeli, who attended with the other members of the House of Commons, 'performed her part with great grace and completeness, which cannot in general be said of the other performers; they were always in doubt as to what came next, and you saw the want of rehearsal.'[1]

The acclamations.

For the first time at a coronation, the Commons were allowed to acclaim their Sovereign after the Peers. The latter had enjoyed the privilege from time immemorial. The Commons now cheered their Sovereign nine times, among them Daniel O'Connell, the Irish leader;[2] but Dean Stanley, who, then a boy, sat in a gallery, thought all the responses and acclamations were feebly given. Towards the close of the ceremony a singular accident befell Lord Rolle, a peer, eighty years old, as he was endeavouring to offer his homage. He 'fell down as he was getting up the steps of the throne.' The Queen's 'first impulse was to rise, and when afterwards he came again to do homage she said, "May I not get up and meet him?" and then rose from the throne and advanced down one or two of the steps to prevent his coming up, an act of graciousness and kindness which made a great sensation.'[3] 'Nothing could be more effective,' wrote Disraeli of this incident.[4] While the peers were doing homage, the Lord Chamberlain and his officers flung medals, specially designed by Pistrucci, for the

The homage.

---

[1] Lord Beaconsfield's *Letters to his Sister* (June 29, 1838), p. 139.
[2] *Gent. Mag.* 1838, ii. 198.   [3] *Greville Memoirs*, 2nd ser. i. 107.
[4] Lord Beaconsfield's *Letters*, p. 139.

spectators to scramble for, and the confusion was not dignified.

At length the ceremonial, which lasted more than five hours, ended. At four the Queen set out for Buckingham Palace. She drove through the streets wearing her crown and all her apparel of state, and looked to spectators pale and tremulous. Carlyle, who was in the throng, breathed a blessing on her: 'Poor little Queen!' he added, 'she is at an age at which a girl can hardly be trusted to choose a bonnet for herself; yet a task is laid upon her from which an archangel might shrink.' *The return to Buckingham Palace.*

But, despite her consciousness of the responsibilities of her station, the Queen still had much of the child's lightness and simplicity of heart. On returning to the palace she hastily doffed her splendours in order to give her pet spaniel, Dash, its afternoon bath.[1] She then dined quietly with her relatives who were her guests, and, after sending a message of inquiry to the unfortunate Lord Rolle, concluded the day by witnessing from the roof of the palace the public illuminations and fireworks in the Green and Hyde Parks. Next morning a great 'coronation' fair was opened by permission of the Government for four days in Hyde Park; and on the second day the Queen paid it a long visit. The coronation festivities concluded with a review by her of five thousand men in Hyde Park (July 9), when she again shared the popular applause with Marshal Soult, in whose honour the display was mainly devised.[2] *Youthful elation.*

Close of the celebrations.

[1] *Recollections*, by C. R. Leslie, R.A., ed. Tom Taylor.
[2] The coronation attracted popular interest throughout Europe, and accounts of it were published in foreign languages. An Italian

The Queen's speeches in Parliament, 1838-9.

A month later, on August 16, the Queen prorogued Parliament in person, and, after listening to the usual harangue on the work of the session from the Speaker of the House of Commons, read her speech with customary clearness. Her grace of utterance grew with practice. When she performed the like ceremony at the opening of the next session in February 1839, Charles Sumner, the future American orator and statesman, happened to be among her auditors, and he paid singular testimony to the excellence of her elocution. 'I had no predisposition to admire the Queen,' he wrote with republican candour, 'but her reading has conquered my judgment. I was astonished and delighted. . . . She pronounced every word slowly and distinctly with a great regard to its meaning. I think I have never heard anything better read in my life than her speech.'[1] Another stranger, who obtained a prominent place on the same occasion near the throne, was Prince Louis Bonaparte, at the moment an exile from France, who was, as Napoleon III., to play a disturbing part in two later decades of Queen Victoria's history.

Crises of 1839.

No sooner was Parliament opened in February 1839 than the peace and contentment which had hitherto

chapbook, entitled *Descrizione della solenne incoronazione di S. M. Vittoria I, regina d'Inghilterra, seguita il dì 28 giugno* 1838, includes an appendix giving by way of contrast (*che potrià servire di confronto*) a full account of the coronation of Queen Mary Tudor in 1553. I owe my knowledge of this little volume, which was published in Foligno, to a friend, who presented it to me on obtaining it from an Umbrian contadino of Amelia, whom he chanced to meet reading it in the summer of 1902.

[1] *Memoirs and Letters of Charles Sumner*, by Edward L. Pierce, i. 59.

encircled the Court were rudely menaced. The Queen was to realise that her popularity was not invulnerable, and that, despite Melbourne's parental care, her position was fraught with difficulty and danger, with which she was as yet hardly fitted to cope. Both the crises through which the Queen and her Court passed in the first half of 1839 were attributable to her youth and inexperience. Problems arose which needed for their due solution greater self-mastery and knowledge of the world than she yet possessed.

The first crisis was the result of a train of circumstances which it was extremely embarrassing for a young girl to be confronted with. In January 1839 Lady Flora Hastings, daughter of the Marquis of Hastings, was lady-in-waiting to the Duchess of Kent at Buckingham Palace. On account of her appearance, she was most improperly suspected by some of the Queen's attendants of immoral conduct. Neither the Queen nor her mother put any faith in the imputation, but Lady Tavistock, a Lady of the Bedchamber, informed Melbourne of the matter, and the Queen assented to his proposal that the unfortunate lady should be subjected by the royal physician, Sir James Clark, to a medical examination. Clark made the examination and signed a certificate denying all allegations against Lady Flora (February 17, 1839). *The episode of Lady Flora Hastings.*

The incident was soon noised abroad. The lady's family appealed directly to the Queen to make fitting reparation. Lady Flora's brother, the Marquis of Hastings, obtained an interview with her. Lady Flora's mother wrote her impassioned letters and *Her family appeals to the Queen.*

begged for the dismissal of Sir James Clark. The Queen made no reply. Melbourne, writing in his own name, stated that the Queen had seized the earliest opportunity of personally acknowledging to Lady Flora the unhappy error, and that it was not intended to take any other step. 'I am sure the Queen does not understand what they betrayed her into,' wrote the injured lady to her uncle, Hamilton Fitzgerald. 'She has endeavoured to show her regret by her civility to me, and expressed it handsomely with tears in her eyes.' But the lady's relatives held that the Queen and the Court had done Lady Flora a wrong which should be publicly admitted and apologised for.

Outcry in the press. The 'Morning Post,' the organ of the aristocratic section of the Conservative party, to which the Hastings family belonged, took the unpleasing topic in hand and greatly disturbed the public mind by its bold presentment of the case. Lady Flora was hailed as 'the victim of a depraved Court.'

Lady Hastings published in the newspapers her correspondence with the Queen and Melbourne, and Clark circulated, through the columns of the London press, a defence of his own conduct. A general feeling of disgust was roused, and the reputation of the Court suffered severely. The situation was rendered worse by the tragic ending of the episode. *Lady Flora's death.* Lady Flora was suffering from a fatal internal disease—enlargement of the liver. On July 4 she was announced to be dying at Buckingham Palace. A royal banquet which was to take place that evening was countermanded.[1] The lady died next day. The Queen was gravely troubled. Society throughout the land was depressed and shocked.

The Queen's advisers had committed a serious blunder and one bad enough to warrant an unmistakable expression of her personal regret, whatever the rules of Court etiquette might urge against any admission of error by a royal personage. But nothing followed. The Queen did not break silence. Blame for her apparent supineness was currently laid on the Baroness Lehzen. Her attitude was doubtless the fruit of innocence and inexperience; but, however cogently it might be explained, it came near proving a national calamity, through the widespread hostility which it provoked against the Court. The Queen looked back on the incident in after years with natural abhorrence. *Hostility to the Court.*

The second Court crisis of 1839 was due to precisely opposite causes—to the Queen's peremptory and unprompted exercise of her personal authority and to her active interposition in business of the State without seeking advice. *The second crisis.*

During the session of 1839 the Whig ministry finally lost its hold on the House of Commons. Colonial questions of moment to the future continued to embarrass them. They were under the obligation of putting into force the great measures for abolishing slavery in the British colonies which had been passed in 1833-4, and their efforts encountered a determined resistance. The emancipation of the slaves in the *Her first ministerial crisis May 1839.*

---

[1] Malmesbury's *Memoirs*, p. 77.

Crown colony of Jamaica led the planters, who owned the slaves, into rebellion, and the Government was now driven to the disagreeable necessity of inviting Parliament to suspend the constitution of that island. The proposal was carried by a majority of only five (May 7). Melbourne felt the position to be hopeless, and placed the resignation of himself and his colleagues in the Queen's hands. The Queen was deeply distressed. When Lord John, leader of the House of Commons, visited her to discuss the situation, she burst into tears.

Melbourne's resignation, 1839.

But she soon nerved herself fully to exert for the first time the Sovereign's traditional power of choosing a successor to the outgoing Prime Minister. Her grief at parting with Melbourne was quickly checked. She asked him for no advice, but, after consulting Lord Spencer, she sent for the Duke of Wellington, and startled him by her self-possession (May 8). He declined her offer to form a ministry on the ground of his age and of the desirability of the Prime Minister being in the House of Commons. Accordingly she summoned Sir Robert Peel, the leader of the Conservative Opposition in the Lower House, who had already filled the office of Prime Minister at the arbitrary bidding of her uncle, William IV., for a few months in 1835. She feared his coldness and severity of demeanour 'after the open and affectionate manner' to which Lord Melbourne had accustomed her, but she was well alive to the obligation that the constitution imposed on her when Parliament transferred power from one party to another.[1]

Peel agrees to take office.

[1] Cf. *Peel Papers*, ii. 391.

The Queen's personal demeanour at Peel's first interview with her was dignified, although very frank. The conversation began with some discussion of the question whether Parliament should be dissolved or the Tory party should accept office in the existing House of Commons. The Queen said 'she had parted with her late Government with great regret,' but deprecated a dissolution of Parliament at so early a date in the life of the existing Parliament. Peel vaguely expressed sympathy with her view, but he declined to pledge himself to forego a dissolution. Finally he agreed to form a Government, and, on leaving the Queen, set about selecting members of his cabinet.

There was already a strong feeling among the Tories that the Queen, who had hitherto shrunk from association with Conservatives, and viewed them, with the sole exception of her old friend Lord Liverpool, with frankly expressed dislike, was hedged in on all sides of her household by the female relatives of her Whig ministers. Peel, in consultation with his friends, decided that the ladies holding the higher posts in the household must be displaced if Conservative ministers were to receive adequate support from the Crown. He had no intention of interfering with the subordinate offices, but deemed it essential to remove some at least of the ladies about the Queen—the Mistress of the Robes and two or three ladies-in-waiting. *The Queen and her Ladies of the Bedchamber.*

Peel formed a high conception of his personal responsibility in all directions. But he was quite willing to consult the Queen's wishes in filling such *The Queen resists change* in her household.

appointments as might fall vacant. Unfortunately he did not define at the outset the precise posts or the number of them which were affected by his proposals. The subject was broached in another personal interview with the Queen on May 9. The Queen was at once alarmed. She feared that she was to be deprived of the companionship of her closest friends, and suspected—quite incorrectly—that the Baroness Lehzen was aimed at. Her mind was made up at once. She declined point blank to entertain any suggestion of change in the female constitution of her household. All her queenly spirit was roused, and she put no curb on her passionate indignation. Peel left her hastily. Thereupon she wrote to Melbourne that the Tories wanted to deprive her of her ladies; they would rob her next of her dressers and housemaids; they thought to treat her as a girl; she would show them she was Queen of England. Finally, she requested her old minister to draft a reply of refusal to Peel's demands.

The Queen's letter to Peel, May 10, 1839.

Melbourne, who feared that Peel had treated the girl harshly, and was chiefly moved by a parental kind of sympathy, expressed no opinion on the merits of the case, but did as he was asked without further inquiry. The Queen's letter to Peel ran: 'Buckingham Palace, May 10, 1839.—The Queen, having considered the proposal made to her yesterday by Sir Robert Peel to remove the ladies of her bedchamber, cannot consent to adopt a course which she conceives to be contrary to usage, and which is repugnant to her feelings.' Peel answered that he feared there was some misunderstanding, and declined to proceed to the formation of a Government.

Peel's decision was received by the Queen with immense relief, and she made no endeavour to conceal her elation at a state ball that took place the same evening. With every sign of satisfaction she appealed to Melbourne to resume power. Although her action was her own, Melbourne had given it a tacit approval by not resisting it when she first informed him of her intention. The old cabinet met on May 11 to reconsider its position; some members argued for advising the Queen to withdraw from the attitude that she had assumed. Lord Grey, Melbourne's former chief, whose son, Lord Howick, was Melbourne's colleague as Secretary at War, thought Peel's attitude not unreasonable, and he told Melbourne that on becoming Prime Minister in 1830 he had made similar changes in the household of the Queen-Consort, but he admitted that there was 'a considerable difference between the situation of a Queen-Consort and a Queen-Regnant.' With some hesitation he advised Melbourne to support the Queen in her struggle with Peel.[1] Lord Spencer insisted that as gentlemen they must stand by her. Palmerston declared that her youth and isolation should have protected her from the odious conditions that Peel sought to impose.

Melbourne's cabinet reconsiders its position.

At length the good-natured Melbourne acquiesced in that opinion. The Whigs returned to office, but they recognised their weakness, and some endeavour was made, with the Queen's willing assent, to

Melbourne supports the Queen.

[1] *Melbourne Papers*, p. 397.

strengthen the ministry's *personnel*. Spring-Rice, the Chancellor of the Exchequer, was replaced by Francis Baring. Lord Glenelg, the very inefficient War and Colonial Minister, was excluded, and his office was transferred to Lord John Russell, formerly the Home Secretary, who was succeeded at the Home Office by the Earl of Mulgrave, afterwards Marquis of Normanby, the old Lord-Lieutenant of Ireland. The most interesting newcomer was Thomas Babington Macaulay, in whose favour Lord Howick retired from the Secretaryship at War.

Melbourne's reconstructed ministry.

The circumstances in which the reconstructed ministry resumed power quickly formed the topic of animated debate in both Houses of Parliament. Peel effectively defended his action in making his assumption of office conditional on permission to change the constitution of the Queen's household. Lord John Russell somewhat lamely endeavoured to prove his demands to be without precedent. Melbourne chivalrously identified himself with the Queen, and was severely handled from different points of view for his alleged pusillanimity both by the Duke of Wellington, who supported Peel, and by Lord Brougham, who deemed Peel and Melbourne equally blameworthy in admitting the Sovereign's personal responsibility; but the debate passed off without seriously damaging the old ministry's position.

Admission of her error.

In point of fact Peel's conduct was amply warranted, and subsequently Melbourne, Lord John Russell, and the Queen herself admitted as much. In 1853 she confided to Lord John that she had taken no advice in the matter. 'No,' she said, ' it was entirely my own foolishness!' Melbourne afterwards remarked characteristically: 'You should take care to give people who are cross time to come round. Peel's fault in that business, when he failed to form a Government, was not giving the Queen time to come round.' But at heart Melbourne seems to have cherished graver misgivings of the significance to be attached to the Queen's display of wilful temper on the occasion. The character and fate of the Queen's ancestress, and one of her historical heroines, Mary Queen of Scots, seems indeed for an instant to have flashed across his mind. It was an involuntary and momentary association of ideas. But Melbourne, with a sardonic touch of humour, which was familiar to his friends, and was commonly kept under restraint in the royal presence, casually remarked to the Queen a little later across the dinner-table, that there were words which Mary Queen of Scots spoke on the scaffold that might not prove on occasion unfitted to her own lips.[1]

The immediate effect of the Queen's act was to extend by more than two years the duration of

Tory attacks on the Queen.

[1] Melbourne's curious passing association of the Queen's name with that of Mary Queen of Scots was made, carelessly and without deliberation, in conversation with the Queen on the evening that the session closed. When the Queen was disrobing after the ceremony of prorogation in the House of Lords, the lady who was waiting on her found difficulty in detaching the crown from her hair. At dinner in the evening the Queen told Melbourne the story, adding: 'To be sure it was very nervous for poor Lady —— to do it before so many people, all looking at her, and never having done such a thing before.' Melbourne quietly replied, '*Your Majesty might have said as Mary Queen of Scots did on the scaffold*, "I am not accustomed to be undressed before so many people nor by such attendants."'

Melbourne's ministry, and to embitter the personal hostility of the Tories towards her. James Bradshaw, the Tory M.P. for Canterbury, made at a Conservative meeting in July so caustic a comment on her reputed feeling of repugnance to his party that the Whig M.P. for Cockermouth, Edward Horsman, challenged him to a duel, which was duly fought. For the time her antipathy to the Tories certainly redoubled. 'The Tories do all in their power to make themselves odious to me,' she openly remarked at Court on reading some acrid remarks on her conduct in a Tory journal.[1]

General effect of the bedchamber crisis.
The permanent outcome of the crisis was beneficial. The Queen never repeated her obduracy, and although she often afterwards asserted her personal predilections when a new ministry was in course of creation, the nineteen changes of government that followed during her reign were effected with comparatively little friction. The 'household' difficulty never recurred. Ladies-in-waiting at once ceased to be drawn from the families of any one political party, and as early as July 1839 the Queen invited Lady Sandwich, the wife of a Tory peer, to join the household. It became the settled practice for the office of Mistress of the Robes alone to bear a political complexion, and for its holder to retire from office with the party to which she owed her appointment. Politics ceased to affect the tenure of office by the other ladies of the royal household, and no serious inquiry was made as to their political predilections.

On the whole, the two crises of 1839, although

---

[1] *Peel Papers*, ii. 405.

they were not without salutary effect on the Queen's developing character, are chiefly interesting as illustrations of traits of her disposition which time and a new environment were alone competent to hold in check. Increase of years and the good counsel of a wise husband were needed to teach the Queen to exercise with greater tact those habits of imperious command and of self-reliance which were natural to her, and to bring under firmer control the impatience and quickness of her temper.

Its testimony to the Queen's character.

VIII

MARRIAGE

Adoption of penny postage.

MELBOURNE signalised his return to power by passing into law as part of the budget proposals a reform which profoundly affected the future prosperity of the Queen's subjects and in a sense brought herself into closer personal relations with all of them. Rowland Hill's scheme for the conveyance and delivery of letters at a uniform minimum rate of one penny throughout the United Kingdom was adopted by Parliament in July 1839. The Post Office had long enjoyed a monopoly as letter-carriers, but the charges had varied, according to the distance to be traversed, from fourpence to one-and-eightpence for each sheet of letter-paper. The reduction of the charge to the uniform rate of one penny gave an enormous impetus to communication among various parts of Great Britain and Ireland for commercial and all other purposes. The usefulness of the new arrangement was greatly increased by the invention at the same time of the adhesive postage-stamp. That device, which was soon afterwards adopted by the Government, bore as its distinguishing mark the Queen's portrait-head, and this rendered her likeness familiar throughout the globe. Improvement in means of communication was perhaps the most striking characteristic of the social history of the country while the Queen reigned over it. All the improvements were the fruit of British ingenuity and originality, and foreign countries were content to follow at a respectful distance in the wake of British invention. But it is doubtful if any legislation of the Queen's reign exerted more beneficial influence on the social progress not merely of England but of the world than the postal reform, which carried as its ensign her own picture and was passed into law by her first Government just after her own obstinate will had given it a new lease of life.

Absorption in the Sovereign's work, the elation of spirit which accompanied the major part of her new experiences, the change from dependence to independence in her private affairs, put marriage out of the Queen's thoughts during the first two years of her reign. But the question was always present to the minds of her kinsfolk. Her official advisers were prudently willing to allow her to follow her own inclination in a matter of so much concern to herself, but they were fully conscious of the momentous consequences to themselves and to the State which marriage in her case involved. *Unreadiness to marry.*

The Queen's uncle, King Leopold, regarded a settlement of the question as within his peculiar province, and he had already resolved on his course of action. He had chosen her first cousin, Albert of Saxe-Coburg-Gotha, for her husband soon after her birth. He had brought his decision to his niece's notice shortly before her accession to the throne, *King Leopold's choice of Prince Albert.*

and he had no intention of quietly letting his choice be thwarted, now that she was Sovereign.

Early in 1838 King Leopold reminded his niece of his matrimonial plan. Her acknowledgment of his reminder was disconcerting. She replied that she and the Prince, who was of her own age lacking three months, were too young to think of marriage yet, and she claimed permission to defer a decision till the end of three years.

Stockmar's co-operation. King Leopold summoned Prince Albert to Brussels in March 1838, and explained the situation to him. Albert assented with some hesitation to the Queen's proposal of delay. He assumed that in her proud elevation she would ultimately seek in marriage a partner of more exalted rank than a younger son of a poor and undistinguished German duke. He somewhat supinely assumed the projected alliance to be beyond his scope. But Albert's cause had in King Leopold's confidential counsellor, Baron Stockmar, a champion as zealous as the King himself, and one probably more astute. He had left the Queen's side at the end of 1838 for the first time since her accession. During the disturbing crises of 1839 he was out of England, and for the Queen's action and inaction of that period he was in no way responsible. He was employing himself to her ultimate advantage abroad. Early in 1839 he accompanied Prince Albert on a tour in Italy with a view to keeping him faithful to King Leopold's matrimonial scheme and to instructing him betimes, in case of need, in the duties of the consort of a reigning English monarch.

Among the English courtiers doubts of the success of the innocent conspiracy, hints of which quickly spread abroad, were freely entertained. Such members of the large Coburg family as visited the Queen at this period were too 'simple' and too 'deutsch' in manner to recommend themselves to her English attendants. 'How unlike an English youth!' remarked a lady-in-waiting of the Queen's cousin, Prince Augustus of Coburg, on his visiting Windsor in August 1839. 'After being used to agreeable and well-informed Englishmen, I fear she will not easily find a foreign prince to her liking,' Lord Palmerston wrote in April 1838. Several names besides Prince Albert's were, too, freely canvassed, from the first days of her reign, as those of suitable candidates for her hand.[1] Another first cousin, Prince George of Cambridge (now Duke of Cambridge), was often in her society. A younger son of the Prussian reigning family, and the Duc de Nemours (brother of the Queen of the Belgians and second son of Louis Philippe), who had been one of her guests during the coronation festivities, were believed to possess attractions both in her sight and in that of some of her advisers. In May 1839 she entertained at Windsor the Tsarevitch of Russia (afterwards Tsar Alexander II.), the nephew of her godfather, Tsar Alexander I., together with Prince William Henry,

English courtiers and German princes.

Reputed suitors.

---

[1] The Duchess of Sutherland, the Queen's first Mistress of the Robes, writing as early as July 29, 1837, of the Queen's possible suitors, remarked: 'There is a young Danish prince come over for a few days, rather genteel, only nineteen. I suppose he has been sent to see and be seen, but I should not think with any chance.' *Stafford House Letters*, ed. Lord Ronald Gower, p. 223.

younger son of King William II. of the Netherlands; the latter had been encouraged by William IV. to regard marriage with her as a fit object of ambition, and his claims were now widely reported to be under her consideration.

Her sense of isolation in 1839.

The solution of the problem was not long delayed. The social and political embarrassments of the first half of 1839 caused the Queen a sense of isolation, which rendered the prospect of marriage more congenial to her than it was before. At the same time she suffered much annoyance from a number of offers of marriage made to her by weak-minded subjects, several of whom forced themselves personally on her notice when she was riding out, or even gained entrance to her palaces. King Leopold, who was her guest at Windsor in September 1839, was not slow to use the opportunity that the varied accidents of the eventful year presented.

Arrival of Prince Albert, Oct. 10, 1839.

The King, on returning to the Continent, directed that Prince Albert and his elder brother Ernest should present themselves at the English Court a month later. Nothing was said to the Queen in the meantime of the objects of the mission. On October 10 the young men arrived at Windsor, bearing a letter from King Leopold commending them to her notice. Many guests were there, besides Lord Melbourne, who was a permanent member of the royal circle.

Engagement to him, Oct. 15.

For four days the princes joined the Queen and a crowded retinue in the ordinary routine of afternoon rides, evening banquets, and dances; but during the entertainments she contrived to have much talk with

QUEEN VICTORIA AT THE AGE OF TWENTY
From the original sketch by Sir Edwin Landseer, *now at Windsor Castle*

Albert, and suddenly a genuine and overpowering affection between them declared itself. On October 15 she summoned the Prince to her room, and, taking full advantage of her royal station, abruptly offered him marriage. It was 'a nervous thing' to do, she afterwards told her aunt, the Duchess of Gloucester; but, she added, it would not have been possible for him to propose to the Queen of England; 'he would never have presumed to take such a liberty.'[1] Melbourne, who had already committed himself to the wise view that in the choice of a husband it was best for the Queen to please herself, seems to have been taken by surprise. His first impression was that Prince Albert was too young and untrained for the position of royal consort. But he complacently hoped for the best and was warm in his congratulations.

The Queen at once sent the information to King Leopold, by whom it was enthusiastically welcomed, but the public announcement was delayed for more than a month. During that interval the Queen and her affianced lover were rarely separated either in public or private. The Prince was conspicuous at her side at a review of the rifle brigade which she held in the Home Park on November 1, when she wore, on her own initiative, a military cap trimmed with gold. *The Queen's letter to King Leopold.*

On the 14th the visit of Albert and his brother came to an end. Next day the Queen wrote with delightful naïveté to all members of the royal family announcing her engagement. Sir Robert Peel saw *The public announcement, Nov. 20.*

---

[1] *Peel Papers*, ii. 414.

the communication she sent to Queen Adelaide, and, although he regarded the match with little enthusiasm, said she was 'as full of love as Juliet.'[1] On November 20 she left Windsor for Buckingham Palace, where on the 23rd she made the official declaration, which Melbourne had drawn up, to an extraordinary meeting of the Privy Council. No less than eighty-three members were present. The Queen wore on her arm a bracelet enclosing the Prince's miniature; although her hand shook, she read her short and simple speech without hesitation. 'It is my intention,' she said, ' to ally myself in marriage with the Prince Albert of Saxe-Coburg and Gotha. Deeply impressed with the solemnity of the engagement which I am about to contract, I have not come to this decision without mature consideration, nor without feeling a strong assurance that, with the blessing of Almighty God, it will at once secure my domestic felicity, and serve the interests of my country.' She subsequently accepted the congratulations of her councillors with great composure.

Reception of the news.

Daniel O'Connell's congratulations.

The news was received by the public with mixed feelings. Daniel O'Connell, who was in temporary alliance with the Whigs, described the coming marriage at a meeting at Bandon in ludicrous hyperboles of joy; he menaced the Tories with violent reprisals from Irish swords if they caused the Queen any renewal of anxiety in this happy crisis of her life.[2]

---

[1] *Croker Papers.*

[2] The contemporary report of O'Connell's oration at Bandon, October 5, 1839, runs thus : ' We must—we are—loyal to our young and lovely Queen—God bless her ! [*Tumultuous cheers.*] We must

O'Connell's anticipations were not unjustified. There were ominous murmurs amid the popular applause. Little was definitely known of the Prince, excepting that he was German and very young. Neither fact was a strong recommendation with the British public. Absurdly erroneous views were hastily formed of him. Some argued that he owed his good fortune to his distaste for affairs of state and his fondness for empty amusement. Others credited him with perilously stirring ambitions. The Tories took for granted that he was of 'liberal' opinions—an assumption which did not please them.[1] Baseless objection, too, was taken to him on religious grounds. Although it was notorious that the Saxe-Coburg house was staunchly Lutheran, two of its members, King Leopold and Prince Ferdinand, had lately married Roman Catholics, and a

Public criticism.

be—we are—attached to the throne, and to the lovely being by whom it is filled. She is going to be married! [*Tremendous applause.*] I wish she may have as many children as my grandmother had—two-and-twenty! [*Immense cheering and laughter.*] God bless the Queen! I am a father, and a grandfather; and in the face of heaven I pray with as much honesty and fervency for Queen Victoria as I do for any one of my own progeny. The moment I heard of the daring and audacious menaces of the Tories towards the Sovereign, I promulgated, through the press, my feelings of detestation and my determination on the matter. Oh! if I be not greatly mistaken, I'd get in one day 500,000 brave Irishmen to defend the life, the honour, and the person of the beloved young lady by whom England's throne is now filled! [*Exulting and protracted cheers.*] Let every man in the vast and multitudinous assembly stretched out before me, who is loyal to the Queen and would defend her to the last, lift up his right hand! [*The entire assembly responded to the appeal.*] There are hearts in those hands. I tell you that, if necessity required, there would be swords in them! [*Awful cheering.*]'—*Annual Register*, 1839, p. 314.

[1] *Peel Papers*, ii. 408–9.

foolish rumour circulated that Prince Albert was a papist. Abroad the match was regarded as anything but brilliant for the Queen. At foreign Courts, and even in his own domestic circle at Coburg, it was felt that the prize the Prince had won was above his station.

The Queen's demands.

The Queen, who saw the situation through the haze of true womanly affection, treated all criticisms with disdain. She especially scorned the foreign point of view. She deplored the sacrifice of family and country which she regarded the Prince as making for her sake. She held that an imperative obligation rested on her to offer him substantial recompense for his expatriation. She pressed her ministers to secure for him wellnigh every honour which she enjoyed, in order to compensate him for what he was surrendering. Like Queen Mary Tudor, she entreated that her husband should be created a king-consort. The ministers hesitated. Melbourne bluntly reminded the Queen that to acknowledge power in the legislature to make a king was to admit its power of 'unmaking' a sovereign. 'For God's sake, madam,' he is reported to have brusquely added, ' let's hear no more of it.' He pointed out that Prince Albert's rank, as well as his household and emoluments, must conform with established precedent. They must correspond with the position accorded the last prince consort, Prince George of Denmark. The Queen was galled by the comparison of her lover with ' the stupid and insignificant husband of Queen Anne,' as she called him, and was ill-disposed to let the matter rest there.

The final decision rested neither with herself nor

with the Prime Minister, but with Parliament, and Melbourne, who somewhat pusillanimously declined to invite a preliminary exchange of views with his political opponents, made no effort to force the hand of either House. The session opened on January 16, 1840, and the Queen, in the speech which she read from the throne, spoke in appropriately simple terms of her approaching marriage and requested the Legislature to make suitable provision. As soon as business began, Melbourne found himself in a difficult situation. While the Queen continued to demand in private intercourse with him a far higher status for her future husband than precedent warranted, a majority in both Houses of Parliament showed plain signs of a resolve to grant far less. Stockmar had just resumed residence with the Queen in order to give her private advice and to watch the position of affairs in the interests of King Leopold and his nephew, Prince Albert. He strenuously urged on Melbourne at the eleventh hour a private consultation between Whigs and Tories so as to avoid the disagreeable consequences of a public wrangle on matters of delicacy which personally affected the Queen. But he gained no hearing and his worst fears were realised.

Melbourne's dilemma.

The ministers confined themselves to a proposal to grant Prince Albert an annuity of 50,000*l.*, the sum granted to the Queen Consorts of George II., George III., and William IV. Objection was taken to the amount on both sides of the House. It was deemed needlessly extravagant by Tories and Radicals alike. Joseph Hume, the Radical spokesman, moved

Ministerial proposals.

I

an amendment to reduce the sum to 21,000*l.* on his habitual ground of economy. This was negatived by 305 to 38. Thereupon Colonel Sibthorp, the veteran M.P. for Lincoln, a Tory of a very pronounced kind, who warmly championed every insular prejudice, moved another amendment to reduce the sum to 30,000*l.* He received powerful support. Sir Robert Peel, the Tory leader, spoke in his favour. Sir James Graham, who had lately deserted the Whigs for the Tories, denied that the parallel with the position of the Queen Consorts could be sustained; the independent status of the Queen Consort, he said, not very logically, was recognised by the constitution, but the Prince Consort stood in no need of a separate establishment. On a division the reduction was carried against the ministry by the large majority of 104, the votes being 262 to 158.

An obvious slight had been passed by the House of Commons not merely on the ministry, but on the Queen and her future husband. Sir Robert Peel and his friends made emphatic protests against insinuations of disloyalty, and denied that the Tories were ' acting from a spiteful recollection of the events of last May.' But Lord John Russell insisted with some justice that the vote was an insult to the Sovereign. Colonel Sibthorp further proposed, as soon as the Bill making provision for the Prince reached the committee stage, that the Prince, in the event of his survival of the Queen, should forfeit the annuity if he remarried a Catholic, or failed to reside in the United Kingdom for at least six months a year. This motion was disavowed by Peel, who admitted that it implied a want of confidence in the Prince, and it was rejected. But the blow that had been struck in the earlier proceedings could not be recalled. The whole episode deeply incensed the Queen, and her uncle, King Leopold, wrote from Brussels that the action of the Commons was intolerable.

The Queen's irritation.

The House of Lords was in no more amiable mood. There the attack was led by no less a personage than the Duke of Wellington. The Duke carried an amendment to the address censuring ministers for having failed to make a public declaration that the Prince was a Protestant and able to take the Holy Communion in the form prescribed by the Church of England. On this point Stockmar had already given the ministers in private satisfactory assurances which they had neglected to divulge. But the Lords were not content with this measure of triumph. When, on January 27, the Bill for the naturalisation of the Prince was introduced into the upper chamber, it contained a clause giving him precedence next after the Queen. The royal Dukes of Sussex and Cambridge had agreed to accept a position below the Queen's husband; but the irreconcilable King of Hanover, who despite his foreign sovereignty was still Duke of Cumberland in the peerage of the United Kingdom, and still cherished the jealous belief that he had been supplanted by his niece on the English throne, bluntly declined to give way to any 'paper royal highness.' His protest found much sympathy in the Lords. Melbourne argued that he was following the precedent set in the case of Philip and Mary, but

Difficulties with the House of Lords.

The Prince's precedence.

was willing to modify the clause so as to give the heir-apparent, when he should arrive, precedence of his father. The concession was deemed inadequate, and the clause was withdrawn.

The Queen's warrant. Thereupon the Naturalisation Bill passed without further opposition, and for the moment the question of the Prince's precedence was suffered to drop. But a few months later Greville, the Clerk of the Council, prepared a paper proving that the Queen could grant her husband by royal warrant what precedence she chose without any appeal to Parliament. On this she acted, giving him under her own signature the next place to herself in all public functions.[1] But the warrant carried no weight outside the Queen's dominions. To her chagrin foreign Courts declined to recognise in the Prince any rank above that of his hereditary honours, and insisted on distinguishing his status from hers with an emphasis that wounded her wifely sentiment.

The Prince's attendants. Another difficulty arose with regard to the choice of the Prince's personal attendants. It was deemed inadvisable to allow him to appoint a private secretary for himself. A German was not reckoned desirable for the post. The Prince deprecated the appointment of an Englishman. Melbourne solved the problem by nominating his own private secretary, George Anson. Happily, neither the Queen nor the Prince had cause to regret the choice.

Meanwhile the marriage was fixed for February 10.

---

[1] Greville's paper on the subject is printed in the Appendix to *Greville Memoirs*, 2nd ser. vol. i.

Before the parliamentary wrangle ended, Lord Torrington and Colonel Grey had been sent to Coburg to invest the Prince with the insignia of the Garter and to conduct him to England. On January 28 the Prince with his father and brother left Coburg.[1] At Brussels he met his uncle Leopold. On February 7 he was at Dover. Next day he was received with much outward enthusiasm in London, and on reaching Buckingham Palace the oaths of naturalisation were administered to him by Lord Cottenham, the Lord Chancellor. On the 10th the wedding took place in the chapel of St. James's Palace. Lord Liverpool was reputed to be the only Tory to whom the Queen sent a personal invitation to attend. After an elaborate breakfast at Buckingham Palace the bride and bridegroom drove to Windsor amid vociferous acclamations. Two days later they were visited by the Duchess of Kent, the Duke of Coburg, and others, and on February 14 returned to London. On February 19 the Queen held a levee, and the Prince stood at her left hand. Despite all temporary annoyance, a period of difficulty and danger in the Queen's career had been brought to a triumphant termination.

Marriage, Feb. 10, 1840.

[1] The Prince's departure caused deep grief to many of his relatives, who had some misgivings of his future. Caroline, the Dowager Duchess of Gotha (Prince Albert's step-grandmother) wrote to a friend (in an unpublished letter in private hands) on February 3, 1840: 'The high position he goes to occupy cannot console me for his leaving, and that position will certainly not be without thorns, although the young Queen's love is for him a most comforting gift. He, too, is sincerely devoted to her, and will ever stand loyally and lovingly by her side.'

IX

PRINCE ALBERT'S POSITION

Prince Albert and his wife.

WITH her marriage a new era in the Queen's life and reign began. From a personal point of view the union realised the highest ideal of which matrimony is capable. The Queen's love for her husband was without alloy, and invested him in her sight with every perfection. He, on his part, reciprocated her affection, and he made her happiness the main object of his life.

His character and influence on the Queen.

Intellectually and morally the Prince was worthy of his position. He was admirably educated; his interests were wide; he was devoted to art, science, and literature; he was a first-rate musician; his life was scrupulously well ordered; he was sagacious, philanthropic, conscientious, and unselfish. His example and influence gave new weight and stability to the Queen's character and temperament, and her knowledge and experience grew. She always regarded the two years and eight months that intervened between her accession and her marriage as, in her own words, 'the least sensible and satisfactory time in her whole life. . . . That life of constant amusement, flattery, excitement, and mere politics had a bad effect (as it must have upon any one) on her naturally simple and serious nature.' All changed, she added, with her marriage in 1840. 'Lord Melbourne was very useful to me,' she told another friend in later life, 'but I can never be sufficiently thankful that I passed safely through those two years to my marriage. Then I was in a safe haven, and there I remained for twenty[-one] years.'[1]

But the situation was not wholly free from anxieties. Outside the domestic circle the Prince was not liked. He was cold and distant in manner, and his bearing, both mental and physical, was held to be too characteristically German to render it acceptable to Englishmen. His temperament was out of harmony with the habitual ease and levity of the English aristocracy. He had no active sense of humour, no enthusiasm for field sports, no vices; his habits were exceptionally regular, he abhorred late hours,[2] and did not conceal his disdain for many of the recreations in which the English leisured classes indulged.

Popular dislike of the Prince.

[1] Prothero, *Life of Dean Stanley*, ii. 127.

[2] Lady Willoughby de Eresby, describing to a correspondent a musical party at Lady Normanby's London house in honour of the Queen and Prince Albert in June 1840, notes: 'Lady Williamson, Lady Barrington, and Lady Hardwicke all sang divinely, supported by Lablache and Rubini. The Queen was charm'd and Cousin Albert looked beautiful, and slept as quietly as usual, sitting by Lady Normanby.' (C. K. Sharpe's *Correspondence*, ii. 524.) Monsieur Guizot, when French Ambassador in London, in 1840, describes in somewhat depreciatory terms a 'stiff' concert, which he attended at Buckingham Palace. 'The Queen' (he wrote) 'took a more lively interest in it than the greater part of her guests did. Prince Albert slept. She looked at him, half smiling, half vexed. She pushed him with her elbow. He woke up, and nodded approval of the piece of the moment. Then he went to sleep again, still nodding approval, and the Queen began again.' (*Une vie d'ambassadrice au siècle dernier—La Princesse de Lieven*, par Ernest Daudet, 1903, p. 285.)

His embarrassed position.

From a more serious point of view his position was fraught with embarrassment. His place in public affairs was undefined. He himself conscientiously believed it his duty to play a prominent part in them. The public held the view that he had no title to associate himself with them at any point. There was indeed a jealous fear abroad that his private influence with the Queen and his foreign prejudices might affect her public action to the national injury. Resentment at any possible interference by him in affairs of state quickly spread. At the Queen's request Melbourne gave her permission to show him official papers, but that concession marked at the outset the limit of his connection with matters of public business. During the first two years of his settlement in England he was deliberately excluded from her interviews with ministers. The Prince consequently felt his position to be one of humiliation. He was 'the husband, not the master of the house,' he wrote in May 1840 to his friend, Prince William of Löwenstein, and his powerlessness to improve his position filled him with deep depression.

His gradual emancipation.

The Queen was in complete sympathy with her husband's aspirations. It was never with her concurrence that he filled a rank in her kingdom or her household subordinate to herself. On December 28, 1841, she wrote in her journal: 'He ought to be, and is, above me in everything really, and therefore I wish that he should be equal in rank with me.' Happily time wrought a welcome cure. By slow degrees the Prince's undoubted abilities and prudence came to be recognised by ministers, and they gradually yielded to the Queen's persuasion to take him into their counsels. His permanent exclusion was clearly impossible. Lord Melbourne, who had hitherto filled the office of her private secretary, prepared the way to his full participation in them: he ceded that important post to the Prince. The cares of maternity were soon to distract the Queen on occasion from the details of public duty, and her dependence on her husband in all relations naturally increased with the widening experience of married life. Ultimately Prince Albert assumed in behalf of his wife in reality, although not in form, nearly all her responsibilities, and his share in the rule of the country through most of the twenty-one years of their married life is indistinguishable from hers.

As soon as the Prince finally settled down to his new life he regarded it as his province (he wrote in 1850 to the Duke of Wellington) to 'fill up every gap which, as a woman, the Queen would naturally leave in the exercise of her regal functions, continually and anxiously to watch every part of the public business, in order to be able to advise and assist her at any moment in any of the multifarious and difficult questions or duties brought before her, sometimes international, sometimes political, or social, or personal.' He claimed to be of right ' the natural head of her family, superintendent of her household, manager of her private affairs, sole *confidential* adviser in politics, and only assistant in the communications with the officers of the Government.' At the same time he was, he pointed out, ' the husband of the Queen, the tutor of the royal children, the private secretary of

The Prince's ultimate position.

the Sovereign, and her permanent minister.' The defect and danger of such a claim lay, according to the constitution of the country, in the fact that the Prince was under no parliamentary control, and his description of himself as the Queen's 'permanent minister' was inexact. Substantially, however, the statement truthfully represented the Prince's functions and occupation during his career as Queen Victoria's consort.

Obstinacy of the public prejudice.

None the less a large section of the public never conquered their first suspicions of him and never willingly acquiesced in his exercise of the authority which he gradually absorbed. Until his death he had to run the gauntlet of a galling and unceasing public criticism, and the Queen, despite her wealth of domestic happiness, was rarely free from the sense of discomfort and anxiety which was bred of a consciousness that many of her subjects viewed her husband with dislike or suspicion. But from 1841 to 1861, the date of his death, the fact is unassailable that Prince Albert's position gave him as good a right as the Queen to be regarded as the ruler of the British realm.

Changes in the palace.

Within the palace a complete revolution in the Queen's personal and domestic entourage followed hard on her marriage. Her mother, the Duchess of Kent, at once removed from her daughter's roof. The Duchess's influence in the royal circle had long been declining, and now came to an end. No less important was the retirement soon afterwards of the Baroness Lehzen from the Queen's service. These changes in the royal household disposed of checks which might have seriously limited the development of Prince Albert's power.

The supersession of both mother and *gouvernante* was effected without friction. The curmudgeonly King of Hanover declined the Queen's request to give up to the Duchess of Kent his apartments in St. James's Palace which he never occupied, and thereupon the Queen rented for her mother Ingestre House, Belgrave Square, at 2,000*l*. a year; but on the death of the Princess Augusta in September, Clarence House, St. James's Palace, was made over to her, together with Frogmore Lodge at Windsor. Hardly a day passed without the exchange of visits. As a rule, the Duchess both lunched and dined with her daughter. The Baroness Lehzen left England in October 1842 for her native country of Hanover, finally settling with a sister at Bückeburg.[1] For many years the Queen found time to write her a letter once a week, an interval which was subsequently lengthened to a month at the Baroness's own considerate request; the correspondence was maintained until the Baroness's death in 1870.[2]

Stockmar alone of the Queen's early confidential attendants retained his position after her marriage; until 1857 he spent the autumn, winter, and spring of each year with the Queen and Prince Albert, and occupied rooms in their palaces. On every domestic

The withdrawal of the Duchess of Kent.

Departure of the Baroness Lehzen.

Stockmar remains at Court.

---

[1] Cf. Bloomfield, *Reminiscences*, i. 215.
[2] As late as 1867 the Queen wrote to Sir Theodore Martin, after reading his translation of Oehlenschläger's play 'Correggio,' saying that the Baroness had often spoken to her of the original work, and asking for a copy of the translation to send to her.

or public question that arose both the Queen and Prince looked to him for private guidance.

First attempt on the Queen's life, June 10, 1840.

Amid the festivities which celebrated the early days of married life general alarm was caused by an attack on the Queen's life. The outrage had no political significance. On June 10 a brainless potboy, Edward Oxford, fired two shots at her from a pistol as she was driving through the Green Park from Buckingham Palace to Hyde Park Corner. She was unhurt, and to all appearance unmoved, and after making a call at her mother's house to assure her of her safety, she composedly continued her customary drive in Hyde Park. The lad was arrested and was mercifully pronounced to be insane. Addresses of congratulation were presented by both Houses of Parliament.

The concert at Buckingham Palace, June 12, 1840.

The incident served to increase the Queen's popularity, and in no way affected her health or spirits. On June 12, 1840—two days after—a concert was given at Buckingham Palace under Costa's direction, and the Queen herself took part in no less than five numbers, singing in a duet with Prince Albert, and in a trio with Signors Rubini and Lablache, and in three choruses.[1] A week or two later a magnificent reception was accorded her at Ascot.

---

[1] The numbers in which the Queen performed were thus entered in the printed programme :—

    Duo, ' Non funestar crudele ' (*Il Disertore*) :
        Her Majesty and Prince Albert . . . *Ricci*
    Coro Pastorale, ' Felice Età : '
        Her Majesty, Lady Sandwich, Lady Williamson, Lady Normanby, Lady Norreys,

PRINCE ALBERT'S POSITION

Next month there was promulgated intelligence of great importance to the future of the monarchy and to the happiness of the Queen's life. The approaching birth of an heir to the throne was formally announced. In such circumstances ministers were anxious to treat any request on the Queen's part in a conciliatory spirit. Consequently, in accordance with her wish, a Bill was presented by the Government to Parliament constituting Prince Albert Regent in the contingency of her death, provided that he did not remarry a Catholic and that he resided in the country.

Approaching birth of an heir.

The fear that such a proposal would be resisted by public opinion was quickly dissipated. The prudence which had distinguished the recent conduct of the Prince and the Queen was well calculated to

The Regency Bill.

    Misses Liddell and Anson; Signor Rubini and Signor Costa; Prince Albert, Lord C. Paget, and Signor Lablache . *Costa*

TRIO, 'Dunque il mio bene' (*Flauto Magico*):
    Her Majesty, Signori Rubini and Lablache   *Mozart*

QUARTETTO, con Coro, '*Tu di grazia*:'
    Her Majesty, Lady Williamson, Lady Sandwich, Lady Norreys, Lady Normanby, Misses Liddell and Anson; Signor Rubini and Signor Costa; Prince Albert, Lord C. Paget, and Signor Lablache . . . . . . *Haydn*

CORO, 'Oh come lieto giunge' (*St. Paul*):
    Her Majesty, Lady Sandwich, Lady Williamson, Lady Normanby, Lady Norreys, Misses Liddell and Anson; Signor Rubini and Signor Costa; Prince Albert, Lord C. Paget, and Signor Lablache
                                 Felix Mendelssohn

Royal advances to the Tories.

silence the opposition that might have been expected from the Tories and from the Queen's uncles. Prince Albert, by the advice of Stockmar, and with the full concurrence of Melbourne, had given ample proofs of an anxiety to relieve the strained relations between the Court and the Tories. Their leaders had been entertained by the Queen, and she had shown them marked civility. With the Duke of Wellington every effort was made to maintain cordial relations, and he reciprocated the advances with alacrity. To the Queen's discomfort her uncle, the Duke of Sussex, maintained a critical attitude, despite the filial civilities she invariably paid him, but he had been partially conciliated by the bestowal, on April 10, 1840, of the title of Duchess of Inverness on his second morganatic wife,[1] and in the same month, when the Queen and Prince Albert attended a great ball at Lansdowne House, the new Duchess was permitted to sup at the royal table.

The nomination of Prince Albert.

The pacific atmosphere which was thus engendered had the agreeable effect of commending to public approval the nomination of Prince Albert to the contingent regency. The Duke of Sussex alone proved refractory. He resisted the Bill in the House of Lords on the ground that the rights of 'the family' were ignored. But the measure became law amid signs of general complacency. On August 11, when the Queen, according to custom, prorogued Parliament in person, the Prince sat for the first time in

---

[1] Lady Cecilia Letitia Underwood, daughter of Arthur, second Earl of Arran, and widow of Sir George Buggin, Knt. She died without issue August 1, 1873.

an armchair next the throne, and, although objection was again feared, none was raised. His predominance was treated as inevitable and was accepted with as good a grace as could be hoped for. On August 28 he received the freedom of the City of London. On September 11 he was admitted to the Privy Council. On February 5, 1841, the Queen ordered his name to be inserted in the Liturgy. His right to share the Queen's ceremonial dignities was not again openly contested.

Meanwhile, on November 21, 1840, the Queen's first child, a daughter, was born at Buckingham Palace. All passed off so well and the Queen's recovery from the confinement was so rapid that the Regency Bill seemed destined to lie dormant. She was able to remove to Windsor for the Christmas holidays. On February 10, the anniversary of her marriage, the child, the Princess Royal of England, was baptized at Buckingham Palace in the names of Victoria Adelaide Mary Louisa. The sponsors were the Prince's father, the Queen's mother, and her uncle, King Leopold, besides her aunts, the Dowager Queen Adelaide and the Duchess of Gloucester, and her uncle, the sour Duke of Sussex whom the Queen treated with irrepressible charity. The Duke of Saxe-Coburg, the Prince's father, was unable to attend in person, and the Queen by her own motion chose the Duke of Wellington to represent him. The last trace of animosity on account of Wellington's open objections to the Queen's marriage was now removed. 'He is,' the Queen wrote in her journal, 'the best friend we have.'

Birth of Princess Royal, Nov. 21, 1840.

The baptism, Feb. 10, 1841.

Political anxieties.

Meanwhile politics were casting clouds on the joys of domestic life. The Queen's lively interest in the fortunes of her foreign kindred brought the business of the Foreign Office, almost to a larger extent than that of any other department of the State, within the range of her personal sympathies, and she was now to suffer, for the first of many times, a conflict of feeling between her private obligations to her foreign kindred and her public obligations to her country. Such conflict, despite her instinctive repugnance to unworthy concessions in the sphere of foreign diplomacy, was naturally liable to involve her in difficulties with her advisers.

The Queen and foreign affairs.

Questions of foreign policy strongly appealed, too, to Prince Albert, and he studied them closely and with intelligence. Melbourne had already assented to the Queen's proposal, which private sentiment rather than public considerations prompted, that her husband should enjoy free access to all the Foreign Office despatches. But the tacit perusal of the papers was barely possible to the Prince's active, well-informed mind, and he soon claimed in behalf of the Queen the full right to a voice in consultation before any action was taken by the Government abroad. Under his guidance the Queen came to regard the supervision of foreign affairs as peculiarly within the Sovereign's province.

The Prince and foreign policy.

Palmerston at the Foreign Office.

The pretension on the part of the Queen or of her husband to influence ministerial decisions required tactful assertion in view of the general constitutional principle which gave Parliament sole supremacy of control in all departments of government. In the existing juncture of foreign affairs it was especially difficult to press the claim without generating friction between the Sovereign and her ministers. Palmerston, the Foreign Secretary in Melbourne's ministry, had held his office (with only four months' interval in 1835, during which the Tories, under Peel, had a fleeting taste of power) for the long period of ten years.[1] He joined Lord Grey's ministry as Foreign Secretary at the end of 1830. In that post he won his main reputation, and was ambitious to wield in it unquestioned authority. His Liberalism in domestic matters was of a vague pattern, which never wholly lost the colour of his early political associations with the Tories, but his views of foreign policy were firmly and confidently held. They were formed under the influence of Canning, and were impregnated by a genuine enthusiasm for popular liberty, by a hatred of political despotism, and by an assertive faith in England's power and right to impose at will on foreign monarchies the political principles that she had herself adopted. Of a masterful temperament, he treated all who offered him counsel with a breezy air of scornful superiority. Carelessly frank in conversation, he was no respecter of persons; his unreadiness to conciliate their idiosyncrasies had earned him the cordial dislike of Queen Victoria's two predecessors on the throne,

His frankness of address.

---

[1] Palmerston had first entered the House of Commons as a Tory at the youthful age of three-and-twenty, thirty years before the Queen came to the throne, and he had filled a subordinate post in no less than five Tory administrations between 1809 and 1828, before he transferred his allegiance in the latter year to the Whigs.

George IV. and William IV. He always affected to ignore the natural and inevitable sympathy which English sovereigns felt with the occupants of foreign thrones.

His impatience of the Prince's counsel.

Personally, Palmerston had in the first years of her reign made himself agreeable to the Queen, who was his junior by thirty-five years. In 1839 he married Lord Melbourne's sister, the widow of Lord Cowper, a union which the Queen thoroughly approved. But in all the circumstances of the case it could only be on sufferance that the Prince, or indeed the Queen herself, could expect to share in Palmerston's management of foreign affairs.

Palmerston and the throne.

Palmerston, at the first entrance of the Prince on the scene, avowed conscientious reluctance to recognise the existence outside Parliament of any check on his independence. His attitude at once caused vexation in the royal circle. None the less he persisted in it unmoved. Prolonged heartburnings followed, and they ultimately led to an open rupture between the Crown and one of the most influential of its constitutional advisers. But much was to happen before that point was reached in the relations of Queen Victoria and Lord Palmerston.

Mehemet Ali and Turkey, 1840.

The earliest immediate cause of divergence (in 1840) between the Queen and her Foreign Minister was due to affairs in the east of Europe, which threatened a breach in the friendly relations of France and England. Egypt under her Viceroy, Mehemet Ali, was seeking to cast off her allegiance to the Sultan of Turkey. France encouraged the act of rebellion, while England and the rest of the Great Powers took

Turkey under their protection. The Queen and Prince Albert loathed the prospect of war with France, with whose sovereign, Louis Philippe, they had, through repeated intermarriages, close domestic relations; and the added likelihood that the dominions of her uncle and political ally, King Leopold, which were under England's protection, would, in case of war between England and France, be invaded by a French army, filled the Queen with alarm. *Political crisis with France.*

Divisions in the cabinet encouraged intervention on the part of the Queen and Prince. Lord John Russell seldom took Palmerston's view of foreign complications, and he raised his voice for the preservation of peace at all hazards. Palmerston, however, peremptorily decided that the best way of dissipating all risk of French predominance in Egypt was to crush Mehemet Ali at once by force of English arms. The Queen appealed with energy to Melbourne. She entreated him to reconcile his divided colleagues, to use his influence against Palmerston, and to seek a pacific settlement with France. But Palmerston stood firm. He summarily issued orders to the British fleet to apply force to Mehemet Ali and compel him to return to his allegiance to the Sultan (November 1840). To all appearance the French King was under an obligation to retaliate by bringing material support to Mehemet Ali's aid. War between France and England seemed to be inevitable. How deeply the episode impressed itself on the Queen's mind is evident from her half-playful remark to her uncle, King Leopold, when she was considering amid the crisis the names to be bestowed on her *Divisions in the cabinet.*

K 2

newly born infant: 'I think our child,' she wrote, 'ought to have, besides its other names, those of Turko-Egypto, for we think of nothing else.'

Palmerston's triumphant action.

The victory remained with Palmerston. The minister's triumph was indeed more rapid and complete than even he anticipated. Louis Philippe, to the general surprise, proved too pusillanimous to take the offensive in behalf of his friend in Egypt, who quickly yielded to English coercion. The French King finally joined the concert of the Powers, who in July 1841 pledged themselves by treaty to maintain Turkey and Egypt *in statu quo*. But the incident evoked in Louis Philippe, in his ministers, and in King Leopold a feeling of bitterness against Palmerston which, despite the preservation of European peace, found a ready echo in the minds of Queen Victoria and the Prince.

Weakness of Melbourne's ministry.

The foreign crisis was not the only political trouble that confronted the Queen at this season. There were sources of anxiety nearer home. The Government was losing its hold on the House of Commons, and the retirement of Melbourne's ministry, which the Queen had long dreaded, was clearly a question of weeks. The prospect of parting with Melbourne, her tried councillor, caused her pain. But, in anticipation of the inevitable event, hints had been given at Prince Albert's instance by the Court officials to the Tory leaders that the Queen would interpose no obstacle to a change of government when it became inevitable, and would not resist such reconstruction of her household as might be needful. The blow fell in May. The agitation for free trade was growing in the country, through the energetic efforts of Cobden, and the Whig ministers introduced a budget which gently tended in the popular direction. For radical changes in the fiscal system of the country Parliament was not prepared, and on the ministry's proposal to reduce the duty on sugar they were defeated by a majority of thirty-six. Sir Robert Peel thereupon carried a vote of confidence against them by one vote. It was open to Melbourne to resign and to advise the Queen to entrust Peel with the duty of forming a government. But, moved by the Queen's feelings, Melbourne forbore to take that step. Instead of resigning, he recommended the Queen to appeal to the country. Parliament was dissolved on June 29.

<small>Defeat of Melbourne, May 1841.</small>

The Queen hoped against hope that th ecountry might decide the trial at issue in favour of her old friend Melbourne. But the signs were not propitious. In June, amid the political excitement, the Queen paid a visit to Archbishop Harcourt at Nuneham, and thence she and Prince Albert proceeded to Oxford to attend Commemoration. The Duke of Wellington, the Chancellor of the University, presided, and conferred on the Prince an honorary degree. The Queen was disturbed by the hisses which were levelled at the Whig ministers who were present. But their threatened loss of popular favour incited her to give further proof of her attachment to them. She seized the opportunity to pay a series of visits among the Whig nobility. After spending a day or two with the Duke of Devonshire at Chatsworth, the royal party was entertained next month by the Duke of Bedford

<small>The Queen at Oxford, June.</small>

<small>The Queen's sympathy with Whig ministers.</small>

at Woburn Abbey and by Lord Cowper, Melbourne's nephew, at Panshanger. From Panshanger they went to lunch with Melbourne himself at his country residence, Brocket Park.

Defeat of the Whigs at the polls.

The general election was proceeding at the time, and the Whigs made the most out of the Queen's known sympathy with them and of her alleged antipathy to their opponents. But, to the Queen's dismay, a large Tory majority was returned, and she recognised that she was face to face with that party in the State which she had hitherto viewed with dislike and distrust.

X

SIR ROBERT PEEL'S ADMINISTRATION

THE new Parliament assembled on August 19, 1841. The Queen made no secret of her disappointment at the results of the recent electoral battle. For the first time in her reign she was absent at the opening of the session, and her speech was read by the Lord Chancellor, an indication that the constitution of the House of Commons was not to her liking. Melbourne's ministry remained in office till the last possible moment, but on August 28 a vote of confidence was refused it by both Houses of Parliament. The same evening Melbourne saw the Queen at Windsor and resigned his trust. She accepted his resignation in a spirit of deep dejection, which he did something to moderate by assuring her of the high opinion he had formed of her husband. On August 30 Melbourne took leave of Prince Albert. The Prince wrote to him later in the day of 'the *real grief* with which he said farewell.' *[The Queen's regrets.]*

In conformity with Lord Melbourne's advice the Queen at once summoned Sir Robert Peel, and invited him to form a government. The lesson she had learnt in 1839 bore good fruit, and she raised no objection to any of his proposals. Although she *[Acceptance of Peel's ministry.]*

spoke freely to him of her grief in separating from her late ministers, she discussed the business in hand with a composure and correctness of manner which aroused Peel's admiration. He promised to consult her comfort in all household appointments, and changes were made with the Queen's full approval. Peel wrote (September 18, 1841) that he was 'met by her Majesty in a very fair and considerate spirit.' The Duchess of Buccleuch replaced the Duchess of Sutherland as Mistress of the Robes, and the Duchess of Bedford and Lady Normanby voluntarily made way for other ladies-in-waiting. By September the new Government was formed, and the Queen had the tact to treat her new ministers with every appearance of amiability. The Council, at which the new officers of state kissed hands on their appointment, was held at Claremont. Gladstone, who joined Peel's government as Vice-President of the Board of Trade, and was made a Privy Councillor, wrote of the proceedings: 'The Queen sat at the head of the table, composed but dejected—one could not but feel for her all through the ceremonial.'[1]

Cordiality between the Queen and Peel.

Prophecies of evil were summarily confuted, and the main credit for the avoidance of disaster must be divided between Prince Albert and Peel. The Prince's influence induced in the Queen's attitude to the machinery of politics a prudent complacency of which her earlier conduct had given no sign. Peel adapted himself to the situation with admirable tact. In the result he and the Queen were soon the best of friends. Accepting Melbourne's hint, he fully yet briefly ex-

[1] Morley, *Life of Gladstone*, i. 242.

ably.¹ Among the new officers of her household she warmly welcomed her early friend, Lord Liverpool, who filled the post of Lord Steward.

Birth of Prince of Wales, Nov. 9, 1841.

A short autumn session closed on October 7. The Queen was absent from the ceremony of prorogation, but her absence was due to personal affairs and to no want of confidence in her new advisers. On November 9, 1841, her second child, a son and heir, was born at Buckingham Palace. The confinement was imminent for several weeks, and, though she hesitated to appear in public, she, with characteristic spirit, continued ' to write notes, sign her name, and declare her pleasure up to the last moment, as if nothing serious were at hand.' ² Sir Robert Peel had accepted an invitation to dine with her on the night of the child's birth.

General rejoicings.

Much public and private rejoicing followed the arrival of an heir to the throne. Christmas festivities were kept with great brilliance at Windsor, and on January 25 the christening took place in St. George's Chapel with exceptional pomp. The boy was named Albert Edward, and more than fifty-nine years later succeeded his mother as King Edward VII. Vague political reasons induced the Government to invite

---

¹ The other members of Peel's cabinet, as first constituted, were: Henry Goulburn, Chancellor of the Exchequer; Lord Ripon, President of the Board of Trade; Sir Henry Hardinge, Secretary at War; Lord Wharncliffe, President of the Council; the Duke of Buckingham, Lord Privy Seal. Gladstone became Vice-President of the Board of Trade without a seat in the cabinet, but he entered the cabinet in 1843 as President of the Board of Trade. Disraeli was bitterly disappointed by Peel's failure to confer any office on him. (Cf. *Peel Papers*, ii.)

² Sir James Graham, ap. *Croker Papers*, ii. 408.

plained to her every detail of affairs. He strictly obeyed the request which she made him as soon as he took up the reins of government to send regularly and promptly a daily report of proceedings of interest that took place in both the Houses of Parliament. The duty which the Queen required of him of constant attendance on her, and of autograph correspondence with her several times a day, seriously taxed Peel's time and patience ; but he faithfully performed it throughout his tenure of office.[1] Melbourne was thenceforth an occasional and always an honoured guest at Court, but the Queen accustomed herself without delay to seek political guidance exclusively from Peel, and the confidence she reposed in him soon equalled that which she had reposed in his predecessor.

Closer acquaintance with Peel's leading colleagues finally dissipated, too, her early antipathy to the Tory party and to Tory principles. The Duke of Wellington joined Peel's cabinet without office, and her relations with him increased in cordiality now that he was in official association with her. With Lord Lyndhurst, the Lord Chancellor, with Lord Aberdeen, the Foreign Secretary, and with Sir James Graham, the Home Secretary, she came in frequent contact, and all treated her with that respectful kindliness and courteous frankness which always won her regard. Lord Stanley (afterwards Earl of Derby), the War and Colonial Secretary, who was thrice to act as her Prime Minister hereafter, also impressed her favour-

Change of attitude to the Tories.

---

[1] Morley, *Life of Gladstone*, i. 297-299.

Inconvenient display of loyalty at Brighton.

homely instincts which were strong in her people. When a week later she went with her young family to stay a month at the Pavilion, the royal residence at Brighton, her presence excited more public demonstration of goodwill than was convenient.[1] Privacy was sought in vain. The Queen and Prince Albert conceived, in consequence, a dislike for the place, and soon sought a more sequestered seaside retreat.

The London season of 1842.

The following season of 1842 combined agreeable with distasteful incidents. The first of a brilliant series of fancy dress balls took place to the Queen's great contentment at Buckingham Palace on May 12; the Prince appeared as Edward III. and the Queen as Queen Philippa. Some feeling was shown in France at what was foolishly interpreted as the celebration of ancient victories won by the English over French arms. The entertainment was charitably designed to give work to the Spitalfields weavers, who were then in distress. A fortnight later the Queen and Court went in state to a ball at Covent Garden Theatre, which was organised in the interest of the same sufferers. But French sensitiveness was too acute to be easily appeased.

The introduction of railways.

In June the Queen first associated herself publicly with that improved mode of locomotion which was revolutionising the social economy of the country. It was in 1825 that the first railway between Stockton and Darlington had been opened, and in 1830 was inaugurated the line between Manchester and Liverpool. During the reign of William IV. the new system of travelling had been steadily growing in all

[1] Lady Bloomfield's *Reminiscences*.

Frederick William, King of Prussia, to be the chief sponsor; the others were the Queen's uncle, the Duke of Cambridge, her aunt, Princess Sophia, and three members of the Saxe-Coburg family. To the King of Prussia, who stayed with the Queen for the christening ceremony from January 22 to February 4, she paid every honour,[1] and her personal intimacy with the Prussian royal house was thus initiated. Subsequently the King of Prussia, who was not gifted with much political insight or strength of purpose, took advantage of the good personal relations he had formed with the Queen to correspond with her confidentially on political affairs with somewhat embarrassing results.

The sponsors.

The King of Prussia.

The preponderance of German guests at the christening of the Prince of Wales caused some unamiable comment. Adverse criticism, too, was excited by the formal bestowal on the little Prince of his father's hereditary title of Duke of Saxony, and by the quartering of his father's hereditary arms of Saxony on his shield with those of England. Such procedure was regretted as a concession by the Queen to her husband's German predilections, but it was in conventional accord with heraldic law. On February 3, 1842, when the Queen opened Parliament, the King of Prussia accompanied her. There was no great display of loyalty in the streets,[2] but she impressed her auditors in the House of Lords by referring in the speech from the throne to the birth of her son as 'an event which has completed the measure of my domestic happiness.' The words appealed to the

Popular fear of German preponderance.

[1] Bunsen, ii. 7. [2] Fanny Kemble's *Records*, ii. 181.

1842] SIR ROBERT PEEL'S ADMINISTRATION 141

parts of the country, but it still provoked almost as much hostility as approval. The superiority of horse-power to steam-power for purposes of haulage had many loud-voiced advocates when the Queen ascended the throne. It was not till the year after her accession that London was first entered by a railway—by the North-Western company's line from Birmingham. Subsequently lines to London multiplied quickly. The battle of the railway was not, however, altogether won till seven years of the Queen's reign had passed, when the last stage-coaches were driven off the southern roads.

The Queen's first experience of railway travelling was an event of no little interest to herself and of no small encouragement to the pioneers of the new mechanical invention. The journey was made on the new Great Western line from Slough to Paddington.[1] Court etiquette required that the Master of the Horse and the coachmen under his control should actively direct the Queen's travels by land, and it was difficult to adapt the old forms to the new conditions of locomotion. But satisfactory arrangements were made, and the Queen thoroughly enjoyed the novel experience. Thenceforth she utilised to the fullest extent the growing railway systems of the kingdom, and especially interested herself in improvements which should secure the safety and comfort of the poorer passengers.

The Queen first travels by rail, June 1842.

Unhappily two further senseless attempts on her life, which took place at the same time, marred her

Second attempt on her life.

The line from Slough to Windsor was first opened on October 8 1849.

sense of security, although they offered her opportunity of proving anew her intrepidity of spirit. In her attitude to the first attempt the Queen and Prince Albert indeed showed a courage which bordered on imprudence. On Sunday, May 29, Prince Albert noticed that a man pointed a pistol at the Queen as she drove past him in her carriage through the Green Park. She and the Prince resolved to pass the same spot on the following afternoon in order to secure the arrest of the assailant, if, as they surmised, he should put in a second appearance. The bold device succeeded. 'She would much rather,' the Queen explained at the moment, 'run the immediate risk at any time than have the presentiment of danger constantly hovering over her.' The man, who proved to be a destitute carpenter named John Francis, fired at her as she passed him for the second time, happily without result, and, being easily captured, was condemned to death, a sentence which was commuted to transportation for life. On the evening following the outrage, the Queen visited the opera to hear the 'Prophète,' and was cheered rapturously.

Third attempt on her life.

But the danger was, unfortunately, not past. A new attempt on the Queen's life followed almost immediately. On July 3, when she was driving in the Mall with the King of the Belgians, who happened to be her guest, a crippled lad, John William Bean, sought in an aimless, half-hearted way to emulate the misdeeds of Francis and Oxford. There was no endeavour in this instance to inflict actual injury, and the offender received only eighteen months' imprisonment; but some new steps were clearly needed to prevent the repetition of cowardly offences so damaging to the repute of the nation. According to the strict interpretation of the existing law, these contemptible outrages could be treated solely as acts of high treason, and the offenders won through their misdeeds a notoriety and a specious importance which were gratifying to their vanity. Peel, immediately after the date of Bean's offence, hastily passed through Parliament a 'Bill for providing for the further protection and security of her Majesty's person.' The terms of the measure made any attempt to hurt the Queen a criminal offence far below the dignity of treason; it was reduced to the rank of a misdemeanour punishable by either transportation for seven years or imprisonment for three, with or without personal chastisement at the discretion of the judge. On the whole the new law worked with good effect. *New legislation for her personal security.*

Signs of unrest were numerous in the country. Chartist riots had long been distracting the nation. The Chartist movement was an outcome of political and social discontent on the part of the working classes. The reformed House of Commons had failed to grapple with social questions so as to relieve the economic distress which had prevailed among the poorer classes of the community since the great war, and the disappointment bred an agitation for a further change in the constitution of the Legislature. The people's charter, which had been drawn up by the leaders of the working men in 1838, demanded manhood suffrage, equal electoral districts, vote by *Chartist agitation.*

ballot, abolition of property qualification for members of Parliament, and payment of members of the House of Commons for their services. Whig and Tory Governments alike declined to treat such proposals seriously. A powerful section among the agitators advocated violent reprisals. Riotous attacks on the police and on wealthy representatives of the middle classes who were especially obnoxious to the Chartists were made, in the Northern and Midland counties especially, during the winter and spring of 1842 The Queen pressed her ministers to employ decisive measures for the preservation of peace, but did not take an unduly serious view of the danger.

During the summer the Queen directed Peel to arrange for her an autumn holiday in Scotland. To her surprise the prudence of a royal progress through the disturbed districts of the north of England was gravely doubted by her ministers. But Peel was anxious to forward the Queen's wish, and after consulting Sir James Graham, the Home Secretary, he came to the conclusion that the expedition to Scotland might be safely and wisely made by sea.

First visit to Scotland, Aug. to Sept. 1842.

It was the first visit that the Queen paid to North Britain, and in the event greatly added to her future happiness. It inspired her with a lifelong regard for Scotland and its inhabitants, and as her years increased, her heart (in her own words) 'yearned to that part of her dominions more and more.' The first portion of the journey, on her first expedition across the border—that from Slough to Paddington—was again made by rail. At Woolwich the royal party embarked on the 'Royal George' yacht on

August 29, and on September 1 they arrived at Granton pier.

There Sir Robert Peel, at the Queen's request, met them. Passing through Edinburgh they stayed with the Duke of Buccleuch at Dalkeith, where on September 5 the Queen held a drawing-room and received addresses. Next day the royal party left for the highlands, and, after paying a visit to Lord Mansfield at Scone, were accorded a princely reception by Lord Breadalbane at Taymouth. A brief stay with Lord Willoughby at Drummond Castle was followed by their return to Dalkeith, and they left Scotland by sea for the return journey on the 15th.

Her Scottish hosts.

Not only was the Queen enchanted with the scenery through which she passed, but the historic associations, especially those connected with Mary Stuart— her 'unfortunate ancestress' as she called her—and with her son, James I., deeply interested her, and she read on the voyage with a new zest Sir Walter Scott's poems, 'The Lady of the Lake' and 'The Lay of the Last Minstrel.'[1] Before embarking she instructed Lord Aberdeen to write to the Lord Advocate an expression of her regret that her visit was so brief, and of her admiration of the devotion and enthusiasm which had been 'evinced in every quarter and by all ranks' of her Scottish subjects.[2] On September 17 she was again at Windsor.[3]

Her affection for Scotland.

The experience left so pleasant an impression that

---

[1] *Leaves from the Queen's Journal*, 1867, pp. 1-28.

[2] *Greville Memoirs.*

[3] In November the Duke of Wellington placed Walmer Castle at her disposal, and she and her family were there from November 10 to December 3.

Second visit to Scotland.

it was soon repeated. Two years later, in 1844, another peaceful autumn holiday was spent in Scotland. On that occasion the Queen and the Prince proceeded by sea from Woolwich to Dundee. Thence they drove to Blair Athol to visit Lord and Lady Glenlyon, afterwards the Duke and Duchess of Athol, to both of whom the Queen became deeply attached. Prince Albert engaged in deerstalking, and the Queen did much sketching. The 'life of quiet and liberty' proved even more enjoyable than before, and bred a resolve to revisit Scotland as often as was practicable. With regret they set out on the return voyage to Woolwich on October 3, when their second Scottish sojourn ended.[1]

The Queen and Peel.

With Peel the Queen's good relations remained uninterrupted. On April 6, 1842, after six months' experience of office, he described his position thus : 'My relations with her Majesty are most satisfactory. The Queen has acted towards me not merely (as every one who knew her Majesty's character must have anticipated) with perfect fidelity and honour, but with great kindness and consideration. There is every facility for the despatch of public business, a scrupulous and most punctual discharge of every public duty, and an exact understanding of the relation of a constitutional sovereign to her advisers.'[2]

The disruption of the Scottish Church.

With the domestic policy of her ministers the Queen thoroughly identified herself. During the autumn of 1842 the schism in the Scottish Church on the question of the right of the local presbytery to reject in certain circumstances the minister whom

---

[1] *Journal*, pp. 29–42.   [2] *Peel Papers*, ii. 544.

the lay patron presented to the benefice led to the disruption of the Scottish Establishment and the formation of the Free Church. The Queen, in a letter to Peel, described 'the demands and assertions' of those members of the General Assembly who sought to limit the exercise of lay patronage as 'extraordinary and inadmissible.' She manifested full sympathy with her Government's declaration against interference with the patron's ancient and hitherto unrestricted rights.[1]

In January 1843 the Queen was deeply concerned at the assassination of Peel's secretary, Edward Drummond, in mistake for himself, and she shrewdly criticised in private the jury's verdict of insanity at the trial of MacNaughten, the assassin.[2] With common-sense wisdom the Queen wrote to Peel, January 25: 'The proofs of the wretch MacNaughten's madness seem to the Queen very slight, and indeed there is and should be a difference between that madness which is such that a man knows not what he does, and madness which does not prevent a man from purposely buying pistols, and then with determined purpose watching and shooting a person.'

The murder of Edward Drummond.

Among Peel's colleagues, Lord Aberdeen, Minister of Foreign Affairs, came after Peel himself into closest personal relations with the Queen and the Prince, and with him she found herself in hardly less complete accord. But elements of difficulty still lurked in her attitude to foreign affairs. She never concealed even from Lord Aberdeen her wish to bring the Foreign Office under the active influence of the

The Queen and Lord Aberdeen.

[1] *Peel Papers*, ii. 568.
[2] Martin, i. 27 ; *Peel Papers*, ii. 553.

Crown. She bade Aberdeen observe 'the rule that all drafts not mere matters of course should be sent to her before the despatches had left the office.' Aberdeen guardedly replied that 'this should be done in all cases in which the exigencies of the situation did not require another course.' She found no practical difficulty in acquiescing in the reservation. Lord Aberdeen's general policy developed no principle from which the Queen or the Prince dissented, and the harmony of their intercourse was undisturbed.[1]

Prince Albert's growing influence.

Peel greatly strengthened the cordiality of his relations with the Sovereign by a full acknowledgment of Prince Albert's position. He permitted the Prince to attend the audiences of ministers with the Queen. He nominated him president of a royal commission to promote the fine arts of the United Kingdom in connection with the rebuilding of the Houses of Parliament which had been burnt down in 1834, and he encouraged the Prince to reform the confused administration of the royal palaces. The Prince's authority consequently increased. From 1843 onwards the Queen, in announcing her decision on public questions to her ministers, substituted for the singular personal pronoun 'I' the plural 'we,' and thus entirely identified her own judgment with her husband's. The growth of his authority was indicated in the spring of 1843 by his holding levees in the Queen's behalf in her absence—an apparent assumption of fresh power which was none too well received by the press or by the public.

Domestic incidents occupied much of the Queen's

[1] Walpole, *Life of Lord John Russell*, ii. 54.

attention. The death of her uncle, the Duke of Sussex, on April 21, 1843, preceded by four days the birth of a third child, the Princess Alice. The coincidence of the two events impelled her, mainly from domestic sentiment, to make some new advances to her unfriendly uncle, Ernest, the King of Hanover, who was now one of the only two surviving sons of George III., the Duke of Cambridge being the other. The Queen asked King Ernest to be a sponsor of her second daughter Alice, together with her half-sister, Countess Féodore, Prince Albert's brother, and Princess Sophia. The King accepted the invitation, but with characteristic awkwardness arrived too late for the christening (June 5). He came soon afterwards, and remained in England for several weeks, apparently to prove that he still regarded his niece as an obstacle in the path of his obsolete ambition of succeeding to his father's crown. A large family gathering followed his arrival, for there was a wedding to be celebrated in the royal circle in July. The Queen's first cousin Augusta, elder daughter of the Duke of Cambridge, married at Buckingham Palace, on the 28th, Friedrich, Hereditary Grand Duke of Mecklenburg-Strelitz.

Domestic incidents, 1843.

The baptism of Princess Alice.

King Ernest, who attended the ceremony in a surly mood, improved the occasion by an unusually brusque effort to disturb the equanimity of his hostess. When the register was to be signed after the wedding, the King made a bold endeavour, by furtively taking up a position next the Queen, to set his autograph in the book immediately after hers and before that of Prince Albert, whom he especially disliked. The Queen herself perceived the manœuvre

The surliness of the King of Hanover.

and foiled it. Suddenly moving to that part of the table where the Prince was standing, she had the book hurriedly passed to her, and, having appended her own signature, at once handed the pen to her husband before the King had time to change his place at the table. By way of marking her resentment of her uncle's unconciliatory demeanour, she gave King Leopold precedence of him at Court. She first consulted the Duke of Wellington as to how she might justify such procedure, and the Duke advised her to follow the example of the Congress of Vienna, at which representatives were arranged in the alphabetical order of the countries whence they came: 'B [i.e. Belgium] comes before H [i.e. Hanover],' he quietly explained.[1] In August two of Louis Philippe's sons, brothers of the Queen of the Belgians, the Prince de Joinville and the Duc d'Aumale, joined the Queen's party, and she extended to them all the solicitous courtesy which she reserved for connections of the Saxe-Coburg House.

Queen's visit to Louis Philippe.

A month later, after proroguing Parliament in person (August 24) and making a short yachting tour on the south coast, the Queen carried out an intention that had long been present in her mind of paying a visit to the King of the French, with whose family her own was so closely connected by marriage. It was not a scheme which the Queen's ministers suggested or even regarded at the first glance with favour. It was the fruit of the Queen's personal intimacy with the Queen of the Belgians, Louis Philippe's daughter, who during her frequent sojourns

[1] Raikes, *Journal*.

at Windsor had long urged on the English Sovereign a visit to France.

The resolve of Queen Victoria and Prince Albert to cross the English Channel was an event of much interest, historic, political, and constitutional. In the first place it was the first occasion on which the Queen had trodden foreign soil. In the second place it was the first occasion on which an English sovereign had visited a French sovereign since Henry VIII. appeared on the Field of the Cloth of Gold at the invitation of Francis I. in 1520. In the third place it was the first time for nearly a century that an English monarch had left his own dominions, and the old procedure of nominating in his absence a Regent or Lords-Justices was now first dropped.

Varied interest of the event.

The question of forming a regency according to precedent during the Queen's projected absence much exercised the minds of the ministers. Neither George III. nor William IV. ever quitted Great Britain while they filled the throne. But George I. and George II. had frequently visited their dominion of Hanover, while George IV. went thither once. It was a settled custom in Georgian days to confer on duly appointed deputies the main executive power of sovereignty so long as the King was absent. The practice was now reconsidered. The Duke of Wellington was emphatic in the opinion that 'the Queen could not quit this country without an Act of Regency,' and to the argument that Henry VIII. had crossed to Calais without any such formality he replied that Calais was then an English possession and was comparable to an English county. The

The question of a regency.

problem was finally submitted to the Crown lawyers, who reported that the nomination of a regency might be safely dispensed with. The ministers adopted their view, and thereby relieved the Sovereign of a somewhat harassing restriction of her personal liberty.[1] Of this relief the Queen in future years took full advantage, and the frequency of her visits to the continent—often in an informal way—was one of the points in which her practice as Sovereign differed from that of her predecessors.

At the Château d'Eu.

Although the French expedition was the outcome of domestic sentiment rather than of political design, Peel and Aberdeen offered no opposition on its first proposal, and ultimately encouraged it in the belief that the maintenance of good personal relations between the English Sovereign and her continental colleagues was a guarantee of peace and goodwill among the nations. The view was also held strongly by Lord Brougham, who differed from contemporary statesmen on almost all other subjects. Louis Philippe and his Queen were staying at the Château d'Eu, a private domain near Tréport. The Queen, accompanied by Lord Aberdeen, arrived there on September 2 in her new yacht 'Victoria and Albert,' which had been launched on April 25, and of which Lord Adolphus FitzClarence, a natural son of William IV., had been appointed captain.

Louis Philippe's hospitality.

Her host met the Queen in his barge off the coast, and a magnificent reception was accorded her. The happy domestic life of the French royal family

[1] Raikes, *Journal*, ii. 368.

strongly impressed her, and she appreciated 'the parental air' with which Louis Philippe treated her.[1] She greeted with enthusiasm, among the French King's guests, the French musician Auber, with whose works she was very well acquainted, and she was charmed by two *fêtes champêtres* and a military review. Lord Aberdeen and M. Guizot, Louis Philippe's minister, who while French Ambassador in London in 1840 had failed to win much favour at the English court, discussed political questions with apparent cordiality, and although their conversations led later to misunderstanding, everything passed off at the moment agreeably. The visit lasted five days, from September 2 to 7, and the Queen's spirit fell when it was over.[2]

On leaving Tréport the Queen spent another four days with her children at Brighton, and paid her last visit to George IV.'s inconvenient Pavilion. But her foreign tour was not yet ended. From Brighton she

The Queen in Belgium.

[1] Peel wrote jestingly to Aberdeen of Louis Philippe's alleged bourgeois notions of hospitality on August 31: 'I see that for the purpose of doing honour to his royal visitors and their companions, he [i.e. Louis Philippe] sent a very large order to England for cheese and bottled beer. I hope you will have had calm weather so that you may all enjoy these delicacies.' *Peel Papers*, iii. 393.

[2] A year later Louis Philippe sent to the Queen at Windsor a char-à-bancs, which he had caused to be built on the model of one of his, which she had admired while at the Château d'Eu. The Queen wrote, on September 6, 1844, to the Queen of the French a long autograph letter of thanks, in French, which is now in the British Museum (MS. Addit. 24023): 'Je ne saurais vous dire (she remarked) *combien* nous pensions ce jour-là, ainsi que tous ces jours, aux doux moments que nous avons passés à Eu, au milieu de vous tous.' A postscript acknowledged the gift of 'le curieux et beau tableau de François II., qui est d'une grande valeur pour notre collection.'

sailed in her yacht to Ostend to pay a long-promised visit to her uncle, the King of the Belgians, at the palace of Laeken, near Brussels. 'It was such a joy for me,' she wrote after parting with him, 'to be once again under the roof of one who has ever been a father to me.' The novelist Charlotte Brontë, who was in Brussels, saw her 'laughing and talking very gaily' when driving through the Rue Royale, and noticed how plainly and unpretentiously she was dressed.[1] Her vivacity brought unwonted sunshine to King Leopold's habitually sombre Court.

First visit to Trinity College, Cambridge.

The Queen reached Woolwich, on her return from Antwerp, on September 21, and the concluding months of the year (1843) were agreeably spent in visits at home. In October she went by road to pay a first visit to Cambridge. Dr. Whewell, the Master of Trinity, who was at the time Vice-Chancellor of the University, had written, on first learning of the Queen and Prince Albert's wish to come to Cambridge, that Trinity claimed on all occasions the honour of receiving the Sovereign or her representatives, and invited the royal party to stay at the Master's Lodge. It is questionable whether the common notion that Trinity Lodge is actually a royal residence rests on firm foundations. But the form of the reception which Whewell accorded the Queen suggests that he acknowledged her authority to be superior to his own within his own college. As Vice-Chancellor he met her outside the College gates and delivered to her

[1] Gaskell, *Life of Charlotte Brontë*, 1900, p. 270. Miss Brontë in *Villette*, chap. xx., paints in very gloomy colours a portrait of King Leopold, 'a nervous, melancholy man,' a victim of that darkest foe of humanity, 'constitutional melancholy.'

his mace. As Master of Trinity he handed to her in the middle of the court all his keys of office.[1] While staying at the Lodge of Trinity College, she held a levee in Trinity Hall. She visited the Senate-house to witness Prince Albert's reception of a doctor's degree from the University. The undergraduates offered her a thoroughly enthusiastic reception.

Next month she gave public proof of her regard for Peel by visiting him at Drayton Manor (November 28 to December 1). Thence she passed once more to Chatsworth, where, to her gratification, Melbourne and the Duke of Wellington were fellow-guests. The presence of Lord and Lady Palmerston, although the latter was Melbourne's sister, was less congenial. At a great ball one evening her partners included Lord Morpeth (afterwards Earl of Carlisle) and Lord Leveson (better known later as Earl Granville), who was subsequently to be one of her most trusted ministers. Another night there was a vast series of illuminations in the grounds, of which all traces were cleared away before the morning by two hundred men, working under the direction of the Duke's gardener, Joseph (afterwards Sir Joseph) Paxton.[2] The royal progress was

At Drayton Manor.

At Chatsworth.

---

[1] *Life and Selections from the Correspondence of William Whewell*, by Mrs. Stair Douglas, 1881, p. 302. Cf. Adam Sedgwick's full narrative of the Queen's visit to Cambridge in 1843 in his *Life and Letters*, by Clark and Hughes, ii. 57-64.

[2] This story recalls, *mutatis mutandis*, one which is reported of Queen Victoria's great predecessor, Queen Elizabeth, when on a visit to another distinguished subject. In 1576, when Queen Elizabeth paid a visit to Sir Thomas Gresham at Osterley Park, 'her Majesty found fault with the court of this house as too great, affirming " that it would appear more handsome if divided with a wall in the

continued to Belvoir Castle, the home of the Duke of Rutland, where she again met Peel and Wellington, and it was not till December 7 that she returned to Windsor.

Death of Prince Albert's father.

On January 29, 1844, Prince Albert's father died, and in the spring the Prince paid a visit to his native land (March 28 to April 11). It was the first time the Queen had been separated from her husband, and she felt the severance keenly. In her husband's absence the King and Queen of the Belgians, of whom she often said that 'next to her husband she loved them best in the world,' came over to console her.

Visit of Tsar Nicholas I., 1844.

On June 1 two other continental sovereigns arrived in the country to pay her their respects, the King of Saxony and the Tsar Nicholas I. of Russia. The King of Saxony was a family acquaintance. To the Tsar, who came uninvited at very short notice, it was needful to pay elaborate attentions. His elder half-brother, the Tsar Alexander, had been the Queen's godfather, and political interests made the strengthening of the personal tie desirable. The Tsar attended a great review at Windsor Park with the Queen, and went with her to Ascot and to the opera. At a grand concert given in his honour at Buckingham Palace, Joseph Joachim, then on a visit to England as a boy, was engaged to perform. A rough soldier in appear-

middle." What doth Sir Thomas, but in the night-time sends for workmen to London (money commands all things), who so speedily and silently apply their business, that the next morning disclosed that court double, which the night had left single before. It is questionable whether the Queen next day was more contented with the conformity to her fancy, or more pleased with the surprise and sudden performance thereof.'—*Fuller's Worthies*, ed. P. A. Nuttall, 1840, ii. 313.

ance and manner, the Tsar treated his hostess with a courtesy which seemed to her pathetic, and, although preoccupied by public affairs, civilly deprecated all likelihood of a divergence of political interests between England and his own country.[1]

At this time domestic politics were agitating the Queen to a greater degree than foreign affairs. The spread of disaffection in Ireland during the repeal agitation distressed her, and, although she was in favour of a policy of tolerance and forbearance in matters affecting religion and land legislation in Ireland, she was always insistent on the strong-handed suppression of violence and disorder. Nor did she regard as justifiable the cry for the repeal of the Union. In the controversy over that question her name was made more prominent than was prudent. The Irish Lord Chancellor, Sir Edward Sugden, asserted in a published letter that the Queen was personally determined to prevent repeal (May 1843). The repeal leader, O'Connell, a chivalric admirer of the Queen, promptly denied the statement. Peel mildly reprimanded Sugden, but truth forced him to admit at the same time that the Queen 'would do all in her power to maintain the Union as the bond of connection between the two countries.'[2] To that aspiration she remained faithful till death.

Political affairs.

The Queen and the Irish Union.

The obstructive policy of the Irish and other members of the Opposition in Parliament at the same time caused her concern. She wrote to Peel on

The Queen on parliamentary obstruction.

[1] Sir Herbert Maxwell's *Memoir of Sir Charles Murray*; Lady Lyttelton's *Letters*.
[2] *Peel Papers*, iii. 52.

August 15 of 'her indignation at the very unjustifiable manner in which the minority were obstructing the order of business;' she hoped that every attempt would be made 'to put an end to what is really indecent conduct,' and that Sir Robert Peel would 'make no kind of concession to these gentlemen which could encourage them to go on in the same way.'[1]

Peel threatens resignation.

Worse followed in the month of the Tsar's visit. On June 14 the Government were defeated on a proposal to reduce the sugar duties. The cause of free trade was rapidly gaining ground in the country, although not apparently in the House of Commons. Peel's fidelity to the opposing cause of protection was waning, and he foresaw that his change of view might force him into a position that his followers would repudiate. To the Queen's consternation, he consequently expressed an intention of resigning at once. Great uncertainty as to the result of his threat prevailed. But happily, four days later, a vote of confidence was proposed and carried, and the crisis passed. The Queen wrote at once to express her relief (June 18). 'Last night,' she said, 'every one thought that the Government would be beat, and therefore the surprise was the more unexpected and gratifying.'[2]

Foreign affairs.

Foreign affairs, despite the hospitalities of the English Court to royal visitors, were soon again menacing the Queen's peace of mind. The jealousy between the English and French peoples might be restrained, but could not be stifled, by the friendliness subsisting between the two Courts, and in the autumn

---

[1] *Peel Papers*, iii. 568.   [2] *Ibid.* iii. 153.

of 1844 the maltreatment by French officials of an English consul, George Pritchard, in the island of Tahiti, which the French had lately occupied, caused in England an explosion of popular wrath against France, which the Queen and her Government at one time feared must end in war. Amid this excitement a second son, Prince Alfred, was born to the Queen at Windsor on August 6, 1844.

Birth of Prince Alfred, August 6, 1844.

Hospitalities to foreign monarchs were not long interrupted. At the end of the month of August the Queen entertained yet another royal personage from Germany, the Prince of Prussia, brother of the King, and eventually first German Emperor. The introduction was fertile in results. There sprang up between the Queen and her new guest a warm friendship which lasted for more than forty years, and was finally cemented by a marriage between the Queen's eldest daughter and the Prince's eldest son.

Later in the same year, with bold impartiality, an equally hospitable reception was given the ruler of the great nation that was the traditional rival of Prussia on the European continent. Louis Philippe returned the Queen's visit. He arrived on October 8, 1844. For the first time a French monarch voluntarily landed on English shores. The event seemed to foreshadow more decisively than any other recent Court entertainment a new reign of peace in Western Europe. The Tahiti quarrel had been composed, and the interchange of hospitable amenities was unclouded. On October 9 the King, vastly to his delight, was invested at Windsor with the Order of the Garter. On the 14th the visit ended, and the Queen and

Louis Philippe's visit to Windsor.

Prince Albert accompanied their well-satisfied visitor to Portsmouth, though the stormy weather ultimately compelled him to proceed to Dover to take the short sea trip to Calais.

The opening of the Royal Exchange, Oct. 28, 1844.

The Queen's activity led to a manifest growth in her general popularity—a sentiment which she liked to trace to public sympathy with her happy domestic life. An elaborate ceremony in London evoked a magnificent display of loyalty. The Queen went in state to the City, on October 28, to open the new Royal Exchange.[1] Of her reception Peel wrote to Sir Henry Hardinge (November 6, 1844): 'As usual she had a fine day, and uninterrupted success. It was a glorious spectacle. But she saw a sight which few sovereigns have ever seen, and perhaps none may see again, a million human faces with a smile on each. She did not hear one discordant sound.'[2] On November 12 the Radical town of Northampton gave her a hardly less enthusiastic greeting when she passed through it on her way to visit the Marquis of Exeter at Burghley House —the historic mansion near Stamford where she had before stayed in girlhood with her mother.

The Queen's visits to the nobility.

It was always congenial to the Queen to repeat in the company of her husband the experiences of her early life, and she constantly encouraged invitations from the nobility, which recalled episodes in the maiden progresses that she had undertaken as Princess under her mother's control. She always requested

---

[1] A finely coloured panoramic plate of the elaborate procession was published at the time and is now rare.

[2] *Peel Papers*, iii. 264.

that the lists of the guests who were invited to meet her should be submitted beforehand for her approval, but rarely suggested change. She did not wish to restrict the parties to old friends, but preferred that she and the Prince should enjoy the opportunity of suitably extending their circle of acquaintance.

Besides the Marquis of Exeter, noble hosts of this winter season included the Duke of Wellington at Strathfieldsaye (January 20–22, 1845). He manifested some unwillingness to invite preliminary royal criticism on the constitution of his house-party. But the Queen was in the humour to yield to his objections, for she had just enjoyed the hospitality of a singularly facile host, the Duke of Buckingham, at Stowe. The Duke, a staunch protectionist, commonly known as 'the Farmer's Friend,' had lately resigned the office of Lord Privy Seal in Peel's Government by way of indicating his dislike of the Prime Minister's benevolent attitude to the agitation for free trade. None the less Peel and Aberdeen were, at the Queen's special request, of the Duke's party. The entertainment at Stowe was of interest in varied ways. The visitors included Disraeli, the brilliant member of the Tory rank and file who was to excite in the Queen hereafter a conflicting succession of emotions—curiosity, distrust, and finally affectionate admiration. At Stowe, in January 1845, the Queen met him in private for the first time. He was smarting at the moment under Peel's indifference to his rare abilities, and was about to retaliate with stinging effect. But a somewhat treacherous peace reigned in the royal presence among all who were gathered at the Duke

<small>At Strathfieldsaye.</small>

<small>At Stowe.</small>

<small>First meeting with Disraeli.</small>

of Buckingham's table. Disraeli wrote with enthusiasm of the sumptuous scene and of the triumphal splendour of the ducal hospitality. 'Her Majesty, Peel, Aberdeen, and all,' he added, when writing to his sister of the treatment accorded to him and to his unconventional wife who accompanied him, 'equally distinguished us by their courtesy.'[1] By a curious coincidence, within a few days of the Queen's meeting Disraeli at Stowe, she entertained Gladstone at Windsor, and was agreeably impressed, as it seemed to observers, by his copious conversation.[2]

[1] Lord Beaconsfield's *Letters*, ed. Ralph Disraeli, 1887, p. 204. There were other ironical features in the protectionist Duke's reception of the Queen besides his inclusion of both Peel and Disraeli among the company. The lavish hospitality that the Duke extended to his Sovereign precipitated a distressing crisis in his own fortunes. He was already deep in debt, and two years later the whole of his vast property was for ever alienated to his creditors, to whom he stood indebted for more than a million pounds.

[2] Lady Lyttelton's *Letters*.

XI

THE QUEEN AND FREE TRADE

BEFORE January 1845 ended the Queen was deeply immersed once more in urgent public affairs. A stormy session of Parliament was on the point of opening. But the Queen had the satisfaction of knowing that in the opinion of her ministers she had by her own tactful influence helped to promote peace in the foreign sphere of politics. When the Queen read her speech at the opening of Parliament, February 4, 1845, she referred with great satisfaction to the visits to her Court of the Tsar Nicholas and of the King of the French, and Peel took an early opportunity of pointing out that the munificent receptions accorded those sovereigns and other royal visitors were paid for by the Queen out of her personal income without incurring any debt. *The session of 1845.*

The session was largely occupied with the affairs of Ireland. The repeal agitation was subsiding and the Government were considering an important measure of conciliation. It was proposed to endow the training college for Catholic priests at Maynooth. Gladstone deemed the proposal inconsistent with the principles to which he had publicly committed himself and withdrew from the Government. The Queen *The Queen and the Maynooth agitation.*

regretted the secession of so promising a supporter of the Prime Minister. On February 3 the Queen granted Gladstone an audience in her private sitting-room at Buckingham Palace. She told him his retirement 'was a great loss.' But she encouraged Peel to press on with the measure, which she regarded as a wise and tolerant concession to the dominant religion in Ireland. The Protestant bigotry which the scheme roused in the country excited her disdain. On April 15, 1845, she wrote to Peel: 'It is not honourable to Protestantism to see the bad and violent and bigoted passions displayed at this moment.'

Court entertainments.

Through the session there was much activity at Court. Another *bal costumé* at Buckingham Palace on June 6, when the period chosen for illustration was the reign of George II., was the chief entertainment of the year; and in the same month (June 21) there was a review of the fleet, which was assembled at Spithead in greater strength than had been seen before. Next month the Queen gave a new proof of her friendly feeling for continental rulers by including the King of the Netherlands among her guests.

Queen's first visit to Germany.

In the autumn the Queen for the second time defied precedent by leaving England for travel in a foreign country. No question of providing a regency in her absence was raised. She was absent for a month. The Minister for Foreign Affairs again bore the royal party company. The chief object of the journey was to visit Coburg and other scenes of her mother's and her husband's youth. A subsidiary object was to pay on their outward road a return visit to the King of Prussia, their elder son's godfather.

The King of Prussia's welcome.

Landing at Antwerp (August 6), the Queen and the Prince were met at Malines by the King and Queen of the Belgians, and at Aix-la-Chapelle by the King of Prussia; thence they journeyed through Cologne to the King of Prussia's palace at Brühl. Much pleasurable recreation was offered them. They visited Bonn to attend both the unveiling of the statue of Beethoven, and a great Beethoven festival concert, while at another concert at Brühl, which Meyerbeer conducted, the artists included Jenny Lind, Liszt, and Vieuxtemps. The regal entertainment was continued at the King's castle of Stolzenfels, near Coblenz on the Rhine, which they left on August 16.

Prince Albert's precedence.

Although the Queen was received with much enthusiasm, and she was deeply interested in the experience, the visit was not without painful incident. The question of the Prince's rank amid the great company caused the Queen deep annoyance. Archduke Frederick of Austria, the uncle of the Emperor of Austria, who was also a guest, claimed and, to the Queen's chagrin, was awarded precedence of the Prince in the King of Prussia's palace. The refusal of Court officials to give her husband at Stolzenfels, in 1845, the place of honour next herself rankled in her memory, and made her long reluctant to accept future offers of hospitality from the Prussian Court.

At Rosenau.

On August 19 the Queen reached the palace of Rosenau, Prince Albert's birthplace, which was the main goal of her journey. Thence they passed through

Coburg, finally making their way to Gotha. At Gotha the Queen was gratified by a visit from her old governess Lehzen, and many pleasant excursions were made in the Thuringian forest. On September 3 they left for Frankfort, stopping a night at Weimar on the way.

A second visit to Louis Philippe.

Thus ended the Queen's first expedition to Germany, the country to which she was linked by ties of blood and wifely affection. Antwerp was reached on September 6, but the Queen and Prince did not come straight to England. On their way to Osborne [1] they paid a flying visit to Tréport to offer their respects anew to Louis Philippe. The state of the tide did not allow them to land from the yacht, and Louis Philippe's homely wit suggested a debarkation in bathing machines, which excited the ridicule of London wits.

The Queen's delight at visiting Coburg.

Next day (September 9) the Queen settled once again at Osborne. Writing thence (September 14, 1845) to her aunt, the Duchess of Gloucester, she said: 'I am enchanted with Germany, and in particular with dear Coburg and Gotha, which I left with the very greatest regret. The realisation of this delightful visit, which I had wished for so many years, will be a constant and lasting satisfaction.' To her uncle Leopold she wrote to the same effect.

Peel and the corn laws.

Before the close of 1845 the Queen was involved in the always dreaded anxiety of a ministerial crisis. The potato crop had completely failed in Ireland, and the harvest in England and Scotland was very bad. Great distress was certain throughout the

---

[1] See p. 199.

United Kingdom during the winter. Thereupon Peel made up his mind that the situation demanded the repeal of the corn laws—a step which he and his party, it was generally assumed, were pledged to oppose, although he had himself already shown a plain inclination to accept the main principles of the free-traders. Most of his colleagues were startled by his change of view, many threatened resistance, but all except Lord Stanley ultimately agreed to stand by him.

The rank and file of the party showed fewer signs of complacence. The Young England party, under the leadership of Disraeli, had already betrayed signs of restiveness beneath Peel's sway, and Disraeli had in the session of 1845 inaugurated that long series of scathing invectives against Peel on the ostensible ground of the minister's indifference to the agricultural interests of the country. The Conservative Government had become, he declared, 'an organised hypocrisy.' The Queen was gravely disturbed. She warmly resented Disraeli's bitterness of tongue, though at a later period of her life she reached the conclusion that there were extenuating circumstances, which rendered his treatment of Sir Robert Peel explicable if not altogether justifiable. She now threw the whole weight of her influence into the Prime Minister's scale. On November 5, 1845, she wrote to Peel of the anxiety occasioned her by his report of 'disagreement in the cabinet at this moment, when every one should be united, and co-operate to remedy the alarming state of scarceness which is threatening.' On November 28,

The Queen supports Peel.

1845, the Queen wrote again from Osborne: 'The Queen is very sorry to hear that Sir Robert apprehends further differences of opinion in the cabinet. At a moment of impending calamity it is more than ever necessary that the Government should be united. The Queen thinks the time is come when a removal of the restrictions on the importation of food cannot be successfully resisted. Should this be Sir Robert's own opinion, the Queen very much hopes that none of his colleagues will prevent him from doing what it is right to do.'[1]

Peel's resignation, December 6, 1845.

But Peel, although greatly heartened by the Queen's support, deemed it just both to his supporters and to his opponents to let the opposite party, which had lately advocated the reform, carry it out. On December 6, 1845, he resigned. The Queen was as loth to part with him as she had formerly been to part with Melbourne. The day before she had written to him, 'Whatever should be the cause of these differences, the Queen feels certain that Sir Robert Peel will *not leave her* at a moment of such difficulty, and when a crisis is impending.' But Peel was resolute.

Lord John Russell summoned.

While regretting his decision, the Queen rose to the situation and prepared to exercise, according to her wont, all the influence that was possible to her in the formation of a new Government. By Peel's desire she sent for Lord John Russell, who was at the moment at Edinburgh, and did not reach Windsor till the 11th. In the meantime she asked Melbourne to come and give her counsel, but his health was

[1] *Peel Papers*, iii. 237–8.

failing, and on every ground prudence urged him to refuse interference.

The Queen's chief fear of a Whig cabinet was due to her and her foreign kinsmen's distrust of Palmerston as Foreign Minister. She feared that no Whig ministry could exclude him, but she did what she could to interpose obstacles to his admission to his old place in the cabinet. At her first interview with Lord John, she promptly requested him to give Palmerston the Colonial Office. Lord John naturally demurred, and asked for time before proceeding further. *Negotiations with Lord John.*

In the extremity of her fear the Queen flung herself with energy into a larger and more intricate series of diplomatic negotiations than she had yet ventured on. She begged Lord Aberdeen, the Foreign Minister in Peel's cabinet, to support in political circles her objections to Palmerston; but since it was notorious in political circles that Palmerston would accept no post but that of Foreign Secretary, Aberdeen could give her little comfort. He merely advised her to make the best of what was inevitable. She might impress Palmerston with her desire of peace with France, and bid him consult her regularly on matters of foreign policy. But it was impossible to exclude him from the post to which long service entitled him. The Queen acquiesced in the advice with grave reluctance. *The Queen's dread of Palmerston.*

On December 13 the Queen had a second interview at Windsor with Lord John, who was now accompanied by the veteran Whig leader, Lord Lansdowne. Prince Albert sat beside her, and she *Lord John's pertinacious appeals.*

let her visitors understand that she spoke for him as well as for herself. Lord John addressed her with great frankness. He asked her to obtain assurances from Peel that the members of his cabinet who were opposed to a free-trade policy were not in a position to form a new Government. If he undertook to repeal the corn laws, it was right, Lord John added, that the Queen should secure for him the full support of Peel and his followers. The Queen consulted Peel, who gave her a vague and guarded answer. Lord John was dissatisfied, and he urged her with characteristic pertinacity to obtain more specific promise of co-operation. The Queen deemed the request unreasonable, but civilly appealed anew to Peel without result. Thereupon she stood aside to await the turn of events.

Lord John's difficulties.

At length, on December 18, Lord John accepted the Queen's command to form a Government. But his difficulties were only begun. There were members of his party who distrusted Palmerston as thoroughly as the Queen distrusted him. Lord Grey declined to join the Government if Palmerston took the Foreign Office, and he at the same time demanded a place in the cabinet for Cobden, the leader of the free-trade agitation. Lord John felt unable either to accept Lord Grey's proposals or to forego his presence in the administration; and greatly to the Queen's surprise he, on December 29, suddenly informed her that he was unable to serve her.

Peel's return to power.

For a moment it looked as if the Queen were to be left without any Government, but she turned once more to Peel, who, at her earnest request, resumed power. To this result she had more or less passively contributed throughout the intricate negotiation. She had tacitly triumphed all along the line, and the issue was completely satisfactory to her. The next day, December 30, she wrote to Peel of his return to office: 'The Queen cannot sufficiently express how much we feel Sir Robert Peel's high-minded conduct, courage, and loyalty, which can only add to the Queen's confidence in him.' Some changes were made in the restored ministry. Gladstone, to whom the Queen felt grateful for his consistent and efficient support of Peel, succeeded, much to her satisfaction, the dissentient Lord Stanley in the office of Colonial and War Secretary.

Thenceforth the Queen identified herself almost recklessly with Peel's policy of corn-law repeal. Melbourne, when dining at Windsor, told her that Peel's conduct was 'damned dishonest,' but she declined to discuss the topic and bade him keep silence. She lost no opportunity of urging Peel to persevere. On January 12, 1846, she wrote of her satisfaction at learning of the drastic character of his proposed measures, 'feeling certain,' she added, 'that what was so just and wise must succeed.' On January 27 Prince Albert attended the House of Commons to hear Peel announce his plan of abolishing the corn laws in the course of the next three years. Strong objection was raised to the Prince's presence by protectionists, who argued that it showed partisanship on the part of the Crown. The Queen ridiculed the protest, but it offended her, and the Prince never went to the Lower House again. On February 4 she told Peel that he would be rewarded with the gratitude of the country, which

The Queen's support of Peel.

'would make up for the abuse he has to endure from so many of his party.' On February 18 she not only sent a letter to congratulate Peel on his speech in introducing the Bill, but forwarded to him a note from the Dowager-Queen Adelaide which expressed an equally flattering opinion.

Regrets for his difficulties.

Gladstone and Lord Lincoln, although they accepted Peel's policy, withdrew from the House of Commons at the opening of the session because, as parliamentary nominees of the Duke of Newcastle, who was a staunch protectionist, they could not honourably vote against his opinions. The Queen expressed sympathy with Peel in his loss of such powerful lieutenants. She pressed Peel to secure other seats for them. 'Where *is* a seat to be found for Mr. Gladstone and Lord Lincoln?' she wrote hurriedly on March 4. Every speech during the corn-law debates she read with minute attention, and she closely studied the division lists. 'The proceedings of each night,' she wrote, 'are of the greatest interest to us.'

Peel's fall.

The birth of the Princess Helena on May 25 was not suffered to distract the royal attention, and the Queen watched with delight the safe passage of the Bill for the Repeal of the Corn Laws through both Houses of Parliament. The sequel, however, disconcerted her. On June 26, the night that the Anti-Corn-law Bill passed its third reading in the Lords, the Protectionists and Whigs voted together against the Government on the second reading of a Coercion Bill for Ireland, and Peel was defeated by seventy-three votes. His resignation followed of necessity, and, at a moment when his services seemed most valuable to her, the Queen saw herself deprived of them, as it proved for ever. She wrote of 'her *deep* concern' at parting with him. 'In whatever position Sir Robert Peel may be,' she concluded, 'we shall ever look on him as a kind and true friend.' Hardly less did she regret the retirement of Lord Aberdeen. When Gladstone delivered up his seals of office on July 6, the Queen said she was 'sorry to receive them.' Her sense of dejection was almost as acute as on the resignation of Melbourne nearly five years before. 'We felt so safe with them,' she wrote of Peel and Aberdeen to her uncle Leopold, who agreed that Peel, almost alone among contemporary English statesmen, could be trusted 'never to let monarchy be robbed of the little strength and power it still may possess.'[1]

Although Peel had not suffered the Queen to exercise more power than the constitution allowed, he had increased her sense of influence by the fulness and frequency of his communications with her on political business. He had thereby created a mutual confidence between Sovereign and minister which stimulated the Queen's interest in the affairs of her people, and induced in her genuine enthusiasm for a reform like the abolition of the corn laws which, her minister readily convinced her, would alleviate her people's sufferings and add to their prosperity. Difficult as Peel's position was when he resolved to give practical effect to the principle of free trade, it would have been almost unendurable had the Queen done other than identify herself with his enlightened action.

The Queen's enthusiasm for free trade.

[1] *Peel Papers*, iii. 172.

XII

THE SPANISH MARRIAGES

Lord John's first ministry, July 1846.

SIR ROBERT PEEL'S defeat in Parliament was so emphatic that the Queen had no alternative but to invite the leader of the Opposition to take his place. At her request Lord John Russell formed a new Government. He insisted on Palmerston's return to the Foreign Office, and with misgivings the Queen assented. It was understood that a general election should take place next year, and decide the length of the new ministry's life. In the event the ministry lasted nearly five years, although the voice of the country at the polls in November 1847 did not declare itself very strongly in its favour. The Liberals in the new House of Commons numbered 325 against 105 Conservative followers of Peel, and 226 Conservative Protectionists, under the leadership of Peel's rival, Disraeli. The numbers failed to establish the Government on very firm foundations, and the Queen marked her indifference to its welfare by absenting herself from the opening ceremony in the newly summoned Parliament.

The Queen and Lord John.

The Queen's third Prime Minister, Lord John, although awkward and unattractive in manner, and wedded to a narrow view of the Queen's constitutional powers, set himself to emulate the example of his predecessors in conciliating the royal favour. She had come into frequent personal intercourse with him at the opening of her reign. He was Home Secretary and leader of the House of Commons in Melbourne's ministry, and he knew all that had passed between her and Melbourne. Closer acquaintance improved his relations with the Queen, and she marked the increase of cordiality by giving him for life Pembroke Lodge in Richmond Park in March 1847, on the death of its former occupant, the Earl of Erroll, husband of a natural daughter of William IV.

Some of Lord John's colleagues greatly interested the Queen. Lord Clarendon, who had been Lord Privy Seal under Melbourne, was at first President of the Board of Trade under Lord John, and in 1847 became Lord-Lieutenant of Ireland. He was out of sympathy with Palmerston's high-handed foreign policy, and, like his brother, Charles Pelham Villiers, was an enthusiastic free-trader. In their views on both home and foreign affairs he and the Queen (and Prince) were at one. Thoroughly disinterested in public life, and in private most considerate and courteous, he gained the Queen's entire confidence and became an intimate friend. Of equally high character was Sir George Grey, who now first took the office of Home Secretary, and filled it almost continuously for nearly twenty years. With him the Queen's relations were uniformly cordial. *Lord John's colleagues.*

She took pleasure at the same time in the society of Macaulay, who joined Lord John's ministry as Paymaster-General. His brilliant conversation, after *Macaulay at Court.*

he had overcome a feeling of shyness in addressing her, interested and amused her, and he, on his side, formed a high opinion of her general intelligence and amiability. On March 9, 1850, when Macaulay dined at Buckingham Palace, he talked freely of his 'History of England.' 'The Queen owned that she had nothing to say for her poor ancestor, James II.' 'Not your Majesty's ancestor, your Majesty's predecessor,' Macaulay returned; and the remark, which was intended as a compliment, was well received.[1] On January 14, 1851, when he stayed at Windsor, he 'made her laugh heartily,' he said. 'She talked on for some time most courteously and pleasantly. Nothing could be more sensible than her remarks on German affairs.'[2]

Difficulties with Palmerston.

But, in spite of her respect for many of its members, the Queen's relations with her third ministry were less amicable than with her first or second, owing to the unaccommodating temper of the most prominent and self-assertive member of it—Palmerston, the Foreign Secretary. Between him and the Crown a continual struggle was in progress for the effective supervision of foreign affairs. The constitution did not provide for the regular control by the monarch of the minister's work in that or any other department of the State. The minister had it in his power to work quite independently of the Crown, and it practically lay with him to admit or reject a claim on the Crown's part to suggest even points of procedure, still less points of policy. For the Crown to challenge the fact in dealing with a strong-willed and

---

[1] Trevelyan's *Life of Macaulay*, pp. 537-8.   [2] *Ibid.* p. 549.

popular minister was to invite, as the Queen and Prince were to find, a tormenting sense of impotence.

At the outset monarch and minister found themselves in agreement. Although Palmerston realised anticipations by embroiling France and England, the breach was deemed, in the peculiar circumstances, inevitable even by the Queen and the Prince. A difference had for some years existed between the two countries in regard to the affairs of Spain. The Spanish throne was occupied by a child of sixteen, Queen Isabella, whose position sufficiently resembled that of the Queen of England at her accession to excite interest in her future at the English Court. It was the known ambition of Louis Philippe or of his ministers to bring the Spanish kingdom under French sway. English politicians of all parties were agreed, on the other hand, that an extension of French influence in the Spanish peninsula was undesirable. Perfectly conscious of the strength with which this view was held, Louis Philippe walked warily. There were rumours that he was ambitious to ally the little Spanish Queen in matrimony with his own family—with his fourth son, the Duc d'Aumale—but he did what he could to allay excitement on that score. In 1843 he announced that the Spanish Queen's matrimonial fortunes were no concern of his. He admitted, however, that his younger son, the Duc de Montpensier, was to be affianced, not to the little Spanish Queen herself, but to her younger sister.

The Spanish marriages.

Queen Victoria received the announcement with equanimity. Lord Aberdeen, then Foreign Minister, saw no objection to such a match provided that the

The Château d'Eu agreement.

marriage should be delayed till the Spanish Queen had herself both married and had issue, and that it should be clearly understood that no member of the French Bourbon house should become the royal consort of Spain. During each of the visits of Queen Victoria to the Château d'Eu the King of the French gave her a distinct verbal assent to these conditions.

Prince Albert and Prince Leopold of Saxe-Coburg.

The Spanish Queen had many suitors, but she was slow in making a choice, and her hesitation kept the Spanish question open. Unluckily for the good relations of France and England, the personal position of Prince Albert in England and his connection with Germany introduced a curious complication into the process of selecting a consort for the Spanish Queen. The Regent Christina, the mother of the Spanish Queen, had no wish to facilitate French ambition. With a view to foiling it she urged her daughter to follow the example alike of the English Queen and of the Queen of Portugal, and marry into the Saxe-Coburg family. In 1841, when the notion was first put forward, Prince Albert's elder brother Ernest, who was as yet unmarried, was suggested as a desirable suitor; but on his marriage to another in 1842, Queen Christina designated for her son-in-law Prince Leopold of Saxe-Coburg, Ernest and Albert's first cousin, whose brother Ferdinand was already Prince Consort of Portugal. Prince Albert, who had entertained the young man at Windsor, was consulted. He felt that his cousin should not be lightly deprived of the opportunity of securing a throne, but recognised a delicacy in urging English statesmen to serve Saxe-Coburg interests, and he and the Queen stood aside to await the passage of events.

France, however, showed at once passionate hostility to the scheme. Guizot, Louis Philippe's Prime Minister, brusquely declared that he would at all hazards preserve Spain from England's and Portugal's fate of a Saxe-Coburg ruler. Accordingly, in the interests of peace, the Saxe-Coburg suit was avowedly dropped by consent both in Spain and England. Yet on May 2, 1846, it was covertly revived by Queen Christina. That lady wrote to Duke Ernest of Saxe-Coburg, who was on a visit to his relatives in Portugal, bidding him seek the personal aid of Queen Victoria in marrying her daughter to his cousin and Queen Victoria's cousin, Prince Leopold. With the embarrassing ignorance which prevailed in continental Courts of English constitutional usages, Queen Christina desired her letter to reach Queen Victoria's hand alone, and not that of any of her ministers. Duke Ernest forwarded it to King Leopold, who communicated it to his niece.

Queen Christina's interference.

Both Duke Ernest and King Leopold came to England in August, and they discussed the Saxe-Coburg aspect of the question with the Queen and Prince Albert. The matter was thoroughly threshed out anew, and the royal conclave reluctantly reached a decision adverse to the Saxe-Coburg prince, on the adequate ground that both English and French ministers had virtually rejected him. Duke Ernest at once wrote to that effect to the Queen-mother Christina, and advised the young Queen to marry a Spaniard.[1]

Family conference at Windsor

---

[1] Duke Ernest of Saxe-Coburg, *Memoirs*, i. 190 seq.

Palmerston's rash despatch.

Almost at the same moment as the royal family had arrived at this understanding, Palmerston returned to the Foreign Office, and in a despatch to the Spanish Government which he wrote in haste and with half knowledge only of the result of the recent Saxe-Coburg conclave, he pressed the Spanish Queen to choose without delay one of three suitors, among whom he included Prince Leopold of Saxe-Coburg. The despatch was communicated to the French ministers, who saw in Palmerston's resuscitation of the Saxe-Coburg offer of marriage a breach of a specific agreement. The renewed mention of Prince Leopold constituted in French eyes a serious grievance against the English Court.

French retaliation.

Retaliation was at once attempted by France. Without seeking further negotiation, the French ministers arranged at Madrid that the young Queen should marry at once, that the bridegroom should be a Spanish suitor, the Duke of Cadiz, and that on the same day the Duc de Montpensier should marry the young Queen's only sister. On September 8 the Queen of the French, in a private letter to Queen Victoria, announced the approaching date of the two marriages. The Queen, in reply (September 10), expressed surprise and regret. Louis Philippe sent an apologetic explanation to his daughter, the Queen of the Belgians, who forwarded it to Queen Victoria. She replied that Louis Philippe had broken his word.

French breach of faith.

Bitter charges of breach of faith abounded on both sides, and the war of vituperation involved not merely both Courts but both countries. The sinister rumour ran in England that the French ministers knew the

Duke of Cadiz to be unfit for matrimony, and had selected him as husband of the Spanish Queen so that the succession to the Spanish crown might be secured to the offspring of Montpensier. In any case, that hope was thwarted; for although the marriage of the Spanish Queen Isabella proved unhappy, she was mother of five children, who were ostensibly born in wedlock. The indignation of the Queen and Prince Albert was intensified by the contempt which was showered by the French ministers and the French press on the Saxe-Coburg family; its endeavours after aggrandisement were alleged to be insatiable. The efforts of Louis Philippe and his family at a domestic reconciliation proved for the time vain.

Palmerston, after his wont, conducted the official negotiation without any endeavour to consult the views or respect the wishes of the Queen or Prince Albert. In one despatch to Sir Henry Bulwer, the English minister at Madrid, he reinserted, to the Queen's annoyance, a paragraph which Prince Albert had deleted in the first draft touching the relation of the issue of the Duc de Montpensier to the Spanish succession; the royal rights of the Duc's heirs should, he argued, be cancelled. King Leopold held Palmerston responsible for the whole imbroglio.[1] But the Queen's public and private sentiments were in this case identical with those of Palmerston and of the English public, and, in the absence of any genuine difference of opinion, the minister's independent action won from the Queen reluctant acquiescence.

The Queen's indignation.

With the Queen's tacit but uninvited assent, the

---

[1] Duke Ernest's *Memoirs*, i. 199.

Popular excitement.

English Government formally protested against the two Spanish marriages. But they duly took place on October 10. English execrations were loud. 'There is but one voice here on the subject,' the Queen wrote (October 13) to King Leopold, 'and I am, alas! unable to say a word in defence of one [i.e. Louis Philippe] whom I had esteemed and respected. You may imagine what the whole of this makes me suffer. . . . You cannot represent too strongly to the King and Queen [of the French] my indignation, and my sorrow, at what has been done.' Then the hubbub, which seemed to threaten war, gradually subsided. The effect of the incident on English prestige proved small, but it cost Louis Philippe the moral support of England, and his tottering throne fell an easy prey to revolution.

XIII

THE YEAR OF REVOLUTION, 1848

At the opening of 1847 the political horizon was clouded on every side; but despite the anxieties at home—threats of civil war in Ireland, and so great a rise in the price of wheat in England that the Queen diminished the supply of bread to her own household—the 'season' of that year was exceptionally lively. Numerous foreign visitors were entertained, including the Grand Duke Constantine of Russia (the Tsar Nicholas's younger son), Prince Oscar of Sweden (afterwards King of Sweden and Norway), and many German princes. On June 15 a state visit was paid to Her Majesty's Theatre in the Haymarket, during the first season of Jenny Lind, who appeared as Norma in Bellini's opera.[1] The Queen applauded eagerly, and wrote to her uncle Leopold: 'Jenny Lind is quite a remarkable phenomenon.' *The season of 1847.*

In the spring the Queen had been much gratified by the election of Prince Albert to the dignified office of Chancellor of Cambridge University. The choice was not made without a contest—'the unseemly contest' the Queen called it—and the Prince won by a majority of only 117 votes over those cast *Prince Albert Chancellor of Cambridge.*

[1] Holland and Rockstro, *Jenny Lind*, ii. 113 seq.

for his opponent, the Earl of Powis. But the Queen wisely concentrated her attention on the result, which she represented to herself and her friends as no gift of hers, but an honour that the Prince had earned independently on his merits.

At Cambridge, July 1847.

In July the Queen accompanied her husband to the Cambridge Commencement, over which he presided as Chancellor. From Tottenham she travelled on the Eastern Counties Railway, under the personal guidance of the railway king, George Hudson, and thereby proved anew her interest in the amazing growth of railway enterprise. As on the occasion of her former visit, she was the guest of Trinity College. On July 5, 1847, in the hall of Trinity College, she received from her husband in his official capacity an address of welcome to the University. In reply she smilingly congratulated the graduates on their wise selection of a Chancellor.[1] Her old friend Melbourne, together with three German princes, who were royal guests—Prince Waldemar of Prussia, Prince Peter of Oldenburg, and the hereditary Grand Duke of Saxe-Weimar—received honorary degrees from Prince Albert's hands.[2] On the evening of the 6th there was a levee at the lodge of Trinity College, and next

[1] *Life of Wilberforce*, i. 398; Dean Merivale, *Letters*; Cooper, *Annals of Cambridge*.

[2] An installation ode, set to music by T. A. Walmisley, was published in the newspapers of July 7, 1847, as 'written for the occasion by the Poet Laureate, by royal command,' but there is no likelihood that Wordsworth, then Poet Laureate, was its author. It seems to have been written by Edward Quillinan at Wordsworth's request, after the Laureate had failed in a reluctant attempt to prepare an ode. Cf. *Poetical Works of William Wordsworth*, edited by William Knight, 1896, viii. 320.

morning the Queen attended a public 'breakfast' or afternoon party in Nevill's Court.

For the third time the Queen spent her autumn holiday in Scotland, where she had now taken a highland residence at Ardverikie, a lodge on Loch Laggan, in the occupation of the Marquis of Abercorn. She and her family travelled thither by the west coast from the Isle of Wight (August 11–14). Pausing at the outset for a night on the Scilly Isles, the Queen and Prince made for the Menai Straits, where they transferred themselves from their yacht 'Victoria and Albert' to the smaller yacht 'Fairy.' Passing up the Clyde they visited Loch Fyne. On the 18th they arrived at Inverary Castle, the seat of the Duke of Argyll, and afterwards reached their destination by way of Fort William. Palmerston was for the most part the minister in attendance, and, amid the deer-stalking, walks, and drives, there was found time for political discussion between him and Prince Albert, in which their views did not prove more reconcilable than hitherto. The sojourn in Scotland lasted three weeks, till September 17, and intensified the Queen's enthusiasm for that country. On the return journey the royal party went by sea only as far as Fleetwood. Thence they proceeded by rail from Liverpool to London.[1]

Third visit to Scotland, 1847.

In the months that followed, public affairs, especially abroad, abounded in causes of alarm for the Queen. The year 1848 was one of revolution in Europe, and the cause of monarchy seemed threatened throughout the world. The period passed without serious

Louis Philippe's dethronement.

[1] *Journal*, pp. 43–61.

disturbance in England, but the Queen's equanimity was rudely shaken by the rebellions that wrought havoc in foreign lands. The dethronement of Louis Philippe in February proved as severe a shock to her as any that she had yet suffered. It wounded her tenderest feelings, and stimulated her liveliest sympathies. Ignoring recent political differences with the King of the French, she thought only of the distress of a fellow sovereign who was bound to her by domestic ties. When his sons and daughters hurried to England, nothing for a time was known of the fate of Louis and his Queen. On March 2 they arrived in disguise at Newhaven, and Louis immediately wrote to the Queen, throwing himself on her protection.

Everything that the Queen could do for his comfort she did with prompt energy. She at once obtained her uncle Leopold's consent to offer the refugee King and Queen his own royal residence at Claremont, and there the exiles found an asylum for the rest of their lives. Prince Albert visited them as soon as they arrived, and on March 6 ex-King Louis came to Windsor to express his gratitude for the protection that the Queen had vouchsafed him. The contrast between the conditions of his present and of his previous visit deeply impressed her. 'If it were not for the generosity of the Queen of England,' remarked the exiled King to a guest shortly afterwards at dinner at Claremont, 'I should not have either this house to cover my head or the plate or anything which is on the table.' [1]

[1] *Memoirs of Sir Edward Blount, K.C.B.*, edited by Stuart J. Reid, 1902, p. 127.

But it was not only in behalf of the ex-King and the ex-Queen of the French that Queen Victoria exerted herself. To all members of the French royal family the Queen showed unremitting attention. To the Duc de Nemours she allotted another royal residence at Bushey. She frequently entertained him together with his brothers, the accomplished Duc d'Aumale, Comte de Paris, and Prince de Joinville. She always treated them with the respect which was due to members of reigning families. *Welcome to his sons.*

Nor was it only in France that the Revolution dealt hardly with the Queen's circle of royal acquaintances and kindred. Her half-brother of Leiningen, who had been in Scotland with her the year before, her half-sister, Princess of Hohenlohe-Langenburg, the Duke of Saxe-Coburg-Gotha (Prince Albert's brother), and their friend, the King of Prussia, suffered severely in the revolutionary movements of Germany, and although their thrones survived they endured much tribulation. In Italy and Austria, too, the safety of kings and princes was rudely menaced. *Revolution in Germany.*

Happily, in England, threats of revolution came to nothing. The Queen faced the possibilities of the situation with great boldness. During the crisis she was temporarily disabled by the birth, on March 18, of the Princess Louise; but at the end of her confinement she wrote to her uncle, King Leopold, with admirable spirit, 'My only thoughts and talk were politics, and I never was calmer or quieter or more earnest. Great events make me calm; it is only trifles that irritate my nerves' (April 4). *Birth of Princess Louise, March 18, 1848.*

Chartist menaces.

The great Chartist meeting on Kennington Common, on April 10, proved abortive. It had been announced that on that day half a million of persons were determined, in spite of the army or the police, to carry to the Houses of Parliament a petition bearing five million signatures and demanding the adoption by the Legislature of all the points of the Charter. London was placed under military protection, and expectations of a serious riot were general.[1] By the advice of ministers the Queen and her family removed from Windsor to Osborne a few days before, but the agitators had exaggerated their power. The meeting at Kennington was thinly attended and dispersed peacefully. The Court returned to London on May 2 to find all prophecies of disaster confuted. Chartism did not long survive the farcical *dénouement* at Kennington.

Quiet restored.

When the infant Princess Louise, to whom the Queen of the Belgians stood godmother, was christened at Buckingham Palace on May 13, the strain of anxiety was at an end. But no sooner was quiet completely re-established in London than the Queen was faced by a new perplexity in the sphere of party politics. In June 1848 Lord John feared defeat in the House of Commons on the old question of a further reduction of the sugar duties. That proposal had already nearly wrecked two Governments, and it was widely assumed that it was about to wreck a third. Although the Queen's confidence in the ministry was chequered by Palmerston's conduct of the Foreign Office, she declared any

[1] Lady Lyttelton's *Letters*.

change inopportune while the social atmosphere was still charged with menaces of revolution. It was therefore unwillingly that she approached the consideration of the choice of Lord John's successor. Demurring to Lord John's own suggestion of Lord Stanley, the Protectionist leader in the Lords, who as a seceder from Peel was not congenial to her, she took counsel for the last time with Melbourne. He advised her to summon Peel. No step could have been more agreeable to her. But the alarm of Lord John proved delusive. The Government was stronger than was anticipated. A small majority in the House of Commons remained faithful to Lord John, and for three years longer he continued in office.

On September 5, 1848, the Queen prorogued Parliament in person, and peace once more reigned in the Parliament and in the country. The ceremony took place for the first time in the Peers' Chamber in the new Houses of Parliament, which had been rebuilt after the fire of 1834. Her French kinsmen, the Duc de Nemours and the Prince de Joinville, were present with her. Popular enthusiasm ran high, and she was in thorough accord with the congratulatory words which her ministers put into her mouth on the steadfastness with which the bulk of her people had resisted incitements to disorder.

Parliament prorogued.

England and revolution.

XIV

PRIVATE LIFE AND RECREATIONS, 1848–54

First stay at Balmoral, 1848.

On the same afternoon she embarked at Woolwich for Aberdeen in order to spend three weeks at Balmoral House, then little more than a shooting lodge, which she now hired for the first time of Lord Aberdeen's brother, Sir Robert Gordon. The climate of the place proved invigorating, her affection for the Highlands redoubled, and it was in tears that she left for the South after the brief sojourn. But the plan which had long been in contemplation, of securing a permanent residence in Scotland, was then finally formed. The main railway systems of Scotland and England were now completed, and rendered communication between the two countries rapid and easy. Owing to bad weather the Queen tried the new experiment of making practically the whole of the return journey to London by rail, travelling from Perth by way of Crewe. The experiment was successful, and thenceforth she travelled to and from Scotland in no other way.[1]

---

[1] Later in the year a distressing accident caused the Queen deep depression (October 9). While she was crossing from Osborne to Portsmouth, her yacht, the 'Fairy,' ran down a boat belonging to the 'Grampus' frigate, and three women were drowned. 'It is a terrible thing, and haunts me continually,' the Queen wrote.

PRIVATE LIFE AND RECREATIONS

Music and the drama at Court.

The Queen, when in London or at Windsor, sought recreation more and more frequently each year in music and the drama. Elaborate concerts, oratorios, or musical recitations were repeatedly given both at Windsor and at Buckingham Palace. On February 10, 1846, Charles Kemble read the words of the 'Antigone' when Mendelssohn's music was rendered, and there followed like renderings of 'Athalie' (January 1, 1847), again of 'Antigone' (January 1, 1848), and subsequently of 'Œdipus at Colonos' (February 10, 1848, and January 1, 1852).

The Queen and Mendelssohn.

During 1842 and 1844 the composer Mendelssohn was many times at Court, and the Queen received him with a delightful cordiality. Of a visit to Buckingham Palace in July 1842 he wrote at length to his mother, and the description presents an idyllic picture of the Queen's private life:—

'Prince Albert had asked me' (Mendelssohn wrote on July 19) 'to go to him on Saturday at two o'clock, so that I might try his organ before I left England; I found him alone, and as we were talking away the Queen came in, also alone, in a simple morning dress. She said she was obliged to leave for Claremont in an hour, and then, suddenly interrupting herself, exclaimed, "But goodness, what a confusion!" for the wind had littered the whole room, and even the pedals of the organ (which, by the way, made a very pretty feature in the room), with leaves of music from a large portfolio that lay open. As she spoke she knelt down and began picking up the music; Prince Albert helped, and I too was not idle. Then Prince Albert proceeded to explain the stops to me, and she said that she would meanwhile put things straight.

Prince Albert and Mendelssohn.

'I begged that the Prince would first play me something, so that, as I said, I might boast about it in Germany; and he played a Chorale, by heart; and the Queen, having finished her work, came and sat by him and listened, and looked pleased. Then it was my turn, and I began my chorus from "St. Paul"—"How lovely are the messengers." Before I got to the end of the first verse they both joined in the chorus. . . . Then the young Prince of Gotha [i.e. Prince Albert's brother Ernest] came in, and there was more chatting; and the Queen asked if I had written any new songs, and said she was very fond of singing my published ones. "You should sing one to him," said Prince Albert; and, after a little begging, she said she would try the "Frühlingslied" in B flat— "If it is still here," she added, "for all my music is packed up for Claremont." Prince Albert went to look for it, but came back, saying it was already packed. "But one might perhaps unpack it," said I. "We must send for Lady ——," she said. (I did not catch the name.) So the bell was rung, and the servants were sent after it, but without success; and at last the Queen went herself, and while she was gone Prince Albert said to me, "She begs you will accept this present as a remembrance," and gave me a little case with a beautiful ring, on which is engraved "V.R. 1842."

The Queen sings to Mendelssohn.

'Then the Queen came back, and said, "Lady —— is gone, and has taken all my things with her. It really is most annoying." (You can't think how that

amused me.) I then begged that I might not be
made to suffer for the accident, and hoped she would
sing another song. After some consultation with
her husband, he said, "She will sing you something of Gluck's." Meantime the Princess of Gotha
[i.e. Prince Ernest's wife] had come in, and we
five proceeded through various corridors and rooms
to the Queen's sitting-room. The Duchess of Kent
came in too, and while they were all talking
I rummaged about amongst the music, and soon
discovered my first set of songs. So, of course, I
begged her rather to sing one of those than the
Gluck, to which she very kindly consented; and
which did she choose?—"Schöner und schöner
schmückt sich!" sang it quite charmingly, in strict
time and tune, and with very good execution. . . . Then
I was obliged to confess that Fanny [i.e. the musician's
sister] had written the song (which I found very hard,
but pride must have a fall), and to beg her to sing
one of mine also. If I would give her plenty of help,
she would gladly try, she said, and then she sang the
Pilgerspruch "Lass dich nur" really quite faultlessly,
and with charming feeling and expression. I thought
to myself, one must not pay too many compliments
on such an occasion, so I merely thanked her a great
many times; upon which she said, "Oh, if only I had
not been so frightened! generally I have such long
breath." Then I praised her heartily, and with the
best conscience in the world; for just that part with
the long C at the close she had done so well, taking
it and the three notes next to it all in the same
breath, as one seldom hears it done, and therefore it

o

amused me doubly that she herself should have begun about it.

Mendelssohn's farewell.

'After this Prince Albert sang the Aerndtelied, "Es ist ein Schnitter;" and then he said I must improvise something before I went, and they followed me with so much intelligence and attention that I felt more at my ease than I ever did in improvising to an audience. The Queen said several times she hoped I would soon come to England again and pay them a visit, and then I took leave; and down below I saw the beautiful carriages waiting, with their scarlet outriders, and in a quarter of an hour the flag was lowered, and the "Court Circular" announced, "Her Majesty left the Palace at twenty minutes past three."'

Actors and actresses at Court.

Great actors and actresses were welcomed by the Queen with hardly less enthusiasm than musicians. The French actress Rachel was invited to recite at Buckingham Palace on more than one occasion, and on February 26, 1851, when the popular actor Macready, the chief of his profession, took farewell of the stage at Drury Lane, the Queen was present.

The drama at Windsor

Meanwhile, to give greater variety to the Christmas festivities, the Queen organised at the end of 1848 dramatic performances at Windsor. Charles Kean was appointed director, and until Prince Albert's death, except during three years—in 1850 owing to the Queen Dowager's death, in 1855 during the gloom of the Crimean war, and in 1858 owing to the distraction of the Princess Royal's marriage—dramatic representations were repeated in the Rubens room at the Castle during each Christmas season. On

December 28, 1848, at the first performance, 'The Merchant of Venice' was presented, with Mr. and Mrs. Kean and Mr. and Mrs. Keeley in the cast. Thirteen other plays of Shakespeare and nineteen lighter pieces followed in the course of the next thirteen years, and the actors included Macready, Phelps, Charles Mathews, Ben Webster, and Buckstone.

To the director, Charles Kean, and his wife, Mrs. Charles Kean, also an actress of note, the Queen showed constant attention. When Kean died, in June 1868, the Queen at once wrote in her own hand to his widow: 'I recall most vividly to my mind the many hours of great intellectual enjoyment which your lamented and talented husband (who did so much for his profession) and you afforded to my dear husband and myself in bygone happy days. They will never be forgotten, and I shall dwell with melancholy pleasure on the recollection of them.'[1] In 1857 William Bodham Donne succeeded Kean as director; but the last performance under Donne's management took place on January 31, 1861, some eleven months before the Prince's death. More than thirty years then elapsed before the Queen suffered another professional dramatic entertainment to take place in a royal palace.

The Queen and Charles Kean.

The most conspicuous encouragement which the Queen and her husband bestowed on art during this period was their commission to eight artists (Eastlake, Maclise, Landseer, Dyce, Stanfield, Uwins, Leslie, and Ross) to decorate with frescoes the Queen's summer house in the gardens of Buckingham Palace. The subjects were drawn from Milton's 'Comus.' The

Patronage art.

---

[1] This letter is now in the Victoria and Albert Museum.

work was completed in 1845. But the Queen was also at the same period generous in commissions to Sir Edwin Landseer and other well-known artists for scenes in which she and her family played prominent parts. Occasionally they painted portraits for her, but her favourite portrait painter in the middle years of her reign was Winterhalter, a German artist, who undertook not only numerous single portraits but many groups of the Queen and members of her family.[1]

Education of the children.
Under Prince Albert's guidance, the Queen's domestic life was now very systematically ordered. The education of the growing family occupied their parents' minds almost from the children's birth. Prince Albert frequently took counsel on the subject with Stockmar and Bunsen, and the Queen consulted Melbourne (March 24, 1842) even after he had ceased to be her minister. In the result Lady Lyttelton, widow of the third Baron Lyttelton, and sister of the second Earl Spencer (who formerly led the Liberal party in the House of Commons as Lord Althorp), was in 1842 appointed governess of the royal children. She had been a lady-in-waiting since 1838, and enjoyed the Queen's full confidence. On Lady Lyttelton's retirement in January 1851, she was succeeded by Lady Caroline Barrington, widow of Captain the Hon. George Barrington, R.N., and daughter of the second Earl Grey, the Prime Minister; she held the office till her death on April 28, 1875. The office of royal governess was thus filled during the Queen's reign by only two holders.

[1] See Appendix II.

To the royal governess was entrusted complete control of the 'nursery establishment,' which soon included German and French as well as English attendants. All the children spoke German fluently from infancy. The Queen sensibly insisted that they should be brought up as simply, naturally, and domestically as possible, and that no obsequious deference should be paid to their rank. The need of cultivating perfect trust between parents and children, the value of a sincere but liberal religious training from childhood, and the folly of child-worship or excessive laudation were constantly in her mind. She spent with her children all the time that her public engagements permitted, and delighted in teaching them youthful amusements. She interested herself in their friends and in their pets, and looked after their health with assiduity. As they grew older she and the Prince encouraged them to recite poetry and to act little plays, or to arrange tableaux vivants, of which the parents were always gratified spectators.

<small>The 'nursery establishment.'</small>

To the education of the Prince of Wales as the heir-apparent the Queen and her husband naturally devoted special attention, and in every way they protected his interests. Very soon after his birth the Queen appointed a commission to receive and accumulate the revenues of the Duchy of Cornwall, the appanage of the heir-apparent, in their son's behalf, until he should come of age, and the estate was administered admirably. For the methods adopted in educating her sons, after their childhood was passed, she disclaimed any personal credit; she

<small>Education of sons and daughters.</small>

assigned it all to the Prince, and declared that public commendation of herself on this score caused her pain. In the matter of the education of her daughters she admitted that she exerted greater responsibility. Although she abhorred advanced views on the position of woman in social life, and vehemently denounced the champions of women's rights, she sought to make her daughters, in what she deemed their fitting sphere, as useful to society as her sons. While causing them to be instructed in all domestic arts, she repudiated the notion that marriage was the only object which they should be brought up to attain.[1] She often expressed regret that, among the upper classes in England, girls were taught to aim at little else in life than matrimony.

The Queen's dislike of London.
The Queen and Prince Albert regulated their own habits and pursuits with much care for their idiosyncrasies. Although public business compelled them to spend much time in London, the Prince rapidly acquired a distaste for it, which he soon communicated to the Queen. As a young woman she was, she said, wretched to leave London; but, though she never despised or disliked London amusements, she came to adopt her husband's view, that peace and quiet were most readily to be secured at a distance from the capital. The sentiment grew, and she reached the conclusion that 'the extreme weight and thickness of the atmosphere' injured her health, and in consequence her sojourns at Buckingham Palace became less frequent and briefer; in later life she did not visit it more than twice or thrice a

[1] *Letters of Princess Alice*, 1874, p. 320.

year, staying on each occasion not more than two days. Windsor came in course of time to be hardly more agreeable to her, but it was never open to such strong objections as London. It was near enough to the capital to enable her to transact business there without inconvenience, and in early married life she resided there for the greater part of the year.

But the Queen's happiest hours were spent beyond the walls of her official palaces, or indeed beyond the reach of towns. The Pavilion at Brighton, George IV.'s favourite home, she soon abandoned altogether, and, after being dismantled in 1846, it was sold to the Corporation of Brighton in 1850 to form a place of public assembly. She had already decided to secure residences in districts of her own choosing, which should be personal property and free from the restraints of supervision by public officials. Her resolve was to acquire private abodes in those parts of her dominions which were peculiarly congenial to her—the Isle of Wight and the highlands of Scotland. *Her love of the country.*

The Queen's residence in the south was secured first. Late in 1844 she purchased of Lady Isabella Blachford the estate of Osborne, consisting of about eight hundred acres, near East Cowes. She had known the spot in very early life, when her mother's friend and counsellor, Sir John Conroy, had lived at Osborne Cottage. Subsequent purchases increased the land which the Queen owned in the Isle of Wight to about two thousand acres. The existing house, Osborne House, proved inconvenient, and the foundation-stone of a new one was laid on *Acquisition of Osborne, 1844.*

June 23, 1845. A portion of it was occupied in September 1846, but the whole was not completed until 1851. In the designing of the new Osborne House and in laying out the gardens Prince Albert took a very active part. In the grounds was set up in 1854 a Swiss cottage as a workshop and playhouse for the children. The Queen interested herself in the neighbourhood, and rebuilt the parish church at Whippingham.[1]

Acquisition of Balmoral, 1848-52.

But greater interest attached in the Queen's eyes to her choice of a private residence in Scotland. In 1848 the Queen leased of the Fife trustees Balmoral House, a small and unpretending building near Braemar, Aberdeenshire. This she visited each year till 1852, when she purchased it of the owner and resolved to replace it by an elaborate edifice of granite. The new Balmoral Castle was completed in the autumn of 1854, and large additions were subsequently made to the estate, so that it finally extended to 25,000 acres. The Duchess of Kent rented in the neighbourhood Abergeldie Castle, which was subsequently leased from time to time by the Queen and was frequently occupied in the autumn by the Prince of Wales. Balmoral was henceforth identified with the Queen's most cherished memories.

Modes of life at Osborne and Balmoral.

Until the Queen's death a part of every autumn was spent at Balmoral; and through her widowhood she spent, in addition, at her highland residence

[1] In July 1902 the Queen's eldest son and successor, Edward VII., made over, with certain reservations, Osborne House and grounds to the nation, and suggested that it should be employed as a convalescent home for invalid officers of the army and navy.

several weeks of the early summer. Three or four annual visits were also paid regularly to Osborne. At both Osborne and Balmoral very homely modes of life were adopted, and, at Balmoral especially, ministers and foreign friends were surprised at the simplicity which characterised the Queen's domestic arrangements. Before the larger house was built only two sitting-rooms were occupied by the royal family. Of an evening billiards were played in the one, under such cramped conditions that the Queen, who usually looked on, had constantly to move her seat in order to give the players elbow-space. In the other room the Queen at times would take lessons in the Scotch reel. The minister in attendance did all his work in his small bedroom, and the Queen would run carelessly in and out of the house all day long, walking alone, visiting neighbouring cottages, and chatting unreservedly with their occupants. Cottage visiting at Balmoral became a fixed practice with her, and she was desirous that the ladies in attendance on her should emulate her example. She usually personally introduced her ladies-in-waiting, on their first arrival at Balmoral, to the cottagers. One of her subsequent complaints of Windsor as contrasted with Balmoral was her inability to go among the poor there with the freedom that was habitual to her on her Scottish estate.[1]

[1] The Queen's relations with Balmoral and her mode of life there are well illustrated in *Recollections of a Royal Parish*, by Mrs. Patricia Lindsay, daughter of the late Dr. Robertson, Commissioner for the Queen in Scotland from 1848 to 1875.

XV

IRELAND AND LOSS OF FRIENDS

First visit to Ireland, 1849.

AFTER identifying herself thus closely with Scotland, it was right for her to make the acquaintance of Ireland, the only portion of the United Kingdom which she had not visited during the first decade of her reign. Peel had entertained a suggestion that the Queen should visit the country in 1844, when she received an invitation from the Lord Mayor of Dublin, and a conditional promise of future acceptance was given. In the early autumn of 1849 the plan was carried out with good results.

State of the country.

The social and political condition of the country was not promising. The effects of the famine were still acute. Civil war had broken out in 1848, and, although it was easily repressed, disaffection was widespread. In June 1849 the Queen's attention was disagreeably drawn to the unsatisfactory condition of the country by a difficulty which arose in regard to recent convictions of Irish agitators for high treason; commutation of capital sentences was resolved upon, but it was found to be impossible to substitute terms of imprisonment for the penalty of death until a new statute had been devised, giving the Crown specific authority to that effect. This was accordingly accomplished in haste, and the Sovereign, for the first time in English history, was placed in a position to abrogate (on the advice of the Home Secretary or Lord-Lieutenant of Ireland) the penalty of death for the supreme crime against the State.

Personal loyalty to the Sovereign was still believed to prevail in Ireland, and the event proved the belief to be true. But the general distress and the political temper of the country precluded a state visit. The Queen went by sea from Cowes to the Cove of Cork, upon which she bestowed the new name of Queenstown in honour of her first landing there on Irish soil.[1] She was respectfully received. Thence she proceeded in her yacht to Kingstown, and took up her residence for four days at the Viceregal Lodge in Phœnix Park, Dublin. She held a levee one evening in Dublin Castle; she received addresses and visited public institutions, and met with a welcome that was all that could be wished. It was 'idolatrous,' ironically wrote Monckton Milnes (Lord Houghton), 'and utterly unworthy of a free, not to say ill-used, nation.'[2] Everything she saw delighted her, and she commemorated her satisfaction by creating the Prince of Wales Earl of Dublin (September 10, 1849). From the Irish capital she went by sea to Belfast, where her reception was equally enthusiastic. Thence she crossed to the Scottish coast, and after a public

Arrival at Queenstown.

[1] In this matter the Queen was following the precedent set by George IV., who on his visit to Ireland in September 1821 caused the port of Dunleary, near Dublin, where he landed, to be renamed Kingstown.

[2] Reid, *Lord Houghton*, i. 485-6.

visit to Glasgow she sought the grateful seclusion of Balmoral.

Last royal water pageant, 1849.

On October 30, 1849, an attack of chicken-pox prevented the Queen from fulfilling a promise to open the new Coal Exchange in Lower Thames Street, and she was represented by her husband. In two ways the incident proved of interest. The Queen's two eldest children there first appeared at a public ceremonial, while the royal barge, which bore the royal party from Westminster to St. Paul's wharf, made its last state journey on the Thames during the Queen's reign.

Deaths in royal circles, 1848-50.

In the large circle of the Queen's family and Court it was inevitable that death should be often busy and should constantly break valued links with the Queen's youth. During 1848 and 1850 few months passed without giving her cause for mourning. Her aunt, Princess Sophia, died on May 27, 1848, and her old minister and mentor, Melbourne, on November 24, 1848, while a year later George Anson, the Prince's former secretary and now his keeper of the privy purse, passed suddenly away. Anson's loss was severely felt by the Queen, who described it as 'irreparable.' But Melbourne's removal severed a tie of older and firmer standing. 'Truly and sincerely,' the Queen wrote in her Journal on hearing the news, 'do I deplore the loss of one who was a most kind and disinterested friend of mine, and most sincerely attached to me. He was indeed, for the first two years and a half of my reign, almost the only friend I had except Stockmar and Lehzen, and I used to see him constantly, daily. I thought much

Melbourne's death, Nov. 24, 1848.

and talked much of him all day.' Two days later she recorded with her customary simplicity of phrase: 'I received a pretty and touching letter from Lady Palmerston [i.e. Lord Melbourne's sister], saying that my last letter to poor Lord Melbourne had been a great comfort and relief to him, and that during the last melancholy years of his life we had often been the chief means of cheering him up. This is a great satisfaction to me to hear.' Another grief was the death, on December 2, 1849, at Stanmore Priory, of the old Queen Adelaide, who was buried in St. George's Chapel, Windsor, beside William IV. on December 13. The old Queen had always treated her young successor with motherly tenderness.

The summer of the following year (1850) was still more fruitful in episodes of mourning. On July 3 Peel succumbed to an accidental fall from his horse. In him the Queen said she lost not merely a friend, but a father. To her uncle, King Leopold, she wrote: 'The sorrow and grief at his death are most touching, and the country mourns over him as over a father. Every one seems to have lost a personal friend.' *Peel's death, July 3, 1850.*

Five days after Peel, died, too, the Queen's uncle, the Duke of Cambridge, whose widow survived him, to a patriarchal age, and was always carefully tended by the Queen. Subsequently death struck down in quick succession both Louis Philippe, the ex-King of the French, whose fate of exile roused the Queen's abiding sympathy (August 26), and the French King's gentle daughter, the Queen of the Belgians, wife of King Leopold (October 10). Every fresh blow that Louis Philippe's family suffered *Louis Philippe's death, Aug. 26, 1850.*

seemed to tighten the bonds that united them with the Queen.

Two assaults on the Queen, 1849-50.

Minor anxieties were caused the Queen by two brutal attacks upon her person : on May 19, 1849, when she was returning from a drive near Constitution Hill, a blank charge was fired at her from a pistol by an Irishman, William Hamilton, of Adare; and on May 27, 1850, one Robert Pate, a retired officer, hit her on the head with a cane as she was leaving Cambridge House in Piccadilly, where the Duke of Cambridge was lying ill. Offences so disgraceful excited universal sympathy, and in spite of the courage with which she faced them, they caused the Queen much suffering.[1]

Prince Arthur and the Duke of Wellington, May 1, 1850.

The last outrage was the more brutal, seeing that the Queen was just recovering from her confinement. Her third son, Arthur, was born on May 1, 1850. The date was the Duke of Wellington's eighty-first birthday. A few weeks before the Duke had delighted the Queen by the injudicious suggestion that Prince Albert should become Commander-in-Chief of the Army in succession to himself. The Prince wisely declined the honour. Apart from other considerations his hands were over-full already, and his health was giving evidence of undue mental strain. But, by way of showing her appreciation of the Duke's proposal, the Queen made him godfather to her new-born son. A second sponsor was the Prince of Prussia, brother of the King. The christening took place on

---

[1] Both Hamilton and Pate were sentenced to seven years' transportation under the Act for securing the Queen's safety passed in 1841.

June 22. The infant's third name, Patrick, commemorated the Queen's recent Irish visit.

At the time, despite family and political cares, the Queen's health was exceptionally robust. On going north in the autumn, after inaugurating the high-level bridge at Newcastle and the Royal Border Bridge on the Scottish boundary at Berwick—two notable feats of engineering—she stopped two days in Edinburgh at Holyrood Palace, where she closely investigated scenes of past history. 'Every step,' she wrote, 'is full of historical recollections, and our living here is quite an epoch in the annals of this old pile, which has seen so many deeds, more bad, I fear, than good.' She was especially interested in the spot where Rizzio was killed and the rooms that Queen Mary Stuart had occupied. On the second day of the visit she climbed Arthur's Seat, the noble hill overlooking Edinburgh. The exploit, although she found it (she wrote), 'after a year's disuse of climbing in England, hard work,' exhilarated her, and cost her little fatigue.[1] When she settled down to her holiday at Balmoral she took energetic walking exercise every day, and showed exceptional physical briskness. It was well that her health was growing in vigour, for annoyances in official life, far graver than any she had yet experienced, were within sight. No little physical strength was needed to enable her to face her coming trials with equanimity.

The Queen's robust health.

---

[1] *Leaves from the Queen's Journal*, pp. 81 seq.

XVI

THE DISSENSIONS WITH PALMERSTON

Differences with Palmerston.

THE habitual attitude to the Crown of Lord Palmerston, who was the Foreign Minister, first in Lord Melbourne's and now in Lord John Russell's administration, always implied a risk of open warfare between the Queen and her ministers. Of late the breach between her and Palmerston had been widening each year. Foreign affairs interested the Queen and her husband with increasing intensity as their years and experience grew. The more complex the foreign problems became, the more closely the Prince studied them. He conscientiously prepared ever-growing sheaves of memoranda with a view to counselling the Foreign Minister. But Palmerston was unmoved by his efforts or interests. He viewed the Prince's industry with undisguised contempt, and rendered his offers of advice abortive by going his own way, without consulting the Court, or, at times, even his colleagues.

Prince Albert's antagonistic views.

The antagonism between Prince Albert's views, with which the Queen identified herself, and those of Palmerston was based largely on principle. Palmerston consistently supported the Liberal movements, which were steadily gathering force abroad, even at the risk of exposing himself to the charge of encouraging 'revolution.' Although the Queen and the Prince fully recognised the value of constitutional methods of government in England, and were by no means averse to their spread on the continent of Europe, their personal relations with foreign dynasties evoked strong sympathy with reigning monarchs. They cherished an active repugnance to revolution, which Palmerston seemed to them to view with a perilous complaisance.

Through 1848, the year of revolution in Europe, the differences between the Prince and the minister were steadily widening. Palmerston treated with unruffled equanimity all the revolutionary riots at Berlin, Vienna, and Baden in 1848-9, and affected to be at a loss to understand why they should stir any active emotion in his royal mistress. He failed to recognise her poignant compassion for those crowned kinsmen or acquaintances whose lives and fortunes were menaced.

Palmerston and the Prince were probably in disagreement as to the past history and future destiny of every country of Europe. In their attitudes to both Italy and Prussia—the two countries whose affairs now commanded most attention—they were as far removed from each other as well could be. When efforts were first made in Italy to secure national unity and to throw off the yoke of Austria, Palmerston spoke with benevolence of the endeavours of the Italian patriots, and was always sanguine of their chances of success. Although the Prince strongly deprecated the cruelties which the Austrian rulers and the smaller native despots practised on their

Their respective attitudes to Italy.

P

Italian subjects, he and the Queen cherished a warm sympathy with the Austrian Emperor, and regarded with dismay the efforts of the North Italians to cast off Austrian rule. The revolutionary endeavour to unite Italy under a single ruler meant for them primarily the suppression of many thrones whose occupants were entitled to their sympathetic regard.

Their respective attitudes to Prussia.
In regard to Germany, on the other hand, the opposition between royal and ministerial opinions was assignable to another train of considerations. The Prince was well disposed to the movement for national unity under Prussia's leadership. His and the Queen's social relations both with the King of Prussia, who was the Prince of Wales's godfather, and with his brother, the Prince of Prussia, who was godfather to Prince Arthur, were growing in intimacy, and whatever tended to improve Prussia's position in Germany and Europe was agreeable to the English Court. Palmerston saw in the Prussian King only a weak man and a reactionary politician. He regarded the Prussian King's allies among the German Princes as deserving of no greater respect than that Sovereign. He consequently looked with suspicion on German nationalist aspirations to which effect must be given, if at all, under such unpromising auspices.

Distrust of the reigning houses both of Prussia and Austria coloured all Palmerston's view of German politics. In the intricate struggle for the possession of the duchies of Schleswig-Holstein, which opened in 1848, he inclined to the claim of Denmark against that of the confederation of German States, whether Prussia or Austria should ultimately be at its head.

Meanwhile the English royal family hopefully anticipated the triumph of Prussia in the final settlement of German rivalries or pretensions in Central Europe.

In point of practice Palmerston was as offensive to the Prince and the Queen as he was in point of principle or policy. He lost no opportunity of indicating to them that their predilections were of no interest to him, and he deprecated their offers of counsel or of regular exchange of views. He frequently caused them intense irritation or alarm by involving the Government in acute international crises without warning the Queen of their approach. In 1848, before consulting her, he peremptorily ordered the reactionary Spanish Government to liberalise its institutions, with the result that the English Ambassador, Sir Henry Bulwer, who was directed to deliver the frank despatch to Queen Isabella's advisers, was promptly expelled from Madrid. Again, in January 1850, to the Queen's consternation, Palmerston, by despatching the British fleet to Grecian waters, coerced Greece into compliance with English demands for the compensation of Don Pacifico and other English subjects who had disputed claims against the Greek Government. France was at the moment embarked in an attempt to mediate in this quarrel, and that country regarded as insulting Palmerston's precipitate action, which practically ignored the pacific tone of French intervention. The French Ambassador was withdrawn from London, and for the third time in the Queen's reign—on this occasion almost before she had an opportunity of learning the cause—Palmerston brought France and

Palmerston's offensive practice.

England to the brink of war. It was only very gradually that the bitter and perilous controversy that was roused between the two countries lost its venomous character.

The Queen's private correspondence.

The Queen's embarrassments were aggravated by the personal intimacies which she cultivated with foreign sovereigns. They cherished a belief that her personal power was far greater than it was, and they maintained with her a vast correspondence which was inspired by that misconception. It was their habit to address to her personally autograph appeals on political affairs, and they were under the impression that privately through her it was possible for them to influence in their own interests the foreign policy of her country. She was wise enough to avoid the snares that were thus laid for her, and she frankly consulted Palmerston, the Foreign Minister, before replying to communications made to her by continental princes who were not her kinsmen. He invariably derided her notion of conciliating the good opinion of foreign Courts. He knew that his name was a word of loathing to them, and he felt under no obligation to diminish their fear of England.

The appeal of the Queen of Portugal, 1847.

The advice which Palmerston often offered the Queen when her foreign correspondence was submitted to him involved her in many mortifying experiences. In 1847, the Queen of Portugal, the Queen's early playmate, and the wife of her first cousin, Ferdinand of Saxe-Coburg, was threatened by her revolutionary subjects with the loss of her throne. She promptly appealed direct to Queen Victoria for protection. Queen Victoria at once consulted Palmerston.

He treated the Portuguese difficulty as a 'Coburg family affair.' He breezily attributed the Portuguese Queen's peril to her reliance on the absolutist advice of one Dietz, a native of Coburg, who stood towards her and her husband, Prince Ferdinand, in a relation resembling that of Stockmar to Prince Albert and Queen Victoria. Palmerston insisted that the Portuguese Queen could only save the situation by assenting to Dietz's summary dismissal. Such counsel was highly offensive to Queen Victoria and to her Saxe-Coburg kinsmen. The latter relieved their feelings by applying to the minister in conversation or correspondence with one another such epithets as 'ill-tempered, coarse, and threatening.'[1] Palmerston, however, dictated a solemn letter, full of constitutional advice and warnings against the iniquities of Dietz, for his royal mistress to copy in her own reluctant hand and forward to her unhappy correspondent at Lisbon.[2]

Later in the same year 1847 the vacillating and pusillanimous King of Prussia emulated the Portuguese Queen's example. He wrote Queen Victoria a private letter, and directed his ambassador at St. James's, Baron Bunsen, to deliver it to her in private audience in the absence of her ministers. The monarch invited Queen Victoria's avowed encouragement of the feeble efforts that Prussia was making to dominate the German federation. Palmerston was never to be safely ignored. He learned from Bunsen of the Prussian King's missive, and told him with great frankness that it was irregular for the

Letter to the King of Prussia, 1847.

---

[1] Duke Ernest, *Memoirs*, i. 288 seq.
[2] Walpole, *Life of Lord John Russell*.

English Sovereign to correspond with foreign monarchs unless they were her relatives. The correspondence must pass through the ministers' hands.[1] Queen Victoria felt her impotence acutely. In concert with Prince Albert Palmerston sketched a colourless draft reply to her royal correspondent. This Palmerston requested the Queen to copy out in her own hand; it 'began and ended in German, though the body of it was in English.' The incident was exceptionally galling to the susceptibilities of both the Queen and her husband. Prince Albert, in frequent private correspondence with the King of Prussia, had already sought to stimulate him to more active assertion of Prussian power in Germany. The apparent discrepancy between the Prince's ardour in the cause of Prussia and the coolness in regard to it which Palmerston imposed on his wife's epistle was peculiarly repugnant to both her and her husband.

Palmerston's obduracy.

But the position of affairs appeared to the Queen and Prince quite incurable. Expostulation with Palmerston seemed vain. In June 1848 Prince Albert bade Lord John remind him that every one of the ten thousand despatches which were received annually at the Foreign Office was addressed to the Queen and to the Prime Minister as well as to himself, and that the replies involved them all. In the following autumn Palmerston apathetically remarked on a further protest made in the Queen's behalf by Lord John, the Prime Minister: 'Unfortunately the Queen gives ear too easily to persons who are hostile to her government, and who wish to

[1] Bunsen, *Memoirs*, ii. 149.

poison her mind with distrust of her ministers, and in this way she is constantly suffering under groundless uneasiness.' To this challenge the Queen answered, through Lord John, October 1, 1848 : 'The Queen naturally, as I think, dreads that upon some occasion you may give her name to sanction proceedings which she may afterwards be compelled to disavow.'[1] Palmerston deemed such an anticipation unworthy of attention.

Unfortunately for the Queen the general lines of Palmerston's foreign policy were vehemently applauded by a majority in Parliament and in the country. His elaborate defence of his action in regard to Greece in the Don Pacifico affair in June 1850, when he nearly involved England in a war with France, elicited the stirring enthusiasm of the House of Commons. There was nothing open for the Queen to do except to exclaim loudly against her humiliation in conversation with political friends like Aberdeen and Clarendon. Lord John, the Prime Minister, offered her cold comfort. He was often as much out of sympathy with Palmerston as she in viewing his treatment of foreign affairs, but he knew the Government could not stand without its popular Foreign Secretary. Consequently the Queen, who was always averse to inviting the perplexities of a change of ministry, often despaired of the situation. But she had no intention of submitting to it meekly.

Popularity of Palmerston's policy.

In March 1850 she and the Prince made some effort to modify Palmerston's pretensions. They drafted a full statement of their grievance, which

The Queen's demands, 1850.

[1] Walpole, *Lord John Russell*, ii. 47.

they proposed to forward to the offending minister. They delayed its actual despatch for three months, and, when in June the statesman appealed with triumphant effect to the House of Commons for an endorsement of the administration of his office, the royal protest seemed inopportune, and it was laid aside for a further period. In the summer Lord John recalled Palmerston's attention to the Queen's irritation, and the Foreign Minister disavowed any intention of treating her with disrespect. But his general conduct remained unchanged.

Her two requests.

At length, on August 12, 1850, the Queen sent Palmerston, through Lord John, two carefully worded requests in regard to his future behaviour: 'She requires,' her words ran, ' (1) that the Foreign Secretary will distinctly state what he proposes in a given case, in order that the Queen may know as distinctly to what she has given her royal sanction. (2) Having once given her sanction to a measure, that it be not arbitrarily altered or modified by the minister. Such an act she must consider as failure in sincerity towards the Crown, and justly to be visited by the exercise of her constitutional right of dismissing that minister. She expects to be kept informed of what passes between him and the foreign ministers before important decisions are taken, based upon that intercourse; to receive the foreign despatches in good time, and to have the drafts for her approval sent to her in sufficient time to make herself acquainted with their contents before they must be sent off.' [1]

Two days afterwards Prince Albert explained

[1] Martin, *Biography of Prince Consort*, ii. 51.

more fully to Palmerston, in a personal interview, the Queen's grounds of complaint. 'The Queen had often,' the Prince said, 'latterly almost invariably, differed from the line of policy pursued by Lord Palmerston. She had always openly stated her objections; but when overruled by the cabinet, or convinced that it would, for political reasons, be more prudent to waive her objections, she knew her constitutional position too well not to give her full support to whatever was done on the part of the Government. She knew that they were going to battle together, and that she was going to receive the blows which were aimed at the Government; and she had these last years received several [blows], such as no sovereign of England had before been obliged to put up with, and which had been most painful to her. But what she had a right to require in return was, that before a line of policy was adopted or brought before her for her sanction, she should be in full possession of all the facts and all the motives operating; she felt that in this respect she was not dealt with as she ought to be. She never found a matter "intact," nor a question, in which we were not already compromised, when it was submitted to her; she had no means of knowing what passed in the cabinet, nor what passed between Lord Palmerston and the foreign ministers in their conferences, but what Lord Palmerston chose to tell her, or what she found in the newspapers.' *Prince Albert on Palmerston.*

Palmerston affected pained surprise and solemnly promised amendment. But he remained in office and his course of action underwent no permanent alteration. *Fresh dissensions.*

A few months later he committed the Queen, without her assent, to new dissensions with the Austrian Government and to new encouragement of Denmark in that country's claims to Schleswig-Holstein. In the first case Palmerston answered the Queen's protest by threatening Lord John with resignation, but he ultimately endeavoured to modify his action in accordance with the royal wish, and gave vague expression to a show of sympathy with Austria in her harassing struggle with her Italian subjects. In regard to Denmark's pretensions to Schleswig-Holstein, Palmerston declined to recant his faith in their justice. At no point did he give plain proof of penitence.

'Papal aggression.'
In the winter of 1850 a distasteful domestic question distracted the Queen's mind from foreign affairs. Lord John had identified the Government with the strong Protestant feeling which was roused by Cardinal Wiseman's announcement of the Pope's revival of the Roman Catholic hierarchy in England. Hundreds of protests from public bodies were addressed to the Queen in person, and she received them patiently. But she detested the controversy and regretted 'the unchristian and intolerant spirit' exhibited by the Protestant agitators. 'I cannot bear,' she wrote privately, 'to hear the violent abuse of the Catholic religion, which is so painful and so cruel towards the many innocent and good Roman Catholics.' When she opened Parliament on February 4, 1851, she resented the cries of 'no popery' with which she was greeted; but the ministry was pledged actively to resist the 'papal aggression.' A bill was introduced making it illegal for Roman Catholic priests to bear

in England ecclesiastical titles. The Queen had no choice but to acquiesce.

It was consequently with comparatively small concern that she saw Lord John's Government—partly through intestine differences on the religious question—outvoted in the House of Commons in February 1851. The immediate question at issue was electoral reform—a topic which the Government was indisposed seriously to entertain. They declined to accept a motion for the assimilation of the borough and county franchise, and it was carried by their supporters against them. Lord John at once resigned, and much difficulty followed. The Queen sent for the Conservative leader, Lord Stanley, afterwards Lord Derby, the leader of the Conservative party in the House of Lords. He declined to assume office in the absence of adequate support in the House of Commons, and strongly advised a reconstruction of the existing ministry on a more comprehensive basis. That course was entirely congenial to the Queen, and she employed her influence in abetting it. On February 22 she consulted Lord Aberdeen with a view to a fusion between Whigs and Peelites, who had now practically broken with the Conservatives, but the combination at the moment proved impracticable.

Ministerial crisis and deadlock.

Perplexed by the deadlock which the refusals of Derby and Aberdeen created, the Queen turned for advice to the old Duke of Wellington. In agreement with the Duke's counsel, she recalled Lord John Russell; Prince Albert had already sent him a memorandum of the recent negotiations with Lord Stanley. Lord John consented with some hesitation

Recall of Lord John.

to resume his post, and managed to get through the session in safety. He secured the passage of his anti-papal Ecclesiastical Titles Bill, although he found it needful completely to emasculate it. It received the royal assent on July 29, 1851, but it was never put into force, and was, to the Queen's satisfaction, repealed in 1870.

XVII

THE GREAT EXHIBITION AND PALMERSTON'S FALL

MEANWHILE the attention of the Court and country turned from party polemics to a demonstration of peace and goodwill among the nations which excited the Queen's highest hopes. It was the inauguration of the Great Exhibition in the Crystal Palace which was erected in Hyde Park from the designs of Sir Joseph Paxton. In origin and execution that design was due to Prince Albert; and it had consequently encountered abundant opposition from high Tories and all sections of society who disliked the Prince. Abroad it was condemned by absolute monarchs and their ministers on unexpected grounds. It was the wish of the Queen and her husband that rulers of all countries of the world or their representatives should be their guests on the auspicious occasion, and invitations were issued with a liberal hand. But many foreign sovereigns regarded an assembly of crowned heads in any one place as an incitement to revolutionary conspiracy to organise attempts on their lives. Such a reunion offered the suggestion, it was urged, to revolutionary agents in Europe to gather together in London on a speciously innocent pretext, and hatch nefarious designs.

_{The Great Exhibition, 1851.}

The Queen was especially desirous that the Prince of Prussia and his son should be among their visitors at the opening of the Exhibition. The Prussian minister, Freiherr von Manteuffel, argued with vehemence against the presence of any prominent member of the Prussian royal family. He wrote to the Prince of Prussia that a number of madmen had collected in London, who were bent on destroying the existing order of affairs; Prussia was especially obnoxious to these revolutionary spirits, and the assassination of the Prince and his son in London, which was well within the limits of possibility, would, by interrupting the succession to the Prussian throne, work the country irretrievable disaster.[1]

Its successful accomplishment.

The result belied all prophecy of evil. The Queen flung herself with spirit into the enterprise. She interested herself in every detail, and she was rewarded for her energy by the knowledge that the realised scheme powerfully appealed to the imagination of the mass of her people. In spite of their censorious fears foreign Courts were well represented, and among the Queen's guests were the Prince and Princess of Prussia and their eldest son. The brilliant opening ceremony, over which she presided on May 1, 1851, evoked a marvellous outburst of loyalty. Her bearing was described on all hands as 'thoroughly regal.'[2] Besides twenty-five thousand people in the building, seven hundred thousand cheered her out-

---

[1] *Unter Friedrich Wilhelm IV.: Denkwürdigkeiten des Ministerpräsidenten Otto Freiherrn v. Manteuffel*, herausgegeben von Heinrich von Poschingen (Berlin, 1901), vol. iii. p. 420.

[2] *Life of Stanley*, i. 424.

side as she passed them on her way from Buckingham Palace. It was, she said, the proudest and happiest day of her happy life. Her feelings were gratified both as Queen and wife. 'The great event has taken place,' she wrote in her diary (May 1), 'a complete and beautiful triumph—a glorious and touching sight, one which I shall ever be proud of for my beloved Albert and my country. . . . Yes! it is a day which makes my heart swell with pride and glory and thankfulness!' In her eyes the great festival of peace was a thousand times more memorable than the thrilling scene of her coronation.

Tennyson, who had been appointed Poet Laureate in November 1850, in succession to Wordsworth, in the noble address 'To the Queen,' which he prefixed to the seventh edition of his 'Poems' (March 1851), wrote of the Great Exhibition:

> She brought a vast design to pass
> When Europe and the scatter'd ends
> Of our fierce world did meet as friends
> And brethren in her halls of glass.

The stanza was not reprinted.

The season of the Great Exhibition was exceptionally brilliant. On June 13 another *bal costumé* at Buckingham Palace illustrated the reign of Charles II. On July 9 the Queen attended a ball at the Guildhall, which celebrated the success of the Exhibition. Everywhere her reception was admirably cordial. When at length she temporarily left London for Osborne, she expressed pain that 'this brilliant and for ever memorable season should be past.' Of

Court festivities.

the continuous display of devotion to her in London she wrote to Stockmar: 'All this will be of a use not to be described: it identifies us with the people and gives them an additional cause for loyalty and attachment.'

<small>The Queen at Liverpool and Manchester.</small>

Early in August the Queen came to Westminster to prorogue Parliament, and she visited the Exhibition for the last time. Throughout the country the people gave new proofs of their devotion to her which she actively reciprocated. In October, on her customary removal to Balmoral, she made a formal progress through Liverpool and Manchester, and stayed for a few days with the Earl of Ellesmere at Worsley Hall. She manifested intelligent interest in the improvements which manufacturing processes were making in these great centres of industry, and the tour was a triumphal progress. Her visit to Peel Park, Salford, on October 10, was commemorated by a statue of her, the cost of which was mainly defrayed by 80,000 Sunday-school teachers and scholars; it was unveiled by Prince Albert, May 5, 1857.

<small>Palmerston and Kossuth.</small>

A month after the closing of the Exhibition the dream of happiness was fading. The death of her sour-tempered uncle, King Ernest of Hanover (November 18, 1851), was not a heavy blow, but Palmerston was still disturbing her equanimity. Kossuth, the leader of the Hungarian revolution, had just arrived in England; Palmerston openly avowed sympathy with him, and his attitude threatened England's good relations with Austria. Both the Queen and Lord John remonstrated. The Queen prepared a note for the perusal of the cabinet, in which the ministers were requested to censure Palmerston's attitude unequivocally; but her appeal was vain.

Relief from the tormenting conduct of Palmerston was, however, at hand. It came at a moment when the Queen had almost abandoned hope of alleviating her lot, and it was due to causes in which she had no hand. On December 2, 1851, Prince Louis Napoleon, President of that French Republic which was created on the expulsion of Louis Philippe, made himself, by a *coup d'état*, absolute head of the French Government, with the avowed intention of re-establishing the imperial Napoleonic dynasty. Palmerston believed in Napoleon's ability, and a day or two later, in casual conversation with the French Ambassador, Walewski, expressed of his own initiative approbation of the new form of government in France. This was the reverse of the sentiment with which recent events in Paris had inspired the Queen. Both she and Lord John viewed Napoleon's accession to despotic power, and the means whereby it had been accomplished, with detestation. Palmerston's precipitate committal of England to a friendly recognition of the new *régime* before he had communicated with the Queen or his colleagues placed her and them alike in a position of intolerable difficulty.

Palmerston and Napoleon III.

Happily Palmerston's own inconsiderate talk untied the Gordian knot that bound him to the Queen. The Foreign Minister's careless display of self-sufficiency roused the temper of Lord John, who had simultaneously assured the Queen that for the present England would extend to Napoleon the coldest neutrality. To the Queen's astonishment,

Palmerston's fall.

but to her unconcealed delight, Lord John, before consulting her, summarily made Palmerston's declaration to Walewski a ground for demanding his resignation (December 19). Palmerston was taken by surprise. He feebly defended himself by claiming that in his intercourse with Walewski he had only expressed his personal views, and that he was entitled to converse at will with ambassadors. Lord John offered to rearrange the Government so as to give him another office, but this proposal Palmerston declined. The seals of the Foreign Office were without delay transferred to Lord Granville, who had been on friendly terms with the Queen since her girlhood, and was of her own generation.

Prince Albert's elation.

The Queen and the Prince made no secret of their joy at the turn of events. They gave full vent to that bitterness of feeling which Palmerston's complacent attitude to revolutionary activity had stirred in them, and they freely betrayed, in their elation at his removal, the torture they had mentally suffered from his supercilious scorn of their natural prejudices. To his brother Ernest, Prince Albert wrote without reserve in a little-known letter of remarkable interest: 'And now the year closes with the happy circumstance for us, that the man who embittered our whole life, by continually placing before us the shameful alternative of either sanctioning his misdeeds throughout Europe and rearing up the Radical party here to a power under his leadership, or of bringing about an open conflict with the Crown and thus plunging the only country where liberty, order, and lawfulness exist together into the general chaos—

that this man has, as it were, cut his own throat. "Give a rogue rope enough and he will hang himself" is an old English adage with which we have sometimes tried to console ourselves, and which has proved true again here.'[1]

The judgment that the Queen and the Prince passed at the moment on Palmerston's conduct and on the circumstances of his removal from office has not stood the test of time. As a matter of fact, Palmerston's dismissal was from the outset a doubtful triumph for the Crown. It was, in the first place, not the Queen's act; it was the act of the Prime Minister, Lord John, who was not greatly influenced by Court feeling, and it was an act that Lord John lived to regret. Furthermore, Palmerston's popularity in the country grew in proportion to his unpopularity at Court, and, in the decade that followed, his power, and ministerial power generally, increased steadily at the expense of the Crown's influence in both home and foreign affairs. The substantive victory lay with the minister. The principle of ministerial responsibility, unfettered and uninfluenced by the Sovereign's will, was too firmly rooted in the country's constitution to be affected seriously by any personal disagreement between minister and monarch.

The peril of dismissing a minister.

[1] Duke Ernest's *Memoirs*.

XVIII

LORD ABERDEEN'S MINISTRY

Palmerston's revenge.

PALMERSTON'S removal did not, in fact, diminish anxiety in the sphere either of domestic or foreign politics at Court for more than a few weeks. The year 1852 opened ominously. The intentions of France under her new and untried Government were doubtful. The old tradition of hostility between the two countries was always liable suddenly to light the torch of war. The need of increasing the naval and military forces was successfully urged on Lord John Russell's Government; but no sooner had the discussions on that subject opened in the House of Commons than Palmerston descended once more into the arena. He warmly condemned as inadequate the earliest proposals of the Government which were embodied in a Militia Bill. The majority of the House of Commons came to his aid and enabled him to inflict a defeat on his former colleagues on February 20, 1852. He carried an amendment against the ministry by 136 to 125. Lord John, recognising that the feeling of Parliament was hostile to the Government, straightway resigned. Within two months of his own dismissal, Palmerston had driven his former colleagues from office. 'I have had my tit-for-tat with

John Russell,' wrote the elated victor on the 24th, 'and I turned him out on Friday last.'[1]

The Queen had no affection for Lord John's ministry, but neither had she much confidence in the Opposition. She now, however, acted strictly according to precedent, and summoned the leader of the Conservative party, who, hitherto known as Lord Stanley, had just succeeded to the earldom of Derby on his father's death. She bade Lord Derby form a Conservative Government. He consented after deliberating with his friends. His acceptance of office meant that his ally, Disraeli, who was the acknowledged chief of the main body of Conservatives in the House of Commons, should enter official life for the first time at almost its apex. Lord Derby nominated Disraeli Chancellor of the Exchequer and leader of the House of Commons.

Lord Derby's first Government.

The new ministry was not strong, despite the ability of its two joint-leaders. With none of its members did the Queen feel real sympathy. Almost all were new to official life, all belonged to the party of protection; but protection seemed to the Queen to have vanished from practical politics, and she was disposed to reproach her new advisers with their delay in discerning the impracticability of the obsolete policy. 'A little more haste,' she said of their past attitude to the question, 'would have saved so much annoyance, so much difficulty.'

Inexperience of its members.

Personal intercourse rapidly overcame her prejudices against Lord Derby and his friends. Lord Derby proved extremely courteous. Lord Malmesbury, the Foreign Minister, kept her thoroughly well

Early impression of Disraeli.

---

[1] Evelyn Ashley's *Life of Palmerston*, i. 334.

informed of the affairs of his office, and was always ready to take her advice. What she knew of Disraeli did not prepossess her in his favour, but the personal difficulty that she and her friends had anticipated from his presence in the cabinet was quietly dispelled. Disraeli had won his prominence in Parliament by his caustic denunciations of the Queen's friend, Peel, whose associates represented him to her as an unprincipled adventurer. Disraeli was perfectly aware of the Queen's suspicions of him, and during the ministerial crisis that preceded his entry into office he expressed himself quite ready to accept a post that should not bring him into frequent relations with the Court. But personal acquaintance with him at once diminished the Queen's distrust; his clever conversation amused her. She regretted his denunciation of Sir Robert Peel, but was captivated by his respectful manner and courteous bearing. She afterwards gave signal proof of a dispassionate spirit by dismissing every trace of early hostility, and by extending to him in course of time a confidence and a devotion far exceeding that which she showed to any other minister of her reign.

Defeat of Derby's Government.

But her present experience of Disraeli and his colleagues was brief. A general election in July, five months after they had taken office, left the Conservatives in a minority. Only 299 Conservatives were returned, against 315 Liberals and 40 Peelites, whose votes were usually at the command of the Liberal party.

In the same month the Queen made a cruise in the royal yacht on the south coast, and a few weeks later paid a second private visit to King Leopold, now a widower for the second time, at his summer palace at Laeken. The weather was bad, but on returning she visited the chief objects of interest in Antwerp, and steered close to Calais, so that she might see the place.

Second visit to Belgium.

When at Balmoral later in the autumn, information reached her of the generous bequest to her by an eccentric subject, John Camden Neild, of all his fortune, amounting to half a million. He had inherited from his father, James Neild, a well-known philanthropist, about half that sum, and the last thirty years of his life had been devoted exclusively to the miserly accumulation of the other half. He was unmarried and had no relations. The Queen accepted the large sum with gratitude. She did not spend the legacy, but suffered it to swell her savings. She increased Neild's bequests to the three executors from 100*l.* to 1,000*l.*, provided for her benefactor's servants, gave an annuity of 100*l.* to a woman who had once frustrated his attempt at suicide, and finally, in 1855, rebuilt the chancel of North Marston Church, Buckinghamshire, in the neighbourhood of which Neild had much property; she also placed a window in the church to his memory.

Neild's bequest.

The elation of spirit which this munificent addition to her private fortune caused her was succeeded by depression on hearing of the death of the Duke of Wellington on September 14. 'One cannot think of this country without " the Duke," our immortal hero,' she wrote in her Journal. ' The Crown never possessed —and I fear never *will*—so *devoted*, loyal, and faithful

Death of the Duke of Wellington.

a subject, so staunch a supporter! To *us* (who, alas! have lost, now, so many of our valued and experienced friends) his loss is *irreparable*, for his readiness to aid and advise, if it could be of use to us, and to overcome any and every difficulty, was unequalled. . . . He was a link which connected us with bygone times, with the last century.'[1] 'He was to us a true friend,' she wrote to her uncle Leopold, 'and most valuable adviser . . . we shall soon stand sadly alone. Aberdeen is almost the only personal friend of that kind left to us. Melbourne, Peel, Liverpool,[2] now the Duke—all gone.'

The Duke's funeral.
The Queen issued a general order of regret to the army, and she put her household into mourning—a mark of regard very rarely accorded by a sovereign to a subject. She went to the lying-in-state in Chelsea Hospital, and witnessed the funeral procession to St. Paul's from the balcony of Buckingham Palace on November 18.

Lord Derby's resignation.
On November 11 the Queen opened the new Parliament. Lord Derby was still Prime Minister, but the position of the Government was hopeless. On December 3 Disraeli's budget was introduced. Suspicion was entertained that it embodied relics of the heresy of protection, and on the 17th it was thrown out by a majority of nineteen. Lord Derby promptly resigned.

Queen's desire for a coalition ministry.
For six years the Queen's Government had been extraordinarily weak. Parties were disorganised, and no leader enjoyed the full confidence of any

[1] *Leaves from the Queen's Journal*, p. 99.
[2] The Queen's early friend, the third Earl of Liverpool, had died October 3, 1851.

large section of the House of Commons. A reconstruction of party seemed essential to the Queen and the Prince. In November she had discussed with Lord Derby a possible coalition of Whigs and Tories. The chief condition she then imposed was that Palmerston should not lead the House of Commons. Derby judged the plan chimerical, but when he resigned the Queen made up her mind to a strenuous personal effort whereby she might give her views effect.

The Queen sent for veteran statesmen on the Whig and Peelite sides, Lord Aberdeen and Lord Lansdowne, both of whom she had known long and fully trusted. The Whig leader, Lord Lansdowne, had been Lord President in the Council under Lord John Russell, had endeavoured to curb, before the great crisis, the independence of Palmerston, and had lately committed himself to the view that the continuance in office of a weakly supported Government injured the country. But he was now seventy-two years old and crippled with gout, so that he was unable to obey the Queen's commands. The Peelite leader Lord Aberdeen came alone. He lent a willing ear to the Queen's proposals. Immediately after her interview with him, on December 19, the Queen wrote to Lord John Russell: 'The Queen thinks the moment to have arrived when a popular, efficient, and durable Government could be formed by the sincere and united efforts of all parties professing Conservative and Liberal opinions.'[1] Lord John was complaisant; other friends were sounded with

Queen's appeal to Aberdeen

and to Lord John.

---
[1] Walpole, *Life*, ii. 161.

satisfactory results. Finally Aberdeen undertook to form a coalition Government, with the Queen's assistance.

Coalition of Peelites and Liberals.

The task was, after a fashion, easier of accomplishment than the Queen contemplated. Lord Aberdeen had little hope of assistance from the Conservative leaders, who still looked coldly on Peel's followers, and were altogether out of sympathy with professed Liberals. If the Queen acquiesced in the exclusion of Conservatives from the projected administration, there was little reason why the scheme should fail. Differences of opinion on domestic questions between Peel's friends, whom Lord Aberdeen led, and the Whigs had been gradually diminishing. Ultimately Aberdeen confined his endeavours to combining in his cabinet the chiefs of the Peelite party with the chiefs of the Liberal party. Four Peelites accepted Aberdeen's invitation to join his Government. Gladstone became Chancellor of the Exchequer, the Duke of Newcastle Colonial Secretary, Sir James Graham First Lord of the Admiralty, and Sidney Herbert Secretary at War. The left wing or Radical section of the Liberal party was conciliatory, and a strong representative of it, Sir William Molesworth, entered the cabinet as First Commissioner of Works. The seven remaining members were Whigs who had served in the last administration.

Aberdeen's Whig colleagues.

Of Lord Aberdeen's Whig coadjutors the most important was Palmerston, whose presence was rightly deemed essential to the stability of the Government; and the Queen, fully recognising the distasteful fact, raised no objection to his appointment to the Home

Office. The Foreign Office was bestowed on Lord John, but he soon withdrew from it in favour of the Queen's firm friend, Lord Clarendon. Lord Lansdowne joined the cabinet without office, Lord Granville became President of the Council, Lord Cranworth Lord Chancellor, the Duke of Argyll Lord Privy Seal, and Sir Charles Wood (afterwards Viscount Halifax) President of the Board of Control (of India).

All the members of the cabinet were men of high ability, and the Queen was well content with the outcome of her suggestion, even though the Conservatives had declined to enter the fold. On December 28 Aberdeen had completed his task, and the Queen wrote with sanguine satisfaction to her uncle Leopold of 'our excellent Aberdeen's success,' and of the 'realisation of the country's and of our own most ardent wishes.' *The Queen's satisfaction.*

Thus the next year opened promisingly, but it proved a calm before a great storm. On April 7, 1853, the Queen's fourth and youngest son was born, and was named Leopold, after the Queen's uncle, King Leopold, who was his godfather. George, the new blind King of Hanover, was also a sponsor, and the infant's third name of Duncan celebrated the Queen's affection for Scotland. The child, to whom the Queen was deeply attached, proved very delicate, and during his life of thirty-one years was a frequent source of anxiety to his mother. *Birth of Prince Leopold, April 7, 1853.*

The Queen was not long in retirement on her youngest son's birth, and public calls were numerous. Military training, in view of possible warlike complications on the continent, was proceeding actively *Military preparations.*

with the Queen's concurrence. Twice—June 21 and August 5, 1853—she visited, the first time with her guests, the new King and Queen of Hanover, a camp newly formed on Chobham Common.[1] In the interval between the two visits the Queen, Prince Albert, the Prince of Wales, Princess Royal, and Princess Alice were all disabled by an attack of measles, and Prince Albert, to the Queen's alarm, suffered severely from nervous prostration. But recovery was not long delayed. On August 11 the navy was encouraged by a great naval review which the Queen held at Spithead.

Second visit to Dublin, 1853.

Before the month ended the Queen paid a second visit to Dublin, in order to inspect an exhibition of Irish industries, which was framed on the model of the Great Exhibition of 1851. A million Irish men and women are said to have met her on her landing at Kingstown. The royal party stayed in Dublin from August 30 to September 3, and attended many public functions. As on the former occasion, the Queen spent, she said, 'a pleasant, gay, and interesting time.'

Napoleon III.'s advances.

Throughout 1852 the Queen persisted in her frank avowals of repugnance to personal intercourse with Napoleon III., Emperor of the French, who had supplanted Louis Philippe on the French throne. Her relations with the exiled royal family of France rendered the usurper an object of suspicion and dislike, and the benevolence with which Palmerston regarded him did not soften her animosity. But she gradually acknowledged the danger of allowing her personal

[1] On August 5, 1901, a granite cross was unveiled on Chobham Common to commemorate the first of these visits.

feeling to compromise peaceful relations with France. Lord Malmesbury, the Foreign Minister under Lord Derby, had known Napoleon in earlier days, and had formed an opinion of him which differed little from Lord Palmerston's. One of the late Conservative Government's last acts was to join the European Powers in formally recognising the new Napoleonic empire (December 2, 1852). At the same time the Emperor was making advances to England of a kind which it involved peril to repel.

The French Ambassador in London had sounded Malmesbury, the Foreign Minister, at the date of the British Government's formal recognition of the empire, as to whether a marriage between the Emperor and Princess Adelaide of Hohenlohe-Langenburg, daughter of the Queen's half-sister, would be acceptable. The Queen was startled by the suggestion. She spoke with horror of the Emperor's religion and morals, and of the fate of consorts of French rulers since the Revolution. She was therefore not sorry that the discussion should be summarily ended by the Emperor's marriage in the following January with Mlle. Eugénie de Montijo. With that lady the irony of fate was soon to connect the Queen in a lasting friendship.

Napoleon's matrimonial plans.

Meanwhile the Queen's uncle, King Leopold, realised the wisdom of promoting better relations between her and the Emperor, whose openly expressed anxiety to secure her countenance was likely to become a source of embarrassment were it hastily ignored. In the early months of 1853 Duke Ernest, Prince Albert's brother, after consultation with King

King Leopold's mediation between the Queen and Napoleon.

Leopold, privately visited Paris and accepted the hospitality of the Tuileries, which was eagerly offered him. The opportunity of conciliating the brother-in-law of the Queen of England was not lost. Emperor and Empress outbid each other in their laudation of Queen Victoria's domestic life. The Empress quite sincerely expressed a longing for close acquaintance with her, her husband, and children. A revolution had been worked, she said, in the conditions of Court life throughout Europe by the virtuous examples of Queen Victoria and of her kinswoman and ally, the Queen of Portugal. Such assurances had their effect. Duke Ernest promptly reported the conversation of the Tuileries to his brother and sister-in-law. The Queen, always sensitive to sympathy with her domestic experiences, was greatly mollified. Her initial prejudices were shaken, and the political situation soon opened a road, which could not be readily avoided, to perfect amity.

Napoleon's importunities.

Napoleon was quick to seize every opportunity of improving the situation. At the end of 1853 he boldly suggested for the second time a matrimonial alliance between the two families, and one of a more practical sort than his contingent offer of his hand to the Queen's niece. With the approval of King Leopold and of Palmerston he proposed a marriage between his cousin, Prince Jerome, who ultimately became the political head of the Bonaparte family, and the Queen's first cousin, Princess Mary of Cambridge, afterwards Duchess of Teck. Princess Mary was a frequent guest at Windsor, and constantly shared in the Queen's recreations. The Queen had no faith in forced political marriages, and at once consulted the Princess, whose buoyant, cheerful disposition endeared her to all the royal family. The Princess rejected the proposal without hesitation, and the Queen would hear no more of it. Palmerston characteristically expressed astonishment at the hasty rejection of the Emperor's plan. He coolly remarked that Prince Jerome was at any rate preferable to a German princeling.

XIX

THE CRIMEAN WAR

Quarrel with Russia.

BUT although Napoleon's first moves led to nothing, an alliance between France and England was at hand. For the first and only time England, under the Queen's sway, was about to engage in war in Europe. It was not France that she was to meet in battle. It was with Russia that she was, beneath Palmerston's spell, to drift into conflict, and it was in alliance with France that she was to draw the sword. In the autumn of 1853 Russia pushed her claims to protect the Christians of the Turkish empire with such violence as to extort from Turkey a declaration of war (October 23). The mass of the British nation held that England was under an imperative and an immediate obligation to intervene by force of arms in behalf of Turkey, her *protégé* and ally. The English cabinet had to decide the issue on which the peace of Europe hung.

Palmerston's resolute views.

Lord Aberdeen's Government was unfortunately divided in opinion, and the hope of firm and decisive action that had been formed of the coalition was not realised. The Prime Minister regarded the conduct of Russia as indefensible, but hoped to avert war by negotiation with the European Powers. Palmerston, then Home Secretary, took, as was only to be expected, a clearer and more popular view. Turkey, he urged, was far too weak to meet Russia single-handed; the maintenance of the integrity of the Turkish empire was a British interest, and no delay in intervention on England's part was justifiable. Aberdeen was not disposed hastily to abandon the cause of peace. On December 16 Palmerston suddenly resigned, on the ostensible ground that he differed from proposals of electoral reform which his colleagues had adopted. The true reason was his attitude to the foreign crisis. Signs that he interpreted the voice of the country aright abounded. An agitation for his readmission to the cabinet menaced the life of the ministry. Lord Aberdeen and his colleagues bowed to the storm. Palmerston was recalled. His resumption of office meant the destruction of the peace of Europe.

To the Court the course of events was from every point of view distressing. The Queen placed implicit trust in Aberdeen, and like him she hoped to avoid war. But Palmerston's restored predominance alarmed her. A sense of the futility of her recent struggles with him, in which she thought for a season that she had come forth victorious, humiliated her. A dread of war oppressed her. *Queen's dread of war.*

In no direction could she find a gleam of hope. Abroad the situation was not more reassuring than at home. The Emperor Napoleon had promptly offered to join his army with that of England, and the King of Sardinia also promised to follow the Emperor's example *Attitude of foreign sovereigns.*

if England would straightway attack Russia. But other foreign sovereigns with whom the Queen was in fuller sympathy privately entreated her with the utmost solemnity and persistency to thwart the bellicose designs which they identified with her most popular minister's name. The Tsar Nicholas stoutly protested to her the innocence of his designs (November 1853). The nervous King of Prussia anxiously petitioned her at all hazards to keep the peace, and even sent her an autograph note by the hand of a special messenger, General von Gröben, adjuring her that any forward step on her part would embarrass his own position in Central Europe. Lord Clarendon, the Foreign Minister, was happily sympathetic, and gave her wise advice regarding the tenor of her replies. She reproached the King of Prussia with his weakness, and told him it was his duty to aid her in the vindication of international law and order, not to persuade her to shirk her duty; were the Great Powers of Europe united with her, Russia would yield to diplomatic pressure (March 17, 1854).

Popular suspicion of Prince Albert.

To all her continental correspondents the Queen's attitude was irreproachable. But the country was growing impatient, and soon the rumour spread that she and her husband were employing their foreign intimacies against the country's interest. Aberdeen's hesitation to proceed to extremities, the known dissensions between Palmerston and the Court, the natural jealousy of foreign influences in the sphere of government, fed the suspicion that the Crown at the instance of a foreign prince-consort was obstructing the due assertion of the country's rights, and was playing into the hands of the country's foes.

The winter of 1853-4 progressed without any signs of decisive action on the part of the English Government. Thereupon popular indignation redoubled and burst in its fullest fury on the head of Prince Albert and the Queen. The Prince was denounced as a chief agent of an Austro-Belgian-Coburg-Orleans clique on the European continent. He was held up to obloquy as an avowed enemy of England, and a subservient tool of Russian ambition. The Tsar, it was seriously alleged, communicated his pleasure to the Prince through the Prince's kinsmen at Gotha and Brussels. 'It is pretended,' the Prince told his brother (January 7, 1854), 'that I whisper [the Tsar's orders] in Victoria's ear, she gets round old Aberdeen, and the voice of the only *English* minister, Palmerston, is not listened to—ay, he is always intrigued against, at the Court and by the Court.'[1] The Queen's husband, in fact, served as scapegoat for the ministry's vacillation. Honest men believed that he had exposed himself to the penalties of high treason, and they gravely doubted if the Queen herself were wholly guiltless.

The Queen took the calumnies deeply to heart, and Aberdeen, who was, she told Stockmar, 'all kindness,' sought vainly for a time to console her. 'In attacking the Prince,' she pointed out to Aberdeen (January 4, 1854), 'who is one and the same with the Queen herself, the throne is assailed, and she must say she little expected that any portion of her subjects would

[1] Duke Ernest's *Memoirs*, ii. 46.

thus requite the unceasing labours of the Prince.' The Prime Minister in reply spoke with disdain of 'these contemptible exhibitions of malevolence and faction,' but he admitted that the Prince held an anomalous position which the constitution had not provided for.

War declared with Russia.

Pity for the Queen's sufferings was soon awakened by the unscrupulous violence of her detractors. When she opened Parliament on January 31, she was respectfully received, and the leaders of both sides— Lord Aberdeen and Lord Derby in the Upper House and Lord John Russell and Spencer Walpole in the Commons—emphatically repudiated the slanders on her and her husband. The tide of abuse thereupon flowed more sluggishly, and it was temporarily checked on February 27, 1854, when the Queen sent a message to the House of Lords announcing the breakdown of negotiations with Russia. War was formally declared next day, and France and Sardinia affirmed their readiness to fight at England's side.

The Queen and the troops.

The popular criticism of the Queen was unwarranted. Her attitude was characterised alike by dignity and common sense. She hated war but never shrank from it when it was inevitable, nor did she believe in pursuing it half-heartedly. Repulsive as the incidents of war were to her, and active as was her sympathy with the suffering that it entailed, she never ceased to urge her ministers and her generals, when war was actually in being, to press forward with dogged resolution and not to slacken their efforts until the final goal of victory was reached. As soon as the fatal word was spoken on February 27, 1854, she spared no effort to give encouragement to all ranks of the army and navy. For months she watched in person the departure of troops. On March 10 she inspected at Spithead the great fleet which was destined for the Baltic under Sir Charles Napier. She faced the situation with cool resolution and discretion. At the opening of the conflict the Government proposed a day of humiliation for the success of the British arms. The Queen was not enthusiastic for the proposal. She warned Aberdeen of the hypocrisy of self-abasement in the form of prayers. At the same time she deprecated abuse of the enemy.

Some alleviation of anxiety was sought in the ordinary incidents of Court life. On May 12 the Queen, by way of acknowledging the alliance into which she had entered with the Emperor, paid the French Ambassador, Count Walewski, the high compliment of attending a *bal costumé* at the French Embassy at Albert Gate. The Queen alone wore ordinary evening dress. Next day she went to Woolwich to christen in her husband's honour a new battleship of enormous dimensions, the 'Royal Albert.' In June the Queen entertained for a month her cousin, the new King of Portugal, Pedro V., and his brother the Duke of Oporto, who afterwards succeeded to the throne as King Luis. Their mother, Queen Maria da Gloria, in whom she was from childhood deeply interested, had died in childbed seven months before (November 20, 1853). The Queen showed the young men every attention, taking them with her to the opera, the theatre, and Ascot. An injudicious

Hospitalities at Court.

suggestion made to them by some courtiers that Portugal should join England in the Crimean war was reasonably rejected by their advisers, but did not affect their relations with their hostess. The chief spectacular event of the season was the opening by the Queen at Sydenham, on June 10, of the Crystal Palace, which had, much to the Prince's satisfaction, been transferred, under his auspices, from Hyde Park after the Great Exhibition.

<small>Queen protests against lukewarmness about the war.</small>

In the summer the Queen confuted signally the slanderous accusations of pusillanimity. She now shared with a large section of the public a fear that the Government was not pursuing the war with requisite energy. When Lord Aberdeen, in a speech in the House of Lords on June 20, argumentatively defended Russia against the violent assaults of the English press, the Queen promptly reminded him of the misapprehensions that the appearance in him of lukewarmness must create in the public mind. Whatever were the misrepresentations of the Tsar's policy, she said, it was at the moment incumbent on her ministers to remember that ' there is enough in that policy to make us fight with all our might against it.'

<small>Prince Albert at St. Omer.</small>

Incessantly did she and the Prince appeal to the ministers to hasten their deliberations and to improve the organisation of the Crimean army. The most hopeful feature of the situation was Napoleon III.'s zeal. In July the Prince accepted the Emperor's pressing invitation to inspect with him the camp at St. Omer, where an army was fitting out for the Crimea. The meeting was completely successful.

The Queen was grateful for the attentions shown her husband, and the good relations of the rulers of the two countries were placed on a surer foundation.

On August 12 the Queen took part for the last time in a ceremony, participation in which had hitherto formed one of the Sovereign's constitutional functions. For the last time she attended Parliament to command its prorogation. From time immemorial it had been customary for the Sovereign to meet members of the House of Commons at the close of each session and to listen to an harangue on the session's work of the House from the lips of the Speaker. The Speaker, Charles Shaw Lefevre, who had performed the office many times during the fifteen years that he had filled the chair of the lower chamber, now reviewed for her benefit the past labours of 'her faithful Commons.' The outbreak of war, he told her, had interrupted the progress of legislation. 'Notwithstanding your Majesty's unremitting endeavour to maintain peace,' he said, ' war has been forced upon us by the unwarrantable aggression of Russia on the Turkish empire.' He proceeded at some length to justify the struggle, and he congratulated the Queen upon sending forth 'fleets and armies complete beyond all former precedent in discipline and equipment.' Although the address was on this as on former occasions quite respectful in tone and comparatively brief, the Queen disliked receiving instruction in public, and being never unwilling to break with precedent which oppressed her, she omitted to prorogue Parliament in person again. The absence of the Sovereign from the ceremony

The Speaker harangues the Sovereign for the last time on Aug. 12, 1854.

relieved the Speaker henceforward of the obligation of delivering his formal lecture, and the Queen thus condemned an ancient custom to desuetude.

Anxieties about the war.

The Crimean war remained the Queen's absorbing anxiety. While at Balmoral in September she was elated to receive 'all the most interesting and gratifying details of the splendid and decisive victory of the Alma.' On leaving Balmoral she visited the docks at Grimsby and Hull, but her mind was elsewhere. From Hull she wrote to her uncle Leopold, 'We are, and indeed the whole country is, entirely engrossed with one idea, one anxious thought—the Crimea.' News of the victories of Inkermann and Balaclava did not entirely remove her apprehensions. 'Such a time of suspense,' she wrote on November 7, 'I never expected to see, much less to *feel*.'

At Hull, Oct. 13.

Inkermann, Oct. 25. Balaclava, Nov. 5.

The winter of 1854-5.

During the winter the cruel hardships which climate, disease, and failure of the commissariat inflicted on the troops strongly stirred public feeling. The Queen was fully alive to the sorrowful situation. She initiated or supported all manner of voluntary measures of relief. With her own hands she made woollen comforters and mittens for the men. On New Year's day, 1855, she wrote to the Commander-in-Chief in the Crimea, Lord Raglan, expressing her sympathy with the army in its 'sad privations and constant sickness,' and entreated him to make the camps 'as comfortable as circumstances can admit of.' No details escaped her, and she especially called his attention to the rumour 'that the soldiers' coffee was given them green instead of roasted.' Although the Queen and the Prince grew every day more convinced of the defective administration of the War Office, they were unflinchingly loyal to the Prime Minister, Lord Aberdeen, who was the target of much public censure. Before the opening of Parliament in January 1855, by way of proof of their personal sympathy, the Queen made him a Knight of the Garter.

But it was beyond her power, had it been her ultimate wish, to prop the falling Government. The session no sooner opened than Lord John suddenly insisted on seceding in face of the outcry in the country against the management of the war. The blow was serious. After an animated debate in the cabinet, January 24, all the ministers tendered their resignation to the Queen. With the greatest eagerness she urged 'that the decision should be reconsidered.' Lord Aberdeen and his colleagues reluctantly yielded to her wish that they should hold on. Complete shipwreck was not long delayed. On January 29 the Government was hopelessly defeated on a hostile motion for an inquiry into the management of the war. Only 148 votes were cast in favour of Lord Aberdeen; 305 were given against him. Aberdeen's retirement was inevitable. On February 7 the Queen addressed him an affectionate letter of farewell, generously acknowledging his past services to her. 'She wishes to say,' she wrote, 'what a *pang* it is for her to separate from *so* kind and dear and valued a friend as Lord Aberdeen has ever been to her since she has known him. The day he became her Prime Minister was a *very happy*

<small>Lord Aberdeen's defeat.</small>

one for her, and throughout his ministry he has ever been the kindest and wisest adviser, one to whom she could apply for advice on all and trifling occasions even. This she is sure he will still ever be—but the losing him as her first adviser in her Government is *very painful.*'[1]

[1] *Lord Aberdeen,* by the Hon. Sir Arthur Gordon (Lord Stanmore), 1893, pp. 291–2.

XX

TRIUMPH OF PALMERSTON AND NAPOLEON III

It was obvious that Lord Aberdeen's retirement left the Queen face to face with a most distasteful obligation. Destiny had ordained that she should confer the supreme power in the State on her old enemy, Palmerston. The situation called for all her fortitude. She took time before submitting. A study of the division lists taught her that Lord Derby's supporters formed the greater number of the voters who had destroyed Lord Aberdeen's ministry. She therefore, despite Aberdeen's warning, invited Lord Derby to assume the government. Derby explained to her that he could not accept the commission without aid from other parties, and a day later he announced his failure to secure extraneous assistance. Disraeli urged Lord Derby to make a more strenuous effort to help the Queen, but he declined to take further part in the negotiation. The Queen's renewed dread of Palmerston.

The Queen then turned to the veteran Whig, Lord Lansdowne, and bade him privately seek advice for her from all the party leaders. Lord Lansdowne thought he might form a government if Gladstone would join it in his former office of Her appeal to Lord John.

Chancellor of the Exchequer. But Gladstone was not yet prepared fully to identify himself with the Whigs, and declined to entertain the proposal.[1] Lord Lansdowne proved no more helpful than Lord Derby. In the result the Queen summoned Lord John Russell, who had contributed largely to Lord Aberdeen's defeat. His followers were in number and compactness second to Lord Derby's, and the Queen pointed out that, in view of Lord Derby's inability to act, it was incumbent on Lord John to form an administration. She could not blind herself to the inevitable course of the discussion, and, suppressing her private feeling, she assured Lord John that she hoped Palmerston would join him. But she had not gone far enough in her approach to Palmerston. Lord John declared that he was not strong enough to accept her commands.

Palmerston's omnipotence.

The business of the country was at a standstill. A continuance of the deadlock was perilous. The Queen confided to her sympathetic friend Lord Clarendon her reluctance to take the next step—the only one she now feared that would end the dangerous crisis. Clarendon convinced her that the dreaded course was alone open to her to follow. He assured her that Palmerston would prove conciliatory if frankly treated, and that none other could take the helm. With grave reluctance she yielded to necessity; she sent for Palmerston, and bade him form an administration.

[1] In later life Gladstone wrote: 'I have always looked back upon [this decision] with pain as a serious and even gross error of judgment.' He thought it helped to substitute Palmerston for Lansdowne in the office of Prime Minister, a result which he deemed calamitous. Cf. Morley's *Gladstone*, i. 529, 530.

Palmerston's popular strength was undoubted, and longer resistance on the part of the Crown was idle if not unsafe. As soon as the die was cast, the Queen with characteristic good sense made the best of a bad situation. She indicated that she would extend to her new Prime Minister the confidence she had extended to his predecessors. On February 15 Palmerston wrote to his brother: 'I am backed by the general opinion of the whole country, and I have no reason to complain of the least want of cordiality or confidence on the part of the Court.' Greatly to the Queen's relief and satisfaction Lord Clarendon remained at the Foreign Office, Earl Granville retained the presidency of the Council, and Sir George Grey, formerly the Colonial Secretary, succeeded Palmerston at the Home Office. Lord Aberdeen had persuaded others of his colleagues to serve temporarily at least under his successor. 'The pain [of parting with Aberdeen],' she wrote, 'has been to a certain extent lessened by the knowledge of *all* he has done to further the formation of this Government in so loyal, noble, and disinterested a manner, and by *his* friends retaining their posts, which is a *great* security against any possible dangers.' But within a few days the Peelite members of the old Government—Gladstone, Sir James Graham, and Sidney Herbert—went out. Lord John Russell and friends of his came in to fill their places. The Queen parted with the Peelite ministers 'with great pain,' and 'spoke of the difficulty of making arrangements for carrying on the Government in the present state of things.' But the withdrawal of the Peelites secured to the new

Queen accepts Palmerston.

Government a practicable unity, and Palmerston's power was freed of restraint.

Wounded soldiers.

Baseless rumours of the malign influence exerted by Prince Albert on the country's destinies were still alive, but no doubt was permissible of the devoted energy with which the Queen was promoting the relief of the wounded. In March she visited the military hospitals at Chatham and Woolwich, and encouraged the invalids by simple words of sympathy. She complained privately that she was not kept informed in sufficient detail by the War Office of the condition and prospects of disabled soldiers on their return home. She was resolved to use all her influence to alleviate their lot.

Napoleon offers to go to the Crimea.

A new difficulty arose with the announcement on the part of Napoleon that he intended to proceed to the Crimea to take command of the French army there. His presence was certain to provoke complications in the command of the allied forces in the field. Gentle objections were raised by the English Foreign Office. Thereupon the Emperor hinted that it might be well for him to discuss the project in person with the Queen. The hint was taken by the Queen and her advisers. The Queen invited the Emperor and Empress to pay her a state visit.

Queen's distrust of her political associates.

On all sides the Queen was thrown into association with men who had inspired her with distrust. Palmerston, 'the man who,' in Prince Albert's words, 'embittered our whole life,' was her Prime Minister. Her closest ally in Europe, whom public obligations compelled her to conciliate and honour, was Napoleon III., whose past history was, in her opinion, infamous. But she yielded her private sentiments at the call of a national crisis with all the cheerfulness and alacrity she could command.

The Queen made every effort to give her imperial guests a brilliant reception. She personally supervised each detail of the programme of the entertainments that were organised in their honour. She drew up with her own hands the lists of guests who were commanded to meet them. On April 16 the Emperor and Empress reached Dover and proceeded through London to Windsor. No elaborate formality that at any time distinguished the reception of sovereigns in England was suffered to lapse, and the Emperor was at once favourably impressed.

Visit of Napoleon III., April 1855.

The ordeal proved far less trying than the Queen feared. At a great banquet in St. George's Hall on the evening of his arrival, the Emperor won the Queen's heart by his adroit flattery and respectful familiarity. She found him 'very quiet and amiable and easy to get on with.' He reminded her of an early meeting with her, when he was a refugee in London, and affected a deep interest in her domestic concerns. Next day, when a review of the household troops in Windsor Park was followed by a state ball, the harmony was confirmed. On the 18th the Queen raised her guest's spirits to the highest pitch of elation by bestowing on him the knighthood of the Garter. Time was not standing still. Louis Philippe, the victim of Napoleon's triumph, had been no less cheered by the gift of the same high distinction from the Queen's hand a short eleven years before.

His agreeable demeanour.

The public warmly seconded the Queen's endea-

His welcome by the people.

vours to render her hospitality attractive to Louis Philippe's successor. A visit of the royal party on the 19th to the Opera House in Covent Garden,[1] which was sumptuously decorated, evoked a great display of popular enthusiasm, and amid similar manifestations the royal party went on the 20th to the Crystal Palace. On the 21st the visit ended, and with every sign of mutual goodwill the Emperor left Buckingham Palace for Dover. Of 'the great event' the Queen wrote: 'On all it has left a pleasant satisfactory impression.' The royal party had talked much of the war with the result that was desired. On April 25 the Emperor wrote to the Queen that he had abandoned his intention of going to the Crimea.

The Queen on the irony of royalty.

But, throughout the hospitable gaieties, the ironies of fate that dog the steps of sovereigns were rarely far from the Queen's mind. Three days before the Emperor arrived, the widowed ex-Queen of the French, who had fallen far from her high estate, visited her at Windsor, whence she drove away unnoticed in the humblest of equipages, and the contrast between her present and past fortunes deeply impressed her hostess. After the great ball in the Waterloo room at Windsor, when the Queen danced a quadrille with the Emperor on the 17th, she noted in her diary, 'How strange to think that I, the granddaughter of George III., should dance with the Emperor Napoleon, nephew of England's great enemy, and now my nearest and most intimate ally, in the Waterloo room, and this ally, only six years ago, living in this country an exile, poor and unthought of!'

[1] Beethoven's opera of *Fidelio* was performed.

Meanwhile proposals for peace between the combatants in the Crimea were under the consideration of a conference of the Powers at Vienna. The consultation proved abortive. The Queen was resolved that, in view of the sacrifices that the war had entailed, none but the best possible terms should be entertained by her ministers. At Vienna Lord John represented England and M. Drouyn de Lhuys represented France. Lord John seemed willing to accept conditions that were to the Queen unduly favourable to Russia. He deemed it needless to insist on the assignment by Russia of material guarantees for the future immunity of Turkey from invasion. The Queen resented her envoy's pusillanimity. She wrote peremptorily on April 25, 1855, to Palmerston, 'How Lord John Russell and M. Drouyn can recommend such proposals for our acceptance is beyond her [our] comprehension.' The conference was dissolved without result. In the months that followed the Queen and Prince were indefatigable in exerting their influence on the cabinet against what they deemed unworthy concessions to Russia. From their point of view the resignation of Lord John on July 16, owing to discontent with his recent diplomatic exploits, rendered the situation more hopeful.

Queen reproves Lord John.

In May the Queen identified herself conspicuously with the national feeling by distributing war medals to the returned soldiers on the Horse Guards' Parade. It was the Queen's own suggestion, and it was the first time that the Sovereign had performed such a function with her own hands. Lord Panmure, Secretary at War, was at her side to

First distribution of war medals, May 18.

assist her through the ceremony, and was not very adroit in the aid he gave her.[1] But of the new experience the Queen wrote in all seriousness: 'The rough hand of the brave and honest private soldier came for the first time in contact with that of their [his] Sovereign and their [his] Queen.' Later in the day she visited the riding school in Wellington Barracks while the men were assembled at dinner.

<small>The Emperor's invitation.</small>

Domestic distress was occasioned the Queen in the summer by an outbreak of scarlet fever in the royal household, which attacked the four younger children. But on their recovery the Queen and Prince redoubled their energies in the public service. The maintenance of the French alliance was now, in their sight, a cause worthy of exertion. With a view to strengthening it, they accepted the Emperor's invitation to pay him a return visit to Paris. Following the example of Prince Albert, the Emperor had organised a great 'Exposition,' and it was his desire that his royal friends should compare it with their own 'Great Exhibition.' No time was lost in acceding to his wish.

<small>Queen in Paris, August 1855.</small>

On August 20, after Parliament had been prorogued by commission (as now was to be the settled custom), the Queen travelled, with the Prince and

[1] Panmure was distinguished by an abnormal slowness of wit. The amusing story is told that at the conclusion of the distribution of medals, when the War Secretary was asked by the Hon. Mrs. Norton, the brilliant authoress, whether the Queen was 'touched,' he replied: 'Bless my soul, no! She had a brass railing before her, and no one could touch her.' Mrs. Norton then said: 'I mean, was she moved?' 'Moved!' answered Lord Panmure; 'she had no occasion to move.'—*Memories of an Ex-Minister* (Lord Malmesbury), p. 363.

her two eldest children, the Prince of Wales and the Princess Royal, from Osborne to Boulogne. There the Emperor offered them a cordial welcome. By an accident they reached Paris rather late, but they passed through it in elaborate procession to the palace of St. Cloud [1] on the outskirts of the city. Although this want of punctuality in the arrival of the royal party caused the Parisians passing annoyance, they were loud in their acclamations of the English Queen when she appeared in their streets. Marshal Magnan declared that the great Napoleon was not so warmly received on his return from Austerlitz.

The occasion was worthy of enthusiasm. It was the first time that an English sovereign had entered the French capital since the infant Henry VI. went there to be crowned in 1422. It proved the most imposing reception that had been yet offered Queen Victoria—either within or without her own country. Splendid festivities were devised for her daily entertainment. The opportunity was also allowed her for private visits, not merely to the Exposition, but to the public buildings of Paris, St. Germain and Versailles. Their historical associations greatly stirred her, especially those which recalled the sad regal tragedies—always fascinating to her—of Marie Antoinette [2] or

Her brilliant welcome.

---

[1] The palace was destroyed by the German invaders in October 1870: only ruins survive.

[2] The Queen was fond of recalling that she had come into indirect association with Marie Antoinette through 'the old Lord Huntly' (i.e. the ninth Marquis of Huntly, who died in 1853 at the age of ninety-two). Lord Huntly had as a young man danced a minuet with the ill-fated Queen of France at the Tuileries before the Revolution. In his old age he joined in a square dance with Queen Victoria. Lord Ronald Gower's *Old Diaries*, p. 116.

James II. When she saw the dilapidated monument above James II.'s grave in the church of St. Germain, she caused it to be restored, and added to the old inscription the pathetic exordium : 'Regio Cineri Pietas Regia.' Napoleon I.'s fate likewise moved her to compassion, and she bade the Prince of Wales, who, clad in Highland costume, had accompanied his mother to the Hôtel des Invalides, kneel at the hero's tomb. A thunderstorm broke out at the moment, and the impressive scene moved to tears the French generals who were present.[1]

First meeting with Bismarck.

Among the official celebrations were a review on the Champ de Mars of 45,000 troops, a state visit to the Opéra, and balls of dazzling magnificence at the Hôtel de Ville and at Versailles. At the Versailles fête, on August 25, the Queen made a fateful addition to her circle of acquaintance. She was introduced by the Emperor for the first time to Count (afterwards Prince) Bismarck, then Prussian Minister at Frankfort, from whose iron will her host, and afterwards her daughter, and to a smaller extent herself, were in course of time to suffer much. The Queen conversed with the resolute statesman in German with great civility. He thought that she was interested in him, but that she lacked sympathy with him. The impression was correct, and her want of sympathy with Bismarck never wore away. Among the eminent Frenchmen she met was Marshal Canrobert, Commander-in-Chief of the French army in the Crimea during the late campaigns; he was impressed

[1] 'Journal du Maréchal Canrobert,' in *Revue Hebdomadaire*, November 1901. A picture of the scene, now at Windsor, was painted for the Queen by E. M. Ward, R.A.

by her amiability in greeting him without the formalities of a presentation.[1]

The French visit ended on August 27. On reaching Boulogne on her way to Osborne, she was accorded a great military farewell by the Emperor, who exchanged with her the warmest assurances of attachment to herself, her husband, and her children. Of the whole episode, which she often recalled in later life with the utmost satisfaction, she wrote a full and buoyant description in her Journal.[2] The immediate effect of the experience was excellent. The anticipations of a permanent alliance between the two countries seemed at the moment assured.

Success of the Paris visit.

These happy prognostications proved too sanguine. The political relations between Napoleon III. and the Queen were soon to be severely strained, and her faith in his sincerity to be rudely shaken. Yet his personal courtesies both at Windsor and Paris left an indelible impression on her. Despite her political distrust she constantly corresponded with the Emperor until his death in autograph letters of dignified cordiality ; and the sympathetic affection which had arisen between the Queen and the Empress Eugénie steadily grew with time and the vicissitudes of fortune.

Relations with Napoleon.

[1] The Queen's costume somewhat amazed the Marshal. 'She wore,' he wrote in his diary, ' a massive hat of white silk, in spite of the great heat. Her dress was white, and she had a mantilla and a parasol of downright green, which seemed to me to be out of harmony with the rest of the costume. In the evening she was in a white *toilette décolletée*, with quantities of geranium blooms all over her.' *Revue Hebdomadaire*, November 1901.

[2] Numerous quotations are given in Sir Theodore Martin's *Life of the Prince Consort*, vol. iii. chap. lxvi.

XXI

THE PEACE OF PARIS

The fall of Sebastopol.

The early autumn of 1855, which was spent at Balmoral, was brightened by two gratifying incidents. On September 10 there reached the Queen news of the fall of Sebastopol, after a siege of nearly a year—a decisive triumph for British arms, which brought honourable peace in sight. Prince Albert himself superintended the lighting of a bonfire on the top of a neighbouring cairn.

The Princess Royal's engagement.

The other episode appealed directly to the Queen's maternal feeling. The Prince of Prussia's eldest son (afterwards the Emperor Frederick III.), who, attended by Count von Moltke, was at the time a guest at Balmoral, requested permission to propose marriage to the Princess Royal. She was not quite fifteen, and he was twenty-four, but there were indications of a mutual affection. The manly goodness of the Prince strongly appealed to the Queen, and an engagement was privately made on September 29. The public announcement was to be deferred till after the Princess's confirmation next year.

Hostility in England.

From the politician's point of view the betrothal had little to recommend it, and Prince Albert at once denied that it had any political significance. A close union between the royal families of London and Berlin was not likely to approve itself to the Queen's late host of Paris. Nor was it specially congenial to the English ministry. To most English statesmen Prussia appeared to be on the downward grade under a Government which was incurably infected with reactionary stolidity. Although Prince Albert and the Queen had faith in the future of Prussia, they were themselves disappointed by the inability of its present ruler, Frederick William IV., the uncle of their future son-in-law, to maintain its supremacy in the councils of Central Europe, or to overcome internal dissensions. The Prussian King had cravenly deserted them in the recent war, but was still weakly seeking their diplomatic influence in private letters to the Queen, which he conjured her not to divulge either in Downing Street or at the Tuileries. His pertinacity had grown so troublesome of late that, to avoid friction, she deemed it wisest to suppress his correspondence unanswered.[1]

It was not, therefore, surprising that, when the news of the betrothal leaked out in England, the public comments should be unpleasing to the Court. The 'Times' on October 3 denounced the arrangement with heat as an act of truckling 'to a paltry German dynasty.' Nor was it more warmly welcomed by statesmen at the Prussian Court. On March 26, 1856, the minister Gerlach wrote to his chief, Manteuffel, 'What do you think of the English match? Bismarck is strongly against it, and so am I. It will

Views of Prussian statesmen.

[1] Duke Ernest's *Memoirs*, vol. iii.

involve us in many things without helping us, and is, besides, very dear.'[1] Russia, too, looked with disfavour on the union. But the King of Prussia was ebullient in enthusiasm, and although his ministers continued to argue that the heir to the Prussian throne ought to have 'preferred a German princess,' they acquiesced in the alliance when they learned that both the English and the Prussian royal families were unalterably pledged to its accomplishment.

Victor Emanuel visits the Queen.

In November, when the Court was again at Windsor, the Queen extended her acquaintance among great kings and statesmen by receiving a visit from her second ally in the Crimea, Victor Emanuel, King of Sardinia, and his minister, Count Cavour. The internal affairs of one more country of Europe were thus closely pressed upon her attention. The King's brother, the Duke of Genoa, had been her guest in 1852, and she had presented him with a riding-horse in words that he interpreted to imply sympathy with the efforts of Cavour and his master to unite Italy under a single king, and to purge the separate States of native tyranny or foreign domination.[2] Victor Emanuel had come to Windsor to seek confirmation of his brother's version of the Queen's sentiment, and to test its practical value. He had just been at the Tuileries, where Napoleon was encouraging, while Palmerston, now Queen Victoria's Prime Minister, was known to sympathise with the Italian aspiration for Italian unity.

[1] Otto Freiherr v. Manteuffel, *Unter Friedrich Wilhelm IV.* iii. 115-6, 267. The princess's dowry was deemed in Germany to be unduly small.

[2] Duke Ernest's *Memoirs*, iii. 22-23.

It was not opportune at the moment for Palmerston to promise King Victor Emanuel material aid. At the same time Prince Albert, however deeply he deplored the misgovernment which it was sought to annul in Italy, deprecated any breach with Austria, the power responsible for rule in North Italy. He and the Queen dreaded, indeed, the kindling of further war in Europe, in whatever cause. Victor Emanuel and Cavour therefore received from the Queen cold political comfort. None the less she paid the Italian monarch every formal honour. His brusque and unrefined demeanour rendered much cordiality impossible. But he was invested with the Garter on December 5, and a great banquet was given him in St. George's Hall in the evening. Prince Albert personally introduced him to both Lord Clarendon, the present Foreign Secretary, and to Lord Malmesbury, the past Foreign Secretary. When the King left Windsor the Queen put herself to the trouble of rising at four o'clock in the morning to bid him farewell. *Queen discourages him.*

Meanwhile satisfactory terms of peace with Russia were arranged in Paris on the part of England and her allies, Turkey, France, and Sardinia. The chief provision declared the Black Sea to be neutral waters, from which all ships of war were to be excluded, while the merchantmen of all nations were to enjoy free access to it; Turkey was admitted to the advantages of the European concert, and future disputes between the Porte and any of the great Powers were to be settled jointly by them all; all conquered territory was to be restored and the boundaries of certain provinces under Turkish suzerainty were to be defined *The peace of Paris, March 30, 1856.*

anew; Christians in Turkey were secured due protection.

General rejoicings.

Amid great rejoicing, in view of the happy ending of the war, the Queen opened Parliament on January 31, 1856. On March 30 the treaty was signed and the encroachment of Russia on Turkey was believed to have been effectively checked. Napoleon had shown a rather suspicious supineness in the negotiations and seemed to be developing a tendency to conciliate the common enemy, Russia. But the Queen exchanged hearty congratulations with him on the settlement, and on April 11 she celebrated the general harmony by conferring the knighthood of the Garter on Palmerston, to whom, with some natural qualifications, she acknowledged the successful issue to be mainly due.

First visit to Aldershot 1856.

Henceforth the army, with which she regarded herself as identified by descent, was the Queen's care to a far larger extent than before. Military engagements she henceforth treated as more binding than any others. A visit to the military hospital at Chatham on April 16 was immediately followed by a first visit to the newly formed camp at Aldershot. There the Queen, for the first of many times, slept the night in the royal pavilion, and next day she reviewed 18,000 men. She was on horseback, and wore the uniform of a field-marshal with the star and ribbon of the Garter. Shortly after she laid two foundation-stones —of a new military (the Royal Victoria) hospital at Netley on May 19, and of Wellington College, Sandhurst, for the sons of officers on June 2. Much of the summer she spent in welcoming troops on their return from the Crimea. On June 7 and 8 the Queen, accompanied by her guests, the King of the Belgians and Prince Oscar of Sweden, inspected a great body of them at Aldershot, and addressed to them stirring words of thanks and sympathy. Thoroughly identifying herself with the heroism of her soldiers and sailors, she instituted a decoration for acts of conspicuous valour in war, to be known as the Victoria Cross (V.C.); the decoration carried with it a pension of 10*l*. a year. A list of the earliest recipients of the honour was soon drawn up, and the crosses were pinned by the Queen herself on the breasts of sixty-two men at a great review in Hyde Park next year (June 26, 1857).

The Victoria Cross.

A melancholy incident had marked her visit to Aldershot on June 8, 1856. While the Commander-in-Chief, Lord Hardinge, who had succeeded on the Duke of Wellington's death to that high office, was speaking to her, he was seized by incurable paralysis, and had to vacate his post.[1] An opportunity seemed thus presented to the Queen of tightening the traditional bond between the Crown and the army, on which recent events had led her to set an enhanced value. Of no prerogative of the Crown was the Queen more tenacious than that which gave her a nominal control of the army through the Commander-in-Chief. It was a control that was in name independent of Parliament, although that body claimed a concurrent authority over the military forces through the Secretary of State for War. Parliament was in course of time, to the Queen's dismay, to make its

The Duke of Cambridge Commander-in-Chief.

[1] He died September 24 following, in his 72nd year.

authority over the army sole and supreme, to the injury of her prerogative. But her immediate ambition was to confirm the personal connection between the army and herself. She therefore induced Palmerston to sanction the appointment of her cousin, George, Duke of Cambridge, as Commander-in-Chief, in succession to Lord Hardinge (July 14, 1856). The Duke had held a command in the Crimea, and the Queen's recent displays of attachment to the army rendered it difficult for her advisers to oppose her wish. But the choice was not in accord with public policy, and, through the public criticisms which it constantly provoked, had the ultimate effect of weakening the military prerogative of the Crown which the Queen sought to strengthen.

Court festivities.

Public and private affairs justified a season of exceptional gaiety. The Princess Royal had been confirmed on March 20, and her betrothal was publicly announced on April 29. In May Prince Frederick William, again accompanied by Von Moltke, paid the Court another visit. The Queen's spirits ran high. On May 7 she gave a great banquet to the leaders of both parties and their wives. She arranged that Whig ministers should have for their partners the wives of Tory ex-ministers, and Tory ex-ministers the wives of the Whig ministers; and she was amused at the signs of discomfort which made themselves apparent. Lord Derby told the Prince that the guests constituted 'a happy family.'[1] Balls were incessant, and at them all the Queen danced indefatigably.

[1] Malmesbury, *Memoirs*, p. 380.

On May 9 the new ball-room and concert-room at Buckingham Palace, which Prince Albert had devised, were brought into use for the first time on the occasion of a ball in honour of the Princess Royal's *début*. On May 27 the Queen attended a ball at the Turkish Ambassador's, and, to the Ambassador's embarrassment, chose him for her partner in the first country-dance. She was still regarded as one of the most graceful performers of the day in minuets and country-dances. At a ball in the Waterloo Gallery at Windsor on June 10 she danced every dance, and finally performed a Scottish reel to the bagpipes.[1] On June 26 the Duke of Westminster gave a great ball in her honour at Grosvenor House, where she equally distinguished herself.

Ball at Buckingham Palace, May 9, 1856.

All who had won renown in the recent war could reckon on a hospitable welcome from her. On June 20 she entertained Sir Fenwick Williams of Kars[2] at Buckingham Palace. On July 9 she gave a state reception to the Guards on their homecoming from the Crimea. In the autumn she received at Balmoral Miss Florence Nightingale, who had reorganised the nursing in the military hospitals of the Crimea; she had sent her in the previous January a valuable jewel as a memento.

Reception of Sir Fenwick Williams and Florence Nightingale.

The round of domestic hospitalities knew no cessation. From August 10 to 28 the Prince and Princess

Domestic hospitalities.

---

[1] Moltke, *Letters*, vol. i. passim; Malmesbury, *Memoirs*, pp. 380 sqq.
[2] He was British Military Commissioner with the Turkish army during the Crimean war, and had heroically defended Kars when it was besieged by the Russians (June–November 1855).

of Prussia, the father and mother of her future son-in-law, were her guests. But in November 1856 the family were plunged in mourning by the death of Prince Leiningen, the Queen's half-brother. It was the first gap in the circle of the younger companions of her youth.

XXII

INDIA AND THE PRINCESS ROYAL

THE next year 1857 involved the Queen in a new and great public anxiety, and the serious side of life oppressed her. Parliament was opened by commission on February 3, and before the end of the month the country heard the first bitter cry of the Indian mutiny. Disaffection among the native Indian troops was spreading rapidly through Central India; little groups of English officials, isolated in scattered rural stations, were soon to be at the mercy of masses of the fanatically stirred native peoples.

Approach of the Indian mutiny.

A month after the earliest news of the coming danger reached the Queen's ears, she was gravely disquieted by the confusion which suddenly involved the political world at home, owing to a conflict which had broken out in another quarter of Asia. Palmerston was defeated in the House of Commons on Cobden's motion condemning his warlike policy in China. The crew of a Chinese ship sailing from Hong Kong under the British flag had been captured and imprisoned by the Chinese authorities at Canton on a charge of suspected piracy. The English consul had demanded their release and had been refused. The English fleet had thereupon been directed to force a

Palmerston's defeat on China question, March 1857.

passage up the Canton river, and a severe encounter followed. Palmerston, on his defeat in the House of Commons, refused to resign. He demanded a dissolution, to which the Queen assented with characteristic reluctance. The self-confident minister had full faith that the majority of the people approved his action, and the faith was justified. His appeal to the country received a triumphant answer, and the new Parliament assembled with a majority of seventy-nine in his favour. It was a signal tribute to his personal popularity, which the Queen acknowledged with mingled feelings.

Birth of Princess Beatrice.

In the Queen's sphere the interest attaching to public affairs was always in urgent competition with that attaching to domestic affairs. The calls of motherhood had not yet ceased. On April 14 the Queen's youngest child, Princess Beatrice, was born at Buckingham Palace. The youngest-born of her nine children proved, in her view, 'the flower of the flock.' Sixteen days after Princess Beatrice's birth, the last personal link that united the Queen to her predecessor, George III., was severed. On the 30th April died her aunt, Mary, the Duchess of Gloucester, the last surviving child of George III.; 'we all looked upon her,' wrote the Queen, 'as a sort of grandmother.'

Grant to Princess Royal.

But domestic interests of another kind were soon to absorb her attention. The marriage of her eldest daughter was approaching. On May 16 the betrothal was formally announced at Berlin, and on the 25th the Queen sent a message to Parliament asking for a provision for the Princess. It was her first appeal to the nation for the pecuniary support of her children, and she felt some anxiety as to the reception with which it would meet. But her fears proved groundless. The Government proposed a dowry of 40,000*l.* and an annuity of 8,000*l.* Roebuck, then a very outspoken Radical member of Parliament, raised the objection that the forthcoming marriage was an 'entangling alliance,' and opposed the grant of any annuity. Sir George Cornewall Lewis, the Chancellor of the Exchequer, called attention to the fact that the Queen's recent expenses in connection with the French visits were defrayed out of her income, and that the eldest daughters of George II. and George III. each received a dowry of 80,000*l.* and an annuity of 5,000*l.* All parties finally combined to support the Government's proposal, which found in its last stages only eighteen dissentients.

The royal betrothal continued to be celebrated by brilliant and prolonged festivities. In June and July Prince Frederick William once more stayed at Court, and Von Moltke, who was again his companion, declared the succession of gaieties to be overpowering.[1] One day (June 15) there was a state visit to the Princess's Theatre to see Charles Kean's spectacular production of Shakespeare's 'Richard II.' Next day the infant Princess Beatrice was baptized. On June 11 the Ascot ceremonies were conducted in full state, and among the royal guests was M. Achille Fould, the Paris banker and Napoleon III.'s Minister of Finance. On the 17th the whole Court attended the first Handel Festival at the Crystal Palace, when 'Judas

Brilliant festivities at Court.

[1] Cf. Von Moltke's *Letters* to his wife and friends.

Maccabeus' was performed; the royal company drove to and fro in nine four-in-hands. On the 18th a levee was followed by a State ball, in which the Queen danced with unabated energy.

Public functions.

Hardly a day passed without an elaborate ceremonial. On June 26 a military review took place in Hyde Park amid extraordinary signs of popular enthusiasm, and the first batch of Victoria crosses was distributed. From June 29 to July 2 the Queen stayed with the Earl of Ellesmere at Worsley Hall to inspect the Art Treasures Exhibition at Manchester. Next month she laid the foundation at Wandsworth Common of the Royal Victoria Patriotic Asylum for daughters of soldiers, sailors, and marines, and before the end of the month time was found for a visit to Aldershot.

Royal guests.

Royal personages from the continent thronged the Queen's palaces. The King of the Belgians brought his daughter, the Princess Charlotte, and her *fiancé* the Archduke Maximilian of Austria, who was later to lay down his life in Mexico under heartrending circumstances. The Prince of Hohenzollern, the Queen of the Netherlands, and the Duke and Duchess of Montpensier arrived in quick succession, and all interested their royal hostess. She was gratified, too, on both personal and political grounds, by a short visit to Osborne of the Grand Duke Constantine of Russia, brother of the reigning Tsar Alexander II. He had been invited to the Tuileries by Napoleon, who was ominously seeking every opportunity of manifesting goodwill to Russia, and the Queen did not wish to be behind her ally in showing courtesies to her recent foes. There was no lack of cordiality on either side.

The constant intercourse of the Queen and the Prince at this moment with the royal families of Europe led her to define her husband's rank more accurately than had been done before. On June 25, 1857, by royal letters patent, she conferred on him the title of Prince Consort. 'It was always a source of weakness,' the Prince wrote, 'for the Crown that the Queen always appeared before the people with her *foreign* husband.' Of that fact there was no room for doubt. Even the closest friends of the Court never overlooked his German proclivities or temperament.[1] But it was doubtful whether this bestowal of a new name effectively removed the embarrassment. The 'Times' wrote sneeringly that the new title guaranteed increased homage to its bearer on the banks of the Spree and the Danube, but made no difference in his position anywhere else. Abroad, at any rate, it achieved the desired result. When, on July 29, the Prince attended at Brussels the marriage of the ill-fated Archduke Maximilian with the Princess Charlotte of Belgium, he was accorded precedence before the Austrian Archdukes and immediately after the King of the Belgians.

Title of Prince Consort.

The English Government still deemed it prudent to cultivate the French alliance, but the Emperor's policy was growing enigmatic, and in the diplomatic skirmishes among the Powers which attended the final adjustment, in accordance with the provisions of the treaty of Paris, of the affairs of the Balkan

Relations with Napoleon III.

[1] Cf. Lord Malmesbury's *Memoirs of an ex-Minister*, p. 323.

peninsula, he and the English Government took opposite sides. The anxiety of the Emperor to maintain good personal relations with the Queen was the talisman which restored harmony. A few informal words with the Queen, the Emperor assured her ministers, would dissolve all difficulties. Accordingly he and the Empress were invited to pay a private visit to Osborne, and they stayed there from August 6 to 10. The French ministers, Walewski and Persigny, accompanied their master, and the Queen was attended by Palmerston and Clarendon.

Differences about the Balkan peninsula.

The blandest amiability characterised the discussion, but from the point of view of practical diplomacy ultimate advantage lay with the Emperor. He had supported the contention of Russia and Sardinia that it was desirable to unite under one ruler the two semi-independent principalities of Wallachia and Moldavia in the Balkan peninsula, which were under the suzerainty of Turkey. The English Government supported Austria's desire to keep the two apart. Napoleon agreed at Osborne to the continued separation of the principalities. At the close of the Osborne visit affectionate compliments passed between the Emperor and the Queen in autograph letters, and the agreement was regarded as final. But two years later the two principalities, by their own efforts, joined together and founded the dominion which was afterwards named Roumania. Napoleon insisted on maintaining the union, and England found it futile to press objection.

No effort was meanwhile spared by either Court to maintain their friendly relations. The Queen and

Napoleon continued to profess the completest mutual amity. The Queen, after parting from him in 1857, wrote with ingenuous confidence of the isolation that characterised the position of a sovereign, but added that fortunately her ally, no less than herself, enjoyed the compensation of a happy marriage. The ostentatious activity with which the Emperor was strengthening his armaments at Cherbourg hardly seemed promising for the continuance of such personal harmony, but the Emperor paradoxically converted the warlike preparations, which were going forward almost within hail of the English shore, into new links of the chain of friendship which was binding the two royal families together. At his suggestion, within a fortnight of his leaving Osborne, the Queen and the Prince crossed in her yacht 'Victoria and Albert' to Cherbourg on August 19 in order to inspect the new dockyard, arsenal, and fortifications. Every facility of examination was given them, although the Emperor was absent; but amid the civilities of the welcome the Queen did not ignore the use to which those gigantic works might be put if England and France came to blows. From first to last the relations of the Queen and Emperor abounded in poignant irony.

Meanwhile the nation was in the throes of the Indian mutiny—a crisis more trying and harrowing than the recent Crimean war. Having smouldered since February, it burst into flame in June, and was in August at its cruel height. The Queen, in common with all her subjects, suffered acute mental torture. She eagerly scanned the news from the disturbed districts, and showered upon her ministers, according to her wont, entreaties to do this and that in order to suppress the rebellion with all available speed. Palmerston resented the Queen's urgency of counsel, and wrote (July 18) with unbecoming sarcasm, to which she was happily blind, how fortunate it was for him that she was not on the Opposition side of the House of Commons. At the same time he reminded her that 'measures are sometimes best calculated to succeed which follow each other step by step.'

Queen's urgency of counsel.

The minister's cavils only stimulated the activity of her pen. But the public was ignorant of her energy and greatly under-estimated her vigilance. She left Osborne for her autumn holiday at Balmoral on August 28. Parliament was still sitting. Her withdrawal to the north before the prorogation, in the midst of the Indian peril, excited adverse criticism. The affairs of the nation had to yield, it was bluntly argued neither for the first nor for the last time, to the convenience of her private affairs. There was small justification for the reproach. Throughout her sojourn at Balmoral little else except India occupied her mind. She vividly felt the added anxieties due to the distance from the seat of danger and the difficulty of communication. She warned Palmerston against his habitually sanguine temper. 'While we are putting off decisions,' she wrote to him on September 18, 'in the vain *hope* that matters will mend, and in discussing the objections to different measures, the mischief is rapidly progressing, and the time difficult to catch up again.'

Happily, while the Court was still in Scotland, events took a more favourable turn. On September 30, Delhi, the stronghold of the mutineers, was captured, and the relief of Lucknow, which was also in their hands, was at length in view. One of the earliest congratulations on the improved prospect came from Napoleon III. It reached the Queen by way of the newly invented telegraph wire. 'L'Impératrice et moi,' were the Emperor's words, 'nous félicitons cordialement sa Majesté de la prise de Delhi.' On December 3, when the Queen silenced her censors by opening Parliament in person, the mutiny was nearing extinction.

Fall of Delhi and relief of Lucknow.

The sudden death at Claremont of the Queen's cousin, Victoria, Duchess de Nemours, in November increased at the time the Queen's depression. A first cousin on the Saxe-Coburg side of both the Queen and Prince Albert, the Duchess had been driven with her husband from France to England on the overthrow of Louis Philippe, her father-in-law. 'We were like sisters,' the Queen wrote; 'bore the same name, married the same year, our children of the same age.'

Death of the Duchess de Nemours.

But the need of arranging for the celebration of her eldest daughter's marriage soon diverted the Queen's attention from all else. The ceremony was devised on a large scale. As many as seventeen German princes and princesses accepted invitations to be present. The festivities were varied and prolonged. They opened on January 19, 1858, with a state performance at Her Majesty's Theatre, when 'Macbeth' was performed, with Phelps and Miss Faucit in the chief parts, and Mr. and Mrs. Keeley's

Marriage of the Princess Royal.

rendering of the farce of 'Twice Killed' followed. At length the wedding took place at St. James's Palace on the 25th, amid appropriate splendour. 'It was the second most eventful day of my life as regards feelings,' wrote the Queen in her Journal. 'I felt as if I were being married over again myself, only much more nervous.' Eight days later the bride and bridegroom left England. The Queen felt severely the parting with her eldest daughter, and dwelt upon her mixed feelings of joy and sorrow in her replies to the addresses of congratulation which poured in upon her. Henceforth the fortunes of Germany, and especially of Prussia, became one of her urgent domestic concerns.

Palmerston and the Orsini conspiracy.

Before the Queen quite reconciled herself to the separation from her daughter, she was suddenly involved in the perplexities of a more than usually embarrassing ministerial crisis. The French alliance which Palmerston had initiated, and had done all that in him lay to confirm, proved a boomerang and destroyed his Government. The Emperor's position in France was never secure, and early in 1858 a desperate attempt was made on his life in Paris. On January 15 an explosive bomb was thrown in the Rue Lepelletier by one Orsini, an Italian refugee, at the Emperor and Empress of the French while they were approaching the Opera House. Though they escaped unhurt, ten persons were killed and 150 wounded. The outrage seemed at first sight in no way to touch the relations between France and England, but it was soon discovered that the plot had been hatched by conspirators in England, and that the bomb had been manufactured there. A strongly worded despatch from the French minister Walewski to Palmerston demanded that he should take steps to restrict the right of asylum which England had hitherto freely accorded to foreign political malcontents. Addresses of congratulation from the French army to the Emperor on his escape, which were published in the official 'Moniteur,' threw the blame of the crime on England, and threatened reprisals. Palmerston ignored Walewski's despatch. No reply was sent to it. But, with a view to conciliating the Emperor Napoleon, he introduced a mild Bill making conspiracy to murder, hitherto a misdemeanour, a felony. The step was approved by the Queen, but it was denounced by the Liberals and by the public generally as a weak truckling to Palmerston's old friend Napoleon.[1] Hostility to the minister was roused, and the Bill was defeated on being submitted to a second reading in the House of Commons on February 19 by nineteen votes. Thereupon Palmerston resigned.

The Queen, who had a natural horror of Orsini's crime, deemed it needlessly punctilious in her Parliament to hesitate about what she regarded as a disavowal of sympathy with the assassin's confederates. For once she found herself in full sympathy with Palmerston, and had no wish at the moment to dispense with his services. She begged him to recon-

Palmerston's fall, February 1858.

[1] By direction of Palmerston's Government Dr. Simon Bernard, a friend of Orsini, had been arrested in London on a charge of complicity in the conspiracy against the Emperor's life. He was brought to trial on April 12, 1858, and was acquitted, to the annoyance alike of the Queen and the Emperor, but to the offensively expressed satisfaction of the greater portion of the English public and press.

sider the situation and remain in office. There was another ground for her anxiety to retain the existing ministry for some time longer. If she could seldom expect to derive much comfort from her association with Palmerston, she had great faith in his colleague Clarendon, the Foreign Minister, and it was her fear that a less congenial and a less able statesman might fill his important place in a new ministry which added force to her appeal to Palmerston to hold on. But Palmerston was never desirous of conciliating his Sovereign, and persisted in resigning.

XXIII

THE RESETTLEMENT OF INDIA

THE Queen had no other course open to her than to summon the Conservative leader, Lord Derby. Although both he and the Queen recognised the parliamentary weakness of a Conservative Government in a House of Commons which was dominated by a large Liberal majority, she was successful in urging him to assume power. Lord Derby found no difficulty in forming a cabinet. Most of the ministers had served in the Conservative Government of 1852, and the Queen was personally acquainted with them. Lord Malmesbury resumed the Foreign Office, and Disraeli was once more Chancellor of the Exchequer and leader of the House of Commons. The newcomer to cabinet office who most interested the Queen was Sir Robert Peel's brother, General Jonathan Peel. It gratified her that he should become Secretary for War. 'His likeness to his deceased brother,' she wrote, 'in manner, in his way of thinking, and in patriotic feeling, is quite touching.' At the end of her life she declared with much deliberation that General Jonathan Peel was the best War Minister she ever had.

Lord Derby's second cabinet.

Friendly relations with France were easily re-established by the new ministry, and the Queen was delighted by the Emperor's choice of the eminent General Pélissier, Duc de Malakoff, to represent France at her Court in place of Persigny, who was no favourite. General Pélissier was constantly at Court, often played with the royal children, and was much liked by all the royal family. When he withdrew, on March 5, 1859, tears were shed on all sides.[1]

Second visit to Cherbourg, August 1858.

Public and domestic affairs soon again impelled her to foreign travel. The need of maintaining at full heat the French alliance called her and the Prince to France in August 1858, when they paid a second visit to Cherbourg. The meeting of the Sovereigns characteristically bore a somewhat equivocal aspect. The Queen in her royal yacht was accompanied by a great escort of men-of-war, while nearly all the ships of the French navy stood by to welcome her. On landing at Cherbourg the Emperor met her, and she joined him in witnessing the formal opening of the new arsenal. Afterwards she climbed up the steep fort La Roule in order to survey the whole extent of the fortifications. The Emperor pleasantly reminded his guest that a century before the English fleet had bombarded Cherbourg, but the cordiality between the two appeared unchanged, and the Emperor repeated, with emotion, his confidence

---

[1] Amable Jean Jacques Pélissier was a veteran French soldier, who had acquired notoriety by his violence in subduing Algiers, and had subsequently distinguished himself in the Crimea in command of the First French Army Corps. He succeeded Marshal Canrobert in the chief command before Sebastopol, and, in recognition of his success in storming the Malakoff (September 8, 1855), was created by Napoleon a Marshal of France and Duc de Malakoff.

in the permanence of the Anglo-French alliance. The Prince, however, thought the imperial ardour cooler than of old.

From France the Queen passed to Germany on a visit to her married daughter, whose fortunes were rarely absent from her parents' minds. The Prince Consort had already spent a few days with her in the previous June, but now he paid her a longer visit in company with the Queen. It was an extended and an interesting expedition, and the Queen renewed personal intercourse with many friends and kinsmen. She and the Prince landed at Antwerp, and at Malines met King Leopold, who travelled with them to Verviers. At Aix-la-Chapelle the Prince of Prussia, her daughter's father-in-law, joined them. Thence they travelled to Hanover to visit the blind King George and his queen at Herrenhausen, and the Queen delighted in the various memorials of her Hanoverian predecessors which she saw for the first time. Her daughter was residing at the castle of Babelsberg, about three miles from Potsdam, and there she arrived on August 13. The family gathering filled the Queen with joy, and the time passed rapidly. In the course of the next few days many visits were paid to Berlin. The Queen inspected the public buildings; spent much time at the tomb of Frederick the Great, in the shadow of whose death her mother had resented being born; and explored the royal palaces of Sans-Souci and Charlottenburg, and the Neues Palais. On the 27th she left for Cologne, and, after a brief visit to places of interest there, arrived at Osborne by way of Antwerp and Dover on the 31st.

Tour in Germany.

At Birmingham and Leeds.

The Queen and the Prince spent their annual rest in the north, but they paused on the journey at Leeds to open the new town-hall. They still faithfully performed each year many arduous engagements in the provinces. Three months earlier the Queen, during exceptionally hot weather, which interfered with her comfort, had made a royal progress to Birmingham in order to open the Aston Park. She and the Prince then stayed with Lord Leigh at Stoneleigh Abbey.

The first submarine cable.

Nor had the foreign tour in any way withdrawn the Queen from business of great moment at home. When she was setting out the country's interest was excited by the completion of the laying of the first submarine cable between America and the United Kingdom—the most effective bond of union between the two countries that science could devise. The Queen sent an elaborate message of congratulation over the wires to the President of the United States, James Buchanan. She described the enterprise as an additional link between nations whose friendship was founded upon common interest and reciprocal esteem. Unfortunately the cable soon ceased to work, and the permanent connection was not established till 1861. But at that date the experiment proved thoroughly successful, and the benefit that the Queen had anticipated from the invention was fully realised.

The resettlement of India.

During her stay in Germany, Indian affairs mainly occupied her Government's attention. While the mutiny was in course of suppression, Parliament decided to abolish the old East India Company, which had governed the greater part of the peninsula in qualified partnership with the British Government since its incorporation by charter of Queen Elizabeth on the last day of the sixteenth century. It was resolved to transfer the whole of the Company's territories and administrative powers to the Crown. India was thenceforth to be administered by a Secretary of State in London assisted by a council of fifteen. The Queen naturally set a high value on the new and direct connection which the measure created between India and herself. She justly felt that it added dignity to the prestige of the British monarchy.

But the Queen was anxious that the royal power over India should be something more than a mere shadow. She argued that the royal prerogative should not be refined away by legislative enactments. In two details the Queen deemed the Bill for incorporating India with the dominions of the Crown to menace the free exercise of the royal power. In the first place the introduction of competitive examinations for appointments in the new Indian Civil Service cancelled the Crown's power of nomination to posts which carried with them a delegation of royal authority. In the second place the Indian army was to be put under the authority of the Indian Council. She insisted that she, as Sovereign, enjoyed supreme control of all military forces of the Crown through the Commander-in-Chief exclusively. To the first objection she attached less weight than to the second. But she laid her views on both points before Lord Derby with her usual frankness. The Government had pledged itself to the proposed arrangements, and Lord Derby informed the Queen that he could

Queen's objections to the Government Bill.

give way on neither point. He threatened to resign if the Queen pursued the argument further. Conscious of her powerlessness, she prudently dropped the first objection, and awaited a more opportune moment for renewing discussion on the second. In the event she was, nominally at any rate, victor in the controversy as far as the Indian army was concerned. In 1860 it was decided to amalgamate the European forces in India with the home army, which remained, nominally at any rate, under the ancient control of the Crown.

Queen's personal interest in India.

The Act for the reorganisation of the Indian Government received the royal assent on August 2, 1858. Thereupon Lord Derby's cabinet drafted a proclamation to the people of India defining the principles which would henceforth determine the Crown's relations with them. The Queen was resolved that her first address to the native population should plainly set forth her personal interest in its welfare.

Her sympathy with the natives.

The Queen had already avowed her sympathy with the people of India. She had thrown the whole weight of her influence against those who defended indiscriminate retaliatory punishment of the native population for the misdeeds of the mutiny. The Governor-General, Lord Canning, who pursued a policy of conciliation, had no more sympathising adherent than the Queen. 'The Indian people should know,' she had written to him in December 1857, 'that there is no hatred to a brown skin, none; but the greatest wish on their Queen's part to see them happy, contented, and flourishing.'

THE RESETTLEMENT OF INDIA

The draft proclamation of her new Indian sovereignty was forwarded by Lord Derby to her at Babelsberg. She disapproved of its wording. It seemed to assert England's power with needless brusqueness, and was not, in her opinion, calculated to conciliate native sentiment. Undeterred by the ill-success which had attended her previous efforts to modify those provisions in the India Government Bill which offended her, she now spoke out again. She reminded the Prime Minister 'that it is a female sovereign who speaks to more than a hundred millions of Eastern people on assuming the direct government over them, and after a bloody civil war, giving them pledges which her future reign is to redeem, and explaining the principles of her government. Such a document should breathe feelings of generosity, benevolence, and religious toleration, and point out the privilege which the Indians will receive in being placed on an equality with the subjects of the British Crown, and the prosperity following in the train of civilisation.'[1]

The Queen especially resented her ministers' failure to refer with sympathy to native religion and customs. The deep attachment which she felt to her own religion imposed on her, she said, the obligation of protecting all her subjects in their adherence to their own religious faith. She desired to give expression to her feelings of horror and regret at the mutiny, and her gratitude to God at its approaching end. Finally she desired Lord Derby to rewrite the proclamation in what she described as 'his excellent language,' and give due prominence to her personal regard for

Her attitude to her Indian subjects.

[1] Martin, *Prince Consort*, iv. 49.

the enlightened principles of toleration and conciliation.

Final form of Queen's proclamation.

The Queen never brought her influence to bear on an executive act of government with nobler effect. Lord Derby accepted the Queen's criticism with a good grace, and his second draft, which was warmly approved by the Queen, breathed throughout that wise spirit of humanity which was the best guarantee of the future prosperity of English rule in India. Her suggestion was especially responsible for this magnificent passage in the proclamation, the effect of which, from the point of view of both literature and politics, it would be difficult to exaggerate: 'Firmly relying ourselves on the truth of Christianity, and acknowledging with gratitude the solace of religion, we disclaim alike the right and the desire to impose our convictions on any of our subjects. We declare it to be our royal will and pleasure that none be in any wise favoured, none molested or disquieted by reason of their religious faith or observances, but that all shall alike enjoy the equal and impartial protection of the law; and we do strictly charge and enjoin all those who may be in authority under us that they abstain from all interference with the religious belief or worship of any of our subjects on pain of our highest displeasure.'

The Order of the Star of India.

By way of completing ceremonially the connection between the Crown and India, the Queen recommended the establishment of a new Order of the Star of India as a decorative reward for those native princes who were loyal to her rule, and for such of her officials in the Indian Government as rendered conspicuous service. The first investiture was held with due elaboration on November 1, 1861, and was regarded as worthily closing the first chapter in the history of India under the Queen's immediate sway.[1]

The reorganisation of the Indian Government reflected lasting honour on Sovereign and country.

Queen's sense of imperial responsibility.

---

[1] The Queen wrote in her own hand, at the close of the mutiny, on the subject of the new Order to Lord Canning, the Governor-General of India, and, although all her proposals were not finally adopted, the letter is of great interest: —

'Buckingham Palace: May 18, 1859.

'The Queen must begin her letter to Lord Canning by expressing her joy and gratitude at the termination of this sad mutiny, which caused her such grief, and so much misery to so many.

'The Queen must also express again her high sense of Lord Canning's services during these most trying times.

'Lord Canning will hear from Lord Derby on a subject in which she takes a personal interest. It is the means of gratifying the personal feelings of the chief number of the native princes, binding them together in a confraternity, and attaching them by a personal tie to the Sovereign.

'These results the Queen looks for in the foundation of a high order of chivalry. The statutes might be similar to those of the Garter, the Thistle, and the St. Patrick. The number of its members to be few, perhaps twenty or twenty-four, the Viceroy to be Grand Master, the Queen the Sovereign of the Order. The members to be invested by the Viceroy in person, and thus do personal homage to him. All existing members to be summoned for the admission of a new one. The day for the investiture to be the anniversary of the assumption of the government of India by the Crown of England.

'The Queen would wish also to obtain the means of conferring honorary Knighthoods (making honorary members) of the Order on Eastern potentates, like the Shah of Persia, the sovereigns of Nepaul, Burmah, &c., as a means of extending influence over them.

'The Queen has entered into all these details in order to give Lord Canning a notion of her ideas on the subject, and to elicit his opinion and views as to whether they will be feasible.' (Cf. Martin, iv.)

The absorption by the Crown of the territories and administrative powers of the old East India Company added nearly two hundred million human beings to those who already owed direct allegiance to Queen Victoria, and more than eight hundred thousand square miles to the existing area of the British dominions. It was an imposing increase of empire. By the noble spirit of justice which the Queen infused into her proclamation of sovereignty over her new subjects and her new territories, she proved, more conspicuously than before, her consciousness of the high responsibilities that imperial rule involved.

XXIV

THE QUEEN'S FEARS OF NAPOLEON III.

In the closing months of 1858 and the opening months of 1859 time forcibly reminded the Queen of its passage. On November 9, 1858, the Prince of Wales, the heir to the throne, who had been confirmed on April 1, 1858, entered on his eighteenth year. That age in the royal family was equivalent to a majority, and the Queen in an admirable letter to her eldest son, while acknowledging that, in the interest of his own welfare, his discipline had been severe, now bade him consider himself his own master; she would always be ready to offer him advice if he wished it, but she would not obtrude it. Majority of Prince of Wales.

No sooner had she set her eldest son on the road to independence than she welcomed the first birth of that second generation of her family which before her death was to grow to great dimensions. On January 27, 1859, a son and heir was born at Berlin to the Princess Royal. The child—'dear little William' as he was long called by the Queen—ultimately became the present German Emperor, William II. For some time the Princess's condition caused grave anxiety to her family. 'The doctors despaired at the first,' the Queen wrote, ' of the child's Her eldest grandchild.

life,' but the crisis happily passed. The Queen thus became a grandmother at the age of thirty-nine. Congratulations poured in from every quarter.

Queen's appeal for peace to Napoleon III.

Among the earliest and the warmest greetings came one from Napoleon III., and the Queen in her acknowledgment took occasion solemnly and frankly to urge him to abide in the paths of peace. 'Your Majesty,' she wrote, 'has now an opportunity, either by listening to the dictates of humanity and justice, and by showing to the world your intention to adhere strictly to the faithful observance of treaties, of calming the apprehensions of Europe, and of restoring its confidence in the pacific policy of your Majesty, or, on the other hand, by lending an ear to those who have an interest in creating confusion, of involving Europe in a war, whose extent and duration it is scarcely possible to foresee, and which, whatever glory it may add to the arms of France, cannot but interfere materially with her internal prosperity and financial credit. I am satisfied your Majesty will not doubt the sincerity of the friendship which alone induces me to write thus unreservedly to your Majesty; and if anything could add to the sorrow with which I should view the renewal of war in Europe, it would be to see your Majesty entering upon a course with which it would be impossible for England to associate herself.'

Napoleon's intervention in Italy.

There was good ground for the Queen's appeal. The persistency with which Napoleon continued to increase his armaments had roused a widespread belief that he was preparing to emulate the example of his great predecessor. For a time it seemed doubtful in which direction the Emperor would aim his first blow. But when the Queen's first grandson was born, she knew that her smooth-spoken ally was about to challenge the peace of Europe by joining the King of Sardinia in an endeavour to expel Austria from Lombardy and Venetia. He was about to promote by force of arms the unification of Italy under the kingship of the royal house of Sardinia. The Emperor accepted the Queen's pacific counsel in good part, but at the same time wrote to her to announce and to defend the projected war.

The Queen was in no complacent mood, but she cherished the notion that Napoleon was not likely to persist in his turbulent purpose. On February 3 she opened Parliament in person, and read with emphasis those passages in her speech which declared that England would be no party to the Emperor Napoleon's ambitious designs. Before the end of April the Queen's hopes of peace were defeated by the unexpected action of Austria, which, grasping its nettle, declared war on Sardinia. There was no delay in the opening of hostilities. Napoleon at once took the field with his ally of Italy. *Austria declares war on Italy.*

The Queen and the Prince were harassed by fear of a universal war, and they had the added mortification of knowing that popular feeling in England in respect of the Italian struggle was entirely antagonistic to their own. English public sentiment regarded Sardinia as the courageous challenger of the absolutist tyranny of Austria. Napoleon was applauded for disinterestedly rendering Sardinia assistance. The Queen and the Prince, on the other hand, while they *Napoleon at war with Austria.*

deplored Austria's precipitancy, cherished sympathy with her as a German power, whose fortunes might be expected to affect immediately those of her neighbour, Prussia. If Austria fell before French aggression, would Prussia be able to resist a like fate?

The Queen's anxiety respecting Prussia.

Solicitude for her newly married daughter redoubled the Queen's desire for the safety of Prussia. Her son-in-law had risen a step nearer the Prussian throne in 1858, when the incapable King, his uncle, had, owing to failing health, been superseded by his father, the Prince of Prussia, who became Prince Regent. The change seemed to bring the affairs of Prussia more fully than before within the Queen's sphere of influence. The new ruler of Prussia was a most intimate friend of Prince Albert and of the Queen.[1] He had much faith in Prince Albert's judgment, and had long been in the habit of freely appealing to them for confidential counsel.

Her efforts to localise the war.

It was now for the Prince Regent of Prussia to decide whether the safety of his dominions required him to throw in his lot with Austria. The English Court, mainly moved by a desire to protect a daughter from the consequences of strife, besought him to stand aside. He assented, and the Queen straightway turned again to Napoleon. In the hope of completely safeguarding Prussia, she appealed to him to keep hostilities within a narrow compass. When the Empress of the French sent the Queen

[1] When he had been their guest at his son's marriage with their daughter in 1858, the Queen, according to her Journal, had petitioned him thenceforth to call her 'du,' a usage in German society which attests the closest intimacy.

birthday congratulations on May 25, the Queen in reply entreated her to persuade her husband to localise the war. The prompt triumph of the French arms achieved that result. To the Queen's relief, although not without continued anxiety, she learned in June that the end of the war was in sight, and that the two Emperors were to meet at Villafranca to negotiate terms of peace.

The Queen's fears of the sequel were greatly increased by the change of Government which took place at home during the progress of the Austro-Italian war. On April 1 Lord Derby's Government, which in the main agreed with her views of the foreign situation, was defeated on its Reform Bill. The Bill had been introduced by Disraeli, but failed to provide for the extension of the franchise on the scale that the Liberal majority of the House desired. The Queen declined to accept the ministers' resignation. She suspected that the sympathy avowed by Palmerston, Lord John Russell, Gladstone, and others of their colleagues with the aspirations of Italy might bring England, if they came into power, into conflict with Austria. With some imprudence the Queen consequently assented to the only alternative to Lord Derby's resignation—a dissolution of Parliament. The elections passed off quietly, but they left the Conservatives in a minority of forty-three.

Lord Derby's resignation.

On June 10 the old Conservative ministers were attacked and defeated in the new House of Commons, and, to the Queen's disappointment, she found herself compelled to accept Lord Derby's retirement. Again Palmerston was the Conservative leader's only

The Queen sends for Lord Granville.

practicable successor. But it was repugnant to the Queen to recall him to power at the existing juncture in foreign politics. She had convinced herself that his sympathy with Italy and his antipathy to Austria were irrepressible. Lord John Russell, too, had identified himself with Italian interests beyond all chance of misconception abroad. His return to the post of Prime Minister she dreaded almost as greatly as Lord Palmerston's return. She therefore invited Lord Granville, a comparatively subordinate member of the party, to extricate her from her difficulties by forming a Government on his own account (June 11). To him she was personally attached, and, although his views were not known to differ materially from those of his older colleagues, he was calculated to prove more pliable than they. She was aware that no Liberal Government could be formed without the admission to it of both Palmerston and Lord John, but she met that fact in her own fashion. In autograph letters addressed to Palmerston and Lord John, which Granville was charged to deliver, she requested those veterans to serve under him.

Her confidence betrayed to the 'Times.'

Naturally her action was mortifying to both statesmen, and by accident it involved her and them in even more embarrassment than might have been anticipated. Owing to some indiscreet talk of Lord Granville with a friend, a correct report of the Queen's conversation with him appeared in the 'Times' next morning (June 12). The Queen was in despair at this betrayal of her confidence. 'Whom am I to trust?' she said as she read the statement in the newspaper: 'these were my own very words.'

In the result Palmerston proved more amiable than Lord John. Palmerston genially agreed to accept Lord Granville's leadership, but Lord John brusquely refused to entertain it. Thereupon Lord Granville withdrew from the negotiation, for which he never felt much heart. The Queen was compelled to take the uncongenial step, against which she rebelled. Nothing remained for her but to appeal to Palmerston, and to accept him as her Prime Minister for the second time.

Lord John's obstinacy.

The Queen's trials were only beginning. Before Palmerston's ministry was constituted she suffered yet another disappointment. Lord John insisted on taking the Foreign Office. As a consequence, Lord Clarendon, whom she now regarded as her only sure friend in the Liberal party and who had good claims to the post, was excluded from the Government.[1]

Palmerston again Prime Minister.

---

[1] Palmerston's cabinet was finally constituted thus:—

First Lord of the Treasury	Viscount Palmerston.
Lord Chancellor	Lord Campbell.
President of the Council	Earl Granville.
Lord Privy Seal	The Duke of Argyll.
Home Secretary	Sir Geo. Cornewall Lewis, Bart.
Foreign Secretary	Lord John Russell.
Secretary of State for Colonies	The Duke of Newcastle.
Secretary of State for War	Sidney Herbert.
Secretary of State for India	Sir Charles Wood, Bt.
Chancellor of the Exchequer	William Ewart Gladstone.
First Lord of the Admiralty	The Duke of Somerset.
President of the Board of Trade	Thomas Milner Gibson.
Postmaster-General	Earl of Elgin.
Chancellor of the Duchy of Lancaster	Sir George Grey.
Chief Commissioner of Poor Law Board	Charles Pelham Villiers.
Chief Secretary for Ireland	Edward Cardwell.

Differences with Lord John on the Italian question.

The Queen's forebodings of difficulty with her new ministers were amply justified. At the hands of Lord John, as Foreign Minister, she endured hardly fewer torments than Palmerston had inflicted on her when he held that office. Lord John and his chief at once avowed a resolve to serve the interests of Italy at the expense of Austria, and won, in the inner circle of the Court, the sobriquet of 'the old Italian masters.'

The peace of Villafranca.

Meanwhile the course of the negotiations between Napoleon and the Emperor of Austria was perplexing alike to the Queen and to her ministers. Napoleon at Villafranca arranged mysterious terms with the Emperor of Austria which seemed to the friends of Italy far too favourable to Austria, although they gave France no advantage. Austria was to lose Lombardy, but was to retain Venetia. France protested unwillingness to take further part in the matter. Sardinia was recommended to rely on her own efforts to obtain whatever other changes she sought in the adjustment of Italy. So barren a result was unsatisfactory to all Italian Liberals, and was deemed by Palmerston and Lord John to be grossly unjust to them. The English ministry opened diplomatic negotiations with a view to a modification of the proposed treaty, and frankly encouraged the Italians to fight their battle out to the end.

Queen's quarrel with her ministry.

The Queen, who was relieved by the cessation of hostilities and by the easy terms offered to Austria, stoutly objected to her ministers' intervention. 'We did not protest against the war,' she told Lord John; 'we cannot protest against the peace.' She insisted that the cry 'Italy for the Italians,' if once raised by the Government, would compel this country to join Sardinia in war. But Palmerston and Lord John were unmoved by her appeals. They refused to stand aside and allow Italy to forfeit the advantage which appeared to them to be justly due to her recent efforts. Palmerston declared that, if the Queen rejected her ministers' advice on foreign questions, they must resign. The Queen retorted that the Prime Minister did not speak for all his colleagues. In August, when the vacation had scattered the ministers, she insisted on the whole cabinet being summoned to London, so that they might learn her unconquerable resolve to observe a strict neutrality on England's part during the progress of what she called 'the Italian Revolution.' Palmerston affected indifference to her persistency, but it had some effect. It helped to cool his ardour and to lend greater caution to his utterances. In the event, Italian affairs were suffered to take their own course without English interference.

Yet the outcome was not agreeable to the Queen. As soon as the treaty of Villafranca was signed in July 1859, Sardinia, aided by Garibaldi, sought at the sword's point, without foreign aid, full control of the independent states of the peninsula outside Rome and Venetia. Although she was aware of the weakness of their cause, the Queen could not resist sympathy with the petty Italian rulers who were driven by the armies of Garibaldi and Victor Emanuel from their principalities. The Duchess of Parma, one of the discrowned sovereigns, appealed to the Queen for protection. Lord John, whose stolidity in such matters widened the breach between him and the Queen,

Struggle for Italian unity.

drew up a cold and bald refusal of help, which she declined to send. Lord Clarendon, however, was at the moment on a visit to her at Windsor. By his advice she contrived to impart a more sympathetic tone to her reply, which better accorded with her private sentiment, yet fell short of openly defying the counsel of her ministers.

Anger with Napoleon III.

But it was not her ministers alone who exasperated her. While she was still in conflict with them she was startled to learn that, with Sardinia's reluctant assent, Napoleon had annexed to France the provinces of Savoy and Nice as the price of his benevolent service to Italy in the past, and by way of a warning that he would tolerate no intrusion in Italian affairs from any foreign power, whether England or Germany, so long as the internal struggle for Italian unity was proceeding. The Queen viewed this episode with especial disgust. That Napoleon should benefit from the confusion into which, in her eyes, he had wantonly thrown Southern Europe roused her indignation to its full height. She bitterly reproached her ministers, whom she suspected of secret sympathy with him, with playing into his hands. Her complaint was hardly logical, for she had herself urged on them the strictest neutrality, and the need of abstaining from any sort of interference in the affairs of the Italian peninsula.

Heated protests against her ministers' supineness.

None the less, on February 5, 1860, she wrote to Lord John, 'We have been made regular dupes, which the Queen apprehended and warned against all along.' Europe ought to stand together to prevent the annexation ; but if that were not to be hoped

for, then at least sympathy with France should be
openly disclaimed by England. 'It is a belief in this
[active sympathy between France and England],' she
wrote to Lord John on March 27, 'which makes the rest
of Europe powerless and helpless [to protest against
Napoleon's unprincipled conduct].' 'All Europe was
paralysed by a fear of England's full acquiescence
in the various schemes of the Emperor.' The other
continental Powers distrusted England and declined
to aid her in diplomatic repression of the wild
ambition of Napoleon, because 'the English press
and general public' encouraged disorder and revolt
everywhere. 'They were favourable,' she said, with
sarcastic allusion to the personal prejudices of Lord
John, her correspondent, 'to the Italian Revolution
and the loss of the Italian provinces by Austria, and
were supposed to be so with regard to the separation
of Hungary from Austria and Poland from Russia.'
In letters to her family she exclaimed with greater
vehemence against France. 'France,' she wrote to
her uncle Leopold (May 8, 1860), 'must needs
disturb every quarter of the globe, and try to make
mischief, and set every one by the ears. Of course
this will end some day in a general crusade against
the universal disturber of the world.'

Outspoken as was the Queen's language to her ministers throughout this session, she ultimately accepted what was inevitable with comparative composure. Nor did her attitude to France and to Napoleon take in permanence the openly hostile colour which her passing indignation lent it. With her ministers her relations naturally remained cool,

The Queen and the Commander-in-Chief.

but she endeavoured to exert greater control over her feelings, and her criticisms proved none the less effective on that account. Later in the year Palmerston and his colleagues gave her further ground for annoyance. They proposed to abolish the post of Commander-in-Chief, and to bring the army entirely under the control of Parliament through the Secretary of State. She protested with deliberate emphasis against the change; she regarded it as an infringement of her prerogative. Her protest was respectfully heard, and for the moment the scheme was dropped.

XXV

THE SECOND VISIT TO COBURG

APART from politics the Queen's life still knew no cloud. Her public duties continued to bring her into personal intercourse with the army which was always congenial to her. On January 29, 1859, she opened Wellington College for the sons of officers, an institution of which she had already laid the foundation-stone.[1] On June 6 she once more distributed Victoria crosses, which had been earned in the Indian mutiny. On August 26 she inspected at Portsmouth the 32nd Regiment, whence the heroes of Lucknow had been drawn.

Military ceremonials.

The suspicions aroused by the Emperor Napoleon had in 1859 provoked great military enthusiasm through the country—a feeling with which the Queen eagerly identified herself. To meet surprises of invasion from France a volunteer force was called into existence by royal command in May 1859, and to this new branch of the service the Queen showed every favour. She held a special levee of 2,500 volunteer officers at St. James's Palace on March 7, 1860, and she reviewed twenty thousand men in Hyde Park on June 23. Her brother-in-law, Duke

The volunteers.

---

[1] See p. 266 supra.

Ernest, who accompanied her on the occasion, did not conceal his contempt for the evolutions of her citizen soldiers, but she was earnest in her commendation of their zeal. On July 2, 1860, she personally inaugurated the National Rifle Association, which was a needful complement of the volunteer movement, and in opening its first annual meeting on Wimbledon Common she fired the first shot at the targets from a Whitworth rifle. She at once instituted the Queen's prize of the value of 250*l.*, which was awarded annually till the end of her reign, and was continued by her successor. When on the way to Balmoral in August 1860, she stayed at Holyrood in order to review the volunteer forces of Scotland.

Domestic life. Domestic life proceeded agreeably. Twice in 1859 her daughter, the Princess Royal, visited her, on the second occasion with her husband. During the autumn sojourn at Balmoral of that year the Queen was exceptionally vigorous, making many mountaineering expeditions with her children. The Prince Consort presided over the meeting of the British Association at Aberdeen in September 1859, and afterwards invited 200 of the members to be the Queen's guests at a highland gathering on Deeside. On her way south, at the close of her northern holiday, she opened the Glasgow Waterworks at Loch Katrine, and made a tour through the Trossachs. She also paid a visit to Colonel Douglas Pennant, M.P., at Penrhyn Castle, near Bangor, and was well received by the workmen at the Penrhyn slate quarries.

Another marriage in the Queen's family was now on her horizon. Soon after she had opened

Parliament in person on January 24, 1860, she entertained a large party at Windsor, including the King of the Belgians and the young German Princes, Louis of Hesse-Darmstadt and his brother. Prince Louis paid the Queen's second daughter, Princess Alice, attentions on which she looked with silent favour. The Princess was barely seventeen, and, although the Queen deprecated marriage at so early an age, she awaited the result with interest. *[margin: Engagement of Princess Alice.]*

At the same time the Queen and her husband were organising for the Prince of Wales a tour through Canada and the United States, which promised well for the good relations of England and the American commonwealth. President Buchanan, in a letter to the Queen, invited the Prince to Washington, an invitation which she herself accepted in his behalf in an autograph reply. At the conclusion of the Prince's tour, the President wrote again to inform the Queen of the warm welcome that had been extended to her son, and of the good impression that he had personally made. The Queen acknowledged the compliment with friendly cordiality. In the letter, which Prince Albert drafted, and she copied out, she expressed anxiety to maintain the best possible relations between England and the United States, 'two nations of kindred origin and character' (November 19, 1860). *[margin: Tour of Prince of Wales in America Feb.–Nov. 1860.]*

In the late autumn of 1860 the royal family paid a second visit to Coburg. A main inducement was to converse once more with Stockmar, who had since 1857 lived there in retirement, in advanced age and failing health. The Queen and the Prince were still actively corresponding with him, and were as *[margin: Second visit to Coburg, 1860.]*

dependent as ever on his counsel. On September 22, accompanied by Princess Alice and attended by Lord John Russell, the Foreign Secretary, they embarked at Gravesend for Antwerp. During the journey they were distressed by the intelligence of the death of the Prince Consort's stepmother, with whom they had both cherished sympathetic intimacy.[1] But they were cheered while passing through Germany by a meeting with members of the Prussian royal family, including their son-in-law.

The Queen and her eldest grandson.

At Coburg they met their daughter and her first-born son, William, with whom his grandmother then first made acquaintance. On September 29 they removed to Rosenau. Among the guests there was Gustav Freytag, the German novelist, who greatly interested the Queen. In his 'Reminiscences' Freytag described her 'march-like gait' and affable demeanour.[2]

Accident to Prince Albert.

On October 1 the Prince met with an alarming carriage accident.[3] The Queen, though she suppressed her emotion, was gravely perturbed, and by way of a thank-offering instituted at Coburg, after her return home, a Victoria-Stift (i.e. foundation), endowing it with 1,000*l.* for the assistance of young men and women beginning life. Happily the Prince sustained slight injury, but the nervous depression which followed led his friend Stockmar to remark that he would fall an easy prey to illness. When walking with his brother on the day of his departure (October 10), he com-

---

[1] Princess Antoinette Frederica, daughter of Alexander Friedrich Carl, Duke of Würtemberg. She died September 24, 1860.

[2] Gustav Freytag, *Reminiscences*, Engl. trans. 1890, vol. ii.

[3] Cf. Lord Augustus Loftus, *Reminiscences*, 1st ser. ii. 89.

pletely broke down, and sobbed out that he would never see his native land again.[1]

On the return journey the Prince and Princess of Prussia entertained the Queen and the Prince at their palace of Coblenz, where slight illness detained the Queen for a few days. Lord John Russell and Baron von Schleinitz, the German minister, spent the time in political discussion, partly in regard to a trifling incident which was at the moment causing friction between the two countries. An English traveller, Captain Macdonald, had been imprisoned by the mistake of an over-zealous policeman at Bonn. No settlement was reached by Lord John in the interview at Coblenz. Palmerston afterwards used characteristically strong language in a demand for reparation. A vexatious dispute followed between the two Governments, and the Queen and the Prince were displeased by the manner in which the English ministers handled the matter. The Queen wisely avoided all open expression of opinion, but shrewdly observed that, 'although foreign governments were often violent and arbitrary, our people are apt to give offence and to pay no regard to the laws of the country.'

Relations with Prussia.

The discussion gradually dropped, and foreign politics took a brighter hue in the Queen's eyes. On January 2, 1861, the death of the paralysed Frederick William IV. placed the Queen's friend, the Prince Regent, finally on the throne of Prussia as King William I. Her son-in-law and her daughter at the same time became Crown Prince and Princess of Prussia. At the moment the Queen

Accession of King Wm. I. of Prussia.

[1] Duke Ernest's *Memoirs*, iv. 55.

cherished the belief that friendship between the two countries, as between the two Courts, was permanently assured. Her wrath with Napoleon, too, was waning. A private visit to Windsor and Osborne on the part of the Empress Eugénie, who had come in search of health, revived the tie of personal affection that bound her to the Queen, and the new year saw the customary interchange of amicable letters between the Queen and Napoleon III. English and French armies had been engaged together in China. But the main burden of the Queen's greeting to the Emperor was an appeal for peace. A further source of satisfaction sprang from the second visit which Prince Louis of Hesse paid to Windsor in November 1860. On the last day of that month he formally betrothed himself to Princess Alice.

XXVI

DEATH OF THE PRINCE CONSORT

CHRISTMAS and New Year 1860-1 were kept at Windsor with unusual spirit, although the death of Lord Aberdeen on December 14 was a cause of grief. Among the many guests were both Lord Palmerston and Mr. Disraeli with his wife. The Queen and Prince had much talk with Disraeli, of whose growing influence they took due account. Their early prejudice against him was fading on closer acquaintance, and they were gratified by his assurance that in foreign affairs his followers might be relied on to support any policy that gave due weight to national interests and national reputation. On more personal questions Disraeli was equally complacent. The Queen was about to appeal to Parliament for the endowment of her second daughter Alice on her marriage. There was always ground for apprehending public censure of grants to the royal family. Disraeli's approval of the appeal was of importance. He delighted his royal hosts by expressing full concurrence with them. He readily agreed to support the Government in granting a dowry of 30,000*l.* and an annuity of 6,000*l.* to Princess Alice on her approaching marriage.

Disraeli and the grant to Princess Alice.

On February 4, 1861, the Queen opened Parlia-

The twenty-first anniversary of her marriage.

ment, and herself announced the happy event. It was the last occasion on which she delivered with her own voice the speech from the throne, for the tenor of her life was to undergo, before the year was out, a terrible disruption. On February 10 she kept quietly at Buckingham Palace the twenty-first anniversary of her marriage. 'Very few,' she wrote to her uncle Leopold, 'can say with me that their husband at the end of twenty-one years is not only full of the friendship, kindness, and affection which a truly happy marriage brings with it, but of the same tender love as in the very first days of our marriage.' Death was to destroy the mainspring of her happiness within the year.

Death of the Queen's mother.

The Queen passed to the crowning sorrow of her life through a lesser grief, which on its coming tried her severely. On March 16 her mother, the Duchess of Kent, who kept her youthful spirit and cheerfulness to the last, and especially delighted in her grandchildren, died at Frogmore after a brief illness of a painful kind. It was the Queen's first experience of death in the inmost circle of her family, and for the time it overwhelmed her. Although she was much broken, the Queen at once sent the sad news in her own hand to her half-sister, to the Princess Royal, and to King Leopold. To her uncle Leopold she wrote: 'On this, the most dreadful day of my life, does your poor broken-hearted child write one line of love and devotion. *She* is gone—that precious, dearly beloved, tender mother, whom I never parted from but for a few months—without whom I cannot imagine life—has been taken from us! It is too dreadful—

but she is at peace—her fearful sufferings at an end!' Princess Alice, who was with the Queen at the moment of the Duchess of Kent's death, first gave proof of that capacity of consolation which she was often afterwards to display in her mother's trials. 'Good Alice was with us all through,' the Queen wrote.

Expressions of sympathy abounded, and the general sentiment was well interpreted by Disraeli, who said in his speech in the House of Commons, in seconding a vote of condolence: 'She who reigns over us has elected, amid all the splendours of empire, to establish her life on the principle of domestic love.' The words fell gratefully on the Queen's ear. *Disraeli's condolence.*

The Duchess's body was laid to rest on March 25 in St. George's Chapel, Windsor, but the Queen resolved that a special mausoleum should be built at Frogmore for a permanent burial-place, and the remains were removed thither on August 17. The Queen's behaviour to all who were in any way dependent on her mother was exemplary. She pensioned her servants; she continued allowances that the Duchess of Kent had made to her elder daughter, the Princess Hohenlohe, and to her grandsons, Prince Victor and Prince Edward of Leiningen (sons of the Duchess's son, Prince Charles of Leiningen). To the Duchess's lady-in-waiting, Lady Augusta Bruce, sister of Lord Elgin, who had shown great devotion, the Queen was herself much attached, and she at once made her her own bed-chamber woman in permanent attendance upon her. *The Queen and her mother's dependents.*

The mourning at Court put an end for the time to festivities, and some minor troubles added to the Queen's depression. In May, when Prince Louis of *Minor troubles.*

Hesse visited Osborne, he fell ill of measles. On July 14 the Queen was greatly shocked by news of the attempted assassination at Baden of her friend the new King of Prussia.

Resumption of hospitalities.

But she gradually resumed the hospitalities and activities of public life. Before the end of the season she entertained the King of the Belgians, the Crown Prince and Princess of Prussia, the King and Prince Oscar of Sweden, and the ill-fated Archduke and Archduchess Maximilian.

Third visit to Ireland, 1861.

On August 21 the Queen, with the Prince Consort, the Princesses Alice and Helena, and Prince Arthur, set out from Osborne to pay Ireland a third visit. The immediate inducement was to see the Prince of Wales, who was learning regimental duties at the Curragh camp. The royal party travelled by railway from Southampton to Holyhead, and crossed to Kingstown in the royal yacht. The Queen took up her residence in the Viceregal Lodge in Phœnix Park on the 22nd. On Saturday the 24th she went to the Curragh to review a force of 10,000 men, among whom her eldest son held a place.

At Killarney.

The Queen was wisely desirous of conciliating her Irish subjects outside Dublin, and she extended her journey to districts far from the capital. On the 26th she and her family went south, travelling to Killarney and taking up their residence at Kenmare House. They were received by the people of the countryside with every mark of enthusiasm. Next day they explored the lakes of Killarney, and removed in the evening to Muckross Abbey, the residence of Mr. Herbert. Among the Queen's guests there was

James O'Connell, brother of Daniel O'Connell the agitator, with other members of the agitator's family. A stag hunt was organised for the royal party, and it proved enjoyable, although no stag was found. On the 29th the Queen left Killarney for Dublin and Holyhead on her way to Balmoral. Nearly thirty-nine years were to pass before the Queen visited Ireland again.

At Balmoral the Queen occupied herself mainly with outdoor pursuits. On September 4, to her delight, she was joined by her half-sister, the Princess Hohenlohe, who came on a long visit. Near the end of October, on the journey south, a short halt was made at Edinburgh to enable the Prince Consort to lay the foundation-stones of a new post office and the industrial museum of Scotland (October 22). Windsor Castle was reached the next morning. This was the last migration of the Court which the Prince Consort was destined to share.

Prince Consort's last visit to Balmoral.

As usual, guests were numerous at Windsor in November, but the deaths of Sir James Graham, who had served under both Peel and Aberdeen, as well as of the Queen's two cousins, Pedro V., King of Portugal, and his brother Ferdinand, damped the spirits of host and hostess.

At Windsor, Nov.

In the middle of November signs that the Prince's health was failing became obvious. A year before he had had an attack of English cholera, and he suffered habitually from low fever; he had shown much nervous depression on his last visit to Coburg. Though the Queen was solicitous on his account, she, like most persons in robust health, was inclined to

Prince Consort's illness.

take a hopeful view of his condition, and not until the last did she realise that a fatal issue was impending.

A serious political crisis suddenly arose to absorb her attention, and for the last time she, by her husband's advice, brought personal influence to bear on her ministers in the interests of the country's peace: In April the civil war in America had broken out, and the Queen's Government had issued a proclamation of neutrality. Public opinion in England was divided on the merits of the two antagonists, but the mass of the people favoured the Confederation of the South. Palmerston, the Prime Minister, Gladstone, Chancellor of the Exchequer, and many of their colleagues made no secret of their faith in the justice of the cause of the South. The Queen and Prince Consort inclined to the opposite side.

Federals' attack on the Southern envoys.

In November the prevailing English sentiment of sympathy with the South seemed on the point of translating itself into actual war with the North. Two Southern envoys, named respectively Mason and Slidell, had been despatched by the Southern Confederates to plead their cause at the English and French Courts. They had run the Northern Federals' blockade of the American coast, and, embarking on the 'Trent,' an English steamer, at Havana, set sail in her on November 8. Next day a Federal ship-of-war fired at the 'Trent.' The Federal captain (Wilkes) boarded her after threatening violence, and captured the Confederate envoys with their secretaries.

Palmerston's peremptory tone.

On November 27 the 'Trent' arrived at Southampton, and the news was divulged in England. The spirit of the Government and the country was roused.

On November 30 Palmerston forwarded to the Queen the draft of a despatch to be forwarded to Washington. In peremptory and uncompromising terms the English Government demanded of the Northern Federals immediate reparation and redress for a wanton breach of international law. The strength of Palmerston's language seemed to place any likelihood of an accommodation out of question.

The Prince Consort realised the perils of the situation. He did not share the Prime Minister's veneration of the Southerners, and war with any party in the United States was abhorrent to him. He at once suggested, in behalf of the Queen, gentler phraseology, and, in spite of his rapidly developing illness, wrote to Lord Palmerston for the Queen (December 1) urging him to recast the despatch. All belief that the assault on the 'Trent' was the deliberate act of the Government of the United States should be disavowed. Let the Prime Minister assume that an over-zealous officer of the Federal fleet had made an unfortunate error which could easily be repaired by 'the restoration of the unfortunate passengers and a suitable apology.' *Prince Albert's intervention.*

This note to Palmerston 'was the last thing' the Prince 'ever wrote,' the Queen said afterwards, and it had the effect its author desired. The English Government had a strong case. The Emperor of the French, the Emperor of Austria, the King of Prussia, and the Emperor of Russia had at once expressed themselves in full sympathy with England. But happily the Prince Consort's wiser counsels prevailed. Palmerston and Russell accepted the Prince's *Prince Consort's advice accepted.*

correction. They substituted his moderation for their own virulence, with the result that the Government of Washington assented cheerfully to their demands. The risk of war between England and the United States was averted by the despatch which the Prince Consort had drafted in the name of the Queen and with her enthusiastic assent.

The gratitude of American democrats.

Both in England and America it was acknowledged that a grave disaster had been averted by the Prince's tact. Leaders of the Northern States afterwards admitted a conviction that the outbreak of war with England in 1861 would have brought in its train the formal recognition of the Southern Confederacy by the great European States. The most earnest democrats among the Northern Federals gratefully recognised that they owed preservation from an imminent calamity to the personal intervention of royalty. Walt Whitman, the poet, in whom the democratic spirit of the United States burnt with full force, wrote some years later of the successful intervention of the Queen and Prince Albert in the 'Trent' affair in such exuberant terms as these:—

Walt Whitman on the Queen's action.

'Very little, as we Americans stand this day, with our sixty-five or seventy millions of population, an immense surplus in the treasury, and all that actual power or reserve power (land and sea) so dear to nations—very little, I say, do we realise that curious crawling national shudder when the "Trent affair" promis'd to bring upon us a war with Great Britain— follow'd unquestionably, as that war would have been, by recognition of the Southern Confederacy from all the leading European nations. It is now certain that all this then inevitable train of calamity hung on arrogant and peremptory phrases in the prepared and written missive of the British Minister, to America, which the Queen (and Prince Albert latent) positively and promptly cancell'd ; and which her firm attitude did alone actually erase and leave out, against all the other official prestige and Court of St. James's. On such minor and personal incidents (so to call them) often depend the great growths and turns of civilisation. This moment of a woman and a queen surely swung the grandest oscillation of modern history's pendulum. Many sayings and doings of that period, from foreign potentates and powers, might well be dropt in oblivion by America—but never *this*, if I could have my way.'[1]

But Prince Albert was never to witness the fruits of his successful intervention in the affair of the 'Trent.' The beneficent result of the action to which his prudence had prompted the Queen and her ministers was never known to him. Before the critical despatch had been finally corrected he had a presentiment that he was going to die, and the presentiment proved true. The Prince did not cling to life. He had none of the

Prince Albert's death.

---

[1] These words form a note which Walt Whitman appended to the following poetic greeting to the Queen :—

'*For Queen Victoria's Birthday.*—An American arbutus branch to be put in a little vase on the royal breakfast table, May 24, 1890.

Lady, accept a birthday thought—haply an idle gift and token,
Right from the scented soil's May-utterance here,
(Smelling of countless blessings, prayers, and old time thanks,)
A bunch of white and pink arbutus, silent, spicy, shy,
From Hudson's, Delaware's, or Potomac's woody banks.'

(Walt Whitman's *Complete Prose Works*, Boston, Mass. 1898.)

Queen's sanguineness or elasticity of temperament, and of late irremovable gloom had oppressed him. During the early days of December his weakness grew, but good hope was entertained of his recovery, when on the 14th he passed away unexpectedly at Windsor in the Queen's presence. He was little more than forty-two years old. The Queen was only his senior by three months. Almost without warning the romance of the Queen's life was at its meridian changed into a tragedy.

XXVII

THE QUEEN'S GRIEF

No heavier blow than the Prince's removal could have fallen on the Queen. Rarely was a wife more dependent on a husband. More than fifteen years before she had written to Stockmar (July 30, 1846) in reference to a few days' separation from the Prince: 'Without him everything loses its interest ... it will always be a terrible pang for me to separate from him even for two days, and I pray God never to let me survive him.' Now that the permanent separation had come, the future for her spelt desolation. As she wrote on a photograph of a family group, consisting of herself, her children, and a bust of the Prince Consort, 'day for her was turned into night.'[1]

The Queen's widowhood.

Her tragic fate appealed strongly to the sympathies of her people, who mourned with her through every rank. 'They cannot tell what I have lost,' she said; but she was not indifferent to the mighty outburst of compassion. Personal sympathy with her in her bereavement was not, however, all that she asked. She knew that the exalted estimate she had formed of her husband was not shared by her

Public sympathy.

[1] Lady Bloomfield, ii. 148.

subjects, and as in his lifetime, so to a greater degree after his death, she yearned for signs that he had won her countrymen's and countrywomen's highest esteem. 'Will they do him justice now?' she cried, as, in company with her friend, the Duchess of Sutherland, she looked for the last time on his dead face.

Tennyson's elegy.

Praise of the Prince was the Queen's fullest consolation, and happily it was not denied her. The elegiac eulogy with which Tennyson prefaced his 'Idylls of the King,' within a month of the Prince's death, was the manner of salve (she said) that best soothed 'her aching, bleeding heart:'—

> 'We know him now: all narrow jealousies
> Are silent; and we see him as he moved,
> How modest, kindly, all accomplished, wise,
> With what sublime repression of himself,
> And in what limits, and how tenderly;
> Not swaying to this faction or to that;
> Not making his high place the lawless perch
> Of wing'd ambitions, nor a vantage ground
> For pleasure; but thro' all this tract of years
> Wearing the white flower of a blameless life,
> Before a thousand peering littlenesses,
> In that fierce light which beats upon a throne
> And blackens every blot: for where is he,
> Who dares foreshadow for an only son
> A lovelier life, a more unstain'd than his?'

The Prince's reputation.

The memorials and statues that sprang up in profusion over the land served to illumine the gloom that encircled her, and in course of years she found in the task of supervising the compilation of his biography a potent mitigation of her grief. Public opinion proved tractable, and ultimately she enjoyed the satisfaction of an almost universal acknowledgment that the Prince had worked zealously and honestly for the good of his adopted country.

Few parallels can be found in history to the length of time during which the actively vivid sense of loss clung to the Queen's heart. 'Here I and sorrows sit,' the words of the bereaved Constance in Shakespeare's play of 'King John,' fitted her lips not for a year but for a generation. No act of hers nor of her children's, however trivial, did she during that period dissociate from the Prince's memory.[1] Nothing that reminded her of him was ever disturbed—no room that he inhabited, scarcely a paper that he had handled. She never ceased to wear mourning for him; she long lived in seclusion, and took no part in Court festivities or ceremonial pageantry. The anniversary of the Prince's death was, until her own death, kept as a solemn day of rest and prayer, and the days of his birth, betrothal, and marriage were held in religious veneration. *Permanence of her grief.*

But, despite the poignancy of her sorrow, and the sense of isolation which thenceforth abode with her, her nerve was never wholly shattered. Naturally and freely as she gave vent to her grief, her woe did not degenerate into morbid wailing. One of its most lasting results was to sharpen her sense of sympathy, which had always been keen, with the distresses of others, especially with distresses resembling her own; no widow in the land, in what- *Queen's sympathy with others' distress.*

[1] Three years after her husband's death she was still signing her letters to her younger children 'your unhappy mama,' and never referred to their present experiences without adding a reminiscence of 'your darling papa.'

ever rank of life, had henceforth a more tender sympathiser than the Queen.[1]

Queen's movements after bereavement.

At the time of the Prince's death, her daughter Alice and her stepsister the Princess Hohenlohe were with the Queen at Windsor, and all the comfort that kindred could offer they gave her in full measure. Four days after the tragic event she drove with Princess Alice to the gardens at Frogmore, and chose a site for a mausoleum, where she and her husband might both be buried together. Her uncle Leopold, in letters forwarded in haste from Brussels, took control of her immediate action, and at his bidding she reluctantly removed to Osborne next day. In the course of December 20 she mechanically signed some papers of State. At midnight her brother-in-law, Duke Ernest, reached Osborne, and, dissolved in tears, she at once met him on the staircase. On December 23, in all the panoply of state, the Prince's remains were temporarily laid to rest in St. George's Chapel, Windsor. The Prince of Wales represented her as chief mourner. Early in January her uncle Leopold came to Osborne to console and counsel her.

Her ministers' reproof.

During the following weeks the Princess Alice and Sir Charles Phipps, keeper of her privy purse, acted as intermediaries between her and her ministers, but before the end of the first month of bereavement her ministers reminded her that she was bound to

---

[1] As early as January 10, 1862, twenty-seven days after the Prince's death, she sent a touching message of sympathy with a gift of 200*l.* to the widows of the victims of a great colliery explosion in Northumberland.

communicate with them directly. Palmerston at the moment was disabled by gout, and the cabinet was under the somewhat severe and pedantic control of Lord John Russell. The reproof awoke the Queen to a sense of her position.

Gradually she controlled her anguish, and deliberately resigned herself to her fate. She had lost half her existence. Nothing hereafter could be to her what it had once been. No child could fill the place that was vacant. But she did not seek to ease herself of her burden. She steeled herself to bear it alone. Hitherto the Prince, she said, had thought for her. Now she would think for herself. His example was to be her guide. The minute care that he had bestowed with her on affairs of State she would bestow. Her decisions would be those that she believed he would have taken. She would seek every advantage that she could derive from the memory of his counsel.[1]

Her resolves for the future.

Now that the grave had closed over the Queen's sole companion and oracle of one-and-twenty years, she felt that a new reign had begun, and must in

The Prince's lasting influence on her.

[1] Most of the expressions employed in this and earlier paragraphs of this chapter are drawn from letters of the Queen sent to friends soon after the Prince's death, or from records of her early interviews with them. There is a remarkable unanimity as to the simple sincerity with which she spoke of her sorrow, her self-possession, and the earnestness with which she faced her future responsibilities. Cf. Clark and Hughes, *Life of Adam Sedgwick*, ii. 382; Morley, *Life of Gladstone*, ii. 89, 90. Of her absolute reliance on the Prince's opinions in the years that followed, Gladstone wrote to his wife while in attendance on the Queen at Balmoral, September 28, 1864: 'Whenever she quotes an opinion of the Prince, she looks upon the question as completely shut up by it for herself and all the world.' Morley, *Life of Gladstone*, ii. 105.

outward aspect—in perpetual signs of mourning and in suppression of ceremonial pomp—be distinguished from the reign that had closed. But the lessons that the Prince had taught the Queen left so deep an impression on her, she clung so tenaciously to his spirit, that her attitude to the business of State and her action in it during the forty years that followed his death bore little outward sign of change from the days when he was perpetually at her side.

XXVIII

FIRST ANXIETIES OF WIDOWHOOD

In the 'two dreadful first years of loneliness' that followed the Prince's death the Queen lived in complete seclusion, dining often by herself or with her half-sister, and seeing for any length of time only members of her own family. But her widowhood rendered her more dependent than before on her personal attendants, and her intimacy with them grew greater. **Her personal attendants in her widowhood.**

Of the female members of her household on whose support she rested, the chief was Lady Augusta Bruce. On Lady Augusta's marriage to Dean Stanley on December 23, 1863, congenial successors to her were found in Jane Marchioness of Ely, who had been a lady of the bedchamber since 1857, and filled that office till April 30, 1889, and in Jane Lady Churchill, who was a lady of the bedchamber from July 4, 1854. Till her sudden death on Christmas day 1900—less than a month before the Queen herself died—Lady Churchill remained in constant attendance on her. **Friends in her household.**

Even from the lower ranks of her household she welcomed sympathy and proofs of personal attachment. She found Scotsmen and Scotswomen of all classes, but especially of the humbler, readier in the **Scottish sympathisers.**

expression of kindly feeling than Englishmen and Englishwomen. When she paid, in May 1862, the first painful visit of her widowhood to Balmoral, her reception was a real solace to her. Her Scottish chaplain, Dr. Norman Macleod, gave her, she said, more real consolation than any clergyman of the south.

John Brown.

The Queen consequently found a satisfaction in employing Scots men and women in her domestic service. John Brown, a son of a farmer on her highland estate, had been an outdoor servant or gillie at Balmoral since 1849, and had won the regard of the Prince and herself. She soon made him a personal retainer, to be in constant attendance upon her in all the migrations of the Court. He was of rugged exterior and uncourtly manners, but she believed in his devotion to her and in his strong common sense, and she willingly pardoned in him the familiarity of speech and manner which old servants are in the habit of acquiring. She came to regard him as one of her trustiest friends.[1]

The Queen's private secretaries.

In official business the Queen derived invaluable assistance in the early years of her widowhood from those who were filling more dignified positions in her

[1] The Queen wrote of him in 1866, in her *Journal of the Highlands*, p. 93, *note*: 'His attention, care, and faithfulness cannot be exceeded; and the state of my health, which of late years has been sorely tried and weakened, renders such qualifications most valuable, and indeed most needful in a constant attendant upon all occasions. . . . He has all the independence and elevated feeling peculiar to the Highland race, and is singularly straightforward, simple-minded, kind-hearted, and disinterested; always ready to oblige; and of a discretion rarely to be met with. He is now in his fortieth year.' Archibald, a brother of John Brown, was valet to the Queen's youngest son, Prince Leopold.

household. The old objections to the appointment of a private secretary to the Queen, now that the Prince who had acted in that capacity was no more, were not revived, and it was at once conferred without debate on General the Hon. Charles Grey, a younger son of the second Earl Grey, who had been since 1846 private secretary to the Prince, and whose sister, Lady Caroline Barrington, was since 1851 the governess of the royal children. Some differences of opinion were held outside Court circles as to his tact and judgment, but until his death in 1870 his devotion to his work relieved the Queen of much pressing anxiety. 'In many, many ways he was most valuable to the Queen,' she wrote, 'and a very devoted, zealous, and very able adviser and friend.'

The Queen also reposed full confidence in Sir Charles Phipps, Keeper of the Privy Purse, who died in 1866, and in Sir Thomas Biddulph, who was Master of her Household from 1851, and after 1867 sole Keeper of the Privy Purse until his death in 1878. No three men could have served her more single-mindedly than Grey, Phipps, and Biddulph. She was especially fortunate, too, in General Sir Henry Ponsonby, Grey's successor as private secretary, who had been equerry to the Prince Consort, and had been brought within the sphere of influence which the Queen deemed the best inspiration for her advisers. Like Grey, he was personally of Liberal politics, but he treated party questions officially with great width of view. Sir Henry remained her secretary for the long period of a quarter of a century— April 8, 1870, to May 1895, when he was succeeded

Grey, Phipps, and Biddulph.

by her last private secretary, Colonel Sir Arthur Bigge.

Dean Wellesley.

Outside her household she derived much benefit from the counsel of Gerald Wellesley, son of Lord Cowley, and nephew of the Duke of Wellington, who had been her domestic chaplain since 1849, and was Dean of Windsor from 1854 until his death in 1882. She was often in consultation with him, particularly in regard to the Church appointments which her ministers suggested to her, and in Mr. Gladstone's view his unvarying prudence was of inestimable value alike to the Crown and the Church. Sir Arthur Helps, who had become Clerk of the Council in 1860, and was an author of repute, was also much in her confidence, and aided and advised her in her private and personal affairs until his death in 1875.

Public business, January 1862.

Public business, in accordance with her resolve, occupied her almost as soon as her husband was buried. On January 9, 1862, she received the welcome news that the authorities at Washington had solved the difficulty of the 'Trent' by acceding to the requests of the English Government. She reminded Lord Palmerston that 'this peaceful issue of the American quarrel was greatly owing to her beloved Prince,' and Palmerston considerately replied that the alterations in the despatch were only one of innumerable instances 'of the tact and judgment and the power of nice discrimination which excited Lord Palmerston's constant and unbounded admiration.' A day or two later she assented to Palmerston's proposal to confer the Garter on Lord Russell, though she would not hear of a chapter of the Order being

FIRST ANXIETIES OF WIDOWHOOD

held, and insisted, contrary to precedent, on conferring the distinction by warrant. On January 11 she presided over a meeting of her Privy Council, and a month later (February 10) she formally instituted the 'Royal Order of Victoria and Albert'—a commemorative decoration to be conferred on ladies of her family and household.

In one direction only did the Queen relieve herself of any of her official work on the Prince's death. It had been her custom to sign (in three places) every commission issued to officers in all branches of the military service, but she had fallen into arrears with the labour of late years, and 16,000 documents now awaited her signature. In March 1862 a Bill was introduced into Parliament enabling commissions to be issued without bearing her autograph, though her right of signing was reserved in case she wished to resume the practice—and this she subsequently did. *Her signature to officers' commissions.*

Two plans of domestic interest which the Prince had initiated she at once carried to completion. It had been arranged that the Prince of Wales should make a tour to the Holy Land with Dr. Arthur Penrhyn Stanley, the late Prince's chaplain. In January 1862 the Queen finally settled the tour with Stanley, who visited her at Osborne for the purpose, and from February 6 till June 14 her eldest son was absent from her on the expedition. There was some inevitable delay, too, in the solemnisation of the marriage of Princess Alice, but it was quietly celebrated at Osborne on July 1. The Queen was present in deep mourning. Her brother-in-law, the Duke of Saxe-Coburg, gave the Princess away. The Queen felt *Prince of Wales in the Holy Land.* *Princess Alice's marriage.*

acutely the separation from the daughter who had chiefly stood by her in her recent trial.

Memorial to the Prince at Balmoral.

During the autumn visit to Balmoral (August 21, 1862) the Queen began that long series of memorials to her dead husband which she encouraged almost to her own death. She laid near Balmoral Castle the foundations of a cairn 'to the beloved memory of Albert the Great and Good, Prince Consort, raised by his broken-hearted widow.' She and the six children who were with her placed on it stones on which their initials were to be carved.

Betrothal of Prince of Wales.

Despite her grief, the Queen directed with eager interest the fortunes of her children. Next month (September 1862) negotiations were in progress for the betrothal of the Prince of Wales, the heir to the throne. His choice had fallen on Princess Alexandra, daughter of Prince Christian of Schleswig-Holstein-Sonderburg-Glucksburg, the next heir to the throne of Denmark, to which he ascended shortly afterwards, on November 15, 1863, as King Christian IX. The Princess's mother, Princess Louise of Hesse-Cassel, was niece of Christian VIII. of Denmark, and sole heiress of the old Danish royal family. Princess Alexandra was thus already a distant connection of the Queen by marriage, for the Queen's aunt, the old Duchess of Cambridge, a member of the princely house of Hesse-Cassel, was also aunt of the Princess's father. The Queen readily assented to the match, and the Princess was her guest at Osborne in November. Her grace and beauty fascinated from the first the Queen as well as the people of England. The Princess's connection with Denmark did not recommend the alliance to the Prussian Government, which anticipated complications with its little northern neighbour, but the betrothal had little political significance or influence, and was universally welcomed in England.

More perplexing was the consideration which it was needful for the Queen to devote in December 1862 to a question affecting the future of her second son, Alfred, who, under the Prince Consort's careful supervision, had been educated for the navy. A sudden offer came to him from the extreme end of Europe. The popular assembly of the kingdom of Greece had driven their King, Otho, a scion of the royal house of Bavaria, from the throne, and they abruptly resolved to confer the vacant crown on Prince Alfred, as a representative of the country which had helped to restore to Greece her independence in 1828. The Queen at first regarded the proposal with unconcealed favour, but her ministers declared its acceptance to be impracticable and to be contrary to the country's treaty obligations with the Powers. *[The throne of Greece.]*

Unhappily for the Queen's peace of mind, the ministers' rejection of the invitation to her second son, in which she soon acquiesced, did not relieve her of further debate on the subject. A substitute for Alfred as a candidate for the Greek throne was suggested in the person of her brother-in-law, Duke Ernest of Saxe-Coburg. He at once came to England to take the Queen's advice, and his conduct greatly harassed her. The Duke had no children, and his throne of Saxe-Coburg would naturally devolve, should he die childless, on his only brother's eldest son, the *[Duke Ernest and the Greek throne.]*

Prince of Wales; but it had already been agreed that, in view of the Prince of Wales's heirship to the English throne, he should transfer to his next brother Alfred his claim to the German duchy. Duke Ernest was quite willing to ascend the Greek throne, but made it a condition that he should be at liberty to retain for an indefinite period after his accession to it his ducal position in Coburg.

His appeal to the Queen.
Such a condition was treated as impossible of acceptance, alike by English ministers and by Greek leaders, but the Duke obstinately urged the Queen to forward his impracticable scheme. From the first she summarily rejected it. It had nothing to recommend it in her eyes. For the Duke to abandon Coburg meant its immediate assignment to Prince Alfred. That event was congenial to the Queen, who was deeply attached to the principality, and was always solicitous of the future fortunes of her younger children. But Duke Ernest was not easily silenced. He querulously complained that his sister-in-law's attitude was ambiguous; she was insufficiently considerate of his interests. Their uncle, King Leopold, added to her perplexities by coming to Duke Ernest's support. The King was also indisposed to sanction the premature transference of the Saxe-Coburg-Gotha duchies to the third generation of the family.

Her replies.
The Queen was embarrassed and displeased. She endeavoured to soothe her brother-in-law with civil phrases, but she resented his querulous pertinacity. On January 29, 1863, she begged him to spare her further reproaches. 'What I can do to remove difficulties, without prejudicing the rights of our children

and the welfare of the beloved little country, you may rely upon. You are sure of my sisterly love, as well as my immense love for Coburg and the whole country. . . . I am not at all well, and this whole Greek matter has affected me fearfully. Much too much rests upon me, poor woman, standing alone as I do with so many children, and every day, every hour, I feel more and more the horrible void that is ever growing greater and more fearful.'[1]

Finally, the Duke realised that the union of Coburg and Greece under a single ruler was impossible of attainment, and his candidature for the Greek throne was withdrawn. He made the Queen what reparation he could for the trouble he had caused her. He admitted that he was wrong in questioning her solicitude for the welfare of his small country, and declared himself reconciled to the ultimate succession of Prince Alfred to his throne. The Greek crown was thereupon placed by England, in concert with the Powers, on the head of George, brother of the Princess Alexandra, who was the affianced bride of the Prince of Wales. The settlement freed the Queen from the worry of family bickerings, and Greece was well contented with her new sovereign.

Prince George of Denmark, King of Greece, March 30, 1863.

Through all ranks of the nation the marriage of the Queen's eldest son, the heir to the throne, aroused abundant enthusiasm. At the Queen's request Parliament readily granted an annuity of 40,000*l.* for the Prince, which, added to the revenues of the Duchy of Cornwall, brought his income to over 100,000*l.* a year, while his bride was assigned an immediate

Marriage of the Prince of Wales, March 10, 1863.

[1] Duke Ernest, iv. 99–100.

annuity of 10,000*l*. and a prospective one of 30,000*l*. in case of widowhood. In accordance with the marriage treaty, which was signed at Copenhagen on January 15, 1863, the marriage took place on March 10, 1863, at St. George's Chapel, Windsor. The Queen played no part in the ceremony, but witnessed it from a gallery overlooking the chancel. The sadness of her situation impressed so unsentimental a spectator as Lord Palmerston, who shed tears as he gazed on her.

Hopes of her reappearance in public life.

The Queen's protracted withdrawal from public life was beginning to excite censure among the people. This trend of public feeling was well within her knowledge, but she had no intention of conciliating it. There was an anticipation that she would make her son's wedding the occasion of ending the period of gloomy seclusion in which she had chosen to encircle the Court. But the hope was very imperfectly realised. After the Prince's marriage the Court resumed something of its old routine; state balls and concerts were revived to a small extent, but the Queen disappointed expectation by refusing to attend Court entertainments herself. She entrusted her place in them to her eldest son and his bride, and to others of her children.

XXIX

THE QUEEN AND PRUSSIA

BUT while ignoring the pleasures of the Court, the Queen did not relax her devotion to the business of State. Her main energy was applied to foreign politics. While anxious that the prestige of England should be maintained abroad, she was desirous to keep the peace, and to impress other sovereigns with her pacific example. Her dislike of war in Europe was fostered to a growing extent by family considerations—by her concern for the interests of her married daughters at Berlin and Darmstadt, and in a smaller degree for those of her ungrateful brother-in-law at Coburg. The fortunes of all, and especially those of the Crown Princess of Prussia, seemed to her to be involved in every menace of the tranquillity of Europe. Into the precise merits of the difficulties which arose among the nations she did not enter with quite the same fulness as her husband. But the safety of existing dynasties was a principle that had appealed to him, and by that she stood firm. *Her views of foreign policy in 1863.*

Consequently, the points of view from which the Queen and her ministers, Lord Palmerston and Lord John Russell, approached the foreign questions that engrossed the attention of Europe from 1863 to 1866 *Disagreements with ministers.*

were invariably divergent. She made no endeavour to study her ministers' idiosyncrasies or make allowance for their personal convictions. She pressed her own counsel on them with unfailing pertinacity, and was often heard with ill-concealed impatience. Constantly she had to acquiesce, however unwillingly, in the rejection of her advice. Nevertheless, she largely fulfilled her purpose of keeping her country free from such European complications as were likely to issue in war. And though she was unable to give effective political aid to her German relatives, she was often successful in checking the activity of her ministers' or of her people's sympathies with their enemies.

The Polish insurrection.

The different mental attitudes in which the Queen and her ministers stood to current foreign events are well illustrated by the sentiments which the Polish insurrection excited in them respectively in 1863. Palmerston and his colleague, Lord John, sympathised with the efforts of Poland to release itself from the grip of Russia, and their abhorrence of the persecution of a small race by a great reflected popular English feeling. The Queen's views of the situation altogether ignored the grievances of the Poles. In 1859 she had taunted Lord John Russell with the distrust that was inspired in her and her Government at foreign Courts by the favour which the Liberal press bestowed on Polish insubordination. She now tacitly identified herself with the oppressors of Poland. The Grand Duke Constantine, who was Governor-General of Poland when the insurrection broke out, had been her guest after the Crimean war. His life was menaced by the Polish rebels, and his modes of tyranny, however repugnant in other circumstances, became in her sight inevitable weapons of self-defence. The question had, moreover, driven France and Prussia into opposite camps. France, affecting horror at Russia's cruelty, invited English co-operation in opposing her. The Queen sternly warned her Government against any manner of interference. Prussia, where Bismarck now ruled, declared that the Poles were meeting their deserts. Maternal duty prompted the Queen to endorse the view of Prussia, her eldest daughter's adopted country and future dominion.

Early in the autumn of 1863 the Queen visited Germany and examined the foreign situation for herself at close quarters. The main object of her tour was to revive her memories of the scenes of her late husband's youth. After staying a night with her uncle Leopold at the summer palace of Laeken, she proceeded to Rosenau, Prince Albert's birthplace, and thence passed on to Coburg. The recent death (on July 9, 1863) of her husband's constant counsellor, Stockmar, at Coburg, intensified the depression in which public and private anxieties involved her, but she took pleasure in the society of the Crown Prince and Princess, who joined her at Rosenau. *Visit Coburg*

The political prospects of the Prince and Princess, however, filled her with fresh alarms. The sovereigns of Germany were meeting at Frankfort to consider a reform of the confederation of the German States. For reasons that were to appear later, Prussia declined to join the meeting, and Austria assumed the leading *Depressed prospects of the Crown Prince.*

place in the conference. It looked probable that an empire of Germany would come into being under the headship of the Emperor of Austria, that Prussia would be excluded from it, and would be ruined by its helpless isolation. The jealousy with which not only Austria, but the smaller German States, regarded Prussia seemed to the Queen to render imminent its decay and fall.

Queen's despair of Prussia.

Maternal instincts spurred her to exert all her personal influence in Germany to set the future of Prussia and her daughter's fortunes on a securer basis. Her brother-in-law, Duke Ernest, was attending the German Diet of Sovereigns at Frankfort. From Rosenau she addressed to him constant appeals to help to protect Prussia from the disasters with which the Frankfort meeting threatened it. On August 29, after drawing a dismal picture of Prussia's rapid decline, she wrote: 'All the more would I beg you, as much as lies in your power, to prevent a weakening of Prussia, which not only my own feeling resists—on account of the future of our children— but which would surely also be contrary to the interest of Germany; and I know that our dear angel Albert always regarded a strong Prussia as a necessity, for which therefore it is a sacred duty for me to work.'

Visit of King of Prussia.

Two days later, on August 31, the King of Prussia, at her request, paid her a visit at Coburg. Bismarck, who had a year before assumed control of the policy of Prussia, and understood the situation better than the Queen, was in his master's retinue. He was not present at the interview, and, by cynically hinting to King William that the ulterior motive of the Queen's intrigue was to make the interests of England predominant in Germany, did what was necessary to render her negotiation abortive. The King's tone was kindly, but he failed to reassure the Queen. He civilly deprecated her interference. She thought he failed to realise his country's and his family's danger.

But the King of Prussia's apparent pusillanimity did not check the Queen's energies. A personal explanation with the ruler from whom Prussia had, in her view, everything to fear, became in her mind essential. Early in September Francis Joseph, the Emperor of Austria, was returning to Vienna from the Diet at Frankfort. She invited him to visit her on the way at the castle of Coburg. On September 3 he arrived there. It was her first meeting with him. She had been interested in him since his accession to the throne in the eventful year 1848. Ten years later, in August 1858, he had sent to her when at Babelsberg a letter regretting his inability to make her personal acquaintance while she was in the neighbourhood of his dominions; and when his son and heir was born a day or two later, on August 22, 1858, she at once wrote a cordial note of congratulation. She had sympathised with him in the indignities which the Emperor of the French had put on him by aiding Sardinia to deprive him of his territory in North Italy.

Interview with the Emperor of Austria.

The Queen met the Emperor of Austria in an earnest spirit, and her interview with him lasted three hours. Only Duke Ernest was present with them. The Queen prudently deprecated the notion

The Queen's earnest appeal to him.

that she desired to enter in detail into political questions, but her maternal anxiety for her children at Berlin impelled her, she said, to leave no stone unturned to stave off the dangers that threatened Prussia. She knew how greatly Prussia would benefit if she won a sympathetic hearing from the Emperor. He heard her respectfully, but committed himself to nothing, and the interview left the situation unchanged.[1] It had as little effect as her conversation with the King of Prussia. But the interest of the episode cannot be measured by its material result. It is a signal proof of the Queen's courageous will and passionate devotion to her family.

At Darmstadt and Balmoral.

Soon after parting with the Emperor Francis Joseph, the Queen set her face homewards, only pausing at Darmstadt to see her daughter Alice under her own roof. Arrived in England, she paid her customary autumn visit to Balmoral, and spent some days in September with her friends the Duke and Duchess of Athol at Blair Athol.

Prince Consort's statue unveiled at Aberdeen, Oct. 13, 1863.

The second year of her widowhood was ending, and she had relaxed none of the strict etiquette of mourning. But before the two years reached their final close she temporarily issued from her seclusion in order to unveil publicly at Aberdeen, on October 13, 1863, a bronze statue of the Prince Consort. It was designed at the expense of the city and county by Baron Marochetti, an Italian sculptor high in the Queen's favour, who had been patronised by Louis Philippe, and had fled from France to England on his patron's fall. In reply to the address from the subscribers the Queen

[1] Duke Ernest, *Memoirs*, iv. 134.

declared through Sir George Grey, the Home Secretary, that she had come 'to proclaim in public the unbounded reverence and admiration, the devoted love that fills my heart for him whose loss must throw a lasting gloom over all my future life.' The occasion was one of severe and painful trial to her; but it proved the first of numerous occasions on which she presided over a like ceremony. The warmth with which she welcomed the multiplication of statues of the late Prince was such that by degrees, as Gladstone said, they 'covered the land.'

XXX

THE SCHLESWIG-HOLSTEIN QUESTION

The Schleswig-Holstein question.

Before the end of the year 1863 there broke out in Central Europe the struggle which had long been threatened by the conflicting claims of Germany and Denmark to the duchies of Schleswig-Holstein. English ministers and the Queen had always kept the question well in view, and knew that at some time or other it would call for the arbitrament of the sword. In 1852 a conference in London of representatives of the various parties had arranged, under the English Government's guidance, a compromise, whereby the relation of the duchies to Germany and Denmark was so defined as to preserve peace for eleven years. The Danes held them under German supervision. But in the course of 1863 Frederick VII. of Denmark asserted new and independent claims on the disputed territory. Although he died just before he gave effect to his intentions, his successor, the Princess of Wales's father, Christian IX., fully accepted his policy.

Opinion in Germany.

Opinion in Germany, while at one in its hostility to Denmark, and in its deliberate resolve henceforth to exclude her from the duchies, ran in two sharply divided currents in regard to their future status and relation to Germany. One German party was desirous that the duchies should form an independent State of the German Confederation; another party was resolved to absorb them altogether in existing German States.

In 1852 Denmark had bought off a German claimant to the duchies in the person of Duke Christian of Schleswig-Holstein-Sonderburg-Augustenburg, but his son Duke Frederick declined to be bound by the bargain, and had, also in 1863, reasserted an alleged hereditary right to the territory, with the enthusiastic concurrence of the smaller German States, who were congenitally jealous of the Prussian kingdom, and of a minority in Prussia, mainly formed of Liberal politicians who were resenting Bismarck's high-handed and illiberal methods of rule. Duke Frederick's claim was sincerely believed by its champions to rest on right and justice. *Duke Frederick's claim.*

Before the end of 1863 an abortive endeavour was made by those who urged the formation of the duchies into an independent unit of the German Confederation, to give effect to their views by force. Two of Duke Frederick's adherents, the Kings of Saxony and Hanover, actually sent troops to drive the Danes from Kiel, the chief city of Holstein, in December 1863, and to put him in possession. But the attempt failed and the situation was not appreciably affected. *Efforts of Duke Frederick's allies.*

The Government of Prussia was hostile to Duke Frederick's pretensions, and was proposing to settle the Schleswig-Holstein problem in its own fashion. Anticipating embarrassments from co-operation with the small German States, most of which cherished aims antagonistic to its own, it took the matter entirely out of their hands. The King of Prussia induced the Emperor of Austria to join him exclusively *Intentions of Prussia.*

in expelling the Danes from the two duchies. It was agreed at the same time that the two Powers, having overcome the Danes, should hold the territories jointly until some final arrangement was reached.

The Queen's divided interests.

There were thus three parties to the Schleswig-Holstein dispute—the King of Denmark, Duke Frederick of Augustenburg with his German champions, and the rulers of Prussia and Austria. With all of these Queen Victoria had more or less close personal relations. Two of the three litigants, the King of Denmark and Duke Frederick, each clamoured for her support and begged without concealment for the intervention of English arms.

Her sympathy with Germany.

The Queen, who narrowly watched the progress of events, and surprised ministers at home and envoys from abroad by the minuteness and accuracy of her knowledge, was gravely disturbed. Her sympathies were naturally German and anti-Danish; the Prince Consort had not recognised the justice of the Danish pretension; but between the two sections of German opinion she hesitated. Family considerations gave each a claim to her active sympathy. Duke Frederick of Augustenburg was the husband of the daughter of her half-sister Féodore; she had entertained him at Windsor and regarded him with affection. The Crown Prince of Prussia was his close friend, and his cause was also espoused by the Queen's daughter Alice and her husband, Prince Louis of Hesse, as well as by her brother-in-law, Duke Ernest of Saxe-Coburg, who was loud in his appeals to the Queen to declare herself on Duke Frederick's side. But while regarding with benevolence and sympathy the pretensions of Duke Frederick of Augustenburg, and pitying the misfortunes of his family, she could not repress the thought that the policy of Prussia, although hostile to Duke Frederick's interests, was calculated, if successful, to increase materially that kingdom's strength and prestige, the promotion of which was for her 'a sacred duty.'

Nor was England at liberty to ignore the arrangements made at the conference of London in 1852, when the claim of Duke Frederick's father to the duchies had been abrogated with his assent. 'You seem quite to overlook the fact,' she wrote to Duke Ernest on January 8, 1864, 'that England is bound by the treaty of 1852, and, greatly as I may deplore the manner in which the treaty was concluded, the Government here has *no other choice* but to adhere to it. Our beloved Albert *could not* have acted otherwise.'

England's treaty obligations.

There were other grounds which impelled her to restrain her impulse to identify herself completely with any one party to the strife. Radical divergences of opinion were alive in her own domestic circle. The Princess of Wales, the daughter of the King of Denmark, naturally felt acutely her father's position, and when, in December 1863, she and her husband were fellow-guests at Windsor with the Crown Prince and Princess of Prussia, who were the friends of Duke Frederick, the Queen treated Schleswig-Holstein as a forbidden subject at her table. To her ministers and to the mass of her subjects, moreover, the cause of Denmark made a strong appeal. The threats of Prussia and Austria against a small power like Denmark seemed to them another instance of brutal oppression of the weak by the strong, far worse than

Differences in her family circle.

Russia's oppression of Poland, or Austria's oppression of Hungary. Duke Frederick's position was deemed futile. The popularity of the Princess of Wales, the King of Denmark's daughter, tended to strengthen the prevailing popular sentiment in favour of the Danes.

Queen's efforts for peace.

In view of interests and opinions so widely divided, the Queen hoped against hope that peace might be preserved. To that end she directed all her energies. In private letters to German friends and relations she frankly denounced as 'rash and precipitate' the action of the small German States—even that of Saxe-Coburg-Gotha—in identifying themselves past recall with Duke Frederick's cause. She declared that they were setting Germany on the road to 'revolution and civil war.' 'Every one must show a disposition to be conciliatory,' she told the querulous Duke Ernest. At any rate she was resolved that England should not directly engage in the strife. If the conflict could not be restrained altogether, she wished to see it restricted to the narrowest possible limits of time and space.

Ministry's support of Denmark.

It was therefore with deep indignation that she learned that active interference in behalf of Denmark was contemplated by her cabinet. Napoleon III. was sounded as to whether he would lend his aid, but he had grown estranged from Palmerston, and answered coldly. The ministers' ardour in behalf of Denmark was not diminished by this rebuff. But the Queen's repugnance to their Danish feeling was strengthened. She made no endeavour to conceal her German sympathies, although they became, to her regret, the subject of reproachful comment in the press. To be attacked on account of her German sympathies, she wrote to Duke Ernest, was all that was needed to make her sad position unbearable. But her unconquerable frankness was responsible for the public censure. Theodor von Bernhardi, the Prussian historian and diplomatist, had an interview with her at Osborne on January 8, 1864. She openly deplored the strength of the Danish party in England, which had won, she said, the leading journalistic organs. She thought that Germany might exert more influence in the same direction. She was dissatisfied, she added, with the position of the Crown Prince, and lamented the depressed condition of the Liberal party in Prussia.[1]

[1] The writer's full account of the interview is of interest. It runs as follows:—

'I found the Queen very cheerful—one might almost say happy—and she welcomed me in the most friendly manner.

'She spoke German—the language of the royal family when alone—and told me that she knew me by name and reputation; the Prince Consort, "who to my desolation is no more," had often spoken of me, and always with great approbation; he had read to her many passages from my works.

'Then she turned the conversation on to the Prince's brother, the Duke of Coburg; asked in what humour and state of mind I had left him, and soon let it be clearly seen that she gave the conversation this turn, and dwelt on it, in order to show me that she thought little of the Duke, that he could achieve nothing with her, that she attached no sort of importance to his advice or views. With womanly wit and womanly penetration she made unsparing merriment over the Duke, his variable quixotic disposition.

'It was so managed as to convey to me that if I wished to keep my post I must take care not to be identified with good Duke Ernest; I must show that I in no way belonged to his party, and knew perfectly well how to estimate him.

'The Queen then asked with interest after Duke Friedrich von Augustenburg, and regretted that public opinion—the prevailing opinion in England—was so decidedly for Denmark and against

Her rejection of Duke Frederick.

At the same time she gave a final and direct refusal to the urgent petitions of Duke Frederick's friends for material assistance or outward show of her

Germany. The Danish party had set itself for many years to win the leading organs of the daily press; in this they had succeeded and influenced public opinion. On the side of Germany that was unfortunately wanting. She thought that German effort should be directed to win weighty support in Parliament and in the press, and to enlighten the public and public opinion on the particular nature and importance of the German-Danish dispute. In short, she said enough to let it be recognised most definitely that she personally stood upon the side of Germany in this dispute, and, so far as she could, took part with Germany.

'I merely followed, allowed myself to be instructed, let it be recognised through a few remarks that I knew how to value the worth of the hint, and naturally made no attempt to go deeper into the subject, or to lead the conversation farther than the Queen wished. There was, indeed, no necessity; we did not need to win her.

'The Queen then spoke of the present disagreeable state of things in Prussia; of the unpleasant and difficult position of the Crown Prince. Under those conditions, under the dominion of the present system, the Crown Prince would naturally wish to hold aloof from the centre of government. His particular desire was to receive a military command in the provinces, that would permit him to settle in some place far from the capital; the general command in Breslau was, he considered, most suitable.

'Here I held it necessary to speak the truth. I said that the Crown Prince's position was undoubtedly a very difficult one, and there was a good deal to say for the provincial command which he desired. But there were also many things to be considered. The general situation might possibly become worse if he remained away for a long time from the centre of things and renounced all influence. The most intelligent of our Liberals, the personal friends of the Crown Prince, had already regretted that the Queen and the Prince had so long stayed away from Berlin; that all had kept away from whom the King might have heard something else than the views of the reactionary party.

'The Queen listened in kindly fashion and with interest to those remarks, and after some talk on trivial matters I was dismissed.'— Bernhardi, *Aus dem Leben*, 1895, pt. v. 276-81.

friendship. Within a few hours of her interview with Bernhardi she wrote to her brother-in-law at Coburg that she had come to see with her Government that Duke Frederick's claim was hopeless. She was resolved to work with her Government for peace alone. Her German relatives were aggravating her difficulties by circulating reports of her differences with her Government. 'The sad tension'—between Germany and England—'which is really to nobody's advantage'—could only be reduced by tactful reticence and moderate courses on all sides.

None the less her ministers' words and acts remained, in their defiance of Germany, hardly more consonant with her own views than the German Princes' tactless outcry. When her ministers introduced, at the opening of Parliament (February 4, 1864), expressions into the Queen's speech which she regarded as committing England to active interference on behalf of Denmark, she insisted on their removal. She substituted for their ambiguous menaces of Germany the following colourless paragraph: 'Her Majesty has been unremitting in her endeavours to bring about a peaceful settlement of the differences which have arisen between Germany and Denmark, and to ward off the dangers which might follow from a beginning of warfare in the north of Europe, and her Majesty will continue her efforts in the interest of peace.' *The Queen's declaration to Parliament.*

A more critical stage in the eventful history of the duchies was reached a few weeks later, when hostilities actually broke out between Austria and Prussia on the one hand, and Denmark on the *The London conference.*

other. German troops invaded the disputed territories. Although the Danes fought bravely, they were soon defeated, and the English Government, with the assent of the Queen, urged on the belligerents not merely an armistice, but a conference in London, so that an accommodation might be reached and the war abridged. The conference met on April 20. The Queen saw many of the envoys, and talked to them with freedom. She energetically recommended mutual concessions. But it was soon seen that the conference would prove abortive. In May it broke up without arriving at any decision.

<small>Queen's zeal for neutrality.</small>

To the Queen's annoyance, before the conference dissolved, the leading members of her Government championed with new vehemence the cause of the Danes, and warlike operations in their behalf were again openly threatened. Palmerston told the Austrian Ambassador, Count Apponyi, that if the Austrian fleet went to the Baltic it would meet the British fleet there. The Queen, through Lord Granville, expressed grave dissatisfaction with the threat, and roused herself to greater efforts. As on a former occasion while Palmerston was Prime Minister, she appealed to the cabinet to aid her against the Prime Minister. She invited, too, in the service of peace, the private support of the leader of the Opposition, Lord Derby. She hinted that, if Parliament did not adopt a pacific and neutral policy, she would have resort to a dissolution, and let the country decide between her and her ministry.

<small>Her tactful correspondence.</small>

In the Queen's foreign correspondence, as the situation developed, she grew more and more scrupulous. Her German relatives continued to complain to her of the encouragement that her ministers and subjects were giving the Danes. She deprecated the notion that she had it in her power to take any course to which her Government was adverse.

The war in Schleswig-Holstein was resumed in June with triumphant results to the German allies, who quickly routed the Danes and occupied the whole of the disputed duchies. Throughout these further operations England maintained the strictest neutrality, despite the occasional threats of public speakers. The credit of upholding in England a neutral policy was laid with justice, in diplomatic circles, at the Queen's door. Gladstone wrote privately from Balmoral early in 1864 that it was 'just' for her to take 'credit to herself for having influenced beneficially the course of policy and of affairs in the late controversy.' Her 'extraordinary integrity of mind' had, it seemed to him, overborne 'all prepossessions and longings, strong as they are, on the German side,' and had enabled her 'spontaneously to hold the balance tolerably even.'[1]

The Queen's triumph

Much of this agitation waged round the Princess

[1] Morley, *Life of Gladstone*, ii. 104, 105, 192. Cf. Duke Ernest's *Memoirs*; Count von Beust's *Memoirs*; Count Vitzthum von Eckstädt's *Memoirs*. The Queen's ministry, although it abstained from active interference, never affected acquiescence in the result of the struggle. At the close of the war, when the Prussian Government formally announced to the English Government the joint occupation of Schleswig-Holstein, and attempted to justify its action, Lord Russell informed Bismarck that the war was an act of unjust aggression and perfectly needless, and that the British Government lamented the advantages that Austria and Prussia had gained by their success in hostilities. He urged that the people of the disputed duchies should still be allowed to choose their own ruler and enjoy 'free constitutional institutions.' Cf. *Politische Briefe von Bismarcks*, 1849–89, iii. 144–9.

Birth of Prince of Wales's son.

of Wales, and while it was at its height a new interest was aroused in her. On January 8, 1864, she became, at Frogmore, the mother of a son (Albert Victor), who was in the direct line of succession to the throne. The happy event gave the Queen, in the heat of the political anxiety, immense gratification. It was soon followed by her first public appearance in London since her bereavement. On March 30 she attended a flower show at the Horticultural Gardens in London. She also permitted her birthday on May 24 to be celebrated for the first time since her widowhood with state formalities.

Garibaldi's visit.

Unhappily, from her point of view, public attention was absorbed during the same months by the visit to England of Garibaldi, the hero of the Italian war of emancipation, with which she was out of sympathy. The English people of all ranks welcomed the Italian general with a passionate enthusiasm which the Queen viewed with ill-concealed disdain. 'She felt half ashamed,' she said impatiently, 'of being the head of a nation capable of such follies.'

Unveiling of Prince Consort's statue at Perth.

In the autumn Duke Ernest and his wife were her guests at Balmoral, and German politics continued to be warmly debated. But she mainly devoted her time in the North to well-earned recreation. She made, as of old, many excursions in the neighbourhood of her highland home. But her thoughts still reverted to the past. For the second time in Scotland she unveiled a statue of the Prince Consort, on this occasion at Perth; and on her return to Windsor she paid a private visit to her late husband's foundation of Wellington College.

XXXI

THE QUEEN'S SECLUSION

A HEAVY addition to her trials was now awaiting the Queen. A feeling was growing throughout the country that her seclusion was unduly prolonged, and was contrary to the nation's interest. Expressions of discontent were growing ominous. *Complaints of the Queen's seclusion.*

It was not within the knowledge of the majority of her subjects that she was performing the routine business of her station with all her ancient pertinacity, in spite of her withdrawal from public ceremonials. She had never failed to give public signs of interest in social and non-political questions affecting the people's welfare. On December 27, 1864, she, on her own responsibility, addressed a letter to the railway companies, calling their attention to the frequency of accidents, and to their responsibilities for the safety of their passengers.[1] In London, in March *Her interest in her subjects' welfare.*

---

[1] The letter contained the following passages:—

'It is not for her own safety that the Queen has wished to provide in thus calling the attention of the Company to the late disasters. Her Majesty is aware that when she travels extraordinary precautions are taken, but it is on account of her family, of those travelling upon her service, and of her people generally, that she expresses the hope that the same security may be insured for all as is so carefully provided for herself. . . . The Queen hopes it is unnecessary for her to recall to the recollection of the railway directors the heavy

1865, she visited the Consumption Hospital at Brompton. She watched with active interest all that passed, not merely on the continent of Europe, but in more distant parts of the globe. The assassination of President Lincoln on April 14 called forth all her sympathy, and she at once sent to the President's widow an autograph letter of condolence, which excited enthusiasm on both sides of the Atlantic, and did much to relieve the tension that English sympathy with the Southern Confederates had introduced into the relations of the Governments of London and Washington.

Her neglect of ceremonial duties.

But at the same time her neglect of the ceremonial functions of her office was patent, and it was held to diminish the dignity of Government. On three occasions she had failed to open Parliament in person. That ceremony most effectually brought into prominence the place of the Sovereign in the constitution; it was greatly valued by ministers, and had in the past been rarely omitted. William IV., who had excused his attendance at the opening of Parliament in 1837 on the ground of the illness of his sister, the Duchess of Gloucester, had been warned that his absence contravened a principle of the constitution; and Lord Melbourne, the Prime Minister, wrote to Lord John Russell that that was the first occasion in the history of the country on which a Sovereign had failed to present himself at the opening of Parliament, except in cases of personal illness or infirmity.[1]

responsibility which they have assumed since they succeeded in securing the monopoly of the means of travelling of almost the entire population of the country.'

[1] Walpole's *Russell*, i. 275.

The Queen was known to be in the enjoyment of good health, and, despite her sorrow, had regained some of her native cheerfulness. Her absence from Parliament seemed to lack adequate justification. When, therefore, early in 1864 the rumour spread that she would resume her place on the throne at the opening of the new session, signs of popular satisfaction abounded. But she did not come, and the disappointment emphasised the popular discontent.

Radicals, who had no enthusiasm for the monarchical principle, began to argue that the cost of the crown was out of all proportion to its practical uses. The press almost unanimously declared her attitude to the public to be a breach of public duty. The Queen, although pained from the first by the outcry, had no intention of yielding to popular clamour. She frankly defied the criticism of her conduct. On April 1, 1864, the 'Times' newspaper in a leading article, after referring to a revived rumour 'that the Sovereign is about to break her protracted seclusion,' declared it to be futile on her part to attempt to exert 'an abiding influence on public affairs without appearing as a factor of them.' 'They who would isolate themselves from the world and its duties must cease to know and to care, as well as to act, and be content to let things take their course. This in effect they cannot do; this they never do; and the only result is a struggle in which they neither live nor die—neither live, as they wish, in the past, nor do their duty in the "working world."'

Vehement attacks.

On April 6, 1864, five days later, the Queen

The Queen's reply.

replied to the 'Times' newspaper by a peremptory denial of the current report that she 'is about to resume the place in society which she occupied before her great affliction; that is, that she is about again to hold levees and drawing-rooms in person, and to appear as before at Court balls, concerts, &c. This idea cannot be too explicitly contradicted.'

Explanation of her position.

'She would not shrink,' she boldly proceeded, 'from any personal sacrifice or exertion, however painful. But there are other and higher duties than those of mere representation which are now thrown upon the Queen, alone and unassisted—duties which she cannot neglect without injury to the public service, which weigh unceasingly upon her, overwhelming her with work and anxiety.' She had worked hard in the public service to the injury of her health and strength. The fatigue of mere state ceremonies, which could be equally well performed by other members of the royal family, she was unable to undergo. 'She would do what she could—in the manner least trying to her health, strength, and spirits—to meet the loyal wishes of her subjects; to afford that support and countenance to society, and to give that encouragement to trade which was desired of her. More the Queen could not do, and more the kindness and good feeling of her people would surely not exact of her.'

Severity of 'The Times.'

The Queen remained steadfast to her resolve, but public opinion was not diverted from the channel in which it had begun to flow, and throughout the year the tide of censure continued to rise. On the third anniversary (December 14, 1864) of the Prince Consort's death, the 'Times' newspaper renewed its attack.

'The living' (the Queen was reminded) 'have their claims as well as the dead; and what claims can be more imperative than those of a great nation, and the society of one of the first European capitals? . . . It is impossible for a recluse to occupy the British throne without a gradual weakening of that authority which the Sovereign has been accustomed to exert. . . . For the sake of the Crown as well as of the public we would, therefore, beseech her Majesty to return to the personal exercise of her exalted functions. It may be that in time London may accustom itself to do without the Palace, but it is not desirable that we should attain that point of Republican simplicity. For every reason we trust that now that three years have elapsed, and every honour that affection and gratitude could pay to the memory of the Prince Consort has been offered, her Majesty will think of her subjects' claims and the duties of her high station, and not postpone them longer to the indulgence of an unavailing grief.' On September 28, 1865, a cartoon in 'Punch' portrayed the Queen as the statue of Hermione in Shakespeare's 'Winter's Tale,' while Britannia figuring as Paulina was represented as addressing to her the words: ' 'Tis time; descend; be stone no more ' (v. iii. 99).

The violence and persistence of the denunciations brought with them a partial reaction; chivalrous defenders pointed to the natural womanly sentiment which explained if it did not justify the Queen's retirement. In the first number of the 'Pall Mall Gazette,' which appeared on February 7, 1865, the day of the opening of a new Parliament, the first article, headed ' The

Partial reaction in her favour.

Queen's Seclusion,' sympathetically sought to modify public hostility.

John Bright's defence of her.

A more influential voice came to her support some months later. At a great Liberal meeting at St. James's Hall on December 4, 1866, after Mr. A. S. Ayrton, member of Parliament for the Tower Hamlets, had denounced the Queen's neglect of public duty in no sparing terms, John Bright, the Radical orator, who was present, brought his eloquence to her defence and said with fine feeling: 'I am not accustomed to stand up in defence of those who are the possessors of crowns. But I think there has been, by many persons, a great injustice done to the Queen in reference to her desolate and widowed position; and I venture to say this, that a woman, be she the Queen of a great realm, or be she the wife of one of your labouring men, who can keep alive in her heart a great sorrow for the lost object of her life and affection, is not at all likely to be wanting in a great and generous sympathy with you.' Mr. Ayrton endeavoured to explain his words, but was refused a hearing.

Her refusal to leave her retirement.

Nevertheless the agitation was unrepressed, and to a small extent the Queen gave way. She opened Parliament in person once again,[1] but she still declined formally to resume her old place in public life, and grew to regard the complaint of her seclusion as unmerited persecution. In her view the public censure was based on misapprehension of the constant work and anxiety which her position imposed on her. Her health suffered from the incessant calls that public

[1] See p. 366.

affairs made on her time and thought. She thought that the criticism of the press would be silenced by a frank statement on the part of friends of her absorption in public and private affairs. Her relatives deeply sympathised with her perturbation. But her confidential advisers deprecated public notice of the journalistic invectives.

XXXII

THE SEVEN WEEKS' WAR

Visit to Coburg, Aug. 1865.

THERE was force in the Queen's contention that she was always hard at work. Apart from public questions, which were rarely absent from her mind, the individual fortunes of her numerous kindred constantly filled her thoughts. In the autumn of 1865 domestic matters largely occupied her. Accompanied by her family, she paid another visit to her husband's native country, in order to unveil, in the presence of his relatives, a statue to him at Coburg (August 26). Twenty-four of her near kinsmen and kinswomen attended the ceremony.

Betrothal of the Princess Helena.

While at Coburg the Queen approved a matrimonial project affecting her third and eldest unmarried daughter, Helena, who had of late years been her constant companion. Largely at the instance of her brother-in-law, Duke Ernest, the Princess was betrothed to Prince Christian of Schleswig-Holstein - Sonderburg - Augustenburg, the younger brother of that Duke Frederick whose claim to the duchies of Schleswig and Holstein had been pressed by the smaller German States on Denmark and on the Prussian-Austrian alliance with results disastrous to himself. After the recent Schleswig-Holstein war

Bismarck had deprived Duke Frederick and his family of their property and standing, and the claimant's younger brother, Prince Christian, who had previously been an officer in the Prussian army, had been compelled to retire. In view of recent events the match was calculated strongly to excite political feeling in Germany. The sympathy felt by the Crown Prince and Princess for the injured house of Augustenburg rendered the match congenial to them; but it was viewed with no favour at Berlin, and the Queen was freely reproached there with a wanton interference in the domestic affairs of Germany. She unmistakably identified herself with the arrangement, and by her private munificence met the difficulty incident to the narrow pecuniary resources of the young Prince.

The Queen returned to England in good health and spirits, meeting at Ostend her uncle Leopold for what proved to be the last time. Events in the autumn unfortunately intensified her sense of isolation. In the summer of 1865 a dissolution of Parliament had become necessary; it was in its seventh year, and the ministry's hold on the House of Commons was slackening. In the result the Liberals slightly increased their majority in the new House of Commons; they numbered 361 to 294 Conservatives. But, before the new Parliament met, it was faced by disaster. Palmerston, the Prime Minister, died on October 18, two days before his eighty-first birthday. The Queen was at the moment at Balmoral, and her unwillingness to shorten her stay there in order to arrange on the spot for the necessary reconstitution of the

Dissolution of Parliament, Aug. 1865.

Death of Palmerston, Oct. 18, 1865.

Government tended to intensify the misgivings of those who feared she was underrating her obligations to the public service.

But the Queen, despite her refusal to come south to meet the emergency, was deeply touched by Palmerston's death. She had known him as a minister of the Crown from almost the hour of her accession, twenty-eight years before, and although she never was in genuine sympathy with him, and had suffered bitter anguish from his conduct towards her, his removal broke for her a strong link with the past. In the presence of death the Queen magnanimously forgot all the trials that the minister had caused her. She only felt, she said, how one by one her servants and ministers were taken from her. She acknowledged the admiration which Lord Palmerston's acts, even those that met with her own disapproval, had roused in his fellow-countrymen, and, justly interpreting public sentiment, she accepted the suggestion, which came in the first instance from Gladstone, that a public funeral in Westminster Abbey should be accorded her dead minister. Afterwards, on her return to London, she paid Lady Palmerston a touching visit of condolence.

Lord Russell Prime Minister.

As soon as the news of Palmerston's death had reached Balmoral, the Queen without hesitation sought his successor in Lord John, the oldest minister in her service. In 1861 he had gone to the House of Lords as Earl Russell. She now bade him take Palmerston's place at the head of the Government. The change was rendered grateful to her, not by any special confidence in the value of Lord John's political views or experience, but because his promotion enabled her to bestow the office of Foreign Secretary, which he had hitherto held, on her trusted friend, Lord Clarendon. Another necessary change in the constitution of the ministry caused her a little anxiety. It was inevitable that Gladstone, the Chancellor of the Exchequer, should become leader of the House of Commons in succession to Palmerston. She had admired Gladstone when he was the active lieutenant of Peel, and she had not yet lost confidence in his judgment or patriotic ardour. But she recognised that his opinions were inclining towards democratic liberalism, a direction which was obnoxious to her. Although she had long known him personally, his new and dignified position brought her for the first time into close personal relations with him, and on nearer acquaintance his manner and tone of thought failed to be congenial to her. At his entrance on the responsible duties of leader of the Lower House, she was prepared to view his conduct with indulgence. After the opening of the session in which he first took the helm in the House of Commons, she wrote to express her gratification 'at the account she hears from all sides of the admirable manner in which he has commenced his leadership'[1] (February 21, 1866). But in the years that were soon to follow, Gladstone was to play a part in the drama of her life not wholly unlike that which Palmerston had abandoned only with his death.

On December 10 the Queen suffered another loss, which brought her acute sorrow—the death of King Leopold. She had depended on him almost since

Death of the King of the Belgians.

[1] Morley, *Life of Gladstone*, ii. 157.

her birth for advice on both public and private questions. Since the Prince Consort's death her reliance on him in her private affairs had steadily increased. In St. George's Chapel, Windsor, she at once placed a monument to his memory, beside the tomb of his first wife, Princess Charlotte, George IV.'s only lawful child, and in the inscription she recorded that he held the place of a father in her affections.[1] There was no member of the Saxe-Coburg family, of which henceforth she was herself the head, who could take her uncle's place. None of her relatives were qualified to fill the position in her circle of advisers which his death left vacant. Her brother-in-law Ernest, who was vain and quixotic, looked up to her for counsel, and in his judgment she put no faith. Of her children she was the mentor who offered advice and sought none in return. In her family circle it was now, more than before, on herself alone that she had to rely.

The Queen opens Parliament, Feb. 10, 1866.

But she recognised that the future had calls upon her as well as the past. The forthcoming marriage of Princess Helena coincided with the coming of age of her second son, Prince Alfred. For her son and daughter the Queen was anxious that due pecuniary provision should be made by Parliament, and the public temper did not give her confidence in the issue. This circumstance, coupled with the fact that a new Parliament was assembling, led her to yield to the pressure of her ministers, and once more, after an interval of five years, she opened the Legislature in

[1] Cf. Saint-René Tallandier's *Le Roi Léopold et La Reine Victoria.* 2 vols. Paris, 1878.

person (February 10, 1866). She came to London from Windsor only for the day, and she deprived the ceremony of its ancient splendour. No flourish of trumpets announced her entrance. The gilded state carriage was replaced by one of more modern build, though it was drawn as of old by the eight cream-coloured horses. The Queen, instead of wearing the royal robes of state, had them laid on a chair at her side, and her speech was read not by herself, as had been her habit hitherto, but by the Lord Chancellor (Lord Cranworth). The old procedure was never restored by the Queen, and on the six subsequent occasions that she opened Parliament before the close of her reign the formalities followed the new precedent of 1866. She was dressed in black, wearing a Marie Stuart cap and the blue ribbon of the Garter. During the ceremony she sat perfectly motionless, and manifested little consciousness of what was proceeding. A month later she showed the direction that her thoughts were still taking by instituting the Albert medal, a new decoration for those endangering their lives in seeking to rescue others from perils of the sea (March 7, 1866).

Later in the year she again forsook her seclusion, and, for the first time after the Prince's death, revisited Aldershot. She went there twice to review troops— on March 13 and on April 5. On the second occasion she gave new colours to the 89th Regiment, which she had first honoured thus in 1833, and she now bestowed on the regiment the title 'The Princess Victoria's Regiment,' permitting the officers to wear on their forage-caps the badge of a princess's coronet.

Visits to Aldershot.

Two marriages.

The summer perceptibly illumined her gloom. It was brightened by two marriages in her immediate circle. Not only her daughter Helena, but her cousin and friend, Princess Mary of Cambridge, had recently become engaged. The latter was betrothed to the Duke of Teck, who was congenial to the Queen by reason of his Saxe-Coburg connections. He was her second cousin, being the son, by a morganatic marriage, of Duke Alexander Constantine of Würtemberg, whose mother, of the Saxe-Coburg family, was elder sister of the Duchess of Kent, and thus the Queen's aunt. On June 12, dressed in deep black, she was present at Princess Mary's wedding, which took place at Kew. On July 5 she attended the solemnisation of marriage at Windsor of her third daughter, Helena, with Prince Christian of Schleswig-Holstein.

Grants to Princess Helena and Prince Alfred.

Parliament had been conciliatory in the matter of grants to her children. Princess Helena received a dowry of 30,000*l*. and an annuity of 6,000*l*., while her second son, Prince Alfred, received an annuity of 15,000*l*., to be raised to 25,000*l*. in case of his marriage. There was, contrary to expectation, no opposition to either arrangement.

War between Austria and Prussia.

But throughout the session the position of the Government and the course of public affairs in Germany filled the Queen with alarm. It was clear that the disputes between Prussia and Austria in regard to the final settlement of the conquered duchies of Schleswig-Holstein were to issue in a desperate conflict between the two Powers. Not otherwise could their long rivalry for the headship of the German States be finally decided. The prospect of war caused the Queen acute distress. The merits of the quarrel were blurred in her eyes by domestic preoccupations. The struggle hopelessly divided her family in Germany. The Crown Prince was identified with Prussia; but her son-in-law of Hesse, her cousin of Hanover, and her brother-in-law of Saxe-Coburg were supporters of Austria. The likelihood that her two sons-in-law of Prussia and Hesse would fight against each other was especially terrifying to her. Her former desire to see Prussia strong and self-reliant was now in conflict with her fear that Prussian predominance meant ruin for all the smaller States of Germany, to which she was personally attached.

In the early months of 1866 the Queen eagerly inquired of Lord Clarendon how best to direct her influence to the maintenance of peace. She bade Lord Russell, the Prime Minister, take every step to prevent war; and in March 1866 her ministry, with her assent, proposed to the King of Prussia that she should act as mediator. Bismarck, however, brusquely declined her advances. In letters to the King of Prussia he heaped terms of contumely on the head of the Queen, whom he regarded as seeking to foil for selfish domestic reasons his policy of humiliating Austria and of giving Prussia the supremacy of Central Europe. He declaimed against the baneful influence she exerted in Prussian affairs. Through her daughter, she dominated the Crown Prince. She prompted the Duke of Saxe-Coburg, who shared (Bismarck asserted) in every intrigue that was likely to undermine Prussian power.[1]

Queen's offer of mediation.

[1] Bismarck's *Politische Briefe*.

Queen and the Reform Bill.

The Queen's perplexities were increased in May by her Government's domestic difficulties. Lord Russell warned her of the probable defeat of the Government on the Reform Bill, which they had lately introduced into the House of Commons. The Queen had already acknowledged the desirability of a prompt settlement of the long-debated extension of the franchise. She had even told Lord Russell that vacillation or indifference respecting it, on the Government's part, now that the question was in the air, weakened the power of the Crown. She thought that the consideration of the whole question might well have been postponed, but now that it had been raised by the Government, it was essential that it should be 'prosecuted to its completion.'

Her defiance of Lord Russell.

In effect the continental complication tended to reduce home politics to small dimensions in the Queen's eye. She declined to recognise a Reform Bill to be a matter of the first importance, and she wrote with heat to the Prime Minister, Lord Russell, that, whatever happened to his franchise proposals in the Commons, she would permit no resignation of the ministers until the foreign peril was averted. Her ministers begged her to remain at Windsor in May instead of paying her usual spring visit to Balmoral, so that she might be at hand in case they were unable to carry on the government. She declined, with the remark that they were bound at all hazards to avert a ministerial crisis.

Lord Russell's resignation.

In June the worst happened, alike at home and abroad. War was declared between Prussia and Austria, and Lord Russell's Government was defeated while its Reform Bill was in committee in the House of Commons. On June 19 Lord Russell forwarded his resignation to Balmoral; he deprecated a dissolution at so early a date after the general election. The Queen was filled with anger. She wrote protesting that she was taken completely by surprise. 'In the present state of Europe,' she said, 'and the apathy which Lord Russell himself admits to exist in the country on the subject of Reform, the Queen cannot think it consistent with the duty which the ministers owe to herself and the country that they should abandon their posts in consequence of their defeat on a matter of detail (not of principle) in a question which can never be settled unless all sides are prepared to make concessions; and she must therefore ask them to reconsider their decision.'[1] Lord Russell quickly retorted that his continuance in office was impracticable, and the Cabinet supported him. On her return to Windsor, June 26, she at once saw the Prime Minister and Gladstone. She repeated her view that the Government was resigning on a 'matter of detail,' and that the 'state of the Continent' rendered their action perilous. She suggested that her opinion should be announced to Parliament, but her ministers deemed her advice impolitic.[2] Lord Russell, after careful reconsideration, declined to retract his own or his colleagues' resignation, and with the ministry's retirement he ended his long public life.

The Queen regarded his withdrawal as amounting to desertion, and her anger did not readily cool.

[1] Walpole, *Lord John Russell*, ii. 415.
[2] Morley, *Life of Gladstone*, ii. 209–211.

Lord Derby Prime Minister.

For some days she suffered the Government to lie in abeyance. At length the Conservative leader, Lord Derby,[1] accepted her command to form a new ministry, with Disraeli as Chancellor of the Exchequer and leader of the House of Commons (July 6, 1866). Disraeli was called anew to the captaincy of a House of Commons which was less than one year old, and in which the party majority against him numbered nearly seventy. The perils of the new Government were consequently great, but the Queen was hopeful of its ability to defend itself. She welcomed back to office with especial warmth Lord Malmesbury, who

[1] The members of the cabinet were as follows:—

First Lord of the Treasury	Lord Derby.
Lord Chancellor	Lord Chelmsford.
President of Council	Duke of Buckingham.
Privy Seal	Lord Malmesbury.
Chancellor of the Exchequer	Mr. Disraeli.
Home Secretary	Mr. Spencer Walpole.
Foreign Secretary	Lord Stanley (son of the Prime Minister).
Secretary for the Colonies	Lord Carnarvon.
Secretary for War	General Jonathan Peel.
Secretary for India	Lord Cranborne (who succeeded as Marquis of Salisbury, 1868).
President of the Board of Trade	Sir Stafford Northcote (afterwards Earl of Iddesleigh).
Chancellor of the Duchy of Lancaster	Lord Devon.
First Commissioner of Works	Lord John Manners (afterwards the Duke of Rutland).
First Lord of the Admiralty	Sir John Pakington (afterwards Lord Hampton).
President of the Poor Law Board	Mr. Gathorne Hardy (afterwards Viscount Cranbrook).

became Lord Privy Seal, and General Peel, who was again Minister of War. Lord Stanley, the Prime Minister's son, became Foreign Secretary, and of him she always cherished grateful recollection.

Meanwhile the Austro-Prussian war was waging in Germany, and many of the Queen's relatives were in the field. The Crown Prince was alone fighting for Prussia, the rest were standing by Austria. She was in constant communication with her kindred on the two sides, and her anxiety was intense. She took charge of the children of Princess Alice of Hesse-Darmstadt at Osborne, and she sent their mother at Darmstadt much linen for the wounded. The result of the conflict was not long in doubt. At the outset, the rapid invasion of Hanover by Prussian troops drove the Queen's cousin, the blind King George, from his throne, and summarily blotted out the kingdom, converting it into a Prussian province, 'It is too dreadful,' she telegraphed to Duke Ernest in reply to his announcement of the distressing news, June 28, 1866 ; ' where is the poor King and his son ? ' The Queen bitterly felt the humiliation involved in the extinction of a kingdom which had long been identified with England. She was deeply interested in arrangements for the future safety of the expelled royal family of Hanover, but came to agree with Disraeli and the King of Prussia that their settlement in England might provoke further tension between England and Prussia.[1] The King of Hanover finally, with the Queen's full assent, made his residence at Paris.

Prussia seizes Hanover

---

[1] Appendix to Bismarck's *Gedanken u. Erinnerungen*, i. 169-170, Letter 193.

But in the welfare of him and of his family, especially of his daughter Frederica, whom she called 'the poor lily of Hanover,' her affectionate interest never waned.

<small>End of seven weeks' war.</small>

Elsewhere Prussia's triumph in the war was as quickly assured. The Austrians were decisively defeated at the battle of Sadowa near Königgrätz on July 3, 1866, and the conflict was at an end seven weeks after it had begun. Meanwhile the Queen suffered more disappointments. Italy had joined Prussia against Austria. Austria was summarily deprived of Venetia, her last hold on the Italian peninsula, and the union of Italy under Victor Emanuel—a project with which the Queen had no sympathy—was virtually accomplished.

Thus Prussia was finally placed at the head of the whole of Western Germany; its accession to the imperial crown of Germany was in sight, and Austria was compelled to retire from the German Confederation. It was with mixed feelings and with more misgiving than gratification that the Queen saw her early hopes of a strong Prussia realised. The price of the victory was abolition of the kingdom of Hanover, loss of territory for her son-in-law of Hesse-Darmstadt, and reduction of power and dignity for the other small German States with which she was lineally associated. Moreover, the undisguised contempt with which Bismarck, who was the minister mainly responsible for Prussia's triumph, treated her daughter and son-in-law, the Crown Prince and Princess, checked in her the elation of spirit that she had thought in earlier days to derive from every conspicuously forward step in the career of Prussian power.

XXXIII

THE PRINCE CONSORT'S BIOGRAPHY

The Queen's withdrawal to the quiet of Balmoral in October gave welcome relief after such severe political strains. She repeated at Dunkeld a short sojourn, which she had made the year before, with the lately widowed Duchess of Athol, a favourite lady of the bedchamber, with whom her sympathy was complete. *[Rest at Balmoral.]*

The Queen was persuaded to take part in two public ceremonials before the end of the year. She opened the Aberdeen Waterworks at Invercannie (October 16, 1866), when for the first time in her widowhood she herself read the answer to the address of the Lord Provost. Another public ceremonial in which she took part after her return south revealed the vast store of loyalty which, despite detraction and criticism, the Queen still had at her command. On November 30 she visited Wolverhampton to unveil a statue of the Prince Consort in the market-place. It was the earliest mark of respect that any English municipality had paid his memory. She expressed a desire that her route should be so arranged as to give the inhabitants, both poor and rich, full opportunities of showing her respect. A network of streets *[The Queen at Aberdeen.]* *[The Queen at Wolverhampton.]*

measuring a course of nearly three miles was traversed. The Queen acknowledged that 'the heartiness and cordiality of the reception' left nothing to be desired, and her spirits rose.

The biography of the Prince Consort.

The perpetuation of her husband's memory was still a main endeavour of her life, and she now enlisted biography in her service. At her wish Sir Arthur Helps edited for her a collection of the Prince's 'Speeches and Addresses' in 1862. She inscribed copies, which she sent to friends, with the words 'from his broken-hearted widow, Victoria.' Subsequently, under her direction her private secretary, General Grey, who had served the Prince in the same position, set to work on a minute account of the early years of the Prince Consort. The Queen designed the volume, which was based on confidential and intimate family correspondence, for private distribution among friends and relatives. It was sent to press in 1866. It brought the Prince's life only to the date of his marriage, but interest was manifested in it, and in 1867 the Queen placed the book at the disposal of the wider audience of the general public. The work, when it was published in the ordinary way, was well received. At the Queen's request Bishop Wilberforce reviewed it in the 'Quarterly.' He described it as a cry from the Queen's heart for her people's sympathy, and he said that her cry was answered.[1]

Choice of (Sir) Theodore Martin as biographer.

The Queen at once resolved that the biography should be continued, but General Grey's heavy occupations did not permit him to proceed further with the task. Thereupon, in August 1866, the Queen

[1] *Life of Wilberforce*, iii. 236.

consulted Sir Arthur Helps respecting the choice of a successor. She wished the biography of the Prince's later life, which so nearly concerned her own, to be, she wrote, ' as *faithful* a representation as it possibly can be.' Sir Arthur recommended Mr. (afterwards Sir Theodore) Martin, who was a German scholar and was free from political bias. Sir Theodore Martin was offered, and with some hesitation undertook, the work. Much of her time was thenceforth devoted to the sorting of her and her husband's private papers and correspondence, and to the selection of extracts for publication. Every chapter as it was completed was carefully read and criticised by the Queen. She was quick to detect and correct errors in dates and names, and to suggest at times tactful modifications of language. But she left the biographer free to map out and develop his narrative as seemed best to him. She was always insistent that at all points the facts should be fully told.

The work was designed on an ample scale, the first volume appearing in 1874, and the fifth and last in 1880. Amazement was felt even by her own children at the want of reserve which characterised their father's biography. The whole truth best vindicated him, she explained, and it was undesirable to wait before telling it till those who had known him had passed away. The German side of his character, which alienated sympathy in his lifetime, could only be apprehended in a full exposition. Both she and he would suffer, she said, were the work not carried through.[1]

Character of the work.

[1] *Princess Alice's Letters*, pp. 333-5.

Her faith in its utility.

As the work progressed her conviction of the wisdom of her plan steadily grew upon her. Memoirs of some of the Prince's contemporaries were appearing, and gave impressions of the Prince's opinion or conduct, which called, in her opinion, for authoritative correction. The record of Stockmar's life, which was published by his son in 1872, dissatisfied her. She deemed that it did scant justice to the trusted mentor of herself and of her husband. Her daughter Alice continued to express doubt of her wisdom in communicating private information to the public; the Queen repeated her assured belief that it was of 'much use to posterity and to princes to see what an unselfish self-sacrificing and in many ways hard and unenviable life beloved papa's was.'[1]

Her dislike of the 'Greville Memoirs.'

At the same time she deprecated indiscretion or levity in writing of the royal family, and in 1874 she was greatly irritated by the publication of the first part of the 'Greville Memoirs.' She judged the work, by its freedom of comment on her predecessors, to be disrespectful to the monarchy. Henry Reeve, the editor, was informed of her displeasure, and she was not convinced by his defence that monarchy had been injured by George IV.'s depravity and William IV.'s absurdity, and had only been placed on a sure footing by her own virtues.[2]

Publication of her 'Leaves from a Journal.'

The Queen was not content to leave the whole of the burden of setting the true facts of her life before her people in the hands of others. She herself attempted authorship in order to help forward that design. To

[1] *Princess Alice's Letters*, pp. 333–5.
[2] Laughton, *Memoir of Henry Reeve*.

illustrate the happy character of her married life, she in 1867 privately issued for circulation among friends some extracts from her own regularly kept diary under the title of 'Leaves from a Journal of our Life in the Highlands from 1848 to 1861.' This she was induced to publish at the beginning of the following year (1868). She derived aid in preparing the manuscript for press from Sir Arthur Helps, who did what he could to remedy the colloquial inaccuracy of her style. She always wrote with great rapidity, and her faults of composition were ineradicable; on one occasion she naïvely confessed to Lord John Russell that she often in writing found herself in the middle of a long sentence from which she saw no chance of extricating herself—a confession on which Lord John bluntly commented: 'Yes, Madam, so I perceive.'[1] But the unaffected simplicity and naïveté of her published journal attracted the public, who saw in the book, with its frank descriptions of her private doings, proof of her wish to share her joys and sorrows with her people. The favourable reviews of the publication in the press greatly moved and cheered her.

The year 1867 abounded in political incidents which distracted the Queen's attention amid her literary occupations. With her new Conservative ministers her relations were invariably cordial. Their views on foreign politics were mainly identical with her own, and there was none of the friction which had marked her relations with Palmerston and Lord Russell. The new ministers' sympathetic tone led her to modify still further her habits of seclusion. She

Cordial relations with Lord Derby's ministry.

[1] C. L. Graves, *Life of Sir George Grove*, pp. 130–1.

bore public testimony to the harmony existing between them and herself by consenting once more to open Parliament in person on February 5. In May she again appeared in public, when she laid the foundation of the Royal Albert Hall, which was erected in her husband's memory. Her voice, in replying to the address of welcome, was scarcely audible. It had been with a struggle, she said, that she had nerved herself to take part in the proceedings. The mental strain which public ceremonials imposed on her was evident to all.

XXXIV

FOREIGN AFFAIRS IN 1867

The chief event of the year in domestic politics was the passage of Disraeli's Reform Bill through Parliament. The Queen encouraged the Government to settle the question, which had been more or less agitating the country for sixteen years. Although she had no enthusiasm for sweeping reforms, and regarded domestic legislation as of small importance compared with movements in foreign diplomacy, her old Whig training inclined her to regard extensions of the franchise with favour. She deemed the widening of the electorate of advantage to the monarchy and to the foundations of her government.

Disraeli's Reform Bill.

But now, as always, foreign affairs were her main concern. The European sky had not grown clear, despite the storms of the previous year. The Queen was particularly perturbed in the early months of 1867 by renewed fear of her former ally, Napoleon III. Although her personal correspondence with him was still as amiable as of old, her distrust of his political intentions was greater than ever, and she employed all her influence to foil what she believed to be his dangerous purposes. It was long generally recognised that he was seeking an opportunity to annex to France

Her distrust of Napoleon III.

the eastern bank of the Rhine, and the Queen in 1863 had plainly warned him against so serious a menace to the peace of Europe. The success of her first remonstrance was generally admitted. King Leopold in 1863 pointed out to the Crown Prince of Germany that the Queen's emphatically expressed disapproval of Napoleon's ambitious design on the integrity of German territory had deterred him from pursuing it. The King of Prussia at the same time assured the sceptical Bismarck that the Queen's calm and prudent conduct had, in the opinion of all her relatives, preserved Germany from French invasion.

The Luxemburg affair.

In 1867 Napoleon was again fomenting disquiet. He professed to detect danger to France in the semi-independence of the frontier state—the duchy of Luxemburg—which lay between France and Germany. The new conditions which Prussian predominance created in North Germany had given that Power the right at will to fortify the duchy on its French border, which had hitherto been unprotected. Napoleon objected to the establishment of any new German armaments on the boundaries of France. He therefore negotiated with the King of Holland, the suzerain of the duchy of Luxemburg, for the annexation of the duchy to the King's dominions, or he was willing to see it annexed to Belgium if some small strip of Belgian territory were assigned to him. Prussia raised protests and Belgium declined to entertain Napoleon's suggestion. Both German and French susceptibilities were excited, and the shadow of war seemed to darken Central Europe. The Queen renewed her action of 1863, and vehemently appealed to her Government to urge on all the Powers concerned the necessity of peace. Her appeal had its effect. A conference met in London (May 11 to 14, 1867), with the result that the independence of the duchy of Luxemburg was guaranteed by the Powers, though all its fortresses were to be dismantled. Napoleon was disappointed by his failure to secure any material advantage from the settlement. He was inclined to credit the Queen with thwarting his ambition.

His relations with her endured a further strain next month when his fatal abandonment in Mexico of her friend and connection, the Archduke Maximilian, became known. In 1864 Napoleon had managed to persuade the Archduke, the Austrian Emperor's brother, who had married the Queen's first cousin, Princess Charlotte of Belgium, and had frequently been a favoured guest at Windsor, to accept the imperial throne which a French army was setting up in republican Mexico. Few of the inhabitants of the country acknowledged the title of the new Emperor, and in 1866, after the close of the American civil war, the Government at Washington warned Napoleon that, unless his troops were summarily withdrawn from the North American continent, force would be used to expel them. The Emperor pusillanimously offered no resistance to the demand, and the French army was withdrawn, but the Archduke declined to leave with it. His wife, Princess Charlotte of Belgium, as soon as she realised her husband's peril, came to Europe to beg protection for him, and to the Queen's lasting sorrow her anxieties permanently affected her intellect. She was thenceforth confined

Murder of Emperor Maximilian, June 20, 1867.

in a lunatic asylum. Meanwhile the inhabitants of Mexico restored the Republic, and the Archduke Maximilian was shot in the city by order of a court-martial on June 20, 1867.

The Queen's horror.

The catastrophe appalled the Queen, whose personal attachment to its victims was great. She wrote a frank letter of condolence to the Archduke's brother, the Emperor of Austria, and spoke of Napoleon as politically past redemption. But political disagreement with the Emperor and disgust at his reckless courses failed to diminish the Queen's affection for the Empress of the French, and she privately entertained her as her guest at Osborne in July, while her sorrow for the fate of the Emperor Maximilian and Empress Charlotte was uppermost in her heart. Nor, when misfortune overtook the Emperor himself in 1870, did she permit her repugnance to his political action or principles to repress her sense of compassion.

Foreign sovereigns at Court.

While the Mexican tragedy was nearing its last scene the second Great Exhibition was taking place at Paris. Napoleon III., despite the universal suspicion that he excited, succeeded in entertaining many royal personages, among them the Tsar Alexander II., the King of Prussia, Abdul Aziz, the Sultan of Turkey, Ismail Pasha, the Khedive of Egypt, and the Prince of Wales. The Queen's ministers recommended that she should renew the old hospitalities of her Court and invite the royal visitors in Paris to be her guests. The Queen of Prussia had spent several days with her in June before the arrival of the Empress Eugénie, but she demurred to acting

as hostess in state on a large scale, or to entertaining
sovereigns who were not already her personal friends.
She was, however, persuaded, with a view to con-
firming her influence in Eastern Europe, which she
always regarded as of importance to British interests,
to entertain Abdul Aziz, the Sultan of Turkey, and to
receive Ismail Pasha, the Khedive of Egypt. The
Khedive had, uninvited, announced his intention of
coming, and was in the country from July 6 to 18.

No Sultan of Turkey had yet set foot on English
soil, and the visit, which seemed to set the seal on
the old political alliance between the two Governments, evoked intense popular excitement. The Sultan
was magnificently received on his arrival on July 12,
and was lodged in Buckingham Palace. Though the
Queen took as small a part as possible in the festivities, she did not withdraw herself altogether from
them. Princess Alice helped her in extending hospitalities to her guest, who lunched with her in state
at Windsor and greatly appreciated her attentions.
A great naval review by the Queen at Spithead was
arranged in his honour, and he accompanied his
hostess on board her yacht, the 'Victoria and Albert.'
The weather was bad, and amid a howling storm
the Queen invested the Sultan with the Order of the
Garter on the yacht's deck. The general effect of
her hospitality was all that was wished. When the
Sultan left on July 23 he exchanged with her highly
complimentary telegrams.

The Sultan's visit, 1867.

At Balmoral, in the autumn, she showed more
than her usual energy. On her way thither she
made an excursion in the Scottish border country,

At Abbotsford, Aug. 22, 1867.

staying for two days with the Duke and Duchess of Roxburghe at Floors Castle, near Kelso (August 21 to 23). On the 22nd she visited Melrose Abbey, and thence proceeded to Abbotsford, the former home of Sir Walter Scott, where she was received by its tenant, Mr. Hope Scott, the husband of Sir Walter's grand-daughter, and was greatly interested in the memorials of the great novelist. In the study, at her host's request, she wrote her name in Scott's journal, an act of which she modestly wrote in her diary: 'I felt it to be a presumption in me to do.' Subsequently she unveiled with some formality a memorial to Prince Albert at Deeside, and in September visited the Duke of Richmond at Glenfiddich.

Continued depression.

Unfortunately, when she returned next month to Windsor, all her old depression was renewed. After the homely freedom of her life at Balmoral, she was harassed by the formal constraint of the court etiquette that was inseparable from residence at Windsor. The passion for seclusion and privacy which her husband's death had roused in her had lost little of its intensity at the close of the six years that had elapsed since her bereavement.

XXXV

DISRAELI'S FIRST ADMINISTRATION

EARLY in 1868 the Queen accepted, for the seventh time in her experience, a new Prime Minister, and one with whom her intimacy was to be greater than with any of his six predecessors. In February Lord Derby resigned owing to failing health. The choice of a successor lay between Disraeli and Lord Derby's son, Lord Stanley. Disraeli's steady work for his party for nearly a quarter of a century seemed to entitle him to the great reward. Since 1850 he had been the chief of the Conservatives in the House of Commons, and by his gifts of speech and dexterous party management had done more than any of his colleagues to strengthen their position in the country. The Queen without any hesitation conferred the prize on him.

Disraeli Prime Minister, Feb. 1868.

As her Prime Minister Disraeli from the first confirmed her recent good opinion of him. Her relations with him had been steadily improving. Though she acknowledged that he was eccentric, his efforts to please her convinced her of his devotion to the Crown. His bearing was invariably courteous, and, despite his cynicism and sardonic temperament, she believed

Queen's growing respect for him.

in his genuine kindness of heart. His deepening enthusiasm for the monarchical principle of government and his growing faith in the imperial destiny of England strongly appealed to her, and by the adroitness of his counsel he increased her sense of power and dignity. His power in Parliament was insecure; his own followers were in a minority, and the Queen was soon face to face with a new ministerial crisis. But in that crisis Disraeli contrived that she should play not unwillingly an unwontedly prominent part.[1]

Gladstone and the Irish Church.

In April Gladstone brought forward his first and main resolution in favour of the disestablishment of the Irish Protestant Church—a measure which had been long clamoured for by the Roman Catholic population of Ireland and had been formally admitted into the official Liberal programme. The Government resisted Gladstone's motion, and on May 1 was sharply defeated by a majority of sixty-five. Next day Disraeli went to Windsor and tendered his resignation to the Queen. He had held the post of Prime Minister barely three months.

Queen's dislike of Disestablishment.

Personally the Queen disliked Gladstone's proposal. She regarded the Established Church throughout her dominions as intimately associated with the Crown, and interference with it seemed to her to impair her prerogative. But as a constitutional sovereign she realised that the future of the Church Establishment in Ireland or elsewhere was no matter for her own decision, whatever were her convictions;

[1] Almost all the members of Lord Derby's cabinet took office under Disraeli. The main change was the substitution of Lord Cairns for Lord Chelmsford in the office of Lord Chancellor.

it was for the decision of her Parliament and people. In the present emergency she desired the people to have full time in which to make up their minds regarding the fate of the Irish Church. But the position of affairs was complex.

The simplest course open to her was to accept Disraeli's resignation, and to confer office on Gladstone. But in that event her Government would be committed instantly to Irish Disestablishment, and this result she resolved, if she could, to avoid. Disraeli pointed out that she could, if not escape, at least defer the evil moment by declining to accept his resignation and by dissolving Parliament. But that course involved especial difficulty. An immediate dissolution was for peculiar reasons undesirable, if not impossible. New constituencies had been created by the late Reform Bill, and all parties wished that the electoral appeal should be made to these. The Scottish and Irish Reform Bills and the Boundary Bills for the whole country which were required to complete the recent measure of electoral reform had yet to pass through their final stages. Consequently the Queen's refusal to accept the existing Government's resignation meant no early dissolution. It meant the continuance of Disraeli in office, in spite of his defeat, during the six months which were fully needed before all the arrangements for the appeal to the newly enfranchised electors could be accomplished.

Disraeli's offer of resignation.

The Opposition might decline to keep the Government in power during that period, but in that case the Sovereign would not be the better disposed to offer them power. She would then in all probability, as

The Opposition.

she always could, insist on a dissolution before the new electoral reform was consummated. To such a step the Opposition had strong objection, for their chance of conspicuous victory in the country depended largely on their securing the suffrages of the new voters.

Queen elects to dissolve Parliament.

Disraeli discussed the situation with the Queen in great detail. Finally he left her to choose between the only two possible alternatives which she or he recognised—the acceptance of his resignation or the refusal of his resignation coupled with a resolve to appeal to the country six months later. After two days' consideration the Queen elected to take the second course.

The Queen was prepared to accept full responsibility for her decision, and when Disraeli announced it to Parliament on May 5 he described, with her assent, the general drift of his negotiations with her, and made it plain that she had determined the issue for herself. Grave doubts were expressed in the House of Commons as to whether his conduct was consistent with that of the ministerial adviser of a constitutional sovereign. In his first conversation with the Queen he had acted on his own initiative, and had not consulted his colleagues. This self-reliance somewhat damped enthusiasm for his action in the ranks of his own party. The leaders of the Opposition boldly argued that the minister was bound to offer the Sovereign definite advice, which it behoved her to adopt; that the constitution recognised no power in the Sovereign to exercise personal volition, and that the minister was faithless to his trust in offering her two courses and abiding by her voluntary selection of one.

The question of constitutional practice was one of delicacy. But the argument against the minister was pushed too far. The Queen had repeatedly exerted a personal choice between a dissolution and a resignation of the ministry in face of an adverse vote in the House of Commons. The new features that the present situation offered were, first, the acceptance of a deferred, not of an immediate, dissolution; and, secondly, Disraeli's open attribution to the Queen of responsibility for the final decision. The first point was accidental and relatively unimportant: the second was crucial. But Disraeli's procedure was no serious breach with precedent; it served to bring into clearer relief than before the practical ascendency, within certain limits, which under the constitution a ministerial crisis assured the Crown, if its wearer cared to assert it. The revelation was in the main to the advantage of the prestige of the throne. It confuted the constitutional fallacy that the monarch was necessarily and invariably an automaton.

Her constitutional powers

But, despite the open assertion of her personal freedom of choice, the Queen had no intention of exceeding her constitutional power. When, immediately after the settlement of the ministerial difficulty, the House of Commons, by an irresistible vote of the Opposition, petitioned her to suspend new appointments within the Crown's control in the Irish Church, and to place royal patronage at the Parliament's disposal, she did not permit any personal predilections to postpone her assent for a day. Alarmists,

Queen's respect for parliamentary power.

Public functions.

who affected to believe that she and her minister were hatching a plot against the independence of Parliament, were thereby silenced.

Disraeli's accession to office was distinguished by the Queen's occasional resumption of public functions. On March 10, 1868, for the first time since her widowhood, she held a drawing-room at Buckingham Palace. On June 20 she reviewed 27,000 volunteers in Windsor Park, and two days later gave a public 'breakfast,' or afternoon party, in the gardens of Buckingham Palace.[1] She appeared to observers to enjoy the entertainment. But these activities were not to be permanently exercised nor to grow in scope. She had no intention of introducing any permanent change into her habitually secluded mode of life.

First visit to Switzerland

By way of illustrating her desire to escape from Court restriction, she in August paid a first visit to Switzerland. She travelled incognito under the name of the Countess of Kent, and forbade any public demonstration in her honour. But she accepted the Emperor Napoleon's courteous offer of his imperial train in which to travel through France. On the outward journey she rested for a day at the English Embassy in Paris,

---

[1] From the early years of the nineteenth century 'breakfasts' were a very popular form of entertainment in fashionable society. Mrs. Bagot, in *Links with the Past* (1901, pp. 13, 286), writes of London society in 1840 : 'In those days garden parties were called "breakfasts," and most of the big houses gave them weekly during the summer months. The Duchess of Bedford's breakfasts at the house known later as Argyll Lodge, at Campden Hill, were very popular entertainments. There was generally dancing after what was in reality a luncheon at those so-called breakfasts, and occasionally some of the male *habitués* not only remained to dinner, but also really breakfasted with their hosts the following morning.'

where the Empress Eugénie paid her an informal visit (August 6). Next day she reached Lucerne, where she had rented the Villa Pension Wallace near the lake. She stayed there, engaged in the recreations of a private pleasure-seeker, till September 9, when she again passed through France in the Emperor's train. She paused at Paris on September 10 to revisit St. Cloud, which revived sad memories of her happy sojourn there thirteen years before. The Emperor was absent, but courteous greetings by telegraph passed between him and the Queen.

Removing, on her arrival in England, to Balmoral, she there gave yet additional proof of her anxiety to shrink from publicity or Court formality. She took up her residence for the first time in a small house, called Glassalt Shiel, which she had built in a wild deserted spot in the hills at the head of Loch Muick, under the shadow of Loch-na-gar. She regarded the dwelling as in all ways in keeping with her condition. 'It was,' she wrote, 'the widow's first house, not built by *him*, or hallowed by *his* memory.' At the end of the year she attended a mournful ceremony which brought some relief to her inveterate sense of desolation. On December 14, 1868, a special service was held in her presence at the new Frogmore mausoleum, where a permanent sarcophagus had now been placed over her husband's coffin. It was destined to hold her own remains as well as those of the Prince. The whole cost of the completed mausoleum was 200,000*l*.

Her retreat of Glassalt Shiel.

While she was still in Scotland the general election took place, under the new Electoral Act, and Disraeli's Government suffered a crushing defeat.

Disraeli's defeat.

The Liberals came in with a majority of 128, and Disraeli, contrary to precedent, resigned office without waiting for the meeting of Parliament. He had enjoyed the highest office in the State for only ten months.

Her special mark of favour to him.

The Queen, although in view of the pronounced results of the elections she deemed 'immediate resignation the most dignified course to pursue and the best for the public interests,' parted with Disraeli regretfully. She was anxious to show him a special mark of favour. He declined her offer of a peerage because he judged it right that he should remain in the House of Commons. But the Queen was aware of his chivalric devotion to his wife, and he welcomed her suggestion that Mrs. Disraeli should receive the distinction which he felt himself unable to accept. Accordingly Mrs. Disraeli became a peeress in her own right as Viscountess Beaconsfield on November 30, 1868.

Appointment of Archbishop Tait.

Despite the Queen's liking for Disraeli, his last official act excited a passing difference of opinion with her. The incident showed how actively she asserted her authority even in her relations with a minister with whose general policy she was in agreement, and with whom her personal relations were unfailingly harmonious. The Archbishopric of Canterbury became vacant on October 28, 1868, owing to the death of Archbishop Longley. The Queen at her own instance recommended for the post Archibald Campbell Tait, Bishop of London since 1856, in whom she had long taken a personal interest.[1] Disraeli had

[1] Tait was a Scotsman, born in Edinburgh December 21, 1811. After a very successful career at Oxford, he was seven years tutor at

another candidate. But the Queen persisted; Disraeli yielded, and Tait received the primacy.

Friendship with Tait.

Tait was the first Archbishop of Canterbury with whom the Queen maintained a personal intimacy. Neither with Archbishop Howley, who held office at her accession, nor with his successors, Archbishops Sumner and Longley, had she sought private association. But with Tait and with his successor, Benson, she cultivated a close friendship.

Queen's attitude to bishops.

With bishops, as a class, she was not in personal sympathy, and no ceremonial function in which she had to take part did she like less than that of receiving the homage of bishops, who were obliged to kiss her hand on their appointment. A feeling of shyness invariably overcame her on the occasion, and her manner often appeared, to the chief actors in the scene, brusque and indifferent. Nor as a rule did she appreciate, with a few conspicuous exceptions, the sermons of bishops. Their tone and manner were rarely simple or homely enough to harmonise with her predilection. Her attitude to bishops was possibly due in part to the Lutheran sympathies which she had derived from the Prince Consort. But to the principle of the episcopal form of Church government she was in no sense

---

Balliol, and was, from 1842 till 1850, head master of Rugby. While Dean of Carlisle, in 1856, he had the misfortune to lose five children from scarlet fever—an experience which aroused the Queen's pity. Lord Palmerston made him Bishop of London in 1856, and in 1862 offered him the Archbishopric of York, which he declined. In 1866 he won the Queen's admiration by his energy in meeting the cholera epidemic in the East of London. A Whig by early conviction, he had resisted the Oxford movement, and given many proofs of an enlightened Protestantism, and of a desire to make the Church of England national and comprehensive.

opposed. Her desire was that it should work with the highest spiritual advantage to her subjects. The misgivings with which many bishops inspired her were mainly attributable to the native simplicity of her religious faith, which made suspicion of worldly pride or parade in spiritual affairs distasteful to her. She was always an attentive hearer of sermons and a shrewd critic of them. She chiefly admired in them simplicity and brevity, and was better satisfied with unpretending language and style than with polish and eloquence. A failure on the part of a preacher to satisfy her sentiment sometimes proved a fatal bar to his preferment.

Queen's view of Church patronage.
Disraeli's experience in regard to the appointment of Tait was not uncommon with preceding or succeeding prime ministers. Throughout her reign the Queen took a serious view of her personal responsibilities in the distribution of Church patronage; and though she always received her ministers' advice with respect, she did not confine herself to criticism of their favoured candidates for Church promotion; she often insisted on quite other arrangements than they suggested.

Interference in Church appointments.
To the choice of bishops she attached an 'immense importance,' and the principles that in her view ought to govern their selection were sound and statesmanlike. She deprecated the influence of religious or political partisanship in the matter. 'The men to be chosen,' she wrote to Archbishop Benson, January 3, 1890, 'must not be taken with reference to satisfying one or the other *party* in the *Church*, or with reference to any political party,

but for their real worth. We want people who can be firm and conciliatory, else the Church cannot be maintained. We want large broad views, or the difficulties will be insurmountable.'

While holding such wise views, she was not unaffected by her personal likes or dislikes of individuals, and she would rather fill an ecclesiastical office with one who was already agreeably known to her than with a stranger, especially if its holder were likely to be brought officially into relations with her. In 1845 she refused to accept Sir Robert Peel's recommendation of Buckland for the Deanery of Westminster, and conferred the post on a personal acquaintance, Samuel Wilberforce, though she did not oppose the bestowal of the deanery on Buckland when Wilberforce vacated it later in the same year to become Bishop of Oxford. Subsequently Dean Stanley owed the same benefice to the Queen's great personal regard for him; while she influenced the choice of Dean Stanley's friend, Dean Bradley, to succeed Dean Stanley because the latter had himself expressed a dying wish to that effect.

While watchful of the interests of her own Church the Queen was tolerant of almost all religious opinions, and respected most of those from which she differed; only the extreme views and practices of Ritualists irritated her, and the tendencies of the High Church party at times caused her alarm. Although never forgetful of her headship of the Anglican Church, she was at the same time proud of her connection with the Presbyterian establishment of Scotland. Without bestowing much attention on the theology peculiar

Her respect for the Scottish Church

to it, she gratefully recognised what she somewhat erroneously took to be its Lutheran tendencies, and she enjoyed its unadorned services and the homely exhortations of its ministers. To her Scottish chaplains she extended a cordiality which was rare in her attitude to her English chaplains.

XXXVI

GLADSTONE'S FIRST ADMINISTRATION

On Disraeli's resignation the Queen at once sent for Gladstone, and he for the first time became her Prime Minister in December 1868. Gladstone had been prominent in the highest walks of public life from almost the opening of her reign, and his loyalty to Peel through his long administration had excited in the Queen much interest in him. She had joined in the chorus of congratulation which had greeted his budget speeches of former years—speeches by which he first earned the confidence of the general public. But he had gradually abandoned his Tory associations. After transferring his allegiance to the Liberal party, he steadily developed advanced opinions on almost all pressing questions of domestic reform. With such opinions the Queen was out of sympathy. Not that her political intuitions were illiberal, but the Liberalism to which she clung was confined to the old Whig principles of religious toleration and the personal liberty of the subject. She deprecated change in the great institutions of government, especially in the army and the Church. The obliteration of class distinctions was for her an idle dream. Radicalism she

Gladstone Prime Minister 1868.

judged to be a dangerous compromise with the forces of revolution.

Divergent views of foreign policy.

Nor did Gladstone share the Queen's view that foreign affairs were of greater practical moment than home affairs. His theory that England had little or no concern with European politics, and no title to exert influence on their course, conflicted with her training and the domestic sentiment that came of her foreign family connections. At the same time Gladstone cherished Palmerston's enthusiasm for those struggles for freedom of oppressed nationalities which the Queen viewed coldly and was always averse from encouraging.

Tendencies to alienation.

The Queen fully recognised Gladstone's abilities, and he always treated her personally with a deferential courtesy to which Palmerston's temperament very often made him a stranger. His early intercourse with her had, indeed, inspired him on his part with warm admiration for her character. 'Her love of truth,' he had written of her while in attendance at Balmoral in 1864, 'and wish to do right prevent all prejudices from effectually warping her.' But this appreciative judgment was now to suffer many severe shocks. As soon as the Queen and Gladstone began to drift apart it was inevitable that the breach between them should widen with the progress of years. From almost his first interview with her in his capacity of Prime Minister Gladstone failed to inspire her with confidence. She detected in his arguments a mutability of political principle and a tendency to move in directions which she regarded as unsafe. She confessed herself 'afraid.' Her nerves were tried, and she showed an irritability of temper in future intercourse with him which at times tended to hinder despatch of public business.[1]

During Gladstone's first ministry he and his colleagues undertook a larger number of legislative reforms than any Government had essayed during her reign, and the obligation which she felt to be

The Government's legislative activity.

[1] Gladstone's first cabinet was thus constituted:—

First Lord of the Treasury, Mr. Gladstone; Lord Chancellor, Lord Hatherley (Page Wood); President of the Council, Lord de Grey and Ripon (created Marquis of Ripon, 1871); Lord Privy Seal, Earl of Kimberley (formerly Lord Wodehouse); Chancellor of the Exchequer, Robert Lowe (created Viscount Sherbrooke, 1880); Home Secretary, Henry Austin Bruce (created Lord Aberdare, 1873); Foreign Secretary, Lord Clarendon; Colonial Secretary, Lord Granville; War Secretary, Edward Cardwell (created Viscount Cardwell, 1874); Indian Secretary, Duke of Argyll; President of the Board of Trade, John Bright; Chancellor of the Duchy of Lancaster, Lord Dufferin; Postmaster-General, Lord Hartington (afterwards Duke of Devonshire); First Lord of the Admiralty, H. C. E. Childers; President of the Poor Law Board, G. J. Goschen (now Viscount Goschen).

In 1870 W. E. Forster, Vice-President of the Privy Council, was given a seat in the cabinet. On Lord Clarendon's death in 1870 Lord Granville became Foreign Secretary; Lord Kimberley, Colonial Secretary; and Lord Halifax (Sir C. Wood), Lord Privy Seal. John Bright retired owing to illness in the same year, and was succeeded by Chichester Fortescue, afterwards Lord Carlingford. In January 1871 Goschen succeeded Childers at the Admiralty, and James Stansfeld became President of the Poor Law Board. In May 1872 Childers succeeded Lord Dufferin as Chancellor of the Duchy of Lancaster; and in October of this year, on the resignation of Lord Hatherley, Roundell Palmer (created Lord Selborne) became Lord Chancellor. In 1873 Lord Ripon and Childers retired; John Bright re-entered the ministry as Chancellor of the Duchy of Lancaster; Gladstone took, in place of Lowe, the Chancellorship of the Exchequer in addition to the Treasury; Bruce (created Lord Aberdare) was made President of the Council; and Robert Lowe, Home Secretary.

imposed on her of studying the arguments in their favour overtaxed her mental strength.[1] New questions arose with such rapidity that she complained that she had not the time wherein to form a judgment. Gladstone, although he was unwearied in his efforts to meet her protests or inquiries, and was (she frankly admitted) 'most ready to enter into her views and to understand her feelings' on public affairs, had not the faculty of brevity in exposition. His intellectual energy, his vehemence in argument, the steady flow of his vigorous language, tormented her. With constitutional correctness she acknowledged herself to be powerless to enforce her opinion against his; but she made no secret of her personal hostility to most of his proposals.

Gladstone's social accomplishments, moreover, were not of a kind calculated to conciliate the Queen in intercourse outside official business, or to compensate for the divergences between their political points of view. The topics which absorbed him in private life were far removed from the Queen's sphere of knowledge or interest.

Gladstone and the Queen's private affairs.

Another seed of alienation had been sown and was likely to prove of fertile growth. In her private affairs the Queen often thought that Gladstone felt 'little interest' or was 'very helpless.' In point of fact Gladstone held far more strongly than any of his predecessors that it was in her own interest and

[1] The six chief legislative enactments for which Gladstone's ministry was responsible between 1869 and 1873 were: Irish Church Disestablishment Act (1869), Irish Land Act (1870), Elementary Education Act (1870), Army Regulation Act (1871), Ballot Act (1872), and Supreme Court of Judicature Act (1873).

ment gave way on certain subsidiary points, and the Bill, to the immense relief of both Gladstone and his sovereign, passed safely its last stages.[1] How much of the result was due to the Queen's interference, and how much to the stress of events, may be matter for argument; but there is no disputing that throughout this episode she by her personal energy oiled the wheels of the constitutional machinery.

While the Irish Church crisis was in progress the Queen did not neglect comparatively unimportant topics of government business. She showed her versatility of mind by discussing through the same months with as much earnestness as she discussed Disestablishment of the Irish Church a very trifling innovation in the navy. In March 1869 she was much moved by a proposal of her half-nephew, Prince Leiningen, captain of the royal yacht, to give sailors in the navy permission to wear beards. She raised objection to the concession, and bade Childers, the First Lord of the Admiralty, in whose control the decision lay, commit himself to nothing without consulting a representative body of naval officers. When Childers agreed to the suggested change the Queen assented reluctantly, and added the proviso that moustaches without beards should be forbidden sailors on the ground that the personal appearance of sailors should be adequately distinguished from that of soldiers.[2]

The Queen and sailors' beards.

During this busy period, when questions of the smallest and the largest importance equally taxed the Queen's thoughts, her public activities were

Public activities, 1869.

[1] *Life of Tait*, ii. passim.
[2] Childers's *Life of Childers*, i. 175 seq.

mainly limited to a review of troops at Aldershot on April 17. On May 25 she celebrated quietly her fiftieth birthday, and at the end of June entertained for a second time the Khedive of Egypt. On June 28 she gave a 'breakfast' or afternoon party in his honour at Buckingham Palace. It was the main festivity in which she took part during the season. In the course of her autumn visit to Balmoral she went on a tour through the Trossachs and visited Loch Lomond. Towards the end of the year, November 6, she made one of her rare passages through London. She opened the new Blackfriars Bridge and Holborn Viaduct, but she came from Windsor only for the day. It was the first public progress through the capital that she had made since her widowhood, and she had looked forward to the ordeal with much nervous apprehension. Her welcome was unexpectedly gratifying. Nothing was said or done that disturbed her equanimity for a moment.

Intercourse with men of letters.

The Queen now occasionally sought a new form of relaxation in intercourse with some of the men of letters whose fame contributed to the glory of her reign. Her personal interest in literature was not strong, and it diminished in later years; but she respected its producers and their influence.

Tennyson.

With Tennyson, whose work her husband had admired, and whose 'In Memoriam' gave her comfort in her grief, she was already in intimate correspondence. This she maintained till his death, and whenever he visited her at Windsor or Osborne she treated him with the utmost confidence.

Carlyle.

Through her friends, Sir Arthur Helps and Dean Stanley, she had come to hear much of other great living writers. Lady Augusta Stanley told her of Carlyle, and she sent him a message of condolence, of which he was duly appreciative, on the sudden death of his wife in 1866. In May 1869 the Queen visited the Westminster Deanery, mainly to make Carlyle's personal acquaintance. The Stanleys' guests also included Grote, the historian of Greece, and his wife, Sir Charles Lyell, the geologist, and Lady Lyell, and the poet Browning. The Queen was in a most gracious humour. Carlyle deemed it 'impossible to imagine a politer little woman; nothing the least imperious; all gentle, all sincere . . . makes you feel too (if you have any sense in you) that she is Queen.'[1] The impression Carlyle made on the Queen was far less agreeable than that which she produced on him. To her he appeared to be gruff-tempered, if not unmannerly. She told Browning that she admired his wife's poetry.[2]

George Eliot and Dickens.

Among the novels she had lately read was George Eliot's 'Mill on the Floss,' and she afterwards read with close attention the same writer's 'Middlemarch,' which she criticised with shrewdness; but Dickens's work was the only fiction of the day that really attracted her in the early and middle years of her reign. In him, too, she manifested personal interest. She had attended in 1857 a performance by Dickens and other amateurs of Wilkie Collins's 'The Frozen Deep' at the Gallery of Illustration, and some proposals, which came to nothing, had been

[1] Froude, *Carlyle in London*, ii. 379–80.
[2] Reid, *Lord Houghton*, ii. 200.

made to him to read the 'Christmas Carol' at Court in 1858.[1] In March 1870 Dickens, at Helps's request, lent her some photographs of scenes in the American civil war, and she took the opportunity that she had long sought of making his personal acquaintance. She summoned him to Buckingham Palace in order to thank him for his courtesy. On his departure she asked him to present her with copies of his writings, and handed him a copy of her 'Leaves' with the autograph inscription, 'From the humblest of writers to one of the greatest.'

Dr. Smiles.

Other writers of whom she thought highly included Dr. Samuel Smiles, whose 'Lives of the Engineers' she presented to her son-in-law of Hesse-Darmstadt in 1865. She was interested, too, in the work of Dr. George Macdonald, on whom she asked Lord Beaconsfield to confer a pension in 1877.

[1] At the sale of Thackeray's property in 1864 she purchased for 25*l*. 10*s*. the copy of the 'Christmas Carol' which Dickens had presented to Thackeray.

XXXVII

ANXIOUS YEARS, 1870-1

In 1870 European politics once more formed the most serious topic of the Queen's thought, and the death in July of her old friend, Lord Clarendon, the Foreign Secretary, increased her anxieties. Despite her personal attachment to Lord Granville, who succeeded to Clarendon's post, she had far smaller faith in his political judgment, and was inclined to regard her own experience as more than a match for his. *Lord Clarendon's death.*

Although she watched events with attention, the Queen was hopeful until the last that the struggle between France and Germany, which had long threatened, might be averted. In private letters to the rulers of both countries she constantly counselled peace; but her efforts were vain, and in July 1870 Napoleon declared war. She regarded his action as wholly unjustified, and her indignation grew when Bismarck revealed designs which he alleged Napoleon to have formed to destroy the independence of Belgium. In the fortunes of that country she was deeply concerned by reason of the domestic ties that linked her with its ruler. *The Franco-German war.*

In the opening stages of the conflict that followed her ruling instincts identified her fully with the cause of Germany. Both her sons-in-law, the Crown Prince *Her sympathy with Germany.*

and Prince Louis of Hesse-Darmstadt, were in the field, and through official bulletins and the general information that her daughters collected for her, she studied their movements with painful eagerness. She sent hospital stores to her daughter at Darmstadt, and encouraged her in her exertions in behalf of the wounded. When crushing disaster befell the French arms she regarded their defeat as a righteous judgment. She warmly approved a sermon preached before her by her friend, Dr. Norman Macleod, at Balmoral on October 2, 1870, in which he implicitly described France as 'reaping the reward of her wickedness and vanity and sensuality.' [1]

Her pity for France.

But many of her subjects sympathised with France, and her own tenderness of heart evoked pity for her French neighbours in the completeness of their overthrow. With a view to relieve their sufferings, she entreated her daughter, the Crown Princess, and her son-in-law the Crown Prince, as well as her friend the Queen of Prussia, to avert the calamity of the bombardment of Paris. On October 2, 1870, the Crown Prince noted in his diary: 'Queen Victoria, who watches our actions with touching sympathy, has telegraphed to his Majesty [the King of Prussia] to urge him to be magnanimous in regard to the proposals of peace [for which the French were already suing], although she has no practical measures to propose.' [2]

Bismarck resents her interference.

Bismarck bitterly complained that 'the petticoat sentimentality' which the Queen communicated to

[1] *More Leaves*, p. 151.

[2] *Diaries of Emperor Frederick*, edited by Margaretha von Poschinger, 1902.

he Prussian royal family hampered the fulfilment of German designs. The Crown Prince's unconcealed devotion to her, and the ready ear he lent to her counsel, wholly compromised him in the eyes of Bismarck. He cynically taunted her son-in-law with his innocent faith in her genuine attachment to German interests.[1] But Bismarck's scorn did not deter the Queen from pressing her ministers formally to offer her mediation with the object not merely of bringing the war to an early close, but of modifying the vindictive terms which Germany sought to impose on France.

Her endeavours were of small avail. English influence was declining in the councils of Europe. Russia had made the preoccupation of France and Germany with their own quarrel the occasion for breaking the clause in the treaty of Paris which excluded Russian warships from the Black Sea. This defiant act was acquiesced in by Gladstone's Government, in spite of the Queen's indignant protest.

Decline of British influence.

Yet the Queen's efforts for France were well appreciated there. Some years later (December 3, 1874) she accepted, with sympathetic grace, at Windsor, an address of thanks from representative Frenchmen for the charitable services rendered by English men and women during the war. She replied in French. The elaborate volumes of photographs illustrating the campaigns, which accompanied the address, she placed in the British Museum.

French gratitude.

Hatred of Napoleon's policy did not estrange her compassion from him in the ruin that overtook him

[1] See the Prince's 'Diary,' edited by Professor Geffcken, in *Deutsche Rundschau,* 1888.

The Queen's care of the Empress Eugénie and Napoleon III.

and his family. Very early in the conflict, the fortune of war turned against him; his empire was brought to a violent end, and a republic was proclaimed in Paris. The Empress Eugénie fled to England in September 1870, and took up her residence at Chislehurst. The Queen at once sent her a kindly welcome, and on November 30 paid her a long visit, which the exiled Empress returned at Windsor five days later. The Empress's calm resignation to her fate excited the Queen's admiration, and she was thankful for the public sympathy generally extended to her unhappy guest. Thenceforth the friendship of Queen and Empress grew closer than before. When, too, Napoleon, on his release from a German prison, joined his wife in March 1871, the Queen lost no time in visiting him at Chislehurst, and until his death on January 9, 1873, openly showed her fellow-feeling with him in his melancholy fate. His misfortune dissipated every trace of her former distrust and animosity, and she fell anew under the spell of his charming courtesy, which had fascinated her at their first meeting in 1855.

Domestic politics.

The course that domestic affairs were taking during 1870 was hardly more agreeable to her than the course of foreign affairs. In January the cabinet resolved to take another great step in their endeavour to conciliate Ireland, by submitting to Parliament a Bill for the reform of Irish land tenure. This measure, which bore notable testimony to the progressive principles which governed his Irish policy, evoked in Gladstone intense enthusiasm. To 'mark the gravity of the occasion,' he implored the Queen to open in person the new session. He tried to persuade himself that, despite her attitude to Irish disestablishment, her sympathies on the land question would be 'in the same current' as his own.[1] But the Queen heard his appeal unmoved, and declined, on the ground of feeble health, to entertain the notion of a visit to Westminster. In April the attempt by a Fenian to assassinate Prince Alfred while on a visit at Port Jackson, New South Wales, greatly disturbed her and further weakened her faith in the wisdom of Gladstone's conciliatory policy towards Ireland. Happily the Prince recovered; and she had no reason to doubt the genuineness of public sympathy which was given her in full measure.

Further political anxiety was caused her by the Government's large scheme for the reorganisation of the army, which had been long contemplated. The first step taken by Cardwell, the Secretary of State for War, was to subordinate the office of Commander-in-Chief to his own. Twice before the Queen had successfully resisted or postponed a like proposal. She regarded it as an encroachment on the royal prerogative. Through the Commander-in-Chief she claimed that the Crown directly controlled the army without the intervention of ministers or Parliament; but her ministers now proved resolute, and she, on June 28, 1870, with ill-concealed reluctance, signed an Order in Council which deposed the Commander-in-Chief from his place of sole and immediate dependence on the Crown.[2]

Dislike of Cardwell's army reforms.

[1] Morley's *Life of Gladstone*, ii. 293.
[2] *Hansard*, ccii. 10 sq.; *Parl. Papers*, 1870 c. 164.

Abolition of purchase in army, 1871.

Next session the Government's plan for reorganising the army was pushed a step further in a Bill for the better regulation of the army, of which a main clause sought to abolish promotion by purchase. The measure passed through the House of Commons by large majorities. In the House of Lords the Duke of Richmond carried resolutions which practically excluded the crucial clause for the abolition of purchase. Characteristically, the Queen deprecated a conflict between the Houses, but the Government extricated her and themselves from that peril by a bold device which embarrassed her. They advised her to accomplish their reform by exercise of her own authority without further endeavour to win the approval of the Upper House. The purchase of commissions had been legalised not by statute, but by royal warrant, which could be abrogated by the Sovereign on the advice of her ministers without express sanction of Parliament. The Queen was in a painful dilemma. She was, on the one hand, required to cancel a royal warrant, the terms of which did not to her judgment seem in need of change. On the other hand, she was expected violently to strain the power of the prerogative against a branch of the Legislature with which she was at heart in sympathy. Lacking all enthusiasm for the proposed reform, she feared to estrange the House of Lords from the Crown by action on her part which circumvented its authority. But the ministerial counsel was imperative, and the Queen accepted it with mixed feelings. At any rate, she had this much consolation. Despite her dislike of the manœuvre, the assertion of the prerogative was never ungrateful to her, and it was well understood that the responsibility for her present exercise of it was her minister's. So that there might arise in the future no doubt on the latter point, she directed the cabinet, immediately after she had signed the warrant, to draw up a formal minute declaratory of the advice they had given her (July 19, 1871).

The Queen's industrious pursuit of public business in private failed to reconcile the people to the continued infrequency of her appearances in public. She alienated sympathy, too, by occasional promises of attendance at formal functions which she at the last moment failed to fulfil. Of the only two public ceremonies in which she engaged to take part in 1870, she figured in no more than one. She opened the new buildings of London University at Burlington House (May 11, 1870); but to the general disappointment, indisposition led her to delegate to the Prince of Wales the opening of so notable a London improvement as the Thames Embankment (July 13, 1870). Throughout the year the galling criticism continued in full force, and she appealed in vain to the Prime Minister, to make some declaration in her defence. The outcry caused Gladstone hardly less anxiety than it caused the Queen, but he conscientiously believed that it could only be met effectively by a more regular and more public resumption of the Queen's ceremonial duties.

Continued complaints of her seclusion.

The feeling of discontent was somewhat checked by the announcement in October 1870 that she had assented to the betrothal of her fourth daughter, Princess Louise, to a subject, and one who was in the

Betrothal of Princess Louise.

eye of the law a commoner. The Princess had given her hand at Balmoral to the Marquis of Lorne, eldest son of the Duke of Argyll. It was the first time in English history that the Sovereign sanctioned the union of a Princess with one who was not a member of a reigning house since Mary, youngest daughter of Henry VII. and sister of Henry VIII., married, in 1515, Charles Brandon, Duke of Suffolk.[1] The Queen regarded the match merely from the point of view of her daughter's happiness, to which she believed it would signally contribute.

Queen opens Parliament, Feb. 9, 1871.

Princess Louise's engagement rendered necessary an appeal to Parliament for her daughter's provision; and as her third son Arthur was on the point of coming of age, and also needed an income from public sources, it seemed politic to conciliate popular feeling by opening Parliament in person. Accordingly, on February 9, 1871, she occupied her throne in Westminster for the third time since her bereavement. The ceremony was curtailed as on the two previous occasions.

Grants to Princess Louise and Prince Arthur.

The Duke of Argyll, the Marquis of Lorne's father, was Secretary of State for India, and Sir Robert Peel, son of the former Prime Minister, denounced as impolitic the approaching marriage of a Princess with a 'son of a member of her Majesty's Government.'[2] But the proposed dowry of 30,000*l*. with an annuity of 6,000*l*. was granted almost unanimously (350 to 1). Less satisfaction was manifested when the Queen requested Parliament to provide for Prince Arthur.

---

[1] James II.'s marriage to Anne Hyde in 1660 did not receive the same official recognition.

[2] *Hansard*, cciv. 359.

An annuity of 15,000*l.* was ultimately bestowed. But, although the minority on the final vote numbered only eleven, as many as fifty-one members voted in favour of an unsuccessful amendment to reduce the sum to 10,000*l.*[1]

Meanwhile the Court cast off some of its gloom. The marriage of Princess Louise took place at St. George's Chapel, Windsor, with much pomp, on March 21, 1871, in the presence of the Queen, who for the occasion lightened her usual mourning attire. With unaccustomed activity in the months that followed she opened the Albert Hall (March 29), inaugurated the new buildings of St. Thomas's Hospital, and on June 30 reviewed the household troops in Bushey Park. At the review the Emperor Napoleon's heir, the young Prince Imperial, joined the royal party.

Princess Louise's marriage.

In the autumn the Queen entertained at Balmoral a large family party, including the Crown Prince and Princess of Prussia and Princess Alice. But her health gave increased cause for anxiety. She suffered severely from rheumatic gout and neuralgia. Her illness caused her intense pain, and she attributed it to worry over public business. As the news of her suffering spread, a more friendly tone characterised the references to her in the press, and she noted the change with pleasure. But she still cherished some resentment at the failure of her ministers to explain to the people that her seclusion was due to the constant demands made on her strength by official work.

Queen's illness, September 1871.

The Queen's anxieties were not destined at present

[1] *Hansard*, ccviii. 570–90.

Illness of the Prince of Wales. to know much diminution. The glimpse of increasing happiness in the royal circle was darkened at the end of the year by a grief almost as great as that which befell it just ten years before. At the end of November the Prince of Wales, the heir to the throne, fell ill of typhoid fever, at his house at Sandringham, and as the illness reached its critical stage, the gravest fears were entertained. The Queen went to Sandringham on November 29, and news of a relapse brought her thither again on December 8 with her daughter Alice, who had been for many months her guest. Both remained for eleven days, during which the Prince's life hung in the balance. Happily, on the fateful December 14, the tenth anniversary of the Prince Consort's death, the first indications of recovery appeared, and on the 19th, when the Queen returned to Windsor, the danger was passed. A week later the Queen issued for the first time a letter to her people, thanking them for the touching sympathy they had displayed during ' those painful terrible days.'

Public thanksgiving. As soon as her son's health was fully restored the Queen temporarily abandoned her privacy to accompany him in a semi-state procession from Buckingham Palace to St. Paul's Cathedral, there to attend a special service of thanksgiving (February 27, 1872). She was dressed in black velvet, trimmed with white ermine. For the last time the sovereign was received by the Lord Mayor with the traditional ceremonies at Temple Bar, the gates of which were first shut against her and then opened.[1] On the following day the

[1] The Bar was removed in the winter of 1878–9, and was sold to Sir Henry Meux, who re-erected it as a lodge gate on his estate of

Queen endured renewal of a disagreeable experience of earlier years. A lad, Arthur O'Connor, who pretended to be a Fenian emissary, pointed an unloaded pistol at her as she was entering Buckingham Palace. He was at once seized by her attendant, John Brown, to commemorate whose vigilance she instituted a gold medal as a reward for long and faithful domestic service. She conferred the first that was struck on Brown, together with an annuity of 25*l*. On the day following O'Connor's senseless act the Queen addressed a second letter to the public, acknowledging the fervent demonstrations of loyalty which welcomed her and her son on the occasion of the public thanksgiving.

That celebration, combined with its anxious cause and the general sympathy evoked by the Queen's own recent illness, strengthened immensely the bonds of sentiment between the Crown and the people. There was a peculiar need at the instant of strengthening these bonds. The formation of a republic in France had greatly stimulated that tendency to disparage monarchical institutions which the alleged self-effacement of the Queen had done much to create. A strong body of latent opinion even in educated society took a serious view of the situation. Lord Selborne, the Lord Chancellor, when the guest of the Queen at Windsor, was bold enough to tell her that if the French republic held its ground it would influence English public opinion in a republican direction.[1] An advanced

Display of Republican tendencies in England.

Popular censure of the Sovereign.

Theobalds Park, Hertfordshire. Its site in Fleet Street was marked by a memorial which is adorned by statues of the Queen and the Prince of Wales, now Edward VII.

[1] Selborne, *Memorials*, vol. ii.

thinker like John Richard Green, the historian, wrote somewhat cynically on December 19, 1871, that the feeling of 'domestic loyalty' engendered by the Prince of Wales's illness—the constant repetition of the statement that 'the Queen is an admirable mother, and that her son has an attack of typhoid'—would not settle the 'question of republicanism.'[1] Despite the modified renewal of the Queen's personal popularity, the cry against the monarchy threatened to become formidable.

Attacks on the Queen's income.

Mob orators prophesied that Queen Victoria would at any rate be the last monarch of England. The main argument of the noisier anti-royalists touched the expenses of the monarchy, which now included large provision for the Queen's children. Criticism of her income and expenditure was developed with a pertinacity which deeply wounded her. Pamphlets, some of which were attributed to men of position, compared her income with the modest 10,000*l.* allowed to the President of the United States. A malignant tract, published in 1871, which enjoyed a great vogue, and was entitled 'Tracts for the Times, No. 1: What does she do with it? by Solomon Temple, builder,' professed to make a thoroughgoing examination of her private expenditure. The writer argued that while the Queen was constantly asking

[1] 'I am sorry,' Green added, 'when any young fellow dies at thirty, and am far more sorry when any mother suffers; but the sentiment of newspapers and town councils over " telegrams from the sick-bed " is simply ludicrous. However, one remembers that all France went mad with anxiety when Lewis the Well-Beloved fell sick in his earlier days, and yet somehow or other '89 came never the later.' *Letters of John Richard Green*, ed. Leslie Stephen, 1901.

Parliament for money for her children she was not spending her official annuity on the purposes for which it was designed. A comparatively small proportion of it was applied, it was asserted, to the maintenance of the dignity of the Crown, the sole object with which it was granted; the larger part of it went to form a gigantic private fortune which was in some quarters estimated to reach already 5,000,000*l*. To these savings the writer protested she had no right; any portion of the Civil List income that at the end of the year remained unexpended ought to return to the public exchequer.

Personally, it was said, the Queen was well off, apart from her income from the Civil List. Besides Neild's bequest [1] she had derived more than half a million from the estate of the Prince Consort, and the receipts from the Duchy of Lancaster were steadily increasing.

The Queen's reputed affluence.

These reports of the Queen's affluence were largely founded on erroneous information. The Queen's savings in the Civil List were rarely 20,000*l*. a year, and her opportunities of thrift were grossly misrepresented. But in the hands of the advocates of a republican form of government the pecuniary argument was valuable, and it was pressed to the uttermost. Sir Charles W. Dilke, M.P. for Chelsea, when speaking in favour of an English republic at Newcastle, on November 6, 1871, complained that the Queen paid no income tax, and the statement added fuel to the agitation throughout the land.

Falsity of public rumours.

Ministers at the Queen's request refuted in detail the

[1] See p. 231.

Official refutations.

damaging allegations. Mr. (afterwards Sir) Algernon West, one of the Treasury officials, was directed by the Prime Minister to prepare an answer to the obnoxious pamphlet, 'What does she do with it?' Robert Lowe, the Chancellor of the Exchequer, announced that income tax was paid by the Queen. Twice at the end of the Session of 1871 Gladstone, in the House of Commons, insisted that the whole of the Queen's income was justly at her personal disposal.[1]

Debate on the Civil List 1872.

But the agitators were not readily silenced. Next Session, on March 19, 1872, Sir Charles Dilke introduced a motion for a full inquiry into the Queen's expenditure with a view to a complete reform of the Civil List. His long and elaborate speech abounded in minute details, but he injured his case by avowing himself a republican, and thus suggesting that he was moved by hostile prejudice. When the same avowal was made by Mr. Auberon Herbert, who seconded the motion, a scene of great disorder in the House of Commons followed. The Prime Minister, Gladstone, denied that the Queen's savings were on the alleged scale, or that the expenses of the Court had appreciably diminished since the Prince Consort's death.[2] Only two members of the House, Mr. G. Anderson and Sir Wilfrid Lawson, voted with Sir Charles Dilke and Mr. Herbert, and their proposal was rejected by a majority of 274.

Causes of her future popularity.

In the event the wave of republican sentiment was soon spent, but the conviction that the people paid an unduly high price for the advantages of the

[1] *Hansard*, ccvii. 1124, ccviii. 158–9.
[2] *Ibid.* ccx. 253 *sq.*

monarchy remained fully alive in the minds of large sections of the population, especially of the artisan class, until the Queen conspicuously modified her habits of seclusion. The main solvent of the popular grievance, however, was the affectionate veneration for her personality which was roused in course of time throughout her dominions by the veteran endurance of her rule, and by the growth of the new and powerful faith that she symbolised in her own person the unity of the British Empire.

XXXVIII

OLD FRIENDS AND NEW

Visit to Germany.

FROM the flood of distasteful criticism in 1872 the Queen escaped for a few weeks in the spring to the continent (March 23 to April 8). She crossed to Germany in order to visit at Baden-Baden her step-sister, whose health was failing. After her return home the German Empress was a welcome guest (May 2). With her the Queen was in thorough sympathy, especially in her dread of a renewal of war in Central Europe. In the same month the Queen sought unusual recreation by attending a concert which her favourite composer, Gounod, conducted at the newly opened Albert Hall.

Assassination of Lord Mayo.

But death was again busy in her circle and revived her grief. The assassination of Lord Mayo, Viceroy of India, startled the world on February 12, 1872. He was suddenly killed by a native Indian while inspecting the convict settlement at Port Blair, in the Andaman Islands in the Bay of Bengal. The Queen had known him as a member of Lord Derby's three administrations, in all of which he filled the office of Chief Secretary for Ireland. He had been nominated by Disraeli to the chief governorship of India on the eve of that minister's resignation in 1868.

He had won the Queen's personal regard, and after his murder, which she was inclined to attribute to neglect of simple precautions, she bore public testimony to the ability of her murdered representative, and to his personal loyalty. Memories of the Indian mutiny crowded to her mind, but happily the crime proved an isolated manifestation of native rancour, and did not disturb the peace of the empire.

Other incidents of the year were equally sad, if less tragic in their circumstance. The Queen had derived immeasurable comfort from conversation with Dr. Norman Macleod, her Scottish chaplain. 'How I love to talk to him,' she said, ' to ask his advice, to speak to him of my sorrows, my anxieties!'[1] but on June 16, 1872, he passed away. Her first mistress of the robes and lifelong friend, the Duchess of Sutherland, had died in 1868, and she now visited the duchess's son and daughter-in-law at Dunrobin Castle (September 6 to 12, 1872), so that she might be present at the laying of the first stone of a memorial to her late companion.

Death of Norman Macleod.

More trying than either of these bereavements was the loss, also in 1872, of her step-sister, the Princess Féodore, the last surviving friend of her youth, who died at Baden-Baden, September 23. There had been no slackening in recent years of the ties of affection that first united them in childhood. Yet another death on the following January 9 intensified the Queen's sense of desolation. On that day died, in his exile at Chislehurst, Napoleon III., ex-Emperor of the French. The amiability which

Death of Queen's step-sister.

Death of Napoleon III.

[1] *More Leaves*, pp. 148–161.

characterised his personal relations with the Queen and her family was never conquered by disaster, and the Queen at once undertook the mournful task of consoling his widow. The sympathy and feeling shown by the nation on the occasion were grateful to the Queen, and she appreciated the 'very generous and kind' terms in which the Empress Augusta wrote to her of the event from Berlin. Pity for Napoleon's sufferings seems to have ultimately blotted out in the Queen's mind all his moral defects. Her final charitable judgment of him was unjustified by his deserts, and was mainly inspired by the unfailing courtesy of his demeanour in social life, which had deeply impressed her on her first introduction to him. She offered a public and practical proof of her regard by providing the sarcophagus which enclosed the ex-Emperor's remains in St. Mary's Church, Chislehurst.

Disraeli declines office.

The year that opened thus sadly witnessed several incidents in public affairs that stirred in the Queen more pleasurable sensations. In March Gladstone's Irish University Bill was rejected by the House of Commons, and he at once resigned (March 11). The Queen accepted his resignation with alacrity, suggested his elevation to the House of Lords, and invited Disraeli to take his place as Prime Minister; but Disraeli declined the invitation in view of the normal balance of parties in the existing House of Commons, where the Conservatives were in a minority. Disraeli was vainly persuaded by the Queen to take another course. Gladstone pointed out to her that the refusal of office on the part of Disraeli, who had brought about his defeat, amounted to an unconstitutional shirking of his responsibilities. But Disraeli was awaiting with confidence an appeal to the constituencies; and although that appeal could not be long delayed, he had no greater desire than Gladstone to invite it at the moment. In face of Disraeli's obduracy, and his own unreadiness to face a dissolution, Gladstone was compelled, however reluctantly, to return for a season at least to the Treasury bench (March 20). His Government was greatly shaken in reputation, but it succeeded in holding on till the beginning of next year.

When the ministerial crisis ended the Queen paid for the first time an official visit to the East End of London in order to open an important extension of Victoria Park.[1] She was received with noteworthy enthusiasm.

Visit to East London, April 2.

The summer saw her occupied in extending hospitality to a political guest, the Shah of Persia, who, like the Sultan of Turkey, was the first wearer of his crown to visit England. The Queen's regal position in India rendered it fitting for her to welcome Oriental potentates to her Court, and the rivalry in progress in Asia between Russia and England gave especial value to the friendship of Persia. The Queen was in full accord with the policy that brought the Persian monarch to her shores. The

First visit of the Shah of Persia.

---

[1] Victoria Park (in the districts of Bethnal Green and Hackney) was originally formed by Act of Parliament in 1842, and named after the Queen. An outer fringe of the land which the Government had acquired was destined for building purposes. This fringe was purchased by public subscription in 1872, and the Queen consecrated it to the public use next year.

Shah stayed at Buckingham Palace from June 19 to July 4, and an imposing reception was accorded him. The Prince of Wales for the most part did assiduous duty as host in behalf of his mother, but she thrice entertained her guest at Windsor, and he wrote with enthusiasm of the cordiality of her demeanour. At their first meeting, on June 20, she invested him with the Order of the Garter; at the second, on June 24, he accompanied her to a review in Windsor Park; at the third, on July 2, he exchanged photographs with her, and he visited the Prince Consort's mausoleum at Frogmore.[1]

Relations with Russia.

Meanwhile the governments of both Russia and England were endeavouring to diminish the friction and suspicion that habitually impeded friendly negotiations between them. At the opening of the year Count Schouvaloff was sent by the Tsar, Alexander II., on a secret mission to the Queen. He assured her that the Russians had no intention of making further advances in Central Asia. Events proved that assurance to be equivocal; but there was another object of Schouvaloff's embassy which was of more immediate interest to the Queen, and accounted for the amiability that she extended to him. A matrimonial union between the English and Russian royal houses was suggested. The families were already slightly connected. The sister of the Princess of Wales had married the Tsarevitch (afterwards Tsar Alexander III.), Tsar Alexander II.'s eldest (surviving) son. It was now proposed that Prince Alfred, the Queen's second son, should be betrothed to the Grand Duchess

[1] *Diary of the Shah*, translated by Redhouse, 1874, pp. 144 sq.

Marie Alexandrovna, the Tsar Alexander II.'s only daughter.

At the date of the Shah's visit the Tsarevitch and his wife came on a visit to the Prince and Princess of Wales at Marlborough House in order to facilitate the project. The match was regarded by the Queen as of political promise, and in July she formally assented to it. Subsequently the Queen chose her friend, Dean Stanley, to perform at St. Petersburg the wedding ceremony after the Anglican rite (January 23, 1874), and she struggled hard to read in the Dean's own illegible handwriting the full and vivid accounts he sent her of his experiences. *Marriage of the Duke of Edinburgh.*

The Queen welcomed the formation of this new tie with the family of England's present rival in Asia and her old antagonist on the field of the Crimea; but she did not exaggerate its power of allaying the turmoil of political dispute between the two Powers. In the following May the coping-stone seemed to be placed on the edifice of an Anglo-Russian peace by the Queen's entertainment at Windsor of the Tsar Alexander II., her new daughter-in-law's father. But the political issues at stake between Russia and England were not of the kind to be affected by social amenities, and within three years the two countries were on the verge of war. *Its small political influence.*

XXXIX

DISRAELI IN POWER

Disraeli in power, 1874.

THE Liberal Government had survived its defeat by nearly ten months, when, in January 1874, the Queen learned 'with some surprise,' although with no regret, of Gladstone's decision to dissolve Parliament. The result was a triumphant victory for the Conservatives. To the Queen's relief, Gladstone's term of office was ended. He resigned office before the new Parliament met. She took formal leave of him with friendly dignity and self-control. 'She felt sure,' she said, 'that he might be reckoned upon to support the throne.' She renewed her offer of a peerage, but this honour was declined from motives which (the Queen wrote) she fully appreciated. At the same time she made no attempt to conceal the gratification with which she recalled Disraeli to power. She saw in the Conservative success proof that the advance of Radicalism, which she feared, was stayed, and that the Conservative instinct of the country had renewed its strength.

Strength of his position.

Her new minister's position was exceptionally strong. He enjoyed the advantage, which no minister, since Peel took office in 1841, had enjoyed, of commanding large majorities in both Houses of Parliament. Despite a few grumblers, he exerted supreme authority over his party, and the Queen was prepared to extend to him the fullest confidence. She had reached the unalterable conviction that he was a man of high character and patriotic ambition. His private and public life now alike evoked her admiration. Since he had last been in office Lady Beaconsfield had died (December 15, 1872). Disraeli's chivalric devotion to his wife, and the marks of respect that he paid to her memory, especially appealed to the Queen; they gave him, in her eyes, a moral force which she deemed rare in the upper class of society.

The more she came to consider Disraeli's political views the more strongly they commended themselves to her. His elastic Conservatism did not run counter to her hereditary whiggish sentiment. His theory of the Constitution gave to the Crown a semblance of strength and dignity which she valued the more after her experience of her recent ministers, who had been loth to listen patiently to her advice. Moreover, his opinion of the Crown's relations to foreign affairs precisely coincided with the belief which her husband had taught her, that it was the duty of a sovereign of England to seek to influence the fortunes of Europe. *Queen's approval of his political views.*

In his social intercourse, of which the Queen was now to enjoy much, Disraeli had the advantage of a personal fascination, which grew with closer acquaintance, and developed in the Queen a genuine affection. He conciliated her idiosyncrasies. He affected interest in the topics which he knew to *His personal fascination.*

interest her. He showered upon her all his arts and graces of conversation. He did what no other minister in the reign succeeded in doing in private talk with her—he amused her. His social charm lightened the routine of State business. He briefly informed her of the progress of affairs, but did not overwhelm her with details.

His recognition of his own responsibilities.

Nevertheless, Disraeli well understood the practical working of the Constitution, and, while magnifying the Queen's potential force of sovereignty, he did not prejudice the supreme responsibilities of his own office. His general line of policy being congenial to her, prolonged argument or explanation was rarely needful; but in developing his policy he was not moved by her suggestions or criticism in a greater degree than his predecessors. Even in the matter of making important appointments he did not suffer her influence to go beyond previous limits. But by his exceptional tact and astuteness he reconciled her to almost every decision he took, whether or no it agreed with her inclination. When he failed to comply with her wishes he expressed regret with a felicity which never left a wound. In immaterial matters – the grant of a Civil List pension or the bestowal of a subordinate post or title—he not merely acceded to the Queen's requests, but saw that effect was given to them with promptness. Comparing his attitude to the Queen with Gladstone's, contrasting the harmony of his relations with her with the tension that characterised his rival's, he was in the habit of saying, 'Gladstone treats the Queen like a public department; I treat her like a woman.'

Disraeli's Government began its work quietly.[1] Its main business during its first session was ecclesiastical legislation, with which the Queen was in full sympathy. Both the Churches of Scotland and England were affected. The Public Worship Regulation Bill, which was introduced by Archbishop Tait, was

Church legislation, 1874.

[1] Disraeli constituted his Cabinet thus:

First Lord of the Treasury	Mr. Disraeli (created Earl of Beaconsfield, August 1876).
Lord Chancellor	Lord Cairns.
Lord President of the Council	The Duke of Richmond.
Lord Privy Seal	The Earl of Malmesbury.
Foreign Secretary	The Earl of Derby.
Secretary for India	The Marquis of Salisbury.
Colonial Secretary	The Earl of Carnarvon.
Secretary for War	Mr. Gathorne Hardy (created Viscount Cranbrook, 1878).
Home Secretary	Mr. Richard Cross (created Viscount Cross, 1886).
First Lord of the Admiralty	Mr. Ward Hunt.
Chancellor of the Exchequer	Sir Stafford Northcote (created Earl of Iddesleigh, 1885).
Postmaster-General	Lord John Manners (afterwards Duke of Rutland).

In July 1876, on the resignation of Malmesbury, Lord Beaconsfield took the Privy Seal in addition to the First Lordship of the Treasury. In August 1877, on the death of Ward Hunt, W. H. Smith, Secretary to the Treasury, became First Lord of the Admiralty. In February 1878, on the resignation of Lord Carnarvon, Sir Michael Hicks-Beach became Colonial Secretary, and Mr. James Lowther Secretary for Ireland, with a seat in the Cabinet; at the same time the Duke of Northumberland became Lord Privy Seal. In April 1878, on the resignation of Lord Derby, Lord Salisbury became Foreign Secretary; Mr. Gathorne Hardy (afterwards Viscount Cranbrook), Secretary for India; and the Hon. Frederick Stanley (afterwards Lord Stanley of Preston and Earl of Derby), War Secretary.

an endeavour to check in England the growth of ritualism, which the Queen abhorred. The Scottish Church Patronage Bill substituted congregational election for lay patronage in the appointment of ministers in the Established Church of Scotland. This last measure was deemed essential to the prosperity of the Established Church of Scotland, which the Queen made a personal concern. She had at an earlier date favoured resistance to this reform, but she had seen with regret the disruption of the Established Church of Scotland to which that resistance had led, and she was not now inclined to dispute the justice of the innovation. Scottish Dissenters, especially those who had left the Church, raised stout opposition to a concession which they regarded as too belated to be equitable. To the Queen's disgust, Gladstone vehemently opposed the measure. His speech against the Bill excited her warm displeasure. She denounced his attitude as mere obstruction. 'He might so easily have stopped away,' she remarked to her friend, Principal Tulloch, when he spoke to her of the great orator's contribution to the debate. But the Bill was carried in spite of Gladstone's protest, and the Queen was content.

<small>Continued irritation with Gladstone.</small>

<small>Prince Leopold's illness.</small>

It was the Queen's full intention to have opened Parliament in person in February 1875, by way of indicating her sympathy with the new ministers; but the serious illness of Prince Leopold, who was suffering from typhoid fever, kept her away.

On her son's recovery, in conformity with the views that she and her Prime Minister held of the obligations of intervention in European politics that lay upon an English monarch, the Queen immersed herself in delicate negotiations with foreign sovereigns. Rumour spread abroad that the Franco-German war was to be at once renewed. Republican France had been pushing forward new armaments. It was recognised that she was bent on avenging the humiliations of 1870-1. The Queen's relatives at Berlin and Darmstadt informed her in the spring of 1875 that Bismarck was resolved to avoid a possible surprise on the part of France by suddenly beginning the attack. Her recent friend, Tsar Alexander II., was travelling in Germany, and she wrote appealing to him to use his influence with the German Emperor (his uncle) to stay violence.

Queen's fear of another Franco-German war.

On June 20, 1875, the Queen addressed herself directly to the German Emperor and offered her mediation. She quoted expressions that she had been informed Field-Marshal von Moltke had used, and begged her old friend to preserve Europe from a great calamity. The King of Prussia replied by denying the truth of her allegations. He thanked her for her suggestion of mediation, but expressed pain that she regarded him as a disturber of the peace of Europe. Her knowledge of his character should have made such an assumption impossible. 'No one is more thoroughly convinced than the writer that he who provokes a war in Europe will have the whole of public opinion against him and will accordingly have no ally, no *neutrale bienveillant*, but rather adversaries. The expressions which the Queen attributes to Field-Marshal Moltke represent an opinion which every one would hold

Her appeals to the King of Prussia.

in case of a quarrel—namely, *de se mettre en avantage*; but no politician, including Moltke, would ever contemplate wantonly plunging Europe into war.' The Queen replied that her fears were not exaggerated. Bismarck was informed of her action and wrote to the Emperor with cynical resentment of her interference. He ridiculed her suspicions. But, in spite of Bismarck's and his master's scornful disclaimer, it is undoubtedly true that there was a likelihood of an outbreak of hostilities between France and Germany in the early months of 1875. An accommodation may have been in progress before the Queen intervened. Although Bismarck affected to ignore her appeals, they clearly helped to incline the political scales of Central Europe in the direction of peace, and the scare of war soon passed away.[1]

End of the correspondence.

The Queen, in a subsequent letter to the Emperor, remarked that, apparently without his knowledge, the views that she had reported had been freely proclaimed in his 'entourage.' 'She will, however, say no more about it' (she wrote), 'as the whole affair is now consigned to oblivion.' The correspondence closed with the Emperor's assurance that as she did not give the names of her informants he would make no further inquiries. Bismarck maintained his attitude of scorn, and satirically expressed sorrow that the matter was suffered to drop so inconclusively.

It was agreeable to the Queen to turn from Euro-

[1] Bismarck, *Recollections*, ii. 191 *sq.*; Appendix to Bismarck's *Recollections*, i. pp. 256–60; Busch, *Conversations with Bismarck*; *Princess Alice's Letters*, p. 339.

pean complications to the plans whereby Disraeli proposed to enhance the prestige of her crown, and to strengthen the chain that, since the legislation of 1858, personally linked her with the great empire of India. Her pride in her relations with India and her interest in the welfare of its inhabitants never waned. Disraeli's first suggestion regarding her personal connection with India was that the Prince of Wales should, as her representative, make a state tour through the whole territory, and should visit the native princes. To this she readily assented. The needful arrangements were rapidly made, and the Queen took an affectionate leave of her son at Balmoral on September 17, 1875. The expedition was completely successful. The Prince returned to England in the following May, when the Queen welcomed him in London. He brought her welcome proof of the loyalty of India to the Crown.

New links with India.

Prince of Wales's Indian tour, Sept. 17, 1875, to May 11, 1876.

Disraeli's Indian policy also included a measure more directly affecting the Queen. He proposed to bestow on her a new title which would declare her Indian sovereignty. The Royal Titles Bill, which conferred on her the designation of Empress of India, was the chief business of the session of 1876, and she fittingly opened it in person amid much popular enthusiasm (February 8). The opposition warmly criticised Disraeli's proposal, but he assured the House of Commons that the new title would only be employed in India and in Indian affairs, and was designed to complete the connection between the Crown and the Indian Empire, which had been inaugurated after the Mutiny. The Bill passed

Empress of India, 1876.

through all its stages before May 1, when the Queen, to her immense satisfaction, was formally proclaimed Empress of India in London. The words which were adopted after much deliberation for the purpose of translating the new title into the Indian vernacular were Kaisar-i-Hind.

The Queen and the Indian chiefs.

By the ruling princes and chieftains in India her acceptance of the Imperial dignity was hailed with enthusiasm, and they expressed their gratification in personal addresses to the Queen that were characterised by exuberant Oriental imagery which greatly amused and interested her. 'This is the third time,' wrote one chieftain of the historical aspect in which the new title presented itself to the native mind, 'that India is going to be ruled by an Empress. The first was the widow of the Hindu King Agniborna; the second was the Rizia Begum, the daughter of the Mohammedan Emperor Altamash; the third is Queen Victoria, the English Sovereign. But something greater has been achieved. Such a powerful Sovereign of so vast a territory never ruled India. This proclamation may consequently be considered superior to all its kind.'[1]

[1] On January 1, 1877, at Delhi, the Governor-General of India (Lord Lytton) officially announced the Queen's assumption of her title of Empress to an imposing assembly of sixty-three ruling princes. Lord Lytton wrote out and sent to the Queen a very full account of the proceedings (see *Lord Lytton's Indian Administration*, 1899, by Lady Betty Balfour, pp. 115-32). Memory of the great ceremonial was perpetuated by the creation of a new Order of the Indian Empire, while a new Imperial Order of the Crown of India was established as a decoration for ladies whose male relatives were associated with the Indian Government. The Queen held the first investiture at Windsor on April 29, 1878.

The Queen herself gloried in her new honour, and, despite Disraeli's assurances, soon ceased to recognise restrictions in its use. She at once signed herself 'Victoria R. & I.' in documents relating to India, and early in 1878 she adopted the same form in English documents of State. In 1893 the words 'Ind[iæ] Imp[eratrix]' were engraved among her titles on the British coinage.

After the close of the session of 1876 the Queen was glad of the opportunity of marking her sense of the devotion that Disraeli had shown her by offering him a peerage (August 21, 1876); his health had suffered from his constant attendance in the House of Commons, and he contemplated resignation. The Queen declined to entertain the notion of his retirement from office, but she was anxious that he should relieve himself, as far as was practicable, of the pressure of public business. Accordingly he entered the House of Lords next year as Earl of Beaconsfield. *Disraeli becomes Earl of Beaconsfield.*

The Queen's cheering relations with Lord Beaconsfield stimulated her to appear somewhat more frequently in public, and she played prominent parts in several military ceremonials in the early days of Disraeli's government. She had narrowly watched the progress of the little Ashanti war on the West Coast of Africa, and at its successful conclusion she reviewed sailors, marines, and soldiers who had taken part in it in the Royal Clarence Victualling Yard at Gosport on April 23, 1874. At the end of the year, too, she distributed medals to the men.[1] On May 2, *Public appearances, 1874-6.*

[1] She suffered a severe shock in the autumn of 1875, when, while crossing to the Isle of Wight, her yacht, the 'Royal Albert,' ran down

1876, she reviewed troops at Aldershot, and in the following September presented at Balmoral colours to her father's regiment, the Royal Scots. She reminded the men of her military ancestry.

London engagements, 1876.

During the early spring of 1876, too, she was more active than usual in London. She attended a concert given by her command at the Royal Albert Hall (February 25). She opened in semi-state a new wing of the London Hospital (March 7). Two days later she inspected in Kensington Gardens the gorgeous Albert Memorial, the most elaborate of the many monuments to her husband; the central space in it is filled by a colossal gilded figure of the Prince. Thence, with her three younger daughters, she went to the funeral in Westminster Abbey of her old friend, Lady Augusta Stanley, whose death, after a thirty years' association, deeply moved her; in memory of Lady Augusta she erected a monumental cross in the private grounds at Frogmore.

Visit to Coburg, 1876.

Later in the season of 1876 the Queen left for a three weeks' vacation at Coburg (March 31 to April 20); she travelled from Cherbourg through France, but avoided Paris, and on the return journey had an interview at La Villette station, in the neighbourhood of the capital, with the President of the Republic, Marshal MacMahon. The meeting was a graceful recognition on her part of the new form of government, and every courtesy was paid her.

On her return to England the German Empress was once more her guest, and she debated anew the

another yacht, the 'Mistletoe,' and thus caused three of its occupants to be drowned in her presence (August 18, 1875).

prospects of the Crown Prince and Princess, which continued to cause her anxiety. While going to Balmoral a few months later she unveiled at Edinburgh yet another Albert Memorial, on August 17. For the first time since the Prince Consort's death, she kept Christmas at Windsor instead of at Osborne, owing to illness in the Isle of Wight, and she transgressed what seemed to be her settled dislike of Court entertainments by giving a concert in St. George's Hall on December 26.

At Balmoral and Osborne.

During the two years that followed, the Queen's mind was absorbed in the intricacies of European politics far more deeply than at any time since the Crimean war. She had now, she often said, more to do and think of than ever before, and bitterly complained of want of rest. A great conflict among the Powers of Europe seemed imminent. The subject races of the Turkish Empire in the Balkans threatened the Porte with revolt in the autumn of 1875. The insurrection spread rapidly, and it was obvious that Russia, to serve her own ends, intended to come to the rescue of the insurgents after the manner of her action in 1854. Beaconsfield adopted Palmerston's policy of that year, and declared that British interests in India and elsewhere required the inviolate maintenance of the Sultan's authority.

Crisis in Eastern Europe.

The course of events was not propitious for the peace of Europe. Turkey endeavoured to suppress the insurrection in the Balkans with great barbarity, notably in Bulgaria; and in the autumn of 1876 Gladstone, who had lately announced his retirement from public life, suddenly emerged from his seclusion

The Queen's efforts for peace.

in order to stir the people of the United Kingdom by the energy of his eloquence to resist the bestowal on Turkey of any English favour or support. Gladstone's interposition exasperated the Queen. One effect of his vehemence was to tighten the bond between her and Lord Beaconsfield. At Christmas 1876 the crisis had reached a very acute stage. The Queen was at Windsor, and Lord Beaconsfield had arranged to spend the holidays with friends in the country. But at the Queen's earnest entreaty he altered his arrangements at the eleventh hour and remained in London. She appealed to him 'not to leave her at this moment.' She 'declared it an act of high imprudence' (the Prime Minister wrote to a friend) 'for myself and Derby [the Foreign Minister] to leave town at this conjuncture.'

The Queen accepted unhesitatingly Lord Beaconsfield's view that England was bound to protect Turkey from injury at Russia's hands, and she bitterly resented the embarrassments that Gladstone's impassioned denunciation of his policy caused her minister. But the Queen did not readily abandon hope that Russia might be persuaded by diplomatic pressure to abstain from interference in the Balkans. The occupants of the thrones of Russia and Germany were her personal friends, and she believed her private influence with them might keep the peace. Princess Alice met the Tsar at Darmstadt in July 1876, and he assured the Queen through her daughter that he had no wish for a conflict with England. Thus encouraged, she wrote to him direct, and then appealed to the German Emperor to use his influence.

She even twice addressed herself to Bismarck in the same sense. But Bismarck disbelieved in her sincerity. He affected to credit her at heart with as rash a passion for active hostilities with Russia as her friend Napoleon III. had cherished for active hostilities with Germany in 1870. He had not forgiven her interference in German affairs in 1875, and urged the German Emperor and Empress to address her in much the same terms as she had addressed them when she denounced Germany's alleged designs on France.[1] Her efforts to restrain Russia from attacking Turkey failed. Russia declared war on Turkey on April 24, 1877, and before the end of the year won a decisive victory.

As Russia's triumph over Turkey became complete, the Queen did not dissemble her disgust and disappointment. Thereupon she identified herself with her minister's aggressive foreign policy as unmistakably as she had identified herself with Peel's Free Trade policy more than thirty years before. She, no less than Lord Beaconsfield, resolved that England should regulate the fruits of Russia's successes. Twice did she openly indicate her sympathy with her minister's anxieties in the course of 1877—first by opening Parliament in person in February, and secondly by paying him a visit in circumstances of much publicity at his country seat, Hughenden Manor, Buckinghamshire. She had honoured Melbourne and Peel in a similar way, but more than a quarter of a century had passed since she was the guest of a Prime

At Hughenden.

---

[1] Appendix to *Bismarcks Gedanken u. Erinnerungen*, ii. 488; Busch, *Conversations with Bismarck*, ii. 277.

Minister. She, with Princess Beatrice, travelled by
rail on December 21, 1877, from Windsor to High
Wycombe station, where Beaconsfield and his secretary,
Mr. Montagu Corry (afterwards Lord Rowton), met
her. The mayor presented an address of welcome.
Driving with her host to Hughenden, she lunched
with him, staying two hours, and on leaving planted
a tree on the lawn.[1] The incident created a powerful
impression both in England and Europe.

The history of the Crimean war

The situation revived at all stages the Queen's
memory of the earlier conflict with Russia, the course
of which had been largely guided by her husband's
influence. She had lately re-studied the incidents of
the Crimean war in connection with the 'Life of the
Prince Consort,' on which Sir Theodore Martin was
engaged under her supervision. At all events she
desired the whole truth to be told without qualification. The Crimean period of the Prince's career was
reached by his biographer before the great crisis of
1877, and a suggestion was made that the marriage
of her second son with a Russian princess called for
the modification of episodes in the narrative in order

---

[1] A poem in *Punch* on December 29, 1877, illustrating a sketch
by Mr. Linley Sambourne, humorously suggested the continental
alarm. One stanza runs:—

> ' Did the CZAR in far Bucharest shiver?
>   Did GORTSCHAKOFF thrill with a dread?
> Did the SULTAN in Stamboul feel less of
>   The storms where he pillows his head?
> As from luncheon in Hughenden Manor
>   The Queen and my radiant Lord B.
> Walked out to the lawn and proceeded
>   To plant a memorial tree!'

to conciliate the Russian royal family. But the Queen scouted such considerations. Facts and documents must be followed at any cost.

At the end of 1877 there appeared the third volume of the biography, which illustrated the intensity of Court and national feeling against Russia when the Crimean war was in its critical stages. The 'Spectator,' a journal supporting Gladstone, censured the volume as 'a party pamphlet' in favour of Lord Beaconsfield, and Gladstone himself—a member of Lord Aberdeen's cabinet which made the war—reviewed it in self-defence. The issue of the volume, for which the Queen was freely held responsible, added fuel to the bitter controversy at home and abroad. *The third volume of the Prince Consort's biography.*

In 1878 the crisis reached its height, and the Queen's activities were incessant. At the beginning of the year the Sultan made a personal appeal to her to induce the Tsar to accept lenient terms of peace. She telegraphed to the Tsar an entreaty to accelerate negotiations; but when the Tsar forced on Turkey conditions which gave Russia a preponderating influence within the Sultan's dominions, she supported Lord Beaconsfield in demanding that the whole settlement should be referred to a congress of the European Powers. *The Queen seeks to protect Turkey.*

Through the storms that succeeded no minister received stauncher support from his sovereign than Lord Beaconsfield from the Queen. The diplomatic struggle brought the two countries to the brink of war, but the Queen scorned the notion of retreat. A congress of the Powers was summoned to meet in *Her support of Beaconsfield's policy.*

Berlin in June 1878. The Queen recommended that Lord Beaconsfield should himself represent England, together with Lord Salisbury, the Foreign Secretary. The Prime Minister warned the Queen before he set out that his determination to prevent Russia from getting a foothold south of the Danube might abruptly issue in active hostilities. The Queen declared herself ready to face all risks. War preparations were set in motion with the Queen's full approval. On May 13, 1878, she held a review on a great scale at Aldershot in company with the Crown Prince of Prussia and the Princess, who were her guests. On August 13 she reviewed at Spithead in inauspicious weather a strong fleet for 'special service.'

The Congress of Berlin.

Meanwhile the Congress of Berlin had, in spite of obstacles, re-established peace. At an early session a deadlock arose between Lord Beaconsfield, the English envoy, and Prince Gortschakoff, who acted as the Russian envoy. Lord Beaconsfield refused to countenance any cession of territory or material influence to Russia south of the great dividing river. Neither side would give way. Lord Beaconsfield threatened departure from Berlin so that the dispute might be settled by 'other means.' Therein he made no empty boast. He acted in accord with the understanding which he had previously reached with the Queen. But Russia yielded the specific point at Bismarck's persuasion, and the pacific treaty of Berlin was soon formulated and signed.

Queen welcomes Lord Beaconsfield.

The material and moral advantages that England derived from her intervention in the Russo-Turkish war of 1877 were long questioned, but the Queen entertained no doubt of the reality of the benefit in both kinds. When Lord Beaconsfield returned from Berlin, bringing, in his own phrase, 'peace with honour,' she welcomed him with unrestrained enthusiasm. On July 22, 1878, she invested both him and his colleague, Lord Salisbury, at Osborne with the Order of the Garter.

Domestic incident during 1878 was hardly less abundant than public incident. On February 22 there took place at Berlin the first marriage of a grandchild of the Queen. Charlotte, the eldest daughter of the Crown Prince and Princess, was then married to the hereditary Duke of Saxe-Meiningen. But it was mainly death or threatenings of death in the Queen's circle that marked the year. Her former ally, Victor Emanuel, had died on January 9. Two attempts at Berlin to assassinate the old German Emperor (May 11 and June 2) gave her an alarming impression of the condition of Germany, where she specially feared the advance of socialism and atheism. On June 4 died her former Prime Minister, Lord Russell, and she at once offered his family, through Lord Beaconsfield, a public funeral in Westminster Abbey; but the offer was declined, and he was buried at Chenies. A few days later (June 12) there passed away at Paris her first cousin, the dethroned and blind King of Hanover. She gave directions for his burial in St. George's Chapel, Windsor, and herself attended the funeral on June 25.

Domestic incident, 1878.

But the heaviest blow that befell her in 1878 was the loss of her second daughter, Princess Alice, who had been her companion in her heaviest trials. The

Death of Princess Alice.

Princess died of diphtheria at Darmstadt on December 14, the seventeenth anniversary of the Prince Consort's death. It was the first loss of a child that the Queen had experienced, and no element of sorrow was absent. The Princess was nursing her own children when she contracted the fatal illness. The people again shared their Sovereign's grief in full measure, and on the 26th she addressed to them a simple letter of thanks describing the dead Princess as 'a bright example of loving tenderness, courageous devotion, and self-sacrifice to duty.' She erected a granite cross to her memory at Balmoral next year, and showed the tenderest interest in her motherless family.

Marriage of Duke of Connaught.

Fortunately the succeeding year 1879 brought more happiness in its train. Amid greater pomp than had characterised royal weddings since that of the Princess Royal, the Queen attended on March 13 the marriage at St. George's Chapel, Windsor, of her third son, the Duke of Connaught. The bride was third daughter of Prince Frederick Charles of Prussia (the Red Prince), a nephew of the German Emperor, and first cousin of the Crown Prince. A new connection was thus formed with the Prussian House, and one that was thoroughly congenial to the Queen.

First visit to Italy, 1879.

Twelve days later the Queen enjoyed the new experience of a visit to Italy. She stayed for nearly a month, till April 23, at Baveno on Lago Maggiore. She delighted in the scenery, and was gratified by a visit from the new King Humbert and Queen Margherita of Italy. On her return to England she learned of the birth of her first great-grandchild, Feodora, the firstborn of the hereditary Princess of

Saxe-Meiningen.[1] The Queen was herself just completing her sixtieth year. It was an early age at which to welcome a third generation of descendants.

Hardly had the congratulations ceased when she suffered a severe shock. On June 19, 1879, the telegraph wires brought her news of the death, in the Zulu war in South Africa, of the Prince Imperial, the only child of her friend the ex-Empress of the French.[2] He had gone to Africa as a volunteer in the English army, and was slain when riding almost alone in the enemy's country. He was regarded with much affection by the Queen and by the Princess Beatrice, and all the Queen's wealth of sympathy was bestowed on the young man's mother, the widowed Empress Eugénie. The Prince's remains were brought to England, and while they were being interred at Chislehurst, the Queen was the Empress's sole companion (July 12).

The Prince Imperial's death.

Nowhere was the political situation promising at the time. The outlook alike in South Africa and India was a source of especially grave concern to the Queen. The Zulu war in which the Prince Imperial met his death was only one symptom of the unrest in South Africa which the Governor of the Cape, Sir Bartle Frere, had brought about in an endeavour to assert British supremacy over the

The Ministry's difficulties.

---

[1] The infant grew up to womanhood during the Queen's lifetime, and married, September 24, 1898, Prince Henry XXX. of Reuss.

[2] The Queen wrote in her *Journal*, June 20, 1879: 'Had a bad restless night, haunted by this awful event, seeing those horrid Zulus constantly before me, and thinking of the poor Empress, who did not yet know it. . . . My accession day, forty-two years ago: but no thought of it in presence of this frightful event.' (*More Leaves*, p. 258.)

whole of that territory. Sir Bartle Frere's policy generally enjoyed the Queen's support and was proved by after-events to be in principle wise and statesmanlike. But it was not attended at the moment by success. Lord Beaconsfield did not conceal his disapproval of many actions of the Governor, but his preoccupation with Eastern Europe had not permitted him to control the South African situation. He felt morally bound to defend all the awkward positions into which the Government had been led by its accredited representative, with the result that the pertinacious Opposition had often the best of the argument.

Indian wars.

Equal difficulties were encountered by Lord Beaconsfield's Government in India, where the rival pretensions of England and Russia to dominate the Amir of Afghanistan had involved the Indian Government, under Lord Lytton's viceroyalty, in two successive wars with the Afghans (November 1878 and December 1879). These wars were represented by the Government's enemies to be acts of wanton aggression. The Queen took a very different view. Throughout his term of office Lord Lytton constantly sent direct to her letters describing the course of events, and she in her replies gave every encouragement to the policy that he was pursuing. When in the late autumn of 1879 the murder of Sir Louis Cavagnari, the English envoy, at Cabul momentarily convulsed the Indian Government and rendered the second invasion of Afghanistan necessary, the Queen at once despatched to Lord Lytton a cheering message of sympathy which he described as 'kind, patriotic, and manly.' 'She is really,' the Viceroy wrote to a friend of this incident, ' a better Englishman than any one of her subjects, and never falls short in a national crisis, when the interests and honour of her empire are at stake.'[1]

The strife of political parties at home greatly complicated the situation of affairs in distant parts of the empire, and gave the Queen additional cause for distress. Gladstone, during the autumn of 1879, in a series of passionate speeches delivered in Midlothian, charged the Government with recklessly fomenting disaster throughout the globe by their blustering imperialism. Oratorical crusades which excited popular feeling were invariably obnoxious to her and the Queen warmly resented Gladstone's Midlothian campaign. Gladstone's persistent attacks on Lord Beaconsfield as the author of the whole evil especially roused her wrath. In private letters she invariably described Gladstone's denunciations of her favourite minister as shameless or disgraceful.

Gladstone's Midlothian speeches.

The Queen's faith in Beaconsfield was now unquenchable. He acknowledged her sympathy in avowals of the strongest personal attachment to her. He was ambitious, he told her, of securing for her office greater glory than it had yet attained. He was anxious to make her the dictatress of Europe. 'Many things,' he wrote, ' are preparing, which for the sake of peace and civilisation render it most necessary that her Majesty should occupy that position.' But there were ominous signs that Beaconsfield's own

The Queen's devotion to Lord Beaconsfield.

[1] *Lord Lytton's Indian Administration*, by Lady Betty Balfour, 1899, p. 360.

lease of power was reaching its close, despite the Queen's anxiety to lengthen it. For the fourth time while he was Prime Minister she opened the last session of his Parliament, on February 5, 1880. The ceremonial was conducted with greater elaboration than at any time since the Prince's death. On March 24 Parliament was dissolved at the will of the Prime Minister, who believed the omens auspicious for his success at the polls. The future fortune of the Queen's favourite minister was put to the hazard of the people's vote.

XL

GLADSTONE RESUMES OFFICE

DEEPLY as the Queen was interested in the result of the coming election, she did not remain in England to watch its progress. Spring holidays had been arranged some weeks before, and, on the day after Parliament was dissolved, she left on a month's visit to Germany. She spent most of her time at the Villa Hohenlohe, her late half-sister's residence at Baden-Baden, but she went thence to Darmstadt to attend the confirmation of two daughters of the late Princess Alice. At the palace at Darmstadt she lived in the rooms that her dead daughter had occupied. Her attention was diverted by intercourse with her grandchildren who gathered round her, and while she was still abroad a domestic incident in the family of her eldest daughter, the Crown Princess, gratified her highly. Her grandson, Prince William of Prussia (now Emperor William II.), in whom the Queen had delighted from his infancy, was just betrothed to Princess Augusta Victoria of [Schleswig-Holstein-Sonderburg] Augustenburg, daughter of Duke Frederick, the claimant to the duchy of Holstein, who had fared so disastrously in the Schleswig-Holstein struggle. Duke Frederick had died in the previous January, crushed by Bismarck's Prussian policy.

Visit to Germany, 1880.

Betrothal of Prince William of Prussia.

The Queen fully sympathised with the sentiment of young Prince William's parents, who acknowledged that poetic justice was rendered to Duke Frederick's memory by the entrance of his daughter into the direct line of succession to the crown of the Prussian ruler's consort.

The general election of 1880.

But, in spite of her joy at her grandson's betrothal and her happy intimacy with Princess Alice's children, her keenest interests were absorbed in the vicissitudes of the general election in England. Telegrams passed constantly between her and the Prime Minister, and her spirits sank when the completeness of the defeat of the Conservative party proved to her that he could serve her no longer. Liberals and Home Rulers had in the new House of Commons a majority over the Conservatives of no less than 166.

Queen's perplexity.

On April 17 the Queen was back at Windsor, and next day had two hours' touching conversation with her vanquished minister. She felt bitterly her isolation. The least agreeable of her past experiences seemed to threaten her anew. As in 1855 and 1859, when a ministerial crisis brought her in view of the mortifying experience of making Prime Minister one whom she distrusted, she carefully and deliberately examined all possible alternatives. For five days she refrained from any overt action. On April 22 Lord Beaconsfield paid her a second visit at Windsor, and when he left, the Queen summoned by his advice Lord Hartington, who was nominal leader of the Liberal party in the House of Commons; for, in spite of Gladstone's activity in agitation through the country, he had never formally resumed the post of leader of the party since his retirement in 1875, when Lord Hartington had been chosen to fill his place in the House of Commons. She invited Lord Hartington to form a ministry 'as a responsible leader of the party now in a large majority.' She emphasised her faith in his 'moderation.' To her own and to Lord Beaconsfield's disappointment, Lord Hartington replied in effect, that Gladstone alone had won the victory and that he alone must reap the rewards. In vain she urged on her listener 'the obligations arising out of his position.' Finally she desired him to ascertain whether or no Gladstone would enter the cabinet in a secondary post under another's leadership.[1] Beaconsfield said that Lord Hartington showed want of courage in hesitating to take office; he 'abandoned a woman in her hour of need.'

On returning to London Lord Hartington called on Gladstone and reported his conversation with the Queen. It was to Lord Granville, the Liberal leader of the House of Lords, and not to Lord Hartington, Gladstone argued, that he had transferred the leadership of the party in 1875, and he was of opinion that the Queen was defying precedent in sending in the first instance for Lord Hartington instead of for Lord Granville. But he had made up his mind to serve under neither the one nor the other. He would enter the new cabinet as its head or remain outside. Next morning (April 23) Lord Hartington went back to Windsor in company with Lord Granville, who was an old friend of the Queen. Against her will they convinced her that Gladstone

Gladstone resumes office, 1880.

[1] Morley's *Life of Gladstone*, ii. 622–4.

alone was entitled to power, and, making the best of the difficult situation, she entrusted Lord Granville with a message to him requesting an interview. Gladstone hurried to Windsor the same evening, and he accepted the Queen's commission to form a government. To him she appeared to be 'natural under effort.' She expressed the hope that the new Government's general action would be 'conciliatory,' frankly confessed that some of his recent expressions had caused her pain, and, when he remarked that his language while in office would differ from that which he had employed while out of it, she quietly retorted that he would 'have to bear the consequences' of his past freedom of speech. Of Lord Beaconsfield the Queen took formal leave at Windsor on April 27. They conversed together in a spirit of deep dejection. She offered the fallen minister as a mark of her esteem promotion to a higher rank in the peerage, but this he declined.

Gladstone's second administration was soon in being. Small heed was paid to the Queen's suggestions as to the allotment of portfolios. Fearful of further changes in the organisation of the army, she recommended that Lord Hartington should become Secretary of War. Gladstone selected Lord Hartington for the India Office, and the Queen accepted Childers's appointment to the War Office with ill-concealed impatience.[1] Nor did she approve the bestowal of a viscounty on Robert Lowe, a prominent member of Mr. Gladstone's first Government for

[1] Lord Hartington was, however, transferred to the War Office in December 1882.

whom no place was found in the second ministry. A barony, the Queen insisted, met all the requirements of the case. She deprecated the introduction into the cabinet of a politician holding opinions so markedly Radical as Mr. Chamberlain held, and when, two years later, Gladstone found it politic to strengthen the Radical element in his ministry by the admission of Sir Charles Dilke to the cabinet, the Queen was vehement in expressions of dissent.

Gladstone at all points remained firm. But, although some of the *personnel* of the new Government was little to the Queen's taste and she disliked the manner in which offices were distributed, she received all her new advisers with constitutional correctness of demeanour.[1]

[1] Gladstone's second Cabinet was constituted thus

First Lord of the Treasury and Chancellor of the Exchequer	W. E. Gladstone.
Lord Chancellor	Lord Selborne.
President of the Council	Earl Spencer, K.G.
Lord Privy Seal	Duke of Argyll, K.T.
First Lord of the Admiralty	Earl of Northbrook.
Home Secretary	Sir W. Vernon Harcourt.
Foreign Secretary	Earl Granville, K.G.
War Secretary	Hugh C. E. Childers.
Colonial Secretary	Earl of Kimberley.
Secretary for India	Marquis of Hartington.
Chancellor of the Duchy of Lancaster	John Bright.
President of the Board of Trade	Joseph Chamberlain.
President of the Local Government Board.	J. G. Dodson (afterwards Lord Monk Bretton)
Chief Secretary for Ireland	W. E. Forster.

Changes were numerous later. Lord Carlingford, who succeeded Argyll as Privy Seal (May 1881), was also President of the Council from March 1883, in place of Lord Spencer, who succeeded Lord

Marriage of King of Hanover's daughter.

Two acts due to the Queen's native kindness of heart involved her in some public censure as soon as the new Liberal Government was installed. She felt lifelong compassion for the family of her exiled cousin, the King of Hanover, and showed great tenderness to his daughter Frederica, whom she called 'the poor lily of Hanover.' She not only countenanced her marriage with Baron von Pawell-Rammingen, who was formerly her father's equerry, but arranged for the wedding to take place in her presence in her private chapel at Windsor (April 24, 1880). The match was deemed to be wanting in dignity, especially in Germany, and to be undeserving of the Queen's countenance, but she lost no opportunity of proving that it received her full sanction.[1]

Memorial to Prince Imperial.

A few months later she, as visitor of Westminster Abbey, urged the erection of a monument there in memory of the late Prince Imperial. The scheme was brought to the notice of the House of Commons, where, in spite of Gladstone's support, it was em-

---

Cowper as Irish Lord Lieutenant (May 1882). Mr. Forster, Irish Secretary, gave way (May 1882) to Lord Frederick Cavendish, on whose murder Mr. (afterwards Sir) G. O. Trevelyan succeeded. Dodson succeeded Bright as Chancellor of the Duchy (July 1882), and Sir Charles Dilke Dodson at the Local Government Board. Gladstone yielded the Chancellorship of the Exchequer to Childers (Dec. 1882), when Lord Hartington became War Secretary, Lord Derby Colonial Secretary, and Lord Kimberley India Secretary. Mr. Trevelyan succeeded Dodson in the Duchy (Oct. 1884), Mr. Campbell-Bannerman becoming Irish Secretary. Lord Rosebery was First Commissioner of Works from 1884 and Privy Seal also (in place of Carlingford) from February 1885.

[1] The Queen published in the *Court Circular*, on April 26, a long list of the Princess's wedding presents, and on April 28 she announced that the Princess's wedding dress and veil, which were fully described, were her own gift.

phatically condemned on the ground alike of the Prince's nationality and of public policy (July 16, 1880). Five days later the Queen reluctantly withdrew the proposal and at once appointed a site for the monument in St. George's Chapel, Windsor.

As soon as the new Government had settled down to its work, the Queen recalled to Gladstone's recollection the character and procedure of Peel's ministry in which he had himself first held high office. She pronounced in a communication to the Prime Minister a 'high eulogy' on Peel's achievements, which she thought Gladstone would do well to emulate. The Prime Minister declared himself in general agreement with the Queen's verdict on past history, and expressed in vague phraseology his desire to tread in his predecessor's footsteps.[1] The Queen was not reassured, and was disinclined to watch events passively. The misgivings with which her new advisers inspired her stimulated her critical activity, and during the five years that they held office there was increase rather than diminution in her energetic supervision of the conduct of public business. She informed Gladstone and his colleagues at the outset that she insisted on a full exercise of her right of 'commenting on all proposals before they are matured.' Ministers must take no decision before their completed plans were before her. She was punctilious to the last degree in requiring of ministers strict conformity with traditional etiquette, and when Gladstone in September 1883 took, without previous communication with her, a holiday cruise in

Active control of ministers.

[1] Morley's *Life of Gladstone*, i. 642, 643.

the North Sea and visited the Danish Court at Copenhagen, the Queen promptly pointed out to him that he had broken a rule requiring the sovereign's permission before a prime minister could visit a foreign land. Gladstone admitted his fault in a letter of apology.[1]

Burials Act.

One of the new Government's first domestic measures—the Burials Bill—caused her disquietude. The bill was designed to authorise the conduct of funerals by Nonconformist ministers in parish churchyards, and the Queen sought the opinion of Lord Selborne, like herself a firm adherent of the Anglican Establishment, respecting the forms of religious service in churchyards that were to be sanctioned.

Distrust of ministerial measures.

More serious perturbation was caused the Queen by the ministry's plans for the further reorganisation of the army, the control of which, despite recent legislation, she persisted in treating as the Crown's peculiar province. No military reform escaped her censorious vigilance. In May she stoutly protested against the proposal for the complete abolition of flogging in the army. She hated the system, she wrote, but she saw no possible alternative 'in extreme cases of cowardice, treachery, plundering, or neglect of duty on sentry.' She objected to the suspension of the practice of giving honorary colonelcies with incomes attached as rewards for distinguished service; any abuse in the method of distribution could be easily remedied. When Childers, the Secretary of War, in the winter of 1880 sketched out a scheme for linking battalions and for giving regiments territorial

[1] Morley's *Life of Gladstone*, iii. 115–117.

designations, she warmly condemned changes which were likely, in her opinion, to weaken the regimental *esprit de corps*. Childers, though he respectfully considered the Queen's suggestions, rarely adopted them, and in a speech at Pontefract on January 19, 1882, he deemed it prudent openly to contest the view that the Crown still governed the army.

During the first months of Gladstone's second Administration the Queen's main energies were devoted to urging on the ministers the duty of spirited and sustained action in bringing to an end the wars in Afghanistan and South Africa, which their predecessors had left on their hands. The Afghan campaign of 1880 she watched with the closest attention. After the defeat of the English troops at Maiwand she wrote to Childers of her dread lest the Government should not adequately endeavour to retrieve the disaster. She had heard rumours, she said, of an intended reduction of the army by the Government. She thought there was need of increasing it. On August 22 she proved her anxiety by inspecting the troopship 'Jumna' which was taking reinforcements to India. But, to her intense satisfaction and gratitude, Sir Frederick (now Earl) Roberts, by a prompt march on Kandahar, reduced the Afghans to submission. The new Amir, Abdur-Rahman, was securely installed on the Afghan throne, and to the Queen's relief he maintained to the end of her reign friendly relations with her and her Government, frequently speaking to his family and court in praise of her character and rule.[1]

Afghanistan, 1880.

Maiwand, July 27.

[1] Amir Abdur-Rahman, *Autobiography*, 1900.

Recall of Sir Bartle Frere.

In like manner the Queen put every obstacle she could in the way of the recall of Sir Bartle Frere, the High Commissioner in South Africa, who was responsible for the forward policy that had of late years been pursued there. The Queen's prepossessions carried no weight with the cabinet; the feeling of the majority of the House of Commons strongly pronounced itself against Sir Bartle's retention of office, and he was accordingly dismissed. The Queen taunted Gladstone with allowing the House of Commons to trench unduly on the business of the Executive.

The Transvaal, 1881.

After the outbreak of the Boer war in December 1880, and the defeat and death of General Colley on February 27, 1881, at Majuba Hill, the Queen was unremitting in her admonitions to the Government to bestir themselves. She recommended General Roberts for the vacant chief command in the Transvaal—a recommendation which the Government made independently at the same moment. Her ministers, however, decided to carry to a conclusion the peace negotiations which had previously been opened with the Boers, and before General Roberts landed in South Africa the war was ended by the apparent capitulation of the Queen's government to the enemy. The ministerial action conflicted with the Queen's views and wishes. She openly contemned it as weak and pusillanimous. The restoration to the Boers of practical autonomy served signally to increase her distrust of ministerial policy.

But, whatever her opinion of her Government's diplomacy, she was not sparing in signs of sympathy with the sufferings of her troops in the recent hostilities. By her desire the colours of the 24th regiment, which were recovered after being temporarily lost during the Zulu war at the battle of Isandhlwana, were brought to Osborne; while speaking to the officers who bore the flag of the bravery of the regiment and its trials in South Africa, she decorated the colours with a wreath (July 28, 1880). During 1882 she once more held a review at Aldershot (May 16), and on August 17, at Parkhurst, Isle of Wight, she presented new colours to the second battalion of the Berkshire regiment (66th), which had lost its old colours at Maiwand in Afghanistan.

Sympathy with the troops.

Discontent with her present advisers intensified the grief with which she learned of the death of Lord Beaconsfield—her 'dear great friend' she called him—on April 19, 1881. For the moment the blow overwhelmed her. She and all members of her family treated his loss as a personal bereavement. Two days after his death she wrote from Osborne to Dean Stanley: 'His devotion and kindness to me, his wise counsels, his great gentleness combined with firmness, his one thought of the honour and glory of the country, and his unswerving loyalty to the throne make the death of my dear Lord Beaconsfield a national calamity. My grief is great and lasting.' To another friend she described the dead statesman as 'my dear valued and devoted friend and counsellor whose loss is so great to the country and to me. . . . Every sympathetic recollection of him is a satisfaction to me.' When the question of a public funeral was raised the Queen said she knew that he would wish to

Death of Beaconsfield, April 19, 1881.

be buried beside his wife at Hughenden, but she directed that a public monument should be placed to his memory in Westminster Abbey.[1]

Marks of respect for his memory.

At the funeral at Hughenden, on the 26th, she was represented by the Prince of Wales and Prince Leopold. Of two wreaths which she sent, one, of primroses, bore the inscription, 'His favourite flower. . . . A tribute of affection from Queen Victoria.' Thus was inaugurated the permanent association of the primrose with Lord Beaconsfield's memory.

Such marks of regard did not, however, exhaust the Queen's public acts of mourning. Four days after the burial, she and the Princess Beatrice visited Lord Beaconsfield's house at Hughenden, and the Queen placed with her own hands a wreath of white camellias on the coffin, which lay in the still open vault in the churchyard. Next year, on the wall above the seat in the chancel of the church which Lord Beaconsfield was wont to occupy—a position chosen by herself—she caused to be set up an elaborate memorial tablet—a low-relief profile portrait of the minister—with an inscription from her own pen: 'To the dear and honoured memory of Benjamin, Earl of Beaconsfield, this memorial is placed by his grateful sovereign and friend Victoria R.I. ("Kings love him that speaketh right."—Proverbs xvi. 13.)

---

[1] *Life of Stanley*, ii. 565. The actual burial of great men in Westminster Abbey never evoked much enthusiasm in the Queen. When in 1873, on the death of Bishop Wilberforce, his family declined the offer of that honour, the Queen remarked that she was very glad, for 'to her nothing more gloomy and doleful [than the Abbey] exists.' Morley's *Life of Gladstone*, ii. 460.

of disorder always won the Queen's admiration, and
she had given every encouragement to W. E. Forster,
Lord Frederick Cavendish's predecessor as Irish Secretary, in his strenuous efforts to uphold the law. She
had made diligent inquiries respecting the *personnel*
of the agitators, of whom she spoke with impatience,
and had urged every effort to protect the law-abiding
landlords and tenants from outrage. The more
conciliatory policy which ultimately prevailed with
Forster's successors awoke in her no enthusiasm.

Happily the Queen found some compensation
for her varied troubles at home in annual travel
abroad, and in other agreeable vicissitudes of private
life. In the spring she spent a vacation abroad for
the first time in the Riviera, staying for a month
at Mentone. Once more, too, a marriage in her
family gladdened her. Her youngest son, Leopold,
Duke of Albany, had become engaged to Princess
Helen Frederica, a princess of the German house of
Waldeck-Pyrmont, whose sister was second wife to
the King of the Netherlands. The Queen had no previous personal acquaintance with the young princess,
and was doubtful of the stability of Prince Leopold's
health, but she gave her consent to the union with
good hope.

First visit to the Riviera.

The marriage compelled the Queen once more
to approach Parliament for a financial settlement on
behalf of the Prince. Precedent was on the Queen's
side and Gladstone was amiable. He invited Parliament on March 23 to increase the Prince's income,
as in the case of his two next elder brothers, from
15,000*l*., which he had enjoyed since he came of

Grant to Prince Leopold.

age, to 25,000*l*. Gladstone pressed the proposal on the House of Commons with tact and zeal, but as many as forty-two members—mainly from Ireland—voted against the proposal. It was ultimately carried by a majority of 345. The customary corollary, that in case of the Prince's death 6,000*l*. a year was to be allowed his widow, happily passed without dissent.

Prince Leopold's marriage, April 27.

Shortly after the Queen's return from Mentone she attended the marriage of Prince Leopold and Princess Helen of Waldeck-Pyrmont, at St. George's Chapel, Windsor. She provided handsomely for her youngest son and his bride. She purchased in perpetuity the Crown property of Claremont, which had been granted her for life by Parliament in 1866 on the death of its former holder, King Leopold, and this estate she generously presented to the newly married pair for their residence.

Epping Forest and the new Law Courts.

Twice during the year she took part in public ceremonies of interest. On May 6 she went to Epping Forest, which the Corporation of London had recently secured for a public recreation ground, and she dedicated it formally to public use. At the end of the year, on December 4, at the request of Lord Selborne, the Lord Chancellor, she inaugurated the new Law Courts in the Strand.

XLI

GENERAL GORDON

THE prevailing note of the Queen's life, owing alike to public and private causes, during the two years that followed was one of gloom. At the close of 1882 she had been deprived by death of another friend in whom she trusted—Archbishop Tait. He gratified her by sending from his deathbed a message by way of 'a last memorial of twenty-six years of devoted service with earnest love and affectionate blessing' for her and her family. An offer was made by the Dean and Chapter of a tomb for the dead prelate in Westminster Abbey, but his daughters preferred that he should lie with his relatives in Addington churchyard. The question of the Primate's last resting-place was submitted by his daughters to the Queen's decision, and she promptly gave her voice for Addington.

<small>Years of gloom, 1883-5.</small>

The Queen was at one with the Prime Minister, Gladstone, in treating as a matter of the highest seriousness the choice of a successor to Tait in the Archbishopric of Canterbury. The topic had formed a subject of discussion between them during Gladstone's first ministry, in 1870, when Tait's recovery from a serious illness looked doubtful and a vacancy

<small>Choice of a Primate, 1883.</small>

in the Primacy seemed imminent. Then the Queen and her minister agreed to offer the great office to Dean Wellesley of Windsor, who was the confidential friend of both and the Queen's constant adviser for many years past in ecclesiastical matters. But the Dean at the time refused to entertain the suggested promotion, and now—just ten weeks before Tait's death—he had himself passed away. The Queen felt keenly the unwonted absence of his counsel. But she faced the situation with active energy. Many names were suggested by the minister. 'Never,' writes Dean Church, 'for hundreds of years has so much honest disinterested pains been taken to fill the Primacy—such inquiry and trouble resolutely followed out to find the really fittest man, apart from every personal and political consideration, as in this case. Of that I can bear witness.'[1] Tait shortly before his death expressed the wish that Dr. Harold Browne should be his successor. Dr. Browne had, on Gladstone's nomination, succeeded Samuel Wilberforce as Bishop of Winchester in 1873, and still held that see. The Queen was not disinclined to act upon Tait's dying recommendation; but Dr. Browne was past seventy years old, and Gladstone pointed out to her that precedents and prudence alike rendered his age an insuperable bar to his appointment. In due time the Queen explained to the Bishop of Winchester, who was made aware of the course of events: 'The Queen feels it would be wrong to ask him to enter on new and arduous duties, which now more than ever tax the health and strength of him

[1] *Life and Letters of Dean Church*, 1895, p. 307.

who has to undertake them, at his age, which, as the Bishop himself says, is the same as that of our dear late friend [Tait].'[1]

Fortunately she found herself ultimately in agreement with Gladstone as to the fitness of Edward White Benson to succeed to the Primacy. He had been the first headmaster of her husband's foundation of Wellington College, and was afterwards first Bishop of Truro. Benson's acceptance of the office was, she said, 'a great support to herself,' and with him her relations were no less cordial than with his predecessor.

Appointment of Archbishop Benson.

At the moment that Benson took the appointment, the Queen suffered a new sense of desolation from the death, on March 27, 1883, of her faithful attendant, John Brown. She placed a tombstone to his memory in Crathie churchyard, and invited suggestions from Tennyson for the inscription, which she prepared herself. At Balmoral she caused a statue of her humble friend to be erected, and at Osborne a granite seat was inscribed with pathetic words to his memory. 'His loss to me (ill and helpless as I was at the time from an accident),' she wrote a few months later, 'is irreparable, for he deservedly possessed my entire confidence ; and to say that he is daily, nay, hourly, missed by me, whose lifelong gratitude he won by his constant care, attention, and devotion, is but a feeble expression of the truth :

Death of John Brown, March 27, 1883.

> 'A truer, nobler, trustier heart,
> More loyal and more loving, never beat
> Within a human breast.'

[1] Kitchin's *Life of Dr. Harold Browne*, p. 456 ; Morley's *Life of Gladstone*, iii. 93–5.

Publication of 'More Leaves.'

An accidental fall on the staircase at Windsor, early in 1883, rendered the Queen unable to walk for many months, and increased her tendency to depression. Even in January, 1884, it was formally announced that she could not stand for more than a few minutes.[1] In the summer of 1883 she consoled herself in her loneliness by preparing for publication another selection from her journal—'More Leaves from a Journal of Life in the Highlands, 1862–1882,' and she dedicated it 'To my loyal highlanders, and especially to the memory of my devoted personal attendant and faithful friend, John Brown.' She still took a justly modest view of the literary value of her work. When she sent a copy to the poet Tennyson she described herself as 'a very humble and unpretending author, the only merit of whose writing was its simplicity and truth.'

Prince Leopold's death.

The public reception of the volume revived her spirits, but they were quickly dashed by the second loss of a child. On March 28, 1884, the Duke of Albany, her youngest and her lately married son, died suddenly at Cannes. His health had caused her constant concern and intensified her affection for him. The trial of his death shook her severely. A great help and support had been taken from her, she said, in her declining years. But she met the blow with courage and with religious resignation. To one message of condolence she replied: 'Yes, God has taken most away who were my dearest, as well as those I most needed as helps and comforts. I am sorely stricken indeed. This is but a pilgrimage, a

[1] *Court Circular*, January 21.

great struggle, and not our real home.'[1] 'Though all happiness is at an end for me in this world,' she wrote to Tennyson, 'I am ready to fight on.' In a letter to her people, dated from Windsor Castle April 14, she promised 'to labour on for the sake of my children, and for the good of the country I love so well, as long as I can;' and she tactfully expressed thanks to the people of France, in whose territory her son had died, for the respect and kindness that they had shown. Although the pacific temper and condition of the Prince's life rendered the ceremony hardly appropriate, the Queen directed a military funeral for him in St. George's Chapel, Windsor, on April 6.

The conduct of the Government during the year (1883–4) gave her small cause for satisfaction. Egypt, which was now practically administered by England, was the centre of renewed anxiety. Since Arabi's insurrection, the inhabitants of the Soudan had, under a fanatical leader, the Mahdi, been in revolt against Egyptian rule, and they were now menacing the Egyptian frontier. During 1883 the English ministry had to decide whether to suppress by force the rebellion in the Soudan, or to abandon the territory to the insurgents and cut it off from Egypt altogether. To the Queen's dismay, the policy of abandonment was adopted, with a single qualification. Some Egyptian garrisons still remained in the Soudan in positions of the gravest peril, and these the English Government undertook to rescue. The Queen recommended prompt and adequate action, but her words fell on deaf ears (January 1884).

The Soudan.

[1] Lord Ronald Sutherland Gower, *Old Diaries*, p. 404.

General Gordon.

The Government, yielding to journalistic clamour, confined itself to sending General Gordon to Khartoum, the capital of the disturbed districts, in order to negotiate with the rebels for the relief of the threatened garrisons. His influence with natives of the Soudan had in the past proved very great, but at once the Queen expressed doubts whether he could possibly execute his present difficult mission single-handed. She watched Gordon's advance towards his goal with the gravest concern, and constantly reminded the Government of the danger he was running.

The Queen's forebodings proved well justified. Gordon's influence with the natives of the Soudan was of small avail. Soon after his arrival at Khartoum, he urged the home Government to nominate Zobeir Pasha, an influential Egyptian slave-dealer and slave-hunter, Governor-General of the Soudan. Expert opinion supported this advice; the Queen pronounced in its favour; but though Gladstone was willing to adopt it, he failed, despite the Queen's entreaty, to remove the scruples of the majority of the cabinet. Gordon's position at once became desperate, and he was soon besieged in Khartoum by the Mahdi's forces. Thereupon the Queen solemnly warned the Government of the obligation it was under of despatching a British expedition to deliver him. The Government feared to involve itself further in war in Egypt, but the Queen was not to be silenced. Public opinion was clearly with her, and in the autumn a British army was tardily sent out, under Lord Wolseley, to attempt Gordon's rescue. The Queen reproached the Government with the delay, which she brought herself to regard as a neglect of public duty. The worst followed. The expedition failed to effect its purpose; Khartoum was stormed, and Gordon was killed before the relieving force reached the city (January 26, 1885).

No disaster of her reign caused the Queen more pain and indignation. On receipt of the news the Queen sent an angry telegram to Gladstone and Lord Hartington (then Minister of War), who happened to be together at the latter's house, Holker Hall, stating that 'it was too fearful to consider that the fall of Khartoum might have been prevented and many precious lives saved by earlier action.' The despatch was forwarded openly, and not in the cipher which was usual in the Queen's telegraphic communication with ministers.[1] In all directions she expressed herself on the catastrophe with unqualified frankness. In a letter, penned with her own hand at Osborne, and addressed to Gordon's sister a very few weeks after the tragedy, she said that she 'keenly felt the stain left upon England' by General Gordon's 'cruel but heroic fate.' She found it difficult to describe the poignancy of her grief at the remembrance that her urgent counsels had not been followed.

The Queen's view of Gordon's death.

'Dear Miss Gordon' (the letter ran),

'*How* shall I write to you or how shall I attempt to express *what I feel*? To *think* of your dear, noble,

The Queen's letter to Miss Gordon, Feb. 17, 1885.

[1] Morley's *Life of Gladstone*, iii. 167-9. Gladstone urged in reply to the Queen's condemnation, that whatever errors had been committed were due to the impossibility of obtaining trustworthy information as to the actual position of affairs in the disturbed districts.

heroic brother, who served his country and his Queen so truly, so heroically, with a self-sacrifice so edifying to the world, . . . is to me *grief inexpressible.* Indeed it has made me ill!

'My heart bleeds for you, his sister, who have gone through so many anxieties on his account, and who loved the dear brother as he deserved to be. You are all so good and trustful to have such strong faith that you will be sustained even now, when *real* absolute evidence of your dear brother's death does not exist, but I fear there cannot be much doubt of it.

'Some day I hope to see you again, to tell you all I cannot express!

'My daughter Beatrice, who has felt quite as I do, wishes me to express her deepest sympathy with you. I have so many expressions of sorrow and sympathy from abroad—from my eldest daughter the Crown Princess, and from my cousin the King of the Belgians—the very warmest.

'Would you express to your other sisters and your elder brother my true sympathy, and what I do so keenly feel—the *stain* left upon England for your dear brother's cruel, though heroic fate?

'Ever, dear Miss Gordon,
'Yours sincerely and sympathisingly,
'V. R. I.'[1]

The gift of Gordon's Bible.

The diary which Gordon kept while he was besieged at Khartoum, as well as his Bible, was ultimately re-

[1] This and the letters quoted below were bequeathed by Miss Gordon to the British Museum, on her death in 1893. The second letter is on public exhibition there.

covered by the relieving force, and was forwarded to
Miss Gordon. She at once presented her brother's
Bible to the Queen. The Queen expressed her gratitude in a letter dated Windsor Castle, March 16, 1885.

'It is most kind and good of you to give me this
precious Bible,' the Queen wrote, ' and I only hope that
you are not depriving yourself and family of such a
treasure, if you have no other. May I ask you during
how many years your dear heroic brother had it with
him? I shall have a case made for it with an inscription, and place it in the library here with your letter
and the touching extract from his last to you.

'I have ordered, as you know, a marble bust of
your dear brother to be placed in the corridor here,
where so many busts and pictures of our greatest
generals and statesmen are, and hope that you will
see it before it is finished to give your opinion as to
the likeness.

'Believe me, always yours very sincerely,
'VICTORIA R. I.'

Gordon's diary at Khartoum was sent by Miss
Gordon for the Queen's perusal in July. The Queen
acknowledged it without delay from Osborne on
July 11, 1885.

Gordon's diary.

'I must myself thank you,' she wrote, 'for the
volume of your dear brother's diary. Beatrice and I
are reading it with the deepest and saddest interest.'

She referred anew to her sense of mortification
in having been unable to persuade her ministers in

due time of Gordon's imminent peril. She signed herself

'Ever yours most sincerely,
'V. R. I.'

The affairs of the Soudan.

The Queen duly placed the bust of Gordon in the corridor at Windsor. His Bible she kept in a case in the corridor near her private rooms, and often showed it to her guests as one of her most valued treasures. Meanwhile the Queen keenly interested herself in the further efforts to rescue the Egyptian garrisons in the Soudan. In February 1885 the Grenadier Guards, who were ordered thither, paraded by her command before her at Windsor. She was gratified by offers of men from the Australian colonies, which she acknowledged with warm gratitude, and was not well pleased that the Government should decline them. At the end of the year she visited wounded soldiers from the Soudan at Netley, and she distributed medals to non-commissioned officers and men at Windsor.

But the later operations in the Soudan brought the Queen cold comfort. They lacked the decisive success which she loved to associate with the achievements of British arms. Against the final decision of the Government completely to abandon Khartoum and the Soudan to the Mahdi and his followers the Queen was warm in protest. She argued that her position in India was thereby seriously imperilled. Gladstone, in justification of the latest phase of his policy, reminded the Queen that even George III. had yielded his convictions in regard to the American colonies when circumstances arose to make a change of view imperative. The Queen retorted, through her secretary, with an obvious innuendo, that George III.'s Prime Minister, Lord North, 'never flinched from his task till it became hopeless, that he then resigned office, but did not change his opinions to suit the popular cry.'[1] Gladstone elaborately disputed the Queen's reading of history, but his argument failed to convince her, and she regretfully saw the Soudan relapse into barbarism.

Home politics had meanwhile kept the Queen closely occupied through the autumn of 1884. In the ordinary session of that year the Government had passed through the House of Commons a bill for a wide extension of the franchise : this the House of Lords had rejected in the summer, whereupon the Government announced their intention of passing it a second time through the House of Commons in an autumn session. A severe struggle between the two Houses was thus imminent. The Queen had fully adopted Lord Beaconsfield's theory that the broader the basis of the constitution, the more secure the crown, and she viewed the fuller enfranchisement of the labouring classes with active benevolence. At the same time 'organic change' in the Upper Chamber, which Gladstone and prominent Radicals threatened, should the Lords persist in opposing the decision of the Commons, was highly objectionable in her eyes. She always regarded a working harmony between the hereditary and elective Houses of Parliament as essential to the due stability of the monarchy. In the existing crisis she was filled with a lively desire

The Queen and the Franchise Bill, 1884.

[1] Morley's *Life of Gladstone*, iii. 179-82.

to settle the dispute between two estates of the realm with the least possible delay and before any distinct constitutional issue respecting the position of the Upper House was publicly raised. Her action was modelled on that which she took in the dispute over the Irish Church Disestablishment in 1869.

Queen mediates between the two Houses of Parliament.

In her private secretary, Sir Henry Ponsonby, the Queen had a tactful counsellor, and she did not hesitate through him to use her personal influence with the leaders of both parties to secure a settlement. Luckily, it was soon apparent that the danger of conflict looked greater than it was. Before her intervention had gone far, influential members of the Conservative party, including Lord Randolph Churchill and Sir Michael Hicks-Beach, had independently reached the conclusion that the House of Lords might safely pass the Franchise Bill, if to it were joined a satisfactory Bill for the redistribution of seats. This view rapidly gained favour in the Conservative ranks, and was approved by some of Gladstone's colleagues, although he himself at first opposed it. The Queen urged on all sides a compromise on these lines. She was indefatigable in correspondence with the leaders of both political parties. With customary frankness she reproved Gladstone and some of his colleagues for using 'strong expressions' in their speeches, while negotiations were proceeding, and she complained that they rendered the 'task of conciliation' which she had undertaken 'a most difficult one.' Her work was well done. Her influence with the Duke of Richmond and leading Conservatives of the House of Lords contributed very largely to a pacific settlement of the dispute. Assurances which proved satisfactory were given by Gladstone to Lord Salisbury and Sir Stafford Northcote, the Opposition leaders. The latter were privately consulted as to the details of a Redistribution of Seats Bill, which the Government solemnly promised to pass through Parliament as soon as the House of Lords accepted the Franchise Bill. Peace was rapidly ratified on these terms. Gladstone thanked the Queen for ' the wise, gracious, and steady influence on her part which has so powerfully contributed to bring about this accommodation and to avert a serious crisis of affairs ' (November 27, 1884). The Queen replied : ' To be able to be of use is all I care to live for now.'[1] It was an immense satisfaction to her thus to see averted, largely through her own influence, the kind of warfare that she most dreaded within the borders of the Constitution.

The Queen still found the most effective relief from political anxiety in the frequent renewal of her intercourse with her German kindred in their own homes. Her devotion to the children of her dead daughter, Princess Alice, was an unfailing resource. In 1884, immediately after Prince Leopold's death, she went on a visit to them at Darmstadt for three weeks. There she attended, on April 26, 1884, the marriage of Princess Alice's eldest daughter, Princess Victoria of Hesse, to her relative, Prince Louis of Battenberg. Next spring was spent at Aix-les-Bains, but she revisited Darmstadt on her return journey, and was

At Darmstadt, 1884–5.

[1] Morley's *Life of Gladstone*, iii. 138.

present at the confirmation of Princess Irene of Hesse, Princess Alice's third daughter.

The Princes of Battenberg.

Prince Louis of Battenberg, who became by marriage a member of the Queen's family, was one of three brothers in whom she felt much interest. They were first cousins of the Grand-Duke of Hesse, and the Queen's care for the Hesse family led to her making their acquaintance. Their father, Prince Alexander of Hesse, was the grand-duke's uncle, and they were his sons by a morganatic marriage with the Countess von Hauke, who was created Countess of Battenberg in 1851. The eldest son, Prince Louis, who was now wedded to the Queen's granddaughter, Princess Victoria of Hesse, had long been a special *protégé* of hers; she had permitted him to join the British navy as a boy, and become a naturalised British subject. He rose to the rank of Commander in 1885, and becoming Assistant Director of Naval Intelligence in 1899, was appointed Director in 1902. Prince Louis' next brother, Prince Alexander of Battenberg, had been appointed by the Powers of Europe, with the Queen's marked approval, Prince of the new State of Bulgaria in 1879. She had entertained him at Windsor, and was attracted by his handsome bearing.

Princess Beatrice's betrothal, November 29, 1884.

The third brother, Prince Henry of Battenberg, was first introduced to the Queen and Princess Beatrice at Darmstadt at the wedding of his brother, Prince Louis, in the spring of 1884. The meeting had important consequences. Prince Henry then won the affections of Princess Beatrice, and at the end of the year (November 29, 1884) their engagement was announced. The match was not popular in England, where nothing was known of Prince Henry except his German origin. Nor was it well received at the Court of Berlin, where the comparatively low rank of the Battenbergs was held to unfit them for close relations with the Queen. Nor, again, was it approved in Russia, where Prince Henry's brother, the Prince of Bulgaria, was cordially disliked on account of his defiance of Russian domination. The Queen, however, anticipated much happiness from her youngest daughter's projected union with Prince Henry, and viewed with indifference the hostile comments which it provoked. In writing of the engagement to her friends, she spoke of Prince Henry's soldierly accomplishment, although, she frankly added, he had not seen active service. The Princess had long been the Queen's constant companion, and it was agreed that the Princess with her husband should still reside with her.

At the Queen's request Parliament, on Gladstone's motion, voted the Princess the usual dowry of 30,000*l*., with an annuity of 6,000*l*. The minority numbered 38, the majority 337. The marriage took place, in a simple fashion which delighted the Queen, at Whippingham Church, near Osborne, on July 23.

The Princess's marriage, July 23, 1885.

All the Queen's nine children had thus entered the matrimonial state. The Queen's mode of life was in no way affected by the admission of Prince Henry into the royal circle. With him she was soon in confidential relations, and she was exhilarated by his gaiety and genial temper. She always enjoyed the society of the young, and in course of time she was cheered by the presence in her household of the children of Princess Beatrice.

The Queen and Prince Henry of Battenberg.

Gladstone's fall, June 8, 1885.

Much besides the Princess's marriage happened to brighten the Queen's horizon in the summer of 1885. In the spring Gladstone had, to her satisfaction, shown unusual resolution in definitely warning Russia against the encroachments that that country was making on the boundaries of Afghanistan. Russia defied the admonition, and for some weeks the Queen believed another Anglo-Russian war to be inevitable. She urged the ministers, whose competence to carry through a great war she gravely doubted, to hasten preparations, and reminded them of the old errors committed in the Crimea with a view to their avoidance, should a war with Russia recur. Ultimately Russia agreed to submit the points in dispute to arbitration, and the peace remained unbroken. The result brought immediate relief of anxiety. But the Queen had no confidence in Gladstone's foreign diplomacy, and it was with unconcealed elation that she witnessed, soon after the Russian crisis, the fall of his Government. The ministry had been too effectually discredited by its incoherent Egyptian policy to maintain its stability long, and it was defeated on its budget proposals on June 8, 1885. Gladstone at once resigned. The Queen, while frankly acknowledging her satisfaction in her own circle, expressed surprise that Gladstone should treat his defeat as a vital question, and she asked what course he would pursue should the leader of the Opposition decline office. He answered indecisively, and caused the Queen some concern by failing to offer his advice in person at Balmoral. But she did not permit differences of opinion to restrain her from once again offering Gladstone, in accordance with prescriptive practice, a peerage in recognition of 'his long and distinguished services.' She pressed on him the honour of an earldom. The magnanimous terms in which she made the proposal 'must,' Gladstone remarked to a friend, 'have cost her much to write.' Gladstone declined the distinction in equally creditable language. He was fully alive, he told her, to all the circumstances which gave her action value.[1]

The Queen without hesitation invited Lord Salisbury, Lord Beaconsfield's successor in the leadership of the Conservative party, to form a ministry. He was at first reluctant to accede to her wish, but at his request she endeavoured to obtain from Gladstone, whose followers had still a nominal majority in the House of Commons, some definite promise of parliamentary support during the next few months. A dissolution of Parliament was fixed for November, in accordance with the provisions of the recent Reform Bill. The Queen's action closely resembled that which she had taken in 1845, when on Peel's retirement she had invited Lord John Russell to take his place in a hostile House of Commons. She flung herself into the negotiations with characteristic energy, and a long correspondence followed. Gladstone replied evasively to the Queen's inquiry as to the aid that he was ready to lend a Tory Government. But the Queen, after many letters had passed between them, at length persuaded Lord Salisbury to

Negotiations between Lord Salisbury and Gladstone.

---

[1] Morley's *Life of Gladstone*, iii. 209. This was the fourth time that the Queen had suggested Gladstone's withdrawal to the House of Lords. She had recommended it twice during his first ministry, and already once during his second ministry early in 1883, when his health showed signs of failure.

Lord Salisbury's first ministry.

rest content with Gladstone's vague assurances. He accordingly took office on June 24.[1]

With Lord Salisbury the Queen was at once on good terms. She regarded him as the wearer of Lord Beaconsfield's mantle. He took her own view of the importance of foreign politics, and she looked forward to a reign of peace in her political world. It was therefore disappointing to her that Lord Salisbury's first tenure of office should be threatened by the result of the general elections in November. Two hundred and fifty Conservative members were then returned against 334 Liberals and eighty-six Irish

[1] Salisbury's Cabinet was constituted thus:

Foreign Secretary	The Marquis of Salisbury.
Lord Chancellor	Lord Halsbury.
President of the Council	Viscount Cranbrook.
Lord Privy Seal	The Earl of Harrowby.
Chancellor of the Exchequer and leader of the House of Commons	Sir Michael Hicks-Beach.
Home Secretary	Sir Richard Cross.
Colonial Secretary	Sir Frederick Stanley (afterwards Earl of Derby).
War Secretary	W. H. Smith.
Secretary for India	Lord Randolph Churchill.
Secretary for Scotland	Duke of Richmond.
First Lord of the Admiralty	Lord George Hamilton.
First Lord of the Treasury	The Earl of Iddesleigh.
Lord-Lieutenant of Ireland	The Earl of Carnarvon.
Lord Chancellor of Ireland	Lord Ashbourne.
President of the Board of Trade	Edward Stanhope.
Postmaster-General	Lord John Manners (afterwards Duke of Rutland).

In January 1886, on the eve of the Government's retirement, Lord Carnarvon resigned the Lord-Lieutenancy of Ireland. W. H. Smith thereupon succeeded to the office of Chief Secretary in the place of Sir William Hart-Dyke, and Lord Cranbrook was nominated to Smith's place at the War Office.

Nationalists. The Nationalists, by joining the Liberals, would leave the Government in a hopeless minority. The Queen gave public proof of her sympathy with her Conservative ministers by opening Parliament in person on January 21, 1886. It proved the last occasion on which she took part in the ceremony. Five days later Lord Salisbury's Government was outvoted. The Queen of necessity accepted his retirement, and faced with as much resignation as was possible to her the inevitable invitation to Gladstone to assume power for the third time.[1] Although, when Gladstone had audience of her on taking office anew, he thought that she evinced 'less of that armed neutrality' which had characterised her attitude to him during his former Administration, their relations were destined to experience a sharper strain than ever before.

[1] Gladstone's Government was constituted thus on February 1:—

First Lord of the Treasury and Privy Seal	W. E. Gladstone.
Lord Chancellor	Lord Herschell.
President of the Council	Earl Spencer.
Chancellor of the Exchequer	Sir William Vernon Harcourt.
Home Secretary	Hugh C. E. Childers.
Foreign Secretary	The Earl of Rosebery.
Colonial Secretary	Earl Granville.
War Secretary	Mr. Henry Campbell-Bannerman.
Secretary for India	Earl of Kimberley.
Secretary for Scotland	Sir George Trevelyan, Bt.
First Lord of the Admiralty	The Marquis of Ripon.
Chief Secretary for Ireland	Mr. John Morley.
President of the Board of Trade	Mr. A. J. Mundella.
President of the Local Government Board	Mr. Joseph Chamberlain.

In March 1886 James Stansfeld became President of the Local Government Board, and Lord Dalhousie Secretary of Scotland, Mr. Chamberlain and Sir George Trevelyan having resigned.

XLII

THE JUBILEE OF 1887

The Session of 1886.

THE session that followed Gladstone's third accession to the highest office in the State was the stormiest the Queen had watched since Peel abolished the Corn Laws in 1846. But her attitude to Gladstone through the crisis of 1886 was the antithesis of her attitude forty years earlier to Peel. Peel had changed front in 1846 on the critical question of Protection, and the Queen had encouraged him with all her youthful enthusiasm to persevere in his new path of Free Trade. Gladstone suddenly resolved to grant Home Rule to Ireland, after having, as it was generally understood, long treated the proposal as a dangerous chimera. To Gladstone's change of front she offered a strenuous resistance.

Queen's hostility to Home Rule.

To the bestowal of Home Rule on Ireland the Queen was uncompromisingly opposed from the early days of her reign. When the new Government was in course of formation she appealed to the Prime Minister to admit into the cabinet no 'separation'—a word the employment of which sufficiently expressed her view of the Home Rule policy. As soon as the ministry was installed, she freely spoke to all who came into intercourse with her of her repugnance to any change in the principle of Irish government.

The grant of Home Rule appeared to her to be a concession to the forces of disorder. It was to her mind a betrayal of the loyalists of Ulster.[1] But what she felt most strongly was that the grant of Home Rule amounted to a practical separation between England and Ireland, and that to sanction the disunion was to break the oath that she had taken at her coronation to maintain the union of the two kingdoms. To Gladstone's arguments she turned a deaf ear. She complained that he had sprung the subject on her and on the country without giving either due notice. The voters, whom she believed to be opposed to it, had had no opportunity of expressing their opinion. Gladstone and his friends contended that the establishment of a Home Rule Parliament in Dublin increased rather than diminished the dignity of the Crown by making it the strongest link which would henceforth bind the two countries together. But the Queen remained unconvinced.

To her immense relief, Gladstone was deserted by a large number of his followers, and the seceders formed themselves into an independent party, which adopted the name of Liberal-Unionist. Through

Gladstone's defeat, June 7 1886.

[1] In the midst of the agitation caused by Gladstone's Home Rule Bill the Queen had occasion to write to Lord Tennyson to condole with him on the mortal illness of his son Lionel (April 26, 1886). Lord Tennyson shared the Queen's horror of Home Rule. 'I cannot in this letter allude to politics,' the Queen wrote, 'but I know what your feelings must be.' On this sentence Tennyson, to the Queen's satisfaction, commented thus: 'Since your Majesty touches upon the disastrous policy of the day, I may say that I wish I may be in my own grave, beyond sight and hearing, when an English army fires upon the loyalists of Ulster.'—Lord Tennyson's *Life of Tennyson*, ii 445-6.

the junction of the Liberal-Unionists with the Conservatives in the division lobby, Gladstone's Home Rule Bill was decisively rejected in the House of Commons by a majority of thirty.

Queen objects to dissolution.

With the result of that vote the Queen was content. She desired the question to sleep. She did not fear the issue of a fresh election; she was confident that the hostility to Home Rule would steadily grow; but she deprecated an immediate appeal to the country. She deemed it a needless disturbance of her own and of the country's peace to involve the people in the excitement of a general election twice within nine months. But Gladstone was resolute. The Parliament, which was barely eight months old, was dissolved without delay.

The general election, 1886.

To the Queen's satisfaction the ministry was heavily defeated. Gladstone fought his battle with unwearied intrepidity, and was not seriously moved by the Queen's reminder that by persisting in oratorical agitation outside his own constituency he was establishing an undesirable and undignified precedent in ministerial etiquette. His efforts proved of no avail. Three hundred and sixteen Conservatives and seventy-eight Liberal-Unionists were returned to oppose one hundred and ninety-one English Home Rulers or Gladstonians and eighty-five Irish Home Rulers. Gladstone resigned without meeting the new Parliament. His farewell audience with the Queen was of the character that might have been expected. Of his Irish policy she could not trust herself to speak, and hardly a word about public affairs passed her lips. 'The conversation was mainly filled up with nothings,' wrote Gladstone. 'Her mind and opinions have,' he added with not unnatural asperity, 'been seriously warped, and I respect her for the scrupulous avoidance of anything which could have seemed to indicate a desire on her part to claim anything in common with me.'[1] It was recognised on both sides that the breach was irreparable. In July Lord Salisbury for the second time was entrusted by the Queen with the formation of a Government.[2]

The Queen's political anxieties were at once diminished. Although the unexpected resignation on

[1] Morley's *Life of Gladstone*, iii. 348.
[2] Lord Salisbury's second Cabinet was constituted thus:

First Lord of the Treasury	The Marquis of Salisbury.
Foreign Secretary	The Earl of Iddesleigh (who was almost immediately succeeded by the Prime Minister).
Lord Chancellor	Lord Halsbury.
President of the Council	Viscount Cranbrook.
Lord Privy Seal	Earl Cadogan.
Chancellor of the Exchequer and leader of the House of Commons	Lord Randolph Churchill.
Home Secretary	Mr. Henry Matthews (afterwards Viscount Llandaff).
Colonial Secretary	Edward Stanhope.
War Secretary	W. H. Smith.
Secretary for India	Lord Cross.
First Lord of the Admiralty	Lord George Hamilton.
Lord Chancellor of Ireland	Lord Ashbourne.
Chief Secretary for Ireland	Sir Michael Hicks-Beach.
President of the Board of Trade	Lord Stanley of Preston (afterwards Earl of Derby).
Chancellor of the Duchy of Lancaster	Lord John Manners (afterwards Duke of Rutland).
President of the Local Government Board	Mr. C. T. Ritchie.

In January 1887 Mr. Goschen became Chancellor of the Exchequer,

Lord Salisbury's second ministry.

December 20, 1886, of the new leader of the House of Commons (Lord Randolph Churchill) roused in her doubts of the stability of the Government, and caused her to scan the chances of yet another dissolution, the crisis passed, and Lord Salisbury's second ministry retained office for a full term of years. Indeed, with an interval of less than three years (1892-5), Lord Salisbury now remained her Prime Minister until her death, fourteen and a half years later. His total length of service during her reign extended over twelve and a quarter years,[1] and almost equalled Gladstone's twelve and a half years' service, which, by the irony of fate, proved by far the longest of all her Prime Ministers' terms of office.

Queen and Lord Salisbury.

The Queen's relations with Lord Salisbury were no less cordial during his second and third long administrations than during his first brief experience of government. She continued to regard him as the former colleague of Lord Beaconsfield and the depositary of her favourite minister's wisdom. With his general views of policy she remained in full accord. His deep interest in, and full knowledge of, foreign affairs assured him her increasing appreciation as years

Lord Randolph Churchill having resigned; Mr. W. H. Smith became First Lord of the Treasury and leader of the House of Commons; Mr. Edward Stanhope, War Secretary; Sir Henry Holland (afterwards Viscount Knutsford), Colonial Secretary. In March Mr. A. J. Balfour became Secretary for Ireland (Sir M. Hicks-Beach having resigned); Lord Lothian became Secretary for Scotland. In April 1888 Sir Michael Hicks-Beach rejoined the Cabinet as President of the Board of Trade in place of Lord Stanley who became Governor-General of Canada.

[1] Lord Salisbury remained Prime Minister nearly eighteen months after the Queen's death, so that the ultimate length of his tenure of power exceeded Gladstone's by fifteen months. He died on August 22, 1903.

went on. Her confidence in his judgment and her admiration of his sturdy common sense steadily grew. Hence there was none of that tension between him and the Queen which was inevitable between her and Gladstone. Lord Salisbury's second and third Governments gave her a sense of security to which Gladstone had made her a stranger during the long periods of his supremacy. She soon placed a portrait of Lord Salisbury in the vestibule of her private apartments at Windsor, face to face with one of Lord Beaconsfield.

Within a few days of the laying of the spectre of Home Rule, the Queen began the fiftieth year of her reign. The entrance on her year of jubilee and the approaching close of a quarter of a century of widowhood conquered some of her reluctance to figure in public life. At length she resumed much of her earlier public activity. It cost her no small effort of will to overcome her aversion to frequent meetings with her people in ceremonial functions. But she resolutely made the effort, and something of her old elation of spirit was roused by the invariable enthusiasm with which she was greeted in public by her subjects. On February 26, 1886, she had listened amid a crowded company to Gounod's 'Mors et Vita' at the Albert Hall. On May 11 she visited Liverpool to open an international exhibition of navigation and commerce. She drove through the city in drenching rain, but was so warmly received that her dread of such experiences was perceptibly weakened. The resumption in advanced life of those public duties which could alone bring her within view of her people, finally

The jubilee of her accession.

K K

stemmed the tide of discontent which her seclusion had fostered. She won anew and in a larger measure than before the respect of her nation and empire.

The growth of imperialism.

Yet the notable change of popular feeling towards the throne which characterised the last years of the Queen's reign was not primarily attributable to any alteration in the personal conduct of her life. There was a fundamental cause of greater historical significance. A potent imperialist sentiment, a new sense of imperial unity, was growing steadily throughout the whole British Dominion. It was strengthening the bonds between the colonies and India and the home country, and was deepening the sense of loyalty by making the crown the symbol of the unity of the Empire. To what source the rapid growth of the new imperialist sentiment is traceable is not easily defined. The Queen's renewed appearance in public was largely timed so as to indicate her sympathy with it. Her action encouraged its diffusion. But she did not inaugurate it. Its origin must be sought in a wider sphere of observation.

With the increased speed of steamships and the spread to every ocean of the submarine electric telegraph, the distance of the home country from India and her colonial settlements had sensibly diminished. Social and trading relations had become easier of maintenance. The unqualified acceptance by the home Government of the autonomous principle of colonial rule had reduced to the smallest dimensions the political friction between the British settlements and the mother-country. The closer intercourse and the improved political understanding dissipated ancient jealousies which had bred mutual disrespect and offence, and in the place of envious and unmannerly rivalry there was beginning to flourish a sense of kinship on the part of the mother-country and of filial affection on the part of the colonies. Such sentiments touched the Queen's heart. But it was involuntarily that she became the central figure of the great imperialist movement. She owed that position to circumstances which lay beyond the scope of any individual control.

Whatever the Queen could do to cherish the spirit of imperialism in the United Kingdom she henceforth did with conscientious zeal. In the early months of 1886 the Prince of Wales had actively engaged in organising a Colonial and Indian Exhibition at South Kensington. In this enterprise the Queen manifested great interest, and on May 1 she visited the exhibition, which drew numerous visitors to England from India and the colonies. On July 2 she attended a review at Aldershot held in honour of the Indian and colonial visitors, whom, three days later, she entertained at lunch at Windsor. On July 8 she received there Indian and other native workmen who had taken part in the exhibition, and she accepted gifts from them. In August, on her way to Balmoral, she visited another international exhibition at Edinburgh, and later in the year she approved the suggestion made by the Prince of Wales to the Lord Mayor of London to commemorate her fifty years of reign by inviting public subscriptions for the erection of an Imperial Institute which should be a meeting-place for visitors to England from India

The Queen's imperialist zeal.

and the colonies, and should exhibit specimens of
the products of every corner of her empire.

The Queen learns Hindustani.

During the next year—her year of jubilee—1887,
the Queen more conspicuously illustrated her attachment
to India, that part of her empire which always
moved her especial pride, by including native Indians
among her personal attendants. From one of these,
the Munshi Abdul Karim, who served her as groom of
the chamber, she began taking lessons in Hindustani.
Although she did not make much progress in the study,
the Munshi remained to instruct her till her death.

Visit to London, March 19-29, 1887.

Since the Prince Consort's death her visits to
London had been few and brief, rarely exceeding two
nights. In order suitably to distinguish the jubilee
year, 1887, from those that preceded it, she spent in
the opening quarter the exceptional period of ten
successive days in her capital. The following month
was devoted to the Continent; the first six days were
spent at Cannes and the following twenty-four at Aix-
les-Bains. On returning to England she paid another
visit to London, and on May 14 opened the People's
Palace in the East End. The enthusiastic loyalty
which was displayed on her long journey through the
metropolis once more greatly elated her.

The jubilee, June 21, 1887.

After her customary sojourn at Balmoral (May
to June) she reached London on June 20 to play her
part in the celebration of her jubilee. On every
detail of the ceremonies which were planned in honour
of the occasion she was consulted by her officers of
state, and she proved fertile in suggestion and in
criticism. During a single day, while the final
arrangements were under consideration, she addressed

to the Lord Chamberlain, Lord Lathom, no fewer than forty-two telegrams.[1] As the day of the chief ceremonial drew near she confessed nervous fears of the part she was to fill in it, and recalled with much agitation her losses and her sorrow. But the celebration proved more congenial than she anticipated. On June 21 the chief ceremony took place, when she passed in procession to Westminster Abbey to attend a special thanksgiving service, which called up vivid memories of her coronation fifty years before. In front of her carriage rode, at her own suggestion, a *cortège* of princes of her own house, her sons, her sons-in-law, and grandsons, thirty-two in all. In other processions there figured representatives of Europe, India, and the British colonies, all of whom brought her rich gifts. From India came a brilliant array of ruling princes. Europe sent among its envoys four kings : those of Saxony, of Belgium, of the Hellenes, and of Denmark, together with the Crown Princes of Prussia, Greece, Portugal, Sweden, and Austria. The Pope Leo XIII. sent a representative, the courtesy of whose presence the Queen acknowledged next year by presenting the Pontiff at the papal jubilee with a rich golden basin and ewer. The streets through which she and her guests passed were elaborately decorated, and her reception almost overwhelmed her in its warmth.[2]

[1] *Letters of a Diplomat's Wife*, by Mary King Waddington, pp. 252, 258.
[2] The Queen's route on the outward journey from Buckingham Palace lay through Constitution Hill, Piccadilly, Waterloo Place, and Parliament Street, and on her return she passed down Whitehall and Pall Mall.

The Queen's elation.

No accident dimmed the glory of the day, and, despite her forebodings, the Queen was never 'more cheerful.' The first message that the Queen received on reaching Buckingham Palace at the conclusion of her progress was an inquiry after her health from her aged aunt, the Duchess of Cambridge. The Queen replied at once that she was 'very tired but very happy.' In the evening there were illuminations on a lavish scale in all the chief cities of her dominions, and at a signal given from the Malvern Hills at 10 P.M. beacon fires were lit on the principal promontories and inland heights of Great Britain from Shetland and Orkney to Land's End.

The women's gift.

Next day the Queen accepted a personal gift of 75,000*l.* subscribed by nearly three million women of England. A small part of this sum she applied to a bronze equestrian statue of the Prince Consort— a replica by Mr. (afterwards Sir) Edgar Boehm of a statue by Marochetti—to be erected on Smith's Lawn, Windsor Park, where she laid the foundation-stone on July 15.[1] The bulk of the women's gift she devoted to the foundation of a sick nurses' institute on a great scale, which was to provide trained attendants for the sick poor in their own homes. The foundation proved of the highest benefit to the humbler classes throughout the country.

Jubilee ceremonials.

Succeeding incidents in the celebration of the Queen's Jubilee, in which she took a foremost part, included, besides court dinners and receptions, a fête in Hyde Park on June 22 to twenty-six thousand poor school children; a visit to Eton on her return

[1] She unveiled the statue May 12, 1890.

to Windsor the same evening; the laying of the foundation-stone of the Imperial Institute on July 6 ; a review at Aldershot on July 9 ; and a naval review on July 29. The harmony subsisting between her and her Prime Minister she illustrated by attending a garden party given by him in honour of her jubilee at his house at Hatfield on July 13. When the jubilee ceremonies were at an end, and the Queen surveyed them in retrospect, she felt grateful for the warmth of feeling which the people had shown towards her. The popular enthusiasm presented itself to her mind as a welcome recognition of the labours and trials which she had endured in recent years.

The processions, reviews, and receptions proved no transient demonstration. Permanent memorials of the jubilee were erected by public subscription in almost every town and village of the empire, taking the form of public halls, clock towers, fountains, or statues. The celebration was of historic import. The mighty outburst of enthusiasm which greeted the Queen, as loudly in the colonies and India as in the United Kingdom, gave new strength to the monarchy. Thenceforth the Sovereign was definitely regarded as the living symbol of the unity not merely of the British nation but of the British Empire.

Significance of the celebration.

XLIII

THE QUEEN AND HER GRANDCHILDREN

Illness of the Crown Prince.

UNHAPPILY amid the jubilee festivities a new cloud was gathering over the royal house. Since the autumn of 1886 the Crown Prince, to whose future rule in Germany the Queen had for nearly thirty years been looking forward with intense hope, was attacked by a mysterious affection of the throat. Early in June 1887 he and the Crown Princess came to England and settled in Upper Norwood in the hope of benefiting by change of environment. He was well enough to play a conspicuous part in the jubilee procession, when his handsome figure and his white uniform of the Pomeranian Cuirassiers attracted universal admiration. Subsequently he stayed in the Isle of Wight and at Braemar, and he did not return to Germany till September 14. The winter of 1887-8 he spent at San Remo, and it there became apparent that he was suffering from cancer.

The Queen's sorrow.

The Queen, who completely identified herself with the happiness of her eldest daughter, was constantly with her and her husband while they remained in England or Scotland, and she suffered greatly from the anxiety. Nor was it lessened when, on March 9, 1888, the Queen's old friend, the Emperor William I., died, and the crown which she and her daughter had through earlier days longed to see on the Crown Prince's head was now at length placed there while he was sinking into the grave. But the Queen did not during this season altogether abstain from rejoicings in another of her children's households. On March 10 she dined with the Prince and Princess of Wales at Marlborough House to celebrate their silver wedding, and at night, on her return to Windsor, she drove through London to witness the illuminations.

On March 22 she left England for a month's holiday at Florence. It was her first visit to the city, and it and its surroundings charmed her. King Humbert, son and successor of King Victor Emanuel, courteously paid her a visit on April 5, and the attention pleased her. On April 20 she started for Germany, where she had resolved to visit the dying Emperor Frederick. On the journey—at Innsbruck—she was gratified by meeting the Emperor of Austria, who had come to cherish a warm personal regard for her. It was their second interview; the first was now nearly a quarter of a century old.[1]

Visits to Italy and Germany.

On April 21 she drove through Berlin to Charlottenburg, her son-in-law's palace. But it was not solely to bid farewell to the stricken Prince that she had come. It was to mediate in a quarrel in her daughter's family, which was causing grave embarrassment in political circles in Berlin, and for which she was herself freely held responsible. The source of the difficulty was the Queen's kindly interest in the young Princes of Battenberg—a sentiment which was shared by her eldest daughter.

Family quarrel in Berlin.

[1] See p. 341, ante.

Prince Alexander of Battenberg.

Of the three brothers of Battenberg, the eldest, Louis, had married her granddaughter, Princess Victoria of Hesse, and the youngest, Henry, was husband of her daughter, Princess Beatrice. The second brother, Alexander, who was still unmarried, and was now no more than thirty-one years old, had had an adventurous career. For seven years he had been Prince of Bulgaria, but he had incurred the distrust of the Tsar, and in 1886, having been driven from his throne, retired to private life at Darmstadt.

His betrothal to Princess Victoria of Prussia.

Prince Alexander of Battenberg, like his brothers, was personally known to the Queen, whose guest he was at Windsor in 1879. She sympathised with his misfortunes, and she played with the fancy that he also, like his brothers, might marry into her family. An opportunity was at hand. The second daughter of the Emperor Frederick, Victoria, fell in love with him, and a betrothal was arranged with the full approval of the young Princess's mother and grandmother. But violent opposition was manifested at the German Court. Prince Bismarck, Chancellor of the Empire, who had always been on hostile terms with the Crown Princess, denounced the match as the sinister work of Queen Victoria, who had taken the Battenbergs under her protection. He declared that such a union was injurious to the interest of the German royal family. Not merely did it humiliate the imperial house by allying it with a prince of inferior social standing, but it compromised the good relations of Berlin with St. Petersburg, where Prince Alexander was heartily disliked. Bismarck even credited the Queen with a deliberate design of alienating Russia and Germany in the hope of bringing about an Anglo-German alliance against the Tsar.

When the Queen reached Charlottenburg this awkward dispute was at its height. The Empress Frederick stood by her daughter, who was unwilling to abandon Prince Alexander. The dying Emperor and his son, the Crown Prince William, in vain endeavoured to move her. Prince Bismarck threatened resignation unless Prince Alexander was summarily dismissed. On April 24 the Queen, after much conversation with her daughter, boldly discussed the question in all its bearings with Prince Bismarck. The statesman forced her to realise the meaning of resistance to his will. She yielded to his power. After parting from him, she used her influence with her daughter and granddaughter to induce them to break off the engagement with Prince Alexander. Reluctantly they gave way; the Crown Prince William, who had stoutly opposed his mother throughout the episode, was by the Queen's persuasion now reconciled to her, and domestic harmony was restored.

The Queen and Bismarck.

On the night of her interview with Bismarck, the Queen attended a state banquet in the Charlottenburg Palace, and the reconciliation was ratified. None the less the Queen always cherished sympathy with Prince Alexander, whose humiliation she deplored; and though she regretted his marriage next year (February 6, 1889) to Fräulein Loisinger, a singer at the Dresden and Darmstadt court theatres, she used no harsh language, merely remarking pathetically, 'Perhaps they loved one another.'[1]

Royal banquet at Charlottenburg.

[1] The Prince survived his marriage barely four years; he died on February 17, 1893.

Death of Emperor Frederick, June 15, 1888.

On June 15, 1888, the Emperor Frederick died, and the Queen's hopes of thirty years were blighted for ever. A week later she wrote from Windsor to her friend, Archbishop Benson: 'The contrast between this year and the last jubilee one is most painful and remarkable. Who could have thought that that splendid, noble, knightly Prince—as good as he was brave and noble—who was the admiration of all, would *on* the *very* day year (yesterday)—be no longer in *this* world? His loss is indeed a very mysterious dispensation, for it is such a very dreadful public as well as private misfortune.'[1]

Public engagements in Scotland.

Court mourning prevented any celebration of the fiftieth anniversary of the Queen's coronation on June 28. But on her visit to Balmoral in the autumn she took part in several public ceremonials. She stayed with Sir Archibald Campbell at Blythswood in Renfrewshire in order to open new municipal buildings at Glasgow, and to visit the exhibition there. She also went to Paisley, which was celebrating the fourth centenary of its incorporation as a borough. In November the widowed Empress Frederick was her mother's guest at Windsor for the first of many times. The Queen suggested to friends that some public demonstration of sympathy with her 'poor dear persecuted daughter' would be grateful to her, but nothing was done. The Queen, however, showed the Empress the unusual attention of meeting her on her landing in England at Port Victoria (November 19).

During 1889 the Queen's health was good and her activity undiminished. Her spring holiday was spent

[1] *Life of Archbishop Benson*, ii. 211.

for the first time at Biarritz, in former days the favoured health resort of the Queen's friend, the Empress Eugénie. On March 27 she made an excursion into Spain to visit the widowed Queen Regent at San Sebastian. This was another new experience for an English sovereign. None before had set foot on Spanish soil, although Charles I. and Charles II. went thither as princes.

<small>The Queen in Spain, March 27, 1889.</small>

On her return to England she was distressed by the death of her aunt, the Duchess of Cambridge, at the age of ninety-one (April 6). The final link with her childhood was thus severed. To the Duchess the Queen had extended from earliest infancy the fullest measure of filial tenderness. She wished the Duchess to be buried at Windsor, but her aunt had left instructions that she should be buried beside her husband at Kew. The Queen was present at her funeral on the 13th and placed a wreath on the coffin.

<small>Death of Duchess of Cambridge, April 6, 1889.</small>

At the end of the month she paid a visit to her eldest son at Sandringham, and on the 26th she witnessed there a performance by Mr. (afterwards Sir) Henry Irving and his company of 'The Bells' and the trial scene from 'The Merchant of Venice.' It was the second time that the Queen had permitted herself to witness a dramatic performance since the Prince Consort's death. The first occasion, which was near the end of her twentieth year of widowhood, was also afforded by the Prince and Princess of Wales, who, when at Abergeldie Castle in 1881, induced the Queen to come there and see a London company of actors perform Mr. (afterwards Sir) Francis Burnand's comedy of 'The Colonel' (October 11, 1881).

<small>Renewed interest in the drama.</small>

Public activity.

Public activity continued to distinguish her life. In May 1889 she laid the foundation-stone of new buildings at Eton (on the 18th), and she reviewed troops at Aldershot (on the 31st). On June 3 she presented at Windsor new colours to the regiment with which she had already closely identified herself, Princess Victoria's Royal Irish Fusiliers; she had presented colours to it in 1833 and 1866.[1] Next day she witnessed at Eton for the first time the annual procession of boats which celebrated George III.'s birthday.

The Queen and her grandchildren.

In the summer came new difficulties which tried her tact and temper. She turned to consider the pecuniary prospects of her numerous grandchildren. Provision had already been made by Parliament for every one of her nine children, and for her three first cousins, the Duke of Cambridge and his sisters; and although the deaths of Princess Alice and Prince Leopold had caused a net reduction of 25,000*l*., the sum annually assigned to members of the royal family, apart from the Queen, amounted to 152,000*l*. No responsibility for providing for the German royal family, the offspring of her eldest daughter, the Empress Frederick, or for the family of the Princess Alice of Hesse-Darmstadt, attached to her; but she had twenty-two other grandchildren—domiciled in England—for whom she regarded it as her duty to make provision.

Queen's request for pecuniary provision.

In July, 1889, events seemed to her to render appropriate an appeal to Parliament in behalf of the third generation of her family. The question had

[1] See pp. 38 and 367, ante.

long been on her mind, and she had more than once
called Gladstone's attention to it. But no suitable
opportunity of bringing it to the notice of Parliament
had presented itself. Now the elder son of the
Prince of Wales was coming of age, while his eldest
daughter was about to marry, with the Queen's assent,
the Earl (afterwards Duke) of Fife. She therefore sent
two messages to the House of Commons requesting
due provision for the two elder children of her eldest
son. The manner in which her request was approached
was not what she wished. New life was given to the
old cry against the expenses of monarchy.

The Queen's financial position still from time to
time excited jealous comments, not only among her
subjects, but in foreign countries. Exaggerated reports of the extent of her fortune were widely current,
and small heed was paid to her efforts to correct the
false impression. In 1885 it was stated with some
show of authority that she had lately invested a
million pounds sterling in ground-rents in the City of
London. Through her private secretary, Sir Henry
Ponsonby, she denied that she had any such sum
at her disposal. At Berlin, Bismarck often joked
coarsely over her reputed affluence, to which he attributed the power she exerted in the Crown Prince's
household. But while the best friends of the Crown
deprecated or ignored such kind of criticism, they
deemed it inexpedient for the country to undertake the
maintenance indefinitely of the Queen's family beyond
the second generation. Both the extreme and the
moderate opinions found free expression in the House
of Commons, and calm observers like Lord Selborne

False reports of her wealth.

perceived in the discussion ominous signs of a recrudescence of republican sentiment.

Parliamentary committee of inquiry.

The Government proposed to appoint a committee representative of all sections of the House to determine the principles which should govern the reply to the Queen's messages. A hostile amendment to refer the whole question of the revenues of the Crown to the committee was moved by Mr. Bradlaugh,[1] who had for thirty years been advocating republican principles and denouncing the wasteful extravagance of the nation in maintaining the throne. He argued that the Queen's savings on the Civil List enabled her unaided to provide for her grandchildren, and that the royal grants were an intolerable burden on the people. The amendment was rejected by a majority of 188, but 125 votes were cast in its favour.

Government's proposal.

On the due appointment of the committee the Government recommended, with the Queen's approval, the prospective allocation to the Prince of Wales's five children of annuities amounting, on their coming of age and marrying, to 49,000*l.*, besides a sum of 30,000*l.* to be divided equally among the three daughters, by way of dowries. The eldest son was to receive an annuity of 10,000*l.*, to be increased to 15,000*l.* on his marriage; and the second son was to receive, on coming of age, an annuity of 8,000*l.*, to be increased on marriage to 15,000*l.*; each daughter was to receive, on coming of age, an annuity of 3,000*l.* The grant immediately payable would thus be 13,000*l.* annually, together with 10,000*l.* for the dowry of the

[1] Member for Northampton.

Princess Louise of Wales. Precedent, it was shown, justified public provision for all the children of the Sovereign's sons. The daughters of former sovereigns had invariably married foreign reigning princes, and their children, not being British subjects, were outside the purview of the British Parliament. The question whether the children of the Sovereign's daughters who were not married to foreign reigning princes were entitled to public provision had not previously arisen.

The Queen and the Government perceived that public opinion was not in the mood to permit lavish or unconditional grants, and it was soon apparent that a compromise on the submitted proposals would be needful. The Queen disliked the debate, but showed a wish to be conciliatory. She at once agreed to forego any demand on behalf of her daughters' children, for whom she undertook to provide herself. She demurred to a formal withdrawal of her claim on behalf of her younger sons' children, but she stated that she would not press it. Gladstone, whose faith in the monarchy was always strong, and who, despite his personal differences with the Queen, respected the royal family as its symbol, was anxious to ward off agitation, and he induced the Government to modify its original proposal by granting to the Prince of Wales a fixed annual sum of 36,000*l*., to be paid quarterly, for his children's support.

Gladstone's intervention.

This proposal was accepted by a majority of the committee; but when it was presented to Parliament, although Gladstone induced Parnell and the Irish Nationalists to support it, it met with

Grants to Prince of Wales's children adopted.

opposition from the Radical side of the House. Mr. Labouchere invited the House to refuse peremptorily any grant to the Queen's grandchildren. The invitation was rejected by 398 votes against 116. Mr. John Morley then moved an amendment to the effect that the manner of granting the 36,000*l*. to the Prince of Wales left room for future applications from the Crown for further grants, and that it was necessary to give finality to the present arrangement. Most of Gladstone's colleagues in the late Government supported Mr. Morley, but his amendment was defeated by 355 votes against 134, and the grant of 36,000*l*. a year was secured.[1]

The Queen's savings.

In the course of the debate and inquiry it was officially stated that the Queen's total savings from the Civil List amounted to 824,025*l*., but that out of this sum much had been spent on special entertainments to foreign visitors. In all the circumstances of the case the Queen accepted the arrangement gratefully, and she was not unmindful of the value of Gladstone's intervention. For a season she displayed unusual cordiality towards him. On July 25, while the negotiation was proceeding, she sent to him and Mrs. Gladstone warm congratulations on their golden wedding. Meanwhile, on June 27, she attended the marriage of her granddaughter, Princess Louise of Wales, to the Duke of Fife in the private chapel of Buckingham Palace.

After the thorny pecuniary question was settled, hospitalities to foreign sovereigns absorbed the Queen's attention. In July 1889 she entertained, for

[1] *Hansard*, 3rd ser. cccxxxvii. cols. 1840 sq.

a second time, the Shah of Persia, and in August she welcomed her eldest grandson, the German Emperor William II., on his first visit to this country since his accession to his throne. The incident greatly absorbed her, and she arranged every detail of the reception. The Queen had been deeply interested in the Emperor from his birth. She always showed him marked affection, which he fully reciprocated, but at the same time she freely asserted her authority in her intercourse with him, and frankly expressed to him any disapproval that action on his part moved in her. The Emperor came to Cowes on his way to Osborne in his yacht 'Hohenzollern,' accompanied by twelve warships. The Queen held a naval review in his honour at Spithead, August 8, and next day reviewed the seamen and marines of the German fleet at Osborne. All passed off happily, and she congratulated herself on the cordial relations which the visit established between the two countries. The young Emperor gave proof of private and public friendship by causing the Queen to be gazetted honorary colonel of his first regiment of Horseguards, on which he bestowed the title of Queen of England's Own (August 12).

Visit of the German Emperor William II.

The Emperor repeated his visit to Osborne next year, when a sham naval fight took place in his presence, and he came back in 1891, when he was officially received in London, as well as in 1893, 1894, and 1895. At the opening of the following year the Queen saw ground in the Emperor's conduct for reproof, and there was three years' interval before he saw her again.

The Emperor's later visits.

XLIV

DOMESTIC AFFAIRS, *1889-96*

Mode of life, 1889-1901.

During the last eleven years (1889-1901) of her long career the Queen's mode of life followed in all essentials the fixed routine. Three visits to Osborne, two to Balmoral, a few days in London or in Aldershot, alternated with her spring vacation abroad and her longer sojourns at Windsor. Occasionally, in going to or returning from Balmoral or Osborne, she modified her route to fulfil a public or private engagement.

Visit to Wales, August 1889.

In August 1889, on her way to Scotland, she made a short tour in Wales, which she had been contemplating for some ten years. Henry Cecil Raikes, the Postmaster-General, who was a resident in Denbighshire, was nominated, contrary to precedent, minister in attendance, although he was not a member of the cabinet. The Queen reached Palé, near Lake Bala, a residence which Mr. (afterwards Sir) Henry Robertson lent her, on August 23, and stayed there four days. On her arrival she spoke a few words of Welsh to a party of tenants of the district who presented her with a walking-stick of native wood. She listened to much choral singing which interested her.

The loyalty shown by the Welsh people was thoroughly congenial.[1]

In later years the Queen illustrated her varied sympathies by carrying out at least six somewhat arduous engagements in the great provincial cities of England. On July 26, 1890, she opened the deep-water dock at Southampton. On February 26, 1891, at Portsmouth, she christened and launched the 'Royal Sovereign,' the largest ironclad in her fleet, as well as the 'Royal Arthur,' an unarmoured cruiser of new design. On May 21, 1891, she laid the foundation-stone of the new royal infirmary at Derby. On May 21, 1894, she revisited Manchester, after an interval of thirty-seven years, in order to inaugurate officially the great ship canal. On May 21, 1897, she went to Sheffield to open the new town hall, and on November 15, 1899, she performed a last function in the English provinces, when she went to Bristol to open the convalescent home which had been erected to commemorate her length of rule.

Provincial engagements.

But although a sense of duty impelled her to these exertions, it was only in her foreign tours that she sought change of scene with any ardour. For the most part she confined her visits to the south of France.[2] On returning from Cimiez in March 1897,

Foreign tours, 1890-9.

[1] On the 26th she paid a visit to Bryntysilio, near Llangollen, the residence of Sir Theodore and Lady Martin. Next year she privately visited another of her subjects. On May 14, 1890, she spent a day at Baron Ferdinand de Rothschild's beautiful Château at Waddesdon Manor.

[2] In 1890 her destination was Aix-les-Bains; in 1891, Grasse; in 1892, Costebelle, near Hyères; and in the five successive years, 1895 to 1899, Cimiez, a suburb of Nice, about two miles from the centre of the town.

while passing round Paris, she was met at the station of Noisy-le-Sec by M. Faure, the President of the French Republic, who greeted her with every courtesy. Next year the President arrived in Cimiez while the Queen was staying there, mainly with the object of paying her a visit. The interview took place in the afternoon of April 13, 1898, and the Queen highly appreciated the civility. Twice in her latest years she renewed her pleasing experience of Italy. Her Italian sojourns belonged to 1893 and 1894. In each of these years she again passed the spring at Florence. Her delight in the city and neighbourhood grew with closer acquaintance. She constantly inspected the chief sights in Florence and its neighbourhood, and her interest was always fresh and keen.[1] Each year King Humbert paid her a visit; and in 1894 Queen Margherita, whose solicitude for the welfare of the Italian people much impressed the Queen, accompanied him.

Last visits to Germany.

On her homeward journey from the south she usually continued to pay brief visits to Germany. Thrice in 1890, 1892, and 1895 she revisited Darmstadt. On her return journey in 1894 she paid a last visit to Coburg, the city and duchy which were identified with her happiest memories. There she

[1] On April 19, 1893, she spent an hour in the monastery of San Marco. 'The Queen arrived at five o'clock. She was wheeled in her chair through the church and the cloisters, but could not, unluckily, inspect the cells on the first floor; but the Queen saw what is most worth seeing in San Marco—namely, "The Last Supper," by Ghirlandaio, and Fra Angelico's great " Crucifixion "—also Sogliani's great fresco, the so-called " Providenza," before which the Queen remained a long time.'—Lord Ronald Gower, *Old Diaries*, p. 196.

was present, on April 19, 1894, at the intermarriage of two of her grandchildren—the Princess Victoria Melita of Coburg, the second daughter of her second son, Alfred, with the Grand Duke of Hesse, the only surviving son of her second daughter, Alice.[1]

On May 5, 1899, the Queen touched foreign soil for the last time when she embarked at Cherbourg on her home-coming from Cimiez. She frequently acknowledged with gratitude the amenities which were extended to her abroad, and sought to reciprocate them. On August 19, 1891, she welcomed the officers of the French squadron, which was in the Channel under Admiral Gervais, and on July 11, 1895, she entertained the officers of an Italian squadron which was off Spithead under the Duke of Genoa.

Gratitude for foreign courtesy.

The Queen's Court in her last years regained a part of its pristine gaiety. Music and the drama were again among its recognised recreations. In February, 1890, there were private theatricals and tableaux at Osborne, in which the Queen's daughters took part, and in their preparation the Queen found much amusement. Next year, for the first time since the Prince Consort's death, a dramatic performance was commanded at Windsor Castle (March 6, 1891), when Messrs. Gilbert and Sullivan's comic opera of 'The Gondoliers' was performed. In 1894 the Italian actress, Signora Eleanora Duse, performed

Revival of drama and opera at Court.

---

[1] This marriage was unhappily dissolved by the Supreme Court of the Grand-Duchy of Darmstadt on December 21, 1901, eleven months after the Queen's death. The ground for the divorce assigned by the Court was ' irreconcileable natural antipathy.' The only child of the marriage, a daughter Elizabeth, born March 11, 1898, died November 16, 1903.

Goldoni's 'La Locandiera' before the Queen at Windsor, and Mr. Tree acted in 'The Red Lamp' at Balmoral. Her birthday in 1895 she celebrated by a performance of Verdi's opera of 'Il Trovatore' in the Waterloo chamber at Windsor Castle. On June 26, 1900, Mascagni's 'Cavalleria Rusticana,' with a selection from 'Carmen,' was given there; and on July 16, 1900, the whole of her favourite opera of 'Faust.'

Betrothal and death of the Duke of Clarence. Domestic incidents continued to bring the Queen alternations of joy and grief in abundant measure until almost the day of her death. In December, 1891, she was gratified by the betrothal of Princess Mary (May), daughter of her first cousin the Duchess of Teck, to the Duke of Clarence, elder son of the Prince of Wales, who was in the direct line of succession to the throne. But death stepped in to forbid this union. On January 14, 1892, the Duke died. The tragedy for a time overwhelmed the Queen. 'Was there ever a more terrible contrast?' she wrote to Tennyson; 'a wedding with bright hopes turned into a funeral!' In an address to her people she described the occasion as 'one more sad and tragical than any but one that had befallen her.' The nation fully shared her sorrow. Gladstone wrote to Sir William Harcourt: 'The national grief resembles that on the death of Princess Charlotte, and is a remarkable evidence of national attachment to the Queen and Royal Family' (February 6, 1892). Lord Selborne foresaw in the good feeling thus evoked a new bond of affection between the Queen and the masses of her people.

On the Duke of Clarence's death, his brother

George, Duke of York, became next heir to the crown after his father; and on May 3, 1893, the Queen assented to his betrothal to the Princess May of Teck. Sorrow was thus succeeded by gladness. The Duke of York's marriage in the Chapel Royal at St. James's Palace on July 6, 1893, which the Queen attended, revived her spirits. She made the event the occasion of a published address to her people, which breathed a joyful spirit of hope and gratitude for her subjects' sympathy.

The Duke of York's marriage.

Another change in her domestic environment followed within the year. On August 22, 1893, her brother-in-law, Duke Ernest of Saxe-Coburg, died. The cordiality of her early relations with him had not been maintained. She had never thought highly of his judgment, and his mode of life in his old age did not commend itself to her. When he passed away, many years had elapsed since they met. His death gave effect to the old-standing arrangement by which the Duchy of Saxe-Coburg-Gotha passed to her second son, Alfred, Duke of Edinburgh. Duke Alfred and his family thenceforth made Coburg their chief home. Thus the German principality, which was endeared to the Queen through her mother's and her husband's association with it, was brought permanently under the sway of her descendants.

The Duchy of Saxe-Coburg-Gotha.

The matrimonial fortunes of her grandchildren occupied an increasing share of her attention. At the time of the Grand Duke of Hesse's marriage with a daughter of the new Duke of Saxe-Coburg, which she herself attended at Coburg (April 19, 1894),[1] she had

The marriage of the Tsar Nicholas II., Nov. 23, 1894.

---

[1] See p. 519.

given warm approval to the betrothal of another granddaughter—Alix, sister of the Grand Duke of Hesse—with the Tsarevitch Nicholas. This was the most imposing match that any of her grandchildren made, or indeed any of her children save her eldest daughter. Her second son was already the husband of a Tsar's daughter. But this union of her granddaughter with the Tsarevitch brought the head of the Russian royal family into far closer relations with her own. Before the marriage took place the bridegroom was elevated by the death of his father, Tsar Alexander III., on November 1, 1894, to the Russian throne. The marriage followed on November 23. The Queen gave an elaborate banquet at Windsor in honour of the event, and made the new Tsar Nicholas II.—now the husband of her granddaughter—an honorary officer of her army, Colonel-in-Chief of the second Dragoons (Royal Scots Greys).

Birth of Prince Edward of Wales, June 23, 1894.

Meanwhile, on June 23, 1894, the birth of a first son (Edward) to the Duke and Duchess of York added a new heir in the fourth generation to the direct succession to her throne. The Queen was present at the christening at White Lodge, Richmond, on July 16.

The Queen preserved her active interest not only in the growing army of her own direct descendants, but in the children and grandchildren of early friends and kinsmen who occupied foreign thrones. In 1895 she gave a hearty welcome to a foreign kinsman in the third generation, Carlos, King of Portugal, friendship with whose father, King Luis, and with whose grandparents (Queen Maria II. and her consort, Prince Ferdinand of Saxe-Coburg), she had warmly cherished through more than half a century. She celebrated King Carlos's visit by conferring on him the Order of the Garter on November 9, 1895.

XLV

THE POLITICAL SITUATION, 1892-6

Gladstone again in office, 1892-4.

POLITICS at home had once more drifted in the direction which the Queen dreaded. At the end of June 1892, the twelfth Parliament of the reign was dissolved after a life of just six years, and a majority of English Liberals and Irish Home Rulers pledged to support Gladstone's scheme of Irish Home Rule was returned (355 to 315). Lord Salisbury, at the Queen's request, and contrary to recent precedents, waited for the meeting of Parliament before resigning, but a vote of want of confidence was at once carried against him, and he retired on August 12. The Queen defied custom by giving public expression to her disappointment at this turn of events. The 'Court Circular' next day contained the unusual announcement that the Queen had accepted Lord Salisbury's resignation 'with much regret.'

No choice was left her but to summon Gladstone [1]

---

[1] Gladstone's fourth Ministry was constituted thus on August 16, 1892:

First Lord of the Treasury and Privy Seal	W. E. Gladstone.
Lord Chancellor	Lord Herschell.
Lord President of Council and Secretary of State for India	Earl of Kimberley.

for a fourth time to fill the post of Prime Minister, and once again a period of irritation opened for her. With the legislation which the new Government projected the Queen found herself in no greater sympathy than on former occasions. Her objections to Home Rule for Ireland were rooted and permanent, and she was greatly depressed by the passage of Gladstone's second Home Rule Bill through the House of Commons (July 27, 1893). But relief was not far distant. The Queen rejoiced at the rejection of the measure by the House of Lords on September 8 by the decisive majority of 378. As far as her reign was concerned, the scheme then received its death-blow. She suffered no further anxieties in regard to it.

The fate of the Home Rule Bill, Sept. 8, 1893.

In 1894 her political horizon brightened further. The session of Parliament, which had begun on January 31, 1893, only ended in the opening days of

Chancellor of the Exchequer	Sir William Vernon Harcourt.
Home Secretary	Mr. H. H. Asquith.
Foreign Secretary	Earl of Rosebery.
Colonial Secretary	Marquis of Ripon.
War Secretary	Mr. Henry Campbell-Bannerman.
Secretary for Scotland	Sir G. O. Trevelyan.
First Lord of the Admiralty	Earl Spencer.
Chief Secretary for Ireland	Mr. John Morley.
Postmaster-General	Mr. Arnold Morley.
President of the Board of Trade	Mr. Mundella.
President of the Local Government Board	Mr. Henry Fowler.
Chancellor of the Duchy of Lancaster	Mr. James Bryce.
First Commissioner of Works	Mr. Shaw-Lefevre.
Vice-President of the Council	Mr. A. H. D. Acland.

The Queen's farewell to Gladstone, March 2, 1894.

March of the following year, and on the eve of its close Gladstone wrote to inform the Queen that the burden of his years and failure of his sight and hearing compelled his withdrawal from her service. On the evening of March 2, 1894, Gladstone went to Windsor formally to resign his office next morning. His relations with the Queen had not grown of late in cordiality. Interviews with him during his last ministry tried her equanimity more than ever before,[1] and she accepted his resignation without any expression of regret. She confined her remarks to three or four perfunctory and colourless sentences. 'There was not one syllable on the past,' wrote Gladstone of the interview, 'except a repetition, an emphatic repetition, of the thanks she had long ago amply rendered for what I had done, a service of no great merit, in the case of the Duke of Coburg.[2] . . . There was the question of eyes and ears, of German *versus* English oculists, she believing in the German as decidedly superior. Some reference to my wife, with whom she had had an interview and had ended it affectionately—and various nothings.'[3] No word of politics escaped the Queen's

[1] The Queen did not conceal the feeling of weariness which her interviews with Gladstone during his last ministry usually caused her. When on March 10, 1893, Madame Waddington, wife of the retiring French ambassador, paid her a private farewell visit at Buckingham Palace, the Queen remarked to Madame Waddington at the outset that Mr. Gladstone, who had just left the palace, had detained her. Madame Waddington, who stood high in the Queen's favour, made some general remark on his intellectual eminence ; the Queen merely replied ' He is very deaf.'—*Letters of a Diplomat's Wife, 1883–1900*, by Mary King Waddington, p. 371.

[2] Gladstone had facilitated the settlement whereby the Coburg Duchy passed the year before to the Queen's second son, Alfred.

[3] Morley's *Life of Gladstone*, vol. iii. book x. p. 514.

lips in taking formal leave of the most conspicuous political personage among her subjects. The critical question of her appointment of a successor in his high office was excluded altogether from the conversation. Later in the day th Queen sent her old minister 'a few lines' acknowledging his own letter of resignation, and stated that she deemed him right in seeking 'to be relieved at his age of these arduous duties,' and wishing him 'peace and quiet.'[1]

There yet followed one brief meeting between these two veterans of the State, whose paths of thought and feeling had diverged so widely in the course of their long lives. In January 1897 the Queen and Gladstone were both wintering at Cimiez, and Gladstone and his family were invited by the Queen's daughter, Princess Louise, to visit the royal party one afternoon. The Queen, according to Gladstone's account, 'did not show the old and usual vitality;' her manner was motionless, but she manifested a kindliness to which Gladstone confessed he had long been a stranger. She gave him her hand, which she had not done before at any period of his life. But all that was said amounted to a few words of routine about Cimiez and the Queen's accommodation in her hotel.[2] Both sovereign and statesman endeavoured to ignore the sense of constraint which their former association bred in them, but freedom of intercourse was impossible.

Last Meeting with Gladstone at Cimiez.

Gladstone and the Queen did not see one

[1] Morley's *Life of Gladstone*, vol. iii. p. 514.
[2] *Ibid.* iii. 524.

another again. On May 19, 1898, he died. She felt sympathy with his relatives, and was grateful for the proofs he had given of attachment to the monarchy. In late years she rarely spoke harshly of him in private. If his name happened to be mentioned to her, she was wont to confine herself to the remark, 'He was always most considerate to me and my family.' When he lay dead, she honestly refrained from any larger avowal of admiration for his public labours. Yet she was fully alive to the exalted view of his achievements which was cherished by a large number of her subjects, and in a telegram to Mrs. Gladstone on the day of her late husband's funeral in Westminster Abbey she wrote with much adroitness of the gratification with which his widow must 'see the respect and regret evinced by the nation for the memory of one whose character and intellectual abilities marked him as one of the most distinguished statesmen of my reign.' The Queen did not commit herself to any personal appreciation beyond the concluding sentence: 'I shall ever gratefully remember his devotion and zeal in all that concerned my personal welfare and that of my family.'

Lord Rosebery Prime Minister, March 3.

On Gladstone's resignation in 1894 the Queen, by her own authority, and without seeking any advice from her retiring minister, promptly chose the Earl of Rosebery to succeed him.[1] She had long

[1] Before Gladstone had his last official audience with the Queen, her secretary, Sir Henry Ponsonby, informally asked his opinion of a rumoured movement 'among a body of members of Parliament against having a peer for Prime Minister.' Gladstone, while deprecating the attachment of importance to such a movement, declined

known him and his family; his grandmother had been invited to join the Queen's household on her accession, and his mother had been one of the Queen's bridesmaids. She admired his abilities, and she appreciated the deferential consideration which he invariably paid her.[1]

But the Government's policy underwent small change on Lord Rosebery's acceptance of the highest office in the State, and with it the Queen remained out of sympathy. The Welsh Disestablishment Bill, which was read a second time in the House of Commons on April 1, 1895, ran directly counter to the Queen's convictions in favour of Church establishments. Although she came to recognise the necessity of the changes at the War Office, which relieved her cousin, the Duke of Cambridge, of the Commandership-in-Chief of the Army, she did not welcome them. By strictly limiting the future tenure of the post to a period of five years, the cabinet in their reorganisation of the War Office gave the death-blow to the cherished fiction that the Commander-in-Chief was the permanent personal deputy of the Sovereign. But Lord Rosebery's Government was not firmly established. His leadership was not acquiesced in with a good grace by many prominent

Queen's want of enthusiasm for his Government.

to discuss the future, unless at the explicit request of the Queen. That request was not made.

[1] Lord Rosebery made little change in the existing constitution of the Cabinet. He resigned the seals of Foreign Secretary, which he bestowed on Lord Kimberley. Mr. Henry Fowler succeeded Lord Kimberley at the India Office; Mr. Shaw-Lefevre succeeded Mr. Fowler at the Local Government Board, and Mr. Herbert Gladstone took Mr. Shaw-Lefevre's place as First Commissioner of Works, without a seat in the Cabinet.

M M

members of the party. Enthusiasm for him in the rank and file was wanting. The ministers were consequently defeated in June in the House of Commons, and Lord Rosebery at once resigned, after only fourteen months' tenure of office.

Lord Salisbury's third Government.

Lord Salisbury, to the Queen's satisfaction, resumed power for the third time on the understanding that he would be permitted an early appeal to the country. In the new ministry the Conservative leaders coalesced with the leaders of the Liberal Unionists, and the dissolution of Parliament was followed by the return of the Unionists in a strong majority. The Unionist party under Lord Salisbury's leadership retained power till her death.

The Queen and Mr. Chamberlain.

With Lord Salisbury and his Unionist colleagues the Queen's relations were to the last harmonious.[1] Her sympathy with the imperialist sentiments, which Mr. Chamberlain's control of the Colonial Office conspicuously fostered, was whole-hearted. As in the

[1] Lord Salisbury's third Cabinet was constituted thus:

Foreign Secretary	The Marquis of Salisbury.
Lord Chancellor	Earl Halsbury.
Lord President of the Council	The Duke of Devonshire.
Lord Privy Seal	Viscount Cross.
First Lord of the Treasury	Mr. A. J. Balfour.
Chancellor of the Exchequer	Sir Michael Hicks-Beach.
Home Secretary	Sir M. W. (afterwards Viscount) Ridley.
Colonial Secretary	Mr. Joseph Chamberlain.
Secretary for India	Lord George Hamilton.
Secretary of War	Marquis of Lansdowne.
First Lord of the Admiralty	Mr. G. J. (afterwards Viscount) Goschen.
Lord Lieutenant of Ireland	Earl Cadogan.
Lord Chancellor of Ireland	Lord Ashbourne.

case of Peel and Disraeli, her first knowledge of him had not prepossessed her in his favour. When he was a leader of a Radical section of the Liberal party she regarded him with active distrust. He had been President of the Board of Trade in Gladstone's second ministry, but he had then rarely come in contact with her, and her conversation with him in his few visits to Windsor rarely passed beyond an inquiry on her part as to the efforts that his department was making with a view to diminishing the risk of railway accidents. But Mr. Chamberlain's steady and strenuous resistance to the policy of Home Rule, and his secession from the ranks of Gladstone's followers, dissipated her fears, and his imperialist administration of colonial affairs from 1895 till her death was in complete accord with her sentiment. She showed him to the end numerous marks of respect, and encouraged him in all his efforts to consolidate her colonial empire.

But, despite the Queen's confidence in her advisers, her energy in criticising their counsel never slackened. She still required all papers of State to be regularly submitted to her; she was impatient of any sign of carelessness in the conduct of public business, and she

Her critical energy.

Secretary for Scotland	Lord Balfour of Burleigh.
Chancellor of the Duchy of Lancaster	Lord James of Hereford.
President of the Board of Trade	Mr. C. T. Ritchie.
President of the Local Government Board	Mr. Henry Chaplin.
President of the Board of Agriculture	Mr. W. H. Long.
First Commissioner of Works	Mr. Akers Douglas.

pertinaciously demanded full time for the consideration of ministers' proposals. She read most of her ministers' speeches in the country, and when these specially pleased her would send an autograph note of congratulation. All appointments to high public offices continued to be submitted to her by the responsible ministers, and she would frankly criticise the qualifications of the selected candidate. At times the minister would admit the justice of her criticism and explain that his choice was the best to be made out of the material available. But she would shrewdly declare herself unconvinced by the apology. She had lately resumed her early practice of signing commissions in the army, and when in 1895 the work fell into arrears and an appeal was made to her to forego the labour, she declined the suggestion. To diplomatic and other commissions she appended her signature to the last. In no case would she countenance the proposal that she should employ a stamp. She would often travel to Osborne or Balmoral with hundreds of boxes filled with documents that required her sign-manual; she would work on them continuously for two or three hours a day, and would sign two or three hundred papers at a sitting.

Her continued interest in the army.
The Queen's resolve to identify herself with the army never knew any diminution. On May 10, 1892, she opened with much formality the Imperial Institute, but participation in civil ceremonial was rare in her closing years. Her public appearances in London and its neighbourhood came to have almost exclusively military associations, and she conspicuously renewed her old relations with Aldershot. On July 4, 1890, she

inspected the military exhibition at Chelsea Hospital. On June 27, 1892, she laid the foundation-stone of a new church at Aldershot, and witnessed the march past of ten thousand men. Next year, to her joy, but amid some signs of public discontent, her son the Duke of Connaught took the Aldershot command. In July 1894 she spent two days there; on the 11th there was a military tattoo at night in her honour, and a review followed next day. In July 1895, July 1898, and June 1899, she repeated the agreeable experience. In 1898, besides attending a review, she presented colours to the 3rd battalion of the Coldstream Guards.

Early in 1896 the military ardour which she encouraged in her immediate circle cost her a sad bereavement. At the end of 1895 Prince Henry of Battenberg, her youngest daughter's husband, who resided under her roof, volunteered for active service in Ashanti, where native races were in revolt against British rule. The Queen was reluctant to part with him. But he wrote to her that he had been brought up as a soldier, and sought the opportunity of proving his devotion to his adopted country. By joining the expedition he would establish his position in a manner that would be to his children's interest. His wife, Princess Beatrice, supported this plea, and the Queen yielded. After taking some part in the operations in Ashanti, the Prince was invalided home with fever, and died on board H.M.S. 'Blonde' on the way to Madeira on January 20, 1896. The Queen declared she had 'lost the sunbeam of her household,' and with painful grief turned to console her widowed

Death of Prince Henry of Battenberg, Jan. 20, 1896.

daughter, her own constant companion. The Prince's body was met on its arrival at Cowes on February 5 by the Queen and the Princess, who accompanied it to its last resting-place in the church at Whippingham where the marriage of the Prince to the Princess took place less than eleven years before.

The Victorian Order.

The Queen always welcomed with warmth signs of her people's sympathy with her domestic sorrows. They afforded her genuine consolation, and she constantly dwelt on them in private talk. It was rarely that the rendering of any personal attention passed from her memory. A few months after Prince Henry's death she sought a method of recording permanently those acts of devotion to herself by which she set especial store. She instituted, on April 21, 1896, a new decoration which she called the Royal Victorian Order. It was to be conferred on 'such persons, being subjects of the British Crown, as have rendered extraordinary, or personal, or important services to her Majesty, her heirs or successors.' The Queen kept in her own hands the control of the Royal Victorian Order, and carefully selected those who were to be admitted to its honours.

Visit of Tsar Nicholas II., Sept. 22–Oct. 5.

In the autumn of 1896 the Queen had the gratification of entertaining at Balmoral the young Tsar Nicholas II. and her granddaughter the Tsaritza, with their infant daughter. The Tsar's father, Alexander III., his grandfather, Alexander II., and his great-grandfather, Nicholas I., had all been her guests in earlier days. The Tsar Alexander I., elder stepbrother and predecessor of the Tsar Nicholas I., had been her own godfather. The rivalry which characterised the political relations of Russia and England during the reign the Queen regarded as inevitable. To the last she deemed it the duty of her statesmen to watch jealously the forward movements of Russia in Asia. But at the same time she felt pride in the lineal ties that united her with the Russian royal house.

XLVI

THE DIAMOND JUBILEE OF 1897

On September 23, 1896, the Queen achieved the distinction of having reigned longer than any other English sovereign. She had worn her crown nearly twice as long as any contemporary monarch in the world, excepting only the Emperor of Austria, and he ascended his throne more than eleven years after her accession. Hitherto George III.'s reign of fifty-nine years and ninety-six days had been the longest known to English history. Hers was now a day longer.

The Diamond Jubilee of 1897.
In 1897 it was resolved to celebrate the completion of her sixtieth year of rule—her 'Diamond Jubilee'—with appropriate splendour. She readily accepted the suggestion that the celebration should be so framed as to emphasise that extension of her empire which was now recognised to be one of the most imposing characteristics of her sovereignty. It was accordingly arranged that prime ministers of all the colonies, delegates from India and the dependencies, and representatives of all the armed forces of the British Empire should take a prominent part in the public ceremonies. The main feature of the celebration was a state procession through London on June 22. The Queen made almost a circuit of her capital, attended by her family, by envoys from foreign

MEDAL COMMEMORATIVE OF QUEEN VICTORIA'S
DIAMOND JUBILEE OF 1897

countries, by Indian and colonial officials, and by a great band of imperial troops—Indian native levies, mounted riflemen from Australia, South Africa, and Canada, and coloured soldiers from the West Coast of Africa, Cyprus, Hongkong, and Borneo.

From Buckingham Palace the mighty *cortège* passed to the steps at the west end of St. Paul's, where a short religious service was conducted by the highest dignitaries of the Church.[1] Thence the royal progress was continued over London Bridge, through the poorer districts of London on the south side of the Thames. Buckingham Palace was finally reached across Westminster Bridge and St. James's Park. Along the six miles' route were ranged millions of the Queen's subjects, who gave her a welcome which brought tears to her eyes. Her feelings were faithfully reflected in the telegraphic greeting which she sent to all parts of the Empire as she set out from the palace: 'From my heart I thank my beloved people. May God bless them!'

Service outside St. Paul's Cathedral.

In the evening, as in 1887, every British city was illuminated, and every headland or high ground in England, Scotland, and Wales, from Cornwall to Caithness, was ablaze with beacons.

The beacons.

The festivities lasted a fortnight. There was a garden party at Buckingham Palace on June 28; a review in Windsor Park of the Indian and colonial troops on July 2; a reception on July 7 of the colonial

The festivities.

[1] In the pavement at the foot of the steps at the west end of St. Paul's Cathedral there were afterwards inscribed in large deeply cut letters these words in commemoration of this ceremony: 'Here Queen Victoria returned thanks to Almighty God for the sixtieth anniversary of her accession. June 22nd, A.D. 1897.'

Prime Ministers, when they were all sworn of the Privy Council; and a reception on July 13 of 180 prelates of English-speaking Protestant peoples who were assembled in congress at Lambeth. By an error on the part of officials, members of the House of Commons, when they presented an address of congratulation to the Queen at Buckingham Palace on June 23, were shown some want of courtesy. The Queen at once took steps to atone for the unintentional slight by inviting the members and their wives to a garden party at Windsor on July 3.

Naval review.

The only official celebration which the Queen's age of seventy-eight years prevented her from attending in person was a great review of battleships at Spithead (June 26), which in the number of assembled vessels exceeded any preceding display of the kind. Vessels of war to the number of 173 were drawn up in four lines stretching over a course of thirty miles. The Queen was represented by the Prince of Wales. Not the least of many gratifying incidents that marked the celebration was the gift to Great Britain of an ironclad from Cape Colony.

The people's passionate loyalty.

On July 18 the close of the rejoicings drew from the Queen a letter of thanks to her people, expressing in simple language her boundless gratitude. The sentiment was common to her and her people. The passion of loyalty which the jubilee of 1887 had called forth reached at the close of the next decade a degree of intensity which had no historic precedent. During the few years of life that yet remained to the Queen it burned with undiminished force throughout the Empire in the breast of almost every one of her subjects, whatever their race or domicile.

XLVII

THE GREAT BOER WAR

THE anxieties which are inseparable from the government of a great empire pursued the Queen and her country in full measure during the rest of her reign, and her armies were engaged in active hostilities in many parts of the world. Most of her energies were consequently absorbed in giving proof of her concern for the welfare of her troops. She closely scanned the many military expeditions which were needed to repress disorder on the frontier of India (1897–99). The campaign of British and Egyptian troops under Lord Kitchener, which finally crushed the long drawn-out rebellion in the Soudan at the battle of Omdurman on September 2, 1898, and restored to Egypt the greater part of the territory that had been lost in 1883, was a source of immense gratification to her. When Lord Kitchener visited Windsor on his return to England to receive her congratulations, she proved the alertness of her memory by reminding him of incidents in former Soudan campaigns, which had passed from his recollection.

In 1898 the Queen indicated the course of her sympathies by thrice visiting at Netley Hospital the

[margin: Military expeditions, 1897–8.]

The Queen's interest in Netley.

wounded men from India and the Soudan (February 11, May 14, and December 3). Weekly reports were now forwarded her from Netley, and she studied them with minute care.[1] One of her favourite recreations was the making of quilts for the hospital where her wounded soldiers were nursed.

Reviews of troops.

She was still active in inspecting troops or in presenting new colours to regiments. At Balmoral, on October 29, 1898, she presented colours to the newly raised 2nd battalion of the Cameron Highlanders. On July 1, 1899, she reviewed in Windsor Great Park the Honourable Artillery Company, of which the Prince of Wales was Captain-General, and a few days later, on July 15, in the courtyard of Windsor Castle, she presented colours to the Scots Guards, afterwards attending a march past in Windsor Park. On August 10, while at Osborne, she inspected the Portsmouth Volunteers in camp at Ashley, and at Balmoral on September 29 she presented new colours to the 2nd battalion of the Seaforth Highlanders.

The Victoria and Albert Museum.

Apart from these marks of regard for her army, the Queen's chief public appearance during 1899 was on May 17, when she laid the foundation-stone of the new buildings of the Victoria and Albert Museum at Kensington. The South Kensington Museum, as the institution had hitherto been named, had been brought

[1] When on one occasion she heard that the convalescents at Netley found agreeable amusement in doing woolwork, she at once caused the materials to be purchased by one of her ladies-in-waiting, and to be forwarded promptly to the hospital.

into being by the Prince Consort after the Great
Exhibition of 1862, and was always identified in the
Queen's mind with her husband's public services.

All other military experiences which had lately confronted the Queen sank into insignificance in the autumn of 1899 in the presence of the great Boer war. Recent events in South Africa had greatly interested her. When Cecil Rhodes revisited England in 1891 to discuss with the Imperial Government the settlement of Mashonaland, she invited him to dine with her at Windsor. Rhodes afterwards expressed surprise at the Queen's knowledge of South African politics, and her clear and statesmanlike remarks on the prospects of Mashonaland. She listened with close attention to his description of the Kimberley diamond mines and the manner in which the stones were prepared for the market.[1] The interview left the Queen one of Rhodes's admirers. Subsequently, when she was talking of him with her ladies, one of them remarked to her that he was a woman-hater. 'Oh, but he was extremely kind to me,' she said with characteristic simplicity.

The Queen and Cecil Rhodes.

With her ministers' general policy in South Africa before the great war she was in agreement, although she studied the details somewhat less closely than had been her wont. Failing sight disabled her after 1898 from reading all the official papers that were presented to her, but her confidence in the wisdom of Lord Salisbury and her faith in Mr. Chamberlain's devotion to the best interests of the Empire spared her any misgivings while the negotiations with the

Negotiations with the Transvaal, 1899

[1] *Cecil Rhodes*, by Howard Hensman, 1902, pp. 192-3.

Transvaal Government were pending. As in former crises of the same kind, so long as any chance remained of maintaining an honourable peace she cherished the hope that there would be no war; but when she grew convinced that peace was only to be obtained on conditions that were derogatory to the prestige of her government she focussed her energies on entreaties to her ministers to pursue the war with all possible promptitude and effect.

The Great Boer War.

From the opening of active operations in October 1899 until consciousness failed her on her deathbed in January 1901, the serious conflict occupied the chief place in her thoughts. The disasters which befell British arms at the beginning of the struggle caused her infinite distress, but her spirit rose with the danger. Fresh defeats merely added fuel to the zeal with which she urged her advisers to redouble their exertions. Sir Redvers Buller's terrible reverse at Colenso in December, which followed hard upon two minor repulses of other commanders—Lord Methuen and Sir William Gatacre—did not long disturb her equanimity. When those round her gave voice to gloomy prognostications, she declared that she would suffer no depression in her house: 'All will come right.'

The Queen and the reinforcements.

It was with the Queen's especial approval that, before the end of December 1899, reinforcements on an enormous scale, drawn both from the regular army and the volunteers, were hurriedly ordered to South Africa under the command of Lord Roberts, while Lord Kitchener was summoned from the Soudan to serve as chief of the staff. In both generals she had the fullest trust.

Offers of assistance from the colonies stirred her enthusiasm, and she sent many messages of thanks. She was consoled, too, by a visit at Windsor from her grandson, the German Emperor, with the Empress, and two of his sons, on November 20, 1899. Of late there had been less harmony than of old between the courts of London and Berlin. A misunderstanding between the two countries on the thorny subject of English relations with the Boer republics of South Africa had threatened early in 1896. The German Emperor had then replied in congratulatory terms to a telegram from President Kruger informing him of the success of the Boers in repelling a filibustering raid which a few Englishmen under Dr. Jameson had made into the Transvaal. The Queen, like her subjects, reprobated the Emperor's interference, although it had little of the deliberately hostile significance which popular feeling in England attributed to it.

Emperor William II.'s visit, November 1899.

The Emperor's visit to the Queen and Prince of Wales in November, 1899, had been arranged before the Boer war broke out, and the Emperor did not permit his display of friendly feeling to be postponed by the opening of hostilities. His meeting with the Queen was most cordial, and his relations with the English royal family were thenceforth unclouded. By way of indicating his practical sympathy with the British army, he subscribed 300*l.* to the fund for the relief of the widows and orphans of the men of the 1st Royal Dragoons who were then fighting in South Africa—the regiment of which he was colonel-in-chief.

Cordiality of the Emperor's welcome

Throughout 1900 the Queen was indefatigable in inspecting troops who were proceeding to the seat of

The Queen's sympathy with her soldiers.

war, in sending to the front encouraging messages, and in writing letters of condolence to the relatives of officers who lost their lives, often requesting a photograph and inquiring into the position of their families. In the affairs of all who died in her service she took a vivid personal interest. She worked with her own hand woollen comforters and caps for the men in South Africa, and expressed annoyance when she was told that her handiwork had been distributed among the officers and not among the privates.

Her Christmas gift.

The Queen's anxieties at Christmas, 1899, kept her at Windsor and precluded her from proceeding to Osborne for the holiday season, as had been her invariable custom, with one exception, for nearly fifty years. On Boxing Day she entertained in St. George's Hall, Windsor, the wives and children of the non-commissioned officers and men of the regiments which were stationed in the royal borough. She caused a hundred thousand boxes of chocolate to be sent as her personal gift to the soldiers at the front, and on New Year's Day, 1900, forwarded greetings to all ranks. When the tide turned at the seat of war, and the news of British successes reached her in the early months of 1900—the relief of Kimberley (February 15), the capture of General Cronje (February 27), the relief of Ladysmith (February 28), the occupation of Bloemfontein (March 13), the relief of Mafeking (May 17), and the occupation of Pretoria (June 5)— she exchanged warm congratulations with her generals and showed the utmost elation of spirit.

The gallantry displayed by the Irish soldiers was

peculiarly gratifying to her, and she acknowledged it in a most emphatic fashion. On March 2 she gave permission to her Irish troops to wear on St. Patrick's Day, by way of commemorating their achievements in South Africa, the Irish national emblem, a sprig of shamrock, the display of which had been hitherto prohibited in the army. On March 7 she came to London, and on the afternoons of the 8th and 9th she drove publicly through many miles of streets in order to illustrate her watchful care of the public interests and her participation in the public anxiety. Enthusiasm ran high, and she was greeted everywhere by cheering crowds. On March 22 she went to the Herbert Hospital, at Woolwich, to visit wounded men from South Africa.

The Irish soldiers.

But the most signal evidence that she gave of the depth of her sympathy with those who were bearing the brunt of the struggle was her decision to abandon for this spring her customary visit to the South of Europe and to spend her vacation in Ireland, whence the armies in the field had been largely recruited. This plan was wholly of her own devising. Nearly forty years had elapsed since she set foot in Ireland.[1] In that interval political disaffection had been rife, and had discouraged her from renewing her acquaintance with the country. At one time she cherished a feeling of exasperation with her disaffected Irish subjects, and she declined to entertain all invitations to visit their land. She had many times definitely refused the suggestion of establishing a royal residence in Ireland, which many ministers had from time to

Fourth visit to Ireland April 1900.

---

[1] See pp. 202, 236, and 314 ante.

time made to her, in the hope of reviving the drooping loyalty of the island.

<small>The sojourn in Dublin, April 4-25.</small>

But now, within a few months of her death, the Queen's recent feeling for Ireland underwent complete revulsion. She spent three weeks in Dublin, staying at the viceregal lodge in Phœnix Park nearly the whole of April—from the 4th to the 25th. Abandoning every mark of her recent alienation, she came, she said, in reply to an address of welcome from the Corporation of Dublin, to seek change and rest, and to revive happy recollections of the warm-hearted welcome given to her, her husband, and children in former days. Her reception was all that could be wished, and it vindicated her renewed confidence in the loyalty of the Irish people to the Crown, despite the continuance of political agitation. The days were spent busily and passed quickly. She entertained the leaders of Irish society, attended a military review and an assembly of fifty-two thousand school children in Phœnix Park, and frequently drove through Dublin and the neighbouring country. She left nothing undone whereby she might show her regard for the Irish troops. On April 5 she gave orders for the formation of a new regiment of Irish guards. On her departure from Ireland on April 26 she thanked the Irish people for their greeting in a public letter addressed to the lord-lieutenant.

<small>Lord Roberts in South Africa.</small>

The war in South Africa was still in progress, and was never long absent from the Queen's mind. After her return to Windsor on May 2, 1900, she inspected the men of H.M.S. 'Powerful' who had been besieged in Ladysmith, and warmly welcomed their commander, Captain Hedworth Lambton. On the 17th she visited the wounded at Netley. Lord Roberts's successes in South Africa relieved her and her people of pressing anxieties during the summer, and ordinary court festivities were suffered to proceed. On May 4 she entertained at Windsor the King of Sweden and Norway, who had often been her guest as Prince Oscar of Sweden. On May 10 she held a drawing-room at Buckingham Palace; it was the only one she attended that season, and proved her last. Next day she was present at the christening of the third son of the Duke of York, when she acted as sponsor. After the usual visit to Balmoral (May 22 to June 20) she gave several musical entertainments at Windsor. On June 11 there was a garden party at Buckingham Palace, and on June 28 at Windsor a state banquet to the Khedive of Egypt, who was visiting the country. Her old friend the Empress Eugénie was once more her guest at Osborne in September.

Apart from the war, she was interested in a political measure which passed during the session through the House of Commons. This was the Australian Commonwealth Bill, which had for its object the creation of a federal union among the Australian colonies in much the same manner as the colonial provinces of North America had, twenty-three years before, been consolidated into the Dominion of Canada. She received at Windsor on March 27 the delegates from Australia, who were in England to watch the Commonwealth Bill's progress. But she avowed characteristic misgivings of the measure in one

The federation of Australia, 1900.

particular. She found the title obnoxious to her. She had an ingrained dislike of the word 'Commonwealth,' which she identified with Cromwell and his republican form of government. She suggested the substitution of the word 'Dominion,' which had been applied to federated Canada. Explanations were furnished her that the signification of 'Commonwealth' was identical with that of 'Dominion,' and had historical associations other than those which she exclusively attached to it. With some reluctance she suffered her objections to drop, but they illustrate her unimpaired vigilance over all that touched the historic dignity of the Crown. With the policy and aim of the projected statute she was in full sympathy.

The inauguration of the Australian Commonwealth, Jan. 1, 1901.

When in the autumn the Bill received the royal assent, she, on August 27, cordially accepted the suggestion that her grandson, the Duke of York, should, with the Duchess, proceed as her representative to Australia in 1901, to open in her name the first session of the new Commonwealth Parliament at Melbourne in the following May. She was meanwhile especially desirous of showing her appreciation of the part taken by colonial troops in the Boer war, and she directed that the inauguration of the Commonwealth at Sydney on January 1, 1901, should be attended by a guard of honour representing every branch of the army, including the volunteers. The force selected comprised 1,000 men, and included representatives of all branches of the service —viz. regulars, militia, yeomanry, and volunteers. They left England on November 12; they played their part in the Sydney ceremonies in January, and before returning to the mother-country they visited, at the invitation of the various Australasian Governments, Victoria, South Australia, Queensland, Western Australia, Tasmania, and New Zealand.

But the situation in South Africa remained a source of concern, and in the late summer it gave renewed cause for distress. Despite Lord Roberts's occupation of the chief towns of the enemy's territory, fighting was still proceeding in the open country, and deaths from disease or wounds in the British ranks were numerous. The Queen was acutely distressed by the reports of suffering that reached her through the autumn, but, while she constantly considered and suggested means of alleviating the position of affairs, and sought to convince herself that her ministers were doing all that was possible to hasten the final issue, she never faltered in her conviction that she and her people were under a solemn obligation to fight on till absolute victory was assured. Owing to the prevailing feeling of gloom, the Queen, when at Balmoral in October and November, allowed no festivities. The usual highland gathering for sports and games at Braemar, which she had attended for many years with keen enjoyment, was abandoned. She never despaired of the final issue of the war, but the sense of its seriousness oppressed her.

Distresses of the war.

She still watched closely public events in foreign countries, and she found little consolation there. The assassination of her friend Humbert, King of

King Humbert's murder.

Italy, on July 29 at Monza greatly disturbed her equanimity. A few days later her disquietude was increased by an anarchist's abortive attempt on the life of the Shah of Persia while he was on a visit to Paris. She regarded the Shah as belonging to her own caste, despite all differences of race and condition of sovereignty, and deemed the menace of his safety one more indication of the progress of antinomian and radical principles. In France, too, a wave of strong anti-English feeling involved her name, and the shameless attacks on her by unprincipled journalists were rendered the more offensive by the approval they publicly won from the royalist leader, the Duc d'Orléans, great-grandson of Louis Philippe, to whom and to whose family the Queen had proved the staunchest of friends. Fortunately for his credit the Duc afterwards sent to the Queen a humble apology for his misbehaviour, and she magnanimously pardoned him. The libels of the French press were indeed less warmly resented by herself than by her children and many of her subjects. The unvarying courtesy which she experienced at the hands of French people on her visits to France she always gratefully remembered. The journalistic abuse in France chiefly defaced anti-republican or clerical newspapers, and hardly warranted the Queen in assigning the ill-feeling (as she was wont to do in conversation) to the spreading influence of Radicalism, which to her mind was a base and perverted sentiment.[1]

The Duc d'Orléans.

[1] To the like Radical influence in France the Queen had attributed the violent assaults made in the French press upon the

In October a general election was deemed necessary by the Government—the existing Parliament was more than five years old—and the Queen was gratified by the result. Lord Salisbury's Government, which was responsible for the war and its conduct, received from England and Scotland overwhelming support. The elected Unionists, who numbered 402, secured a majority of 134 over the Liberals and Home Rulers, who numbered respectively 186 and 82. The election emphatically supported the Queen's view that, despite the heavy cost of life and treasure, hostilities must be vigorously pursued until the enemy acknowledged defeat.

The new Unionist House of Commons, October 1900.

When the Queen's fifteenth and last Parliament was opened in December, Lord Salisbury was still Prime Minister; but he resigned the Foreign Secretaryship to Lord Lansdowne, formerly Minister of War, and he made, with the Queen's approval, some changes in the constitution of the ministry, which did not impress the country favourably.[1] The policy of the Government remained unaltered.

Changes in the ministry.

Empress Frederick when she paid a somewhat ill-advised visit to Paris and Versailles in February 1891. The Queen hardly seems to have appreciated the political situation in France at the time, and was disappointed by the failure of the English ambassador to secure for the German Empress a welcome from M. Carnot, the President of the French Republic, or from Madame Carnot.

[1] Changes were made in the following offices. The new holders of them were:

Privy Seal	The Marquis of Salisbury.
Foreign Secretary	The Marquis of Lansdowne.
Home Secretary	Mr. C. T. Ritchie.
Secretary for War	Mr. Brodrick.

The Queen's latest bereavements.

Death had again been busy among the Queen's relatives and associates, and cause for private sorrow abounded in her last years. Her cousin and the friend of her youth, the Duchess of Teck, had passed away on October 27, 1897. Another blow was the death at Meran, on February 5, 1899, of her grandson, Prince Alfred, only son of the Duke of Saxe-Coburg-Gotha. The throne of the Duchies of Saxe-Coburg-Gotha was thus deprived of an heir. The Diet of the Duchies eventually offered the reversion to the Queen's third son, the Duke of Connaught; but, although he temporarily accepted it, he, in accordance with the Queen's wish, renounced the position in his own behalf and in that of his son a few months later. The Duke of Albany, the posthumous son of the Queen's youngest son, Leopold, was proposed in his stead. To the Queen's satisfaction, the little Duke of Albany was adopted on June 30, 1899, as heir-presumptive to the beloved principality. This arrangement unhappily took practical effect far earlier than was anticipated. A mortal disease attacked Alfred, the reigning Duke of Saxe-Coburg, the Queen's second son, and before a fatal issue was expected he died suddenly at Rosenau on July 30, 1900.

The last bereavement in the royal circle which the Queen suffered was the death, on October 29, 1900,

First Lord of the Admiralty	Earl of Selborne.
President of the Board of Trade	Mr. Gerald Balfour.
President of the Local Government Board	Mr. W. H. Long.
President of the Board of Agriculture	Mr. Hanbury.
Postmaster-General	The Marquis of Londonderry.

of her grandson, Prince Christian Victor of Schleswig-Holstein, eldest son of Princess Helena, the Queen's second daughter. The young man fell a victim to the Boer war. He had contracted enteric fever on the battlefields of South Africa. But even more distressing was it for the Queen to know that her eldest child, the Empress Frederick, was the victim of an incurable malady that was making slow but fatal progress. Although the Empress was thenceforth gravely disabled, she survived her mother rather more than six months.

Prince Christian Victor's death.

Empress Frederick's malady.

It was amid these griefs that the Queen's long life reached its final stage. On November 7, 1900, the Queen returned to Windsor from Balmoral in order to console Princess Christian on the death of her son, and twice before the end of the month she took the opportunity of welcoming home a few of the troops from South Africa, including colonial and Canadian detachments. On each occasion she addressed a few grateful words to the men. On December 12 she made her last public appearance by attending a sale of needlework by Irish ladies at the Windsor Town Hall. Among other purchases that she made was a screen embroidered with violets, the Napoleonic badge, which she sent as a Christmas present to her faithful friend of past and present days, the Empress Eugénie. On December 14 she celebrated the thirty-ninth anniversary of the Prince Consort's death at Frogmore with customary solemnity. On the 18th she left for Osborne. It was the last journey of her life.

Final migrations of the Court.

XLVIII

THE QUEEN'S DEATH

<small>The Queen's health in old age.</small>

THROUGHOUT life the Queen's physical condition was robust. She always believed in the efficacy of fresh air and abundant ventilation, and those who waited on her had often occasion to lament that the Queen never felt cold. She invariably drove out twice a day for one hour and a half in the morning and two hours in the afternoon. She was extremely careful about her health, and towards the close of her career usually consulted her resident physician, Sir James Reid, many times a day.

<small>Her ailments.</small>

Although she suffered no serious ailments, age told on her during the last five or six years of her life. Since 1895 she suffered from a rheumatic stiffness of the joints, which rendered walking difficult. She could only support herself with difficulty with a stick, and was usually wheeled about in a chair indoors. From 1898, too, incipient cataract greatly affected her eyesight. The growth of the disease was steady, but it did not reach the stage which rendered an operation expedient. In her latest years she was scarcely able to read, although she could still sign her name and could write letters with difficulty.

Ministers were requested, when writing to her, to use broad pens and the blackest possible ink.[1]

It was not till the late summer of 1900 that symptoms menacing to life made themselves apparent. The anxieties and sorrows due to the South African war and to deaths of relatives proved a severe strain on her nervous system. She manifested a tendency to aphasia, but by a strong effort of will she was for a time able to check its growth. She had long justly prided herself on the strength and precision of her memory,[2] and the failure to recollect a familiar name or word irritated her, impelling increased mental exertion. No more specific disease declared itself, but loss of weight and complaints of sleeplessness in the autumn of 1900 pointed to a general physical decay. She hoped that a visit to the Riviera in the spring would restore her powers, but when she reached Windsor in November her physicians feared that a journey abroad might have evil effects. Arrangements for the removal of the Court to the Riviera early next year were, however, begun. At Osborne

Physical decay in 1900.

---

[1] When Gladstone last conversed with the Queen at Cimiez in January 1897, he remarked that 'her peculiar faculty and habit of conversation had disappeared;' but Gladstone's presence doubtless caused her constraint, for which he failed to make allowance.

[2] Lord Ronald Gower relates that, in 1893, 'the Queen spoke of Leslie's picture of her coronation [painted fifty-four years before and containing hundreds of portraits], and on my saying that I believed only three persons who appeared in that painting still lived the Queen immediately corrected me, and said that, besides herself, the Duchess of Cleveland, the Duke of Cambridge, and the Duc de Nemours were the survivors. The "duc" appears in the picture next to the Duke of Cambridge. This shows the marvellous memory of the Queen.'

her health showed no signs of improvement, but no immediate danger was apprehended.

<small>Last days at Osborne.</small>

On Christmas morning her lifelong friend and lady-in-waiting, Jane Lady Churchill, passed away suddenly in her sleep. The Queen was greatly distressed, and at once ordered a wreath to be made for the coffin. On January 2, 1901, she nerved herself to welcome Lord Roberts on his return from South Africa, where the command-in-chief had devolved on Lord Kitchener. She managed by an effort of will briefly to congratulate him on his successes, and she conferred on him an earldom and the Order of the Garter. But she was greatly affected, and her weakness was very perceptible. On the 11th Mr. Chamberlain, the Colonial Secretary, had a few minutes' audience with her, so that she might understand the immediate prospect of South African affairs. She seemed collected and alert. This was her last interview with a minister. It was fitting that the future of her colonial empire should be almost the last business that should be brought to her attention in life. Three days later she gave a second audience to Lord Roberts. She then engaged in an hour's talk with him and showed acute anxiety to learn all details of the recent progress of the war. She appeared to stand the exertion well, but a collapse followed the general's departure.

<small>The Queen's death, Jan. 22, 1901.</small>

The widowed Duchess of Saxe-Coburg-Gotha arrived on a visit on the same day, and, accompanied by her, the Queen drove out on the 15th for the last time. By that date her medical attendants recognised her condition to be hopeless. The brain was failing, and life was slowly ebbing. On the 19th it was publicly announced that she was suffering from physical prostration. The next two days her weakness grew, and the children who were in England were summoned to her deathbed. On January 21 her grandson, the German Emperor, arrived, and in his presence, and in the presence of two sons, the Prince of Wales and the Duke of Connaught, and three daughters, Princess Helena, Princess Louise, and Princess Beatrice, she passed away at half-past six in the evening of Tuesday, January 22.

The Queen was eighty-one years old and eight months, less two days. Her reign had lasted sixty-three years, seven months, and two days. She had lived three days longer than George III., the longest-lived sovereign of England before her. Her reign exceeded his, the longest yet known to English history, by nearly four years. It was only exceeded in European history by the seventy-one years' reign of Louis XIV. of France. *Her age and length of reign.*

On the day following her death the Queen's elder surviving son met the Privy Council at St. James's Palace, took the oaths as her successor to the throne, and was on the 24th proclaimed King under the style of Edward VII. *Accession of Edward VII.*

The Queen named as the executors of her will her younger surviving son, the Duke of Connaught, her youngest daughter, Princess Henry of Battenberg, and her latest Keeper of the Privy Purse, Lieutenant-Colonel Sir Fleetwood Edwards. To them she committed detailed orders for the arrangement of her funeral, even indicating the music that was to be *Her funeral.*

played at the final ceremony. In accordance with a dominant sentiment of her life, the Queen commanded a military funeral. On February 1 the royal yacht 'Alberta,' passing between long lines of warships which fired a last salute, carried the coffin from Cowes to Gosport. Early next day the remains were brought to London, and were borne on a gun-carriage from Victoria station to Paddington. In the military procession which accompanied the *cortège*, every branch of the army was represented, while immediately behind the coffin rode King Edward VII., supported on one side by his brother, the Duke of Connaught, and on the other by his nephew, the German Emperor. They were followed by the Kings of Portugal and of Greece, most of the Queen's grandsons, and members of every royal family in Europe. The funeral service took place in the afternoon, with imposing solemnity, in St. George's Chapel, Windsor. On Monday, February 4, the coffin was removed to the Frogmore mausoleum. The royal family followed on foot. The whole route from the castle was lined by crowds of people in mourning. At Frogmore the coffin was placed in the sarcophagus which already held the remains of Prince Albert.

The universal sorrow.

No British sovereign was more sincerely mourned. As the news of the Queen's death spread, impassioned expressions of grief came from every part of the United Kingdom, of the British Empire, and of the world. Native chieftains in India, in Africa, in New Zealand vied with their British-born fellow-subjects in the avowal of a personal sense of loss. The Legislatures of Canada and of other colonies appointed the

Queen's birthday (May 24) to be a permanent public holiday, so that her name might be held in memory for all time.

Causes of the loyalty to her person.

The demonstration of her people's sorrow testified to the spirit of loyalty to her person and position which had been evoked by her length of life and reign, her personal sorrows, and her recent manifestations of sympathy with her subjects' welfare. But the vital strength and popularity, which the grief at the Queen's death proved the monarchy to enjoy, were only in part due to her personal character and the conditions of her personal career. A force of circumstances which was not subject to any individual control largely contributed to the intense respect and affection on the part of the people of the Empire which encircled her crown when her rule ended. The passion of loyalty with which she inspired her people during her last years was a comparatively late growth. In the middle period of her reign the popular interest, which her youth, innocence, and simplicity of domestic life had excited at the beginning, was exhausted, and the long seclusion which she maintained after her husband's death developed in its stead a coldness between her people and herself which bred much disrespectful criticism.

The Queen and imperial unity.

Neither her partial resumption of the external functions of public life nor her venerable age fully accounts for the new sentiment of affectionate enthusiasm which greeted her declining days. It was largely the outcome of the new conception of the British monarchy which sprang from the development of the colonies and dependencies of Great Britain, and the sudden strengthening of the sense of unity between them and the mother-country. The crown after 1880 became the living symbol of imperial unity, and every year events deepened the impression that the Queen in her own person typified the common interest and the common sympathy which spread a feeling of brotherhood through the territories that formed the British Empire. She and her ministers in her last years encouraged the identification of the British sovereignty with the unifying spirit of imperialism, and she thoroughly reciprocated the warmth of feeling for herself and her office which that spirit engendered in her people at home and abroad. But it is doubtful if, in the absence of the imperial idea, for the creation of which she was not responsible, she could under the constitution have enjoyed that popular regard and veneration of which she died in unchallenged possession.

XLIX

THE QUEEN'S POSITION AND CHARACTER

THE practical anomalies incident to the position of a constitutional sovereign who is in theory invested with all the semblance of power, but is denied any of its reality or responsibility, were brought into strong relief by the Queen's personal character and the circumstances of her life. Possessed of no commanding strength of intellect, but of an imperious will, great physical and mental energy, and an exceptional breadth of sympathy, she applied herself to the work of government with greater ardour and greater industry than any of her predecessors. No sovereign of England was a more voluminous correspondent with the officers of State. She laboriously studied every detail of Government business, and on every question of policy or administration she formed for herself decided opinions, to which she obstinately adhered, pressing them pertinaciously on the notice of her ministers. *Her attitude to business of State.*

Although the result of her energy could not under the constitution be commensurate with its intensity, her activity was in the main advantageous. The detachment from party interests or prepossessions, which her elevated and isolated position came to foster in her, gave her the opportunity of detecting *The benefits of her experience and detachment.*

in ministerial schemes any national peril to which her ministers might at times be blinded by the spirit of faction, and her persistence led to some modifications of policy with happy result. Her length of sovereignty, too, rendered in course of years her personal experiences of government far wider and far closer than those of any of her ministers, and she could recall much past procedure of which she was the only surviving witness.

Her loyalty to the Constitution.

Absolutely frank and truthful in the expression of her views to her ministers, she had at the same time the tact to acquiesce with outward grace, however strong her private objections, in any verdict of the popular vote, against which appeal was seen to be hopeless. In the two instances of the Irish Church Bill of 1869 and the Franchise Extension Bill of 1884 she made personal efforts, in the interest of the general peace of the country, to discourage an agitation which she felt to be doomed to failure. She shrank from no exertion whereby she might influence personally the machinery of the State, and was always ready to face the risk of complete failure in her efforts to enforce her opinions or her wishes. With the principle of the constitution which imposed on the monarch the obligation of giving formal assent to every final decision of his advisers, however obnoxious it might be to the private sentiments of the sovereign, she had the practical wisdom to avoid any manner of conflict.

The Queen's personal influence was far greater at the end of her life than at her accession to the throne. Nevertheless it was a vague intangible element in the political sphere, and was far removed from the solid remnants of personal power which had adhered to the sceptre of her predecessors. Partly owing to the respect for the constitution in which she was educated, partly owing to her personal idiosyncrasies, and partly owing to the growth of democratic principles among her people, the positive force of such prerogatives as the Crown possessed at her accession was, in spite of her toil and energy, diminished rather than increased during her reign. Parliament deliberately dissolved almost all the personal authority that the Crown had hitherto exercised over the army. The prerogative of mercy was practically abrogated when the Home Secretary was virtually made by statute absolute controller of its operations. The distribution of titles and honours became in a larger degree than in former days an integral part of the machinery of party politics, from participation in which the sovereign was almost entirely excluded.

Increase of royal influence and decay of royal power.

Some outward signs of the sovereign's formal supremacy in the State lost, moreover, by her own acts some of their old distinctness. Conservative as was her attitude to minor matters of etiquette, she was self-willed enough to break with large precedents if the breach consorted with her private predilections. During the last thirty-nine years of her reign she opened Parliament in person only seven times. During the last fifteen years of her reign she never once appeared within the walls of the Houses of Parliament. She did not prorogue Parliament once after 1854, although no less than forty-seven sessions were brought to a close before the end of her reign. It had been the

Her absence from Parliament.

rule of her predecessors regularly to attend the Legislature at the opening and close of each session, unless they were disabled by illness. Her defiance of this practice tended to weaken her semblance of hold on the central force of government.

<small>Her foreign travels.</small>

Another innovation in the usages of the monarchy, for which the Queen, with a view to increasing her private convenience, was personally responsible, had a like effect. Of her three immediate predecessors on the throne only one, George IV., left the country during his reign, and then he merely visited his own principality of Hanover. Very rarely had earlier sovereigns of modern times crossed the seas while wearing the crown. In their absence they were invariably represented at home by a regent or by lords-justices, to whom were temporarily delegated the symbols of sovereign power, while a responsible minister was the Sovereign's constant companion abroad. Queen Victoria ignored nearly the whole of this procedure. She repeatedly visited foreign countries ; no regent nor lords-justices were called to office in her absence ; she was at times unaccompanied by a responsible minister, and she often travelled privately and informally under an assumed title of inferior rank. The mechanical applications of steam and electricity which were new to her era facilitated communication with her, but the fact that she voluntarily cut herself off from the seat of government for weeks at a time—in some instances at seasons of crisis—seemed to prove that the sovereign's control of government was in effect less constant and essential than of old, or that it might,

THE QUEEN'S POSITION AND CHARACTER 565

at any rate, incur interruption without in any way impairing the efficiency of the Government's action. Her withdrawal from Parliament and her modes of foreign travel alike tended to enfeeble the illusion which is part of the fabric of a perfectly balanced constitutional monarchy, that the motive power of government at all seasons resides in the sovereign.

In one other regard the Queen, by conduct which must be assigned to her personal feeling and care for her personal comfort at the cost of the public advantage, almost sapped the influence which the Crown can legitimately exert on the maintenance of a healthy harmony among the component parts of the United Kingdom. Outside England she bestowed markedly steady favour on Scotland. Her sojourns there, if reckoned together, occupied a period of time approaching seven years. In Ireland, on the other hand, she spent in the whole of her reign a total period of less than five weeks. During fifty-nine of her sixty-three years of rule she never set foot there at all. Her visit in her latest year was a triumph of robust old age and a proof of her alertness of sympathy. But it brought into broad relief the neglect of Ireland that preceded it, and it emphasised the errors of feeling and of judgment which made her almost a complete stranger to her Irish subjects in their own land during the rest of her long reign. *The Queen and Ireland.*

The Queen's visits to foreign lands were intimately associated with her devotion to her family which was a ruling principle of her life. The kinsmen and kinswomen with whom her relations were closest were German, and Germany had for her most of the *The Queen's foreign relations.*

associations of home. She encouraged in her household many German customs, and with her numerous German relatives maintained an enormous and detailed correspondence.

It was the Queen's cherished conviction that England might and should mould the destinies of the world, and her patriotic attachment to her own country of England and to her British subjects can never be justly questioned. But she was much influenced in her view of foreign policy by the identification of her family with Germany, and by her natural anxiety to protect the interests of ruling German princes who were lineally related to her. It was 'a sacred duty,' as she said, for her to work for the welfare of Prussia, because her eldest daughter had married the heir to the Prussian crown. As a daughter and a wife she felt bound to endeavour to preserve the independence of the duchy of Saxe-Coburg-Gotha, whence her mother and husband sprang. Her friendship for Belgium was a phase of her affection for her uncle, who sat on its throne. The spirit of patriotic kingship was always strong enough in her to quell hesitation as to the path she should follow when the interest of England was in direct conflict with that of her German kindred, but it was her constant endeavour to harmonise the two.

Her views of war. Although the Queen disliked war and its inevitable brutalities, she treated it as in certain conditions a dread necessity which no ruler should refuse to face. Thoroughly as she valued peace, she deemed it wrong to purchase it at the expense of national rights or dignity. But she desired that warfare should be practised with all the humanity that was possible, and she was deeply interested in the military hospitals and in the training of nurses.

The Queen's wealth of domestic affection was allied to a tenderness of feeling and breadth of sympathy with mankind generally which her private sorrows accentuated. She spared no exertion personally to console the bereaved, to whatever walk of life they belonged, and she greatly valued a reciprocation of her sympathy. Every instance of unmerited suffering that came to her notice stirred her to indignation. The persecution of Captain Dreyfus in France evoked strong expressions of disgust in her latest years.[1] Nor were animals—horses and dogs—excluded from the scope of her compassion. To vivisection she was strenuously opposed, denouncing with heat the cruelty of wounding and torturing dumb creatures. Against the orders issued by the Home Office for the muzzling of dogs in the late years of her reign she constantly protested, and she vainly urged the Home Secretary to introduce legislation that should prohibit butchers from killing calves for veal in what she held to be a barbarous mode, which was ordinarily followed in order to make the flesh white.

Her temperament

The Queen countenanced no lenity in the punishment of those guilty of cruel acts. In many instances she expressed disapproval of remissions of punishment which her Home Secretaries, acting according to statute in her name, but really on their own responsibilities, granted persons convicted of

[1] Lord Russell of Killowen, the Lord Chief Justice, wrote at her request an account of Dreyfus's second trial at Rennes, at which he was present. It is printed in Mr. Barry O'Brien's *Life of Lord Russell of Killowen*.

criminal offences against women and children. She paid scant attention to the provocative circumstances which attended the crime and justified the interference of the Home Office. Wife-murder and child-desertion were outrages which in her eyes always demanded the severest penalties known to the law.

Her wide sympathies. The Queen was not altogether free from that morbid tendency of mind which springs from excessive study of incidents of sorrow and suffering. Her habit of accumulating sepulchral memorials of relations and friends was one manifestation of it. She deplored, too, the decay of mourning for the dead, and the growing custom of shortening the interval between death and burial. But the morbid tendency was ultimately held in check by an innate cheerfulness of disposition and by her vivacious curiosity regarding all that passed in the domestic and political circles of which she was the centre. She was interested in the families and personal history of all who served her — especially of the ladies who were in regular attendance on her. She was deeply concerned in the welfare of her servants. She was an admirable hostess, personally consulting her guests' comfort and studying their tastes.

Her recreations. The ingenuousness of youth was never wholly extinguished in the Queen. She was easily amused, and was never at a loss for recreation. Round games of cards or whist which had attracted her in early life she abandoned in later years. But she pursued the gentler of her early amusements until the end; she sketched, played the piano, sang, or did needlework, especially crochet and woolwork. Her serious temperament led her to deprecate excessive devotion to sport, and she came to view many popular games with impatience. The attraction of golf was, she admitted, quite beyond her comprehension. It was new to her experience.

The Queen's artistic sense was not strong. In furniture and dress she preferred the fashions of her early married years to any other. She was not a good judge of painting, and she bestowed her main patronage on portrait painters like Winterhalter and Von Angeli, and on sculptors like Boehm, whose German nationality was for her a main recommendation. 'The only studio of a master that she ever visited was that of Sir Frederic (afterwards Lord) Leighton, whose "Procession of Cimabue" the Prince Consort had bought for her, and whom she thought delightful, though perhaps more as an accomplished and highly agreeable courtier than as a painter.' The sketches with which she occupied herself late in life exhibited no great skill. Yet her robust common sense was at times of service in matters of art.

Her attitude to art.

In music she showed greater taste and had far greater knowledge. Staunch to the heroes of her youth, she always appreciated the operas of Rossini, Bellini, and Donizetti. To the end she was devoted to Mendelssohn and Beethoven, who had won her early admiration. Gounod and Sullivan fascinated her later. Gounod's 'Faust' was her favourite opera, and his setting of the Lord's Prayer was one of the pieces which she ordered to form part of her funeral service. Wagner's merit she was not slow to recognise. She placed his 'Lohengrin' only second to Gounod's 'Faust.'

Her tastes in music.

Much recent German music was by no means uncongenial to her, but she preferred compositions which were characterised by simpler melody.[1] Bach and Handel bored her, because, she said, she had been forced to hear too many of their oratorios in childhood. She was always fond of listening to piano-playing, and it was an essential qualification for those who wished to become ladies-in-waiting that they should be competent executants. When she was alone, she had music in her apartments every evening after dinner.

Her devotion to the drama.

The Queen was devoted to the theatre from girlhood, and all her enthusiasm revived when in her last years she restored the dramatic performances at Court, which her mourning had long interrupted.

Her taste in literature.

Literature did not excite in her the same enthusiasm. She was not well read; but she emulated her husband's respect for literature, was well acquainted with German poetry, and took a serious view of reading as an amusement. In her later years a book was usually read aloud to her late at night before she retired to rest, and although she enjoyed novels of various kinds, especially those of a melodramatic complexion, she deemed it right to alternate fiction with works of more earnest aim. Among works

---

[1] Wide currency has been given to the story that on one occasion, when the Queen was told that a very involved piece of modern German music, to which she was listening with impatience, was a 'drinking song' by Rubinstein, she remarked, 'Why, you could not drink a cup of tea to that.' (*Quarterly Review*, April 1901.) The facts are that Rubinstein's Melody in F was on the occasion in question being played to the Queen, who for the moment forgot what the piece was. She asked a lady-in-waiting, who inappropriately suggested that it was a drinking song. The Queen at once perceived the error, and was heartily amused by it. Nothing further was said.

of that kind which greatly interested her in her last years were Dean Bradley and Mr. R. E. Prothero's 'Life of Dean Stanley' and Slatin Pasha's 'Fire and Sword in the Soudan' (1896). Among recent novelists, the simple pathos of Miss Florence Montgomery's tales attracted her. Mr. Merriman's 'Sowers' gave her much pleasure. But probably she derived as much satisfaction from Mr. Marion Crawford's books as from those of any contemporary writer of fiction. On one occasion, when at Cimiez, she looked forward to meeting Mr. Crawford, to whom she said she owed many delightful hours, but by an accident the interview did not take place. Nevertheless, on the whole, she regarded novel reading as a dangerous distraction from the solemn interests of life. Some great efforts in fiction which she studied carefully she criticised from a serious and pragmatic point of view, which ignored their æsthetic quality.

The Queen dressed simply and without much taste. She was in sympathy with Prince Albert's contempt for fashionable ladies' extravagant expenditure on their wardrobe. But she knew the weakness of her sex and sometimes humoured it by a flattering comment on the attire of a female guest or an attendant at a drawing-room. Despite her small stature and ineffective costume, the Queen always bore herself with grace and dignity, and impressed with her regality of carriage all who came into personal relations with her. She never entirely lost an innate shyness, but she controlled displays of it by force of will.

The Queen's dress and carriage.

In talk she appreciated homely wit of a quiet

Her conversation.

kind, and laughed without restraint when a jest or anecdote appealed to her. Subtlety or indelicacy offended her, and sometimes evoked a scornful censure. Her own conversation had often the charm of naïveté. Gladstone, a somewhat rigorous critic, when recalling late in life her 'peculiar faculty and habit of conversation,' remarked that 'it was a faculty not so much the free offspring of a rich and powerful mind as the fruit of assiduous care with long practice and much opportunity.'[1] Her memory was unusually sound, and errors which were made in her hearing on matters familiar to her she corrected with briskness and point.

Her dislike of obsequiousness.

Although she naturally expected courtesy of address, and resented brusque expression of contradiction or dissent, she was not conciliated by obsequiousness. 'It is useless to ask ——'s opinion,' she would say; 'he only tries to echo mine.' Always frank and absolutely truthful in her own written or spoken word, she desired to be addressed in the same spirit by all who came into personal intercourse with her; and the fear that statements made to her represented what the speakers believed she would like to hear, rather than what was precisely true, caused her frequent annoyance. 'No one can tell,' she remarked to an intimate friend, 'of what value it is to me to hear the truth.'

Her sense of her public services.

The Queen welcomed and appreciated public acknowledgments of her devotion to the public service, and warmly resented criticism of her seclusion, which was, she urged, to a large extent a result of

[1] Morley's *Life of Gladstone*, iii. 524.

the imperative calls of public business. To praise on the score of industrious solicitude for the public welfare she deemed herself fully entitled. She distinguished it from adulation. Of the eulogy which abounded in the newspapers on the occasion of her jubilee in 1887 she wrote, 'That is not flattery, which the Queen hates.' Yet she felt the public applause tended in her last years to exaggeration, and would modestly interrupt the perusal of some extravagant journalistic panegyric with the remark, 'If they only knew me as I am!'

The Queen's religion was simple, sincere, and undogmatic. Theology did not interest her, but in the virtue of religious toleration she was an ardent believer. When Dr. Creighton, the last Bishop of London of her reign, declared that she was the best Liberal he knew, he had in mind her breadth of religious sentiment. On moral questions her views were strict. She was opposed to the marriage of widows. To the movement for the greater emancipation of women she was thoroughly and almost blindly antipathetic. For women to speak in public or associate themselves with public movements was in her sight almost unpardonable. She never realised that her own position gave the advocates of Women's Rights their strongest argument, and when that point of view was pressed on her attention in conversation, she treated it as an irrelevance. With a like inconsistency she regarded the greatest of her female predecessors, Queen Elizabeth, with aversion, although she resembled Queen Elizabeth in her frankness and tenacity of purpose, and might, had the constitution

Her religion.

Her dislike of Women's Rights.

574   QUEEN VICTORIA

of the country in the nineteenth century permitted it, have played as decisive a part in history.

Her Stuart sympathies.

Queen Victoria's sympathies were with the Stuarts and the Jacobites. She declined to identify Prince Charles Edward with his popular designation of 'the Young Pretender,' and gave in his memory the baptismal names of Charles Edward to her grandson, the Duke of Albany. She was deeply interested in the history of her ancestress Mary Stuart. In 1850 she placed a window in Carisbrooke Church in memory of Charles I.'s daughter Elizabeth, and six years later she directed a marble tomb by Marochetti to be erected above her grave in the neighbouring church of St. Thomas at Newport. She restored James II.'s tomb at St. Germain.

Her reliance on her personal sentiment.

But such likes and dislikes reflected purely personal idiosyncrasies. It was not Queen Elizabeth's mode of rule that offended Queen Victoria: it was her lack of feminine modesty. It was not the Stuarts' method of government that appealed to her: it was their fall from high estate to manifold misfortune. Queen Victoria's whole life and action were, indeed, guided by personal sentiment rather than by reasoned principles. But her personal sentiment, if not altogether removed from the commonplace, nor proof against occasional inconsistencies, bore ample trace of courage, truthfulness, and sympathy with suffering. Far from being an embodiment of selfish whim, the Queen's personal sentiment blended in its main current sincere love of public justice with staunch fidelity to domestic duty, and ripe experience came in course of years to imbue it with much of the force of patriarchal wisdom, even with 'something like prophetic strain.' In her capacity alike of monarch and woman, the Queen's personal sentiment proved, on the whole, a safer guide than the best-devised systems of moral or political philosophy. Nature and circumstance met together to endow it in no sparing measure with what Shakespeare called

>   the rare king-becoming graces,
> As justice, verity, temperance, stableness,
> Bounty, perseverance, mercy, lowliness,
> Devotion, patience, courage, fortitude.

APPENDIX

APPENDIX

I

THE QUEEN'S DESCENDANTS

QUEEN VICTORIA and Prince Albert had nine children, four sons—Albert Edward, Prince of Wales, afterwards King Edward VII., Alfred, Duke of Edinburgh, and afterwards Duke of Saxe-Coburg-Gotha, Arthur, Duke of Connaught, and Leopold, Duke of Albany—and five daughters—Victoria, Crown Princess of Prussia, afterwards the Empress Frederick, Alice, Grand Duchess of Hesse, Helena, Princess Christian of Schleswig-Holstein, Louise, Marchioness of Lorne, afterwards Duchess of Argyll, and Beatrice, Princess Henry of Battenberg. *[The Queen's children.]*

Two sons—Leopold, Duke of Albany, and Alfred, Duke of Saxe-Coburg-Gotha—and one daughter—Alice, Grand Duchess of Hesse—died in the Queen's lifetime.

The Queen was survived by two sons—the Prince of Wales (now Edward VII.), and Arthur, Duke of Connaught—and by four daughters, Victoria, Empress Frederick; Helena, Princess Christian; Louise, Duchess of Argyll; and Beatrice, Princess Henry of Battenberg. The eldest daughter, Victoria (Empress Frederick), died on August 5, 1901, nearly seven months after her mother, at her seat, Friedrichshof, near Frankfort. *[Surviving children.]*

All the Queen's children were married, and all except the Princess Louise had issue. The Queen's grandchildren

580   APPENDIX

Grandchildren and great-grandchildren.

numbered forty; of these thirty-one survived at the date of her death; nine died in her lifetime. Her great-grandchildren numbered thirty-seven.

Marriages of grandchildren.

Seventeen of her grandchildren were married before her death. In two instances there was intermarriage of first cousins. The Grand Duke of Hesse (Princess Alice's only surviving son) married Princess Victoria Melita (Prince Alfred's second daughter). Prince Henry of Prussia (the Crown Princess of Prussia's second son) married Princess Irene Marie (Princess Alice's third daughter). The first of these marriages was dissolved on December 21, 1901.[1]

Her grandchildren and the reigning families of Europe.

Other marriages of her grandchildren connected the Queen with the chief reigning families of Europe. The third daughter of the Crown Princess of Prussia (Empress Frederick), Princess Sophie Dorothea, married in 1889 the Duke of Sparta, son of the King of Greece. Princess Alice's youngest daughter (Princess Alix Victoria) married, in 1894, Nicholas II., Tsar of Russia, while Princess Alice's second daughter (Elizabeth) married the Grand Duke Serge of Russia, a younger son of Tsar Alexander II., and uncle of Tsar Nicholas II. Prince Alfred's eldest daughter (Princess Marie) married, in 1893, Ferdinand, Crown Prince of Roumania. Princess Maud, youngest daughter of the Prince of Wales, married in 1896 Prince Charles of Denmark.

Marriages in England.

Only one grandchild married a member of the English nobility—the Prince of Wales's eldest daughter, Louise, who became the wife of the Duke of Fife. Another grandson, Prince George, Duke of York (now Prince of Wales), only surviving son of the Prince of Wales (now Edward VII.), married his second cousin, Princess Mary of Teck, daughter of the Queen's first cousin, Princess Mary of Cambridge, by her husband, the Duke of Teck.

Marriages in Germany.

The remaining seven marriages of grandchildren were contracted with members of princely families of Germany. The German Emperor William II. (the Crown Princess's

[1] See p. 519, note 1.

eldest son) married Princess Victoria of Augustenburg. The Crown Princess's daughters—the Princesses Charlotte, Frederika Victoria, and Margaretta Beatrice—married respectively the Hereditary Prince of Saxe-Meiningen (in 1878), Prince Adolph of Schaumburg-Lippe (in 1890), and Prince Frederick Charles of Hesse-Cassel (in 1893). Princess Alice's eldest daughter (Victoria) married, in 1884, Prince Louis of Battenberg. Prince Alfred's third daughter (Alexandra) married, in 1896, the Hereditary Prince of Hohenlohe-Langenburg. Princess Helena's elder daughter (Louise Augusta) married, in 1891, Prince Aribert of Anhalt, but this union was dissolved by the sovereign decree of the husband's father, the Duke of Anhalt, on December 13, 1900.

There was one marriage in the Queen's lifetime in the fourth generation of her family. On September 24, 1898, the eldest of her great-grandchildren, Feodora, daughter of the Hereditary Princess of Saxe-Meiningen (the Crown Princess of Prussia's eldest daughter), married Prince Henry XXX. of Reuss.

Marriage in the fourth generation.

II

THE QUEEN'S PORTRAITS

Defects of the portraits.

THE Queen's portrait was painted, drawn, sculptured, and photographed several hundred times in the course of the reign. None of the portraits are satisfactory presentments. The Queen's features in repose necessarily omit suggestion of the animated and fascinating smile which was the chief attraction of her countenance. Nor is it possible graphically to depict the exceptional grace of bearing which compensated for the shortness of her stature.

Before accession.

Before her accession the chief paintings or drawings of her are those by Sir William Beechey, R.A. (with the Duchess of Kent), 1821; by Richard Westall, R.A., 1830; by Sir George Hayter, 1833; and by R. J. Lane, A.R.A., 1837.

After accession.

After her accession the chief paintings and drawings are by Alfred Chalon, in state robes (engraved by Cousins), 1838; by Sir George Hayter, 1838; by Sir David Wilkie, 1839 (in Glasgow Gallery); by Sir Edwin Landseer (water-colour sketch presented by the Queen to Prince Albert, and reproduced in the present volume from the original at Windsor Castle by permission of King Edward VII.), 1839. Portraits of the Queen and Prince Albert, which were deemed very successful, were painted by John Partridge in 1840, and were exhibited at the Royal Academy in 1841; that of the Queen is now in the King's private drawing-room at Buckingham Palace; it was engraved in line by John Henry Robinson, R.A. In 1842 Partridge was appointed 'Portrait-painter Extraordinary' to her Majesty, and painted a second portrait of her, of somewhat inferior merit to the first.

THE QUEEN'S PORTRAITS 583

After her marriage many portraits were painted from 1845 onwards by F. Winterhalter. In one she figures in a group with Prince Arthur and the Duke of Wellington, 1848. Sir Edwin Landseer painted a portrait as late as 1866. In 1875 Baron H. von Angeli painted a portrait, of which many replicas were made for presents; a copy by Lady Abercromby is in the National Portrait Gallery, London. Baron von Angeli painted other portraits in 1885 and in 1897 (the latter is reproduced in the present volume from the original at Windsor by permission of King Edward VII.). Mr. W. Q. Orchardson, R.A., introduced the Queen into a group with the Prince of Wales (now King Edward VII.), Duke of York (now Prince of Wales), and Prince Edward of York (now Prince Edward of Wales), in 1900; and M. Benjamin Constant in the same year painted a last portrait. There are several miniatures by Sir W. C. Ross, R.A., and one by Robert Thorburn, A.R.A. (with the Prince of Wales—now King Edward VII.—as a child). A clever caricature lithographic portrait was executed by Mr. William Nicholson, 1897.

After marriage.

Every leading episode in the Queen's life was commemorated by a specially commissioned painting in which her portrait appears. Most of these memorial paintings, many of which have been engraved, are at Windsor; a few are at Buckingham Palace or Osborne. They include Sir David Wilkie's 'The Queen's First Council,' 1837; C. R. Leslie's 'The Queen receiving the Sacrament at her Coronation,' 1838, and 'The Christening of the Princess Royal,' 1841; Sir George Hayter's 'Coronation,' 1838, 'The Queen's Marriage,' 1840, and 'Christening of the Prince of Wales,' 1847; F. Winterhalter's 'The Reception of Louis Philippe,' 1844; E. M. Ward's 'The Queen investing Napoleon III. with the Garter' and 'The Queen at the Tomb of Napoleon,' 1855; G. H. Thomas's 'Review in Paris,' 1855; J. Phillip's 'Marriage of the Princess Royal,' 1859; G. H. Thomas's 'The Queen at Aldershot,' 1859; W. P. Frith's 'Marriage of the

Paintings of ceremonials.

584 APPENDIX

Prince of Wales,' 1863; G. Magnussen's 'Marriage of Princess Helena,' 1866; Sydney P. Hall's 'Marriage of the Duke of Connaught,' 1879; Sir James Linton's 'Marriage of the Duke of Albany,' 1882; R. Caton Woodville's 'Marriage of the Princess Beatrice,' 1885; Laurenz Tuxen's 'The Queen and Royal Family at the Jubilee of 1887'; Sydney P. Hall's 'Marriage of the Duchess of Fife,' 1889; Tuxen's 'Marriage of the Duke of York,' 1893.

Sculptures. The sculptured presentations of the Queen, one or more examples of which are to be found in almost every great city of the empire, include a bust at Windsor by Behnes, 1829, which was always considered a good likeness; a good equestrian statue by Marochetti at Glasgow; and a statue by Sir Edgar Boehm at Windsor; a large plaster bust by the same sculptor is in the National Portrait Gallery, London; there is a statue at Winchester by Mr. Alfred Gilbert, R.A., and a statue at Manchester by Mr. Onslow Ford, R.A., 1900.

National memorial. A national memorial in sculpture has been designed on a vast scale, sixty feet high, by Mr. Thomas Brock, R.A., and is to be placed in the Mall opposite Buckingham Palace. It includes a seated figure of the Queen, surrounded by allegorical figures of Justice, Truth, and Charity, and surmounted by one of Victory, supported by Constancy and Courage. Mr. Aston Webb, A.R.A., has designed an architectural setting for the monument, of which the main features are a screen of columns between the monument and Buckingham Palace and a semicircular screen of columns between the monument and St. James's Park, with some corresponding embellishment of the overlooking façade of the palace. The Mall is to be widened, and to be opened out at its further end into Parliament Street. Public subscriptions for these purposes have been received from all parts of the empire, and exceed the sum of 200,000l.

The coinage. The portrait head of the Queen on the British coinage followed three successive types in the course of the reign. Soon after her accession William Wyon designed from life a head which appears in the silver and gold coinage with the hair simply knotted, excepting in the case of the florin, where the head bears a crown for the first time since the coinage of Charles II. In the copper coinage a laurel wreath was intertwined with the hair. In 1887 Sir Edgar Boehm designed a new bust portrait, showing the features in mature age with a small crown and veil most awkwardly placed on the head. This ineffective design was replaced in 1893 by a more artistic crowned presentment from the hand of Mr. Thomas Brock, R.A.

Of medals on which the Queen's head appears the majority commemorate military or naval achievements, and are not of great artistic note.[1] Many medals commemorating events in the reign were also struck by order of the Corporation of London.[2] Of strictly official medals of the reign the chief are: the medal struck in honour of the coronation from designs by Pistrucci in 1838 ; the Jubilee medal of 1887, with the reverse designed by Lord Leighton, and the obverse bearing Boehm's unsatisfactory bust as on the coinage ; and the Diamond Jubilee medal of 1897, with Wyon's design of the Queen's head in youth on the reverse, with the noble inscription : 'Longitudo dierum in dextera eius et in sinistra gloria,' and Mr. Brock's design of the head in old age on the obverse. **Medals.**

The adhesive postage-stamp was an invention of the Queen's reign, and was adopted by the Government in 1840. A crowned portrait head of the Queen was designed for postage-stamps in that year, and was not modified in the United Kingdom during her lifetime. In most of the colonies recent issues of postage-stamps bear a portrait of the Queen in old age, and recent issues of post-cards in England anterior to Edward VII.'s accession are similarly adorned. **Postage-stamps and post-cards.**

[1] Cf. John H. Mayo's *Medals and Decorations of the British Army and Navy*, 1897.

[2] Cf. Charles Welch's *Numismata Londinensia*, 1894, with plates.

III

PUBLISHED SOURCES OF INFORMATION[1]

General authorities.

THE outward facts of the Queen's life and reign are best studied in the 'Annual Register' from 1837 to 1900, and in 'The Times' newspaper. Hansard's 'Parliamentary Debates' and the collected edition of 'Punch' are supplementary sources of information of the first importance.

Sir Theodore Martin's biography of the Prince Consort.

The only portion of the Queen's career which has been dealt with fully is her married life, 1840-61, the beginning of which is treated in General Grey's 'Early Years of the Prince Consort' (1868), and the whole in Sir Theodore Martin's exhaustive 'Life of the Prince Consort' (5 vols., 1874-80). Sir Theodore Martin's book is an authority of the highest importance. The account there given of the Queen's private and public experiences during the years in question is largely drawn from her and her husband's journals and letters. Both General Grey and Sir Theodore

---

[1] No full life of Queen Victoria has yet been published. An interesting and elaborate sketch in French dealing mainly with the political questions in which the Queen played a part, by M. Abel Chevalley (Paris, 1902), is the most ambitious of existing monographs. M. Chevalley makes generous acknowledgment of his indebtedness to the present writer's article in the supplement to the *Dictionary of National Biography*. There are more or less slender sketches by Mr. R. R. Holmes, librarian at Windsor (with elaborate portrait illustrations, 1887, and text alone, 1901), by Mrs. Oliphant, by the Rev. Dr. Tulloch, Principal Tulloch's son (for young readers), by the Marquis of Lorne (afterwards fourth Duke of Argyll), by Sarah Tooley, by G. Barnett Smith, by J. Cordy Jeaffreson (1893, 2 vols.), and by Mrs. M. G. Fawcett (1901).

Martin write from the Queen's point of view, and they occasionally ignore the evidence of writers with whom the Queen was out of sympathy. Some memoirs published since the appearance of these valuable volumes also usefully supplement General Grey's and Sir Theodore Martin's information. But for the period it covers Sir Theodore Martin's work is a monument of labour and authentic intelligence. Two books, the first of which is used only to a small extent, and the second is not used at all, in Sir Theodore's volumes merit a place beside them. The three series of the 'Greville Memoirs' (1817–60), which are outspoken but in the main trustworthy, are a complementary authority for the general course of the Queen's life and for her relations with political history down to 1860. The Duke Ernest of Saxe-Coburg's 'Memoirs' (4 vols., Eng. transl., 1888–90) throw invaluable side-lights on the Queen's personal relations with Germany and German politics, and print many of her letters; they carry events from her marriage in 1840 down to 1870. *Greville Memoirs and Duke Ernest of Saxe-Coburg's Memoirs.*

The early years of the same period are covered by the 'Memoirs of Baron von Bunsen' and by the 'Memoirs of Baron von Stockmar' (by his son, English transl., 2 vols., 1872). Important hints from the German side may also be gleaned for both early and late periods of the reign, from Wilkinson's 'Reminiscences of King Ernest of Hanover;' 'Tales of my Father' (equerry to King Ernest before his accession to the throne of Hanover), by A. M. F. (1902); Th. von Bernhardi, 'Aus dem Leben,' pt. v. 1895; 'Memoirs of Count von Beust;' 'Memoirs of Count Vitzthum von Eckstädt;' Von Manteuffel's 'Correspondence' (1901); Moltke's 'Letters to his Wife and other Relatives' (ed. Sidney Whitman, 2 vols., 1896); Margaretha von Poschinger's 'Life of the Emperor Frederick' (English transl. edited by Sidney Whitman, 1901); 'Diaries of the Emperor Frederick' (1902); Bismarck's 'Reflections and Reminiscences' (2 vols., 1898, English transl.); the long series of *German memoirs.*

Bismarck's 'Politische Briefe,' 1849-1889 (4 vols., 1889-93); and the ample 'Appendix' of letters to his 'Gedanken und Erinnerungen' (3 vols., 1901-2); and Busch's 'Conversations of Bismarck' (3 vols., 1897).

Relations with France.

For the English relations with Napoleon III. (1851-68) De la Gorce's 'Histoire du Second Empire' (5 vols.) is the best book; and the Queen's relations with Belgium are treated at great length, although mainly on the basis of Stockmar's 'Memoirs,' in 'Le Roi Léopold et la Reine Victoria' by St.-René Taillandier (Paris, 1878, 2 vols.).

English memoirs of early days.

A vast library of memoirs of contemporaries touches at one point or another the whole of the Queen's career in England. For the years before and immediately after the accession, see Mrs. Gerald Gurney's 'Childhood of Queen Victoria' (1901); Tuer's 'First Year of a Silken Reign;' 'Memoir of Gabriele von Bülow' (Engl. transl., 1897); Earl of Albemarle's 'Fifty Years of my Life;' 'Stafford House Letters' (1891, pt. vi.; extracts from the Duke of Sutherland's papers); and Sir Charles Murray's papers of reminiscences in the 'Cornhill Magazine,' 1897, which reappear in Sir Herbert Maxwell's 'Life of Sir Charles Murray.'

Domestic memoirs, 1838-97.

The Queen's domestic life from 1838 to 1870 may be traced in 'Letters from Sarah Lady Lyttelton,' 1797-1870 (privately printed for the family, 1873); from 1842 to 1882 in the Queen's 'Leaves' (1868) and 'More Leaves' (1883) from her own 'Journal in the Highlands;' from 1863 to 1878 in the 'Letters' of Princess Alice, with memoir by Dr. Sell (Engl. transl. 1884); and from 1850 to 1897 in Mr. Kinloch Cooke's 'Life of the Duchess of Teck' (2 vols. 1900).

Diplomatic affairs.

Both court and diplomatic affairs (1837-68) are sketched in Lady Bloomfield's 'Court and Diplomatic Life' (1883, 2 vols.), and diplomatic affairs alone (1837-79) in the two series of Lord Augustus Loftus's 'Reminiscences' (4 vols. 1892-4).

For home politics during the reign, see Torrens's 'Life

of Lord Melbourne;' Thomas Raikes's 'Journal;' the **Political** 'Croker Papers;' the 'Peel Papers' (a specially valuable **memoirs.** work); Sir Spencer Walpole's 'Life of Lord John Russell' (a most useful biography); Bulwer and Ashley's 'Life of Lord Palmerston;' Lord Malmesbury's 'Memoirs of an Ex-Minister;' Benham and Davidson's 'Life of Archbishop Tait' (1891); Lord Selborne's 'Memorials;' Gladstone's 'Gleanings,' vol. i.; Childers's 'Life of Hugh C. E. Childers' (1901), and Sir Algernon West's 'Recollections.'

Personal reminiscences of the Queen in private life **Personal** abound in Donald Macleod's 'Life of Norman Macleod' **reminiscences.** (2 vols., 1876); Mrs. Oliphant's 'Life of Principal Tulloch' (1888); Clark and Hughes's 'Life of Adam Sedgwick;' Bradley and Prothero's 'Life of Dean Stanley;' Lord Tennyson's 'Memoir of Lord Tennyson;' and Benson's 'Memoirs of Archbishop Benson.' The last three print interesting letters from the Queen.[1]

Slighter particulars are met with in Trevelyan's 'Life of **Minor** Macaulay;' Ashwell and Wilberforce's 'Life of Bishop Wil- **notices.** berforce' (3 vols., 1879); Wemyss Reid's 'Lives' of Lord Houghton and of W. E. Forster; Fanny Kemble's 'Records;' Andrew Lang's 'Life of Lord Iddesleigh;' Sir Herbert Maxwell's 'Life of W. H. Smith;' Sir Theodore Martin's 'Life of Helena Faucit, Lady Martin' (1900); Sir John Mowbray's 'Seventy Years at Westminster;' Laughton's 'Life of Henry Reeve' (1899); and Lord Ronald Gower's 'Reminiscences' and 'Old Diaries.'

A valuable account of the *personnel* of the Queen's **The** household throughout the reign may be found in Mr. W. A. **royal** Lindsay's 'The Royal Household,' 1897. **household.**

Of the private sources of information respecting the Queen to which the writer has had access some account is given in the preface of this volume.

[1] A character sketch of the Queen in the *Quarterly Review*, April 1901, is not accurate in all its details, although it is based on the reminiscences of one who was well acquainted with the Queen.

IV

GROWTH OF THE BRITISH EMPIRE, 1837–1901

Extent of the acquisitions.

THE accompanying map of the British Empire indicates the extent of imperial territory as it stood at the time of the Queen's death on January 22, 1901.[1]

Population and area.

At the Queen's accession, the total area of the British Empire (outside the United Kingdom) was about 8,114,035 square miles, with an estimated population of 96,000,000, which has since grown to 116,000,000. At her death the area (excluding Egypt and the Soudan) was reckoned at 12,111,310 square miles, with an estimated population of 240,000,000. The additions approach in area four million square miles, with an estimated population of 124,000,000. It must be borne in mind that the territorial additions made to the British Empire during the Queen's reign mainly affect Africa and India. Of these four million square miles of new territory, more than three million square miles are in Africa, and seven hundred thousand square miles in India and Burma. Less than three hundred thousand of the added four million square miles are situated in other parts of Asia or the rest of the world. One hundred and ten millions of the estimated population, which became subject for the first time to the Queen's sway, belong to India and Burma. Outside India and excluding Egypt and the Soudan, the number of persons who yielded allegiance

---

[1] The map has been prepared by Messrs. W. & A. K. Johnston. The information given in this chapter is partly derived from the preface to the 'British Empire Atlas' (1897) by Mr. C. P. Lucas, C.B., the author of the standard work on the British colonies.

to the English crown for the first time during the Queen's reign do not probably exceed fourteen millions.[1]

Europe. In Europe the only territorial changes have been the acquisition of the island of Cyprus in 1878, and the cession of the Ionian Isles to Greece in 1864 and of Heligoland to Germany in 1890.

Asia, outside India. In Asia, outside India, the account of the chief acquisitions stands thus :

The peninsula of Aden was acquired in 1839, and additions were made to it in 1868 and 1882. The Kuria Muria Islands off the south-east coast of Arabia were taken over in 1854 ; the island of Perim in the Red Sea in 1857 ; the island of Bahrein in the Persian Gulf in 1861 ; and the island of Socotra in the Arabian Sea in 1886.

The island of Labuan, near Borneo, was taken over in 1846. The British North Borneo Company was formed in 1881 to administer the northern peninsula of Borneo, and a British protectorate over the whole of Borneo was established in 1888.

The Straits Settlements, which had been separated from India and formed into a Crown colony in 1867, were enlarged in 1874 ; and Christmas Island in the Indian Ocean was annexed to the Settlements in 1888. The Cocos or Keeling Islands, also in the Indian Ocean, became a British possession in 1857.

In China, the island of Hong Kong was taken over in 1841, and neighbouring territory of Kowloon, on the mainland, was annexed to it in 1860 and 1898. Wei-hai-wai, off the coast of China, was acquired in 1898, but an intention of fortifying it was abandoned in 1902 ; Port Hamilton, an island off Korea, was occupied in 1885, but was soon evacuated.

In the Malay peninsula, British residents were esta-

[1] The population of the United Kingdom, which approached 26,000,000 in 1837, and was 40,000,000 in 1901, increased in the interval by almost the identical number.

592   APPENDIX

blished in many of the native States from 1874 onwards, and these States were formed into a confederation under British control in 1896. A protectorate over the Malay State of Johore was inaugurated in 1885.

India. In India, the administration of which was transferred from the East India Company to the Crown in 1858, Sind was annexed in 1843; Tranquebar and Serampore were purchased from the Danes in 1845; the district between the Sutlej and the Rávi rivers was acquired in 1845; the Punjaub in 1849; Lower Burma in 1852; the Central Provinces (Satara, Jhansi, and Nagpore) in 1853; the Berars in 1853; Oudh in 1856; the Dooabs (incorporated in Bengal and Assam) in 1865; the Nicobar Islands, 1869; and Upper Burma and the Shan States, 1885. Several small States on the N.W. frontier were consolidated 1895–7.

Africa. In Africa four spheres of advance are to be noticed: The West Coast, the East Coast, the South Coast, and the Centre.

At the opening of the Queen's reign Cape Colony (extending over 110,000 square miles) and Sierra Leone (extending over 4,000 square miles) were the only organised British settlements in Africa. At the end of the Queen's reign the territory under the British flag had multiplied thirty times. This calculation takes no account of Egypt and the Egyptian Soudan, on the north side of the continent, with a total population probably exceeding 15,000,000, and an area of some 1,300,000 square miles; these countries still remain under the nominal rule of the Khedive, although the country has been administered since 1882 by English officers, military and civil, who are chosen by the English Government.

West Africa. In Africa, on the West Coast, the Gold Coast Colony and Protectorate was formed in 1843 to take over a few old mercantile settlements; Accra and the neighbourhood was purchased of the Danes in 1850; and the castle of Elmina and other forts of the Dutch in 1871; while the wars with the Ashantis in 1874 and 1896 brought the neighbouring native district under British control. Lagos, which adjoins the Gold Coast, was acquired in 1861, and was successively enlarged in 1882, 1885, and 1887, both along the coast and inland, while the regions abutting on the banks of the River Niger, in the same quarter of Africa, were committed to the administration of a chartered company in 1879, were gradually extended in all directions, and finally acquired by the British Government in 1899. On the West Coast, to the north of the Gold Coast, an existing settlement on the Gambia was formed in 1850 into British Combo, of which the boundaries were defined in 1891 ; Sierra Leone was greatly extended by the acquisition both of neighbouring islands and of districts on the mainland in 1861, 1876-7, and 1886.

On the East Coast of Africa an enormous tract of territory known as British East Africa (1,200,000 square miles in extent) was acquired in 1888 by the chartered company called the Imperial British East Africa Company. A British protectorate over Uganda, part of this company's territories, was proclaimed in 1894, and all the company's territory was made over to the British Government in 1895, when the company was dissolved. Further north of British East Africa a British protectorate was established over Somaliland in 1887, while to the south of British East Africa Zanzibar accepted a British protectorate in 1890. **East Africa.**

In South Africa Natal was formed into a British colony in 1842, and the adjoining St. Lucia Bay was ceded by Zululand at the same time ; absorption of much neighbouring native territory to the south took place in 1866. **South Africa.**

In 1847 the district in the extreme east of Cape Colony was taken from the Kaffirs, was converted for the time into the province of British Kaffraria, and was incorporated with Cape Colony in 1863. The islands of Ichaboe and the Penguin Islands, off the north-west coast of Cape Colony, were added to the colony in 1874. In 1880 Griqualand West, to the north, where the Kimberley diamond fields had been discovered in 1870, was also absorbed in Cape Colony ;

Walfisch Bay, on the north-west coast, was absorbed in 1884; Pondoland, to the extreme east, in 1894; Basutoland, to the north-east of the colony, between Natal and the Orange Free State, was annexed to Cape Colony in 1871, but this was made a separate Crown colony in 1884.

The Transvaal and Orange Free State.

A declaration of British sovereignty, made in 1848 over the territories north-east of Cape Colony, between the Orange and Vaal rivers, was withdrawn in 1854, when the independence of the Orange Free State was recognised. In 1852 the right of self-government was granted to the Dutch farmers beyond the Vaal river, in the land known as the Transvaal. The Transvaal republic was annexed to the British Empire in 1877, was restored in 1881, and was finally re-annexed, together with the Orange Free State, during the great Boer war, in 1900. Zululand, on the coast north of Natal, was proclaimed a British colony in 1887; and Amatongaland, to the north of Zululand, was made a British protectorate.

Central Africa.

Nearer the centre of the continent, Bechuanaland, in the interior, to the north of Cape Colony, became a British colony in 1885; and the chartered British South Africa Company, which was formed in 1889, obtained control of the more northerly and more central interior territories of Matabeleland and Mashonaland. A further province at nearly the heart of the continent, north of the River Zambesi and extending to Lake Tanganyika, has been formed into the British protectorate of Central South Africa. These central districts, including Matabeleland, Mashonaland, and Central South Africa, bear the general name of Rhodesia, after Cecil Rhodes, the guiding spirit of the British South Africa Company.

North America.

In North America the extensions have been mainly on the Pacific side of Canada. Vancouver Island was placed under a British colonial governor in 1849; while the neighbouring mainland territory of British Columbia was formed into a colony in 1858, and Vancouver Island was combined with it in 1866. After the confederation of the North

BRITISH EMPIRE, 1837-1901   595

American colonies in 1867, the old chartered Hudson's Bay Company surrendered its territories to the Dominion Government, and out of them were formed the province of Manitoba in the centre of the continent, and the great tract to the north-west called the North-west Territories.

In Australasia the continent of Australia, although very imperfectly explored, had passed nominally under British control before the Queen came to the throne. But its permanent settlement followed her accession. New South Wales was ultimately subdivided into the three independent colonies of New South Wales, Victoria (1851), and Queensland (1859). South Australia and Tasmania became self-governing colonies in 1856. Western Australia was similarly constituted in 1890. The New Zealand islands were an acquisition of the Queen's reign; they were ceded to the Crown by the native chiefs in 1840, and became a self-governing colony in 1852.

Australasia.

Extensions of territory during the Queen's reign in Australasia, apart from New Zealand, mainly affect islands in the Pacific Ocean. The Fiji Islands were ceded by the chiefs in 1874 and became a new British colony. A British protectorate was proclaimed in 1884 over the south-east coast of New Guinea and the adjoining islands, which lie to the north of the Australian continent, and British sovereignty over all was declared in 1888. In 1887 the Kermadec Islands, to the north-east of New Zealand, were annexed to that colony. Numerous other Pacific islands have been recently annexed to the Crown or placed under British protectorates. Christmas Island, Fanning Island, and Penrhyn Island were annexed in 1888. Over the Cook and Hervey Islands, the Union group, and the Phœnix group, a British protectorate was proclaimed in 1888-9. Suwarrow Island was annexed in 1889; and the Gilbert Islands, the Isles of Danger, Nassau Island, the Ellice group, and the Southern Solomon Islands were placed under a protectorate in 1892-3.

The Pacific Islands.

INDEX[1]

ABBOTSFORD, 386
Abdul Karim, The Munshi, 500
Abercorn, Marquis of, 185
Abercromby, Lady, (App.) 582
  Speaker, 65
Aberdare, Lord, 401 n
Aberdeen, 190, 306, 343
  Lord, 137, 145, 147–8, 162, 169, 173, 215, 219, 253, 315, 447; visit to France, 152–3; and the Spanish marriages, 177; his ministry, 228–39; and the Crimean war, 240–9; his defeat, 249–52; letter from the Queen, 249; 'The Life of,' 250 n; death, 311
  Waterworks, 375
Abergeldie Castle, 200, 509
Abingdon, Earl of, 36
Accra, (App.) 592
Acland, A. H. D., 525 n
Acts of Parliament:
  Royal Marriage Act, 4 n
  Conferring the regency on the Duchess of Kent, 29
  Transferring the royal prerogative of mercy to the Home Secretary, 57–8
  Reform Bills, 297, 370–1; of 1832, 74; of 1867, 381, 389, 394; of 1884, 483–5, 489, 562
  Civil List Bill, 80–1
  Prince Albert's annuity, 113–4
  Naturalisation Bill, 115–6

Acts of Parliament—cont.
  Regency Bill, appointing Prince Albert, 125–7
  Bill for her Majesty's personal security, 143, 206
  Corn Law Repeal Bill, 172
  Bill for the commutation of death sentences for treason, 203
  Ecclesiastical Titles Bill, 220
  India Bill, 288
  Irish Reform Bill, 389
  Scottish Reform Bill, 389
  Boundary Bill, 389
  Irish Church Disestablishment Act, 1869, 401 n, 484
  Irish Land Act, 1870, 401 n
  Elementary Education Act, 1870, 401 n
  Army Regulation Act, 1871, 401 n, 416
  Ballot Act, 1872, 401 n
  Supreme Court of Judicature Act, 1873, 401 n
  Public Worship Regulation Bill, 435
  Scottish Church Patronage Bill, 435
  Royal Titles Bill, 439–40
  Burials Act, 462
  Australian Commonwealth Bill, 547–9
Adare, 206
Addington, 473
Adelaide, Queen of William IV., 30, 47, 49; as Princess of Saxe-

[1] This index, the fulness of which will, it is hoped, increase the usefulness of the volume, has been compiled by Mr. W. J. Williams.

ADELAIDE

Adelaide, Queen—*cont.*
Meiningen, 5; marriage to the Duke of Clarence, 5; and the Duchess of Kent, 16, 33, 46; at the coronation 31; reception of Prince Albert, 42; death of the King, 48; removes from Windsor to Marlborough House, 72; annuity as Queen Consort, 78; godmother to the Princess Royal, 127; letter to Peel, 172; death, 205

Aden, (App.) 591

Adolphus Frederick. *See under* Cambridge, Duke of

Adye, Sir John, 468

Afghan war, 452, 463

Afghanistan, Abdur Rahman, Amir of, 463; his autobiography, 463 *n*; and Russia, 488

Agniborna (Hindu King), 440

Aix-la-Chapelle, 165, 285

Aix-les-Bains, 485, 500, 518 *n*

Albany, Leopold, Duke of, 485, 510, 552; birth, 235; his valet, 328 *n*; illness, 436; at Beaconsfield's funeral, 466; marriage, 471–2; annuity, 471; death, 476–7
Duchess of, 471–2
Leopold Charles Edward, Duke of, 574, (App.) 579, 584; adopted as heir presumptive to the duchies of Saxe-Coburg-Gotha, 552

Albemarle, Earl of, 23, 51; 'Fifty Years of my Life' quoted, 23 *n*, 31 *n*, (App.) 588

Albert, Prince Consort: parentage, 8; birth, 13, 14; considered as a suitor, 26, 43; death of his mother, 32; visit to the Duchess of Kent, 42–4; engagement and marriage, 105–17; his position, 118–34; letter to Wellington, 121; letter to Melbourne, 135; and the attempt on the Queen's life, 141–2; visits to Scotland, 143–5; growing influence, 148; visit to France, 150–4; at Cambridge, 155; death of his father, 156; visit to Germany, 164–6; question of precedence, 165; supports Peel in the House of Commons, 171; and Palmerston's foreign policy, 176–7; and the

ALBERT

Albert, Prince Consort—*cont.*
Spanish marriages, 168; chancellor of Cambridge University, 183–4; and Mendelssohn, 191–4; his children's education, 197–8; and the designing of Osborne House, 200; opens the Coal Exchange, 204; declines the post of Commander-in-Chief, 206; differences with Palmerston, 208–20, 254; and the Great Exhibition of 1851, 221–7; unveils a statue of the Queen at Peel Park, 224; letter to his brother on Lord Palmerston's fall, 226–7; and the Crimean war, 240–50; popular suspicions of, 242–3, 254; at St. Omer, 246; visit to Paris, 258–61; on the Princess Royal's engagement, 262; and Italian unity, 265; plans the ballroom at Buckingham Palace, 69, 269; receives the title of Prince Consort, 275; visits to Cherbourg, 277 284; tour in Germany, 285; at Birmingham and Leeds, 286; fears for Prussia, 296; presides at the meeting of the British Association at Aberdeen, 306; second visit to Coburg, 307–9; in a carriage accident, 308; last visit to Balmoral, 315; failing health, 315–6; intervenes in the affair of the 'Trent,' 317–9, 330; death, 320; his reputation, 321–3; biography, 321, 376 seq.; funeral, 324; his lasting influence on the Queen, 325–6 395; memorial at Balmoral, 332; statue at Aberdeen, 342; statue at Perth, 354; statue at Coburg, 362; statue at Wolverhampton, 375; his 'Speeches and Addresses,' 376; Deeside memorial, 386; his estate, 423; statue on Smith's Lawn, Windsor, 502; founds the South Kensington Museum, 541; (App.) 579, 582; 'Life' of, by Sir Theodore Martin, quoted, 146, 182, 216, 261, 289, 291

Albert Edward, Prince of Wales. *See under* Edward VII.

Albert Hall, 380, 419, 426, 442, 497
Medal, institution of the, 367

INDEX

ALBERT

Albert Memorial at Edinburgh, 443 in Kensington Gardens, 442
Albert Victor, Prince. *See under* Clarence, Duke of
'Alberta' yacht, 558
Albertazzi, Madame, 70
Aldershot, 266–7, 274, 367, 407, 442, 448, 465, 499, 503, 510, 516, 533
Alexandra, Queen : betrothal to the Prince of Wales, 332 ; marriage, 335 ; annuity, 335–6 ; and the Schleswig-Holstein question, 347–8, 353 ; birth of a son, Albert Victor, 354 ; her sister's marriage, 430–31 ; celebration of her silver wedding, 490 ; at Abergeldie Castle, 509
Alfred, King, 1–3
Alfred, Prince. *See under* Saxe-Coburg-Gotha, Duke of
Algiers, 284 *n*
Alice, Princess. *See under* Hesse-Darmstadt, Princess Louis of
Alma, battle of the, 248
Altamash (Mohammedan Emperor), 440
Althorp, Lord. *See under* Spencer, Earl
Amatongaland, (App.) 594
America. *See under* United States of
American Civil War, 316–9, 383, 410
Amorbach, Germany, 10
Andaman Islands, 426
Anderson, G., 424
Angeli, Baron H. von, 569, (App.) 583
Angelico, Fra, 518 *n*
Anglesey, Marquis of, 35
Anhalt, Prince Aribert of, (App.) 581
Anne, Queen, 2, 54, 62, 112
'Annual Register' 75 *n*, 111 *n*, (App.) 586
Anson, Miss, 125 *n*
— George, 116, 204
'Antigone,' 191
Antwerp, 154, 165, 166, 231, 285, 308
Apponyi, Count, 352
Arabi Pasha, 467 seq., 477
Arabia, (App.) 591
Arabian Sea, (App.) 591

AUSTERLITZ

Ardverikie, Highland residence, 185
Argyll, Duchess of (Princess Louise) : birth, 187 ; betrothal to the Marquis of Lorne, 417 ; dowry and annuity, 418 ; marriage, 419 ; at Cimiez, 527 ; at the Queen's death, 557 ; (App.) 579, 586 *n*
— third Duke of, 185, 235, 299 *n*, 401 *n*, 403, 417–8, 459 *n*
— fourth Duke of (Marquis of Lorne), engagement to Princess Louise, 418 ; marriage, 419, (App.) 586 *n* Lodge, 392
Army, abolition of purchase in the, 416
— reform, 462–3
— Regulation Act, 1871, 401 *n*, 416
— signing of commissions in the, 331, 532
Arran, Arthur, second Earl of, 126 *n*
Art, royal patronage of, 195–6
Art Treasures Exhibition, Manchester, 274
Arthur, Prince. *See under* Connaught, Duke of
Arthur's Seat, 207
Ascot, 40, 87, 124, 156, 245, 273
Ashanti war of 1873–4, 441, (App.) 592 ; of 1895–6, 533, (App.) 592
Ashbourne, Lord, 490 *n*, 495 *n*, 530 *n*
Ashford, 26
Ashley camp, 540
Asquith, Mr. H. H., 525 *n*
Assam, (App.) 592
Aston Park, 286
'Athalie,' 191
Athol, Duke of, 145, 342
— Duchess of, 145, 342, 375. *See also under* Glenlyon, Lord and Lady
Auber, musician, 153
Augusta, Princess (daughter of George III.), 12, 16, 123
Augustus, Prince (the Queen's first cousin), 9 *n*
Aumale, Duc d', 150, 177, 187
'Aus dem Leben,' 349–51 *n*, (App.) 587
Austerlitz, 259

AUSTRALIA

Australia offers men for the Soudan war, 482; and the Diamond Jubilee, 537; (App.) 595
Australian Commonwealth Bill, 547–9
Austria, 209–10, 218, 224, 265, 276, 339; at war with Italy, 295–7; and Napoleon III., 300, 303; and the Schleswig-Holstein question, 344–54
 The Austro-Prussian war, 368–74
 Charlotte, Archduchess of, 314, 383–4. *See also under* Belgium, Princess of
 Crown Prince of, 501
 Francis Joseph, Emperor of, 165, 210, 341, 384, 536; at Villafranca, 297, 300; and the 'Trent' affair, 317; meeting with the Queen at Coburg, 341–2; and the Schleswig-Holstein question, 345; meets the Queen at Innsbruck, 505
 Frederick, Archduke of, 165
 Maximilian, Archduke of, 274, 314; marriage, 275; death, 383–4
Avoyne House, 41
Ayrton, A. S., 360

Babelsberg, Castle of, 285, 289, 341
Bach, 39, 570
Back, Captain, 37
Baden, 314
 riots, 209
Baden-Baden, 426–7, 455
Bagot, Mrs., 'Links with the Past,' 36 *n*, 392 *n*
Bahrein, (App.) 591
Bala, lake, 516
Balaclava, victory of, 248
Balfour, Mr. A. J., 496 *n*, 530 *n*
 Lady Betty, 440 *n*, 453 *n*
 Mr. Gerald, 552 *n*
 of Burleigh, Lord, 531 *n*
Balkan peninsula, 275–6, 443
Ballater, 17
Balliol College, 395 *n*
Ballot Act, 1872, 401 *n*
Balmoral House, 190, 200–1
 Castle, 201 seq.; building of, 200–1

BEACONSFIELD

Bandon, 110
Bangor, 306
Barez, M., 22
Barham, Lady, 63 *n*
 Rev. Richard, 88
Baring, Francis, 100
Barrington, Lady Caroline, 63 *n*, 119 *n*; as royal governess, 196, 329
 Captain the Hon. George, 196
Basutoland, (App.) 594
Bath, 34
Battenberg, Countess of, 486
 Prince Alexander of (afterwards Prince of Bulgaria), 486–7, 506–7
 Prince Henry of, marriage, 486–7; death, 533
 Prince Louis of, 485–6, 506, (App.) 581
 Princess Henry of (Princess Beatrice), 273, 446, 451, 466, 506, 533, (App.) 579, 584; birth, 272; and the death of Gordon, 480–1; marriage, 486–7; dowry and annuity, 487; at the Queen's death, 446; co-executrix of the Queen's will, 557
 Princess Victoria of, 506
Baveno, 450
Beaconsfield, Viscountess (Mrs. Disraeli), 311; created peeress in her own right, 394; death, 433
 Earl of (Benjamin Disraeli), 138 *n*, 251, 372, 410, 483, 489–90, 496–7, 531; his 'Sybil,' 51 *n*; member for Maidstone, 76; at the Queen's coronation, 90; 'Letters to his Sister,' 90*n*, 161 *n*; meeting with the Queen at Stowe, 162; denunciation of Peel, 167; leader of the Conservative Protectionists, 174; Chancellor of the Exchequer, 229–30, 232, 283; relations with the Queen, 230; his Reform Bill, 297, 381; and the grant to Princess Alice, 311; leader of the House, 372–4; his

INDEX

BEACONSFIELD

Beaconsfield, Earl of—*cont.*
    first ministry, 387–98;
    declines a peerage, 394;
    refuses office, 428–9; in
    power, 432–54; Royal
    Titles Bill, 439–40; created
    Earl of Beaconsfield, 441;
    dissolves Parliament, 454;
    enters the House of Lords,
    441; the Queen's visit to
    Hughenden, 445–6; at the
    Congress of Berlin, 447–8;
    the Queen takes leave of
    him, 458; death, 465; the
    Queen's memorial, to, 466;
    Letters of, 162 *n*

Bean, John William, 143

Beatrice, Princess. *See under* Battenberg, Princess Henry of

Beaumaris, 35

Bechuanaland, (App.) 594

Bedford, Duchess of, 136, 392 *n*
    Duke of, 133

Beechey, Sir William, (App.) 582

Beethoven, 165, 256, 560

Behnes, sculptor, (App.) 584

Belfast, 203

Belgians, Leopold I., King of the (Prince of Saxe-Coburg), 7 *n*, 13–17, 25–6, 42–3, 62–4, 127–32, 142, 150–6, 165–6, 172, 182–7, 205, 232–8, 248, 274–5, 285, 302–14, 382, 472, 480; death of his first wife (Princess Charlotte Augusta of Wales), 4; becomes King of the Belgians, 32; visits the Queen at Windsor, 72, 108; and the Queen's marriage, 105–17; visits of the Queen to, 153–4, 231, 339; and the Spanish marriages, 179–82; gives up Claremont to Louis Philippe, 186; at Aldershot, 267; advises the Queen on the death of the Prince Consort, 324; and the throne of Greece, 334; last meeting with the Queen, 363; death, 365; 'Le Roi Léopold et la Reine Victoria,' by St. René Taillandier, (App.) 588

Leopold II., King of the, 502

BISMARCK

Belgians, Louise, Queen of the, 72, 107, 150, 156, 165, 180, 188, 205

Belgium, 382, 411
    Princesse Charlotte of, 274; marriage, 275. *See also under* Austria, Archduchess of

Bellini, musician, 183, 569

Belper, 35

Belvoir Castle, 44, 156

Bengal (App.), 592

Benson, Archbishop, 395–6, 475; letter from the Queen, 508; 'The Life of,' 508 *n*, (App.) 589

Berars (App.), 592

Berkshire Regiment (66th), 465

Berlin, 263, 272, 285, 293, 337, 342, 351 *n*, 363, 428, 437, 486, 505, 511, 543
    Congress, 448
    riots, 209

Bernard, Dr. Simon, 281

Bernhardi, Theodor von, 349; 'Aus dem Leben' quoted, 349 *n*–350 *n*, (App.) 587

Berwick, 207

Bessborough, third Earl of, 60 *n*

Beust, Memoirs of Count von, 353 *n*, (App.) 587

Biarritz, 509

Biddulph, Sir Thomas, 329

Bigge, Colonel Sir Arthur, 329

Birmingham, 35, 141, 285

Bishopsthorp, 41

Bismarck, Prince, 382; introduced to the Queen, 260; on the engagement of the Princess Royal, 263; and Poland, 339; at Coburg, 340; and the Schleswig-Holstein question, 345, 353 *n*, 363, 456; declines the Queen's mediation in the Austro-Prussian war, 369, 374; and the Franco-German war, 411–13 seq., 437–8; and the Russo-Turkish war, 445; at the Congress of Berlin, 448; on the betrothal of Princess Victoria of Prussia, 506–7; on the Queen's reputed wealth, 511; Busch's 'Conversations' of, 438 *n*, 445 *n*, (App.) 588; 'Reflections and Reminiscences' of, 373 *n*, 438 *n*, 445 *n*, (App.) 587–8; 'Politische Briefe,' 353 *n*, 369 *n*, (App.) 588

INDEX

Blachford, Lady Isabella, 199
Black Sea, 265, 413
Blackfriars Bridge, opening of, 408
Blair Athol, 146, 342
Bloemfontein, occupation of, 544
'Blonde,' H.M.S., 533
Bloomfield, Lady, 'Court and Diplomatic Life,' 123 *n*, 140 *n*, 321 *n*, (App.) 588
'Blount, Memoirs of Sir Edward,' 186 *n*
Blythswood, 508
Bodleian Library, 36
Boehm, Sir Edgar, 502, 569, (App.) 584–5
Boer war of 1881, 463–4; of 1899–1902, 539–53
Bohemia, Frederick, King of, 2
Bonaparte, Prince Jerome, 238–239
Bonn, 165, 309
Borneo, 537, (App.) 591
Boulogne, 259, 261
Boundary Bills, 389
Bourdin, Mdlle., 23
Bradlaugh, Mr., 512
Bradley, Dean, 397; Bradley and Prothero's 'Life of Dean Stanley,' 571
Bradshaw, James, 102
Braemar, 200, 504, 549
Brand, Mrs., 63 *n*
Breadalbane, Lord, 145
Bright, John, 401 *n*–403, 459 *n*, 460; in defence of the Queen's seclusion, 360
Brighton, Corporation of, 199
  Pavilion, 70, 140, 153, 199
Brinckman, Rowland, 'Historical Records of the 89th Regt.,' 38 *n*
Bristol, 517
British Colombo (App.), 593
  Columbia (App.), 594
  East Africa (App.), 593
  Empire Atlas (App.), 590 *n*
  Kaffraria (App.), 593
  Museum, 413
    Addit. MSS., 13 *n*, 153 *n*
  North Borneo Co. (App.), 591
  South African Co. (App.), 594
Broadstairs, 26
Brock, Thomas, (App.) 584–5
Brocket Park, 134
Brodrick, Mr., 551 *n*
Brompton Hospital for Consumption, 356

Bromsgrove, 36
Brontë, Charlotte, 154
Brougham, Lord, 63, 81, 100, 152
Brown, Archibald, 328
  John, 318, 421, 475–6
Browne, Dr. Harold, 474; Kitchin's 'Life' of, 475 *n*
Browning, Robert, 409
Bruce, Lady Augusta, 313, 327. *See also under* Stanley, Lady
  Henry Austin. *See under* Aberdare, Lord
Brühl, 165
Brunswick, Duke Wm. of, 43
  Prince of, 2
Brussels, 6, 106, 115, 117, 154, 243, 275, 324
Bryce, Mr. James, 525 *n*
Bryntysilio, 517
Buccleuch, Duchess of, 136
  Duke of, 145
Buchanan, James (President U.S.A.), 286, 307
Bückeburg, 123
Buckingham, Duke of, 138 *n*, 161–2, 372 *n*
Buckingham Palace, 91 seq.; the Queen takes up her residence at, 69 seq.; innovations at, 71; coronation festivities at, 88
Buckland, Rev. William, 397
Buckstone, actor, 195
Buggin, Sir George, 126 *n*
Bulgaria, 443
  Prince of, 486–7. *See also under* Battenberg, Prince Alexander of
Buller, Charles, 85
  Sir Redvers, 542
'Bülow, Memoir of Gabriele von,' 25 *n*, 30 *n*, (App.) 588
Bulwer, Sir Henry, 181; expelled from Madrid, 211
Bunsen, Baron von, 196, 213; 'Memoirs' of, 49 *n*, 67 *n*, 71 *n*, 139 *n*, 214 *n*, (App.) 587
Buonaparte, Prince Louis. *See under* France, Napoleon III. of
Burials Act, 462
Burke, Thomas Henry, 470
Burlington House, 417
Burmah, 291 *n*, (App.) 590–1
  Upper and Lower, (App.) 592
Burnand, Sir Francis, 509

INDEX

Bushey, 187
Buxted Park, 36, 44
Byron, Lord, 60 *n*

CABUL, 452
Cadiz, Duke of, 180–1
Cadogan, Lord, 495 *n*, 530 *n*
Cairns, Lord, 388 *n*, 435 *n*
Calais, 151, 160, 231
Cambridge, 154, 155 *n*
    Cooper's 'Annals' of, 184 *n*
    University, 183–4
    Adolphus Frederick, Duke of, 4, 56 *n*, 57 *n*, 115, 139, 149; marriage, 5; death, 205–6
    Augusta, Duchess of, 5, 73, 332, 502, 509
    George, Duke of, 510, 555 *n*; early association with the Queen, 107; Commander-in-Chief, 267–8, 529
    Mary, Princess of, 238, (App.) 580; betrothal, 368. *See also under* Teck, Duchess of
Cameron Highlanders, 2nd battalion of, 540
Campbell, Lord, 299 *n*
    Hon. Mrs. G., 63 *n*
    Sir Archibald, 508
Campbell-Bannerman, Sir Henry, 460 *n*, 491 *n*, 525 *n*
Campden Hill, 392 *n*
Canada, 17, 77, 547, (App.) 594–5; the revolt of, 82–7; the Prince of Wales's tour in, 307; and the Diamond Jubilee, 537; and the Queen's death, 558
Cannes, 476, 500
Canning, Lord, 288; letter from the Queen to, 291 *n*
    George, 11, 59, 129
Canrobert, Marshal, 260–1 *n*, 284 *n*
Canterbury, 102
Canton, 271
    river, 272
Cape Colony, (App.) 592–4; presents an ironclad to Great Britain, 538. *See also under* South Africa
Cardiff, 25
Cardwell, Edward (afterwards Viscount Cardwell), 299 *n*, 401 *n*, 415

Carisbrooke Church, 575
Carlingford, Lord, 401 *n*, 459 *n*, 460 *n*
Carlisle, Dean of, 394 *n*
    Earl of, 155
Carlyle, Thomas, 91, 409
'Carmen,' 520
Carnarvon, Earl of, 372 *n*, 435 *n*, 490 *n*
Carnot, Mons., 551 *n*
    Madame, 551 *n*
Caroline, Princess, 4 *n* (afterwards Queen)
Carroll, George, 77
Cassel, 5
Cavagnari, Sir Louis, 452
'Cavalleria Rusticana,' 520
Cavendish, Hon. Miss, 63 *n*
    Lord Frederick, 460, 470–1
Cavour, Count, 264–5
Central Africa, (App.) 594
    South Africa, (App.) 594
Chalon, Alfred, (App.) 582
Chamberlain, Mr. Joseph, 459, 491; his relations with the Queen, 530–1; and the Boer war, 541–553; last audience with the Queen, 556
Champs de Mars review, 260
Chaplin, Mr. Henry, 531 *n*
Charlemont, Countess of, 63
Charles I., 509, 575
    II., 22, 509, 585
Charles Edward, Prince, 574
Charlotte, Queen, 3
Charlotte Augusta, Princess (afterwards Princess Leopold of Saxe-Coburg), 4, 5, 7, 11, 13, 43, 366, 520
Charlottenburg, Palace of, 285, 505, 507
Chartist riots, 144, 188
Château d'Eu, 152–3; agreement, 177–8
Chatham, 254, 266
Chatsworth, 35, 133, 155
'Chatterton, Memoirs of Georgina, Lady,' 39 *n*
Chelmsford, Lord, 372 *n*, 388 *n*
Chelsea, 26, 423
    Hospital, 232, 533
Chenies, 449
Cherbourg, 277, 442, 519
Chester, 35
Chevalley, M. Abel, ' Monograph on the Queen,' 586 *n*

INDEX

CHILDERS

Childers, Hugh C. E., 401 *n*, 407, 458, 459 *n*, 460 *n*, 463, 491; on the control of the army, 462-3; and the Egyptian war, 468; the 'Life' of, 407 *n*, 469, (App.) 589

China, 310, (App.) 591
    question, 271-2

Chislehurst, 414, 427-8, 451

Chobham Common, 236

Christ Church College, Oxford, 36, 76 *n*

Christians in Turkey, 240, 266

'Christmas Carol,' 409

Christmas Island, (App.) 591, 595

Church, Dean, 474; 'Life and Letters' of, 474 *n*

Church patronage and appointments, 396, 435

Churchill, Jane, Lady, 327, 556
    Lord Randolph, 484, 490 *n*, 495 *n*, 496

Cimiez, 517 *n*, 519, 527, 555 *n*, 571

Civil List Bill, 77-81
    Debates, 422-4, 512

Claremont, in Surrey, 13, 25, 136, 191-2, 279; Louis Philippe's residence at, 186; presented by the Queen to the Duke of Albany, 472

Clarence, Albert Victor, Duke of: birth, 354; coming of age, 511; proposed annuity, 512; betrothal and death, 520
    Adelaide, Duchess of. *See under* Adelaide, Queen
    William, Duke of. *See under* William IV.
    House, 123

Clarendon, Lord, 175, 215, 252, 265, 276, 369, 401 *n*, 403; as Foreign Secretary, 235, 253, 365, 399 *n*; and the Crimean war, 242; the Queen's faith in, 282, 299, 302; death, 411

Clark, Sir James, 93-4

Cleveland, Duchess of, 555 *n*

Clive, Lady Harriet, 63 *n*
    Lord, 30
    Edward. *See under* Powis, Earl of

Clyde river, 185

Coal Exchange, opening of the, 204

Cobden, Richard, 133; leader of the free trade agitation, 170; and the China question, 271

CORNHILL

Coblenz, palace of, 165, 309

Coburg, 64, 112, 117, 213, 521; the Queen's visits to, 164-6, 305-10, 338-42, 362-3, 442-3, 518-9

Cockermouth, 102

Cocks, Hon. Caroline, 63 *n*

Coercion Bill for Ireland, 172

Coldstream Guards, 3rd Battalion, 533

Colenso, battle of, 542

Colley, General, 464

Collins, Wilkie, 'The Frozen Deep,' 409

Cologne, 165, 285

Colonial and Indian Exhibition, 499

Commissions in the army, Queen's signature of, 331, 532

Congress of Berlin, 447-8

Connaught, Arthur, Duke of: birth, 206-7; his godfathers, 210; visit to Ireland, 314; coming of age, 418; annuity, 418; marriage, 450; in the Egyptian war, 468; takes over the Aldershot command, 533; declines the succession to the duchies of Saxe-Coburg-Gotha, 552; at the Queen's death, 557; co-executor of the Queen's will, 557; at the Queen's funeral, 558; (App.) 579, 583-4

Conroy, Sir John, 19, 199; co-executor to the Duke of Kent's will, 14-15; master of the household to the Duchess of Kent, 33-41; retires, 63-4

Conroy, Miss, 19

Constant, M. Benjamin, (App.) 583

Contadino, Umbrian, 92

'Contrast,' the, 75

Conyngham, Lord, 48

Cook Islands, (App.) 595

Cooke, Mr. Kinloch, (App.) 588

Cooper's 'Annals of Cambridge,' 184 *n*

Cooper, Fenimore, 71

Copenhagen, 336, 462

Copley, Lady Charlotte, 63 *n*

Cork, Cove of (afterwards Queenstown), 203

Corn Law Repeal Bill, 172

Corn laws, 166-71, 492; abolition of, 172-3

'Cornhill Magazine,' (App.) 588

Cornwall, duchy of, 78–9, 197, 335
Corporation of London, 46, 472, (App.) 584
Corry, Montagu (afterwards Lord Rowton), 446
Costa, Signor, 70, 125 *n*
Costebelle, France, 518 *n*
Cottenham, Lord, 51, 117
'Court Circular,' 194, 460 *n*, 476 *n*, 524
Cousins, engraver, (App.) 582
Coutts, bankers, 78
Covent Garden Theatre, 140, 256
Cowan, Sir John, 77
Cowden-Clarke, Mrs., 13 *n*
Cowes, 203, 515, 534, 558
  East, 38, 199
Cowley, Lord, 330
Cowper, Lord, 130, 134, 460
Craig Gowan, 469
Cranborne, Lord. *See under* Salisbury, Marquis of
Cranbrook, Lord, 490 *n*, 495 *n*. *See also under* Hardy, Gathorne
Cranworth, Lord, 235, 367
Crathie, 475
Crawford, Mr. Marion, 571
Creighton, Dr., 573
Crewe, 190
Crimean war, 194, 238–50, 277, 488; history of the, 447
Croker Papers, 34 *n*, 50, 54 *n*, 74, 110 *n*, 138 *n*, (App.) 589
Cromwell, Oliver, 548
Cronje, General, capture of, 544
Cross, Mr. Richard (afterwards Viscount Cross), 435 *n*, 490 *n*, 495 *n*, 530 *n*
Crystal Palace, 221 seq., 246, 256, 273
Cumberland, Ernest Augustus, Duke of. *See under* Hanover, King of
Curragh Camp, 314
Cyprus, 537, (App.) 591

DALHOUSIE, Lord, 491
Dalkeith, 145
Danger Island, (App.) 595
Danube river, 275, 448
Darlington, 140
Darmstadt, 337, 342, 373, 412, 437, 444, 450, 455, 485–6, 506–7, 518–19 *n*

Dash, the Queen's pet spaniel, 91
Daudet, Ernest, 119 *n*
Davys, Miss, 63 *n*
  Rev. George, 21, 30, 40
Dee river, 35
Deeside, 306, 386
Delhi, 440 *n*
  the fall of, 279
Denmark, 210, 218, 332; and the Schleswig-Holstein question, 344–54
  Alexandra, Princess of. *See under* Alexandra, Queen
  Charles, Prince of, (App.) 580
  Christian VIII. of, 332
    IX. of, 332, 501; and the Schleswig-Holstein question, 344 seq.
  Frederick VII. of, 344 seq., 362
  George, Prince of, 112 (afterwards King of Greece)
  Louise, Queen of, 332
Derby, fourteenth Earl of (*see also under* Stanley), 236, 244, 251–2, 268, 426, 444; his first government, 230–4; second cabinet, 283–97; and the India Bill, 287–8; drafts the Queen's proclamation to India, 289–90; resignation, 297; and Schleswig-Holstein, 352–3; third administration, 372–3, 379; resigns, 387–8 *n*
Derby, fifteenth Earl of, 435 *n*, 460 *n*. *See also under* Stanley
Derby, sixteenth Earl of, Frederick Stanley, Lord Stanley of Preston. *See under* Stanley
Derby Infirmary, 517
Dering, E. H., 39 *n*
'Deutsche Rundschau,' 413 *n*
Devon, Lord, 372 *n*
Devonport, 38
Devonshire, Duke of, 35, 133, 155, 530 *n*
  See also under Hartington, Lord
Diamond Jubilee, 1897, 536–8, (App.) 585
Dickens, Charles, 'Christmas Carol,' 409–10
'Dictionary of National Biography,' (App.) 586 *n*

INDEX

Dietz (Portuguese minister), 213
Dilke, Sir Charles W., 423–4, 459–60 n
Dillon, Hon. Margaret, 63 n
Disraeli, Benjamin and Mrs. *See under* Beaconsfield, Earl and Viscountess
    Ralph, 162 n
Dodson, J. G. (afterwards Lord Monk Bretton), 459 n, 460 n
Don Pacifico, 211, 215
Doncaster, 41
Donizetti, composer, 569
Donne, William Bodham, 195
Dooabs, (App.) 592
Douglas, Mr. Akers, 531 n
Douglas, Mrs. Stair, 155 n
Dover, 42, 117, 160, 255–6, 285
Drama at Windsor, the, 194–5
Drayton Manor, 155
Dresden, 507
Dreyfus, Captain, 567
Drouyn, M., 256–7
Drummond Castle, 145
    Edward, assassination of, 147
Drury Lane Theatre, 194
Dublin, 202–3, 236, 314–5, 493, 546
    Earl of (*see under* Edward VII.)
Dufferin, Lord, 401 n
Dundee, 146
Dunkeld, 375
Dunleary Port (afterwards Kingstown), 203
Dunrobin Castle, 427
Durham, Countess of, 63 n, 85
    Earl of, mission to Canada, 85–6
Duse, Eleanora, 519
Dyce, William, artist, 195

Ealing, 6, 15
East Africa, (App.) 593
East Cowes, 38, 199
East India Company, 286–7, 292, (App.) 592
Eastern Counties Railway, 184
Eastlake, artist, 195
Eaton Hall, 35
Ecclesiastical Titles Bill, 220
'Eckstädt, Memoirs of Count Vitzthum von,' (App.) 587
Eddystone lighthouse, 39
Edinburgh, 145, 168, 207, 315, 394 n, 443, 499
    Duke and Duchess of. *See under* Saxe-Coburg-Gotha, Duke and Duchess of
Edward III., 140
Edward VII. and the duchy of Cornwall, 79 n; birth and christening, 138–9; created Duke of Saxony, 139; early education, 197; at Abergeldie Castle, 200; presents Osborne House to the nation, 200 n; created Earl of Dublin, 203; his godfather, 210; visit to Paris, 259–60; attains his majority, 293; tour in America, 307; at Curragh Camp, 314; at Prince Albert's funeral, 324; tour in the Holy Land, 330; engagement to Princess Alexandra of Denmark, 332, 335; his claim to the duchy of Saxe-Coburg transferred to Prince Alfred, 334; marriage, 335; annuity, 335–6; birth of his son, Prince Albert Victor, 354; at the Paris Exhibition of 1867, 384; opens the Thames Embankment, 417; illness, 420–2; his statue at Temple Bar, 420; entertains the Shah of Persia, 429; receives the Tsarevitch, 430; tour in India, 439; at Lord Beaconsfield's funeral, 466; organises the Colonial and Indian Exhibition, 499; suggests the erection of the Imperial Institute, 499; celebration of his silver wedding, 505; entertains the Queen at Sandringham, 509; provision for his children, 511–14; represents the Queen at the great naval review (Diamond Jubilee), 538; Captain-General of the Honourable Artillery Company, 540; at the Queen's death, 557; accession to the throne, 557; at the Queen's funeral, 558, (App.) 579–80, 582–3
Edward Augustus. *See under* Kent, Duke of
Edwards, Lieut.-Colonel Sir Fleetwood, 557
Egypt, 130–2, (App.) 592; the war in, 467–70, 477–82

Egypt, Ismail Pasha, Khedive of, 384–5, 408, 547
Elbersdorf, Count Reuss XXIV., von, 12
Elementary Education Act, 1870, 401 *n*
Elgin, Earl of, 299 *n*, 313
Eliot, George, 'Mill on the Floss,' 409; 'Middlemarch,' 409
Elizabeth, Princess (daughter of James I.), 2
 (daughter of Charles I.), 575
 (daughter of George III. afterwards Princess of Hesse-Homburg), 56 *n*; 'Correspondence' of, 57 *n*
Elizabeth, Queen, 30, 54, 155–6 *n*, 287, 573
Ellesmere, Earl of, 224, 274
Ellice Island, (App.) 595
Elmina, Castle of, (App.) 592
Ely, Jane, Marchioness of, 327
Emancipation of slaves, 95–6
'Emerald' yacht, 39
Epping forest, 472
Ernest Augustus. *See under* Cumberland, Duke of
Erroll, Earl of, 175
'Es ist ein Schnitter,' song, 194
Esher, 13, 25
Esterhazy, Nicholas, 47
Eton, 76 *n*, 510; 'montem,' 87
Eugénie. *See under* France, ex-Empress of
Euston Hall, 42
Exeter, 39
 Marquis of, 41, 161
Exhibition of 1851, 221–7, 236, 246, 258, 541

F., A. M., 'Tales of my Father, Equerry to the King of Hanover,' 57 *n*, (App.) 587
'Fairy' yacht, 185; in collision, 190 *n*
Fanning Island, (App.) 595
Faucit, Miss, 279. *See also under* Martin, Lady
Faure, M., 518
'Faust,' 520, 569
'Fidelio,' opera, 256
Field of the Cloth of Gold, bat of the, 151

Fife, Earl of (afterwards Duke of), marriage to Princess Louise of Wales, 511, 514, (App.) 580, 583
Fife trustees, 200
Fiji Islands, (App.) 595
Fitzalan, Lord, 47
FitzClarence, Lord Adolphus, 152
FitzClarence family, 73
Fitzgerald, Hamilton, 94
Fitzwilliam, Lord, 41
Fleetwood, 185
Floors Castle, 386
Florence, 505, 518
Foligno, 92 *n*
Forbes, Viscountess, 63 *n*
Ford, Onslow, (App.) 584
Forster, W. E., 401 *n*, 459 *n*, 460 *n*, 471; 'Life' of, by Wemyss Reid, (App.) 589
Fort William, 185
Fortescue, Chichester. *See under* Carlingford, Lord
Fould, M. Achille, 273
Fowler, (Sir) Henry, 525 *n*, 529 *n*
France and Egypt, 130–2, 468; and the Spanish marriages, 177–82; revolution in, 185–187; Palmerston's relations with, 211–2, 215, 237; English alliance with, 240; and the Crimean war, 244–250; and the Vienna Conference, 256; the treaty of Paris, 265–6; strained relations between England and, 279–84, (App.) 588; and the peace of Villafranca, 300, 302; fears of invasion from, 305; and the Polish insurrection, 339; at war with Germany, 382–3, 411–14, 436–7
 Eugénie, ex-Empress of, 237–8, 254, 296–7, 509, 553; visits to the Queen, 310, 384, 547; visits the Queen in Paris, 393; exile in England, 414, 451
 Louis XIV. of, 557
 Louis Philippe, King of, 8, 9 *n*, 32, 87, 107, 131–2, 149–50, 225, 236, 255, 279, 342, 550, (App.) 583; receives the Queen at Château d'Eu, 152–3, 166;

FRANCE

France, Louis Philippe—*cont.*
visits the Queen at Windsor, 159-60, 163; and the Spanish marriages, 177-182; dethronement of, 185-7; on the Queen's generosity, 186; death, 205

Marie Antoinette, Queen of, 259

Marie Christine, Princess of, 9 *n*

Marie Clémentine, Princess of, 9 *n*

Napoleon I., Emperor of, 260

Napoleon III., Emperor of, 92, 225, 273-4, 279, 284, 341, 384, 392-3, 418, 444, (App.) 583, 588; his relations with the Queen, 236-40, 277, 310, 445; and the Crimean war, 240-50; visits the Queen, 255-6; entertains the Queen in Paris, 259-61; and Italian unity, 264; the treaty of Paris, 266, 275-6; attempt on his life, 280-1; alliance with England, 285; the Queen's fears of, 293-305, 381-4; at war with Austria, 295-6; the peace of Villafranca, 297, 301; and the 'Trent' affair, 317; and Schleswig - Holstein, 348; at war with Germany, 381-3, 411-14; death, 427

Prince Imperial of, 420, 460; death, 451

Queen of (Louis Philippe's Queen), 152-3, 186, 256

Francis I., 151

Francis, John, 142

Franco-German war, 382-3, 411-414; threatened renewal of, 436-437

Frankfort, 166, 260, 339-41, (App.) 579

Frederick, Prince. *See under* Wales, Prince of; York, Duke of; the Great, 7, 285

Frederick VII. *See* Denmark, King of

Free trade, 158, 161, 445, 492; the Queen and, 163-73

Frere, Sir Bartle, 451, 464

GERMANY

Freytag, Gustav, 308
Friedrichshof Palace, (App.) 579
Frith, W. P., (App.) 583
Frogmore, 123, 311-3, 324, 354, 393, 430, 442, 553, 558
Froude's 'Carlyle in London,' 409 *n*
'Frühlingslied,' song, 192
Fryer, Rev. Victor, 13
Fuller's Worthies, 156 *n*
Fyne, Loch, 185

GAISFORD, Dean, 36
Gambia, (App.) 593
Gardiner, Lady, 63 *n*
Garfield, President, 467
Garibaldi, General, 301, 354
Gaskell's 'Life of Charlotte Brontë,' 154 *n*
Gatacre, Sir William, 542
Geffcken, Professor, 413 *n*
General election of 1837, 74; 1841, 133-5; 1847, 174; 1852, 230; 1857, 272; 1859, 297; 1865, 364; 1868, 393; 1874, 432; 1880, 456; 1885, 490; 1886, 494; 1892, 524; 1895, 530; 1900, 550
Genoa, Duke of, 264, 519
'Gentleman's Magazine,' 90 *n*
George I., 2, 3, 56, 151
II., 3, 113, 151, 164, 273
III., 1, 12, 56 *n*, 78, 88, 113, 149, 151, 256, 273, 510, 536, 557; descent from King Alfred, 3; marriage and family of, 3-5; death, 14; loss of the North American Colonies, 83, 482-3
IV., 14, 15, 21, 26-7, 69, 78, 89, 130, 151, 199, 203, 366, 378, 564; as Prince Regent, 4, 11-12; death, 29; erection of the Brighton Pavilion, 70, 153
George Frederick, Prince. *See under* Wales, Prince of
Gerlach (Prussian minister), 263
Germany (*see also under* Prussia), Queen's visits to, 164-5, 285-6, 308, 339 seq., 426, 455-505, 518-19; Palmerston's views on, 210; the Queen's interest in, 280; dispute with England, 309; and Schleswig - Holstein,

GERMANY

Germany—*cont.*
344–54, 368; relations with France, 382–3; Franco-German war, 411–14; Heligoland ceded to, (App.) 591

Charlotte, Princess of, 449, (App.) 581

Emperor Frederick of, 159, 222, 308–9, 314, 339, 363, 419, 443, 448, 455; engagement to the Princess Royal, 262, 268–9, 273–4; marriage, 279–80; visit to the Queen, 306; entertains the Queen at Coblenz, 309; and Schleswig - Holstein, 346–7; and the war with Austria, 368, 374; in the Franco-German war, 411–413; at the Queen's Jubilee, 501; illness, 504–6; accession, 505; death, 508, (App.) 579–80, 583; 'Diaries' of, 413 *n*; 'Life' of, (App.) 587

Empress Frederick of, 194, 236, 314, 337–9, 347, 363, 412, 419, 443, 455, 480, 504, 507–10, 551 *n*; birth, 127; visit to Paris, 259; betrothal to Prince Frederick of Prussia, 262, 268–9; dowry and annuity, 273–4; marriage, 159, 279–80; birth of a son (afterwards Emperor William II.), 293–4; visits to the Queen, 306; meets the Queen at Coburg, 308; becomes Crown Princess of Prussia, 309; marriage of her daughter Charlotte, 449; fatal illness, 553

Prince Frederick Charles of, 450

Princess Frederika Victoria of, (App.) 581

Prince Henry of, (App.) 580

Princess Margaretta Beatrice of, (App.) 581

Sophia Dorothea of, (App.) 580

Victoria of, 506

GLADSTONE

Germany, Emperor William I. of, 159, 206, 210, 222, 269, 285, 368, 372, 382, 384, 437, 444; as Prince Regent, 296; accession, 309; attempted assassination of, 314, 449; and the 'Trent' affair, 317; visits the Queen at Coburg, 340–1; and the Franco-German war, 412; death, 504–5

Empress William I. of, 222, 269, 384, 412, 426, 443

Emperor William II. of, 507, 511; birth, 293–4; meets the Queen at Coburg, 308; betrothal, 455; visits to the Queen, 514–15, 543; at the Queen's death and funeral, 557–8, (App.) 580

Empress William II. of, 543

Gervais, Admiral, 519

Ghirlandaio, artist, 518 *n*

Gibbon (quoted), 13

Gibraltar, 6, 17

Gibson, Thomas Milner, 299 *n*

Gilbert, Alfred, (App.) 584

Gilbert, W. S., 519

Gilbert Islands, (App.) 595

Gladstone, Mrs. W. E., 514, 528

Herbert, 529 *n*

William Ewart, 76, 251–3, 330, 343, 371, 414–5, 417, 497; in Peel's Government, 135–8; entertained by the Queen at Windsor, 162; and the Maynooth grant, 163–4; Colonial and War Secretary, 171–2; Chancellor of the Exchequer, 234, 299; sympathy with Italy, 297; and the American civil war, 316; on the Queen's influence in the Schleswig-Holstein controversy, 353; leader of the House of Commons, 364 seq.; and the Irish Church, 388 seq.; first administration, 399–410; and the Queen's income, 424; resignation, 428–31; Disraeli on, 434; and the Scottish Church,

R R

GLADSTONE

Gladstone, William Ewart—*cont.*
436; and Bulgaria, 443; reviews the Prince Consort's 'Life,' vol. iii., 447; Midlothian speeches, 453; resumes office, 457–72; choice of a Primate, 473–4; and the war in Egypt, 478 seq.; and the Franchise Bill, 483; and the grant to Princess Beatrice, 487; defeated, 488–9; third ministry, 491–4; defeat of his Home Rule Bill, 492–494, 524–5; length of service, 496; and the grants to the Prince of Wales's children, 513–4; on the death of the Duke of Clarence, 520; fourth ministry, 524–6; the Queen's farewell to, 526–527; death, 528; Morley's 'Life of,' 136–7 *n*, 252 *n*, 325 *n*, 353 *n*, 365 *n*, 371 *n*, 403–4 *n*, 406 *n*, 415 *n*, 457 *n*, 461 *n*, 475 *n*, 479 *n*, 483 *n*, 485 *n*, 489 *n*, 495 *n*, 526 *n*, 527 *n*, 572 *n*; 'Gleanings,' (App.) 589

Glasgow, 204, (App.) 584
    Exhibition, 508
    Waterworks, 306

Glassalt Shiel, 393
Glenelg, Lord, 100
Glenfiddich, 386
Glenlyon, Lord and Lady, 146. *See also under* Athol, Duke and Duchess of

Gloucester, Duchess of, 12, 109, 127, 356; letter from the Queen, 166; death, 272

Gluck, musician, 193
Gold Coast Colony, (App.) 592–3
Goldoni, dramatist, 520
Golf, 569
Gorce, De la, 'Histoire du Second Empire,' (App.) 588

Gordon, General, 473–91; besieged in Khartoum, 478, 480; death, 479; the Queen on, 478–82
    Hon. Sir Arthur. *See under* Stanmore, Lord
    Miss, 479–82

GREY

Gordon, Sir Robert, 190
Gortschakoff, Prince, 446 *n*, 448
Goschen, G. J. (now Viscount Goschen), 401 *n*, 495 *n*, 530 *n*
Gosport, 441, 558
Gotha, 165–6, 243
    Caroline, Duchess Dowager of, 117 *n*
Goulburn, Henry, 138 *n*
Gounod, M., 426, 497, 569
Gower, Lord Ronald, 555 *n*; 'Reminiscences,' 555 *n*, (App.) 589; 'Old Diaries,' 259 *n*, 477, 518, (App.) 589; 'Stafford House Letters,' 107 *n*
Grafton, Duke of, 42
Graham, Sir James, 114, 137–8, 144, 234, 253, 315
'Grampus' frigate, 190
Grandineau, M., 22
Granton pier, 145
Granville, Earl, 353, 401 *n*, 403, 405, 457, 459 *n*, 491; Foreign Secretary, 226, 411; President of the Council, 235, 253; summoned by the Queen, 297–9. *See also under* Leveson, Lord
Grasse, 518 *n*
Graves, C. L. 'Life of Sir George Grove,' 379 *n*
Gravesend, 308
Great Exhibition of 1851, 221–7, 236, 246, 258, 541
Great Western Railway, 141
Greece, coerced by Palmerston, 211; the throne of, 333–5; Ionian Isles ceded to, (App.) 591
    Crown Prince of, 501
    George, King of, 335, 501, 558, (App.) 580. *See also under* Denmark, Prince of
    Otho, King of, 333
Greek Christians in Turkey, 240, 266
Green, John Richard, 422; 'Letters' of, 422 *n*
Gresham, Sir Thomas, 155–6 *n*
'Greville Memoirs,' 27 *n*, 30 *n*, 41 *n*, 46 *n*, 66 *n*, 90 *n*, 116 *n*, 145 *n*, 378, (App.) 587
Grey, Colonel, 117
    General the Hon. Charles, private secretary to the Queen, 329; 'Early Years

GREY

Grey, Colonel—*cont.*
    of the Prince Consort,' 7 *n*, 25 *n*, 376, (App.) 586–587
    Sir George, 175, 253, 299 *n*, 343
    Lord, 35, 59, 99, 129, 170
    2nd Lord, 85, 196, 329
Grey and Ripon, Lord de. *See under* Ripon, Marquis of
Grimsby, 248
Grisi, Madame, 39, 70
Griqualand West, (App.) 593
Groben, General von, 242
Grosvenor, Lord, 35
    House, 269
Grote, Mr. and Mrs., 409
Grove, 'Life of Sir George,' 379 *n*
'Guelph, Miss,' 34
Guildhall, 77, 223
Guizot, M., 119 *n*, 153, 179
Gurney, Mrs. Gerald, 'Childhood of Queen Victoria,' (App.) 588

HALIFAX, Lord, 401 *n*
Hall, Sydney P., (App.) 584
Hallam's 'Constitutional History,' 71
Halsbury, Lord, 490 *n*, 495 *n*, 530 *n*
Hamilton, Lord George, 490 *n*, 495 *n*, 530 *n*
    William, 206
Hanbury, Mr., 552 *n*
Handel, composer, 39, 570
    Festival, 273
Hanmer, Major W. E., 19 *n*
Hanover, House of, 1–3, 9; throne of, 56
    Ernest, King of, 4 *n*, 15, 49, 56–7 *n*, 75, 115, 123, 149, 224; 'Tales of my Father, Equerry to the King of Hanover,' by A. M. F., 57 *n*, (App.) 587
    Frederica, Princess of, 374, 460
    George, King of, 4 *n*, 235–6, 285, 345, 368, 460; loss of his kingdom, 373–4; death, 449
    Sophia, Electress of, 2
    Queen of, 236, 285
Hansard's 'Parliamentary Debates,' 20 *n*, 30 *n*, 415, 418–9, 424, 514, (App.) 586

HESSE

Harcourt, Archbishop, 41, 133
    Colonel Francis N., 41
    Sir William Vernon, 459 *n*, 491, 520, 525 *n*
Hardinge, Lord, 267–8
    Sir Henry, 138 *n*
Hardwicke, Lady, 119
Hardy, Gathorne, 372 *n*, 435 *n*. *See also under* Cranbrook, Lord
Harrowby, Lord, 490 *n*
Hart-Dyke, Sir William, 490 *n*
Hartington, Lord (afterwards Duke of Devonshire), 401 *n*, 456–9, 460 *n*, 479
Hastings, Lady Flora, 93–5
    Marquis of, 93
Hatfield House, 503
Hatherley, Lord, 401 *n*
Hauke, Countess von (afterwards Countess of Battenberg), 486
Havana, 316
Hawes, Benjamin, 80
Haydn, composer, 125 *n*
Hayter, Sir George, 37, (App.) 582–3
Helena, Princess. *See under* Schleswig-Holstein, Princess Christian of
Heligoland, (App.) 591
Helps, Sir Arthur, 330, 376–9, 408–410
Henry I., 1–2
    II., 3
    VI., 259
    VII., 418
    VIII., 151, 418
Hensman, Howard, 541 *n*
Her Majesty's Theatre, 183, 279
Herbert, Auberon, 424
    Hospital, 253, 545
    Sydney, 234, 253, 299 *n*, 314
Herrenhausen, 285
Herschell, Lord, 491, 524 *n*
Hervey Islands, (App.) 595
Hesse, Grand Duke of, 486, 519–22, (App.) 580
    Prince Alexander of, 486
    Princess Alexandra of, 522, (App.) 580
        Elizabeth of (afterwards Grand Duchess Serge of Russia), 519, (App.) 580
        Irene of, 485, (App.) 580

HESSE

Hesse, Princess Victoria of (afterwards Princess Louis of Battenberg), 485, (App.) 581
Hesse-Cassel, Frederick Landgrave of, 5
    Prince Frederick Charles of, (App.) 581
    Princess Louise of. *See* under Denmark, Queen of
Hesse-Darmstadt, Prince Louis of, 346, 368, 410; engagement to the Princess Alice, 307, 310; visit to Osborne, 313–4; loss of territory, 373; in the Franco-German war, 412
    Princess Louis of (Princess Alice), 324–5, 337, 342, 346, 373, 378, 385, 404, 412, 419, 420, 444, 455–6, 485, (App.) 579–80; birth, 149; illness, 236; betrothal, 307, 310; visit to Coburg, 308; dowry and annuity, 311; visit to Ireland, 314; marriage, 331; death, 449, 510; 'Letters' of, 198 *n*, 377–8 *n*, 438, (App.) 588
Hesse-Homburg, Frederick, Landgrave of, 56
Hewell Grange, 36
Hicks-Beach, Sir Michael, 435 *n*, 484, 490 *n*, 495–6 *n*, 530 *n*
High Wycombe, 37, 446
Hill, Lord, 38, 51
    Rowland, 104
Hindustani, the Queen's study of, 500
Hohenlohe-Langenburg, Prince von, 32
    Hereditary Prince of, (App.) 581
    Princess Adelaide of, 237
        Féodore of, 20, 88, 149, 312–315, 324, 346, 426; marriage, 32; death, 427; 'Letters' of, 428 *n*
'Hohenzollern' yacht, 515
Hohenzollern, Princess of, 274
Holborn Viaduct, opening of, 408
Holker Hall, 479
Holkham, 42
Holland. *See under* Netherlands, King of

INDIA

Holland, Sir Henry (afterwards Viscount Knutsford), 496 *n*
Holmes, R. R., (App.) 586
Holyhead, 314–5
Holyrood Palace, 207, 306
Homburg, 56 *n*
Home Rule Bill, 492–4, 497, 524–5
Hong Kong, 271, 537, (App.) 591
Honourable Artillery Company, 540
Horsman, Edward, 102
Hôtel de Ville, 260
    des Invalides, 260
Houghton, Lord, 203; 'Life' of, 203 *n*, 409 *n*, (App.) 589
Houses of Parliament rebuilt, 189
Howick, Lord, 99–100
Howley, Archbishop William, 12, 40, 48–9, 395
Hudson, George, 184
Hudson Bay Company, (App.) 595
Hughenden Church, 467 *n*
Hughenden Manor, 445–6, 466, 470 *n*
Hull, 248
Humboldt, 25
Hume, Joseph, 80, 113
Hungary, 303, 348; revolution in, 224
Hunt, Leigh, 24
    Ward, 435 *n*
Huntly, 9th Marquis of, 259 *n*
Hyde, Anne, 418 *n*
Hyères, 518 *n*

Ichaboe Islands, (App.) 593
Iddesleigh, Lord, 372 *n*, 490 *n*, 495 *n*; 'Life' of, (App.) 589. *See also under* Northcote, Sir Stafford
'Idylls of the King,' 322
'Il Trovatore,' 520
Ilchester, Lord, 38
Imperial British East Africa Co., (App.) 593
    Institute, 499, 503, 532
Imperialism, growth of, 498–500, 559–60
'In Memoriam,' by Tennyson, 408
India, the Mutiny in, 271, 277–9; fall of Delhi and relief of Lucknow, 279; resettlement of, 286–292; East India Company abolished, 286–7; the India Bill, 287–288; the Queen's Proclamation to,

INDEX

INDIA

India—*cont.*
288–9; institution of the Order of the Star of India, 290–1; the Queen proclaimed Empress of, 438–40; the Prince of Wales's tour in, 439; creation of the Orders of the Indian Empire and the Crown of India, 440 *n*; the Afghanistan war, 452; and imperialism, 499–500; ruling Princes of, at the Jubilee, 501, 503; representatives at the Diamond Jubilee, 536–8; frontier war, (1897–9), 539; and the Queen's death, 558, (App.) 590–2
Ingestre House, 123
Inglis, Sir Robert, 29
'Ingoldsby Legends,' 88 *n*
Inkermann, victory of, 248
Innsbruck, 505
Inveraray Castle, 185
Invercannie, 375
Inverness, Duchess of, 126
Ionian Islands, (App.) 591
Ireland, 77, 157, 163–6, 414; Coercion Bill for, 172; threats of civil war in, 183; the Queen's visits to, 202–3, 236, 314–5, 545–6; Gladstone and the Church in, 388 seq.; disaffection in, 470–1; Home Rule Bill for, 492–4, 497, 524–5
— Dr. John, 89
Irish Church Bill, 401 *n*, 404–7, 484, 562
— Guards, raising of the, 546
— Land Act (1870), 401 *n*
— Reform Bill, 389
— University Bill, 428
Irving, Sir Henry, 509
Isabella. *See under* Spain, Queen of
Isandhlwana, battle of, 465
Isle of Wight, 28, 33, 38, 185, 199, 442, 465, 504
Italy, 209–10, 264, 518; at war with Austria, 295; England's sympathy with, 297–302; and the Austro-Prussian war, 373; the Queen's visits to, 450, 505
— Humbert, King of, 450, 505, 518; assassination of, 549–550

KENT

Italy, Margherita, Queen of, 450, 518
— Victor Emmanuel, King of, 505. *See also under* Sardinia, King of

JAMAICA, 96
James I., 2, 145
— II., 2, 176, 260, 418 *n*, 574
James, Lord, 531 *n*
Jameson, Dr., 543
Jeaffreson, J. Cordy, (App.) 586 *n*
Jenkinson, Lady Catherine, 36, 41
Jhansi, province of Central India, (App.) 592
Joachim, Joseph, 156
Johnston, W. & A. K., (App.) 590 *n*
Johore, (App.) 592
Joinville, Prince de, 150, 187, 189
Jordan, Mrs., 73
Jubilee of 1887, 492–503, 538, 573, (App.) 583; medal for the, (App.) 584
— of 1897 (Diamond), 536–38; medal for the, (App.) 585
'Judas Maccabeus,' 273–4
'Jumna' troopship, 463

KANDAHAR, the march on, 463
Karim, the Munshi Abdul, 500
Kars, defence of, 269 *n*
Katrine, Loch, 306
Kean, Mrs., 194
— Charles, 194, 273
Keeley, Mr. and Mrs., 195, 280
Keeling Islands, (App.) 591
Kelso, 386
Kemble, Charles, 47, 191
— Fanny, 68; 'Letters' of, 68 *n*, 139 *n*; 'Records' of, (App.) 589
Kenmare House, 314
Kennington Common, 188
Kensington Palace, 10–24, 37–48, 61, 67 seq.
Kent, Edward Augustus, Duke of, 1, 4, 15–16; marriage, 5–9; military career, 5–6; financial difficulties, 6, 10; death, 14; his Radical sympathies, 17 *n*; his debts paid by the Queen, 81

KENT

Kent, Mary Louisa Victoria, Duchess of, 6, 13, 20–47, 66, 71, 93, 117, 123, 127, 193, 312–3, 368, (App.) 582; first marriage (to Ernest Charles, Prince of Leiningen), 7; family connections, 8–9; marriage to the Duke of Kent, 7–9; her position and pecuniary difficulties, 14–6; resigns the Regency of Leiningen, 17; her relations with William IV., 31–46; touring with Princess Victoria, 34–42; annuity, 81; at the Queen's coronation, 89; death, 194

Kermadec Islands (App.), 595

Kew, 368, 509

Palace, 9

Khartoum, 478–9, 480–2

Kiel, 345

Kimberley, relief of, 544

diamond mines, 541, (App.) 593

Earl of, 401 n, 459 n, 460 n, 491 n, 524 n, 529 n

'King John,' 323

Kingstown, 203, 236, 314

Kitchener, Lord, at Omdurman, 539; in the Boer war, 542 seq.; the chief command in South Africa, 556

Kitchin's 'Life of Dr. Harold Browne,' 475 n

Knight, Charles, 23

William, 184 n

Knutsford, Viscount, 496 n

Königgratz, 374

Korea, (App.) 591

Kossuth, leader of the Hungarian revolution, 224

Kruger, President, 543

Kuria Muria Islands (App.), 591

'LA LOCANDIERA,' 505

La Roule, fort of, 284

La Villette, railway station, 442

Lablache, Luigi, 39–40, 70, 119, 125 n

Labouchere, H., 514

Labuan, (App.) 591

Ladysmith, relief of, 544, 546

Laeken, 154, 231, 339

LESLIE

Laggan, Loch, 185

Lagos, (App.) 592

Lambeth, 538

Lambton, Captain Hedworth, 547

Lancaster, duchy of, 78–9, 423

Land's End, 502

Landseer, Sir Edwin, 22, 195–6, (App.) 583

Lane, R. J., (App.) 582

Lang, Andrew, 'Life of Lord Iddesleigh,' (App.) 589

Lansdowne, Marquis of, 11, 49, 51, 169, 233, 235, 251, 530 n, 551

Marchioness of, 63

House, 126

'Lass dich nur,' song, 193

Lathom, Lord, 501

Laughton's 'Life of Henry Reeve,' 378 n, (App.) 589

Law Courts, opening of the new, 472

Lawson, Sir Wilfrid, 424

'Leaves from the Journal,' 145 n, 185 n, 207, 232, 328, 410; publication of, 378

Leeds, 286

Lefevre, Charles Shaw, 247

Lehzen, Baroness (the Queen's first governess), 20–25, 48, 66, 95, 98, 122; the Queen on, 20, 204; retirement, 123; visits the Queen at Gotha, 166

Leicester, Earl of, 42

Leigh, Lord, 286

Leighton, Lord, 569, (App.) 584

Leiningen, Prince of, 407

Princess of. *See under* Kent, Duchess of

Prince Charles of, 19, 37, 72, 88, 270, 313

Prince Edward of, 313

Prince Edward Charles of, 7

Princess Féodore of. *See under* Hohenlohe-Langenburg

Prince Ferdinand of, 8–9 n

Prince Victor of, 313

Leo XIII., Pope, 501

Leopold. *See under* Belgians, King of the

Prince. *See under* Albany, Duke of

Leslie, C. R., 91 n, 195, 555 n, (App.) 583

LESTER

Lester, Miss Harriet, 63 *n*
Leveson, Lord, 155. *See also under* Granville, Earl of
Lewis, Sir George Cornewall, 273, 299 *n*
Lhuys, M. Drouyn de, 257–8
Lichfield, Lord, 36
Liddell, Miss, 125 *n*
Lieven, Prince, 12
Lieven, Princess, 119 *n*
Lincoln, 114
    Lord, 172
    Mrs., 356
    President, assassination of, 356
Lind, Jenny, 165 ; as Norma, 183
    'Life' of, 183 *n*
Lindsay, Mrs. Patricia, 'Recollections of a Royal Parish,' 201 *n*
Lindsay, W. A., 'The Royal Household,' (App.) 589
'Links with the Past,' by Mrs. Bagot, 36 *n*, 392 *n*
Linton, Sir James, (App.) 584
Liszt, musician, 165
Liverpool, 140, 185, 224, 497
    third Earl of, 11, 12, 36, 41, 44, 97, 117 ; in Peel's Government, 138 ; death, 232
Llandaff, Viscount, 495 *n*
Llangollen, 516 *n*
Loch Muick, 393
Loch-na-gar, 393
Loftus, Lord Augustus, 'Reminiscences,' 308 *n*, (App.) 588
'Lohengrin,' 569
Loisinger, Fräulein, 507
Lombardy, 295, 300
Lomond, Loch, 408
London and North Western Railway, 141
    Corporation of, 46, 472, (App.) 584
    Hospital, 442
    the Queen's dislike of, 198–9
    University, 417
Londonderry, Lord, 552 *n*
Long, Mr. W. H., 531 *n*, 552 *n*
Longley, Archbishop, 394–5
Lorne, Marquis of. *See under* Argyll, fourth Duke of
Lothian, Lord, 496 *n*
Louis Napoleon, Prince. *See under* France, Napoleon III. of

MALINES

Louis Philippe, King. *See under* France, King of
Louise, Princess. *See under* Argyll, Duchess of
Lowe, Robert. *See under* Viscount Sherbrooke
Lowenstein, Prince William of, 120
Lowther, Mr. James, 435 *n*
Lucas, C. P., (App.) 590 *n*
Lucerne, 393
Lucknow, relief of, 279 ; heroes of, 305
Luxemburg, duchy of, 382–3
Lyell, Sir Charles and Lady, 409
Lyndhurst, Lord, 29, 51 *n*, 137
Lynn, 42
Lyttelton, Lady, 63 ; as royal governess, 196 ; 'Letters from Lady Sarah Lyttelton,' 22 *n*, 71 *n*, 101 *n*, 107 *n*, 157 *n*, 162, 188
Lytton, Lord, 71, 440 *n*, 452–3

MACAULAY, Thomas Babington (afterwards Lord), 76, 100, 175–6 ; Trevelyan's 'Life' of, 176 *n*, (App.) 589
'Macbeth,' 279
Macdonald, Captain, 309
    Dr. George, 410
Maclean, Roderick, 470
Macleod, Dr. Norman, 328, 412, 427 ; 'Life' of, by Donald Macleod, (App.) 589
Maclise, artist, 195
MacMahon, Marshal, 442
Macnaughten, assassin, 147
Macready, actor, 194–5
Madeira, 533
Madrid, 180–1, 211
Mafeking, relief of, 544
Magee, Dr., 405
Maggiore, Lago, 450
Magnan, Marshal, 259
Magnussen, G., (App.) 583
Mahdi, the, 477 ; besieges Gordon in Khartoum, 478
Maiwand disaster, 463, 465
Majuba hill, 464
Malakoff, Duc de, 284
    storming of the, 284 *n*
Malay peninsula (App.), 591
Malibran, vocalist, 39
Malines, 165, 285

MALMESBURY

Malmesbury, Lord, 229–30, 236, 257 n, 265, 283, 373, 435 n; 'Memoirs of an Ex-Minister,' 95 n, 258 n, 268–9, 275, (App.) 589

Malvern, 34
    hills, 502

Manchester, 140, 224, 274, (App.) 584
    Art Treasures Exhibition, 274
    Ship Canal, 517

Manitoba, (App.) 595

Manners, Lord John, 372 n, 435 n, 490 n, 495 n. *See also under* Rutland, Duke of

Mansfield, Lord, 145

Mansion House, 42

Manteuffel, Otto Freiherr von, 222, 263; 'Correspondence,' (App.) 587

Marie Antoinette, Queen, 259

Marlborough House, 72, 430, 505

Marochetti, Baron, 342, 502, 574, (App.) 584

Martin, Lady, 517. *See also under* Faucit, Miss
    Sir Theodore, 123 n; undertakes the 'Life of the Prince Consort,' 376 seq., 446; entertains the Queen at Bryntisilio, 517 n; biography of the Prince Consort quoted, 147 n, 182, 216, 261, 289, 291, (App.) 586–7; 'Life of Helena Faucit, Lady Martin,' (App.) 589

Martin Patchett, 37 n

Martineau, Harriet, 89

Mary I., 92 n
    II., 2, 112
    Queen of Scots, 101, 145, 207, 574

Mascagni, composer, 520

Mashonaland, 541, (App.) 594

Matabeleland, (App.) 594

Mathews, Charles, 195

Matthews, Henry (afterwards Viscount Llandaff), 495 n

Maximilian. *See under* Austria, Archduke of

Maxwell, Sir Herbert, 'Life of Sir Charles Murray,' 157 n, (App.) 588
    'Life of W. H. Smith,' (App.) 589

MISTLETOE

Maynooth grant, 163–4

Mayo, Lord, 426
    John H., 'Medals and Decorations of the British Army and Navy,' 582 n

Mecklenburg-Strelitz, Augusta, Duchess of, 149
    Charles Louis Frederick, Duke of, 3
    Frederica, Princess of, 4 n
    Frederick, Duke of, 149

Mehemet Ali, 130–1

Melbourne, 548

Melbourne, Lady, 60 n

Melbourne, Lord, 51, 54, 75–9, 98, 108, 119–21, 126–37, 155, 168, 173, 175, 189, 196, 208, 356, 445; and the Canadian revolt, 82–5; first audience with the Queen, 49–50; instructor to her Majesty, 58 seq., 71, 74, 93–4; opinions and character, 59–60; resignation, 96; return to office, 99 seq., and the Queen's marriage, 109–16; resignation, 135; letter from the Prince Consort, 135; on Sir Robert Peel, 171; at Cambridge, 184; death, 204, 232; 'Papers,' 63 n, 99 n; 'Life' of, by Torrens, (App.) 588

Melbury, 38

Melrose Abbey, 385

Menai Bridge, 35
    Straits, 185

Mendelssohn, Fanny, 294
    Felix, 125 n, 569; visit to the Queen, 191–4

Mentone, 471

Meran, 552

'Merchant of Venice,' 191, 509

Merivale, Dean, Letters of, 184 n

Merriman, H. S., 'The Sowers,' 571

Methuen, Lord, 542

Meux, Sir Henry, 420 n

Mexico, 274, 383–4

Meyerbeer, musician, 165

'Middlemarch,' 409

Military Exhibition, 533

Militia Bill, 228

'Mill on the Floss,' 409

Milnes, Monckton, 203. *See also under* Houghton, Lord

Milton's 'Comus,' 195

'Mistletoe' yacht, 442

INDEX

MOLDAVIA

Moldavia, 276
Molesworth, Sir William, 234
Moltke, Count von, 262, 268, 273, 437–8; 'Letters to his Wife,' 269 *n*, 273 *n*, (App.) 587
'Moniteur' newspaper, 281
Montefiore, Sir Moses, 77
Montgomery, Miss Florence, 571
Montijo, Mdlle. Eugénie de, 237. *See also under* France, Eugénie, ex-Empress of
Montpensier, Duc de, 177–81, 274
    Duchess of, 274
Monza, 550
'More Leaves from the Journal,' 412 *n*, 427 *n*, 451 *n*, (App.) 588; publication of, 476
Morley, Arnold, 525 *n*
    John, 491, 514, 525 *n*; 'Life of Gladstone,' 136–7 *n*, 252 *n*, 325 *n*, 353 *n*, 365 *n*, 371 *n*, 403–4 *n*, 406 *n*, 415 *n*, 457 *n*, 461 *n*, 475 *n*, 479 *n*, 483 *n*, 485 *n*, 489 *n*, 495 *n*, 526 *n*, 527 *n*, 572 *n*
'Morning Post,' 94
Morpeth, Lord (afterwards Earl of Carlisle), 155
'Mors et Vita,' 497
Mowbray, Sir John, 'Seventy Years at Westminster' (App.), 589
Mozart, composer, 124
Muckross Abbey, 314
Mulgrave, Countess of, 63. *See also* Normanby, Marchioness of
    Earl (afterwards Marquis of Normanby), 74, 100
Mundella, Mr. A. J., 491, 525 *n*
Murray, Miss Amelia, 63 *n*
    Sir Charles, 'Life' of, 157 *n*, (App.) 588
Music and the drama at Court, 191–5

NAGPORE, (App.) 592
Napier, Sir Charles, 245
Napoleon I. and III. *See under* France, Emperors of Buonaparte, 256–9
Nash, John, 69–70
Nassau Island, (App.) 595
Natal, (App.) 593–4
National Gallery, 47

NORTHUMBERLAND

National Portrait Gallery, (App.) 582, 584
    Rifle Association, 306–7
Naturalisation Bill, 115–6
Neild, James, 231
    John Camden, 423; his bequest to the Queen, 231
Nelson, Lord, 88
Nemours, Duc de, 9, 72, 107, 187, 189, 555 *n*
    Victoria, Duchess of, 9 *n*, 72, 279
Nepaul, 291 *n*
Netherlands, King of the, 382, 471
    King William II. of the, 108, 164
    Prince William Henry of the, 107–8
    Queen of the, 274
Netley Hospital, 265, 482, 539–40, 547
Neues Palais, 285
New Guinea, (App.) 595
    Lanark, 17–8 *n*
    South Wales, 83 *n*, 415, (App.) 595
    Zealand, 83 *n*, 549, 558, (App.) 595
Newcastle, 207, 423
    Duke of, 172, 234, 299 *n*
Newhaven, 186
Newport, I.W., 574
Nice, 302, 517 *n*
Nicholson, William, (App.) 583
Nicobar Islands, (App.) 592
Niger Company, (App.) 592
    river, (App.) 592
Nightingale, Miss Florence, 269
Noisy-le-Sec railway station, 518
Norfolk, Duke of, 47
Normanby, Marchioness of, 119, 124–5 *n*, 136
Norreys, Lady, 124–5 *n*
Norris Castle, 33, 38
North, Lord, 483
    Marston Church, 231
    West Territories, (App.) 595
Northampton, 160, 512 *n*
Northbrook, Earl of, 459 *n*
Northcote, Sir Stafford, 371 *n*, 435 *n*, 485. *See also under* Iddesleigh, Lord
Northumberland, Duchess of, 30, 35
    Hugh Percy, third Duke of 30 *n*

NORTHUMBERLAND

Northumberland, Duke of, 435 *n*
Norton, Hon. Mrs., 258 *n*
Novello, Mary Victoria (afterwards Mrs. Cowden Clarke), 13 *n*
— Vincent, 13 *n*
Nuneham, 133
Nuttall, P. A., 156 *n*

OAKLEY Court, 36
O'Brien, R. Barry, 'Life of Lord Russell,' 567
O'Connell, Daniel, 51, 77, 90, 157, 315 ; speech at Bandon on the Queen's betrothal, 110-11 *n*
— James, 315
O'Connor, Arthur, 421
'Œdipus Coloneus,' 191
Oehlenschläger's 'Correggio,' 123 *n*
Old Bailey, 57
Oldenburg, Prince Peter of, 184
Oliphant, Mrs., 586 *n*; 'Life' of, by Principal Tulloch, (App.) 588
Omdurman, battle of, 539
Oporto, Duke of. *See under* Portugal, King Luis of
Orange, Prince of, 2, 43
— Alexander, Prince of, 43
— Free State, (App.) 594
— river, (App.) 594
Orchardson, W. Q., (App.) 583
Orkney, 502
Orléans, Duc D', 550
Orleans, Louise Marie, Princess of, 9 *n*
Orsini, assassin, 280-1
Osborne, 166 seq.; the Queen acquires the estate of, 199-201
— House, 38
Ostend, 154, 363
Osterley Park, 155
Oudh, (App.) 592
Owen, Robert, 17 ; Autobiography of, 17-18 *n*
Oxford, 36-7, 133, 394 *n*
— Edward, 124, 142
— Movement, 395 *n*

PADDINGTON, 141, 144, 558
Paganini, violinist, 39
Paget, Lord C., 125 *n*
— Hon. Matilda 63 *n*

PARIS

Pakington, Sir John (afterwards Lord Hampton), 372 *n*
'Pall Mall Gazette' on the Queen's seclusion, 359
Palmer, Roundell. *See under* Selborne, Lord
Palmerston, Lady, 155, 205, 364
— Lord, 50, 53, 64, 82, 99, 107, 233, 268, 379, 395 *n*, 399-400, 443, 531; as Foreign Secretary, 129-32, 174-9, 188 seq.; meetings with the Queen, 155 ; the Queen's dread of him, 169-170, 251 ; and the Spanish marriages, 180-2; in attendance on the Queen, 185 ; differences with the Queen on foreign policy, 208-25 ; his fall, 225-7 ; revenge, 228-9 ; as Home Secretary, 235 ; and Napoleon III., 237-9; and the war with Russia, 240-50 ; his ministry, 251-261 ; and Italian unity, 264-5, 297-8 ; and the treaty of Paris, 266, 276 ; defeated on the China question, 271-72 ; and the Indian mutiny, 278 ; and the French alliance, 280-1 ; resignation, 281-2 ; his second cabinet, 299 seq.; dispute with Germany, 309; at Windsor, 311; and the affair of the 'Trent,' 316-9 ; his reproof of the Queen, 324-5 ; at the marriage of the Prince of Wales, 336 ; disagreements with the Queen, 337-8 ; and Napoleon III., 348 ; and Schleswig-Holstein, 352 ; death, 363-4, 403 ; Bulwer and Ashley's 'Life' of, 50 *n*, 82 *n*, 230, (App.) 589
Panmure, Lord, 258
Panshanger, 134
Papal aggression, 218-9
Paris, 225, 240, 263, 280, 374, 384, 393, 442, 449, 518, 550-1; Queen's visit to, 259-61 ; bombardment of, 412; Republic formed in, 414

INDEX

Paris, Comte de, 187
    Exposition of 1855, 257–9;
        of 1867, 384
    treaty of, 262–70, 413
Parkhurst, 465
Parliament, rebuilding of the Houses, of, 189
    the Queen's last prorogation of, 247
Parma, Duchess of, 301
Parnell, Charles Stewart, 513
Partridge, John, (App.) 582
Pasta, vocalist, 39
Pate, Robert, 206
    Hall, 516
Pawell-Rammingen, Baron von, 460
Paxton, Sir Joseph, 155, 221
Peel, General Jonathan, 283, 373
    Sir Robert, 59, 74, 76, 98, 109, 114, 129, 157–67, 189, 234, 283, 315, 364, 398–9, 432, 445, 461, 489, 492; on the Queen's inexperience, 53–54; defeats Lord Melbourne's ministry, 133; his administration, 135–162; visited by the Queen at Drayton Manor, 155; and the corn laws, 166–8; resignation, 168; return to power, 170–2; defeat, 173–4; and the Queen's visit to Ireland, 202; death, 205, 232; 'Peel Papers,' 63, 96, 102, 109, 111, 138, 147, 153, 157, 158, 160, 168, 173, (App.) 589
Peel Park, 224
Pélissier, General (afterwards Duc de Malakoff), 284
Pembroke Lodge, 175
Penguin Islands, (App.) 593
Pennant, Colonel Douglas, 306
Penny postage, introduction of, 104–5
Penrhyn Castle, 306
    Island, (App.) 595
People's Palace, 500
Perim Island, (App.) 591
Persia, Shah of, 291 n, 429–30, 515, 550
    'Diary' of, 430 n
Persian Gulf, (App.) 591
Persigny (French Ambassador), 276, 284

Perth, 190, 354
Phelps, actor, 195, 279
Philippa, Queen, 140
Phillips, J., (App.) 583
Phipps, Sir Charles, 324, 329
Phœnix Islands, (App.) 595
    Park, Dublin, 203, 314, 546
Pierce, Edward L., 92 n
Pistrucchi, artist, 90, (App.) 584
Pitchford House, 36
Pitt, Hon. Harriet, 63 n
Plas Newydd, 35
Plymouth, 38
    Lord, 36
Poland, 303, 348; insurrection in, 338–9
Pondoland, (App.) 594
Ponsonby, General Sir Henry, private secretary to the Queen, 329, 484, 528 n; and the reports of the Queen's wealth, 511
    Lady Caroline (afterwards Lady Melbourne), 60 n
Pontefract, 463
Poole's 'Life of Stratford-Canning,' 50 n
Pope Pius IX., 218; Leo XIII., 501
Port Blair, 426
    Hamilton, (App.) 591
    Jackson, 415
    Victoria, 508
Portman, Lady, 63 n
Portsmouth, 38, 160, 190 n, 305, 517
    volunteers, 540
Portugal, Crown Prince of, 501
    Carlos, King of, 8 n, 522–3, 558
    Ferdinand, Prince Consort of, 178, 212–3, 315, 523
    Luis, King of, 8 n, 245, 522
    Maria II. (da Gloria), Queen of, 8, 27–8, 178, 238, 522; appeals to the Queen for protection, 212–3; death, 245
    Pedro I., King of, 28
    V., King of, 8 n, 245, 315
Poschinger, Heinrich von, 'Unter Friedrich Wilhelm IV.,' 222 n, 264 n
    Margaretha von, 'Diaries of Emperor Frederick,' 412 n; 'Life of Emperor Frederick,' (App.) 587

INDEX

Potsdam, 285
'Powerful,' H.M.S., 546
Powis, Earl of, 30 n, 36, 184
    Castle, 35
Pretoria, occupation of, 544
Prince Consort, The. *See* under Albert
    Imperial, 418, 460; death, 451
Princess Victoria's Regiment (89th), 38, 367, 510; 'Historical Records' of, 38 n
Princess's Theatre, 273
Pritchard, George, 159
'Prophète,' opera, 142
Prothero, R. E., 571
'Proverbs' quoted, 466
Prussia (*see also under* Germany), 209–11, 222, 263; the Queen's interest in, 280, 296, 566; and Denmark, 332–3; and the Polish insurrection, 339; the position of, 340 seq.; and Schleswig-Holstein, 344–354; at war with Austria, 368–74
    Crown Prince and Princess of. *See under* Germany
    Princess Royal of, 4 n
    Frederick William II., King of, 4 n, 139
        IV., King of, 164–5, 210, 213, 242, 263–4, 296, 309, 412
Public Worship Regulation Bill, 435
'Punch,' 359, 446 n, (App.) 586
Punjaub, (App.) 592

'QUARTERLY Review,' 73, 376, 570 n, 587 n, (App.) 589 n
Queen of England's Own (German Horse Guards), 515
Queensland, 83, 549, (App.) 595
Queenstown, 203
Quillinan, Edward, 184

RACHEL, French actress, 194
Raglan, Lord, 248
Raikes, Henry Cecil, 516
    Thomas, 43 n, 87; 'Journal,' 43–4 n, 87–8 n, 150 n, 152 n, (App.) 589

Railways, introduction of, 140–1; growth of, 184
Ramsgate, 26, 42, 44
Ravi river, (App.) 592
Red Sea, (App.) 591
Redhouse's 'Diary of the Shah,' 430 n
Redistribution of Seats Bill, 485
Reeve, Henry, 378; Laughton's 'Life' of, 378 n, (App.) 589
Reform Bills, 297, 370–1; of 1832, 74; of 1867, 381, 389, 393; of 1884, 483–5, 489, 562
Regency Bills, 29, 125–7
    question, 150–1, 164
Regiments:—24th, 465
    Princess Victoria's Regiment (Royal Irish Fusiliers, 89th), 38, 367, 510; 'Historical Records' of, 38 n
    Berkshire (66th), 465
    Queen of England's Own (German Horse Guards), 515
    Royal Scots Greys (2nd Dragoons), 17, 442, 522
    Coldstream Guards, 533
    Cameron Highlanders, 540
    Grenadier Guards, 482
    Honourable Artillery Company, 540
    Scots Guards, 540
    Seaforth Highlanders, 540
    Royal Dragoon Guards (1st), 543
    Irish Guards, 546
Reid, Sir James, 554
    Stuart J., 186 n
    Wemyss, Lives of 'Lord Houghton' and 'W. E. Forster,' 409 n, (App.) 589
Rennes, 567 n
Reuss, Prince Henry XXX. of, 451 n, (App.) 581
'Revue Hebdomadaire,' 260–1 n
Rhine, 165, 382
Rhodes, Cecil, 541, (App.) 594; 'Life' of, 541 n
Rhodesia, (App.) 594
Ricci, musician, 124
'Richard II.,' the play, 273
Richmond, 522
    Park, 175
    Duke of, 386, 416, 435 n, 484, 490 n

INDEX

RIDLEY

Ridley, Sir Matthew White, 29
    Sir Matthew White (afterwards Viscount), 530 *n*
Ripon, Marquis of, 138 *n*, 401 *n*, 491, 525 *n*
Ritchie, Mr. C. T., 495 *n*, 531 *n*, 551 *n*
Riviera, 471, 555
Rizia Begum, 440
Rizzio, 207
Roberts, Lord, march on Kandahar, 463; and the Boer war of 1881, 464; in the Boer war of 1899–1902, 542 seq.; the Queen's welcome to, 556
Robertson, Dr., 201 *n*
Robertson, Sir Henry, 516
Robinson, John Henry, (App.) 582
Roebuck, J. A. (radical M.P.), 273
Rogers, Samuel, 47
Rolle, Lord, 90–1
Rome, 301
    Popes of, 218, 501
Rosebery, Countess of, 63
    Earl of, 460 *n*, 491, 525 *n* succeeds Gladstone as Prime Minister, 528–9
Rosenau, Palace of, 13, 165, 308, 339–40, 552
Ross, Sir W. C., 195, (App.) 583
Rossini, composer, 569
Rothschild, Baron Ferdinand de, 517 *n*
Roumania, 276
    Ferdinand, Crown Prince of, (App.) 580
Rowley, Vice-Chancellor, 36
Roxburgh, Duke and Duchess of, 386
Royal Academy, 47
'Royal Albert' yacht, 245, 442 *n*
'Royal Arthur' cruiser, 517
Royal Border bridge, 207
    Clarence Victualling Yard, 441
    Dragoons (1st), 543
    Exchange, opening of the, 160
'Royal George' yacht, 144
Royal Guelphic Hanoverian Order, 57 *n*
    Irish Fusiliers (89th, Princess Victoria's Regiment), 38, 367, 510; 'Historical Records' of, 38 *n*
    Marriage Act, 4 *n*

RUSSIA

Royal Order of Victoria and Albert, 331
    Patriotic Asylum, 274
    Red Cross (for nurses), 470
    Scots Greys (2nd Dragoons), 17, 442, 522
    Society, 78
'Royal Sovereign' ironclad, 517
Royal Titles Bill, 489
    Victoria Hospital, Netley, 266
    Victorian Order, institution of, 533–4
Rubini, vocalist, 39, 119 *n*, 125 *n*
Rubinstein, musician, 570 *n*
Rugby, 394
Russell, Lord John, 50, 54, 70, 74, 96, 100, 114, 131, 169–70, 208, 214–6, 233–5, 243, 249, 356, 379, 489; at the Queen's first Privy Council, 50; his hopes of the young Queen, 54–5; first ministry, 174 seq., 189; the Queen's gift to him for life of Pembroke Lodge, Richmond Park, 175; and the reduction of sugar duties, 188; the Queen's appeal to, 251–2; in Palmerston's Government, 253; at the Vienna Conference, 257–8; and Italian unity, 297–8; Foreign Secretary, 299 seq.; with the Queen to Coburg, 308 seq.; and the 'Trent' affair, 317; Order of the Garter, 330; disagreements with the Queen, 337–8; and the Schleswig-Holstein question, 353 *n*; succeeds Lord Palmerston as Prime Minister, 364, 370–1; resignation, 370; death, 449; Sir Spencer Walpole's 'Life' of, 55, 148, 213, 215, 233, 356, 371, (App.) 589
    Rev. Thomas, 21
    Lord (of Killowen), 567 *n*
Russia and the Crimean war, 239–250, 429, 488, 506; and the Vienna Conference, 257–8; and the treaty of Paris, 265–6, 276; and Poland,

RUSSIA

Russia—*cont.*
338–9; breaks the treaty of Paris, 413; relations with England, 430–1; at war with Turkey, 443–6; and the Berlin Congress, 447–8; and Afghanistan, 488

Alexander I., Tsar of, 11, 107, 156, 534

—— II., Tsar of, 107, 274, 384, 430–1, 437, 534, (App.) 580; assassination of, 467

—— III., Tsar of, 430, 534, death, 522

Constantine, Grand Duke of, 183, 274; Governor of Poland, 338

Marie Alexandrovna, Grand Duchess of. *See* under Saxe - Coburg - Gotha, Duchess of

Nicholas I., Tsar of, 156–8, 163, 183, 534; and the Crimean war, 242 seq.; and the 'Trent' affair, 317

—— II., Tsar of, (App.) 580; marriage, 521–522; visit to the Queen, 534

Russo-Turkish war, 443–8

Rutland, Duke of, 41, 156. *See also under* Manners, Lord John

SAAL, 6
Saalfeld, 6
Sadowa, battle of, 374
St. Cloud, Palace of, 259, 393
St. George's Chapel, 461, 467 *n*, 472, 477
St. Germain, 260, 574
St. James's Hall, 360
—— Palace, 27–51, 68–9, 117, 123, 280, 305, 521, 557
St. Leonards-on-Sea, 39
St. Lucia, 5
—— Bay, (App.) 593
St. Omer, 246
St. Patrick, Order of, 291 *n*
St. Patrick's Day, 545
'St. Paul' oratorio, 192
St. Paul's Cathedral, 54, 232, 420, 537

SAXE-COBURG-GOTHA

St. Petersburg, 431
St. Simon's Memoirs, 549
St. Thomas's Hospital, 419
Sale, John Bernard, 22
Salford, 224
Salisbury, Marquis of, 372 *n*, 435 *n*, 485; at the Berlin Congress, 448–449; first cabinet, 489–91; second ministry, 495–7, 524; entertains the Queen at Hatfield, 503; third ministry, 530 seq.; and the Boer war of 1899–1902, 541 seq.; again in power, 550 seq.
Sambourne, Linley, 446 *n*
San Marco monastery, 518
San Remo, 504
San Sebastian, 509
Sandhurst, 266
Sandringham, 420, 509
Sandwich, Lady, 102, 124–5 *n*
Sans Souci, Palace of, 285
Sardinia, 341; and the treaty of Paris, 265–6, 276; and the peace of Villafranca, 300–301; and Napoleon III., 302

—— Victor Emanuel, King of, and the Crimean war, 241; visits the Queen, 264–5; at war with Austria, 295–6; and the struggle for Italian unity, 300–1, 374; death, 449. *See also under* Italy, King of

Satara, province of Central India, (App.) 592
Savoy, province of, 302
Saxe-Coburg-Gotha, Duchess Dowager of, 25, 32

Dukes of, 7 *n*

Albert, Prince of. *See under* Albert, Prince Consort

Alexandra, Princess of, (App.) 581

Alfred, Duke of (formerly Duke of Edinburgh): birth, 159; offered the throne of Greece, 333–5; becomes heir to the duchy of Saxe-Coburg, 334; coming of age, 366–7; annuity, 368; attempted assassination of, 415; marriage, 430; marriage of his daughter,

SAXE-COBURG-GOTHA

Saxe-Coburg-Gotha—*cont.*
Princess Victoria Melita, 519; succeeds to the duchy of Saxe-Coburg, 521, 526; death of his only son, 552; death, 552, (App.) 579–80

Alfred, Prince of (only son of above), death, 552

Ernest, Duke of (father of Prince Albert), 26, 72, 108, 117, 127; death, 156

Ernest, Duke of (brother of Prince Albert), 42, 149, 192, 226, 237, 243, 308–9, 337, 366, 368, 373; and the Spanish marriages, 178 seq.; at the volunteer review, 306; at Osborne, 324; at Princess Alice's wedding, 331; and the throne of Greece, 333–5; at Frankfort, 340–1; and Schleswig-Holstein, 346 seq.; at Balmoral, 354; and the betrothal of Princess Helena, 362; death, 521; 'Memoirs' (1840–70) quoted, 179, 181, 213, 227, 243, 263–4, 309, 335, 342, 353, (App.) 587; Wilkinson's 'Reminiscences' of, (App.) 587

Duchess Ernest of, 193

family, 139, 178, 181, 348

Ferdinand Augustus, Prince of, 27–8, 72, 111, 178–9, 212–3

Leopold, Prince of. *See under* Belgians, King of the

Marie, Duchess of (formerly Duchess of Edinburgh), 430, 467, 556

Marie, Princess of, (App.) 580

Victoria Melita, Princess of, 519, (App.) 580

Saxe-Coburg-Saalfeld, Duchess of, 11–12

Francis Frederick Antony, Duke of, 6, 7 *n*, 13

Saxe-Gotha-Altenburg, Princess of, 8

Saxe-Meiningen, Feodora, Princess of, 450, (App.) 581

SCOTT

Saxe-Meiningen, George Frederick Charles, Duke of, 5
Louise, Duchess of, 49
Hereditary Prince and Princess of, 449, 581

Saxe-Weimar, Grand Duke of, 184

Saxony, Duke of. *See under* Edward VII.
King of, 156, 345, 501

Scare of 1847, 183–4

Schaumburg-Lippe, Prince Adolphe of, (App.) 581

Schleinitz, Baron von, 309

Schleswig-Holstein, Duchess of, 210, 218
question, 344–54, 368

Schleswig - Holstein - Sonderburg-Glucksburg, Augusta Victoria, Princess of (now Empress of Germany), 455, (App.) 581

Prince Christian of. *See under* Denmark, Christian IX. of

Prince Christian of, 345 seq.; engagement to Princess Helena, 362–3; marriage, 368

Princess Christian of (Princess Helena), birth, 172; visit to Ireland, 314; betrothal, 362–3; marriage, 366–8; dowry and annuity, 368; death of her eldest son, 553; at the Queen's death, 557, (App.) 579, 581, 584

Prince Christian Victor of, death, 553

Duke Frederick of, 345 seq., 455–6

Louise Augusta, Princess of, (App.) 581

'Schöner und schöner schmückt sich,' song, 193

Schouvaloff, Count, 430

Scilly Isles, 185

Scone, 145

Scotland, 143 seq.; volunteer forces of, 306; Industrial Museum of, 315; the press of, 419; the Queen's preference for, 563

Scots Guards, 540

Scott, Hope, 386

SCOTT

Scott, Sir Walter, 24, 71, 145, 386;
    Lockhart's 'Life' of, 24 *n*
Scottish Church, 147
    Church Patronage Bill, 436
    Reform Bill, 389
Seaforth Highlanders, 540
Sebastopol, fall of, 262, 284 *n*, 469
Secret Service Fund, 78–80
Sedgwick, Adam, 73; Clarke and Hughes's 'Life' of, 73 *n*, 155 *n*, 325 *n*, (App.) 589
Selborne, Lord, 401 *n*, 459 *n*, 552 *n*; on Republicanism, 421, 511; and the Burials Act, 462; opening of the new Law Courts, 472; on the death of the Duke of Clarence, 520; 'Memorials' of, 421 *n*, (App.) 589
Sell, Dr., 'Memoir of the Princess Alice,' (App.) 588
Serampore, (App.) 592
Shakespeare, William, quoted, 575; Plays, 195, 273, 323, 359
Shan States, (App.) 592
Sharpe, C. K., 'Correspondence,' 119 *n*
Shaw-Lefevre, Mr., 525 *n*, 529 *n*
Sheffield, 517
Sherbrooke, Lord, 36, 401 *n*, 424, 458; 'Life' of, 37 *n*
Shetland, 502
Shrewsbury, 35
Shugborough, 36
Sibthorp, Colonel, 114
Sidmouth, 14, 16
Siebold, Madame, 13
Sierra Leone, (App.) 592–3
Sind, (App.) 592
Slatin Pasha, 'Fire and Sword in the Soudan,' 571
Slavery, abolition of, 95–6
Slidell (South American Envoy), 316
Slough, 141, 144
Smiles, Dr. Samuel, 'Lives of the Engineers,' 410
Smith, G. Barnett, (App.) 586 *n*
    Sydney, 54
    W. H., 485 *n*, 490 *n*, 495–6 *n*; 'Life' of, by Sir H. Maxwell, (App.) 589
Socotra, Island of, (App.) 591
Sogliani, artist, 518 *n*
Solomon Islands, (App.) 595

STANLEY

Somaliland, (App.) 593
Sophia, Princess (daughter of George III.), 16, 21, 139, 149; death, 204
Soudan, 542, (App.) 592
    war of 1883, 467–70, 477–82; of 1898, 539–40
Soult, Marshal, 88, 91
South Africa, 451, 464, 537, (App.) 593–4
South African war, 541 seq.
South Australia, 83 *n*, 549, (App.) 595
South Kensington Museum, 540
Southampton, 314, 316
    deep-water dock, 517
'Sowers, The,' 571
Spain, the Queen's visit to, 509
    Christina, Queen Regent of, 178–9
    Isabella, Queen of, 177, 212
Spanish marriages, 174–82
Sparta, Duke of, (App.) 580
'Spectator,' 446
'Speeches and Addresses' by the Prince Consort, 375
Spencer, Lord, 96, 99, 196, 459 *n*, 491, 525 *n*
Spithead, 164, 236, 245, 385, 448, 515, 519, 538
Spree river, 275
Spring-Rice, Miss Mary, 63 *n*
Spring-Rice (Chancellor of the Exchequer), 100
'Stafford House Letters,' 101 *n*, (App.) 588
Stamford, 41–2
Stanfield, artist, 195
Stanhope, Edward, 490 *n*, 495–6 *n*
Stanley, Dean, 397, 408–9, 428 *n*, 431, 465; at the Queen's coronation, 90; marriage, 327; tour in the Holy Land with the Prince of Wales, 331; Bradley and Prothero's 'Life' of, 89 *n*, 119 *n*, 222 *n*, 466 *n*, 571
    Lady Augusta, 409, 442; marriage, 327. *See also under* Bruce, Lady Augusta
    Lord, 137, 167, 171, 189, 219. *See also under* Derby, 14th and 15th Earls of

Stanley, Sir Frederick (Lord Stanley of Preston; *see also under* Derby, 16th Earl of), 435 *n*, 490 *n*, 495 *n*

Stanmore, Lord, 250 *n*
   Priory, 205

Stansfeld, James, 401 *n*, 491

Stephen, Sir Leslie, 'Letters of J. R. Green,' 422 *n*

Stephenson, Mr. (American Ambassador), 74

Steward, Thomas, 21

Stockmar, Baron von, political adviser to the Queen and Prince Albert, 64–5, 113, 115, 123–6, 204, 213, 224, 243, 321; touring in Italy with Prince Albert, 106; in retirement at Coburg, 307–8; death, 339; 'Memoirs' of, 378, (App.) 587–8

Stockton, 140

Stolzenfels Castle, 165

Stoneleigh Abbey, 286

Stowe, 161–2

Straits Settlements, (App.) 591

Strathfieldsaye, 161

Strutt's cotton mills, 35

Submarine cable, the first, 286

Suffolk, Charles Brandon, Duke of, 418
   Mary, Duchess of, 418

Sugar duties, 157, 188

Sugden, Sir Edward, 157

Sullivan, Sir Arthur, 519, 569

Sumner, Charles, 92; 'Memoirs and Letters' of, 92 *n*
   Archbishop, 395

Supreme Court of Judicature Act, 1873, 401 *n*

Sussex, Augustus Frederick, Duke of, 4 *n*, 11, 49, 73 *n*, 115, 126–7; death, 149

Sutherland, Duchess of, 63, 107 *n*, 136, 322; death, 427
   Duke of, 'Stafford House Letters,' (App.) 588

Sutlej river, (App.) 592

Sutton, Dr. Manners (Archbishop of Canterbury), 12

Suwarro Island, (App.) 595

Swan River Settlement, 83 *n*

Swanage, 39

Sweden, Crown Prince of, 501
   Oscar II., King of, 183, 267, 314, 547

Switzerland, the Queen's visit to, 392–3

Sydenham, 246

Sydney, 548–9

Tahiti, Island of, 159

Taillandier, St. René, 366 *n*, (App.) 587

Tait, Archibald Campbell, Archbishop of Canterbury, 394–5, 405–6, 435, 473–5; Benham and Davidson's 'Life' of, 407 *n*, (App.) 589

'Tales of my Father, Equerry to King Ernest of Hanover,' by A. M. F., 57 *n*, (App.) 587

Tamburini, Signor, 39, 70

Tanganyika lake, (App.) 594

Tasmania, 83 *n*, 549, (App.) 595

Tavistock, Marchioness of, 63, 93

Taymouth, 145

Teck, Duke of, 368, 468, (App.) 580
   Duchess of, 239, 468, 520, 552; 'Life' of, (App.) 588. *See also under* Cambridge, Princess Mary of
   Princess Mary (May) of, 520–521, (App.) 580. *See also under* York, Duchess of

Telegraphy, introduction of, 279; first submarine cable, 286

Tel-el-Kebir, battle of, 469

Temple Bar, 77 *n*, 420

Tennyson, Lord, on the Great Exhibition, 223; eulogy of the Prince Consort in 'Idylls of the King,' 322; friendship with the Queen, 408, 475–7, 493 *n*, 520; 'In Memoriam,' 408; 'Life' of, 493 *n*; (App.) 589
   Lionel, 493 *n*

Thackeray, W. M., 410 *n*

Thames, the last royal water pageant on the, 204
   Embankment, 417

'The Bells,' play, 509

'The Colonel,' comedy, 510

'The Frozen Deep,' by Wilkie Collins, 409

'The Gondoliers,' comic opera, 519

'The Red Lamp,' play, 520

S S

THEOBALDS

Theobalds Park, 421 *n*
Thistle, Order of the, 291 *n*
Thomas, E. H., (App.) 583
Thorburn, Robert, (App.) 583
Thuringian forest, 166
Thynne, Lord John, 89
'Times' on Buckingham Palace, 69; on the betrothal of the Princess Royal, 263; on Prince Albert's position, 275; report of the Queen's interview with Lord Granville, 298; on the Queen's seclusion, 357-8, (App.) 586
Tooley, Sarah, (App.) 586 *n*
Torquay, 39
Torrens's 'Life of Lord Melbourne,' (App.) 588-9
Torrington, Lord, 116-7
Tottenham, 184
Tower Hamlets, 360
'Tracts for the Times,' No. 1, 422, 424
Tranquebar, (App.) 590
Transvaal, 464, (App.) 594
    war of 1881, 463-4; of 1899-1902, 541-53
Tree, Mr. Beerbohm, 520
'Trent' (English steamer), the affair of the, 316-9, 330
Tréport, 152-3, 166
Trevelyan, Sir G. O., 460 *n*, 491, 525 *n*; 'Life of Macaulay,' 176 *n*, (App.) 589
Trinity College, Cambridge, 154-155, 184-5
Trossachs, 306, 408
Tuer's 'First Year of a Silken Reign,' (App.) 588
Tuileries, the, 237, 259 *n*, 263-4, 274
Tulloch, Principal, 436, 586 *n*;
    'Life' of, (App.) 589 *n*
    Rev. Dr., (App.) 586 *n*
Tunbridge Wells, 39, 41
Turkey and Egypt, 130-2; at war with Russia, 238-50, 256; and the treaty of Paris, 265-6, 276; and the Balkans, 443-6
    Abdul Aziz, Sultan of, 384-5, 429
    Abdul Hamid II., Sultan of, 443, 447
Turton, Thomas, Bishop of Ely, 89 *n*
Tuxen, Laurens, (App.) 584
'Twice Killed,' farce, 280

VICTORIA

Uganda, (App.) 593
Ulster loyalists, 493
Underwood, Lady Cecilia Letitia (afterwards Duchess of Inverness), 126 *n*
Union Islands, (App.) 595
United States of America, 83, 467; and Canada, 84; first cable from England to, 286; Prince of Wales's tour in, 306; and the affair of the 'Trent,' 316-9, 330; President's allowance, 422
University College, Oxford, 36
'Unter Friedrich Wilhelm IV.,' 232 *n*, 264 *n*
Upper Norwood, 504
Uwins, artist, 195
Uxbridge, 37

Vaal river, (App.) 594
Van Diemen's Land, 83 *n*
Vancouver Island, (App.) 594
Vansittart, Nicholas, 11
Venetia, 295, 300-1, 372
Verdi, composer, 520
Versailles, 259-60, 551 *n*
Verviers, 285
Victor Emanuel. *See under* Sardinia, King of
Victoria, Queen: parentage and birth, 1-18; her descent from King Alfred, 1; her place in the succession, 11; death of her father, the Duke of Kent, 14; childhood, 19-28; settlement at Kensington, 19; knowledge of her rank, 24; visit to George IV., 26; heir to the crown, 29-47; her governess, 30; William IV.'s treatment of her, 33, 44; provincial tours, 36-7; confirmation, 40; first meeting with Prince Albert, 42; coming of age, 46; accession to the throne, 48-55; her first Privy Council, 49; her name as sovereign, 52; the tuition of Lord Melbourne, 56-68; the private secretaryship to, 60; her preference for the Whigs, 61; formation

VICTORIA

Victoria, Queen—*cont.*
of her household, 62; her foreign advisers, 64–6; first speech from the throne, 67; removal to Buckingham Palace, 69; attitude to her kinsfolk, 72; opening her first Parliament, 77; the first settlement, 79; the Queen pays her father's debts, 81; the coronation, 87–91; resists change in her household, 97; admission of her error, 100; unreadiness to marry, 105; suitors, 107; engagement to Prince Albert, 108; the Prince's precedence, 115; marriage, 117; popular dislike of the Prince, 119; first attempt on her life, 123; birth of the Princess Royal, 127; change of attitude to the Tories, 137; birth of the Prince of Wales, 137; her first journey by rail, 141; second and third attempts on her life, 141–2; legislation for her personal security, 142; first visit to Scotland, 144; baptism of Princess Alice, 149; visit to Louis Philippe at Château d'Eu, 152–3; and the Irish Union, 156; birth of Prince Alfred, 159; first meeting with Disraeli, 161; first visit to Germany, 162; her dread of Palmerston, 169, 251; birth of Princess Alice, 172; enthusiasm for free trade, 173; family conference at Windsor on the Spanish marriages, 179; her indignation with Palmerston, 182; her reception of the exiled Louis Philippe and his sons, 186; birth of Princess Louise, 187; first stay at Balmoral, 190; Mendelssohn's visit, 191; education of her children, 196; dislike of London,

VICTORIA

Victoria, Queen—*cont.*
199; acquisition of Osborne, 200; first visit to Ireland, 202; last royal water pageant, 204; deaths of Lord Melbourne and Sir Robert Peel, 204–5; two assaults on the Queen, 206; birth of Prince Arthur, 206; differences with Palmerston, 208; popularity of Palmerston's policy, 215; the Great Exhibition, 221; Court festivities, 223; Palmerston's fall, 225; Lord Derby's cabinet, 229; early impressions of Disraeli, 229; Neild's bequest, 231; death of the Duke of Wellington, 231; her desire for a coalition ministry, 232–5; birth of Prince Leopold, 235; Napoleon III.'s advances, 236; King Leopold's mediation, 238; opening of the Crystal Palace, 246; anxieties about the Crimean war, 248; battles of Inkerman and Balaclava, 248; Palmerston's omnipotence, 252; the wounded soldiers, 254; and Napoleon III.'s visit, 256; first distribution of war medals, 258; in Paris, 258: first meeting with Bismarck, 260; the fall of Sebastopol, 262; the Princess Royal's engagement, 262; treaty of Paris, 265; first visit to Aldershot, 266; institution of the Victoria Cross, 267; birth of the Princess Beatrice, 272; brilliant festivities at Court, 273; title of the Prince Consort, 275; visits to Cherbourg, 277, 284; the Indian mutiny, 279; fall of Delhi and relief of Lucknow, 279; marriage of the Princess Royal, 279; tour in Germany, 285; first submarine cable, 286; her personal interest in

s s 2

VICTORIA

Victoria, Queen—*cont.*
India, 288; proclamation to India, 290; Order of the Star of India instituted, 290; majority of the Prince of Wales, 293; her first grandchild, 293; appeal for peace to Napoleon III., 294; and Italian unity, 300; quarrel with her ministry, 300; and the Commander-in-Chief, 303; and the volunteers, 305; engagement of Princess Alice, 307; the Prince of Wales in America, 307; second visit to Coburg, 307; accident to Prince Albert, 308; twenty-first anniversary of her marriage, 312; death of her mother, 312; at Killarney, 314; the Prince Consort's illness, 315; and the affair of the 'Trent,' 316; Walt Whitman on the Queen's action, 319; Prince Albert's death, 319; the Queen's grief, 321-6; the Prince's reputation, 322; her ministers' reproof, 324; the Prince's lasting influence on her, 325; Scottish sympathisers, 327; John Brown, 328; her private secretaries, 328-9; her signature to officers' commissions, 331; Prince of Wales in the Holy Land, 331; Princess Alice's marriage, 331; memorial to Prince Albert at Balmoral, 332; betrothal of the Prince of Wales, 332; Duke Ernest and the throne of Greece, 333-4; marriage of the Prince of Wales, 335; disagreements with ministers, 337; visit to Coburg, 339; her despair of Prussia, 340; interview with the Emperor of Austria, 341; and the Schleswig-Hol-

VICTORIA

Victoria, Queen—*cont.*
stein question, her divided interests, 344 seq.; birth of the Prince of Wales's son, 354; complaints of the Queen's seclusion, 355 seq., 417; her reply, 358; refusal to leave her retirement, 360; betrothal of Princess Helena, 362; death of Palmerston, 363; death of King Leopold, 365; marriage of Princess Helena, 367; grants to Princess Helena and Prince Alfred, 368; her offer of mediation in the Austro-Prussian war, 369; and the Reform Bill, 369; the biography of the Prince Consort, 376; publication of 'Leaves from the Journal,' 378; her distrust of Napoleon III., 381; her horror at the murder of Emperor Maximilian, 384; continued depression, 386; growing respect for Disraeli, 387; her constitutional rights, 391; visit to Switzerland, 392; her special mark of favour to Disraeli, 394; her view of Church patronage, 396; Gladstone in office, 399; her mediation with the Lords on the Irish Church Bill, 404; intercourse with men of letters, 408-10; the Franco-German war, 411 seq.; and the Empress Eugénie, 414; betrothal of Princess Louise, 417; grants to Princess Louise and Prince Arthur, 418; Princess Louise's marriage, 419; the Queen's illness, 419; illness of the Prince of Wales, 420; attack on the Queen's income, 422-424, 511; visit to Germany, 426; death of Napoleon III., 427; marriage of the Duke of Edinburgh, 430

VICTORIA

Victoria, Queen—*cont.*
cordial relations with Disraeli, 432-4; irritation with Gladstone, 436; Prince Leopold's illness, 436; Prince of Wales's tour in India, 439; Empress of India, 439; visit to Hughenden, 445; third volume of the Prince Consort's biography, 447; death of the Princess Alice, 449; marriage of the Duke of Connaught, 450; visit to Italy, 450; the Prince Imperial's death, 451; Indian wars, 452; Gladstone resumes office, 457; Maiwand disaster, 463; Majuba Hill, 464; death of Beaconsfield, 465; war in Egypt, 467; battle of Tel-el-Kebir, 469; fifth attempt on the Queen's life, 470; visit to the Riviera, 471; grant to Prince Leopold on his marriage, 471; death of John Brown, 475; publication of 'More Leaves,' 476; Prince Leopold's death, 476; and General Gordon's death, 479; her mediation between the two Houses of Parliament, 484; betrothal and marriage of the Princess Beatrice, 486; her hostility to Home Rule, 492; Lord Salisbury's second ministry, 495; Jubilee of her accession (1887), 497 seq.; she learns Hindustani, 500; family quarrel in Berlin, 505; death of the Emperor Frederick, 508; visit to Spain, 509; grants to the Prince of Wales's children, 513; her savings, 514; visit to Wales, 516; revival of the drama and opera at Court, 519; betrothal and death of the Duke of Clarence, 520; the Duke of York's marriage, 521; the duchy of Saxe-Coburg-Gotha, 521; birth of Prince Edward of York, afterwards Wales, 522; Gladstone again in office, 524; fate of the Home Rule Bill, 525; Gladstone's death, 528; Lord Rosebery as Prime Minister, 528; Lord Salisbury's third Government, 530; death of Prince Henry of Battenberg, 533; institution of the Victorian Order, 534; the Diamond Jubilee of 1897, 536-8; military expeditions, 539; interview with Cecil Rhodes, 541; the Great Boer war, 542 seq.; her Christmas gift to the troops, 544; the successes in South Africa, 544; fourth visit to Ireland, 545; inauguration of the Australian Commonwealth, 548; distresses of the war, 549; her latest bereavements, 552-3; last journey to Osborne, 553; her ailments, 554; Lord Roberts's audiences, 556; Mr. Chamberlain's audience, 556; death, 556; her age and length of reign, 557; funeral, 557; universal sorrow, 558; her position and character, 561-75; her descendants, (App.) 579-581; portraits of the Queen, (App.) 582-5; authorities for her biography (App.), 586-9; growth of the empire during her reign, (App.) 590-5

'Leaves from the Journal' quoted, 146, 185, 207, 232, 261, 328, 378, 410, (App.) 588

'More Leaves from the Journal' quoted, 412, 427, 451, (App.) 588

Speeches:—
In Parliament, 77, 92, 113

VICTORIA

Victoria, Queen—*cont.*
 135, 139, 163, 295, 312, 351-2, 366
 in presenting colours to the Royal Scots, 17
 before the Privy Council announcing her engagement, 110
 at Invercannie, 374
 in laying the foundation-stone of the Royal Albert Hall, 379
 to the troops from Egypt, at Windsor, 470
Victoria Adelaide Mary Louise, Princess Royal. *See under* Germany, Empress of
Victoria, Australia, 52, 83, 549, (App.) 595
 Bridge, 35
 Cross instituted, 267; first distribution of, 274; those earned in the Indian mutiny, 305
 Gate, Hyde Park, 70
 Park, 429
 Station, 52, 558
Victoria-Stift (founded at Coburg by the Queen), 308
'Victoria and Albert' yacht, 152, 185, 277, 385
 Museum, 195 *n*, 540-1
Victorian Order, institution of, 583-4
'Victory,' 38
Vienna, 341
 Congress of, 56, 150, 257-8
 Riots, 209
Vieuxtemps, 165
Villa Hohenlohe, 455
Villa Pension Wallace, 393
Villafranca, 297; the treaty of, 300
Villiers, Charles Pelham, 175, 299 *n*, 467
Vivisection, 567
Volunteer movement, 305
 review, 392

WADDESDON Manor, 517 *n*
Waddington, Mary King, 'Letters of a Diplomat's Wife,' 501 *n*, 526 *n*
Wagner, composer, 569

WELLINGTON

Wakefield, Edward Gibbon, 85
Waldeck-Pyrmont, Princess Helen Frederica of (now Duchess of Albany), 471-2
Wales, the Queen's tours in, 35, 516-7
 Albert Edward, Prince of. *See under* Edward VII.
 Prince Edward of Wales, formerly York: birth, 522, (App.) 583
 Frederick, Prince of, 3
 George Frederick, Prince of: annuity, 513; marriage, 521, (App.) 580, 583; birth of Prince Edward, 522; the christening of his third son, 547; visit to Australia, 548
 Princess Louise of: dowry of, 513; marriage, 514, (App.) 580
 Princess Maud of, (App.) 580
Walewski (French Ambassador), 225-6, 276; entertains the Queen, 245; and the Orsini incident, 281
Walfisch Bay, (App.) 594
Wallachia, 276
Walmer Castle, 42, 145
Walmisley, T. A., 184 *n*
Walpole, Sir Robert, 71
 Sir Spencer, 244, 372 *n*; 'Life of Lord John Russell,' (App.) 589
Wandsworth Common, 274
Wangenheim, Baron, 5
Ward, E. M., 260 *n*, (App.) 583
Washington, 307, 317-8, 330, 356, 383
Water pageant, the last state, 204
Waterloo day, 87
Webb, Mr. Aston, 584
Webster, Ben., actor, 195
Wei-hai-wei, (App.) 591
Weimar, 166
Welch, Charles, 582 *n*
Wellesley, Gerald (Dean), 330, 474
Wellington, Duke of, 11, 30 *n*, 88, 96, 100, 126-7, 133, 137, 150, 151, 219, 330; at the Queen's first Privy Council, 49-50; and the Queen's marriage, 115; lends Walmer Castle to the Queen,

WELLINGTON

Wellington, Duke of—*cont.*
145; at Chatsworth, 155; at Belvoir Castle, 156; visited by the Queen at Strathfieldsaye, 161; godfather to Prince Arthur, 206; death, 231-2, 267; (App.) 583
    Barracks, 258
    College, Sandhurst, 266, 305, 354, 475
Welsh Disestablishment Bill, 529
Wentworth House, 41
West, Sir Algernon, 424; 'Recollections' (App.), 589
West Africa, 441, 537, (App.) 592-3
Westall, Richard, 22, (App.) 582
Western Australia, 83 *n*, 549, (App.) 595
Westminster Abbey, 31, 39, 442, 449, 460, 466, 473, 501, 528
    Deanery of, 397, 409
    Duke of, 269
Wetherall, General, 14
Weymouth, 38
Wharncliffe, Lord, 138 *n*
'What does she do with it?' 'Tracts for the Times,' No. 1, 422, 424
Whewell, Dr. William, 154-5; 'Life and Correspondence' of, 155 *n*
Whippingham, 38
    Church, 200, 487, 534
White Lodge, 522
Whitman, Sidney, (App.) 587
    Walt, on the affair of the 'Trent,' 318-9
Whitworth rifle, 306
Wilberforce, Samuel, Bishop, 376, 397, 466, 474; 'Life' of, 184 *n*, 376 *n*, 404 *n*, (App.) 589
    William, 24; 'Life' of, by R. I. and S. Wilberforce, 24 *n*
Wilkes, Captain, 316
Wilkie, Sir David, 33, (App.) 582-3
Wilkinson's 'Reminiscences of King Ernest of Hanover,' (App.) 587
William the Conqueror, 1
    III., 2
    IV., 4, 10-15, 27-30, 56, 69, 96, 108, 113, 130, 140, 151-152, 175, 205, 356, 378; marriage, 5; his two

WÜRTEMBERG

William IV.—*cont.*
daughters, 27 *n*; coronation, 31, 89; attitude towards the Duchess of Kent, 31-47, 61; offers the Queen 10,000*l.* a year, 47; death, 48; dismissal of Melbourne's ministry, 59; family by Mrs. Jordan, 73; colonial expansion during the last years of his reign, 83; coronation expenses, 87
Williams of Kars, Sir Fenwick, 269
Williamson, Lady, 110, 124-5 *n*
Willis, N. P., 40; 'Pencillings by the Way,' 40 *n*
Willoughby de Eresby, Lady, 119 *n*
Willoughby, Lord, 145
Wilson, Mrs. Cornwell Baron, 35
    Sir Samuel, 470 *n*
Wimbledon Common, 397
Winchilsea, Earl of, 26
Winchester, (App.) 584
Windsor, 26, 45, 48; the Queen takes up residence at, 70 seq.; the Queen's preference for, 199 seq.
    Town Hall, 553
Winterhalter, F., 196, 569, (App.) 582
Wiseman, Cardinal, 218
Woburn Abbey, 134
Wodehouse, Lord. *See under* Kimberley, Earl of
Wolseley, Sir Garnet (now Viscount Wolseley), in the Egyptian war, 468; in the Soudan, 478
Wolverhampton, 35, 375
'Woman's Rights,' 573
Wood, Sir Charles, 235, 299. *See also under* Halifax, Lord
    Alderman Matthew, 10
    Page. *See under* Hatherley, Lord
Woodville, R. Caton, (App.) 584
Woolwich, 144, 146, 154, 190, 245, 545
    Military Hospital, 254, 545
Wordsworth, William, 184 *n*, 223
Worsley Hall, 224, 274
Würtemberg, Alexander, Prince of, 37

WÜRTEMBERG

Würtemberg, Alexander Constantine, Duke of, 368
    Alexander Frederick Charles, Duke of, 8, 308
    Antoinette Ernestina Amelia, Duchess of, 8–9 n
    Antoinette Frederica, Princess of, 308
    Ernest, Prince of, 37
    Friedrich Wilhelm, Duke of, 9 n
    Queen of, 12
Wyon, William, 77 n, (App.) 584–5
Wytham Abbey, 36

ZULULAND

York, 41
    Duke and Duchess of. *See under* Wales, Prince and Princess of
    Frederick, Duke of, 4 n, 11–14; death, 27
Yorke, P. C., 57 n

Zambesi river, (App.) 594
Zanzibar, (App.) 593
Zobeir Pasha, 478
Zulu war, 451, 465
Zululand, (App.) 593–4

PRINTED BY
SPOTTISWOODE AND CO. LTD., NEW-STREET SQUARE
LONDON